A People in Revolution

A People in Revolution

The American Revolution and Political Society in New York, 1760–1790

Edward Countryman

W. W. Norton & Company
New York • London

First published as a Norton paperback 1989 by arrangement with The Johns Hopkins University Press.

The clothbound edition of this book was brought to publication with the generous assistance of the National Endowment for the Humanities.
Paperback edition published with the assistance of the New York State Commission on the Bicentennial of the United States Constitution.

Library of Congress Cataloging in Publication Data

Countryman, Edward.
A people in revolution: the American Revolution and political society in New York, 1760–1790: with a new introduction / Edward Countryman.
p. cm. — (Norton paperback)
Reprint. Originally published: Baltimore: Johns Hopkins University Press, 1981. (Johns Hopkins University studies in historical and political science: 99th ser., 2)
Bibliography: p.
Includes index.
1. New York (State)—Politics and government—Revolution, 1775–1783. 2. New York (State)—Politics and government—1775–1865. I Title. II. Series: Johns Hopkins University studies in historical and political science; 99th ser., 2.
E263.N6C68 1989
974.7'02—dc20 89-8530
CIP

ISBN 0-393-30606-2

W. W. Norton & Company, Inc., 500 Fifth Avenue, New York, N.Y. 10110
W. W. Norton & Company Ltd., 37 Great Russell Street, London WC1B 3NU

1 2 3 4 5 6 7 8 9 0

For the Memory
Of My Parents and Brother
And for the Future
Of My Son

Contents

Preface to the Norton Edition

When the hardcover edition of *A People in Revolution* was published, my major goal was to demonstrate how different the New York of 1760 was from the New York of 1790. I wanted as well to show how long and tangled was the path that led from the one to the other. I did suggest then that I would be surprised if the questions I was asking did not apply to most other places. But I made no attempt to generalize beyond the experience of New York itself.

Eight years later the historiographical landscape is different. It turned out that I was one of many historians who were developing the argument that the Revolution was genuinely revolutionary. We understand now that people of many sorts took part in the revolutionary movement, all over the country. They had their own separate reasons for doing it, and the large movement makes no sense unless we can grasp those reasons. We have learned that as people changed their political situation they also changed themselves and their relations with one another. The argument that the revolution was genuinely revolutionary now seems unchallengable.[1]

Others have carried the argument even further than I was prepared to in 1981. I wrote at the end of *A People* that women and black people gained little from the Revolution, but I was wrong, as such scholars as Mary Beth Norton, Linda Kerber, and Gary B. Nash have shown.[2] Their subjects did not experience the Revolution the same way as mine, but they experienced it nonetheless and took their first steps toward forging their own freedom. I wrote about events as civilians experienced them, and left the Revolution's military dimensions almost wholly aside. But historians like John Shy, Charles Royster, E. Wayne Carp, and Stephen Rosswurm have considered how Americas' military experience was also revolutionary experience.[3] The more we think about it, the more revolutionary the American Revolution seems.

The question that now seems to me to be important is what difference the Revolution made. My guess is that it is precisely because the American Revolution was genuinely revolutionary that the American Republic was able to develop as it subsequently did. At the very end of *A People* I write in grand terms about the Revolution "firmly laying the foundations of a liberal bourgeois society" and "sweeping away the contradictions of the past." To some extent I was simply "letting go" as the book came to its conclusion. But other work suggests that my rhetorical flourish in fact possesses some substance.

Three of the best examples focus on New York itself. One is Mary P. Ryan's account of development in the Mohawk Valley between the Constitution and the Civil War. The second is Sean Wilentz's study of New York City during the same years. The third is Paul A. Gilje's account of the changing social meaning of popular violence in New York City during the late eighteenth and early nineteenth centuries.[4] All three trace the experience of enormously vibrant and volatile societies; all three show New York becoming a fully capitalist society, with all the creativity, exploitation, and inequality which that process entailed. All three speak as well to themes that *A People in Revolution* raises.

I began the work that led to *A People* with the hypothesis that internal division was not important in New York's revolution. Contact with the sources quickly changed my mind, for what I found was both extensive dispute and change in the terms on which people disputed. On two separate occasions during the Revolution, conflict threatened the existence of the state itself. One came in the war years, when British invasion and Vermont secession forced a radical redefinition of New York's political geography. The British withdrew at the end of 1783, but Vermont was gone forever. The other occasion came in 1788, when there was a serious threat that New York City would leave the state if the state's Anti-Federalist majority rejected the Federal Constitution.

I discuss the wartime crisis fully in the text. It seems appropriate here to expand somewhat on what happened in 1788. It seems appropriate especially to ask why the fact that New York *did* ratify—despite the overwhelming majority that Anti-Federalists enjoyed in its ratifying convention—did not cause yet more disruption.

Two centuries after ratification it is difficult to realize how hostile most of New York's people were to the Constitution. We are bedazzled by the enduring success of the document itself. We are bedazzled as well by the historical reputations of leading New York Federalists like Robert R. Livingston, John Jay, and especially Alexander Hamilton. We forget the powerful arguments of New Yorkers who took the other side: Abraham Yates, Jr., the "rough hewer" of Albany; Melancton Smith, who made some of the most cogent Anti-Federalist arguments; and especially Governor George Clinton.

But the fact of the matter was that in 1788 most of the state's people were happy as they were, especially outside the immediate region of New York

City. Their convention did finally ratify because, by the time the issue came to a vote, the only question was whether New York would join the federal republic, not whether the republic would exist. Had New Hampshire's convention voted against ratification, as it was expected to do, or had close votes gone the other way in Virginia and Massachusetts, New York's convention would have faced a wholly different situation, and the union might never have come into being at all.

Why did so many of the state's people want in 1788 to stay out of the union? It could not have been that they feared the presidency or the strength of a bicameral congress; they already lived with their own strong governorship and state senate. Indeed, their own state institutions, defined by their constitution of 1777, formed one of the main models for the ones that the Federal Constitution set up. My guess would be that their Anti-Federalism in 1788 sprang directly from what they had achieved in their revolution. In like manner, the Federalism of New Yorkers who did want the Constitution sprang from their sense that the achievement was not enough.

Going further, my guess is that the heart of the dispute lay in questions of power and its use. The Constitution is the great charter of American republicanism. It established the political institutions that still govern us. It is also the great charter of the national American economy, establishing a vast common market on the principles of the legal equality of all participants and the supremacy of federal law.

In order to establish that common market, the Constitution took long steps towards destroying the economic and social autonomy of the separate states and of the smaller communities within them. In New York the desire for such autonomy had found strong expression in the laws passed by a state government that the state's rural majority controlled. This was especially the case with regard to such sensitive areas as taxation, finance, and loyalism. The Constitution would put an end to that majority's ability to run the state's affairs as it chose.

But to the people of commercial New York City, whether they were blacksmiths or bankers, it mattered less to maintain local autonomy than to seize the opportunity that the Constitution opened for a greatly improved position in the Atlantic world. They wanted political institutions that could serve them in a large-scale competitive world. Hence the possibility of their secession if the Federalist drive to create such institutions was defeated.

These people showed their values in the enormous parade they staged to celebrate ratification when it did come. As they marched they made it plain that to them the Revolution's achievement lay in the intertwined themes of military victory, republicanism, and productive prosperity. Anti-Federalists quarreled with none of these. But to them it was still possible to be prosperous without being immersed in the world of long-distance trade. They saw no reason to sacrifice the state autonomy that was so central to the Revolution *they* had experienced

The Constitution, then, did not repudiate the achievements of New York's revolution. Instead, it marked the triumph of what New Yorkers of one kind had decided they wanted from the Revolution. The issue of the Federal Constitution was divisive, and it was hard fought. But it was unlike the loyalist–patriot split of 1776, for it was divisive in terms of what had already been worked out in the Revolution. The issue at stake was serious: the meaning and outcome of all that the Revolution had wrought. But it was not a matter of fundamental identity or, to the Anti-Federalists, a question on which defeat was unacceptable. When they lost, it was a loss with which almost all of them could live.

By accepting the Constitution, whether willingly like most of the people of New York City or reluctantly like most of the people outside it, New Yorkers accepted that their revolution was over. Henceforth they would live under institutions whose legitimacy was not to be challenged, whatever might be said about policies or office-holders. With their republicanism and their national political identity assured, New Yorkers, like other Americans, could turn to other questions, the ones that scholars like Ryan and Wilentz have explored.

Borrowing from another scholar of New York in the early national period, Daniel Calhoun, I asked in the original preface to this book, "What if it should be true that these things do hang together?"[5] Then I was concerned only with the validity of the interpretation of New York's American Revolution that I had worked out. Eight years later I remain sure of that interpretation, not least because it fits with what so many other scholars have found. The question is how the revolution which we now see "hangs together" with the larger course of American history, as the early United States embarked on the great transition that lay before it. Drawing, as usual, on the insights of others, I have offered some suggestions here. They seem to me to be at least an item on the next agenda for students of the American Revolution.

E.C.

New Haven, Connecticut
March 1989

NOTES

1. Edward Countryman, *The American Revoluton* (New York: Hill & Wang, 1985).

2. Mary Beth Norton, *Liberty's Daughters: The Revolutionary Experience of American Women, 1750–1800* (Boston: Scott-Foresman, 1980); Linda K. Kerber, *Women of the Republic: Intellect and Ideology in Revolutonary America* (Chapel Hill: University of North Carolina Press, 1980); Gary B. Nash, *Fording Freedom: The Formation of Philadelphia's Black Community, 1720–1840* (Cambridge, Mass.: Harvard University Press, 1988); Ira Berlin and Ronald Hoffman, eds., *Slavery and Freedom in the Age of the American Revolution* (Charlottesville: University Press of Virginia, 1983).

3. John W. Shy, *A People Numerous and Armed: Reflections on the Military Struggle for American Independence* (New York: Oxford University Press, 1976); Charles Royster, *A Revolutionary People at War: The Continental Army and American Character, 1775–1783* (Chapel Hill: University of North Carolina Press, 1979); E. Wayne Carp, *To Starve the Army at Pleasure: Continental Army Administration and American Political Culture, 1775–1783* (Chapel Hill: University of North Carolina Press, 1984); Steven Rosswurm, *Arms, Country and Class: The Philadelphia Militia and the "Lower Sort" During the American Revolution, 1775–1783* (New Brunswick, N.J.: Rutgers University Press, 1987); see also Ronald Hoffman and Peter J. Albert, eds., *Arms and Independence: The Military Character of the American Revolution* (Charlottesville: University Press of Virginia, 1984).

4. Mary P. Ryan, *Cradle of the Middle Class: The Family in Oneida County, New York, 1790–1865* (New York: Cambridge University Press, 1981); Sean Wilentz, *Chants Democratic: New York City and the Rise of the American Working Class, 1788–1850* (New York: Oxford University Press, 1984); Paul A. Gilje, *The Road to Mobocracy: Popular Disorder in New York City, 1763–1894* (Chapel Hill: University of North Carolina Press, 1987).

5. Daniel Calhoun, *The Intelligence of a People* (Princeton: Princeton University Press, 1973), p. xii.

Preface

Ever since its French counterpart provided a first basis for comparison, students of the American Revolution have remarked on the ease and the smoothness with which their subject accomplished itself. Not for Americans the years, even decades of disorder; not for them the succession of constitutions and provisional governments, the Bonapartes of the Right and the Left, the terror and counterterror that have plagued others seeking to emerge from revolution. On the contrary, accounts both old and new tell us that crowds were well-disciplined and single-minded, that effective state governments went into operation at the very moment of independence, and that when these proved inadequate a suitable remedy was found in the Constitution. "Americans," "radicals," "revolutionaries," "Whigs," and "colonists" formed a single cohesive group. The American Revolution, it seems, had very little in common with other events to which we apply the term *revolution*. American uniqueness begins with the birth of the republic.

But throughout the sources there is evidence that cannot be explained within such a framework, evidence that there took place a real revolution, lost to most historians, and certainly to general consciousness. Take a series of cases in New York, the place whose experience over the decades 1760–90 is the subject of this study. In May 1766 a crowd led by Sons of Liberty sacked the theater in New York City. They tore down the building and carried the pieces to the common for burning, shouting "Liberty!" as they went. Early in 1774 another crowd staged exactly the same parade with the casks from which they had just dumped tea into New York Harbor. In the autumn of 1777 and the winter of 1777/78 the state legislature carried on a long debate over whether it should recognize the extralegal power still being exercised by revolutionary committees. Meanwhile one of those committees, in Albany County, resolved that despite the state constitution, it would not disband, and women in Ulster County seized goods from country stores, paying for them at a price that they, and not the storekeeper, thought just. In 1779, after popular committees and crowds had reappeared all over the state, New York's legislature made a dramatic turnabout in its policies on royalism, taxation, and the money supply. Six years later, in the winter of 1784/85, that legislature found its members splitting the same way on vote after vote, almost without regard to the issue at stake.

By itself each of these pieces of evidence is ambiguous. Yet none of them can be explained in terms of a paradigm that stresses agreement and continuity. Taken together they reinforce a tendency, present in each of them and in many other sources, that requires us to raise again the question of the Revolution's internal dimensions. Crowds, committees, and partisanship all played a part in the events of the independence period. How were they related? What sparked the popular energy that loosed itself in the streets and the fields and what became of it? Why did committees of safety appear, flourish, and disappear? Why were people who had agreed on independence in 1776 dividing bitterly on partisan issues in 1786? How different was New York at the end of the Revolution, in 1790, from what it had been on its eve, in 1760?

None of these questions applies only to New York. On the contrary, in recent historiography each of them has been raised in other contexts. Dirk Hoerder has argued that crowds that were both fully of the eighteenth century and fully revolutionary appeared in Massachusetts.[1] From a different perspective, Pauline Maier has studied the relationship between those crowds and their "leaders" and, more recently, has probed those leaders' lives for the connections that bound them to "the people."[2] Gary B. Nash has traced the domestic reasons why the three great colonial cities formed the Revolution's crucible.[3] Richard Alan Ryerson has examined the development of the radical committees of Philadelphia and has explored the complexities of the way those committees took and transformed power.[4] Eric Foner's study of Tom Paine places its subject in relation to the crowds, the mechanics, and the angry men of Philadelphia. It shows how Paine's vivid prose spoke to and for people whom the Revolution had brought into the public arena.[5] Ronald Hoffman's book on Maryland demonstrates that for that state's new government to consolidate its power required far more than simply proclaiming the state's constitution.[6] Stephen Patterson has considered partisanship in Massachusetts after independence, and Jackson Turner Main has done the same for all the states.[7] Gordon Wood's book on the creation of the republic demonstrates that between 1776 and 1787 Americans used a shared language and conceptual framework to argue out very real differences.[8] Taken together with many of the anthologies that the bicentennial decade produced,[9] these studies command that a student of the Revolution confront what was revolutionary about it. They show, if I may be pardoned, that this revolution was no tea party.

But no single book as yet has brought crowds, committees, radical ideas, and partisanship together in one account. Virtually no study has treated the decades from 1760 to 1790 as a whole, as a time in which men and women raised a set of fundamental political and social problems, developed their complexities, and ultimately resolved them. No historian has expressly drawn the connections between the agonized destruction of British colonialism and the equally difficult erection and stabilization of American republicanism in its place. To do those things is my goal in *A People in Revolution*. The book is a monograph, not a synthesis. Its concern is with one state, not with the whole of the United States. But I have tried in it to crystallize and bring together insights that I have taken from the research of other students on other places, as well as from my own encounter with the primary sources. I would not expect a study on a comparable scale of any other state to reveal precisely the configuration and the processes that I have found in New York. But I would be very surprised if each of the questions that I raise here did not also prove applicable to most other places.

My central organizing concept is political society. The term is loose; though used frequently enough, it does not even have an entry in the *International Encyclopedia of the Social Sciences*. I employ it as a two-word catch phrase to suggest the study's principal concerns. The first of these is to establish the locations and the uses of political power during a time of upheaval and transformation. The second is to explore the changes that took place during that time in the relationships between power wielders and people affected by power.

My large argument is that during the last years of the old order power wielders found themselves profoundly out of harmony with the needs of the society that they claimed a mandate to govern. This led to a situation in which both society and politics were highly unstable. That instability brought the collapse of existing political relationships and of many existing social ones during the independence crisis. New Yorkers who chose independence then created in place of the old order not only new institutions but a new way of doing things within those institutions. Both the new institutions and the new practices were free of most of the contradictions of the past. The result of this "revolutionary redefinition of New York" was a situation in which society was able to embark on a long period of dynamic development and in which politics became something qualitatively different from what New Yorkers had been used to. Taken together, these changes amounted to a democratic revolution with a deep, though complicated, social content.

The book is informed from several different perspectives. My debt to the work of such European historians as E. P. Thompson, Albert Soboul, George Rudé, Christopher Hill, and Eric Hobsbawm will be apparent immediately. Without their discussions of crowds and of class relations in preindustrial Western society my own analysis would have been impossible. I owe a great deal also to thinkers who have dealt more abstractly with the meaning and process of revolution. Those figures include Marx and Lenin, but they also include such scholars as Samuel P. Huntington, Ted Robert Gurr, Harry Eckstein, and J. P. Nettl. The combination is curious, to put it mildly, but it is not simply idiosyncratic. I explain my reasons for using it in part II. For the moment, it is enough to say that all of them have helped sensitize me to the problem of what happens to power during a revolution and that I have invoked their ideas because they have helped me to make sense of evidence that otherwise would have gone unexplained.

The third influence that has shaped my thinking can be found among students of the Russian Revolution. To press a comparison between the American and the Russian events too hard would be ridiculous, but each revolution did lead to a swift consolidation of new power, at least by comparison with what happened in France or China or Latin America. Moreover, I found that study of the popular committees of the late 1770s made much more sense against the background of the work of Trotsky and of Oskar Anweiler on the soviets, the popular councils of 1905–21.[10] I do not think that my use of the Russian comparison is outrageous. I mean it as a device to throw into bold relief the fact that a revolution did take place in America. Perhaps I can sum up my intent by borrowing the question put by another recent student of New York history: "What if it should be true that all these threads do hang together?"[11]

The study is divided into three parts. In the first three chapters I consider the old order in New York, seeking to find the background reasons for the crisis of legitimacy that arose at independence. I find those reasons in the problems posed by social and economic development, in the crowd actions of the late 1760s and the early 1770s, and in the contradictions of the colonial political system. Part II explores the crisis to which these things led. It asks what separated New Yorkers who made different political decisions between 1774 and 1777. It shows how existing relationships of power and obligation collapsed during those same years. It shows that establishing a workable order in their place was a slow and complicated process that required both fundamental change and a subtle combination of the carrot and the stick. This was not a question of "restoring order"; a well-disciplined army might have done that. Rather it meant the incorporation into the new institutions of the popular participation that had destroyed the old ways. But it also meant the end of the coalition for independence that had formed in 1774 and 1775 and had shaped the new state's institutions.

Part III asks what happened to that coalition and to the popular energy that had been embodied in the crowds and the committees of the 1760s and 1770s. It finds the answer in legislative and electoral politics, as coalition gave way to partisanship. It traces the making of a partisan culture in the 1780s, showing how republican politicians learned to recognize their friends and their enemies and to act accordingly. It shows the loss of power by the conservative republicans, who had had so central a part in the events of the mid-1770s. It describes their replacement at the center of events by new men whose political practice and ideas had been shaped in the popular revolutionary movement, and it shows how those men formed themselves into a party. It also demonstrates that in their relationships with their constituents these politicians continued the participatory spirit of the late 1770s. Finally, it looks at the emergence of a conservative party bent on unseating the radicals and on undoing much of what they had done. Though those conservatives were happy enough with both independence and republicanism, they were most unhappy with the men who had gained power, with what power had enabled them to do, and with the participatory politics within which they operated. The Constitution, to which their work led, thus both affirmed and rejected the Revolution, for the movement to create it sprang from disagreement and struggle over what the Revolution itself had been about. Neither side in that final debate of the era could claim that the Revolution was wholly its own, for the members of each had taken part in the events that had freed and transformed America. But one side rejected precisely what was most revolutionary about those events, precisely what identifies the American Revolution with those of other peoples. The measure of the conservatives' triumph is the extent to which we have forgotten those revolutionary qualities, and our forgetting has helped to legitimate the hostility that our government has often shown to revolutions elsewhere. The excitement and the adventure in writing this book has lain in the rediscovery of those things.

Acknowledgments

If nothing else, this project has taught me how social an enterprise scholarship is. The interpretation of New York's revolution that this book offers may be my own, but if I develop it with any sophistication and express it with any grace, the credit belongs to the many people who have helped, stimulated, and befriended me. Some of them, at least, are people with whose own arguments I would quarrel rather than agree.

These are my principal debts. James Morton Smith supervised the doctoral thesis from which the book has grown and taught me that to recapture times past requires expending an enormous amount of time present. Robert Jay Christen introduced me to the study of early America. Joel Silbey helped me get through the thickets of quantitative method, asked endless tough questions, and read the whole project at various stages. Alfred F. Young encouraged me to develop my interest in how ordinary Americans made their revolution, and both he and Richard Alan Ryerson took the time and the care to give me sympathetic but very demanding readings of drafts. Jack P. Greene encouraged my conscious use of theory. Pauline Maier read the final version. Meg Beresford and Susan Deans both read drafts through. Henry Tom and Joanne Allen were most patient and thorough editors.

Chapter drafts and parts of the argument were criticized (often) and praised (sometimes) by Oskar Anweiler, Jeanne Chase, Mary Hedge, Dirk Hoerder, Michael Kammen, Barbara Karsky, Samuel T. McSeveney, Mary Beth Norton, J. R. Ravetz, and Luke Trainor. Conference papers in which I developed my ideas were the subjects of commentaries by Patricia U. Bonomi, Ted Robert Gurr, Ronald Hoffman, Mary Jo Klein, Bernard Mason, George Rudé, Richard Alan Ryerson, and Gordon S. Wood. The members of splendid symposia at Cambridge, Massachusetts (1975), Cologne (1976), and Washington, D.C. (1979), gave me concentrated attention and stimulating criticism. Thanks to Duncan Macleod, Jackson Turner Main, John M. Murrin, Carl Prince, and Joel Silbey, I had chances to discuss my ideas informally with sophisticated audiences. C. Edmund Alford showed me material that, in a small way, made my story that of my own roots. Without encouragement at a critical time from the late Hannah Arendt I might never have seen the project through at all.

I typed it myself, but my computing would have been infinitely more time-consuming (in all senses) without the patient professional advice of Keith Halstead and Rachel Countryman, both programmers at the University of Warwick. Rachel endured and shared much else besides my ability to make every possible computing error during the decade and more that she, this book, and I lived together. And finally, thanks to my son Sam, for everything.

Part I

The Waning of an Old Order, 1760–1775

The changes that Britain began to impose on the American colonies after 1763 affected well-developed places, not empty wilderness. Each province had its own ways of doing things and its own set of problems. It was in relation to what they had learned from those ways and those problems that Americans framed their responses to the imperial challenge. The lives that some had led told them there was no problem. Such people either became royalists or entered the Revolution only when the weight of evidence had overwhelmed them. The lives of others had sensitized rather than deadened them to political questions. These people blended their response to the imperial issue with their concern about many other things. These were the ones whose energy and anger changed that response from a debate to a movement. Still others were so concerned about their own difficulties that the imperial issue passed them by until the independence crisis. That does not mean they were irrelevant to the Revolution. On the contrary, their concern with domestic issues had a major part in causing the crisis to strike at the whole system of colonial life and not simply at the tie to Britain.

The pains of New York's eighteenth-century development were felt differently by different people, but in 1765 they were strong enough to cause the province to pass into a decade of general discontent. People's anger expressed itself in many types of crowd action. There were crowds of mixed social composition whose concern was primarily with the imperial issue. There were lower-class urban crowds that had domestic problems in mind. There were other crowds of lower-class city people who were learning to think independently about what the tie to Britain meant in their lives. In the countryside men rioted in protest against a set of economic, social, and political relations with which they could make no quarter. In doing so, they generated a staying power and self-organization that would contribute weightily to the way that New York transformed itself between 1774 and 1780.

The third element in the waning of the old order was the internal weakening of its government. The provincial political structure began to weaken in the mid-1760s, and by the time of the coercive acts it was in serious trouble. Its problems came from its own internal contradictions and corruption, which made it less and less able to wield effective power over its subjects. As its power weakened, the government itself became the subject of ridicule and criticism that questioned not only the propriety of its actions but the rightfulness of power's remaining any longer with the men and the institutions that held it.

The net effect of all three factors—social development, popular militance, and political decay—was to put New Yorkers in a situation of readiness for a thoroughgoing revolution by 1773 or 1774. That revolution would not have broken out without the renewal then of the British issue, but the way in which New Yorkers responded to that renewal was conditioned by much else besides tea, the Intolerable Acts, and the redcoats at Lexington.

Chapter 1

The Pains of Development

I

In October 1770 Hugh Gaine's newspaper *The New York Gazette and the Weekly Mercury* carried an advertisement inviting readers to buy copies of a large map of New York City. The map had been drawn by Bernard Ratzer, a British officer stationed in the city, and it had been printed in London.[1] It carried a florid dedication to Sir Henry Moore, the governor when the map was drawn, but it was in fact an extravagant tribute to the men who controlled the prosperous city that New York had become. William Smith, Jr., the historian of the province, had commented thirteen years earlier that New York was perfectly sited for commercial success,[2] and anyone who saw Ratzer's map would think Smith's judgment borne out. It was a huge document, measuring 90 by 120 centimeters, lavishly decorated with a gold border. Hand-coloring picked out fields, orchards, woodlands, water, meadows, and built-up areas. It showed many particular buildings. The motif where the dedication was printed was full of symbols of the province's prosperity, symbols that now form the city's seal: a gentleman talking to an Indian, the beaver over whose skin the two were bargaining, the sails of a windmill, and hogsheads and bales of goods ready for shipment. At the bottom of the map a panoramic view showed the city as seen from Governor's Island, with more gentlemen conversing in the foreground, no fewer than sixteen vessels in sight, and the spires of seven churches dominating a skyline where much taller towers, raised to the honor of a different god, would later rise.

Map 1. Ratzer Map of New York City, 1770

Ratzer completed his picture of prosperity by showing in precise detail the country estates that ranged north of the city, some fronting on one of the rivers, some at the end of long, tree-lined avenues that branched off the Bowery. He drew the trees that lined those avenues individually, casting their shadows to show that it was early afternoon, and he pinpointed houses, outbuildings, gardens, and orchards. Their owners were men like Oliver DeLancey, Andrew Elliott, and John Morin Scott, whose estates he identified by name. The first was a great merchant who had built his share of a greater family fortune during the Seven Years' War and who sat on the provincial council. The second, the brother of an English baronet, had used his family's connections to climb from the proprietorship of a small store in Philadelphia to the heights of imperial placemanship. The third was a lawyer and a pamphleteer with burning ambitions to be a popular politician.[3]

Ratzer reinforced his picture of the city's vibrant commercial life by showing enough of Long Island to illustrate some of the differences between it and Manhattan. Western Long Island was well settled, scarcely an acre in Kings and Queens counties lying waste,[4] but its development was almost wholly agricultural. There were no real centers of population; the village of Brooklands had a mere thirteen houses, and the settlement of Bedford was about the same size. There was a slightly larger settlement at the Brooklyn end of the East River ferry, where John Rapalje was starting to turn his fertile farmland into townscape,[5] but in 1770 the process was just beginning. A mere three holdings in Kings were singled out by their owner's name; one belonged to Rapalje, the other two to members of the Livingston family.

By contrast, New York City appeared on the map as a mass of masonry stretching more than a mile northwards from the Battery and, at its widest, running east and west for nearly the same distance. The city was expanding towards the northeast, with a grid pattern of streets platted for another three-quarters of a mile beyond the solidly built-up area and construction going forward on them. The legend on the map identified thirty-seven places where men, and sometimes women, might meet. These included seventeen churches, a synagogue, five markets, King's College, a theater, a prison, a poorhouse, Fort George, City Hall, and the Merchants' Exchange. The map itself showed still more: pleasure gardens at Ranelagh and Vauxhall; the large common, usually called the Fields; places of work, such as the tanyards and shipyards and docks on the East River; and geographical points, such as Golden Hill, which was named not for the metal but for the shower of grain from passing wagons that colored its streets yellow. The merchants, lawyers, and placemen who were in a position to buy Ratzer's map could look at it and feel proud of what they and their fathers had built.

Other, harder sources confirm that their New York had become a major trading city. In the late 1710s and early 1720s its officially recorded trade with Britain had been small, but by the 1760s population growth, internal development, and war had changed the picture. Between 1760 and 1762 the port annually received an average of 176 ships, totaling some 10,000 tons of burden from British and foreign ports. It freighted annually an average of 278 ships, totaling nearly 15,000 tons, many of which it had built itself. In 1768 and 1769 the port authorities entered 462 vessels from all ports, displacing nearly 22,000 tons. They cleared 480 vessels, totaling 23,573 tons. In monetary terms the face value of trade had multiplied many times. In 1720 New York had legally imported British goods worth £37,397, but in 1764 it brought in British goods worth £515,416. That was higher than the value of the imports of Pennsylvania, Virginia, or all the New England provinces together.[6]

At the end of the decade, in 1769, the British authorities assembled in minute detail the trading records of their colonies. Although the year was one of depression, these records show precisely how differentiated and far-flung the legitimate, unsmuggled trade of New York had become. In that year the province exported goods worth £189,277 to the world and legally imported goods worth £90,632 from southern Europe and the West Indies; the value of imports from the British Isles was not recorded. The export trade varied wildly; New Yorkers shipped thirty-four different commodities to Britain, thirty-five to the West Indies, nineteen to southern Europe, and fifteen to Ireland. Some were in ridiculously small quantities, such as the dozen hens that went to the West Indies, the forty-two hides sent to Britain, or the one tun and fifty-seven gallons of Azores wines that went to Ireland. Some of these goods, such as the Azores wines, mahogany, or cotton, were reexports. Some of the items marked a tiny counterbalance against a huge import trade; New York received 117,995 gallons of West Indies rum, but it returned to the islands 1,578 gallons of the product of its own distilleries.

But the figures also demonstrate that some goods were exported in huge quantities. Ireland received 157,893 bushels of flaxseed and 356,970 barrel staves. The West Indies took hundreds of thousands of board feet of timber, nearly a million staves, and some 800,000 shingles. Close to fifteen hundred tons of pig iron went to Britain. The province exported a total of 111,830 bushels of grain and 4,756 tons of bread and flour to all customers. And as a reminder of the significance of that beaver on its seal, it shipped 183 packs of fur to Britain.[7]

Whatever else they may show, these official trade statistics suggest where the money that built the estates, institutions, and streets shown on Ratzer's map came from. Complexity and differentiation were the essence of the late provincial economy, just as they were the pride of the men who ran it. The pot and pearl ashes, the staves, the shingles, and the lumber came from forests that were being turned into farmland, and many of the staves had been hewn by Hudson Valley slaves. The grain and bread were likewise up-province products, as was most of the iron. The 145 bushels and 34,417 ropes of onions that were sent to the West Indies came from the market gardens of Kings, Queens, and Richmond counties and perhaps from the small plots that the ladies of Albany made it their business carefully to tend.[8] But New York City was the port for all of them, and its shipyards, tanyards, distilleries, mills, and foundries were themselves major sources of value.

By the 1760s the city's economy was complex internally as well as in its external relations. Merchants, lawyers, and heirs with money to invest were putting it into city property, sometimes by the thousands of pounds. Oliver DeLancey, who administered the New York holdings of his sister, Lady Susannah Warren, had control for two and a half decades of a fund that at its largest stood at £14,387 New York currency. During his trusteeship he put his sister's money out at interest to fellow merchants, to tenants on the Warren lands in the north, and to himself. Some of the loans were secured by personal bonds, and others by mortgages, and they varied between £10 and £1,285. The chances were good that a large borrower would be favored with a low rate of interest; thus in 1743 Lady Susannah's husband, Admiral Sir Peter Warren, loaned £1,200 to Nicholas Bayard at 6 percent instead of the usual 7 percent. In 1759 DeLancey granted a similar boon to himself.[9] John Wetherhead, a merchant and political figure, had at the time of independence £7,592 in city real estate, £5,591 more in bonds, and £3,434 in book debts. William Axtell, a member of the provincial council, had nearly half of his fortune of £45,707 currency invested in the city, with £2,889 in real property and £18,781 in book debts.[10] In the absence of banks, the credit advanced by such men was a major factor in guiding the city's development. Their ability to extend it depended on their success in an economy compounded of roughly equal measures of confidence in the imperial trading system and land speculation under the royal governor's favor. Was it mere happenstance that each of these men became a royalist in 1776? Not all of the elite did so, of course. What separated protoroyalists, these men for example, from men such as the merchants James Beekman and Isaac Roosevelt or the rising lawyers John Jay, James Duane, and Robert R. Livingston, who chose independence?

By the early 1770s perhaps 20,000 people lived within New York City; 21,863 were counted in the census of 1771. In 1766 they lived in 3,223 houses.[11] Even without knowing the city, someone looking carefully at Ratzer's map might have guessed that not all of those houses were equal. He would have seen that in Montgomerie Ward, hard by the East River, there were narrow little streets like Race Street, Skinner Street, Batavia Lane, Jacob Street, and Gold Street. Some of these surrounded a large tannery, and others lay near the shipyards. Here were the houses of the men who worked in those places. In the same neighborhood, perhaps on Water Street, which had its frontage on the river, there were boardinghouses and taverns that catered to the merchant sailors who manned the ships and the longshoremen who loaded and unloaded them. These little streets were close to the Moravian and Anabaptist meeting houses and to the new Lutheran church. An observer might have concluded that at least some of the people who dwelt there were enthusiastic dissenters and perhaps of German rather than British descent. Among those Germans was the baker Frederick Brautigan, who had come to America in 1756.[12] Brautigan, like DeLancey or Wetherhead, became a royalist, but his choice stands in contrast to that of most of the mechanic, or artisan, class, of which he had been part.

The closeness of St. George's Chapel to the meaner streets shows that the Anglican Church was reaching out to the working class, but those streets lay at some distance from City Hall, the Merchants' Exchange, Trinity Church, King's College, and Fort George. These were the places where the elite gathered to carry on political life and business, to worship, and to learn. The distance was not so great from the houses of the humble to John Street, where there stood a theater, symbolic of the upper class's growing sophistication. The prison and the poorhouse, which faced the Fields, were also close. So was the upper barracks, one of the two places in the city where British troops were housed. The Ranelagh gardens, Vauxhall, the theater, and the Fields joined Fort George and the upper barracks as focal points for crowd action after 1764. That crowds gathered where the governor and the redcoats lived is understandable, for the Revolution was about independence. But why did ordinary people show open hostility also to the symbols of the good fortune of the better sort? Moreover, what is the relationship between that class hostility and the class cooperation necessary to win independence?

An observer might have been pardoned for thinking that the people of Montgomerie Ward, where the small streets lay, were not rich and that they had less weight in the scheme of things than the owners of the country estates to the north. He could not have guessed that in 1772 there were 425 men, women, and children in the poorhouse, all of them required to wear the letters *NY* in red on their clothing. Nor could he have guessed that the rate of serious crime had been rising since 1750 and that the city's courts displayed little ability to do anything about it.[13] But his general surmisings, made from a careful look at a map designed as a tribute to New York's rich, would have been correct. Lavish townhouses, country mansions, imposing public buildings, and invisible patterns of investment all bore witness to the Ratzer Map's silent insistence that New York City was a rich place.

But development had not brought the same benefits to all.

On the contrary, New York City, like Philadelphia and Boston, had witnessed a widening of the gap between rich and poor since the turn of the eighteenth century. Everywhere poor relief, for instance, had risen markedly, in both absolute and relative terms. In the second decade of the century Boston had spent on its poor an annual average of £18 per thousand people, and New York had spent an average of £32 per thousand. In the 1750s, when Boston's annual spending had risen to an average of £77 per thousand, New York spent an average of only £39 per thousand. In the following decade, however, New York's spending climbed to £92 per thousand, and from 1771 to 1775 it spent annually £123 per thousand on its poor. This was still less than Boston's £158 or Philadelphia's £136, but such a drastic jump from the minuscule 1750s figure is clear evidence of widespread poverty, evidence that the city was stratified as well as differentiated.[14]

Perhaps this increase in spending betokened a new humanitarian attitude towards poverty as much as it did more poverty itself. But in any case, by 1773 there were between six hundred and eight hundred "lower class New Yorkers" who "were too poor to survive without public assistance," whether they received that assistance as inmates of the poorhouse or on out-relief. The rate of dire poverty, which had stood at nine per thousand in the late 1740s, had climbed fourfold, to thirty-six per thousand, and this does not even speak to the problem of how many people lived their life on the edge of poverty, cutting every possible cost and constantly dreading the disaster that would push them over.[15]

Nor does it speak to the problem of the urban middle levels, whose people were to be very visible in the politics of revolutionary New York but are much harder to find in its social records. Even defining them is not easy. One might describe them in terms of their property, locating them among the four-fifths of New Yorkers who were in neither the top nor the bottom decile of property holders. In 1730 that group held just half of the city's wealth, but by the early 1770s its share had without doubt dropped precipitously. In Boston the equivalent group's holdings had fallen from 51.1 percent of property in 1687 to 36.5 percent in 1771, and in Philadelphia, from 51.8 percent in 1693 to only 26.6 percent in 1774. Or they might be defined in terms of function and prestige; either way, the broad category "middle group" conceals enormous variety. "Artisans," or "mechanics," which is to say men who worked with their hands, might include everyone from an out-of-work journeyman to a prosperous silversmith like Abraham Brasher or a baker like Abraham P. Lott. Lott was well enough off in 1770 to join various politicians and merchants in a syndicate that was buying a permanent home for the Sons of Liberty. If "artisans" seems too narrow a term and one uses instead the contemporary phrase "middling sort," one finds it extending upwards to include small merchants like Isaac Sears and Jacobus Van Zandt and downwards to include people clinging precariously to respectability.[16]

Whatever their differences, these people had much in common. Mechanics and laborers wore long trousers, not the knee breeches that signified gentility. Had New Yorkers spoken French rather than English, we might now know these men as sans-culottes, the name for the equivalent group in eighteenth-century Paris. People outside the ranks of the elite could not expect to be accorded the titles of respect—Esquire, Mister, Gentleman—that went with membership in it. Even small merchants such as Isaac Sears and

Alexander McDougall were addressed as "Captain," in honor of their sailing days, rather than with the more honorific "Mister."[17]

Precisely where the boundaries between classes—defined by occupation, sorts; defined by property and status, and political loyalties; defined in 1776 by painful choice—intersected is hard to establish. A sizable majority of the pre-Revolution chamber of commerce were rich men who chose royalism and whose trade crossed the Atlantic. But among the members were some Sons of Liberty, many of whom traded up and down the Atlantic seaboard and to the West Indies. The fortunes of such men did not depend on the Anglo-American stability of law and credit that the empire provided. The essentially American quality of their economic interests was one link between them and the mechanics, for New York's artisans were likewise more concerned about a healthy domestic economy than about imperial trade. The artisans generated such organizations as the Society of House Carpenters and the Body of Mechanics partly for the sake of advancing that concern.[18]

This "middling sort" did not form a class, but their common concern with American rather than with transatlantic affairs provided one basis for coalition among them. That basis was strengthened after 1763, when depression settled on New York's economy. The depression stemmed from the end of the wartime boom, in which New Yorkers of all sorts had waxed from the business of supplying British troops and ships; indeed, the greatest merchant fortunes, like Oliver DeLancey's, stemmed directly from that boom. The depression meant a direct loss to West Indian traders like James Beekman, the value of whose imports dropped from an annual average of £5,116 before 1764 to one of £2,045 after it. It meant similar problems for the street leader Isaac Sears. Beekman was a Dutch Calvinist of old New York descent, and Sears a Yankee Anglican from Massachusetts, but they joined in resigning from the chamber of commerce in 1772 and in working for resistance and then revolution.[19]

Their problems were akin to those of the city's artisans and laborers, for they too felt the effects of the depression. Men and women who worked with their hands were not cripples and incompetents, incapable of self-help. They were proud of what they produced and of how they lived, and they had reason to think that their lives had more merit than those of placemen, moneychangers, and landlords. But in 1764 and 1765 they also knew that there was much less market for their wares than there had been and that it was in the interest of the great transatlantic merchants to compete with them in that market by importing cheap British goods.

For all of these people social and economic questions might easily meld with political ones. An Alexander McDougall could attend the provincial assembly eagerly, but he had no reason to think he would ever cross from its visitors' gallery to its floor. An artisan faced with depression could blame it on the Stamp Act. He could demand that New York's port be opened in defiance of the act in the hope of stimulating exports and that New Yorkers themselves consume the products of local industry. A merchant seaman could focus the anger that sprang from his hateful lot on the customs men and the naval officers who personified British authority in his world. A laborer could grow irate when off-duty troops and naval sailors took scarce work from him. In the anger of such men, as chapter 2 will show, was the making of the city's revolutionary coalition.

The impression given by Ratzer's map, then, was not wholly accurate. New York City had matured into the capital of a prosperous, developing province, and members of the ruling class, whom that map celebrated, were in a position to enjoy that maturity. *Their* houses, *their* coaches, *their* ties of interest and family across the Atlantic, *their* writings, *their* churches, *their* theater, *their* cultural life, *their* college—all testified, as did the map itself, that New York had come of age. What in 1700 had been the dull focal point of a conquered province was now a lively city. Local boosters, like William Smith, anxiously kept saying so, and visiting Europeans and New Englanders freely admitted that it was true.[20] But as Michael Kammen has stressed, prosperity had been bought at the price of a serious problem of community. The imperial problems that the British inflicted on the city after 1763 struck a place whose people had reason for quarreling among themselves. Their quarrels became intimately bound up with the way that they responded to what the British did.

II

Nine years after Ratzer's map was published, another geographer dedicated another lavishly colored map of New York to another governor (see map 2). By 1779 New York had been rent by civil and imperial warfare, but the only hint of that on Claude Joseph Sauthier's map is the fact that the governor to whom it was inscribed had become Major General William Tryon instead of simply Mr. Tryon, as he had been when he first took up his office in 1772. Sauthier's map shows the whole province, and it claims to identify all the towns, manors, patents, and counties into which it was divided. But the cartographer's real concern was to show the private grants of land in the valleys of the Hudson and the Mohawk and in the northeastern corner, on both sides of Lakes George and Champlain. Sauthier provided little detail about Long Island, long settled and untroubled by land disputes, but for the strife-torn northern areas he gave very precise information.[21]

Like Ratzer's map of the city, Sauthier's map of the province is thus a significant social document. Carefully read, it offers clues about both the way New York's land had been divided and the way landowners were developing their property. It shows the great estates of the east bank of the Hudson, but it also shows the smaller tracts that covered Orange and Ulster

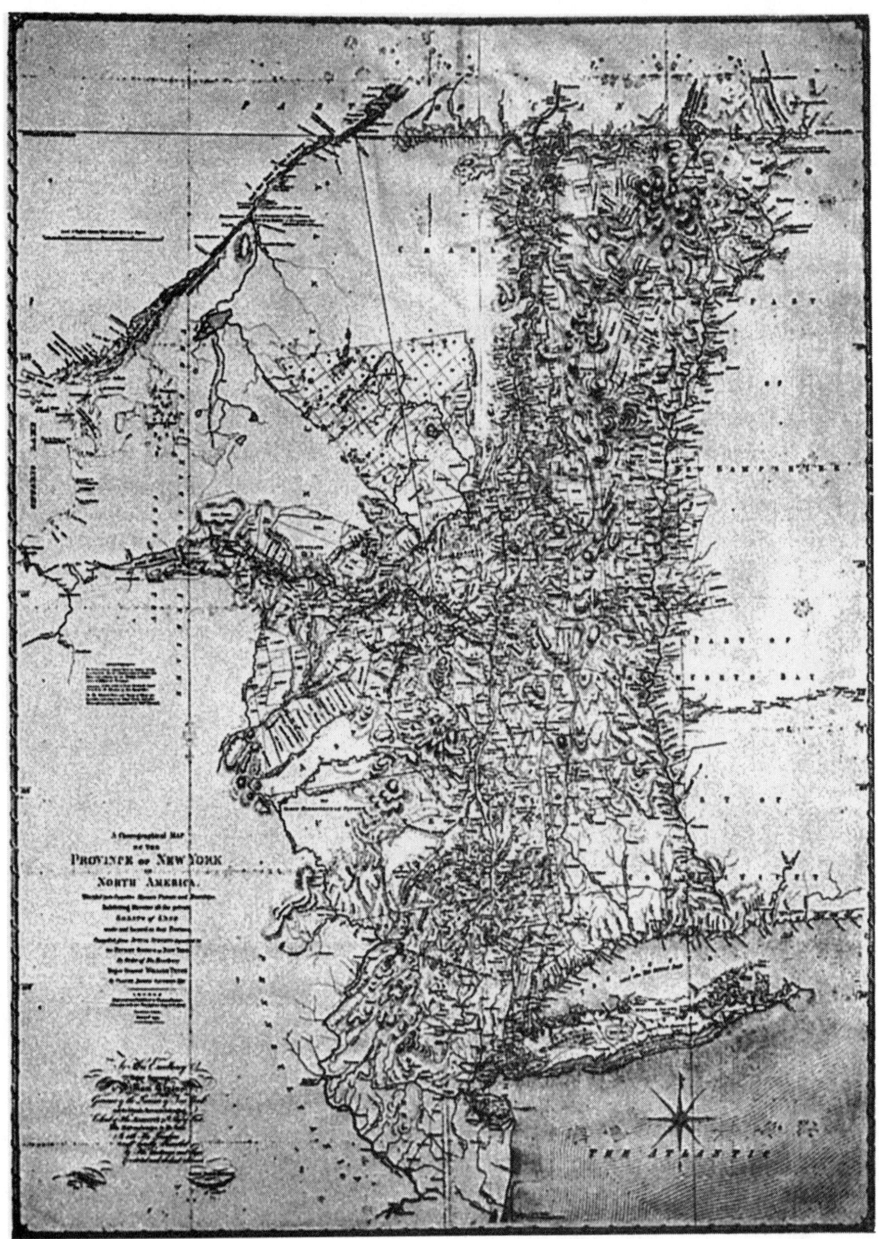

Map 2. Sauthier Map of New York, 1779

counties, across the river. It outlines some huge holdings on the western frontier. Some of those, like Sir William Johnson's Kingsborough and Kingsland or James Duane's Duanesburgh, bore names reminiscent of the Hudson Valley estates, but most were identified simply by their owner's last name, suggesting that they were only speculations.

The map showed more great holdings north of Albany, like Philip Skene's Skenesborough and Philip Schuyler's Saratoga, and it also showed many smaller divisions, often held by men with military titles. In that region there were townships, like New Perth and Argyle, that had been established under New York authority, but the map showed many more with their name underscored to indicate that they had been founded by New Hampshire. That province had claimed the Green Mountains until only a few years before the map was drawn. These New England towns and the New York grants overlapped, but a straight line extending from the northwest corner of Massachusetts to Lake Champlain would have roughly separated them. New York acknowledged no such line, claiming that above Massachusetts the Connecticut River was its proper eastern boundary.

Settled estates, speculative tracts, communal villages, and broad stretches full of individualistic yeomen were all part of the peopling of New York, and historians have long debated their significance. Reechoing an indictment that originated with Cadwallader Colden, some have seen among the great landlords an American feudal aristocracy, and among their tenants an oppressed class of peasants.[22] But taking their cue from St. John de Crevecoeur and from what the landlords said of themselves, others have stressed the legal and physical difficulties faced by land developers and have seen tenancy as a mild, halfway status on the road to a freehold farm.[23] Very few historians have tried to look at New York land practices in systemic, developmental terms and to balance evidence from one section against evidence from another. But John Murrin and Rowland Berthoff have made a suggestive start in that direction with their proposition that eighteenth-century America experienced a "feudal revival" as increasing population and growing opportunities for wealth made it worthwhile to reinvigorate legal privileges granted in the seventeenth century that were relics of medieval practice.[24]

Not more than a tiny number of New York's great grants carried formal, legally defined feudal privileges, and of these only Philipse Manor and Cortlandt Manor, in Westchester, and Rensselaerwyck and Livingston, in Albany, were important units by the 1760s. All of these places, save possibly Philipsburgh, were under stress by that time. The hostility of the crown to the great tracts of New York, whether they were real manors or merely patents without feudal overtones, had been known since the turn of the eighteenth century. Hardly any of them enjoyed firm, certain borders either with other tracts or with the New England provinces. Tenants who thought the king was on their side and who knew that the landlord's claim was fraudulent had good reason to dismiss landlord pretensions out of hand.[25] But to treat the few grants that had both feudal privileges and great size as anachronistic exceptions misses the point. The historical problem of the manors lies in the extent to which they provided a social model that after 1750 was becoming more rather than less salient, more rather than less desired by the owners of the many other great estates that were not technically manorial.

There is evidence that that was very much the case. Sir William Johnson, as a baronet of the United Kingdom, enjoyed an unmistakable symbol of aristocracy along with his great wealth and power in the Mohawk Valley. Yet in the winter of 1769/70 he sought to have his estate Kingsborough formally erected into a manor. Would he have done so had he thought the title empty? His venture failed, and he was told that the failure was because in Britain itself the king could not "now erect a Mannor since the abrogation of feudal tenours" and "if so a Governor can less do it." Sir William had more than just his personal prestige in mind when he sought the title. It fitted with his plan for developing the Mohawk Valley without disturbing Indian relations, by creating a consolidated, ordered community of tenants whose lives would focus on the amenities and institutions that he would provide for them. But though he had to settle for having his lands "erected into a Township with privileges of Market and Fairs," his last decades were very much those of the gentleman whose rank gave him dominion and imposed on him obligations. If he could not gain the legal right to hold a court leet and a court baron, which was one of the privileges that manorial status brought, he still knew that the judges and justices of the ordinary county court were his creatures and that they conducted their business in a courthouse that was his personal property.[26]

Nor, in Sir William's view, would Kingsborough be the only such estate. As a mark of favor, the crown itself granted Johnson another huge tract further west and exempted it from quitrents. He named it Kingsland, said that he would never alienate it, and began to develop it in the same way. After his death in 1774, his son, Sir John Johnson, and his nephew, Colonel Guy Johnson, fully intended to carry on his tradition. Sir John declared after the Revolution that "he had never sold or intended to sell" any land at either Kingsborough or Kingsland. If anything, they went further than Sir William in their claims to dominion. Like any intelligent Tory, Sir William had known when and how to take political advice, but neither of his heirs conceded the slightest legitimacy to undeferential demands from below. Guy Johnson summed up their attitude when he dismissed a revolutionary gathering as having "been called by an itinerant New England Leather Dresser and conducted by others if possible more contemptible." He and Sir John were above the "absurdities" of such men.[27]

The Johnsons' friend Philip Skene was attempting something similar at Skenesborough, his tract at the southern end of Lake Champlain. In 1772

Skene was maintaining a baronial household of forty-four persons and was seeking to have Skenesborough made the county town of Charlotte County, just as Johnstown was of Tryon. Like Sir William, Skene lived on the tract he was trying to develop, but, again like the baronet, he had transatlantic contacts and thought nothing of traveling to England to attend to his interests.[28]

To be a landlord one needed tenants. Skene had seventy-one in 1772, and the Johnsons had one hundred fifty on Kingsborough, as well as another fifty to sixty on Kingsland. These were frontier estates, but such numbers compared favorably with the tenant forces of the Hudson Valley. At the outbreak of the war Beverly Robinson had 173 on his share of the Philipse Highland patent, in southern Dutchess County. Roughly equal numbers paid rent to that tract's other owners, Roger Morris and Philip Philipse.[29] On Philipse Manor there were some 280 tenants.[30] A tenanted estate was thus a massive operation; the families of Philipse Manor could not have totaled less than eleven hundred people and probably numbered closer to fifteen hundred. The Johnson tenants' families totaled between eight hundred and a thousand.[31] There were of course many smaller landlords, like Captain William Houghton, who had four tenants on his land at Lake George. There were landholders like the New York City merchant Isaac Low, who was utterly uninterested in putting his lands under tenancy, seeing them strictly as a speculation. There were sizable tracts, like the Minisink patent, in Ulster County, whose owners' efforts to develop them foundered on bureaucratic snags.[32] But the dominant social model to which ambitious country gentlemen aspired was the one provided by the Philipses, the Livingstons, the Van Rensselaers, and the Johnsons.

The central question is, How did those great landlords and their tenants relate to one another? Their relationships were complicated, involving culture and politics as well as economics. They were varied, for not all landlords behaved in the same way. But most important, they changed and developed; between 1750 and 1790 one can find an ever-increasing tendency for landlord-tenant relations to be defined in terms of money.

After the war, two of those great landlords petitioned the British government for compensation for the loss of their estates, which the revolutionaries had confiscated. Both Frederick Philipse and Beverly Robinson provided minute detail about how their estates had been run, and their claims illustrate the range of possibilities open to a New York landholder. Less complete records for other tracts, including the Beekman patent in Dutchess, Philip Schuyler's Saratoga lands, and the Johnson preserves, bear out the picture of contrast and change that emerges from the Philipse and Robinson claims. They also show how a mild paternalism, which characterized Philipse, was giving way to a hard-nosed acquisitiveness, typified by Robinson.

Frederick Philipse held Philipsburgh as a life tenant rather than in freehold. His claim was thus for less than the total value of the estate, but even his annual income was considerable, averaging more than fifteen hundred pounds sterling. That, when added to his life interest in the manor, his book debts, his freehold property elsewhere, and lesser sources of money, made him a very rich man. Even without the freehold his claim came to £40,216 sterling, and one witness testified that with existing conditions the freehold would have been worth at least £100,000.

The British commissioners questioned Philipse and other witnesses closely about what tenants had paid and owed and what landlords could do to them. The rent of a Philipse tenant was not extortionate; it could vary from as little as £1.10 currency to as much as, in two cases, £150 and £200. But for most tenants a high rent was in the range of £15, and a normal rent about half that. Some of the tenants were in Philipse's debt; they accounted for 56 of the 114 entries on his debt roll. The principal owed by people on that roll varied between £6 and £275, and the interest due between £4.4 and £246. But the colonel was in no hurry to collect what was owed him; in some cases the principal had fallen due as early as 1763 and was never called in.

Philipse Manor was a settled, well-developed place on the eve of the Revolution. It had sawmills, three sets of gristmills, a demesne of three thousand acres, and "not an acre of land on the estate except the domain" that was not tenanted. The mills were lucrative; two of the gristmills were run by tenants, and it was these that fetched rents of £150 and £200 per annum. Such mills, the docks jutting into the Hudson, and the landlords' sloops, which carried the products of their estates to New York City, show that there was no necessary conflict between the interests of landlords and those of merchants. Rather, a great landlord was a trader in his own right, selling, besides grain, staves, timber, potash, and even iron. He took as full a part in the money economy as any member of the city's chamber of commerce.

Unlike many holdings, Philipsburgh had no boundary difficulties to make its territory uncertain and no conflicting Indian titles to lower its value. But it was not Colonel Philipse's to do with as he liked. Rather, it was pervaded by a hierarchical communitarianism that imposed restrictions on the landlord and gave significant benefits to the tenants.[33] The greatest of these was a customary rule that Philipse could not evict his tenants, save for nonpayment of rent. Evidence about the strict legal form of the tenants' position conflicts. Some witnesses said that they were tenants-at-will, and others that they had leases for three lives, or 99 years, or 999 years, or eternity. But it was agreed that the landlord "could not turn off a tenant because he did not like his face."[34] Moreover, Colonel Philipse's tenants had won the right to sell their tenure, and a number of expert observers commented that this was altering the whole legal structure of the manor. John Watts observed that "they have no such thing as a copyholder's state in America, but many farms on Mr. Philip's estate seem to be tending towards a copyhold." James DeLancey said that "he himself should have thought the tenants were something in the nature of copyhold tenants." John Tabor Kempe, former attorney general of the province, testified that his "own private opinion was that Mr. Philips's estate was not copyhold, but that it was verging very fast towards a copyhold and in process of time would have become so."[35]

Philipse further tied his own hands when he promised, after doubling rents in 1760, not to raise them again in his lifetime. How binding the promise was is an open question. One witness thought that despite "some agreement with the tenants," Philipse could "raise the rents when he pleased," and another commented that though Philipse could not arbitrarily evict his tenants, "he had at the same time the power of raising their rents which was tantamount to it." But Philipse himself acknowledged that he had made the promise, and he lived by both its letter and its spirit, despite a comment after the war that he "had it in agitation to have raised the rents," which "he should have doubled. . . with great ease." The long-overdue debts that tenants owed him tell us that he likewise took no advantage of his position as their creditor. Though one witness said that Philipse had gotten tenants "into his debt, and he would throw them immediately into jail and so get rid of them," another, who was perhaps better placed to know, had "never heard of his putting his tenants in prison."[36] In other words, Philipse was a paternalist.

There were ways to recoup some of paternalism's costs. One was to extort a third of the purchase price when a tenant sold his tenure, and a sixth of the price on subsequent sales of the same property. Like the guarantee against eviction, this was never put into writing; it was Philipse's customary right, just as security of tenure was the tenant's. This practice brought Philipse an average of five hundred pounds currency annually. But Philipse was restrained by entail from selling his land as its value grew, by his promise from raising the rents, by powerful custom from evicting unproductive tenants, and by the fullness of the manor from making speculative gains on unoccupied land. He knew how much this cost; one witness had no doubt that if Philipse "had been possessed of the fee simple," he could have done as he chose with the estate and its occupants. Then the estate "would have been worth £450,000 or £500,000 pounds, New York Currency." The landlord gained, however, by the restrictions under which he lived. Despite them his manor was "the most productive of rents of any" in America. Because of them he and his father "were always considered as very mild landlords." Their estate never suffered from tenant unrest, and an unusual proportion of Frederick Philipse's tenants followed him into active royalism. The connection between those facts and the paternalist way he had done things seems unmistakable.[37]

Beverly Robinson, Philipse's brother-in-law, ran his share of the Highland patent on wholly different principles. Robinson spent much of his time there, though some thought that this was so he could economize under a mountain of debt. Profit was the whole story of his relations with his tenants, as the rise in his income before independence shows. The tract was divided into three great lots, the first of which had seventeen tenants at independence, the second seventy-five, and the third fifty-four. In 1755 the first lot had brought a total rental of £26.15, the second £131.10, and the third £161, for a total of £319.5. By 1768 the income had more than doubled, to a total of £791.9. The rentals that Robinson expected in 1777 came to £1,257.4. That was fully 56 percent, allowing for the conversion from currency to sterling, of what Colonel Philipse received from rents, though it came from an estate on which the soil was poorer and which had only 53 percent of Philipsburgh's tenant force. In addition, between 1768 and 1777 Robinson realized £1,599.1 from the share that he required when tenants sold their rights.[38]

Though Robinson's tenant force grew somewhat over this period, his rent roll shows that most of the gains came from rent increases rather than from expansion of the estate. Some of these increases were small; Thomas Williamson's farm went for £1.10 in 1755 and for only £3 in 1777. In other cases the rent never rose; the farms of the widow Arkle and of Jacob Mandiville were let for the same amount in the last year of the rent roll as in the first. But by 1777 the rent on 119 of the tenancies had been raised at least once. The increases followed the rule of whatever the traffic would bear; they varied from as little as £1 to as much as from a total of £15 for three farms in separate hands to £100 for the same farms under a single tenant. In one part of the estate, a part that a witness called "the best square of 4 miles in [Dutchess] county," typical increases ran from £5 to £48.4, from £2 to £13, from £5 to £34, from £4 to £40, and from £2 to £20.[39]

Robinson himself stressed that profit was his goal. He was the witness who told the royalist claims commisioners who were hearing Colonel Philipse's case that even a landlord who lacked the power of eviction had "the power of raising their rents which was tantamount to it." Speaking to his own claim, he said that there was no doubt "that the Rents would (had no troubles happened) have increased in a greater proportion than they had hitherto done." Another witness said that the value at which Robinson's land was estimated reflected the probability of capital gains rather than increased productivity.[40]

Money relationships permeated the estate. Robinson was creditor to his tenants to the amount of £8,529, principal and interest, and he was not the only man to whom they were in debt. John Kane, who was both Robinson's tenant and his associate, acted on the estate as agent for monied men of New York City who made loans to the tenants. Most of Robinson's rents were collected in kind, but that was no favor to the tenants, as a list of persons "whose Rents by their Leases are Payable in Wheat" but who "for Temporary Indulgence" were allowed to pay in money shows. The total wheat due from them was 442 bushels per year, which was equivalent to £132.15. Their rents in money came to only £99.13. The other 126 tenants received no such indulgence. Unlike Philipse, Robinson could and did evict tenants arbitrarily. In 1766 such an eviction sparked off a tenant rising that spread from Westchester to Albany.[41]

These two estates can be distinguished from each other in many ways. One was wholly settled, the other still, if slowly, expanding. The location of one was so close to New York City's port facilities that men regarded it as the most valuable single holding of its kind in America. The other tract lay in the highlands of southern Dutchess, and though it had a river port at Peekskill, it was further from the main arteries of commerce. Both estates, however, were part of the Atlantic world, producing wheat and other commodities that would be sold in the West Indies and in Europe as well as in New York City. The central difference between them is the way in which local custom at Philipsburgh inhibited the landlord there from taking full, selfish advantage of his position in that world. Colonel Philipse was not the only paternalist landlord. Sir William Johnson acted in the same spirit at Kingsborough. In 1764, when tenants whom he was assisting got into difficulty, he threw their debtor bonds into his fire. The Johnson lands, like Philipsburgh, were untroubled by pre-Revolution tenant strife, and two decades after Sir William burned those bonds Guy Johnson could tell the British claims commissioners that the tenants had rarely absconded and had "in general complied with the conditions" of their tenure.[42]

But in general Robinson's mentality, not Philipse's, prevailed. The owners of Livingston Manor and Rensselaerwyck had always calculated for maximum gain, and they reaped their reward in the tenant rioting and guerrilla warfare that plagued them for a century after 1740. Despite Sir William's concern to create a stable social order in the Mohawk Valley, his heirs were unruffled when tenants absconded without paying their rents, because it was "an advantage to the owner—as the improvements generally paid the arrear of Rent and enabled the owner to let at an advanced rent." William Bayard, a city man who had extensive property in New Jersey and in Orange County, felt similarly. His tenants on the Kakiate and Chesecock patents in Orange could expect to have their rents doubled or tripled "according as it might happen" when their leases expired, and he turned his tenants out when he pleased. John Kane, a second-rank Dutchess landlord, had land on lease in the 1770s for three lives, of which two had passed; he was looking forward to raising the rent when the third expired. Even Sir William's development of the Kingsland estate was based after 1769 "on Rents increasing at the expiration of every ten years."[43]

The details brought forth so far come from royalist sources, but landlords who chose independence or who died before it behaved in much the same way. The leases that they granted between 1740 and 1800 show them requiring ever less of tenants in terms of behavior but ever more in terms of payment. Staughton Lynd comments that "a series of leases from 1742 to 1787 in the Gilbert Livingston Land Papers shows the transition towards the cash nexus,"[44] and the same thing can be seen in leases granted by the widow Catharina Pawling, in northern Dutchess, and by Philip Schuyler, at Saratoga.

"Mother Pawling's" leases of the 1750s can be taken as the starting point. They imposed significant restrictions and obligations on the tenants. Joseph Simson, who put his mark to a lease for 160 acres in 1750, committed himself to building a house with a dug, stone-walled cellar, to having all his grain ground at the landlady's mill, to obeying "all reasonable orders" in regard to fences and roads, and to planting fruit trees. He bound himself not to cut wood for charcoal or to peel bark for tanning, and the landlady was to have first refusal of the purchase of his crops. Other leases of the period followed much the same pattern.[45] The daughter of one Henry Beekman and the sister of another, the widow Pawling had had enough tutelage in the ways of landlordism to make her a formidable person of affairs, but the ethos within which she operated was as much concerned with governing the tenants' behavior as it was with extracting money from them.

Philip Schuyler, as hard-headed a land developer as anyone in the late eighteenth century, shows the opposite pole. Between 1764 and 1775 he was busy opening his lands at Saratoga, north of Albany. Unlike Pawling, he imposed few positive obligations on the tenants whom he settled there. The restrictions he imposed were for the sake of maximizing his own chance to make capital and developmental gains. In general he cared very little about receiving "fatt" hens, having fruit trees planted, or having his tenants' houses rest on stone-walled cellars. Rather, he wanted to be free to make the most of the land, whatever the eventual personal cost to the tenant. Henry Mynert, who took out a lease in 1764, was forbidden to mine or to violate the landlord's water and mill rights, and he could not sell his tenure without "the leave and Permission of the said Philip Schuyler . . . signifying his . . . will, terms and conditions." Every successive purchaser would bear the same obligations.[46] Leases that Schuyler granted in the next decade included clauses requiring several days of riding, reserving to the landlord himself the right to flood a tenant's land if building a millpond required it, and reserving as well the right to take firewood and timber from tenants' woods for mill construction and operation. The leases specifically denied mill rights to the tenants and pledged the tenant not to interfere with anything that Schuyler might do in accord with his own rights. The printed forms automatically specified the class difference between the esquire who was granting the lease and the yeoman who was receiving it.[47]

The French writer St. John de Crevecoeur, in his *Letters From an American Farmer*, suggested that it was normal for landlords like Pawling and Schuyler to assist new tenants with periods of free rent and with grants of animals and building materials. Several students have drawn on

Crevecoeur's idyllic picture to suggest that landlords were beneficent capitalists and that their grateful tenants, equally bourgeois in spirit, had little reason to protest against the things that were required of them.[48] But a close look at practice shows that landlords granted such favors only when their estates were young and in need of tenants. In the 1750s Sir William Johnson was granting rent-free periods of five years at Kingsborough, and in the 1740s Catharina Pawling gave periods of between one and six years on her land in Dutchess. Philip Schuyler's Saratoga leases from the 1770s gave at most one year of grace and often none, and there is no mention of any such favor at all on the part of Frederick Philipse or Beverly Robinson in the maturity of their estates.[49] A landlord's indulgence to a new tenant, in other words, was a device to begin the accrual of the capital gains that settlement would bring. It was not a customary right that a prospective tenant could demand.

Not all New York leases were onerous; some were as mild as one filed in Mistress Pawling's papers that gave an unspecified amount of land on a 999-year lease, requiring a rent of three bushels of wheat a year and imposing no serious restrictions on what the tenant might do.[50] But several generalizations seem possible. One is that whether they were opening new land or settled on old, established tracts, few tenants found themselves in the fortunate position of the ones who served Colonel Philipse. Sir William's tenants on Kingsborough might be the only comparable group. Another is that the gains made by tenants as landlords gradually ceased to enforce or even to write restrictive clauses were offset by the ever greater concern of those same landlords for getting more money, whether through increased rents, alienation fines, or capital gains. By the 1770s New York's land system had come to maturity in the Hudson and Mohawk valleys. Maturity meant that just as much as trading houses in New York City, the great estates had become part of an impersonal, profit-oriented commercial network. That fact was as important as uncertain boundaries, the hostility of the crown, and New England immigration in causing both tenant unrest in the 1750s and 1760s and an explosive mixture of popular royalism and popular revolutionism in the late 1770s.

Drawing on Cadwallader Colden's criticisms of landlordism, other students have suggested that the system retarded the province's population growth. They have seen landlords deliberately holding land back from settlement in order to make capital gains and have attributed to that the fact that growth in New York lagged behind growth in Pennsylvania, Virginia, and Massachusetts.[51] Who would go to a leasehold in New York when he could get a freehold elsewhere? The point cannot stand. However unstable and unjust the society the landlords had created, it was in their interest as a class to stimulate, not prevent, the province's peopling. Rents and mill tolls could come only from tenants' labor. Capital gains could come only when tenants built sturdy houses, opened roads, cleared fields, and planted fruit trees and when the landlord had customers for his mills. That was why leases required such things. In fact, until the Revolution the landlord-ridden counties of the east bank of the Hudson were the most attractive in New York. Their attractiveness lay in the safety they provided from the French and the Indians during six decades of warfare, in their relatively good soil, and in the access to market that the river provided. Landlords did not create those factors; they merely took advantage of them.

Because of the inherent attractiveness of their situation, the counties of landlordism sustained the highest growth rate in eighteenth-century New York. Overall, the province's population grew at an annual rate of 3.2 percent between the census of 1695 and that of 1771, a rate slightly above that for the Colonies as a whole. In some parts of the province, the rate stood well below that figure; thus in Kings it was 0.8 percent, in Queens 1.6 percent, and in Richmond 1.9 percent. The Yankees of Suffolk County, on Long Island, sustained an annual rate of 2.2 percent, and New York City grew at only 2.1 percent. In yeoman Ulster, on the west bank of the Hudson, the rate was 3.1 percent, about the same as that of the whole province. But of the four counties where the rate was well above that of the whole province only one, Orange, lacked serious landlordism. There the rate was 5.4 percent.

The province's growth was really sustained in Westchester, Dutchess, and Albany, the counties where landlordism was strongest. Westchester's overall rate from the first census to the last was 4.2 percent per annum, and in the first census interval, from 1698 to 1703, its rate was 13.2 percent. Albany, which until the end of the period included the land that would become many other counties and the state of Vermont, grew at an overall rate of 4.8 percent. The rate of growth in Dutchess was spectacular. The 445 people who were there at its first census, in 1714, had become 22,404 by 1771. Their overall rate of increase was 7.1 percent, and until 1746 it never fell below 8 percent. For the census interval from 1731 to 1737 it was 12.1 percent, and for that from 1737 to 1746 it was 11.1 percent. These figures should demolish forever any argument that landlordism retarded population growth.[52]

But it was precisely in these counties where growth was greatest and the system of great estates most secure that social strife ran highest after 1750 and that social relationships came most asunder during the Revolution. No tenant analyzed his situation in precisely the terms applied here of course, but tenants did generate an independent political consciousness and an ability to carry on sustained militant action. Would they have done so had landlordism not been moving towards a relationship based on exploitation for cash and had a rapidly growing population not thrown into sharp relief the differences between the mansions and the cottages? Would the Livingstons have evicted tenants in the 1750s, and would Beverly Robinson have precipitated the great rising of 1766 by evicting more, had there not been a reserve of would-be tenants waiting to take the evictees' places? Can the differences between landlords and tenants be glossed over by calling the latter "simply bourgeois"?[53] It seems unlikely in each case, and the events of the Revolution show that judgment to be correct.

III

Landlordism and tenantry were not the only social formations in rural New York. The Long Island counties knew a mixture of Dutch and English peasant culture, and there were many places characterized less by wide differentials in "tone," power, and wealth than by relative participation and equality. The political experience of those places would be very different from that of the counties of landlordism during the Revolution.

The material difference between landlord society and yeoman society can be seen even within one of the landlord counties, Westchester. In 1763 officials there made a list of freeholders who possessed estates worth more than sixty pounds; the list presents a marked contrast between the manors of the western half of the county and the townships that lay to their east. Morrisania was represented on the list by only two men. One was the third holder of the lordship of the manor, and the other was his close kinsman. Pelham Manor contributed fourteen men to the list, of whom six bore the surname Pell. Scarsdale, originally the preserve of Caleb Heathcote, was represented by Heathcote's surviving son-in-law and by fifteen others. From the nonmanorial half of Westchester representation on the list was very different. Rye, wedged up against Long Island Sound by an arm of Connecticut, had 150 freeholders with sixty pounds. Bedford and North Castle, also hard by the Connecticut line, had 107 and 106, respectively. Even New Rochelle, carved out of Pelham Manor as a refuge for Huguenots who had fled France, had 57.[54]

The 1763 list allows a comparison of the top ends of the respective social structures of specific Westchester communities. It shows that in the manorial parts of the county the "better sort" were akin to a sharp thin spire, while in the nonmanorial towns and precincts they resembled a low, rounded dome. Although the list gives no specific property figures, it seems probable that the sixty-pound freeholders of Morrisania or Pelham in fact possessed fortunes far in excess of that figure. The Morrises, for instance, though far from being the greatest landlords in the province, held immense political power. That, and the fact that one of their sons, after crossing to Britain, married a dowager duchess and became a ranking British general and Member of Parliament, shows how far removed their lives were from those of ordinary folk.[55]

But in the eastern towns of the county the sixty-pound freeholders lived in comfort rather than in luxury, and they based their political life on participation rather than on the prominent among them. Jackson Turner Main comments that in one of those towns, North Castle, society resembled the egalitarian frontier in its "equal distribution of property, the virtual absence of a ruling class, and the large proportion of medium sized farms."[56] The 1763 list demonstrates that to take all of Westchester as one's unit of analysis is to miss very significant local variations, even without reference to the "great" manors of Cortlandt and Philipsburgh, none of whose tenants appear on the list. These variations were in terms of the prestige and the potential power that went with being a sixty-pound freeholder. It is almost certainly the case that there were tenants on the manors who were as easy in the world as men who were named on the list. But the difference between them was important, for only the freeholders on the list were eligible to do jury service, and it was to establish a panel of jurors for a difficult land case involving tenants and landlords that the list was made.

The difference between egalitarian Rye and stratified Philipsburgh is, in broad terms, the distinction between the societies of the west and east banks of the Hudson, as tax lists from the 1760s show. Assessment rolls done on Rensselaerwyck show a society in which the overwhelming majority was concentrated at the bottom of the economic ladder but a few people were assessed at very different rates. There were 495 people rated on property valued at under £10. Twenty-seven others had estates worth from £11 to £20. Twenty-one had property worth from £21 to £30. Ten were rated between £31 and £40, and ten more above £40. The last group included some men of remarkable wealth. Stephen Van Rensselaer was assessed at £270. His kinsman Abraham Ten Broeck was rated at £100, Rensselaer Nicol at £88, and Johannes Van Rensselaer at £125. These sums were the ratable values of the holdings that the men controlled personally. They did not reflect their residual wealth as members of the family that owned the manor.[57]

In Orange and Ulster counties, as on Rensselaerwyck, the property of most people was concentrated in the range under £10. In Newburgh, for instance, of 240 persons assessed in 1767, 233 fell into that category. The day-to-day life of these people, as measured by their clothes, their houses, their possessions, and the rhythm of their work and play, cannot have been very different from that of a Rensselaerwyck tenant rated at the same level. But in these places there were none of the really high ratable values that distinguished the manorial elite. The highest assessment on the Newburgh roll was £19.4. In 1775 the highest assessment in Goshen, inland from the river in Orange County, was £21.12. Clearly there was a significant spread in these towns; the contrast between the seven Newburgh taxpayers rated above £10 and the ninety-three rated at £1 or less must have been visible in every aspect of daily life. But it was nothing like the contrast between Stephen Van Rensselaer, with his demesne rated at £270, and the 158 Rensselaerwyck tenants rated at £1 each.[58]

Material artifacts tell the same story. It is difficult to imagine an heiress of Orange or Ulster marrying, as did a Philipse woman, under a crimson canopy, the tenantry, "gathered as on rent day," looking on from a respectful distance. It is equally difficult to imagine anyone on the west bank erecting thrones in the local church "for himself and his dame," as did Frederick Philipse.[59] Architecture tells the story as well. No colonial New Yorker, not even a Philipse, could have built a country palace to match the ones that the Whig *nouveaux riches* were erecting in eighteenth-century England. Indeed, the earliest houses put up by the east-bank landlords were comfortable, not elaborate. Thus in the original Livingston manor house, built in 1699, "the walls as in all well-built houses of the period were built for protection and were so thick that the windows looked like mere indentations. It was low ceiled and heavy raftered."[60]

The coming of wealth and of a sizable tenantry to awe awoke different needs in the landlords. Frederick Philipse determined to make his "Manor Hall a showcase of English gentility." He added ornate woodwork and an intricately molded plaster ceiling to the interior and a fenced deer park and formal garden to the exterior, hiring European gardeners to tend his flower beds and shrubs. Philip Schuyler followed suit with the Pastures, south of Albany. Sir William Johnson abandoned the semi-military rigor of Fort Johnson for the Georgian beauty of Johnson Hall. Chancellor Robert R. Livingston's final version of Clermont measured 104 feet by 91 feet. "Surmounted with a balustrade of remarkable beauty," it had four pavilions attached to it and was set in grounds that were exquisitely landscaped. These were stately homes, and their owners intended them most of all as devices to set themselves, people who lived in the grand manner, apart from others who did not.[61] It does not matter that most of those owners were parvenus; so was much of the Whig aristocracy in England. What counts, as the writer Marcel Proust recognized in his long study of aristocrats and bourgeoises in turn-of-the-century France, is that people who behave like an aristocracy are well on their way to becoming one.

But in the west-bank counties such places did not exist. The Bronck house at Coxsackie, the Schoonmaker and Kiersted houses in Saugerties, and the buildings in Kingston and Newburgh that became, respectively, the first state capitol and George Washington's headquarters, were the dwellings of men who had reached the top in Orange and Ulster. They are solid, stone structures. They were designed for comfort and durability, not for the purpose of striking awe in the tenants or showing off newly gained wealth. They crystallize the spirit of a society of roughly equal men.

Ulster and Orange counties had few of the great tracts that characterized Dutchess, Westchester, and Albany. There were some large holdings: the Great Hardenbergh patent, set back from the river in the Catskill Mountains, Kakiate and Chesecocks, closer to the Hudson in southern Orange, and Minisink, sprawling westward across the Shawangunk Mountains to the New Jersey border. But for the most part division in the west-bank counties was along different lines. The most intensely divided part of Orange and Ulster appears on Sauthier's map roughly as a large right triangle, its hypotenuse running along the Hudson between Kingston and Haverstraw. The apex of the triangle was at Mamecoting, due west of Newburgh beyond the Shawangunk Mountains. In its western stretches the triangle shows the names of many individual proprietors, most of them participants in the Minisink patent who had taken out their separate shares. One of those shares, belonging to "P. J. Schuyler and Company," compared in size with, say, Henry Beekman's patent in northern Dutchess, and the owners of the others included a fair number of provincial notables. But most of the individual holdings within the triangle were of the order of the lands of F. Blagg, who had a tract near West Point. Blagg's land measured about one mile by four miles and thus included between twenty-five hundred and three thousand acres. This was a generous amount—the Morris manor held less—and Blagg may well have had tenants on it. But land division on this scale did not carry the burden of political, social, and economic organization that was the essence of east-bank society.

The owners of even the larger west-bank tracts saw their lands in speculative terms rather than as estates to be kept whole. Profits would come from selling when the price became right, not from rents, mill tolls, and alienation fines. As early as mid-century the patentees of Minisink were demonstrating how anxious they were to sell off. Their original joint partnership, formed to obtain a grant "without incurring the burdensome and costly procedure of the fee system," had been divided into separate holdings in order to let them dispose of the land "with a clear title." Individual Minisink patentees advertised land at fetching prices and enticed purchasers with attractive terms and with facilities such as roads and mills. Even Chancellor Robert R. Livingston, who was loath to sell any land, readily forgave his post-Revolution tenants on the Hardenbergh tract their arrears of rents and charged them only half the alienation fine that he demanded of tenants at Clermont, his home estate.[62]

Landowners in such places had to offer good terms to entice settlers, for Minisink, Kakiate, and the Hardenbergh patent were set well back from the Hudson. Their land was rough; getting its produce to the river and then to market was difficult; worst of all, angry Indians could raid it whenever they chose. But not all west-bank land was like that. Between the Minisink patent and the river lay thirteen different places that the Sauthier Map identified as towns rather than as land grants held by individuals. These towns had developed in different ways, and they were already diverging onto the paths that would take a few of them towards the "urban threshold" but would lead others to perpetual sleepiness. The best-studied of them are Kingston, in Ulster County, and Orange-Town, in Orange. The former, commanding the hinterland drained by Esopus Creek, by 1770 was showing the dynamism that would make a small city of it in the nineteenth century.

But the latter, trapped on swampy soil and hemmed in by the Hudson Highlands and the Ramapo Mountains, would remain a backwater until it became an exurb of New York City.[63]

Though some of these towns were founded in the eighteenth century by Britons and New Englanders, many of them were Dutch and dated from much earlier. The Dutch towns had grown out of collective land grants made in the seventeenth century to men whose desire was to settle, not to speculate. Orange-Town developed out of the Tappan patent, granted by Governor Dongan in 1686 to a group of "ordinary farmers" who had already begun to settle there on land they had bought from the Tappan Indians. Newburgh was founded in 1677 by a group led by Abraham Hasbrouck, whose direct descendant and namesake would help lead Ulster County into independence. These Dutch towns bear more than a passing resemblance, in cultural and economic terms, to the peasant communes that the Puritans created in seventeenth-century New England. One of the first things that Abraham Hasbrouck and his twelve associates did after settling at Newburgh was to organize a Calvinist Walloon Protestant Church. The founders of Orange-Town did the same thing.[64]

If their founders wanted to establish places where they might live quietly in their own way, they chose their sites well. Orange-Town lay on the river, but its rugged terrain and its lack of room for expansion meant that the developing money economy of the eighteenth century passed it by. Its recent historian suggests that "lacking currency," its people "exchanged services and commodities on a barter basis" and that their "requirements were simple and in most cases could be satisfied either at the farm itself or through trading and sharing with the neighbors." No eighteenth-century Americans could live wholly without money; there were some goods, such as salt and ironware, for which even the people of Orange-Town had to trade outside. But here was a community of the "subsistence farmers" whom Jackson Turner Main has characterized as a major element in the social structure of early America. The way they lived may be suggested by the fact that when the twenty-seven shareholders of the patent were listed in 1725, twelve could not sign their names.[65]

In Hudson Valley communes, as in Massachusetts ones, the distribution of land was the prime social problem for the founding generation. Their people solved it in the spirit, if not in the exact manner, of the New Englanders. In Marbletown, land distribution was the task of a group called the "twelve men." No record exists of any challenge to their decisions, which suggests either that the townspeople placed a high value on internal harmony or that the twelve did their job exceedingly well. They sold the land rather than granted it for free, and in 1703 they adopted a policy of charging twelve pence per acre for lowland and sixpence for highland. They specified, however, that wood and stone on unfenced land, private or common, would be available for common use.[66]

Groups like the "twelve men" became institutionalized during the eighteenth century as boards of trustees. The task of these boards was the disposal of the common land of a town, and unlike the town meetings, which performed the same function in New England, the trustees made no claim to purely political power. Legally they were private parties, and "if their orders were disobeyed, it is presumed they must necessarily have sought redress through the courts of sessions existing in the county." Nonetheless, until 1709 the trustees were the sole officers of Rochester, Ulster County. The town's separate civil identity grew only slowly, as other offices appeared on a piecemeal basis.[67] Boards of trustees continued to be chosen in these places until into the nineteenth century. Their importance gradually withered away, but their continuance suggests that these towns continued to hold land in common for up to three generations and did not distribute it all by the time the first generation of settlers was dying. Though in Orange-Town, at least, population density had reached 33.6 persons per square mile as early as 1738, it was not until 1786 that overcrowding caused the town to pass an ordinance disclaiming responsibility for needy strangers and making whoever might be host to such people responsible for "all Expence of Keeping and removing" them.[68]

Their behavior shows that these Hudson Valley people tried to realize the same values of communalism and internal harmony as did the New Englanders. The two groups shared attitudes about relative egalitarianism in distributing land; about the importance of keeping contention out of a community's internal life; and, since both were made up of Calvinist Protestants, about God, humankind, and the world. There were three main differences between them. First, the Dutch, unlike the Puritans, had lost their struggle against expanding British power. Since the third quarter of the seventeenth century they had been a conquered people. Second, their church, being disestablished, stood in a different relationship both to the state and to other churches than did New England Congregationalism. Third, the Dutch were a people with far less concern for literacy, either Bible-based or secular.[69]

The social structure of the Hudson Valley was thus riven in several different directions. The class line that separated aristocratic landlords from their tenants was of great importance. Though its effects varied from estate to estate, the landlords as a group faced many occasions when they had to rely on stronger means than paternalism and conspicuous elegance to secure their position. But the line that ran down the river was perhaps equally important, for it separated a society that was built around hierarchy from one that was not. Small freeholding farmers had much in common with tenants, but the important relationships in their lives were with people who were roughly their equals. They may have borne the great landlords no love. They may occasionally have found themselves in struggle with would-be landlords, as the patentees of Orange-Town once did with the absentee owners of Kakiate.[70] But though they had little reason to identify with what the landlords stood for, they had not much more reason to see the tenants' problems as in any way their own. For these people or their representatives to join in political action with either the landlords or the tenants would require the building of a coalition. In the mid-1770s they built such a coalition around the independence issue with the Whigs among the landlords, but in the 1780s they built a very different coalition centered on domestic problems with the representatives of angry tenants.

IV

Most of this study will be concerned with relations between ordinary people and their rulers at the level of first the provincial and later the state government. But local government was a significant factor in eighteenth-century New York, sometimes socializing people into the ways of a participatory society and sometimes repressing just such participation. Like the economics and the demography of the colonial period, it presented both problems and opportunities.

Patricia Bonomi has properly argued that local government in colonial New York could be as open as town government in New England. There was in the province no single local system; its chartered cities, manors, townships, precincts, and counties, though a marvel of simplicity by comparison with English local administration, presented a far more complicated picture than either Virginia's county oligarchies or New England's towns.[71] Yet the point is that all of these local units existed and functioned; even the counties were administered by elected boards of supervisors, a home-grown device. The charters of Albany and New York City likewise provided for popular involvement, for though the governor appointed their mayors, their freeholders and freemen elected their boards of aldermen and common councils.

At the local level the existence of the boards of trustees, which made town policy; of posts as town supervisors, fence-viewers, superintendents of highways, and overseers of the poor; and of the annual town meetings, which elected trustees and officials, meant that political power was close to people's daily lives. Ordinary men stood an excellent chance of wielding it in a day-to-day manner as officials as well as in a symbolic way at the polls. Bonomi has found, for instance, that in Kingston "members of 64 different families served as trustees in the years 1711 to 1726." Moreover, in the late 1720s more than two-fifths of all of the freeholders of the town sat as a trustee at some point in their life. Even in the great manors it was precinct meetings, required by provincial law, and not landlords that chose such important officials as assessors.[72]

But that the towns met annually does not mean that their gatherings served the same social functions as did those in New England. Puritan villages may or may not have been the consensual communities described by Michael Zuckerman, and they certainly were not the middle-class democracies postulated by Robert E. Brown,[73] but it is certain that very few, if any, places exactly identical to them existed in the Hudson and Mohawk valleys.[74] Town-meeting practice itself in New York differed significantly from that in New England. The law provided for annual meetings for elections and to make ordinances, but these never took on the self-consciousness of their Yankee counterparts. This may have been because of New York's lack of New England's utopian spirit, and it may also have been because the towns were not units of representation, save on the county boards of supervisors. Given the lack of the representative function, there was never any reason for town meetings to get into the habit of drawing up instructions to their representatives and thus of involving themselves in wider-ranging affairs.

Yet another difference, in many places, was a lack of local control over the method of land distribution. In Orange and Ulster counties the boards of trustees did have such power, and in the seventeenth century collective land grants were made, as has been shown.[75] But there could be no question on the east bank of the Hudson or in the Mohawk Valley of precinct meetings' deciding how land would be handed out, and Sauthier's map shows that even on the west bank most of the land was in the hands of individuals, not communities. The same point applies to towns that were set up under New York authority in the Green Mountains. The town of Kingsland was granted in 1772 as an endowment to King's College, and it was the college's governors, not the townsmen, who decreed that the town would be laid out in a nucleated village pattern and who specified the size of farm and town lots. Had the town developed as the governors planned, it would have looked like any New England village, but as a result of very different factors from the ones that shaped Dedham, Massachusetts or even Kent, Connecticut.[76]

The image of political socialization presented by local government practice is one of profound contradiction. This emerges most clearly from evidence that dates from after 1760 for the Mohawk Valley and for Westchester County. The formal channels of popular involvement were open, but that openness was complicated by other factors. In Westchester, a particularly convoluted court case, turning on the boundaries of Cortlandt Manor, led to the listing in 1763 of the 801 residents who were qualified, by a freehold tenure worth sixty pounds, to serve as jurymen. Taken as a whole, these freeholders were a cross section of colonial society. They included yeomen, tavernkeepers, professional men, and artisans of all descriptions, including one bricklayer.

Nonetheless, their number excluded between three-quarters and four-fifths of the adult white males in the county. It specifically excluded the tenants at will on Philipse Manor and tenants who acknowledged the landlordship of the owners of Cortlandt Manor. The list did include people from the manors of Morrisania, Pelham, and Scarsdale, but their tiny number compared with those from the nonmanorial towns has been noted. The occupations given on the list are likewise deceptive. The vast majority were listed as "yeomen," but a yeomanry that included Frederick Philipse and Lewis Morris was a curious yeomanry indeed. Whatever kinds of local participation people in Westchester had available to them, only a small percentage of them could sit on the juries that decided weighty cases, whether of land tenure or, after the 1766 rising, of human life.[77] And if the percentage of sixty-pound freeholders is any guide, the men who had the forty-pound freehold requisite for the provincial suffrage could not, in Westchester at least, have totaled anything resembling the 65 percent of adult white males estimated in some studies.[78]

Despite the battering that critics have administered to Carl Becker's ideas on the subject,[79] the other limitation on popular involvement was the power and prestige of the grandees. A recent analysis of a 1773 election return in Tryon County shows how completely Sir William Johnson ruled in the area west of Schenectady. The poll was for five constables in Tryon's Mohawk District, a perfect instance of the sort of local election that generated involvement elsewhere. There was no shortage of qualified electors; at least four hundred men in the district possessed the franchise. But only fourteen turned out for the election, and all of them voted for the same five candidates. Every one of the fourteen voters has been shown to have been closely tied to Sir William, whether by interest, patronage, or economic dependency. This was local democracy in a county where the jail, the courthouse, and the Anglican church were all the personal property of one man and where that man received letters headed "May it Please Your Lordship."[80]

In terms of its political sociology, local government in colonial New York was thus a complicated affair. Through its channels large numbers of men came in contact with power and learned to wield it. In many places its operations meant that the most salient working model of a political system was one that stressed closeness to the people and perhaps even responsiveness to popular desires. As a result, the political education of ordinary New Yorkers provided important training for the "explosion of political participation" that would be the Revolution. But there were things that local government could not do, whether in terms of participation or in terms of secular achievement. The laws of the suffrage meant that it could not bring nonfreeholders, even if they were white, adult, and male, to the polls. In some counties, the realities of life meant that even qualified voters would not oppose choices that in fact had been made by their "betters." Both the terms of leases and the law of taxation meant that assessors could tax only a landowner's demesne; undeveloped land, however valuable, would go untaxed, and tenants would pay the rates on their farms. Local government could do nothing about conditions of land tenure in the countryside, and little about poverty and shortage of work in the city. For these reasons the chance for involvement that it provided was as likely to lead to frustration as to satisfaction.

V

In the seventh and eighth decades of the eighteenth century New York was thus a complicated, tangled place. It was far removed from the raw simplicity that had characterized it in 1700. Its dominant feature was a vibrant, dynamic commercial economy that included the rural counties as well as New York City. That economy reached different New Yorkers in different ways, however. Some urban merchants, and the people who served them, drew their prosperity, or sustenance, from linkages of trade that ran parallel to the British Empire's linkages of authority. Others found their livelihood in ties with Britain's other colonies or with non-British dominions. Urban artisans and laborers, who were separated in many ways from the merchant and professional elite, had reason to be more concerned about a healthy internal trade in New York itself. These conflicting interests were of importance in bringing out the angry crowds that drove the Revolution forward in the city from 1765 to 1775.

The great landlords who dominated the rural economy were as much a part of the world of commerce and money as any merchant. But their version of preindustrial capitalism was complicated by several factors. One was the feudal hangover that permeated their ethos and, for a few of them, provided an additional source of power and prestige. Most of them were affected by this, as their unwillingness to sell any part of their home estates and their hankering after the bauble of a manorial title shows. A second complication was the problem of whether to be acquisitive or paternalistic in their dealings with their tenants. A third complication was the existence of those tenants. They needed them, and a man or woman launching a new estate had every reason to be generous to them. The landlords brought people from Europe, from Long Island, and from New England to join the descendants of the Dutch and the early British who had settled on their land first. But there came a point when the landlord was wealthy enough, and prospective tenants were available enough, that he no longer had to pay much regard to them. Tenants, in their turn, began to muse on the meaning of Indian titles that conflicted with the landlord's, and on border uncertainties. They began to recall cultural traditions that made of landlordism an anathema. The result to which these things led was violent. Along with the crowds of the city, the land rioters of the countryside will be discussed in the next chapter.

Other parts of New York found themselves less torn by the advancing commercial ways of the province. On the west bank of the Hudson lay two counties, Orange and Ulster, that did not know the tension of landlord and tenant, at least in the way that Dutchess, Westchester, and Albany did. Kings, Queens, and Richmond were thoroughly oriented to the market, lightly populated, and utterely placid. Suffolk, stretching east on Long Island to Montauk Point, was virtually an outpost of New England. These places would enter or not enter the Revolution from starting places very different from those of the east-bank counties and New York City. It was in the city and in the landlord counties, however, that New York's revolution began, and it was there that it went furthest. Both its beginning and its development were shaped as much by the kinds of places those counties had become as by the dispute with Britain.

Chapter 2

Riots in the Streets and Fields

Popular uprisings were part of life in provincial New York. Their history extended throughout the colonial period, and the culture that justified them in the minds of the people who rioted had deep roots on both sides of the Atlantic.[1] But between 1764, the year of the Sugar Act, and early 1775, just prior to the outbreak of war with Britain, rioting in New York demonstrates how complicated was the role of ordinary people in the events of the revolutionary era. People closed official courts and tried offenders before popular ones. They tore down buildings, sacked whorehouses, and destroyed crops. They rioted in New York City, in the Hudson Valley, and in the far northeastern region, now the state of Vermont. Some riots were spectacular, involving thousands of people, wholesale violation of the law, massive destruction of property, wounds and death. Others would not deserve a historian's attention were they not, like more notable riots, pieces of a larger jigsaw puzzle and were it not the whole puzzle, rather than the pieces, that made sense. Some crowds that rioted contained members of only one social group, and others had greater heterogeneity. Authoritative, rich, and powerful people regarded some with fear and trembling but looked on others more easily. Rioting was encouraged, and sometimes led, by self-conscious radicals and even by members of the provincial elite, but rioters could also organize and lead themselves. Some rioters acted for "social" reasons, and some for "political." Some affirmed New York's integrity, and some denied it. Some would become patriots in 1776, some royalists, and some would care not a damn. But their net impact was to stretch the fabric of New York until it rent even while they helped do the same thing to the British Empire.

Despite some among their number, they generated the "sustained militancy" required for the "fully revolutionary politics" that was needed to drive New York's reluctant leading Whigs towards independence.[2] And in so doing they also generated much of the energy that would leave New York transformed almost beyond recognition by the mid-1780s.

I

The complexity of New York's revolutionary crowds can be shown by answering some very simple questions. First, what did rioters do? Second, why did they do it? Third, to the extent that it can be answered at all, who were they? And fourth, how did men of power and prestige view rioters of different sorts? Let us answer the first question with a run-through of popular actions, great and small, during the eleven years under discussion.

1764 *15 January:* British soldiers break into the New York City jail, rescuing an officer who is held for debt. A few persons are hurt, and a sergeant is killed.[3]

10 July: Fishermen who "supply the markets" are impressed aboard H.M.S. *Chaleur*, which is operating in New York Harbor. A few days later, when the captain goes ashore, a crowd seizes and burns his barge. The captain orders the fishermen released.[4]

17 August: The sheriff of Albany County reports that land rioters have driven farmers at "Hoseck" from their property, seizing cattle and crops. The rioters are led by men claiming to exercise the offices of deputy sheriff and justice of the peace by New Hampshire authority.[5]

1765 *6 June:* The second of a series of summer concerts is given in the pleasure gardens at Ranelagh, in New York City. It is interrupted, however, by the invasion of a "number of disorderly persons (in a Riotous Manner)."[6]

22 July: Vessels from local, coastal, and transatlantic ports entering New York Harbor are having hands impressed by H.M.S. *Hawke*. "One of the Officers who pursued a Vessel to the Town, was pretty roughly handled by some of the populace."[7]

23 October: Two thousand people gather at the Battery as the ship bearing New York's consignment of stamps under the Stamp Act approaches. The stamps are landed secretly.[8]

31 October: On the day before the Stamp Act is to take effect, people in New York City wear mourning. "A mob in three squads went through the Streets crying 'liberty,' at the same time breaking the Lamps and threatening particulars that they would the next night pull down their Houses. Some thousands of windows Broke. Major James of the Royal Artillery threatened to be buried alive."[9]

1 November: In response to the Stamp Act's going into effect, two thousand "Rabble or rather Rebels" assemble in New York City. They break open "the Governor's Coach house," seize a chariot, a chair, and two sleighs, "which they burnt in the Bowling Green with effigies and Gallows." Marching on Fort George, whose cannon are trained on the city, some of them try to scale its walls. Meanwhile "300 Carpenters belonging to the mob" wait to destroy the gate if the garrison within opens fire. "From thence they proceeded to Major James's House," which they thoroughly sack, breaking windows, cutting down shutters and partitions, and destroying wine and goods to the value of £1,500.[10]

3–5 November: The garrison in Fort George is forced to spike its guns. The captain of the ship that brought the stamps flees. Placards in the city streets threaten "the lives of particulars. Many strangers thronging in with arms." A particular target of placards is Captain Archibald Kennedy, master of the Royal Navy's duty ship in the harbor, son-in-law of a great New York family, and owner of an appreciable amount of city real estate. As five thousand people watch, Lieutenant Governor Colden delivers the stamps to the safekeeping of the corporation of the city of New York.[11]

26 November–1 December: A mass meeting of some twelve hundred people adopts "petitions and resolves" calling on New York City's representatives in the provincial assembly to seek "all necessary Relief, prayed for and solicited by proper Agents, in the most respectful and constitutional Manner." The meeting fails to adopt a stronger motion calling on the assembly to invoke its own institutional prestige against the Stamp Act and to adopt a positive policy of opposition to it. The stamp distributors for Nova Scotia, Canada, New Hampshire and for Maryland are forced by New York crowds to resign their posts, the crowds crossing over to Long Island to catch the last. "A Son of Liberty stabbed with a Bayonet by one of the Royal Artillery."[12]

16–17 December: The streets are placarded, and effigies of Lord Colville, George Grenville, and General Murray are paraded. The effigies are hung on a gallows that has been carried through the streets. John Holt's newspaper notes that "twas observed upon this Occasion that there appeared two Parties, who opposed each other, though each of them were professed enemies to the Stamps." Householders donate candles under threat of crowd action.[13]

23–31 December: A crowd boards a ship believed to be carrying Connecticut's consignment of stamps. The mayor disperses a crowd "collected to destroy Captain Kennedy's house." Another crowd considers burning an effigy of General Thomas Gage, British Commander in Chief in North America, but the threat of military intervention stops it.[14]

1766 *7 January:* A British officer surveying New York City on General Gage's orders acts "*sub rosa* as observations might endanger ones house and effects if not ones life."[15]

14 January: Popular protests erupt against allowing sailors from naval ships wintering in the harbor to work at the dockyards when off duty. The sailors will take a lower rate of pay than will New Yorkers. Meanwhile "children nightly trampouze the Streets with Lanthorns upon Poles and hallowing but allowed of."[16]

20–23 January: A suspected stamp distributor is found in New York City. A crowd gathers and "followed the custom of most places in America, of shewing their resentment against his Effects, by defacing his House, destroying some Furniture in it, and drawing his Winter Carriages thro' the Streets in flames." Stamp Act disturbances take place in Albany. The local stamp distributor, Henry Van Schaack, is asked to swear that he never had and never would seek the office that the British had given him. He objects to the proffered oath, and his house is partially sacked. The following day "notes were found on many public Places, desiring the Sons of LIBERTY. . .and all that had any Business with them to meet. . .to consult Measures to treat the Cause of LIBERTY." Van Schaack then takes the oath, as the Sons of Liberty had demanded.[17]

14–15 February: "A great riot" occurs in daylight in front of the houses of men who are believed to be secretly doing business with stamps. The riot is led by Isaac Sears, Joseph Allicocke, and John Lamb. The suspected gentlemen are brought to the common with the intention of putting them in the pillory, but clergymen intervene. No houses are pulled down, partly "owing to some Gentlemen present" and partly because the house occupied by one of the offenders "belonged to Mr. DeL[ance]y." The march to the common is led by two ship carpenters "who. . .it seems can either raise or suppress a mob instantly."[18]

6 March: A procession carries through the streets a figure of Lieutenant Governor Colden "mounted on a cannon drilling the vent." The parade is "attended by a large concourse of People."[19]

19 March: An officer of the newly arrived H.M.S. *Garland* remarks publicly on the licentiousness of John Holt's newspaper. Two popular leaders board the ship, but the officer will not speak to them. Demonstrations take place on the shore.[20]

27 March–April 1: Little boys who have held street marches all winter continue their demonstrations. They resolve "that no private property should be touched." The magistrates of the city either "approve of it, or do not dare to suppress it tho' children." The Sons of Liberty meet to debate whether a theatrical company should be allowed to perform in the city.[21]

24–30 April: Land rioting breaks out in the Hudson Valley, with the dispossession by three hundred farmers of a shopkeeper on Beverly Robinson's estate. The rioting spreads quickly to "lands belonging to Mr. Courtlandt at West Chester." The urban Sons of Liberty "will not suffer any Lamb to be brought to market or eat, under penalty of having the offenders house pulled down." The upstate rioters march on New York City with a view to pulling down the townhouses of several landlords. They encamp north of the city, demanding that "Mr. Courtlandt. . . give them a grant forever of his lands." Other upstate rioters are reported to be turning out families who had taken the places of evicted tenants and restoring the original occupants.[22]

5 May: A new play opens in the theater in Chapel Street. The first performance is "soon interrupted by the multitude who broke open the doors and entered with noise and tumult." Driving out players and audience, they "immediately demolished the House, and carried the pieces to the Common, where they consumed them in a Bonfire." The skull of one boy is fractured, and several others are "dangerously hurt."[23]

17–20 May: The tenant insurgency spreads to Livingston Manor. The tenants "are in arms to dispossess some and maintain others in their own, without rent or taxation." Reports arrive from Crown Point, on Lake Champlain, that "some scores of Families" are squatting there. "They declare that possession is eleven points in the Law and that they will take the advantage of these Disturbances." They are migrant New Englanders.[24]

8 June: Justices of the peace in the Hudson Valley are "treated ill and beat by the levellers for executing their offices."[25]

28 June–2 July: Some five hundred "levellers" rise on Livingston Manor, two hundred "of which had marched to murther the Lord of the Manor and level his house, unless he would sign leases for 'em agreeable to their form." "Their form" would free them of rent, taxes, or the coming of new tenants. The tenants, armed only with sticks, are dispersed by forty men bearing guns. "Seventeen hundred of the Levellers with fire arms are collected at Poughkeepsie. All the jails broke open through all the countries" below Albany on the east side of the river. A skirmish takes place on Rensselaerwyck between "some settlers. . . who were fixed there without title" and a posse led by the sheriff of Albany. One member of the posse and two settlers are killed, and eight people, including the sheriff, are wounded.[26]

21 July: Tenant rebels fortify a house near Poughkeepsie. They are assaulted by regular British troops who are supplied with a six-pound cannon and a howitzer.[27]

11–21 August: The liberty pole in New York City is cut down by soldiers. A crowd of between two and three thousand people, "chiefly Sons of Liberty," gathers. The soldiers fix their bayonets, and brickbats are thrown. Tension remains high in the next few days. On 12 August the Sons of Liberty resolve to have satisfaction and not to permit the soldiers to "beat their Retreat and Tattoo through the Streets at their peril." Innkeepers and inhabitants are asked to have no intercourse with the soldiers. Papers circulate calling for an abolition of the garrison, and the Sons of Liberty propose a boycott of the soldiers in the market. A merchant named Barker attempts to break up a parade by the soldiers and is assaulted by one of them with the butt of a musket. Two old Dutch women take axes to the canopied pew in the Dutch Church that is set aside for the mayor, recorder, and alderman of the city.[28]

29 September: A crowd gathers "without the least Tumult, Noise or Previous Notice" to free the arrested tenant leader William Prendergast from his imprisonment in Poughkeepsie. He declines to be released, and the company disperses quietly.[29]

23 October–6 November: Troops from the garrison who believe that they have been mistreated by "ladies of pleasure" sack several whorehouses in the city. Later, soldiers assault "Caspar Hart, a Cartman," wounding him and hamstringing his horse.[30]

1767 *26 March:* Soldiers again cut down the liberty pole, and a street brawl ensues.[31]

1768 *2 February:* John Holt's newspaper reports that an apprentice has been assaulted by a soldier. The apprentice, not his assailant, is placed under arrest.[32]

February–March: The provincial assembly is dissolved, and a spectacular election is fought in New York City. A candidate is vilified as homosexual, religious prejudice is evoked, and many newspaper essays play on popular hostility to lawyers.[33]

31 March: The wages of journeymen tailors are reduced, and they go on strike. On 21 April they offer their services directly to the public.[34]

14 November: Effigies of Governor Bernard of Massachusetts and Sheriff Greenleaf of Boston are paraded in the streets and publicly burned.[35]

1769 *12 December:* Commissioners are sent to survey lands in the Green Mountains belonging to James DeLancey and other prominent New York City figures. Armed men resist the commissioners and force them to stop surveying.[36]

December: A case under Britain's White Pine Law is brought before the New York Vice-Admiralty Court. The defendants are residents of Windsor, a town just west of New York's claimed boundary on the Connecticut River. The trial is frustrated by action of Samuel Wells, a Windsor resident and a judge of New York's court of common pleas for Cumberland County. Prisoners are taken, but they are released by a crowd "who behaved in a very hostile Manner and swore they would have the prisoners or pull down the house." Judge Wells affirms his determination to assist the men who have been taken prisoner.[37]

1770 *15–20 January:* Soldiers attempt, without success, to cut down the newest liberty pole and succeed in ransacking a tavern frequented by Sons of Liberty. A broadside appears protesting against employers who hire soldiers instead of inhabitants and against taxation for support of the garrison. The soldiers publish a manifesto of their own, but Sons of Liberty interfere with its distribution. Street brawls break out. The soldiers finally succeed in destroying the heavily armored liberty pole, and two days of street fighting in Golden Hill, at the top of John Street, and in Nassau Street ensue.[38]

9 August: John Grout, an attorney in Cumberland County who had been involved in the White Pine Act affair at Windsor, is victimized by a crowd of some forty persons while he is in service with a sheriff's posse. The posse had been organized to recapture prisoners who had been rescued already by a riot, but its members are captured instead. The crowd demands from the sheriff a bond of five hundred pounds, "to be forfeited if the matters for which the said Sheriff was then attempting to take the prisoners were any further prosecuted." The bond would also be forfeited if any inhabitant of Windsor should be prosecuted at the next court session. Grout is kept prisoner for six days.[39]

1771 *27 February:* John Munro, a justice of the peace of the town of Shaftesbury, in Albany County, describes how settlers in the Green Mountains under New Hampshire auspices frustrate New York authority. Their tactics include assault on New York constables who are serving writs, attempts to rescue prisoners from the custody of New York officers, and threats of bloodshed. Munro mentions that the rioters disguise themselves by blackening their faces.[40]

30 May: John Munro describes rioting in the New Hampshire grants for a second time: "They assemble themselves togither in the night time and throws down all the Yorkers fences etc. as we are called and Drives the cattle into the Filds and Meadows and destroys both Grass and Corn, and do every Mischief they can think of." On the same day, Constable Samuel Willoughby describes how he was forced by grants rioters to "carry off" a writ of ejectment that he had served upon a woman.[41]

11 June: Another run-in takes place between soldiers and civilians in New York City.[42]

August: A riot takes place "near Argyle town," in Albany County, in which fifteen men assault and dispossess "Donald McIntyre and other complainants of Lands granted to them by this government."[43]

21 September: Samuel Gardinier, of Wallumscock, Albany County, tells of conflict over his land with a man claiming it under a New Hampshire title. He finds that his fences have been pulled down and that cattle have been allowed into his grain. One night he was terrorized by armed men disguised in Indian blankets and women's caps. His fences have been pulled down as many as three times in a single week. The rioters warn him that "they had applied to him civilly, but that if he did not do as he was ordered, they would come the next time Devil like." He flees, and his fences and haystacks are destroyed. He fears violence to himself if he tries to return.[44]

30 September–7 October: The New York Provincial Council receives a deposition telling of people in the Green Mountains who were dispossessed of their homes at midnight, and the houses pulled down. The assailants are identified as notable New Hampshire grants leaders. The Albany County sheriff, who has a large but unarmed posse with him, fails in an attempt to evict a New Hampshire grantee from his farm near Bennington.[45]

12 November: Ethan Allen and some nine other men dispossess Charles Hutchesson, a sometime corporal in a Highland regiment who has settled in northern Albany County, at New Perth. They burn Hutchesson's house, and Allen tells his victim that "that morning they had resolved to offer a burnt Sacrifice to the Gods of the world."[46]

1772 *29 January:* More than seventy men break into a storehouse at Putney, Cumberland County, and rescue the goods of a man against whom a New York court had rendered judgment. The group is reported ready to pull down the county jail at Chester. Governor Tryon is advised against appointing a justice of the peace at Windsor on the grounds that the justice's writs would not run and that it would be better to have no authority than to have an empty claim.[47]

10 May–5 June: Governor Tryon proposes negotiations with the grants rioters and offers to meet their representatives, save for a few men whom he names. The rioters' reply stresses the illegality of actions taken by Yorkers against them.[48]

24 November: Two counterfeiters are placed in jail in Cumberland County. They are immediately freed by a crowd that goes on to destroy a potash works belonging to the judge who had jailed them.[49]

1773 *20 February:* David Wooster reports a confrontation with New Hampshire claimants to his military land grant on Lake Champlain. His opponents have organized themselves into military companies with recognized captains. They declare their intention to resist forcibly both ejectment from their farms and any exercise of New York authority.[50]

April: Philip Nichols, a farmer at Socialborough, Cumberland County, is dispossessed by grants people. His adversaries pull down his fences, lay waste his field, and take possession of his land.[51]

August: The Yorker village of Otter Creek, on Lake Champlain, is sacked by a crowd of about a hundred men. Houses are burned, crops are destroyed, the gristmill is "all put down," and the millstones are broken and thrown into the creek.[52]

22 August: Justice of the Peace John Munro is warned that "in a few days the whole of my property should be burnt to ashes." Even ashes are not safe if they belong to him, for his whole stock of pot and pearl ashes has been destroyed. The men who sacked Otter Creek are now publicly identified as the Green Mountain Boys.[53]

December: Two New York justices of the peace are tried at Bennington by a popular court. One is sentenced to have his house burned. The other is to have the roof of his house removed, and some corn destroyed. The first had actually exercised his post, but the second had merely accepted a commission.[54]

1774 *2 February:* Benjamin Hough and others of the town of Durham ask Governor Tryon for armed protection from the Green Mountain Boys. Civil officers have been intimidated, and two New York magistrates have been tried before judges "appointed by their own authority" for executing their offices. The undersheriff of the county has been warned against executing any legal processes "within what they call their district." A constable has been fined by one of their courts for executing a legal process, and the crowd has also interfered in private disputes and rescued prisoners held for debt.[55]

22 April: The ship *London* enters New York Harbor bearing tea. Her captain denies the presence on board of the "contraband," but his lie is discovered. Crowds watch from the shore while a party of "Mohawks" costume themselves and prepare to dump the tea, but before this "official" party can act men without disguise board the ship and destroy the leaf. Another ship bearing tea returns to Britain without unloading in order to avoid similar action.[56]

24 August: A town meeting at Manchester resolves that any person attempting to exercise New York authority or taking a New York civil commission should be "deemed an Enemy to their Country and Common Cause."[57]

1775 *7 March:* Benjamin Hough describes how he was seized in January and held under guard by grants rioters. After being kept prisoner he was tried on charges of executing New York authority, of dissuading people from joining the insurgency, and of complaining of the insurgents' actions to the New York government. He is sentenced to receive two hundred lashes on his bare back. After the punishment is inflicted he is exiled from the New Hampshire grants, bearing a passport from his tormentors.[58]

18–23 March: It is reported that crowd action in the Green Mountains precludes the execution of any legal process for debt in Charlotte County. The crowds will not, however, protect "friends of government" who get into legal difficulties. The court of Cumberland County is violently closed following reports that "the Rioters had threatened" not to let it open. Following those reports, the sheriff gathers a posse of about twenty-five men armed with staves, but the courthouse is occupied by between eighty and ninety men who are armed with guns. The sheriff's party equips itself similarly, fire is exchanged, and the rioters are evicted. More Green Mountain Boys appear, however, and the posse is in its turn dislodged. The victorious rioters declare that the judges will "make satisfaction" and that they will pull down the courthouse. During the riot one man is killed, and several are wounded. The rioters take the officers of the court as prisoners to the jail at Northampton, Massachusetts.[59]

Such was rioting and popular upheaval in New York during the decade in which Americans moved from resistance to revolution. As George Rudé and other scholars have pointed out, American crowds shared a great deal with their counterparts in Europe and especially in England. Pulling down of houses, breaking open of jails, blacking of faces for disguise, and brawls with the military could just as easily have happened in the city of York or in Hampshire as in New York City and the New Hampshire grants. Nor were the similarities restricted to actions. British crowds could be just as political as American crowds; while New Yorkers rioted over the Stamp Act, Londoners took to the streets for "Wilkes and Liberty." But even though Stamp Act and Wilkes rioters each could identify their cause with the other, one suspects that the American urban rioters developed more staying power and ultimately more identification with a Grand Cause than did English ones.

Moreover, upstate rioters raised fundamental questions about social structure and about political authority, questions that rural rioters in the mother country either ignored or did not articulate. The rioters of eighteenth-century America cannot be understood without reference to the findings of students of crowds in eighteenth-century Europe. But no single model of European crowd action can be applied mechanically to the American situation.[60]

The range of crowd experience in New York just before independence suggests instead that certain incidents that seem merely puzzling if taken by themselves, such as the sacking in 1766 of the Chapel Street theater, are really clues to an unexplored aspect of the major political riots of the period. It suggests as well that a least two distinct patterns of upheaval were working themselves out. One was urban, turning on political, social, and imperial discontent. The other was rural, springing primarily from problems of land ownership and the local dominion that went with it. Only slowly did the latter become "politicized," in the larger sense of the term involving the imperial conflict.

Moreover, the evidence shows that crowds of several different sorts were active in His Majesty's province. Some were single-dimensional, drawn largely from one social group with one primary concern. Others reflected class collaboration in a common cause rather than class conflict. Some crowds were made up of people who wished to change a hated state of affairs, and others of people who wished to stave off change that could only be for the worse. Frequently New York crowds were socially "mixed," and there were times when rioters had the support and even the leadership of their social "betters." But there were also times when rioters were led by poor and humble men and when what they said and did were evidence of their independence rather than of their being either "mobilized" or manipulated.

It was precisely this complexity that made the situation in New York revolutionary. As Samuel P. Huntington puts it, "It takes more than one revolutionary group to make a revolution. . .one social group can be responsible for a coup, a riot, or a revolt, but only a combination of groups can produce a revolution."[61] In 1765 New Yorkers of many sorts had grievances enough to make them turn to violence. Even in that year many of them associated their grievances with one or another or all of the political structures that ruled them. A decade later far more of them were drawing the connection, with far less ambiguity. One result was explosive street politics in New York City and to some extent in Albany. Another was the Hudson Valley tenant rising of 1766. A third was guerrilla warfare in the Green Mountains. The urban "mob," the Hudson Valley "levellers," and the Green Mountain Boys had different aims, different methods, and different effects on the fabric of New York. But they did have in common their being made up of people who were refusing to stay in "their place." And in their different ways they were three of the most significant in the combination of revolutionary groups that forced New York's reluctant patriot leaders into the fire of independence and hammered out a revolution in its flames.

II

The questions of who different rioters were and why they did what they did are hopelessly intertwined, and they are best answered by treating rural and urban crowds separately. In the Hudson Valley and the Green Mountains we are dealing with land riots, not bread riots, which immediately sets them off from their counterparts in urban America and western Europe. The problem behind rural crowd action was not provisions or whorehouses or pressgangs or smallpox victims; it was how, under what conditions, and by whom a limited amount of land would be owned and occupied. In the Hudson Valley the issue behind both the 1766 rising and the decade and more of turmoil that preceded it was the very existence of the manors and patents that made New York's land system unique in colonial America. Not all of the great tracts erupted; Philipsburgh, Robert R. Livingston's Clermont, and Sir William Johnson's Kingsborough were notable exceptions. There were times when the trouble was the tendency of a tract's ill-defined borders to grow or the temptation to make them shrink, and there were times when the rioters might have been satisfied simply to reinstate people whom the landlords had evicted. But for many reasons, the question had a way of escalating to one of whether there ought to be great tracts at all.

Those reasons included conflicting Indian titles to the land, claimed by the Indians themselves; the known hostility to the tracts of British officialdom; the problem of where New York ended and where New England began; and the common knowledge that many of the tracts had been obtained by blatant fraud.[62] History, political geography, and bureaucracy combined to put the landlords under heavy pressure. But the problem had roots in the essence of landlordism, as well as in its accidental qualities. Even the most paternalistic of the great owners, such as Frederick Philipse, Henry Beekman, and Sir William Johnson, designed to have their land occupied by tenants. They might offer attractive terms to newcomers, and they might sell off outlying speculations, but on their home estates they had no intention of granting freehold ownership to anyone. And where the watchword of the owners was profit rather than paternalism, as on Livingston Manor and the Philipse Highland patent, there was little camouflage in front of the basic antagonism.

In the far northeast, conditions were somewhat different but not fundamentally so. The Green Mountains were claimed, until 1764, by both New Hampshire and New York, and by the time the crown had resolved the dispute in New York's favor the two provinces had made many overlapping grants. The insurgency that wracked the district after 1764 sprang from the resistance of New Hampshire grantees, who knew that submitting to New York would mean losing much of their land to New York City speculators. The grantees knew, too, that any land they might hold under New York title would be subject to a far heavier quitrent than that due under a New Hampshire deed. The area at stake was enormous: by 1776 New York's royal governors had granted 2,115,610 acres in the region, all but 180,620 of them in direct defiance of a royal order of 1767 prohibiting anyone to make grants there. The order, which followed on the confirmation of New York's basic claim, had been given in the hope that forestalling the greed of New York speculators might induce New Hampshire grantees to accept the province's political control. But the mainspring of political control in colonial America was the power to grant land, and New York politicians had not struggled to have their claim ratified merely for an empty sovereignty.[63] Neither in the New Hampshire grants nor in the Hudson Valley could the basic issue be compromised; either the land would be held by or from the great landlords and the New York grantees or it would not. In both cases the better legal position may have been on the side of the big owners. The institutions of the province certainly were.

Moreover, both the Hudson Valley and the Green Mountains were in the midst of complicated social changes. In the Hudson Valley the combination of rapid development and medieval technicalities was leading towards a society in which seigneurial dominion was to be combined with high profits and capital gains. In the Green Mountains settlement was far less advanced, and most New York owners were absentee owners; a few signs, however, suggest what landowners there had in mind. One sign was the way in which Philip Skene maintained his household of forty-four persons at Skenesborough, east of the southern arm of Lake Champlain. They were supported by the labors of seventy-one tenants, nearly as large a force as worked Robert R. Livingston's Clermont. And years later the diarist Anne Grant would reminisce ruefully about her father's ill-founded plans for establishing a Green Mountain estate. There, it had been thought, "simple felicity" would "prevail among the amiable and innocent tenants we were to have."[64] The Hudson Valley levelers and the Green Mountain Boys were, in short, responding to structural conditions basic to their existing societies and to major trends in their development.

The landlord-tenant relationship lay at the heart of both movements, but, that much said, the movements diverge. The problem in the Hudson Valley was to escape tenancy. Hence the insistence of Livingston Manor rioters in 1766 that they would have "leases for 'em agreeable to their form" and that under these leases they "would neither pay Rent, taxes etc., nor suffer other Tenants." Hence, too, the declaration of Cortlandt Manor rioters that they would pull down their landlord's townhouse if he did "not give them a grant forever of his Lands."[65] Tenants, not squatters, lay behind much of the trouble. In 1752 the manor lord Robert Livingston, Jr., complained that "sundry" of his tenants had gone to Boston to seek title to land they had rented from him; in 1753 whole groups of his tenants were doing the same. In the same year one man who had rented Livingston land for at least six years and had been evicted seized the land he had hired and planted a crop on it. Michael Hallenbeck, who was a leading figure in the Livingston Manor disturbances of the 1750s, had been a tenant for upwards of thirty years. Robert Noble, around whom turmoil swirled for a decade in Rensselaerwyck, was a longstanding tenant of John Van Rensselaer's. Joseph Paine, who "girdled, and cutt down several thousands" of trees belonging to Robert Livingston and told the lord's servants "that the trees were his. . . and Robert Livingston kiss his a–s" was a long-term tenant. Jacob Knight, involved in a raid that abducted some of Livingston's ironworkers, was identified as the manor lord's "servant." William Rees, who lost his life in 1755 at the hands of a party led by John Van Rensselaer, had been a tenant of three generations of his killer's family. What these people had in common was a status that they hated.[66]

By contrast, in the Green Mountains the goal of all but a few of the rioters was to maintain themselves as freeholders. Some Green Mountain settlers—Anne Grant gives them scathing mention[67]—did accept a grant from a New York landlord, only to join landlordism's enemies. But most of the Green Mountain rioters were more akin to artisans struggling against losing their status as skilled workers than to proletarians who had nothing to lose but their chains.[68] On that count Green Mountain crowds were socially more "mixed" than were those in the Hudson Valley. They included small and middling land speculators, such as their leader, Ethan Allen. The Onion River Land Company, owned by Allen and his various brothers, stood to gain much if New York's attempt to impose its titles and its authority could be resisted. But perhaps more typical of grants settlers were the young couple Benedict and Rebecca Alford, who married and settled there during the Revolutionary War. Throughout the 1770s and 1780s they bought and sold land in towns like Pittsford, Rutland, and Manchester, sometimes in his name and sometimes in hers. Between 1775 and 1787 they were parties to at least twelve sales of land, buying eight parcels and selling four. The tracts ranged between £35 and £450 in value and between fifty and six hundred acres in size. Precisely how much a listing of their property and a description of its character would tell about either Allen or the Alfords is of course an open question. Ethan Allen was as much a backwoods Tom Paine, pouring his energy into the rationalist tract *Reason the Only Oracle of Man* and into guerrilla warfare, as he was entrepreneur. And if James Henretta's daring suggestions about the rural American *mentalité* are correct, the Alfords may have done their buying and selling for the sake of the family line rather than for the sake of their private selves.[69] But it takes no imagination to see why Allens and Alfords alike would resist "tenantization."

Although the two groups of rioters viewed landlordism from quite different perspectives, there was much that they shared. For example, they shared a distinct tendency to explain what they were doing in terms of class. A man named Moss Kent, giving testimony when the tenant leader William Prendergast was on trial for his life in 1766, declared that farmers evicted by the landlords "had an equitable title but could not be defended in a Course of Law because they were poor. . . and poor men were always oppressed by the rich." Referring to the tenants' abortive march on New York City, he told the court that "when they went to New York they expected to be assisted by the poor people there." Prendergast himself was quoted as saying that "it was hard they were not allowed to have *any property*" and that he pitied poor people who were turned out of possession, for "there was no law for poor men." And Ethan Allen described his Green Mountain followers as "a poor people. . . fatigued in settling a wilderness country." Their enemies, by contrast, were "a number of Attorneys and other gentlemen, with all their tackle of ornaments, and compliments and French finesse."[70]

Moreover, it is true that the New Hampshire grants and the eastern reaches of the Hudson Valley alike were full of migrant New Englanders. By contrast, the victims of rural crowd action—whether landlords like Robert Livingston, Jr., "loyal" tenants like Johannes Van Deusen of Livingston Manor, or the Scots settlers, many of them retired soldiers, who invaded the Green Mountains under New York auspices—were hardly ever of New England descent. This fact has led several students to see the starting point for understanding the riots in the presence, not of two classes, but rather of two cultures, Yorker and Yankee. Friction and violence developed, they suggest, because land-hungry New Englanders pushed their way into New York and, once there, tried to impose their own way of doing things on Yorkers, both tenant and landlord. Kim carries the point even further, seeing the root of the insurgency of the 1750s on Livingston Manor and Rensselaerwyck as a conspiracy involving Berkshire Mountains landjobbers and the General Court of Massachusetts.[71]

Baldly stated, the point cannot stand. Though the Green Mountain Boys were exclusively New Englanders in their make-up (which explains their absolute refusal to allow prospective victims the option of joining them), the Hudson Valley crowds were ethnically mixed. The leader of the 1766 rising, William Prendergast, had migrated, not from Connecticut or Massachusetts, but from Ireland and had married a Dutchess County Quaker woman. Some half of the persons positively identified as rioters during the 1750s in the extensive records in O'Callaghan's *Documentary History* bore names that were obviously Dutch rather than English. During their insurgency these people asked for aid from Boston, claimed that their lands really lay in Massachusetts, and tried to found New England towns. But both sides took advantage of the uncertainty of New York's border with Massachusetts; while tenant rebels were pulling it closer to the Hudson in order to diminish Livingston Manor and Rensselaerwyck, New York landowners were pushing it towards the Connecticut River in order to establish a "patent of Westonhook." The political boundary was vague, which no doubt encouraged men to challenge the manors that lay on the New York side of it, wherever it was. But the important point is that the challengers lived west, not east, of the Berkshire Mountains, on ground that the landlords called their own.[72]

Dutch tenants like Michael Hallenbeck mingled, however, with many genuine New England migrants, like Josiah Loomis. The ethnically mixed Hudson Valley migrants, the Green Mountain Boys, and other rural rioters whose ranks included New Englanders behaved in remarkably similar ways—and popular behavior is usually rooted in popular culture.[73] If one stresses the culture rather than the simple ethnicity or the supposed greed of those New Englanders who did riot, then the trail blazed by Dixon Ryan Fox and followed by Bonomi and Kim can lead to some noteworthy insights. The sparkling collection of recent studies on the social and cultural history of early New England gives a basis for relating Yankee popular culture to the riots.

The most important point is New England's self-conscious traditionalism. When they were founded in the seventeenth century as "closed, corporate, Christian utopian communities"—to use Kenneth Lockridge's phrase—New England towns were intended to be refuges from the greed, the disruption, and the tensions of pre-Revolution England. Their way stressed consensus, harmony, internal agreement, and a focus on the whole rather than on the individual. During the seventeenth century their static, noncommercial lifestyle was more or less in harmony with such values. By 1700, however, their attempt to escape from the course of Western history was failing. Open-field farming gave way to enclosed farms and to nonagricultural business. New wealth and new poverty appeared, and overcrowding brought heavy pressure on the land. Meanwhile the monopoly of faith once held by the Congregational Church was in full flight, as Anglicans, Baptists, Quakers, Presbyterians, and sectarians established themselves.

These changes, and parallel ones in politics, meant the destruction of the communal way of life that had supported the early values of harmony and stability, but the old ways of thinking and feeling died hard. As a number of scholars have shown, family and emotional ties kept many men and women in the old communities despite the bleak future that they offered, despite the fact that "New England society had to expand geographically or it would die."[74] Those who did move north or west continued to organize themselves in towns. Much emphasis properly has been laid on the fact that at the outset, these towns were owned by speculators and not by community builders, but once a town was incorporated absentees were excluded from its public life, and community decision-making was once again possible. Kent, Connecticut, at its founding in 1738 hardly had the fullness of utopianism that had been present in Dedham, Massachusetts, a century earlier. But the political stability and insularity that were to be found in both Kent and nearby Windham in succeeding years lead one to think that, in an attenuated form at least, the old values were there. Even the tumultuous religious revival of the 1740s—the Great Awakening—included a strong thrust towards recapturing the fraternity that was draining out of New England.[75] The suggestion here is that although by mid-century the old New England order was moribund, Yankee popular culture included a real disposition towards resistance to change away from it.

But seventeenth-century Puritanism had been radical as well as nostalgic. It produced wild men and women who turned the English world upside down, as well as the contented inhabitants of utopias in Massachusetts; it produced Anne Hutchinson as well as John Winthrop. Puritan radicalism likewise survived. Anne Grant, who reminisced lovingly about the ways of the pre-Revolution New York grandees and who hated New Englanders, noted it when she complained that "Obadiah or Zephaniah from Hampshire or Connecticut. . .came in without knocking; sat down without invitation; and lighted their pipe without ceremony; then talked of buying land; and finally began a discourse on politics which would have done honour to Praise God Barebones, or any of the members of his Parliament."[76] Both radicalism and nostalgia showed themselves in the land riots, for both in the Hudson Valley and in the New Hampshire grants there was a conjuncture of the seemingly contradictory themes of private property and individualistic acquisition, which were the essence of the coming American social order, with those of community and fraternity. The large speculations of Ethan Allen and the small ones of Benedict and Rebecca Alford say much about the expectations of the Green Mountain Boys. But other, equally important goals are suggested by the fact that the Alfords and the others who founded the Vermont town of Chittenden in 1780 platted it on the traditional New England basis of a nucleated village surrounded by farmers' fields.[77]

Once in the New Hampshire grants, the settlers found themselves in confrontation with New York institutions and practices that negated both private ambition and the New England way. The prospect of absentee ownership and tenancy, stiff quitrents, and government by county courts filled with men like Philip Schuyler, Philip Skene, and William Duer explains the determination of the New Hampshire grantees to hold onto both their titles and their political institutions. In the Hudson Valley matters were much more complex, but the contradictions were equally sharp. As Alice Kenney has stressed, the Dutch of New York had their own communitarian ethos, likewise emphasizing the primacy and the collective liberty of the whole rather than the individual. The cooperation of Dutch and Yankees in the land riots gives evidence that on some deep level the two groups found affinities, which may not be really surprising. Language, costume, the architecture of their homes, and religion set eighteenth-century American ethnic groups apart, but lurking behind such differences there may well have been a general rural way of viewing the world of which New England communalism was only one form. The evidence hints that even when country people settled on dispersed farms rather than in nucleated villages, their social thought was couched in terms not of rugged individualism but of families extending through time and religious and ethnic communities extending through space. Whether rural insurgents envisaged a future of freehold family farms or one of tidy villages may be less important than the contradiction between any of their views and the blending of seigneurialism and capitalism that was represented by Beverly Robinson, Robert Livingston, Jr., and James Duane.[78]

Scraps, hints, suggestive vignettes, and borrowed arguments—one can make sense of these bits of information from widely scattered sources in only a very tentative way. There is, however, good evidence that some insurgents were thinking consciously along some of these lines. The demands of the tenants for actual or virtual abolition of the great manors and William Prendergast's comment that the rioters of 1766 sought "the good of the country" speak, though in a fuzzy and ambiguous way, to the point. Several of the Green Mountain sources raise the theme of communalism more explicitly. "The Vision of Junus, the Benningtonite," a mock Biblical essay published late in 1772, spoke of the "holy Hill of Bennington," of "the People of the L--d" who dwelt there, and of the hatred that the heathen Albanians, Schanachidyans, and Kinderhookites felt for them. Parody, surely, but coming from a people who would soon give rise to Joseph Smith and William Miller, the founders, respectively, of Mormonism and Seventh-Day Adventism, it is not to be lightly dismissed. And when the Reverend Aaron Hutchinson addressed the founders of Vermont in 1777 he stressed the need of the new state's leaders to cherish the internal love and harmony that bound their community together. The need of the Vermonters was to protect these precious qualities against both outside enemies and internal divisiveness. Belief in God's special blessing on one's own community, fear of outsiders, and a cherishing of social harmony are themes that could have fitted perfectly into the New England towns that have been called "peaceable kingdoms."[79]

Even the old question of whether the Hudson Valley tenants and the grants settlers were peasants may be reopened. The term "peasant" resounds strangely in an American context, but it needs to be stressed that to be a peasant is not necessarily to be a feudal serf, that peasant grievances can extend to far more than rack rent, and that peasant protest does not necessarily take the form of a jacquerie. As Samuel Huntington puts it, in an argument that bears extended quotation, a peasantry caught up in rapid development can be a force of enormous revolutionary potential.

> In agrarian society, a more equitable distribution of *ownership* is the prerequisite to economic growth. . . . It is precisely for this reason that the tensions of the countryside are potentially so much more revolutionary than those of the city. The industrial worker cannot secure personal ownership or control of the means

> of production; this, however, is precisely the goal of the peasant. The basic factor of production is land; the supply of land is limited if not fixed; the landlord loses what the peasant acquires. Thus the peasant. . .has no alternative but to attack the existing system of ownership and control.[80]

A good case has already been made for applying the term to early New Englanders, and the Hudson Valley landlords certainly envisaged their tenants as playing the role of a peasantry. The New Hampshire grantees even described themselves as "hard labouring, industrious, honest peasants." Moreover, some of the rioters showed the classic peasant belief that the king, if only he could know, would be on their side. "Junus the Benningtonite," for example, spoke of the rioters' enemies "[James] Duane and [John Tabor] Kemp," who strove to set "the Lord's anointed against his people, falsely accusing them before the Court of Great Britain." Despite the realities of Anglo-American politics, such beliefs may not have been wholly misplaced. The royal proclamation of 1767 ordering New York to cease granting Green Mountain land and the royal pardon of 1766 that saved William Prendergast from the brutal death to which a New York Court sentenced him demonstrate the point.[81] And most important, the problem in both cases was the classic question in peasant revolution, Who would have the land and the political and social power that went with it? On that count perhaps it makes little difference ultimately whether the rioters themselves saw their model of an alternative to landlord domination in the communal life of early Dedham, in the burgeoning individualism of early Pennsylvania, or, as seems most likely, in an uneasy mixture of the two.

The common problem that rural rioters faced helps to explain their most striking similarity: the way they behaved. Both in the Hudson Valley and in the Green Mountains rioters created durable, well-organized, and disciplined movements that lasted for years and that chose their targets carefully. The Hudson Valley rioters were the less structured, but their movement lasted through the whole of the 1750s, erupted in the great revolt of 1766, fed into dissident politics in the late 1760s, and led to a tortuous pattern of popular royalism and popular revolution in the 1770s. Even in its first phase, when it consisted of not much more than turmoil in the border country, it had clearly recognized leaders, such as Michael Hallenbeck, Josiah Loomis, and Robert Noble, and as the first wave was subsiding in 1762 "the Club" was still self-conscious enough to appoint "an agent to go for them to New York City in order to procure title from the Governor for the land at Taghkanick." The great rising of 1766 was preceded by the choice of a general leader, the setting up of a committee to aid him, the formation of militia companies, and the election of captains for them. When they took to the field, the rioters tried captured enemies before their own courts. And they knew the importance of solidarity, for "it was the resolution of the Mob that if any Tenants setld without the Rest they should be destroyed."[82]

The Green Mountain insurgents had the advantage of starting with the New England town structures that New Hampshire had created, and as Yankees poured into the region, they developed the full spirit of New England local life. Men leading rioters identified themselves to Yorkers as militia officers, constables, sheriffs, and justices of the peace. Committees were coordinating insurgents' actions as early as 1769, and during 1772 and 1773 the rioters took formal shape as the Green Mountain Boys. By the latter year they were following the example of the rising of 1766, establishing courts "appointed by their own authority." The case of the wretched Yorker who suffered two hundred lashes for acting as a justice of the peace shows how well the rioters had learned the lessons of cruelty taught by more conventionally appointed courts in the eighteenth century.[83]

Land rioters created countergovernments that exercised, or tried to exercise, almost all of the functions that government was expected to carry out in the eighteenth century. When they rioted and held popular trials, they attacked landlords, smaller men who supported what the landlords stood for, and courts and law officers that executed the landlords' will. Though land rioting took place only on the east bank of the Hudson and in the far northeast, it nonetheless challenged New York's geographical definition, one of its fundamental institutions, and the power and profits of much of its elite. It is hardly to be wondered at that the elite—whether DeLancey or Livingston, protoroyalist or protorepublican, moderate or firebrand on the question of how to resist Britain—viewed land rioters with the utmost seriousness.

III

The behavior, the make-up, and the concerns of urban crowds were different. Instead of attacking sheriffs, courthouses, landlords, and landlords' dependents, urban folk rioted over stamps, destroyed personal property, brawled with British soldiers, sacked houses, and tore down the Chapel Street theater. It is the attack on the theater that poses the puzzle. The actors playing in it had nothing to do with British policy, which had been the main surface issue during the preceding months, in late 1765 and early 1766. They even included a "song in praise of Liberty" in their program. But Captain John Montresor blamed the sacking on the political radicals who had fought the Stamp Act, and he reported that the crowd shouted "Liberty! Liberty!" as they carried pieces of the demolished building to the common for burning.[84] Taken by itself it is a mere incident, but to place it in context requires exploring a dimension of New York City popular life that has been largely neglected.

There is little "hard" evidence to bear the feeling out, but one senses that crowds of several different sorts rioted in New York City during the late 1760s. The distinction is perhaps more analytical than demographic, for the same people must have been on the streets in most affairs. But it seems that leadership, precise make-up, and motivation varied rather than held constant. It also seems that crowd action had threatening implications for the provincial elite as well as for the civil and military British authorities.

The starting point is the fact that from 1763 until well after 1770 New York City suffered a massive trade depression. This was just as much a cause of worry as the Stamp Act, the Townshend Acts, the New York Suspending Act, customs racketeering, and the presence of troops; indeed, it blended with the imperial issues in a way that even contemporaries may not have fully appreciated. The pages, for instance, of John Holt's newspaper,[85] which was a major voice of the radical movement, show as much concern about trade, unemployment, and poverty as they do about imperial politics. The ways in which these concerns were expressed, in which they led directly to some crowd actions, and in which they fed into uprisings that on the surface seem concerned purely with the question of British imperialism involve a deep background of urban corporatism and a more shallow background of changing relations between men who had wealth, power, and prominence and men who had none of such things.

The corporatism of eighteenth-century New York, inherited from both Dutch and English urban traditions, implied mutual responsibilities on the part of rich and poor, rulers and ruled. The word *corporatism* sums up a collective expectation that men of power and wealth would act to remedy problems of popular concern, an expectation that must have gone some distance towards legitimating the privileges that such men had. But in some circumstances it also legitimated the idea that "the people" could act to remedy wrongs for themselves. Its most important and complete expression was in the way that the authorities of both New Amsterdam and New York controlled the supply, distribution, and quality of food and fuel.[86]

Throughout the colonial period, controlled markets, in which quantity, quality, and price could be guaranteed, were the prime urban means of distributing staples. As early as 1648 Peter Stuyvesant's government established a market and fair after the manner of Amsterdam. After the British conquest, Governor Thomas Dongan renewed "the benefit of ye Markett" and limited the sale of provisions to the area within its bounds. In 1684 the city council legislated against the market offenses of "forestalling," or buying provisions that were on their way to market; "regrating," buying in the market with intent to sell again; and "engrossing," contracting with farmers to buy in bulk before crops were even gathered. In 1742 these laws were renewed, the government having promulgated very detailed regulations for the marketing of grain and meat in the previous year. By 1776 there were five controlled markets in the city. Until well into the nineteenth century one of the tasks of the city fathers was to establish the assize of bread, which was the maximum price at which an ordinary brown loaf might be sold. Their charge was to calculate a price that would balance a fair return for the bakers against people's need for food they could afford. Though the bakers might protest, as they did in 1763, that the price set on brown bread was too low, "the leading citizens" agreed "that in all populous Cities the Regulation of the public Markets respecting the Price of Provisions hath ever been esteemed a Matter of great Importance to the Inhabitants and worth the Attention of the Public." The authorities again emphasized the importance of the grain supply when they exempted millers, along with public officials, schoolmasters, and ironworkers, from military service.[87]

Social welfare was not the only reason for such regulations; they also reflected the need of ever-marching armies for supplies and the requirement that New York's produce have a reputation for full weight and good quality in the markets of the West Indies and Europe. But when the Dutch government regulated taverns in 1657 it exempted wine, which was "not so necessary for the common people," from price controls but set a maximum price on beer. When in 1741 the provincial council forbade the export of wheat it was because "the poor, both in town and country, were distressed." Seven years later, in 1748, the city fathers asked the governor for another embargo on wheat because "great and Unusual Exportation. . .to foreign markets" had made provisions "most excessive dear, to the very Great Oppression of all Degrees of People, but more especially to the industrious Poor." In 1760, when prices rose again, the magistrates set up a public subscription and used the proceeds "for the relief of the poor." And in 1740 the funeral of the wife of Lieutenant Governor George Clarke was marked by the distribution of a loaf of bread "to every poor person who would receive it." It had been "a pleasure" to the lady "in her life to feed the hungry." If popular direct action was to be prevented, these were things the elite had to do.[88]

Generally the elite enforced the regulations, and popular risings did not take place. But newspaper accounts from Europe and popular memory kept the tradition of legitimate direct action alive, and there were times when people did demonstrate. In the winter of 1753–54, when the city's merchants effectively revalued the province's coinage by refusing any longer to accept halfpence at the old rate, it became "the popular cry that the Merchants did it, with a design to sharp them away." Processions wound through the streets in protest, the marchers led by a drummer and armed with clubs and stones. A decade later a newspaper warned that "if unreasonable Restraints are laid upon Liberty, if Property is invaded, Care and Industry distressed, so that the People are poor, discontented, and unhappy; then it is evident to Demonstration, that there is something amiss in the Government, which must either be reform'd or the Destruction of that Government will be the inevitable Consequence." This may not be a complete skeleton, but enough bones have been dug up to expose an American version of the "moral economy of the English crowd" that Edward Thompson has reconstructed.[89] This is one key to the secrets of popular action in New York during the decade before independence.

But there are other keys as well. New York's revolutionary crowds also included respectable mechanics, artisans, and small merchants. For these, starvation in the winter or freezing for lack of firewood were unlikely prospects. If the genuinely poor had few ways besides protest of making themselves visible, the "middling sort" had far more opportunities. They could vote, and politicians eagerly solicited their support whenever a poll was near. During the late colonial period polls came often—ten times between 1740 and 1775 for the provincial assembly—and they were sometimes hard fought. Although everyone could see how a man voted in these viva-voce elections, and although, as Stanley Katz comments, voters often may have been indifferent, naive, and deferential, elections were still fought on the strategy of lustily inviting the public to have its say.[90] John Peter Zenger, who may have pioneered popular political journalism in America, published such verses as this "Song Made Upon the Election of New Magistrates for this City":

To you good lads that dare oppose
  all lawless power and might,
You are the theme that we have chose,
  and to your Praise we write;
You dared to show your faces brave
In spite of every abject slave;
    with a fa la la
And though the Great ones frown at this,
  what need have you to care?
Still let them fret and talk amiss,
  you'll show you boldly dare
Stand up to save your country dear,
In spite of usquebaugh and beer;
    with a fa la la.[91]

"Usquebaugh," which was whiskey, beer, and fa la las there were aplenty, at New York elections, but there were also appeals for people to vote on higher grounds. Morrisites, Cosbyites, DeLanceys, and Livingstons joined in a tradition of inviting the middling sort to act as members of the political community that went back to Jacob Leisler. The invitations were usually cynical; politicians who fought their way into office on the principle of being friends of "the country" rather than of "the court" behaved once in power "no differently than had their erstwhile opponents, many of whom were now their allies."[92] But their appeals to principle had many effects. One was to stimulate voter turnout, which at times ran to over half of the white male population of the city. Another was to get people used to thinking in terms of issues as well as personalities. And a third, perhaps reflected in the intermittent agitation for a secret ballot, was to lay the groundwork for a cynicism among electors about those whom they chose that would match the cynicism of politicians themselves. Colonial political practice was shot through with paradox; people who could meet the property requirement were invited to think for themselves and vote accordingly, but no one seriously expected that the rhetoric of election time would have any real impact on the behavior of politicians who had used it to gain office. Nor did anyone expect that between elections the "Great ones" would treat voters with the respect and bonhomie that they might show at election time.

Poor people who believed that tradition could justify direct action and middling people who were neither in nor out of the political community were the constituent elements of New York City's revolutionary crowds. But what they did cannot be understood without reference to the imperial crisis and to the emergence during it of the Sons of Liberty as an organized and disciplined cadre. Pauline Maier, in her study of the colonial radicals, and Roger Champagne and Robert Christen, in their discussions of Alexander McDougall and Isaac Sears, have shown that what drove the militants was concern that New York should respond energetically to Britain's challenge. The Sons of Liberty cannot be understood either as a vanguard of the lower classes or as domestic revolutionaries bent on changing New York itself.[93]

But it remains true that the Sons of Liberty were men on the make, the successful children of oyster catchers, milkmen, and indentured servants. Men of their type had played no significant political role, beyond voting, prior to the Stamp act, and their emergence as popular leaders was a political novelty of no small dimensions. It also remains true that they had far more affinity with popular concerns in the late 1760s than did the gentlemen, the merchants, and the lawyers who dominated established politics. Whether or not they meant to, their emergence helped begin an internal revolution.

One can find their affinity with popular concerns in the people among whom they lived. Thus Isaac Sears, himself a sometime sea captain, was the son-in-law of the publican who ran the tavern where many merchant sailors drank. One can find it in the things they wrote and in the way they wrote them. Tom Paine epitomized this with his creation of a language, at the same time sophisticated and popular, that could express the thoughts of people who had discovered a new political identity. In 1765 Paine's *Common Sense* was still more than a decade away, but while some colonists were pondering the recondite arguments against the Stamp Act of a Daniel Dulaney others were reading articles such as an essay that appeared in the *New York Mercury*. Its language was purple ("It is enough to melt a stone or even the harder heart of a villain, when he views this wretched land. . . . Methinks the guardian angel of America rises to my view! Indignation and the most poignant grief cloud his lovely face."), but it spoke to the fact that concern about the Stamp Act was not restricted to the Whig elite. And it threatened the province's malefactors that "misery, even in this life, shall be your portion."[94]

But the radicals and the established elite also diverged in the way they responded to domestic popular concerns. My argument here must be constructed from bits of circumstantial evidence that are scattered through the record of the crisis decade, and it could easily be overstated. But it suggests that corporatist feeling stood to city rioters as nostalgic communalism did to rural ones. It suggests as well that after 1765 the bundle of beliefs that the word *corporatism* tries to encompass was losing its power in the minds of elite New Yorkers. The fury and variety of urban crowd action were, in other words, what popular culture made legitimate when the elite proved unresponsive to popular needs.

The initial response of the powerful in New York to the depression that followed the Seven Years' War was what tradition demanded. In 1764, when newspapers began to report that the slump had "reduced very many Families and poor People to great Distress," a plan was launched to end unemployment by domestic manufactures. Its sponsor was "The Society for the Promoting of Arts, Agriculture and Oeconomy," and the scheme was given the most prominent possible billing in the newspapers. This publicity was accompanied by a campaign against general extravagance. Thus in January 1765 it was reported that a gentleman had appeared at the funeral of his only son without displaying the expensive imported mourning regalia that the custom of his class required. New Yorkers were told not to eat lamb and to boycott butchers who slaughtered sheep so that the society's workers could have wool to spin. When nonimportation was introduced as a weapon against the Stamp Act, one important effect was even further stimulation of home manufactures. Domestic products would be sold, it was announced, in the controlled markets, which symbolized the traditional way of doing things. Townsmen and townswomen were urged to buy only there and not from "hawkers and strollers."[95]

But the development after 1765 of a glittering pattern of conspicuous consumption suggests that some New Yorkers had begun to take the rhetoric of mutual responsibility less than seriously. In June 1765 summer nights began to be graced by concerts in the elegant pleasure gardens at Ranelagh, named in imitation of a similar spot in London. In October of the same year a third coach maker went into business, advertising that his wares were "in the genteelest taste, and equal to any made in Europe." He offered coaches, chariots, phaetons, and chairs to his customers. The Chapel Street theater began its new productions in May 1766. Towards the end of the same year one Yorker proudly informed a London newspaper that "notwithstanding the great complaints of the distressing times, we have here no less than four coaches which were brought hither from London in the last ship." In 1767, during the worst of the depression, the "Gentlemen Officers of the Army" gave a "grand entertainment and Ball" for the city gentry. At the festivity "there was the most numerous and brilliant appearance of both sexes that ever was known in this place." In the same year patrons planning on an evening's Shakespeare were given specific traffic directions in order to prevent "accidents by coaches." By 1770 there were eighty-five pleasure vehicles in town; these included twenty-six coaches, thirty-three chariots, and twenty-six phaetons, owned by only sixty-two people.[96]

The same popular newspapers and the same Sons of Liberty that demanded militance against the Stamp Act and the Townshend Acts roundly condemned such display. By April 1766 the Sons of Liberty would "not suffer any Lamb to be brought to market nor eat, under penalty of having the offenders house pulled down." Readers of John Holt's pages saw article upon article criticizing the selfishness of the rich. Satires castigated fashionable youth who would not give up their finery. Discourses opposed the imprisonment of insolvent debtors. In February 1766 a long article written against usurious creditors attacked the way that relations between landlords and tenants had deteriorated: "our Landlords (or rather house usurers)" were raising rents outrageously and were safeguarding their illegitimate profits by making tenants responsible for taxes and repairs. But though "avarice of landlords" might lead to evictions, "no well wisher to the public" would bid so much on the vacant property "as the present tenant."[97]

Holt printed accounts of the popular risings with which the poor of London responded to the engrossment of grain there. One of his writers, styling himself "a Tradesman," asked in 1767 why the paper's coverage of "our distressed situation" had lessened. "Are our Circumstances altered? Is Money grown more Plenty? Have our Tradesmen full Employment? Are we more frugal? Is Grain cheaper? Are our Importations less? – Not to mention the Playhouse and Equipages, which it is hoped none but People of Fortune frequent or use." What had become of the "youthful Vigour" of the Society for Promoting Manufactures? What would become of people who were faced with a long winter "unprovided with Firewood, or Money to buy it?" Meanwhile piece after piece condemned the playhouse. Let "Philander," who remarked with shock that he had heard of as much as fifty pounds being paid for a season ticket, while poor people starved, stand for them all.[98]

Such rhetoric provides the context for such actions as the disruption of the second of Ranelagh concerts in 1765 or the sacking of the theater a year later. It was reported before the attack on the playhouse that advertisements for its opening had given offense to "many of the Inhabitants of this City, who thought it highly improper that such Entertainments should be exhibited at this time of public distress, when great Numbers of poor people can scarce find means of subsistence." But it partially explains as well the fury of the attack on the property of Lieutenant Governor Colden and Major James during the Stamp Act distrubances. Both men had provided the people with ample excuse for hating them. Even without his intransigence on the matter of the stamps, Colden's conduct of provincial politics was utterly maladroit. Though he was a skillful placeman, a pioneering anthropologist, and a eminent natural scientist, he was an abysmal judge of human affairs. His needless provocation of the issues of judicial tenure and jury trials, both by attacking cherished common-law practices and, covertly, by threatening the tenure of the great landlords, just prior to the Sugar Act opened New York's "prologue to revolution," and his enemies seized the chance he had given them to vilify him. James was the sort of British officer who wore his hat at a "damn my eyes cock," and he threatened publicly to cram the stamps down New Yorkers' throats and "drive them out of town for a pack of rascals." He was also the officer who carried out Colden's order to train the guns of Fort George on the city rather than towards the harbor.[99] But carriages like Colden's and houses like James's were prime symbols, in their time, of wealth and, in the context of the depression, of social irresponsibility. The property of Colden and James was politically "safe," like that of Thomas Hutchinson, in Boston, or Martin Howard, in Newport. But it seems a fair suspicion that it stood surrogate for the property of many other wealthy men.

Nine years after the Stamp Act crisis Gouverneur Morris observed that what worried his sort was not that the crowd existed but that "the mob" was beginning "to think and to reason." But the people whom Morris dismissed as "poor reptiles" in his often quoted letter to Mr. Penn had always thought and reasoned. A good part of what Morris was trying to explain stemmed from the divergence between an elite that was moving rapidly towards a laissez-faire understanding of the world and ordinary people, both middling and poor, for whom corporatist ways would retain their appeal for two generations to come. On social questions the plebs and the better sort were thinking and reasoning in different ways. But Morris's astute comments also suggest that the decade of crisis had seen a quantum jump in the ability of people in the crowd to think and to reason for themselves on political questions. Some evidence suggests otherwise. John Montresor acidly observed several times that the crowd was merely being manipulated. When the Stamp Act riots were subsiding he noted that lawyers and people of property had been "at the bottom of this disloyal Insurrection." In February 1766 he wrote in his diary that "the Libertines" were much concerned "that the Gentlemen of Fortune" were hanging back in public from commitments they had made in private. Cadwallader Colden took a similar view, likewise blaming the judges and lawyers for arousing common people.[100]

But even Montresor and Colden provide evidence that not all crowds were led by gentlemen in disguise. Sometimes the evidence is direct. When "a great riot" erupted in mid-February 1766 as a result of secret transactions involving stamps, its two "general officers. . . were Tony and Daly two ship carpenters who it seems. . . can either raise or suppress a Mob instantly." The first time Yorkers demonstrated against the felling of their liberty pole by British troops, Montresor commented that "the principal Townspeople (for a wonder)" were "not immediately at the bottom of this." And a street parade that carried Governor Bernard of Massachusetts and Sheriff Greenleaf of Boston in effigy was opposed rather than led by "the discreet inhabitants."[101] Other evidence is more circumstantial. Late in November 1765 John Montresor described current popular goals: "Having their assembly first to have the Stamp Act repealed. To repeal an act passed by them for no one to trespass on another man's ground with arms, to detain the Lieut. Governor's revenue towards defraying the damages Major James's house sustained." These hardly seem the desires of a manipulative elite. Two weeks previously, at the end of the first wave of Stamp Act riots, General Gage had reported that "the people of property" were alarmed and that "the citizens" were concerned "for the Safety of the Town." And when the newly arrived Governor Sir Henry Moore embarked on a moderate program in order to cool the Stamp Act disturbances, he sent for Isaac Sears, hardly one of the elite, "to preserve the peace of the city."[102]

The purpose of this elaborate discussion is to argue that understanding New York City's revolutionary crowds requires probing in several directions. No single explanation, be it the beastliness of mankind, agitation by radicals, upper-class manipulation, or simple resentment against the British, can account for all that must be understood. Corporatist popular culture taken by itself would be no more satisfactory. I have given it such emphasis because it resolves some questions in the tangled mass of crowd behavior that would otherwise go without solution and because it provides a more powerful understanding of well-known events. The overall model being offered includes not only corporatism but also the more familiar explanations mentioned above, not excluding the capacity of people for behaving horribly to their fellows.

To see how the many factors that motivated New York's crowds came together, let us return to one of the most violent incidents, the Battle of Golden Hill, in January 1770. The events are fairly straightforward: late in that month two days of street fighting took place between civilians, including a large number of merchant seamen, and soldiers of Britain's Sixteenth Regiment of Foot. The riots followed upon proclamations and counter proclamations, the destruction by the troops of the latest in a long series of liberty poles, and the sacking by the same soldiers of a tavern that was popular with radicals and working men. The riots in Golden Hill and Nassau Street were the last incidents in a long series of contretemps between New Yorkers and soldiers, and they were the culmination of particularly strong bitterness that centered on the Sixteenth Regiment. Historically they are far less well known than the King Street riot in Boston, usually called the Boston Massacre, which took place six weeks later. Whereas until independence Bostonians commemorated what had happened in their city with speeches and demonstrations, New Yorkers, in public at least, preferred to forget.

And historians ever since have followed the lead the two separate cities gave.

As Lee Boyer has shown in the first serious published study of these riots, "the violence took place against a backdrop of constitutional rhetoric and a felled liberty pole, as well as local poverty and unemployment, and was, partly, the upshot of a vigorous labor market rivalry between troops and populace."[103] Both the rhetoric that swirled around the affair and the half-decade of strife between town and garrison that preceded it involved not only the actual combatant groups of those two January days but also the provincial authorities and the city's economic leaders. The willingness of New Yorkers to brawl with the soldiers represents, in other words, a particular focus and a politicization of far broader grievances.

Standing armies were never popular in early America, but until the end of the Seven Years' War they at least had the rationale of being there to fight the French. Thereafter the British forces, both military and naval, seemed to be there to raise difficulties. Trouble began in New York in 1764, when soldiers broke into the city prison to rescue one of their officers, who was imprisoned for debt, and when the H.M.S. *Chaleur* harassed fishermen in the harbor. In the following year the H.M.S. *Hawke* harassed the ocean traffic on which the city depended for its livelihood, while townsfolk smarted under the arrogance of such officers as Major James and Captain Montresor, who dismissed Americans as "boorish peasants." Enlisted men's attitudes began to match their officers', and it was reflected in such actions as the stabbing of a Son of Liberty with a bayonet. How people responded is shown by the readiness with which Stamp Act rioters gathered before Fort George, by what happened to James's house, and by talk at the end of 1765 of sacking the house of Captain Archibald Kennedy, commander of the navy's duty ship in the harbor, owner of considerable city property, and a son-in-law of the Schuyler family.

Between 1766 and 1770 tension between town and garrison focused symbolically on the succession of liberty poles erected in the fields to commemorate American resistance. These stood directly in front of the upper barracks, where many of the troops lived, and successive regiments made it a point of honor to cut them down. They often succeeded, but at a high price. The first time they cut down a pole, a crowd of more than two thousand, led by Isaac Sears, assembled to protest. The fight that followed precipitated a month of street battles. Thereafter New Yorkers made it an equal point of honor to break the soldiers' ranks as they marched in the streets and to bar them from inns and the market.[104]

Inns and markets were not the only places from which New Yorkers tried to bar soldiers. The troops themselves were lower-class Britons, and they were both ill-rewarded for their service and intensely aware that however much civilians might value them in wartime, they were reviled in time of peace. As the Sixteenth Regiment collectively explained in a broadside on the eve of the Golden Hill rioting,

> God and a Soldier all Men doth adore,
> in time of War, and not before:
> When the War is over, and all Things righted,
> God is forgotten, and the Soldier slighted.

The provincial assembly drove home what their hosts thought of the soldiers with its celebrated refusal in 1767 to implement Parliament's Quartering Act. Politically its refusal to vote the supplies for the troops that the act commanded was popular. Ideologically it was easily justified. But to the soldiers it was injury as well as insult.[105]

Ever since there had been a garrison in New York, custom had permitted off-duty troops to supplement their wretched pay by taking casual work. They would labor at very cheap prices, and without question their extra income meant for them the difference between an utterly frugal standard of living and one with some comfort. But the depression of the late 1760s made even menial jobs valuable to native New Yorkers, and complaints about unfair competition from enlisted men became even more common than threats against the opulence of their officers. As early as 1766 Montresor recorded that people were "complaining of the Injustice done them by the Captains of the Stationed Ships of War . . . for suffering their men to hire themselves out to work at the Dockyards which means they serve for less than other Men and lower the price of workmanship." And in January 1770, in what may have been the major spark igniting the Golden Hill affair, "Brutus" drove home what the taking of work by soldiers did to civilians. "Whosoever seriously considers the impovrished state of this City; especially of many of the poor inhabitants of it, must be greatly surprised at the Conduct of such of them as Employ the Soldiers, when there are a number of [city people] that want Employment to support their distressed Families." "Brutus" has been identified as both John Lamb and Alexander McDougall, and no matter which it was, the broadside underscores the connection between the Sons of Liberty and the city's working people.[106]

Both early analysts of the riots and their most recent student agree that that essay, by inciting people to drive soldiers out of their jobs at the "flax seed and Flour stores," was "the original cause of the battles." But what needs stress is that though the crowd's anger was directed at the soldiers, it had many causes and many possible targets. "Brutus" said that the "just Reproaches of the Poor" might fall on Yorkers who hired soldiers, as well as on the troops themselves. Such "just reproaches" had already fallen in ample quantity on Major James and on the company of actors.[107]

The issue of the soldiers spilled over to that of the political elite, as well as to the economic issue. Provincial politicians gained great credit in 1767 by refusing to implement the Quartering Act. But over the next two years they showed themselves as cynical about their refusal to supply the troops as New York politicians had ever been on any issue. The Livingstons, who controlled the assembly until 1768, won the initial kudos but then retreated before the threat of Parliament's act suspending the assembly. The DeLanceys, who poured scorn on that retreat to great effect in the election campaigns of 1768 and 1769, themselves retreated as soon as they were safely in power. And Alexander McDougall's famous broadside of December 1769, "To the Betrayed Inhabitants of the City and Colony of New York," pointed popular grievances about the troops towards the rulers of the province. McDougall's concern was constitutional and ideological rather than with the soldiers' taking work from civilians, but even more effectively than "Brutus" he fused imperial and domestic concerns. It was true, he wrote, that "a free people" ought "not to grant the troops any Supply whatsoever," for they were "kept here, not to protect but to enslave us." It was true that British officers like "the audacious, domineering and inhuman Maj[or] Pullaine" were undermining the American movement by providing military protection for violators of nonimportation. But what was most true was that the conduct of the province's own assembly in voting supplies was "BASE [and] INGLORIOUS" and that the province's greatest enemies were its own rulers. The assembly's angry response to the broadside, which included imprisoning McDougall when his authorship was discovered and browbeating him as he stood at its bar, provoked yet more demonstrations. But in 1770 the time for a frontal assault on the assembly was still a half-decade away.[108]

In the final analysis crowd action in New York City formed an unbroken whole. Popular leaders implied as much by their unwillingness to condemn their followers for getting out of hand: New York saw nothing equivalent to the distinction that Boston leaders drew between "legitimate" rioting, like the Stamp Act demonstrations of 14 August 1765, and "illegitimate" affairs, like the sacking of Thomas Hutchinson's house twelve days later.[109] On the contrary: radical newspapers indiscriminately mixed articles about the imperial crisis and protests about domestic depression; Sons of Liberty led the assault on the Chapel Street theater as well as that on Fort George; radical pamphleteers attacked the presence of soldiers because they took New Yorkers' bread, as well as because they threatened liberty; and the same pamphleteers abused the prominent New Yorkers who employed and supplied the soldiers, as well as the soldiers themselves. Rioting was precisely analogous to the "public theater" of elections, costume, ceremonial, conspicuous property, courts, executions, and responsiveness to popular needs by which the old elite had long maintained its control. On both stages the play was sometimes very much for real, with lives and property being destroyed as the plot unfolded. But in the late 1760s the plot was far more complicated than it had ever been before. Among its elements were hostility to the British, a social tradition that was under strain, and the feelings of middling New Yorkers who could identify at least partly with the poor and who could smart at the scorn of the rich. And among them too were the numerous ways—propaganda and manipulation but also assessment of their own situation—by which "the mob" learned "to think and to reason." Both the writings of men close to "the mob" and its members' own actions show that the thinking and the reasoning extended to far more than purely imperial concerns.

IV

"When they went to New York they expected to be assisted by the poor people there." So said Moss Kent to the court that was trying William Prendergast in 1766. There were enough reasons for the rural rioters to expect such assistance, despite John Montresor's remark that the urban Sons of Liberty were "great opposers to these Rioters as they are of opinion that no one is entitled to Riot but themselves." Montresor had his point; the radical lawyer John Morin Scott, rather than aiding the country folk, sat on the court that condemned them. But there were connections between the two waves of violence that occurred during the twelve months between October 1765 and October 1766.[110]

Governor Sir Henry Moore was probably near the mark when he informed Secretary Conway that the example of the city's tumultuous winter had been one cause of the Hudson Valley's eruption. And not all city people were as hostile to the "levellers" as was John Morin Scott. John Holt's newspaper carried a significant number of essays and news items that were sympathetic. The "Thoughts on Usury" that Holt published on 6 February 1766 were just as much an attack on landlord practices as on the extortion of interest by moneylenders, and though the author was talking of city landlords, his discussion could have applied just as well in the Hudson Valley. In May, when the tenant insurgency was at its hottest, Holt noted an action of the Dutchess County Sons of Liberty without bothering to distinguish them, it they could be distinguished, from the land rioters. In July his paper published a request for an "impartial narrative" of what was happening to the north. When William Prendergast was on trial Holt noted approvingly that Lady Moore, the wife of the governor, had supplied bail for most of the rioters. His paper stressed the heroic behavior of Prendergast's own wife, who may have saved her husband's life by dashing to New York City to seek a stay of his death sentence while he appealed to the crown. And in August the paper carried an essay that boldly favored the rioters: it spat on "their High Mightinesses. . .the Landlords (as they are called)," and it pointed out that "it is an easy Matter for Men of Wealth and Power to brand with odious Appelations those whom they intend to oppress and injure."[111]

But the fact remains that the rioters got no aid from the city when they wanted it. That may bear out this chapter's contention that land rioters and urban rioters operated in response to different problems and within different traditions. But the lack of cooperation in 1766 also points towards the fact that men in authority took different sorts of rioters with very different degrees of seriousness.

Pauline Maier, Edward Thompson, and Dirk Hoerder have shown separately many reasons why traditional urban crowds were regarded as institutions rather than as aberrations. Some of these reasons involved the relationships of classes, and some turned on the weaknesses of ruling institutions. Crowd action within the corporatist model posed no serious danger to the hegemony of whoever ruled. It did not challenge property relations, and its expectation that the ruling people would act could only confirm their power if they did act. Even where the elite was impotent it could at least give a crowd legitimacy, for what was a posse or a militia unit but a crowd drawn into ranks and given official backing? What, conversely, was a crowd that rioted in a disciplined way to conserve precious grain or to drive out a press-gang but a posse without official sanction? Such crowds acted as informal extensions of a government that by itself could do hardly anything to defend the community; the vast number of unresolved cases before the courts of colonial New York is a measure of how impotent institutions were. In a province where courts could not enforce the law and whose normal annual budget, beyond the governor's salary, was less than three thousand pounds there were many times when it took a posse to enforce the law and when it took a crowd to enforce hallowed custom. Crowds that enforced the moral law when the courts could not enforce the common law or the statute law had a good case for being regarded as legitimate. And such crowds might embody the whole of a threatened community, with gentlemen donning the plain man's long trousers and plain hair instead of their own knee breeches and wigs.[112]

Two things, however, were changing in the 1760s. One was the increasing disaffection of the gentry from the economics of corporatism. Their disaffection showed itself in actions more than in words, though the rationalization for those actions would be articulated by the 1770s and 1780s. But the reaction that theaters and carriages drew from the radical press and from rioters between 1765 and 1770 showed how things were moving. The drift is clearer now than it could have been to an observer then: the Society for Promoting Manufactures, the contents of at least some of the press, and the cool-headedness with which Governor Moore rode out the Stamp Act disorders counterbalanced the overt selfishness represented by those theaters and carriages.

The other thing that changed was popular political awareness, a cause for deep concern in the eyes of men close to power. In January 1766 John Montresor noted two reports in his diary. One was that at a meeting in Hartford, Connecticut, "some were for choosing a Protector as in Oliver

Cromwell's time." And the other was that in Philadelphia a blank book had been found bearing the inscription "G[eorge] by the Cu[r]se of G[o]d, us[ur]per of G[rea]t B[ri]t[ain] and Dest[ro]y[e]r of the Faith." Possibly neither report was true, and certainly neither report referred to New Yorkers. But Montresor was worried, for even if these were just rumors, they indicated that either Americans were bringing forth a new radicalism or else they were reviving memories of the Puritan Commonwealth of the seventeenth century.[113]

In November 1768, when effigies of Governor Bernard and Sheriff Greenleaf were paraded and burned, both Governor Moore and his adviser William Smith took great alarm. The alarm is surprising, since Smith's diary indicates that neither of them displayed any great concern or panic at earlier affairs, including the Stamp Act disturbances. Smith made a long entry in the diary about this demonstration, and he described his own efforts to quell it. His efforts included an attempt to recruit "the discreet inhabitants," eighty firemen among them, in opposition. Smith also interested himself deeply in the wording of a proclamation that the government issued against the demonstration. Moore, meanwhile, made efforts publicly to minimize the riot's significance. His official proclamation dismissed the demonstrators as "a rabble of Negroes and Children." He addressed the assembly about the riot, saying that it "was disapproved by the inhabitants in general" and that it was "imputable only to the indiscretion of a very few persons of the lowest class." But Moore's anxious efforts to rob the riot of significance, like Smith's backstage maneuvers, seem to be a sign of deep concern. Moore's and Smith's fear was not of crowd action by itself; it was of a crowd that could demonstrate on purely political issues and that was turning its attention from imperial to colonial politics.[114]

By contrast, there had never been a time when land rioters and men of power had not taken one another with the greatest seriousness. In 1749, when central New Jersey was torn open by land riots that had much in common with those in the Hudson Valley and the Green Mountains, one of the rioters said that he "wis'd they (meaning the Authority) had fired upon them the said Rioters, for if they had they never should have seen such work, for...*they would have destroy'd them all* and drove them into the sea." When William Prendergast was cautioned that requiring a victim of the 1766 tenant riots to swear an oath "might be ag[ains]t the King," he replied that "if the King was there he would serve him...that Mobs had overcome Kings before and why should they not overcome." Urban rioters may have risen to defend the law, but the uprising that Prendergast led saw "all the jails" on the east bank of the Hudson between New York and Albany "broke open." Colonel Nathan Stone, of the Connecticut Valley town of Windsor, warned in 1771 that he was determined "no writs or precepts" from New York courts should have any effect there. The men who closed the Cumberland County court in 1775 "would not, under the present circumstances, suffer any Magistrate at all," and about the same time the Green Mountain leader Remember Baker explained that his people lived "out of the bounds of the law." And as Ethan Allen put it to Charles Hutchesson while his followers were burning poor Hutchesson's house, "God damn your Governour, Laws, King, Council and Assembly."[115]

Men of power responded to rural rioting with equally powerful words and with powerful actions. This was true throughout eighteenth-century America, and it was as true after independence as before it. Philadelphia panicked when the Paxton Boys approached in the winter of 1763–64, and even Quakers armed themselves. Authorities used armed force to suppress the Carolina Regulator movements in the 1760s, rural royalist insurgency in both the northern and southern states during the War of Independence, Shays's Rebellion in Massachusetts in 1786, and the Whiskey Rebellion in Pennsylvania in 1794. New York's rulers acted in the same spirit. Governor Moore, who could find it in himself to negotiate with the urban crowd leader Isaac Sears at the end of the Stamp Act disturbances, put both regular troops and militia on alert when upcountry rioters approached the city in April 1766 and offered rewards for the capture of their leaders. In June he ordered a regiment of regulars into action to suppress the continuing rising in Dutchess County. General Gage, the commander in chief of the army, urged the officer actually in charge to give the rebels "a good dressing," and after a skirmish in which three soldiers were wounded the troops took pleasure in doing exactly that. Meanwhile landlords in Albany County worked out a stratagem to bring about bloodshed so that the troops could be summoned to their aid. As Kim suggests, "Governor Moore and the council were most eager to support the landlords' cause," and in July and August two detachments fell upon the rebels, plundering the village of Nobletown and conducting other operations according to the principle of search-and-destroy.[116]

Remembering how successful their use of troops against the Hudson Valley rioters had been, New York officials begged Generals Gage and Frederick Haldimand for more redcoats to use against the Green Mountain Boys in 1773 and 1774. Their appeal was unsuccessful, for by that time the British commanders were realizing that they had other worries, but in 1774 the province enacted a special riot-and-treason law for the region. The law was modeled directly on the infamous Black Act, with which Parliament itself had responded to rural disturbances in southern England in the 1720s, and on the laws that were passed in response to the Jacobite uprisings in Scotland in 1715 and 1745. The act declared forfeit the lives of eight of the leaders of the Green Mountain Boys, who were identified by name, if they did not surrender themselves. And it imposed the death penalty for a long list of offenses if they were committed in the troubled area, even though the offenses carried lighter penalties if they were committed outside the area. Urban rioting may have been quasi-legitimate, provided it was without domestic political content, but the offering of a hundred pounds for William Prendergast's capture, the deployment of troops equipped even with artillery against his followers, the death sentence that was imposed on him when the rioting was over, the attempt to send more soldiers to the Green Mountains, and the passage of the special riot act all demonstrate that in the eyes of the authorities rural uprisings were another matter. The seriousness with which they were taken is a sign of how fundamental were the questions that rural insurgents were asking. A grievance over rent, like a traditional urban grievance over food supplies, might have been susceptible to compromise. But a dispute over title to the land could only be wholly won or wholly lost.[117]

During the quarter-century before independence, crowd action stretched and rent the fabric of New York society. Nearly continuous land rioting in one place or another built up a tradition of rural protest that was utterly outside what other New Yorkers regarded as acceptable ways of doing things. Though urban crowds were much more functional within the old order, the decade of imperial strife saw them transformed and politicized. By 1774 both the words and the actions of ordinary people showed that they thought about their place in the world in ways very different from those of ordinary people of only a decade before. There was no single lower-class movement, and few rioters, urban or rural, could have started out with anything resembling revolutionary intentions. Carl Becker's generalization about the Revolution's becoming a struggle in these years over "who should rule at home" only begins to suggest the complexity of what was happening. Nobody knew in 1765 or even in 1770 what lay ahead, but people did get used to deliberately resisting authority, to challenging official policy, and to trying to change social practice. It was within, and in part at least because of, the tangle of complexities described in this chapter that ordinary people took part in the gathering revolutionary crisis. As a result, independence would transform New York itself, as well as sever the British tie.

Chapter 3

A Political System in Decay

James Fenimore Cooper's novel *Satanstoe* is a tract for its author's own times. Cooper wrote it to show to the rent rioters of the 1840s the evil of their ways. But he set the tale nearly a century earlier, in the 1750s, and he tried in it to give an authentic picture of life when New York was still His Majesty's province. The novel's minor characters, in particular, tell a good deal about the old order's patterns of authority. The father and an uncle of the protagonist are at odds early in the book. Their dispute turns on whether the people at large have any right to take part in government. The uncle, a raving radical, believes that "the subject" has "the right to know in what manner every shilling of the money raised by taxation is expended," but the father, a member of the provincial assembly, disagrees. To him, such accountability smacks of "very obviously improper interference with matters that do not belong" to "the rabble." Both the father and the uncle, however, approve when children and slaves flock out of New York City to watch the stately arrival of the "Patroon of Albany," come down from his northern domain. The young can learn "the profitable lesson of honouring their superiors and seniors," and the slaves can "see the manner in which the Patroon has his carriage kept and horses groomed." An old Dutch militia officer and politician is, in his own words, "a colonel and a memper; my fa'ter was a colonel and a memper; and my grandfa'ter woult have peen a colonel and a memper, but dere vast no colonels and no mempers in his time." Almost needless to say, his son would be "a colonel and a memper" when his own time came.[1] In Cooper's old New York, rulers ruled and simple folk, children, and slaves obeyed.

Like the novel's Cornelius Littlepage and Abraham Van Valkenburgh, the real rulers of provincial New York believed that they held their power virtually as a matter of right. But how, and in whose interests, did they exercise that power? Were their "subjects" as acquiescent as they, like Cooper, thought they should be? Answering such questions makes us realize that the old order was filled with contradictions. From those contradictions much else flowed, for they had a significant part in the way that the conjuncture of imperial issues and postwar depression generated a massive internal political crisis for New York itself.

The formal political structure of provincial New York was small. It had a governor, a lieutenant governor, and a provincial council appointed from England, together with a provincial assembly, courts at the county and provincial levels, and a handful of officials. The combined membership of the assembly and council totaled less than that of a committee in the modern U.S. House of Representatives.[2] Yet the province's institutions were expected to cope with the many political demands created by a growing population, increasing social stratification, uncertain provincial boundaries, and, until 1763, endemic war. The assembly was elected by a sizable proportion of the province's free adult males,[3] and even more had a voice in picking local magistrates and officials. The rhetoric of political discussion told New Yorkers that the relationship between elected and electors was close and that the people's representatives were the best agents of the people's good. Yet once in office, the provincial assemblymen could be as imperious as any royal placeman, and in the last years of the colonial period they were passing laws whose class bias had about it not the slightest subtlety. At the same time that those laws were being enacted, political commentators were vilifying the assembly, rather than the British, as the greatest single threat to New York's well-being.

The nonpopular members of the system, the governor and the council, were supposed to stand for the interests of the crown and thus for those of the greater whole that was the British Empire. But throughout the provincial years, their incumbents gave away the crown's land on a grand scale, without regard to either the king's instructions or New York's own peace. Mainstream writers told the public that the royal councillors brought to New York the wisdom and stability that in theory the Lords gave to Britain. Yet the unresponsiveness and secrecy of the councillors collided with rising demands for the popular involvement that Cooper's Littlepage dismissed as "improper interference." It was these contradictions that were to rip the internal system of the province apart when the empire collapsed in 1775. New Yorkers could have joined in declaring independence had they not been afflicted by them, but even that is doubtful, given that in the province's last years its rulers chose royalism in overwhelming numbers. What is certain is that the internal tensions contributed markedly to making the final crisis into a revolution.

I

Look first at how the system actually worked. The colonial assembly was small and ill-apportioned. At its maximum size, which it enjoyed for less than half a decade, it comprised only thirty-one men, chosen in an idiosyncratic patchwork of constituencies. The busy, populous city of New York had four members, but every other county, no matter how small or empty, was able to choose at least two. This meant that tiny Kings and Richmond had between them as many votes (two each) as the city itself. The assembly thus imitated practice in the unreformed House of Commons, where Old Sarum enjoyed representation but Leeds and Manchester did not. By another carry-over from Westminster, the privilege of electing a single member each was given to five special constituencies. These were the Hudson Valley manors of Rensselaerwyck, Livingston, and Cortlandt, the county borough of Westchester, and the town of Schenectady. Until 1775 voters in these places had the legal privilege of voting in elections for county delegates as well.

There was thus a rough-and-ready system of apportionment, for growing Westchester had four members, and Albany, the most populous county in the province, had five. But the absence of representation for the rest of the manors, for such nonmanorial great patents as Sir William Johnson's estate or the Beekman patent, and for significant towns like Poughkeepsie, Kingston, and Newburgh suggests the system's irrationality. So does the way the assemblymen were paid. All salaries came out of the provincial treasury, but at rates that were fixed when a constituency's members first took their seats. By 1773, representatives from some counties were being paid twice as much as representatives from others.[4] Such practices, and the presence of generation after generation of Livingstons, Morrises, DeLanceys, and Van Rensselaers, suggest that we may best understand the assembly, not as a modern representative institution, but as one of those "constituted bodies" of the *ancien regime* in which Robert Palmer sees the tendency as "more toward the *Geburtstand* than toward free association."[5]

The other major parts of the provincial government were the council and the governorship. The number of the councillors could vary from seven to twelve. They were appointed in England, and they normally included absentees as well as residents; as late as the 1750s a former lieutenant governor, long since retired to Cheshire, was one of them. The council's functions blended those of the House of Lords and the Privy Council. It advised the governor; it sat with him as the highest court in the province;[6] it sat without him as an upper legislative house. In the last capacity it could do anything the assembly could do, save initiate money bills. Only three councillors had to be present to make a quorum, and each councillor enjoyed the right to issue public dissents from decisions that had been secretly taken. That right was copied from the practice of the House of Lords.[7]

In purely formal terms, the governorship was the most powerful of New York's institutions. The governor, or in his not infrequent absences, the lieutenant governor or president of the council, could call, prorogue, adjourn, or dissolve the assembly. Until 1743, when a septennial act was passed, he could keep an assembly in being for as long as he wanted. Even thereafter he was required to call an election only once in seven years. He could make temporary appointments to the council, and these easily became permanent. In 1767, for instance, Governor Sir Henry Moore and William Smith, Jr., conducted an elaborate maneuver to secure the resignation of Smith's father from the council and the appointment of the son in his stead.[8] The man who held the chief magistracy was generally a well-connected Briton like the earls of Bellomont and Dunmore, Viscount Cornbury, or Admiral George Clinton, who was son to an earl of Lincoln. The only colonial to hold it was Sir Henry Moore, a Jamaican. Some of these men proved good at the job, some mediocre, and some atrocious, but New Yorkers had no voice in their selection and little chance to remove them.[9] The lieutenant governor, who often ruled in the governor's place, usually was a minor British placeman, like George Clarke or Cadwallader Colden, or a provincial climber, such as James DeLancey. DeLancey, an imperial politician of consummate skill, was connected by kinship, marriage, and economics to Admiral Sir Peter Warren of the British navy, to Sir William Johnson, and to several members of Parliament. In addition, by the time he became lieutenant governor, his old Cambridge tutor had become archbishop of Canterbury. DeLancey had little reason to feel himself anyone's inferior in the busy world of Anglo-American politics.[10]

Any attempt to explain this system was bound to end in paradox and confusion. The hallowed doctrine of virtual representation could justify the fact that there was a seat for Cortlandt Manor but none for Philipsburgh, or one for Schenectady but none for Newburgh. That doctrine, as the Englishman Thomas Whately explained to protesting colonials in 1765, held that special interests could be represented just as well by a delegate from one group that possessed them as by a delegate from another.[11] On the other hand, the equality, with two seats each, of empty Richmond or Charlotte and of thriving Ulster or Dutchess could be explained in terms of representing the corporate political whole, which in New York was the county. "If a County was made and there were but 5 Freeholders in it, I would vote for a representation" for it, observed William Smith, Jr.[12] Virtual representation and corporate equality did not sit easily together, but both principles had to be invoked if the workings of the assembly were to be understood.

The old order was not a closed system, a "black box" within which arbitrary decisions were taken. On the contrary, there were numerous ways in which the people at large could find out what their rulers, especially their representatives, were doing and put pressure on them. Moreover, these mechanisms increased in number and in strength as the provincial period drew to its close. As early as 1754, when the question of the day was whether the proposed college in New York City should be Anglican or secular, the assembly decided that its own best course was prudence. It postponed deliberations and ordered that the bill before it be published so "that. . . we may have the opportunity of knowing the general sentiments of our Constituents, on this great and important concern." Nor was this the only occasion when it invited public debate.[13]

The assembly's journal was available to general readers, and between 1750 and 1775 the amount of significant information that it contained increased strikingly. In the late 1750s the clerks recorded very few roll-call votes, and the information they provided about these gave very little idea of the content of the division. But by the 1770s the assemblymen were dividing frequently – fifty votes were recorded in the last session alone – and the text of the journal gave a good picture of what they were doing. From 1769 onwards, the assembly chamber was open to the public, and it was by sitting in its gallery that the radical Son of Liberty Alexander McDougall gathered the information that he used in his important broadside "To the Betrayed Inhabitants of the City and Colony of New York."[14] At the end of the colonial period an observer who lived close enough to New York City to attend meetings and who had the time to do it could know the assembly's business fully. Assemblymen who sponsored bills that clearly were calculated to build electoral support showed that they knew as much as any modern politician about pork-barrel politics. In April 1769 Lewis Morris, threatened with expulsion from his seat for the borough of Westchester, immediately acted to build his popularity by introducing bills to compensate the builders of a free bridge across the Harlem River and to release dissenters in Westchester from taxation for the support of the Anglican Church. Morris lost the seat, but the first act of the man who replaced him, John DeLancey, was to bring in another bill favoring the builders of the free bridge.[15]

The most important opening of all came at the polls. For the last three decades of the old order, assembly elections had to be held every seven years at least, and at shorter intervals if the death of a king or the action of a governor dissolved a sitting house. The paradoxes and contradictions of the province's political life were manifest at election time. The prime paradox is that though a large proportion of the province's adult males held the franchise and though many factors stimulated the voters' interest, there was no real popular control over politicians in office. Electors were invited to think about issues and to choose among competing candidates, but they were choosing among men who saw their task in terms of ruling the public, not in terms of serving its wishes.

The basic election law extended the provincial suffrage to men who held a freehold worth forty pounds free of encumbrances and to the freemen of the cities of New York and Albany. The concept of freehold was interpreted liberally, extending to lands under mortgage and to tenancies that ran for a whole life or a series of lives. To be without the vote a man had to be very poor, a slave, a son living with his parents, a wanderer, or a tenant who held his farm at will rather than by a firm lease. The most sizable group of such disenfranchised tenants-at-will lived on Philipsburgh; on nearly every other great estate written leases qualifying the holder for the vote were the rule. The studies of Nicholas Varga, Milton Klein, Staughton Lynd, and Roger Champagne all confirm that at least half, and perhaps many more, of the province's white adult males did have the vote. But the law's restrictions did bite, for poor men, slaves, sons living at home, wanderers, and tenants-at-will made up an appreciable portion of the people, and their number was probably growing.[16]

New Yorkers voted against the background of a long history of political competition. From the time of the Leislerians and the Anti-Leislerians to that of the DeLanceys and the Livingstons, politicians courted the people's favor. Passions ran so high in the earliest of these confrontations, in the 1690s, that they brought the judicial murder of the losers, and throughout the colonial period the province's politicians fought with a viciousness unparalleled elsewhere in America. Open competition took place most frequently in New York City, but the rural counties also saw it. In 1737 a young Westchester man named John Thomas began his political career by challenging the eminent Frederick Philipse for his seat. Thomas lost, and Philipse gave him a public reprimand, but seven years later he won the place that he had coveted. Preparations in Albany for the general election of 1761 included the nomination of two competing tickets. The candidates jockeyed for support and endorsements, and hopefuls found themselves double-crossed by prominent men. In 1768 and again in 1769 Justice Robert R. Livingston was defeated in Dutchess County by a middle-class challenger named Dirck Brinckerhoff, who found in the bitterness left over from the great tenant rising the making of his own political career. In 1769 the election in Orange was fought so energetically that the losers carried charges of corruption to the assembly itself for a verdict.[17]

It is convenient to speak of parties when describing such conflicts, but the term is not wholly satisfactory. Part III of this study will show that after independence, in the 1780s, a partisan culture of a new sort emerged in New York. It will also show that this was of major importance in resolving the questions that the Revolution had raised by then. One reason for doubting that the concept of party really applies to the conflicts of the colonial period is the family names by which the contending groups were known. Admittedly, the usage was a shorthand; to be a "Livingston" or a "DeLancey" one did not have actually to belong to the family in question. In the early 1770s the Livingston party centered within the assembly on the Ulster delegate George Clinton, who had ties of neither blood nor marriage to the manor Livingstons. Similarly, the DeLanceys in that session included John DeNoyelles, of Orange County, and Dirck Brinckerhoff, of Dutchess. Resting her analysis of those two groups on the rhetoric of the elections of 1768 and

1769, Patricia Bonomi has argued that they ought respectively to be identified as "moderate" and "popular" Whigs rather than by family names. If one keeps one's focus firmly on these two elections, the argument is persuasive.[18]

But family names were the labels that provincials themselves used, a fact that is significant on several levels. It indicates that however much politicians invited people to make choices, they did not encourage them to think in terms of mass organizations. Family labels proclaimed that the men who bore them identified with narrow groups, still based on kinship as much as on anything, rather than with broad groups based on class or region or policy. To be called a DeLancey was very different from calling oneself an antifederalist. Moreover, the family labels point to the unstructured maneuvering and interest-mongering that might precede the final publication of a ticket. In 1761 the aspirant Abraham Yates was approached by four different men, including the lord of Livingston Manor, about standing for an Albany County assembly seat. Yates was as much a parvenu as any man in New York, and the Livingstons' seeking him out should destroy any notion that they sought to keep high politics to themselves. But when Yates finally made up his mind to make the race, he found that one of his putative magnate backers, Abraham Ten Broeck, had withdrawn his support and that Sir William Johnson's enmity was costing him even Robert Livingston's backing. Similarly, during the build-up to the hardest fought election of all, that of 1769 in New York City, the DeLanceys actively courted the popular Philip Livingston.[19] Parties, in other words, were small groups of men whose main concern was to hold office themselves or to control the men holding it. Their lack of mass organization or of cohesive principles explains the agility with which New York politicians, once in office, could abandon anything they might have said while seeking election. That very cynicism, however, became a factor in the decay of colonial politics after 1770.

My use of the word *party,* then, to describe New York's preindependence political formations is intentionally loose. Though there was competition and cleavage in New York's politics, there was very little of the organized accountability and responsiveness that eventually would come to be associated with partisanship. The absence of that responsiveness is one major qualification to any argument that the existence of a broad electorate made provincial New York democratic.

Another qualification is the fact that elections were run on the principle of publicly announcing one's choice rather than secretly registering it. Open voting was the norm in early America, and as Chilton Williamson has observed, only in New York did a "demand for secret elections become a major electoral issue." That demand sprang from New York's competitive politics and its hierarchical society. Competitiveness meant that every vote might well count. Hierarchy meant that landlords and great men could coerce tenants and lesser folk into staying away from the polls or into voting as they were told. The local election return of 1773 from Tryon County's Mohawk District, discussed in chapter 1, is good evidence that coercion took place. So is the fact that the secret ballot became a live issue in the late colonial period. But coercion did not always work, as Justice Robert R. Livingston learned when he lost in the Dutchess County elections of 1768 and 1769. His defeat in the second was attributed specifically to tenants' unwillingness to vote for him.[20]

The door between the people and the politicians that elections provided was thus either half-open or half-closed, depending on one's point of view. The breadth of the franchise and the chance to choose that competition provided must be measured against coercion, the absence of really responsive partisan structures, and the cynicism of politicians themselves. In other ways, too, day-to-day practice and operative customs kept New York's political nation small. The assembly journal, for instance, was sold rather than distributed to localities. Privileged men like Sir William Johnson read it with great interest and discussed the affairs of the house in their correspondence. Sir William himself, noted however, that his neighbors in the Mohawk Valley "have no knowledge of what is doing at the Capital" and that their representatives "reside at a distance and have contrary interests."[21]

More important, the representatives showed many times that they considered criticism of either themselves or their institution to be a crime; in this they were at one with assemblymen throughout America.[22] Their insistence that they were above ordinary men showed in such small things as their frequently repeated warnings that "no other person" besides their official printer should "presume to print" the record of their business. It also showed in larger things, like the treatment meted out to writers, printers, and even private correspondents who did criticize them, whether by intention or by inadvertence. In 1756 the assembly resolved that its official printers, by publishing a letter in their newspaper, had tried "by false and malicious Representations, to irritate the People. . . against their Representatives." It found both the author and the printers guilty of "a high Misdemeanour and a Contempt of the Authority of this House." The printers had to creep to obtain the assembly's pardon. One declared that he "humbly confesses his Fault. . . had no Design to give Offence. . . promises to be more circumspect for the future, and humbly begs the Pardon of the Honourable House." His sycophancy saved his official appointment, but though the cringing printer acknowledged that he had "long experienced the Kindness of the Honourable House," the assembly let him languish in jail for another full week after his self-abasement.[23] Other offending writers were forced to bow equally low.[24]

During the 1760s the assembly responded in shrill terms to any criticism. It declared that one piece was "Libellous, scandalous and Seditious, containing many indecent and insolent Expressions, highly reflecting on the Honour, Justice and Authority of and an high Insult and Indignity to this

House."[25] It announced that a mild pamphlet published outside the province by the wretchedly unpopular lieutenant governor Cadwallader Colden "tended to destroy the confidence of the People in two of the Branches of the Legislature...to render the Government odious and contemptible; to abate that due respect to Authority so necessary to Peace and good order."[26] Early in 1770, it imprisoned and tormented Alexander McDougall for writing his broadside "To the Betrayed Inhabitants of the City and Colony of New York." McDougall tried to gain his freedom with a writ of habeas corpus from the supreme court, but the assembly's response was to order a search of the records of the House of Commons in order to prove by precedent that "the Prisoners committed by us, cannot be taken from us."[27] The assemblymen, in other words, balanced their election-time rhetoric about citizenship and participation with actions that better suited the public's masters than its servants.

The other two branches of the government, the governorship and the council, did not pretend to be "popular," for the governor was the king's vicegerent, and the council kept its proceedings secret. The diary that William Smith, Jr., kept from 1763 to 1775, when he was a councillor and a confidant to several governors, demonstrates how one high official thought those branches ought to act. Smith, son of another councillor, codifier of New York's laws, historian of the province, and author of outspokenly Whiggish essays, was no defender of arbitrary authority.[28] Nonetheless, he believed that the distance between the rulers and the ruled ought to be great. In 1772, when the council passed a bill to prevent justices of the peace from holding trials in taverns, he and Governor William Tryon shared a good laugh at "the thought of our submitting to humour the Tavern Keepers." A sheriff who was turned out of office in 1769 despite petitions for his retention was told that "the Petitions should be of no service for the People had no Right to interpose with respect to Offices." Smith thought that "sound doctrine." The newly appointed Governor Tryon told Smith in 1772 that "he meant to consult the Interest of the Province but should not steer by the Popular Voice," and Smith responded that the governor was correct. *Noblesse* could, of course, *oblige*. During a dispute on a minor point that same year, Smith told his fellow councillors that "it greatly magnified an Admn. to promote the public good unsolicited by the People, and still more, when thro' Blindness they opposed what being for their Good, they would afterwards approve." But in 1775, when the legislature passed laws to benefit New York City construction tradesmen and Scots immigrants, Smith noted scornfully that "these two Bills owe their Success to Condescensions to the Carpenters and seceders to get votes at the next Elections – shameful Principles to act upon."[29]

Officials and men in positions of social and political privilege regularly employed the public machinery to achieve their private ends, sometimes with disastrous public results. Many officials considered their office as their private possession, that they held for their own good rather than for the service of either king or country. In 1764 Lieutenant Governor Colden involved himself in a nasty squabble with the captain of a sloop of war over a seizure that the sloop had made in New York Harbor. Such raids caused great distress and popular anger in the city. But that was not what upset Colden; rather, it was that the captain had informed him that "he intended to claim one half for himself, officers and crew." Colden's reply was that "by the statute by which the ship and cargoe are forfeited one third is given up to the Governor and that I could not consent to give up the Rights of the Governor."[30] Nor could he consent to give up his share of the booty. Six years later, when Colden yielded command to the earl of Dunmore, he and the noble lord had a set-to over whether Dunmore should have half of "the Emoluments of Government received by [Colden] since the date of [Dunmore's] Commission."[31] When Dunmore himself was transferred to Virginia he disgraced himself before his successor and the council in a drunken tirade, shouting, "Damn Virginia—did I ever seek it? Why is it forced upon me? I asked for New York—New York I took, and they have robbed me of it without my consent."[32]

One reason for Dunmore's anger at losing New York can be found in what Colden did in 1774 and 1775, when he was once again in charge. The tea crisis had broken, and the empire was at the point of collapse, but much of Colden's time was spent with other things. In an effort to quiet the conflicts in the New Hampshire grants, the Board of Trade had forbidden New York to make any further land grants there. But when Colden resumed control, he announced to the council that he would distribute Green Mountain lands freely. "Observe this well," noted William Smith, who hated Colden and was only too glad to have evidence that the lieutenant governor was a crook. Smith remonstrated again and again in the council against granting the lands; not only did it break the king's instructions but by putting New York grantees into the area, it would ruin whatever hope there was of settling the region's civil war. For the next year, Smith's diary recorded his lonely opposition to grants for the speaker of the assembly, for the governor's son-in-law, and for the members of most of New York's great and aspiring families. Even where he stood to gain himself, he voted against the grants.[33] But at the very beginning of the land grab, writing to his friend Philip Schuyler, Smith demonstrated the limits of his sense of a king's servant's proper role:

> Colden is granting Lands in the Face of the last Instructions. . . the seal is ready if the money is laid down—I intend to sport away about £1000 as I suppose it will be the last chance. . . . I shall buy lands that I opposed the Grant of—Is there any Thing Wrong in this? Have I not discharged my Duty when I voted agt. a Petition in which I was myself concerned. . . . apply soon, for the next Packet may close the present Scene in which the Kings Property is to be disposed of agt. his will—let all this be a secret.[34]

Lord Dunmore, himself heavily involved in northern New York speculations, had known what he was losing.

The whole program of the majority DeLancey party in the last assembly, from 1769 to 1775, rested on assumptions similar to those of Colden, Dunmore, and Smith. The party moved quickly to consolidate its power after the election of 1769, using for its own purposes both the letter of the law and the privileges of the house. Though in technical terms much of what it did was progressive, the problem lay in the spirit in which it was done. A law that prevented justices of the supreme court from sitting in the assembly was a step towards the separation of powers, but its purpose was to exclude one man, Justice Robert R. Livingston, from the seat to which he was repeatedly elected.[35] Another law, requiring representatives to live in their constituencies, presaged future American practice, but it was passed solely for the sake of excluding two other Livingstons. In 1775 the DeLanceys abolished the privilege that the voters of Livingston Manor, Rensselaerwyck, and Schenectady enjoyed of voting for the Albany County members as well as for their special delegates. But these were traditional areas of Livingston strength, and the law did not abolish the double vote in Cortlandt Manor and the borough of Westchester, where the DeLanceys had more sway.[36] In the name of parliamentary privilege, the DeLanceys bullied opposition candidates who challenged elections and even electoral officials who presented the returns from opposition constituencies. They defended all that they did as "an Exertion of the Right which the Constitution had lodged in the Representatives of the People."[37]

Lesser officials, too, considered office as private property. One step taken by the DeLanceys when they gained power in 1769 was to sack officeholders in order to make room for their own men. This was hardly unique in American political history; what is significant is William Smith's comment that one of those fired, the sheriff of Westchester County, was "a Widow's Son" who had acquired the shrievalty "by the resignation of his Uncle." This, thought Smith, gave the sheriff a legitimate claim; Smith himself, after all, had gained his seat on the council by the resignation of his father.[38] Similarly, when residents of southern Albany County complained that the assembly's nomination of a Van Rensselaer as their road commissioner would aid the nominee's "extravagant Claims and Encroachments" against "their ancient Township," the protest had no effect.[39]

Such practices might be dismissed as corruption in the simple sense of theft and hubris, which can infect any political system.[40] But public policy as well as daily practice reflected the interests of the elite at the expense of ordinary people. Historians have paid great attention to the spectacular battles that were fought by the factions of colonial New York, and they have fought some spectacular battles themselves over how many people enjoyed the franchise. They have spent much less effort, however, on understanding what provincial politicians did with power when they had it. A complete study of the laws they passed is impossible here, but a careful look at two sensitive categories, taxation and tenancy law, shows a persistent pattern of class legislation, regardless of who was in control.

Look first at taxation. The day-to-day expenses of colonial New York were met from three permanent taxes. The first was an import duty, the second an excise on various commodities, and the third a license fee paid by hawkers and peddlers. The impost could be quite significant. It reached £10,346 in 1760, when many goods were being brought in for the army, and it stood at £5,200 in 1774. As the historian of colonial taxation suggests, this reliance on imposts and excises meant that the burden of supporting the government rested on consumers in a way quite unrelated to their actual ability to pay. Under such a regressive system, poor and middling people paid much more, proportionately, than the rich.[41]

The province resorted to land taxes only in time of war, when loans had to be floated. But war was a constant fact of life in early America, and land taxes were in use throughout the eighteenth century; between 1759 and 1762 the assembly voted them to a total of £252,000. Throughout the colonial period these taxes were based on the principles established in a law of 1693. They were set out on a county-quota basis, and each time a new tax was passed, each county's quota was determined by bargains and alliances within the assembly. Usually this logrolling meant that the two cities, New York and Albany, bore disproportionate amounts of the tax; in 1693, £1,450 out of a total tax of £6,000 was due to be paid by New York City, and in 1759 the metropolis was billed for £3,000 out of a total tax of £9,000. By contrast, the large, populous, valuable county of Dutchess paid a mere £642 in 1759, barely more than it had paid in 1693, when it had been the rawest of frontiers. In percentage terms its share had dropped considerably.[42] Within the counties taxes were assessed "on estates real and personal," and assessors always took "real estate" to mean improved real estate. The vast empty tracts held by speculators and on great estates would be liable to no taxes until they were settled, and then the terms of leases would require tenants, not landlords, to pay them.[43]

Colonial New Yorkers made sporadic attempts to tighten this ramshackle system, but they always did it on a piecemeal basis. In 1758, for instance, a law established one single method of assessment for all of New York City in order "that persons of Equal Estates in the different Wards may be rated in their assessments at Equal Sums."[44] Another law, passed in 1764, tried to equalize taxation in Orange County by requiring a stringent oath from assessors, but when it required the assessors to rate estates "according to the Value by Improvements thereon," it guaranteed that unsettled land in Kakiate, Minisink, and Wawayanda would continue tax-free. That, no doubt, pleased the past and future assemblymen, the urban merchants, and the Whig attorneys who owned large shares in those patents. Yet another attempt at reform, in 1775, provided a stiff rate on improved lands in Orange but again imposed no taxes on land held for capital gains. These laws were typical: none applied to the whole province, and though they tried to cope with the tax system's inefficiency, none attacked its structural inequities.[45]

Tenancy was another area of class legislation. The tenancy laws of the late colonial period were in no way the basis of even procedural equality between landlord and tenant. Most notable was an act of 1774 "for the better security and more easy recovery of Rents, and Renewal of Leases, and to prevent Frauds committed by Tenants." Its chief effect was to allow landlords to distrain the goods, chattels, and crops (whether harvested or growing) of tenants who owed them rent. The goods were to be appraised and sold at vendue, the proceeds going to the landlord. The law dealt with "rescues" of goods that had been seized by allowing the landlord triple damages. It also allowed triple damages for any breach of impoundment. Tenants could claim double damages if unlawful acts were committed by persons distraining their goods, but such unlawful acts would not make a seizure itself illegal. Moreover, the tenant would be entitled to no damages if the landlord made "tender of amends." A tenant caught rescuing distrained goods would enjoy no equivalent privilege; he would pay his triple damages. Goods taken off the tenant's premises were subject to distraint for up to thirty days after their removal, and the law allowed a landlord, in the company of a constable, to break open and enter any place where he believed a tenant's goods were hidden. The law also provided that any tenant refusing to deliver up his land at the end of a lease would be liable to double rent. And "whereas great Inconveniencies may happen to Lessors and Landlords by reason of the many niceties that attend re-entries at Common Law," those niceties were wiped out as far as tenants were concerned. Instead, a very simple procedure would allow the landlord to serve his notice and evict the tenant.[46]

This act took its place in a barrage of bills in 1773, 1774, and 1775 all having in direct object the establishment of a secure position for New York's landlord class. One act, "for the Recovery of Possessions by Ejectment upon a Title under Sixty Years" of age, was rejected by Governor Tryon. William Smith, who had married into the landholding Livingston family, took issue with the veto. He complained that the governor's only objections were "that a Right of Action over and over again for the same lands, would force the poor occupant to give up to the Rich Plaintiff and that at this Juncture the Ministry would consider the bill as a Mean to ruin and distress the Claimants [in the Green Mountains] under New Hampshire." These reasons, thought Smith, were not enough. Smith's enemy James DeLancey, the son of the former lieutenant governor, knew the bill's importance, for he had been told that it was "requisite to enable the Proprietors of the Manor of Cortlandt to recover old possessed lands." DeLancey himself had a sizable interest in that manor.[47] Another law with a striking class content was the drastic riot act of 1774, by which New York tried to put down the insurrection in the Green Mountains. The law, with its capital attainder on Ethan Allen and seven of his fellows and its imposition of the death penalty for riotous acts committed in the area, was passed at precisely the same time that

Lieutenant Govenor Colden was exacerbating the issue by granting more land.[48] As a final gesture in that session, the assembly enacted a law forbidding the crown the challenge any land title once sixty years had elapsed since the original grant. Both the frauds that lay at the basis of many of the great rural tracts and the hostility of the crown to those tracts were known,[49] but by passing the law, the assembly made the landlords secure against attacks from above as well as from below. The year, however, was 1775.

The prime effect of Britain's imperial policy after 1763 was to put in danger the autonomy of this colonial political system. The Sugar Act, the Stamp Act, and the Townshend Acts all threatened the assembly's control over provincial finance. The revamping of the customs service introduced an alien bureaucracy, and the stationing of British troops was intended to give that bureaucracy the strength to enforce its will. The New York Restraining Act, which suspended the province's assembly until it voted the supplies for the troops that Parliament required of it, drove home that in British eyes the colonial government existed largely for British convenience.

The effect of these imperial policies upon New Yorkers was complex, however, rather than simple. The colonial elite recognized that the institutions in which their power was embodied and legitimated were under attack. They responded with resolves and statements in the most ringing terms. The goal of their rhetoric was to rally mass support behind them, to unite Americans in defense of their institutions and their established ways. That New Yorkers rallied is beyond question. From 1764 to 1775 ordinary people expressed their loathing for what the British were doing, and without their crowd actions New York's resistance would not have amounted to much. But resistance was one thing, revolution was another. The institutions that the elite called upon ordinary people to defend were very much the institutions of a ruling class rather than of a participatory democracy. There was much about them, especially in the open competition that went on at election time, that ordinary people could call theirs, but the contradiction between a rhetoric of involvement, virtue, and public liberty and a reality of exclusion, corruption, and class interests was becoming increasingly visible. The last decade of the old order brought that contradiction into bold relief. Appreciating that fact is necessary if we are to understand the striking changes in political rhetoric that took place during that decade and the equally striking fate of the old institutions at the end of it.

II

The pamphleteers, essayists, and broadside writers of colonial New York produced as prolifically as any in British America. Like writers in the other colonies, they worked within an intellectual milieu compounded of the Atlantic republican tradition, provincial emulation of whatever was being said in Britain, and observation with a local focus.

Their local observation and commentary was the most pertinent of the three elements that went into their writing, for within it two different and mutually exclusive developments took place. Between roughly 1730 and roughly 1765 New York's intellectuals articulated the problems of their society in a way that bolstered the power of that society's elite. Their writings stressed the unity of New Yorkers' interests in the face of all outsiders and the propriety of expressing and acting upon those interests by means of the provincial assembly. But after 1765 the content and the orientation of public discourse shifted. Writers began discussing the differences among New Yorkers rather than their common interests. They poured scorn rather than praise upon the province's institutions and customs. They did so in much the same language that their predecessors had used, but in a way that undermined rather than bolstered the hegemony of the provincial elite. Moreover, they put into their writing an angry passion that had not been there before. By no means did all of the writers who took part in this debate intend to create an internal ideological crisis. Their net effect, however, was to do so. Thus over the same ten years in which Americans everywhere were learning to repudiate the empire and its paraphernalia, New Yorkers, at least, were learning to repudiate the institutions through which their own rulers had governed.

Public discussion about government and political society began in the 1730s, with the events surrounding the famous trial for seditious libel of the printer John Peter Zenger. The charges against Zenger sprang in part from a series of highly abstruse essays that he had published about the powers of the governor to adjourn, prorogue, and dissolve the assembly. It is enough to note that these articles demonstrated the ability of colonial intellectuals both to belabor even the finest of technical points and to turn such technicalities into matters of real import. Underlying the debate was the fact that general acceptance of the case being made in Zenger's paper would have invalidated the actions of many sessions of the assembly.[50] Zenger's defense was conducted not by a New York lawyer but rather by the Philadelphian Andrew Hamilton. In his argument, which was quickly published, Hamilton made a major statement about the assembly's autonomy and its power in relation to that of the governor. Hamilton said that though the king could do no wrong, his governors in the colonies might become as corrupt and tyrannical as any minister in Britain. Then he posed the problem of what provincials could do about it. In theory the courts in Westminster offered them a remedy, but that was open only to the few, and it was useless if an entire people was aggrieved. However, Hamilton said, "when the representatives of a free people are. . .made sensible of the sufferings of their fellow subjects in the hands of a governor they have. . .declared that they were not obliged by any law to support a governor who goes about to destroy." Governors might well use patronage and abuse prerogative to make an assembly bow, but "a House. . .composed of honest freemen" would see "the general bent of the people's inclinations" regardless of "all the craft, caressing, and cajoling made use of by a governor to divert them." In other words, Hamilton had shifted the terms of the debate from freedom of the press to the power and legitimacy of the assemblymen. Whether or not his argument aided Zenger, it certainly told New Yorkers that their elected rulers were at one with themselves.[51]

That his newspaper had said exactly that was one of the reasons why Zenger had come to grief. He had published a statement from voters in Orange County to their representative, Colonel Vincent Mathews. The constituents told Mathews that "the love and esteem of your neighbours will give more real satisfaction and pleasure than the favor of any man however great." Mathews' interest as a good representative "is the same with that of the people amongst whom you live." The ideal assembly was both a defender and a microcosm of the people it represented, and Zenger's paper was saying was saying that New York's assembly was ideal.[52]

Such arguments stood firmly in the tradition of republican thought that has been expounded most subtly by J.G.A. Pocock. That tradition did more than argue that representative institutions were the best defense against tyranny. It drew a complex set of links between the public liberty to take part, the private liberty to make the most of oneself, and the development and well-being of society. New York writers, like their transatlantic mentors, insisted that political representation and social development were intertwined. In 1738 some of them said so in a memorandum to the Board of Trade in London, which was considering a bill that the assembly had passed to require elections at least every three years. The authors of the memorandum maintained that their assembly had two major tasks to perform. One was to give speedy redress for whatever grievances the people might have. The other was positively to promote the development and enrichment of the province. It would take an active assembly to stimulate the exploitation of New York's rich stocks of iron ore and to promote and protect the fur trade. The knowledge that the assembly was doing such things, and that it was frequently elected as well, would be a stimulus to settlement by hard-working European Protestants. Thus a triennial bill would bring positive benefit to the whole province, stimulating both its economy and its peopling.[53]

That memorandum foreshadowed the arguments that William Smith, Jr., William Livingston, and John Morin Scott published in 1752 and 1753 as *The Independent Reflector*. This "New York Triumvirate"[54] symbolized a new maturity in the province's culture and society. Its members were articulate intellectuals strongly imbued both with a close identity with the province and with faith in its future, and they found outlets for their energies and enthusiasm both as lawyers and as writers.[55] They were provincial enough to make wholesale borrowings from such British writers as John Trenchard and Thomas Gordon, whose *Cato's Letters* and *Independent Whig* provided them with models. But while gloom and foreboding pervaded the work of the English Commonwealth men, Smith, Scott, and Livingston bent their talents towards proving that New York was a good place to live and that it could get better.[56] The powers of the assembly, and the benefits that the right use of those powers could bring, formed a major burden of their argument.

They developed that point in a long series of essays that grew out of the controversy over whether the proposed college in New York City should be under the control of the Anglican Church. Presbyterians all, Livingston, Scott, and Smith were at least partly responsible for politicizing a religious issue that would add heat to New York politics until after independence. But their concern, so they said, was about the effect that the college would have on the province rather than about benefit to their own sect. The college's graduates would form the next generation of New York's ruling elite. They would "appear on the Bench, at the Bar, in the Pulpit and in the Senate." New York was a pluralist society, not a monolithic one, and the institution that would shape the minds of the leaders of such a society ought to be under no single group's control. For that reason, they argued, the college ought to be a secular institution. For the same reason, it ought to be founded by the assembly rather than by the king. A legislative act would be "more permanent, better endowed, less liable to Abuse and more capable of answering its true End" than would a royal charter. It would put the college under the assembly's control and thus, by implication, under the control of the community. "Should the College be founded upon an Act of Assembly, the Legislature would have it in their Power, to inspect the Conduct of its Governours, to divest those of Authority who abuse it, and appoint in their Stead, Friends to the Cause of Learning and the General welfare of the Province. Against this, no Bribes, no solicitations would be effectual." The assembly ought to name the college's trustees and to confirm their choice for its presidency. The act of incorporation ought to contain "as many Rules and Directions for the Government of the College as can be foreseen to be necessary." The assembly ought to have the power to confirm the college's bylaws. The assembly was, in other words, the only institution fit to control the shaping of the men who would rule the province in the future. Only if these men were educated under the assembly's guidance could New Yorkers be sure that their rising leaders would acquire the public spirit that New York's conditions required. Once again, the effect was to bolster the assembly's claim that it alone stood consistently for the province's good.[57]

A decade later, one of the triumvirate, Scott, wrote a significant series of essays against the greatest single challenge that the assembly had ever faced to its autonomy and its hegemony, the Stamp Act. Scott had to defend the assembly, not against a governor or an established church, but against the mother of parliaments, which had had half a millennium to surround itself with the illusion that its members spoke for the interests and liberties of all Britons everywhere. Scott's concern was to show that it was the assembly, rather than the House of Commons, that spoke for the specific interests of New Yorkers, and that it alone could exact taxes from them. He argued that it was vital that the interest of a representative "be consistent with that of his Constituent" and that the representative have "an exact knowledge" of the constituent's "Circumstances and all his concerns." For that reason, New Yorkers could be represented only by other New Yorkers. Scott had to deal with the ministry's argument that the Colonies did enjoy a virtual representation in Parliament, in the same way that Philipse Manor and Poughkeepsie enjoyed it in the assembly, for if that argument held, Parliament had every right to impose the Stamp Act. He disposed of it by pointing out that whatever the inequities of borough representation in England, every square inch of British soil was represented directly by the two members who sat for each shire. By contrast, not a single bit of American soil enjoyed such representation.[58]

Scott thus put the matter in the simplest of terms: New Yorkers were not Britons, and they could not count on the mere good will of Britons' representatives to protect them when their interests clashed with those of Parliament's own constituents. He did not need to elaborate on the assembly's role in the way that his predecessors had done. He could take it for granted that his readers accepted what writers had been saying since the 1730s, that New Yorkers' own elected representatives could do nothing other than serve the good of the province, for which reason their power ought to be defended. As long as New Yorkers continued to believe that, the power of the assembly and the power of the class whose members filled it were safe. But over the next ten years New Yorkers found themselves being told that there was less and less reason to believe any such thing.

III

Between 1765 and 1775 New York writers subjected their province's government, and especially its assembly, to a barrage of criticism, abuse, and ridicule. They directed their attack both at the things the government did and at the men who filled it. Some of the battles in this war of words have become famous; one instance is the storm that developed from Alexander McDougall's diatribe of December 1769, "To the Betrayed Inhabitants of the City and Colony of New-York." Most of the other pieces in question proved far more ephemeral, but the result of this stream of pamphlets, broadsides, and newspaper articles was to bring about a drastic change in the tone of political discourse on the eve of the Revolution.

The war of words began during the Stamp Act crisis. At the same time that John Morin Scott was defending the right of the assembly, rather than Parliament, to tax New Yorkers, anonymous radicals in the city were becoming discontented with the assembly's response to Parliament's challenge. Since 1761 the assembly had been controlled by the Livingston party, and the party leaders had no desire to see their power endangered by a general election. They had responded to the Sugar Act the year before with a strongly worded representation to Parliament, but over 1765 and 1766 they did little more than lend their support to the Stamp Act Congress. Out of doors, their leaders were equally loath to take militant action. As Jesse Lemisch has shown, they headed off a radical plan to open the port of New York without the use of stamps by persuading a mass meeting to pass a set of petitions and resolves that had the air but not the substance of radical resistance.[59]

Not all New Yorkers were fooled. Three years later, when a general election did come, the Livingston politicians, John Morin Scott among them, paid the price for their temporizing. The issue was first raised, however, as early as November 1765, only a few weeks after the city's first Stamp Act riots. The assembly had just convened for the first time in thirteen months, and on 29 November its clerk presented to it two letters that had been left for him. Both were signed "Freedom." The first instructed the clerk to read the second "in the open assembly. . .and whare of fail not at your perrel." The second demanded that the assembly pay for the damage that the Stamp Act crowds had done by deducting the costs from Lieutenant Governor Colden's salary. Any Livingston politician would have been happy at least to toy with that idea; none of them had reason to be happy with the rest of the letter. It demanded the repeal of "the Gunning Act" and said "then thare will be a good Militia but not before." It also demanded that a law restricting materials used in building not go into effect "for thare is no Supply of Some Sort of the Materials Requir'd." But the letter did more than just blend domestic issues with imperial ones. It warned the assemblymen to "be not so conceited as to say or think that other People know noting about Government. You have made these laws and say they are Right but they are Rong & take a way Leberty, Oppressions of your Make Gentlemen make us Sons of Liberty think you are not for the Public Liberty, this is the General Opinion of the People for this part of your Conduct."[60]

The assembly published the letters in its journal, but it never discovered who had written them. Four years later it had better luck, but with a far worse result, in the affair of Alexander McDougall. McDougall's broadside "To the Betrayed Inhabitants. . ." was written in the same spirit as were the letters from "Freedom." As chapter 2 showed, McDougall focused anger over the issue of the British troops in New York City onto the assembly itself. Though he published the piece under a pseudonym, the assembly discovered his identity and had him arrested. Its court case against him collapsed when the only person who could testify to his direct involvement in the broadside's production died, but the assembly hauled him before its own bar, where its members browbeat him.

The attack was led by John DeNoyelles, newly elected as a member for Orange County and a man whom William Smith once singled out as the DeLanceys' "mouth" in the provincial Assembly.[61] During the first of his several interrogations, McDougall refused to answer DeNoyelles's questions, on the ground that the court case against him was still pending and that anything he said might prejudice his fair trial. DeNoyelles responded by threatening him with the "long, hard penalty" of being crushed to death. Another member, associated with the Livingston minority, laconically replied to DeNoyelles that the house might throw its prisoner "over the Bar, or out of the Windows, but that the public would judge of the justice of it."[62] That member was George Clinton, of Ulster. Seven years later, when DeNoyelles was dead and his associates were royalists, Clinton's responsiveness to public opinion would make him the first governor of the independent state.

After his ordeal was finished, McDougall published a long narrative account of it. The effect of this new broadside was to bring the assembly into even worse repute than his original publication had done. But even while McDougall was still in jail, his allies and supporters were making his case a *cause célèbre*. The parallels between what was happening to him and the story of John Wilkes in England the previous decade were striking, and a combination of Livingston politicians and Sons of Liberty made sure that everyone in New York was aware of them. Referring to the forty-fifth number of Wilkes's radical paper, *The North Briton*, whose suppression had sparked off massive protests in England, forty-five Sons of Liberty feted him. They drank forty-five toasts in his honor. Forty-five songs were sung to entertain him. The affair thus provided street theater of the first order, and every toast, every song, every march reinforced McDougall's point that the assembly was as much an enemy of New York's interest as was any British minister or placeman.[63]

While the McDougall affair was underway the DeLancey majority was consolidating its power by expelling from the assembly as many of its opponents as it could. The DeLanceys' hatchet man was McDougall's tormentor John DeNoyelles. It was DeNoyelles who moved the expulsion of two of the major figures in the opposition ranks. One victim was the former speaker Philip Livingston, who had been defeated in New York City but had been elected from the manor of Livingston. The other was Lewis Morris, who sat for the borough of Westchester. Neither man actually lived in his constituency, which placed both of them in violation of the election law, and it was on that basis that their expulsion carried. The Westchester seat was filled by the runner-up in the election, John DeLancey, but there had been no contest in Livingston Manor, so a new election had to be called.

The DeLanceys approached a former member for the manor, Peter R. Livingston, about resuming his seat; apparently they were willing to forget that he was as much a resident of New York City as was Philip. But the Livingston family councils decided that the new assemblyman would be Robert R. Livingston, former member for Dutchess County, justice of the provincial supreme court, and father of the future chancellor and diplomat. The DeLanceys responded by passing a resolution to forbid members of the high court to sit as assemblymen and then by refusing to admit Livingston to his seat when he presented himself. Livingston Manor being as much a pocket borough as could be found in America, its voters elected the justice to the vacant seat again and again. But acting under its resolution, the house again and again refused to seat him.[64] Not until 1774 did the Livingstons give up the struggle.

Despite the fact that it had no intention of admitting him to the seat, the assembly allowed Justice Livingston to address it in support of his claim each time he was elected. He, of course, intended the speeches as much for popular consumption as for the advancement of his immediate claim, and he published each of them. In the speeches, he developed in cooler and more temperate language the points that had been made by "Freedom" in 1765 and by McDougall in 1769 and 1770. Justice Livingston was no democrat; no one in his position as a landlord and a politician could have been. His thoughts on representation and on power were thoroughly Whiggish, but within their frame of reference his criticisms were devastating. "It is well known," he said, "that every Man and Body of Men, are desirous of Power; this is natural to humanity, for none fear the abuse of Power in their own Hands." That was just as true in the case of the New York assembly as it was for the British ministry. The principle of representation was no guarantee against the temptations that power presented. Rather, thought the justice, the best parallel to what the assembly was doing was the unrestrained House of Commons during the English Revolution. He described how the Commons took more and more power to itself, until "at last, we find the Commons assuming all Power, turning the Government into what was called a Common Wealth, though it was a real *Tyranny.*" The tyranny had begun when the Commons had sent "*out of their House all such as refused to join them.*" What the Commons had done, the assembly was doing, by stepping between the people of a constituency and the man they had chosen to represent them. If it was "at their Option to receive a Member legally chosen," the justice would "not hesitate to affirm that the Liberties of this Country are at an end."[65]

Justice Livingston was saying nothing new, but he was lending his prestige and his mastery of conventional thought to an assault on an ideological position that men like himself had been building up for decades. His voice was grave and respectable, but like the new generation of popular pamphleteers, he was telling New Yorkers to be as wary of their own rulers as they were of the British.

Early in 1772 another of the popular pamphleteers entered the fray with a series of letters "to the Majority of the General Assembly of Liliput."

Their authorship cannot be traced, but they were printed by John Holt, who was the foremost Whig publisher in the province. The letters stemmed clearly enough from the tribulations of McDougall and of Justice Livingston. Their theme was simple: "the power of the crown is no longer dreaded by the subject," and instead the assembly itself had become "the sole object" of public fears. Livingston was saying much the same thing, but he, a good Whig, looked to the principles of aristocracy and monarchy to check the assembly's power. By contrast, the "Freeholder of Liliput" who wrote these essays told the people that they must look to themselves.

The most notable point about the letters is not anything specific that they said, but their tone. Their author vilified the assembly as had never been done before. Addressing the assemblymen, he said that he would "not refer you to reflection, lest it should consign to you a task for which nature, and long disuse, have rendered some of you unfit, and cruelly anticipate the future punishment of others." He found comfort, though, in the fact that "in the weakness of your heads we find some security against the malignity of your hearts." He told the assemblymen that "you attempted, under the vile pretext of privilege, to stop the courts of justice" and that "after having made us miserable at home, and contemptible abroad, you would add oppression to slavery by denying us the benefits of law and the enjoyment of property." He catalogued "every of [their] misconducts" and told the assemblymen that "we must not . . . be surprised at a vote perpetuating your power, dismembering your House, and declaring the inutility of the other branches of the legislature." Like Livingston, he called up the memory of the uncontrolled Commons: "These measures are by no means unauthorized by precedent, they are legibly written in the Journals of that House, who formerly destroyed the constitution, oppressed the people, and murthered their Prince." But the assembly's trampling on "the established Prerogatives of the CROWN and the sacred rights of the PEOPLE" would be redressed. The author could not teach the assemblymen "to avoid the infamy of your crimes," but he could warn them "to fly the resentment of your injured constituents." The time approached when "a free people" would "awake from their lethargy" and cast the assemblymen out.[66]

Early in 1774, just as the movement towards independence was gaining momentum again, the assembly received yet another public battering. This time, the dispute turned on a proposal by Alexander McDougall's old tormentor, John DeNoyelles, to divide his constituency of Orange County into two parts. DeNoyelles was a shady figure who had come to New York as a mercenary with the British army in the 1750s. Because he had been born in continental Europe, he had to seek naturalization, and when he first did so his petition was denied. The denial involved him in a dispute with Lieutenant Governor Colden before the Board of Trade in which each accused the other of wrongdoing.[67] But by the end of the 1760s DeNoyelles had not only his citizenship but also a seat in the assembly and the political friendship of the DeLancey family. The way the man operated may be indicated by the fact that as soon as he took his seat he introduced legislation to resolve the boundaries of a large Orange County tract in which he had an interest.[68]

An informal political rule in Orange had long provided that one of the county's assemblymen should come from the largely Dutch community that lay south of the Hudson Highlands and the other from the English-speaking area to their north. In 1772 DeNoyelles introduced a bill to regularize this practice by formally dividing the county into two sections, but his bill failed. In 1774 he made another proposal, this time to divide Orange into two parts, each of which would send two members. The bill generated fierce debates, and it was finally defeated by the most narrow of margins.

The bill's opponents attacked it and its author in print, most notably in a long essay that raised yet again the problem of the fit relationship between a representative and his constituents. The essay started with the assumption that direct democracy, not parliamentary representation, was the best form of government. If the complications and size of society required representation, it remained true that "a personal exercise of that Power. . . would be most conformable to our natural Liberty." Any representative was to be mistrusted, because "representative Legislation is naturally exposed to Corruption, a Foe the most dangerous because the most insidious." From that the author went on to a most disingenuous justification of the check imposed upon the Commons by the House of Lords. He had, however, made his central point: the people ought to regard their representatives not as their guardians and benefactors but rather as their most probable enemies.[69]

The same issue brought DeNoyelles himself into open ridicule. Already lampooned as the "Prince of Orange," he now became the butt of heavy-handed humor because of his thick accent and bombastic speaking style. A broadside published the text of a "speech" made by him, quoting him as saying things like "I am sure it was a mistake in dot Bill—because I know it was my Opinion, and I believe de sentiments of dis Ouse, dot a West line would split the Mountains and we taught it would split the Mountains—but dere was a *Mistake* for now a sou *West* line will do better in de course of dem Mountains." The broadside assured its readers that the speech was "performed with that great vehemence, Energy, and Propriety of Voice and Action, peculiar to himself, and for which he hath obtained so much reputation and regard."[70] Never before had a member of the assembly been subjected to so gross a public humiliation or made the object of such personal mockery. That it could happen and that the authors could go unpunished provides a measure of how the assembly's power had deteriorated since the middle of the century.

IV

The abuse that New York writers poured on their province's assemblymen between 1765 and 1774 took many forms and came from many sources.

Some of the writers, like the author of the "Freedom" letters of 1765, were at best half-educated, and others, like Judge Livingston, were sophisticated and polished. Some, like Alexander McDougall, were committed radicals, and others, like the author of the main attack on DeNoyelles's plan to divide Orange County, were as cynical as any politician in power. Some were breaking through old modes of thought, and others were wholly conventional. Some wrote in tones of anger, and others in tones of mockery. But their work had a cumulative effect. It introduced into political consciousness a criticism of the province's own rulers. That ideological criticism matched the criticism that the people of New York City, the Hudson Valley, and the Green Mountains acted out in crowd politics. The criticism sprang from the contradictions of the provincial political system and of practice within it. Like crowd action itself, it meant that political debate during the crisis decade pitted New Yorkers against New Yorkers as much as it pitted Americans against Britain.

The debate reached its conclusion in 1775 in a series of remarkable attacks on the DeLancey politicians and then on the principle of the assembly itself. These attacks were not couched in the language of Whiggery. Their authors did not try to check a too-powerful assembly by aristocratic or monarchical power. Rather, they wrote in the tones of democratic republicanism, arguing that popular participatory power was the best check on the representatives.

The first attack came early in 1775. The DeLanceys, now moving towards an open commitment to royalism, were still in charge of the assembly, and they refused to allow it even to consider the proceedings of the First Continental Congress. In response, an anonymous radical published a full statement of the ties of business interest, of office, and of family that bound New York's rulers to the British Empire. He showed that the speaker was uncle to members both of Parliament and of the provincial council. Other assemblymen held judgeships and militia commissions at the crown's pleasure. One councillor who was a brigadier in the militia was connected by marriage to two knighted Britons. Others had marital ties to ranking officers in the army and navy. Members held contracts to victual the British forces. With leaders like that, it was small wonder that the province was dragging its heals. What had gone wrong? Were New Yorkers neglecting their liberties, or did this dismal record show the success of the British in "biassing our members"? Whatever the cause, the effect was to state in a most serious way what the opposition pamphleteers had been saying for a decade, which was that New York's political elite was thoroughly corrupt and that the only interests its members upheld were their own.[71]

Ten months later, in December 1775, New York voters were faced for the last time with an election for the provincial assembly. As part II will show, those ten months had seen the emergence of a revolutionary counter government based on popular committees and provincial congresses. Though in formal terms the old institutions still existed, they had less and less real power. Governor Tryon, himself ensconced on a British man-of-war riding in New York Harbor, called the election in a last effort to restore vigor to the colonial government. His hope was that the poll would expose the rhetoric and actions of New York's radicals as the hollow pretense of a vociferous minority and that the voters would elect to the new assembly men similar to those whose tenure was ending.

The radicals recognized what the governor was doing and decided to play his game. In New York City they put up a ticket that included John Jay and Alexander McDougall, and all over the province they worked to elect men of their own stamp. The election showed how wrong was Tryon's judgment that the majority would support him, for men committed to the British side won only four seats. For that reason, the new assembly never met.[72]

But even had it met with a royalist majority, Tryon's scheme would not have worked. The most indubitable feature of a working government is its monopoly of public power, resting on the willingness of its subjects to accept its decisions. By the end of 1775 the provincial government of New York enjoyed neither power nor consent. The radicals in the provincial congress and the committee network did not confine their preparations for the election to putting up their own candidates. Instead, they made ready to frustrate the assembly itself if the election went the wrong way. As the poll drew near, the committee of safety, which was sitting in the provincial congress's place, sent a circular letter throughout the province calling for a full representation in the congress when the new assembly gathered. A full congress could "awe a corrupt Assembly (should we be so unfortunate in that representation) from interfering with political subjects."[73] When men could calmly plan to frustrate the assembly's authority, that authority no longer existed.

The point that the old order was at its end and that something else was taking its place was driven home at the same time in an attack on the principle of holding an assembly election at all. The writer explained that the election was useless, because the assembly itself was as corrupt an institution, as much the tool of tyranny, as Parliament. There was no hope for it, and the people had superseded it by something better, the system of committees and congresses. In these, "the people" had "all the weight and influence they ought to have."[74] Whiggery, the writer was saying, had given way to democracy, and the change was for the good.

Taken by itself, the antigovernment rhetoric that became commonplace in New York after 1765 might not signify much. In any political society there are people who are happy to grumble about their rulers. But taken in context, it signifies a great deal. If ideology means the appropriation of the general conceptual structure of a culture for the benefit of certain groups within that culture, the decade witnessed a major ideological shift. New Yorkers were as worried about uncontrolled power in 1775 as they had been in 1765. But in 1765 their intellectuals had been telling them that the danger posed by power came from outside, from the British government and its agents, and that the provincial assembly was the best check upon it. The effect was to legitimate the assembly and thus to secure the power of the men who occupied it. By 1775, in contrast, the assembly had been exposed to years of blistering criticism. The men who made it up, the things they did, the ways they did them, and the principles on which they operated had been analyzed, mocked, and held up as inimical to New York's welfare. The result was to destroy the assembly's legitimacy and with it the Whiggish analysis of politics on which that legitimacy rested. The change meant that New Yorkers were being told that liberty's best defense was no longer to be found in a virtuous elite operating as the people's representatives. Rather, it lay in the people's taking as direct a part in politics as they could.

That ideological change may be recognized as part of the process by which the power of the old order decayed.[75] It meant that by 1774 and 1775 the old institutions had very little moral claim to authority, that their power rested on little more than whatever physical force they could command. They showed as much by their inability after 1770 to punish the pamphleteers and broadside writers who were lambasting them. At the height of its power the provincial assembly had abased men for publishing inadvertent misprints. But as the McDougall affair showed, after 1765 any attempt to terrorize critics into silence only made things worse. Thus the fact that the assembly did nothing about McDougall's later writings, the letters to the assembly of Liliput, or the campaign against John DeNoyelles must be taken as evidence of inability rather than of an unwonted liberality. The assembly did not act because it could not act.

The impotence of the assembly on matters of its own authority was symptomatic of the larger inability of New York's institutions to cope in a creative way with the changes that the crisis was bringing. Those changes would not have taken place so rapidly had there been no confrontation with Britain, but they had internal causes as well as external ones. The greatest of those causes was the explosion of popular interest and involvement in public affairs, whether over the imperial crisis, matters of the market, land tenure, or employment. But the blustering in the assembly of a John De Noyelles, the crushing of the Hudson Valley rising by redcoats, the attempt to obtain troops to suppress the Green Mountain insurgency, and the passage of the New Hampshire grants riot act all show that the only response politicians could consider was to assert their own dubious strength.

They could think of nothing else because by that time the men who traditionally had held power were treating it as something that existed for nothing more than their own good. The Livingstons showed as much by their anxious maneuvers to prevent a dissolution between 1765 and 1768. The DeLanceys showed it by their conduct after winning power in 1769. Under both parties, the assembly showed it by its ramshackle tax policies and by its passage of such laws as the 1774 Tenancy Act. The governor and council showed it by their handling of the Green Mountain land problem. Provincial bureaucrats, like the corrupt provincial treasurers Abraham De-Peyster and John Watts, showed it by the way they diverted public funds to their private businesses. At the basic task of enforcing the law the whole government showed it; Douglas Greenberg has demonstrated that the government was woefully lacking in the power even to punish criminals and adjudicate disputes.[76] Even unsuccessful attempts to reform, like those propounded by William Smith and, earlier, by Archibald Kennedy, showed it, for the roads to the great revolutions are littered with the names of similar reformers, likewise astute and likewise impotent.

The problem, in other words, was systemic. It sprang from contradictions that were inherent in the political structure and the political culture of provincial New York. Those contradictions came to a head during the imperial crisis, as the opposition writers of that decade realized and explained. Their maturation meant that independence would require both angry conflict among New Yorkers and a sharp change from the old ways.

Part II

The Revolutionary Crisis, 1774–1782

Despite the turbulence that New York had known through the five years after 1765, it seemed a stable place by the summer of 1773. Only the troubles in the New Hampshire grants and the running propaganda against the DeLanceys in the assembly disturbed the peace. But by the summer of 1776 its people found themselves in the midst of a crisis that shattered or put in the gravest doubt almost every aspect of the way they lived. That crisis was still in full force three years later, in the summer of 1779, with two counties in secession, five more under British occupation, and civil war and an unstable government in what was left. If "normality" began to return over the ensuing year, it was to a place that was forever different and it was only because politicians had begun making changes in political practice on a scale grand enough to match the cataclysm in political society.

Though the independence crisis was forced on New Yorkers from outside, it came upon a province ready to split open. Had that not been so, its people would not have suffered their enormous problems of royalism and "disaffection." Those problems began to appear as 1773 passed into 1774. Over the next few years Americans would have to make a series of major political decisions: to refuse the East India Company's tea, to support Massachusetts in its hour of need, to join in the Continental Congress's program of economic resistance, to wage war, to become independent, to support or repudiate the republican governments that their leaders gave them. In New York, each of these decisions split some men away from others, each rent the fabric of colonial political society, and each contributed to the weaving of a new fabric, from very different material.

The problem of fundamental loyalty—Was one American? British? a New Yorker at all?—shattered what had been the province. It divided the old ruling elite into republican conservatives, who could live with what the crisis portended even if they did not like most of it, and royalist reactionaries, who could not. It separated counties of overwhelming royalism from counties whose people became predominantly republican. In other counties the split was internal. The ways in which different men and different groups chose their sides can be understood only in terms of their previous relationships with one another. Though some men of every kind—merchants, landlords, artisans, tenants, yeomen, Englishmen, Dutchmen, Germans, Scots, Yankees—could be found on both sides, men's choices were not mere happenstance. Rather, each person's, each group's choice made sense in terms of what the people who had counted in that person's, that group's life were doing.

The division into Tory and revolutionary was not the only split in the province. The British imposed one division when their conquering army seized first Staten Island and then Long Island and Manhattan. From the late summer of 1776, when the brothers Howe invaded, to the end of 1783, when Sir Guy Carleton sailed away with his redcoats and with thousands of Tories and escaped blacks, all of the southern district save Westchester was in enemy hands. Meanwhile, a separate split developed in the far north. While the Howes' ships were disgorging their passengers in New York Harbor, the Green Mountain insurgents were declaring their own independence. The southern counties would eventually be restored to republican New York, but Vermont never would. In geographical terms as well as in matters of imperial loyalty, the independence crisis thus forced New Yorkers to form a whole new set of answers to the question of just who they were.

It also brought a basic redefinition within what remained after the royalists and the Vermonters were gone, for New York may well not have gained independence at all if it had not also undergone revolution. The resistance of the established authorities to the movement was intense at every level. Carrying through the decisions that led to independence meant getting rid of those authorities as much as it did breaking free of Parliament and the king. The energy to oppose all three foes—Parliament, king, and their own rulers—came from "the people," both in crowds and in the revolutionary committees that gave political form and direction to what the members of the crowds wanted. Between the end of 1774 and the summer of 1776 those committees did in New York what similar bodies would do in Paris between 1789 and 1792 and in Russia in 1917. They created a countergovernment on radically different lines from the old one, took power to themselves until the old institutions were hollow shells, and then destroyed in name what they had drained of power in fact.

But the story of the committees did not end there. The committee movement was more than just a convenient device for resisting the British. It sprang out of and crystallized the experience and the ideas of the people whom the movement had politicized. It did not die at independence, or even when the new state constitution was proclaimed a year afterwards. Its end did not come until 1779. When it finally gave up power, it was because the concerns that had driven it and the energies that it had embodied were becoming part of the political practice of the new state. Those concerns, those energies, and the fundamental changes in political society to which they led went a long way towards making the state a democracy as well as a republic. The farthest-reaching transformation of all was not the cutting of the British tie or the inevitable loss of Vermont or the splitting of Yorkers into royalist and republican; it was in the way that patriot New Yorkers lived with one another as a political community.

Chapter 4

Rebels, Royalists, and Frightened Men

The decisions that Americans had to make in the mid-1770s were fundamental. They turned on questions that men could not compromise. They brought those men, and sometimes the women who lived with them, to the point of killing, robbing, imprisoning, and waging war on each other; of sending neighbors into exile and confiscating, burning, and looting what they owned and wreaking vengeance on their parents and children. What caused those things to happen is the subject of the next two chapters, but first, who were the people who carried them out, and who suffered them?

Because every social group in New York had members who chose both independence and the empire, the sources for answering that question are full of contradiction. They are so unamenable to ready analysis that it is tempting not to try to understand them but to settle simply for knowledge. There were many royalists, more revolutionaries, and a great number of people who tried desperately just to keep out of it. Merely to know that broad, simple categories like geography, ethnicity, or class by themselves explain nothing is to have made some gain.

Yet the very complexity of all three groups—the revolutionaries, the royalists, and the people caught between them—presents a way to understand them. Each group was a coalition rather than a simple unity. Each was made up of people who chose their position in relation to the people who figured large in their lives. Within all three groups, and between each the other two, there were points of both opposition and union. The counties of the province sorted themselves into three kinds, according to the political decisions that their people made. In Kings, Queens, and Richmond feeling was overwhelmingly royalist. These were the counties of Tory consensus. In Ulster, Orange, and Suffolk the feeling was almost as unanimous for resistance and then independence. These were the counties of revolutionary agreement. In New York, Westchester, Dutchess, Albany, and Tryon, however, people agreed only that they could no longer agree. These were the counties of conflict. The Tory counties had certain things in common, as did the three that were largely revolutionary. Together, however, all six shared characteristics that separated them from the counties of conflict. The problem of why some counties split and others did not is as important as that of why men chose the sides they did. Both problems can be grasped only in terms of the kinds of relationships within which their people had lived.

This is equally true of the groups that went different ways within the counties of conflict. Class was important in all of those counties, but in no simple way. Rich and powerful men went to both sides, as did the poor, the middling sort, and the weak. It is not enough to say that there was class warfare, though there was, or that classes split, though they did, or that there was class collaboration, though that could be found as well. Rather, every single group must be seen in terms of the other groups that filled its own world. An elaborate counterpoint of likes and opposites, of things shared and not shared, was working itself out. The choices made by rich landlord patriots have to be seen in relation both to the choices of other, different rich men who became Tories and to those of poorer men who wanted to challenge landlord dominion. The same applies to the bearers of every other salient social characteristic. Wealth and poverty, high status and low, power and impotence, and every kind of ethnicity could all be found on both sides of the divide. Abstract characteristics did not count; what counted were the relationships among the people whom they characterized.

I

The counties of royalist consensus and those of revolutionary agreement shared two major characteristics. One was a certain social sluggishness, reflected in their demographic history, their economic life, and their pre-Revolution politics. The other, at least when these counties are compared with the counties that broke apart, was a decided lack of internal differentiation.

Let us return to the census figures touched upon in chapter 1. In all of the counties of consensus except Orange, the rate of population growth was either below or barely equal to that of the province as a whole. In the royalist counties it was far below. Although the provincial growth rate for the whole period from 1698 to 1771 stood at 3.2 percent yearly, in Kings it was 0.8 percent, in Queens 1.6 percent, and in Richmond 1.9 percent. In the counties of revolutionary agreement the figures were somewhat higher. Suffolk's annual growth rate stood at 2.2 percent, Ulster's at 3.2 percent, and Orange's at 5.4 percent. Orange, in fact, showed the least consensus of the six counties, though it did not suffer the problems of an Albany or a Dutchess. In all of these counties the actual size of the population at the end of the colonial period was small. Kings and Richmond had 3,623 and 2,847 people, respectively, in 1771, which meant that both of them were smaller than many a good-sized Massachusetts village. The others were of a different order: Queens had nearly 11,000, Orange just over 10,000, and Suffolk and Ulster both between 13,000 and 14,000. But their dynamism still is not overwhelming.[1]

These six counties were places of yeoman freehold farming, and of relatively narrow distance. They were places that had a history of social peace rather than of social strife. In none of them did the people know what it was like to be dominated by a few great landlords. They did not know the contrast between great house and cottage. Their memories were not scarred by land riots or vicious, angry elections. As in population, Orange is the half-exception. In 1769 its people were treated to a bitter campaign between two sets of candidates for the assembly. The losers were so angry about the result that they appealed the election to the assembly itself, though without achieving what they wanted. Both losers became active revolutionaries, but the winners went another way. One, Samuel Gale, was forced into royalist exile, and though the other, John DeNoyelles, was dead by 1776, the position he would have taken is not hard to guess.[2] But in the way these counties did their business such competition was the exception.

Given the relative tranquillity of all six counties, why did the people of three go to the crown and the people of the other three to Congress? Ethnicity has often been cited as the key to the secrets hidden behind New York affairs, but by itself it offers no solution here. Royalist Kings was heavily Dutch, so much so that people there still spoke the Dutch language. Patriot Suffolk, peopled by Puritans from Connecticut, was largely Yankee, and the villages that dotted it could have been found in New England. Tory Queens, however, was settled by both groups. So was revolutionary Ulster.[3] Demography may make more of a difference. Of the Tory counties, only Queens had a population greater than ten thousand, whereas in all three of the revolutionary counties the population was greater than that. Moreover, the growth rate of each of the patriot counties was larger than that of any of the royalist counties.

There were significant economic differences between the two sorts, stemming largely from where the counties lay. The three Tory counties fronted on New York Harbor and the East River. With nothing more than a short ferry ride to the markets of New York City, their people enjoyed automatic membership in the world of Atlantic commerce. Whatever they grew was destined for the city. On the Ratzer Map and in travelers' accounts these counties project an image of placid prosperity,[4] and the image is supported in the detailed descriptions of the estates of individuals who had lived in these counties that can be found in the royalist claims in the British Public Records Office.[5] These claims show societies where people were prosperous but where even the rich were not enormously wealthy. They show fortunes based not on trade, debts outstanding, great holdings, tenancy, or slavery but rather on rising land values, closeness to market, and the beginnings of urbanization.

Three claims illustrate the point. One was filed by John Rapalje, who had been a provincial assemblyman from Kings. Rapalje had lived directly across the East River from New York City. The farm on which he had dwelled contained only 190 acres, but its location gave it immense value. Its assessed worth of £16,875 sterling accounted for most of Rapalje's total loss of £20,611. Rapalje mentioned neither tenants nor slaves in his claim, and since the claims commissioners were very interested in whether a person had either, the fact that he mentioned neither may indicate that he worked the farm with the help of his family and with hired labor. He knew that the farm's value came as much from its capacity for development as from the crops that its soil could produce. When the war came, the farm had five good houses, including the owner's stone mansion. There were also two blacksmith shops and three barns, and Rapalje was beginning to let part of it for house lots. The Ratzer Map shows a tract of housing, confirming Rapalje's statements, and witnesses agreed that its land was of great value. One testified that soil nearby was worth one hundred pounds per acre.[6]

The second case is that of another former assemblyman, Christopher Billopp, of Richmond. Billopp owned a tract much bigger than Rapalje's farm, totaling 1,078 acres. He lived on it in a house that his grandfather had built. Because Staten Island was at the far end of the bay, rather than just across the East River, its land was worth less, and Billopp claimed only £13,500 currency for his whole estate.[7] But like Rapalje, he mentioned neither tenants nor slaves, and at roughly £10 per acre his farm was worth much more than a comparable amount of land in some more distant county.[8]

The third case is that of John Polhamus, of the town of Jamaica, in Queens. Unlike Rapalje and Billopp, who can be reckoned among the premier men of their counties, Polhamus was just an ordinary New Yorker when the Revolution came. Unlike them, he had little to say to the claims commissioners about either his past or his plans for the future. But he valued his 180-acre farm at £2,000 currency, which meant that acre for acre it was worth more than Billopp's land.[9] Polhamus was the only "typical" man among these three; Rapalje and Billopp had too much of property, fame, and power. But the claims that they made confirm that their societies were prosperous and commercial and that wealth in them was based on the rising values of small amounts of land rather than on vast tracts or on the exploitation of other men.

The economic life of the three revolutionary counties was much less tied to the market, much more a matter of modest comfort rather than of fat prosperity. Orange and Ulster of course fronted on the Hudson River, and they had Newburgh and Kingston to serve as commercial centers. But when travelers like the Marquis de Chastellux or Patrick McRobert described the Hudson Valley, they saved their descriptions of prosperity for the east bank, where the landlords lived. The most famous account of west-bank society, that by St. John de Crevecoeur, pictures the west bank as a land of happy mediocrity rather than of richness.[10] Even now, the countryside along U.S. Route 9-W south of Catskill seems rougher and poorer than that through which Route 9 runs below the city of Hudson. Stony rises cut the interior off from the river, whereas across the river rich plateaus end in bluffs that fall to the riverbank. Suffolk, in its turn, was surrounded by ocean. There were harbors at its far end and on the north shore, but none was a deepwater haven, and the whole of its south coast was blocked by the sand spits of Fire Island. Much of its southern half, in fact, was sandy waste. Whether its people looked to New York City, to Newport, or to Boston to do their trading, going to market meant a long, difficult journey.

Thus land in these counties could not reach the high values that it could reach in the counties near the city. Academic studies confirm that the economies of these counties were based on isolated, self-contained villages, where people grew for themselves and bartered more than they bought and sold and where the idea of capital gains had little meaning. Carl Nordstrom's account of the riverfront town of Nyack, in Orange, suggests that a subsistence economy prevailed there until after 1800 even though the town was not more than fifty miles above New York City. Stuart Blumin's book on Kingston demonstrates that it was not until well into the nineteenth century that Kingston passed the "urban threshold."[11] Because the people of these places did not become royalists, they did not file the claims that tell us about a Rapalje, a Billopp, or a Polhamus. But the tax lists discussed in chapter 1 bear out the picture that Nordstrom and Blumin present.

Modern studies also show that there were differences in how the people of the royalist counties and those of the revolutionary counties did their public business. Patricia Bonomi's portrait of eighteenth-century Kingston shows a community whose people involved themselves actively and constantly in politics. A man who lived there stood a good chance to exercise public office at some point in his life. If he did gain a post, it was because his fellow townsmen, gathered in their annual meeting, decided that he ought to have it. Though he might start off as a fence-viewer or as overseer of a short stretch of highway, the chance was good that eventually he would find himself at the center of town policy as a trustee, town clerk, assessor, or supervisor. If he did become supervisor he would also serve as a county legislator. By contrast, Jessica Erlich's analysis of the Queens County village of Newtown reveals a society in which public life atrophied over the eighteenth century. People there did less and for themselves and relied more and more on higher authorities to make their decisions for them. They even gave up on such matters as where roads would be built. Justices of the peace, appointed by the governor, and the distant grandees who sat in the assembly made the Newtowners' decisions.[12]

Local government thus had completely different effects on the people of Kingston and on those of Newtown. In Kingston it provided a working "base for republicanism," educating the people who lived with it in the ways of an egalitarian, participatory society, But in Newtown its quiet effect was to tell the people who lived under it that they could not control their own lives, that greater men had to do it for them. Why this happened is uncertain, given that early in the century the people who settled there resisted in the name of their Calvinist heritage the imposition of an Anglican establishment.[13] But the difference had a telling effect, for the two towns met the independence crisis in very different ways. Though Kingston was no hotbed of revolutionary fervor in the 1760s, its people responded to the Continental Association of 1774 by forming a committee of observation to enforce it. The gesture was unnecessary, since New York City controlled the commerce of the whole Hudson Valley and the committee there could observe well enough, but that makes the gesture all the more telling as a sign of solidarity. The people of Newtown, however, did nothing.[14]

It can be seen that there were both similarities that spread across the consensus counties as a whole and differences between those that were largely Tory and those whose people chose revolution. All six were quiet by comparison with the noise of New York, Dutchess, or Albany. Their populations grew slowly. Their citizens did not know great extremes of wealth and poverty. Their political life went forward without bitter enmities or hard social conflict. But the Tory counties were part of the money economy and were places where land values were high, sometimes very high. They were places where population growth was close to nil, as opposed to merely slow. They were places where people went about their private business and let authority speak to them from above, rather than places where people chose others and were chosen themselves to wield day-to-day power. In none of the six were tensions great enough to tear society apart over whether to resist and to become independent and republican. But these differences aid in understanding why in Kings, Queens, and Richmond republican independence proved unthinkable, whereas in Ulster, Orange, and Suffolk men turned to it readily.

II

Whether one looks at their demography, their economic life, their class structure, or their political style, the counties of conflict were an altogether different matter. They were far more populous than any of the counties where agreement ruled. Westchester had 21,745 people in 1771. Albany, including the districts that were about to be separated from it as Tryon, Charlotte, Cumberland, and Gloucester counties, had 42,706. Dutchess had 22,404. New York City had 21,863. Over the eighteenth century only in the latter had the growth rate been lower than the provincial rate of 3.2 percent; there it worked out to 2.1 percent per annum. Westchester since 1698 had grown at 4.2 percent every year, Albany at 4.8 percent, and Dutchess since 1712 had grown at a staggering 7.1 percent.[15] Whether their growth stemmed from immigration or from natural increase, the people of these counties knew both greater density and much more dynamic growth than did any who lived in the counties of consensus.

Their people also knew the world of commerce much more directly than did those of at least the solidly revolutionary counties. New York City and Albany were trading cities. Their artisans knew that a flood of cheap British goods could drive them out of business. Their newspapers told readers what was happening at distances of hundreds and thousands of miles. In rural Albany County and in Westchester and Dutchess long-distance trade and its consequences were part of people's lives. The landlords of the great estates took the wheat that was paid to them in rent and the remainder of the crop, which they had forced their tenants to offer to them first, and shipped it in their own sloops to New York City. They may have ground it already in their own mills, but in any case it would leave the city as flour and biscuit to be exported all over the Atlantic basin. The hundreds of pounds of rent that Frederick Philipse received for the two mills that he leased came from millers who were grinding for distant customers as well as for Philipse's tenants. The iron that Robert Livingston's forgemen smelted was made to be sold, not simply to be used by Livingston's tenants. The people of these counties all lived in a world where trade meant long-distance commerce conducted in the language of money rather than local exchange conducted in that of community.

These were counties where class meant the visible differences between merchants in their coaches and periwigs and artisans in their leather aprons and long trousers, or between a landlord in his mansion and a tenant in his cottage. The range of wealth within them was far greater than in any of the counties of consensus. The £20,000 lost by John Rapalje is a small amount by comparison with the losses of royalists like the New York merchants William Bayard (£75,141 sterling) and Oliver DeLancey (£115,100) or the landlords Sir John Johnson (£103,000) and Roger Morris (£68,384). Christopher Billopp's 1,000 acres seems a tiny amount by comparison with Philipse Manor or the 16,000-acre speculation that the merchant Samuel Hake owned in Tryon County. On the patriot side there were men of equal weight: James Duane, with Duanesburgh in Albany County and his land in the Green Mountains; the patroon of Rensselaerwyck; Robert Livingston, Jr.; Philip Schuyler; the sugar refiner Isaac Roosevelt. Very few New

Yorkers of any political tendency lived at that level, but these fortunes defined the upper limit of society and accounted for much of its total wealth.[16]

The counties that split had long histories of strife. Sometimes it was electoral. New York City's tradition of vicious politics went back to the time of Jacob Leisler. Westchester saw challenges to the Morris family as early as the 1730s, and in the early 1770s it was Frederick Philipse, not the latest Lewis Morris, who was in charge there. In Dutchess the assembly election of 1768 was fought starkly in class terms. In Albany the former shoemaker Abraham Yates learned painfully what Sir William Johnson's enmity meant when he ran for the assembly in 1761.[17] But as often as not, strife in these counties was physical: the conflict of landlord and tenant in the Hudson Valley, guerrilla warfare in the Green Mountains, street rioting both in Albany and in New York, and frontier war along the Mohawk. For the people who lived in these places competition and violence were simply part of life.[18]

Let us look at nine men among them. Five of them, Thomas Ryan, Peter Angevine, Andrew Reber, Samuel Sly, and Isaac Deane, were nobodies. Ryan had come to New York City from Ireland in 1762 and had worked since then as a cartman. Angevine had inherited part of his father's tenancy on Philipse family lands. Reber had a small share in a piece of land that lay west of Albany, and Sly, a yeoman of New Windsor, in Ulster County, had served a few terms as overseer of roads. Deane was just one of Beverly Robinson's tenants. The other four, Frederick Philipse, Sir John Johnson, Philip Schuyler, and Pierre Van Cortlandt, were somebodies of the first order. Before independence all nine of these men had lived enmeshed in a complex web of relationships with one another. For the "somebodies" those relationships were often personal: they knew one another face-to-face; they might intermarry; they might be partners in speculation or enemies at the hustings. For the "nobodies," and between them and the greater men, the ties were the invisible but no less binding ones of social structure and class relations.[19]

Yet during the independence crisis many of those ties snapped. Ryan and Angevine, Philipse and Johnson became royalists, and when the Revolution was over, all four found themselves telling their tales of pain and loss to the British commissioners and hoping for aid. For Reber and Sly, the Revolution meant active involvement as committeemen in destroying the old order and shaping the new. For Deane it meant service as a republican militiaman. For Van Cortlandt it meant the lieutenant governorship of the state. For Schuyler it meant one swift bound from being a mere provincial notable to puissance at the national level. Understanding the choices and the fates of these men, as well as those of the many others for whom they can stand, means thinking again in terms of the links and the conflicts among them.

A crisis of the magnitude of independence might be expected to split the counties where such men lived in a much more simple way, along the line that separated the rich from the rest, the powerful from the impotent. Why, instead, did men of all types choose both sides? Why, in the first place, did the ruling elite split so badly that half of its members left New York forever?

Certainly one reason is that many of those great men who chose Britain were powerful and honored as well as rich, and they owed power, honor, and wealth alike to the tie with the mother country. When the connections that bound New York's high judges, councillors, and assemblymen to British power were published in February 1775, they showed how much of the government was in the hands of what men called the "court interest." Of the forty-two men listed, only two did not have ties of marriage, family, office, or commerce with the British. Not all of those ties would prove binding. Among the men who had them were George Clinton, clerk of Ulster; Philip Schuyler, first judge of Charlotte; and Dirck Brinckerhoff, colonel of the Dutchess militia, all three of whom became ardent advocates of independence. Nor were all the ties of great moment; many were no more than a justiceship of the peace or a distant connection by marriage to some underling in the British army. But there were many in the group with direct connections to the heights of power and profit, men tied by blood to English peers or members of Parliament or by money to the East India Company, the army, and the navy.[20]

Modern historians have traced similar connections between such men's interests and their politics. According to Esmond Wright, New York's royalists included a "very large component of royal officials, 'friends of the government,' 'men of business,' [and] 'men of connection.' " James Kirby Martin has shown that every one of the councillors, the high judges, and the ranking executive officials of the province lost his post when independence came. Of the nineteen whom he cites, all but one became royalists, giving New York the highest percentage of royalist officials of any place in America. Its rate was almost twice that of the colonies as a whole.[21]

Not all of these ranking officials were rich men. The claims that were filed by such people as David Mathews, mayor of New York City, who organized a plot to kidnap George Washington; George Duncan Ludlow, justice of the supreme court; or J. H. Cruger, councillor, militia officer, and chamberlain of New York City, show us men who were comfortable rather than strikingly rich. Many of the Tory officials were people for whom officeholding was a way of making a living rather than a perquisite and a responsibility that accompanied a great fortune.[22] But at the highest levels, power and pelf were linked in a chain that ended in London. Thus John Rapalje was a militia colonel and an assemblyman as well as one of the richest figures in Kings County. Frederick Philipse was an assemblyman from Westchester as well as tenant-for-life of the most valuable single estate in the province. James DeLancey was both an assemblyman and a merchant with a fortune of nearly £54,000. James Jauncey, another assemblyman, had a mercantile fortune nearly as great. The largest claimant of all, Oliver DeLancey, was a member of the council, and others like him, such as William Bayard or Sir John Johnson, either had been or could expect to become officers. Honors, offices, and connections all made these men aware that they were not just rich. They were movers and shakers in the great world of Anglo-American politics, which gave them good enough reason to keep that world in existence.[23]

Many of them stressed how much they had done to defend their world. Christopher Billopp claimed credit for Richmond County's decision against sending delegates to the Second Continental Congress and for keeping the county quiet until the British troops came. John Rapalje told the commissioners that his "zeal and Activity. . .made him so obnoxious that, fearing his Influence among his Constituents, the Insurgents took him prisoner." Councillor William Axtell, a Long Island farmer who styled himself a "private gentleman" who had been "brought up to no kind of Business and always lived upon the Profits rising from his own Estates," had written a Tory pamphlet. Many other eminent men, such as Frederick Philipse, Sir John Johnson, Colonel Guy Johnson, Oliver DeLancey, Mayor Mathews of New York, and Mayor Cuyler of Albany, told similar stories.[24]

The great merchants of New York City went largely with the crown. Esmond Wright and Robert East have shown that "of the 104 members of the New York Chamber of Commerce living in 1775, 57 became loyalists, 21 were neutral, and 26 became whigs."[25] The men in whose hands the city's commercial wealth had been concentrated chose, by a ratio of three to one, to make either an active commitment to the old order or to make no decision, which the rebels regarded as the same thing. Only a quarter of them chose the Revolution.

For some of these men—merchant-politicians like James Jauncey, James DeLancey, or Hugh Wallace—the choice was simply a matter of continuing along a path on which they were already far advanced. The fate of the DeLancey party, its transformation from the "popular whigs" of 1768 to the core of royalism by 1775, may well have been set when its leaders made their deal with Lieutenant Governor Colden at the end of 1769. They would give him their votes on the unpopular question of supplying the garrison if he would keep alive an assembly that they dominated. It was no more than the last in a long line of cynical trade-offs between men like themselves and a governor. The difference was simply that this time circumstances would eliminate any chance to change, for by the time of the final crisis in 1774 and 1775, they had made too many public gestures of support for Britain. Moreover, their enemies, the Livingstons, were too closely bound up with the Sons of Liberty.

For other great merchants too the world of political strife had a momentum of its own. John Wetherhead, who lost a fortune totaling £36,119 sterling, did not come to public life until 1775, when he was made foreman of the grand jury of New York City. Wetherhead had a thoroughly conservative view of what the grand jury ought to be and to do. In his words, it "until then always had and at such a time more especially ought to have been chosen from amongst the most considerable and respectable" people, "whose principles and resolutions were to be depended upon." But Wetherhead found that such men had been driven out and that he was charged to lead a jury made up largely of active revolutionaries. The jury had to deliberate on a number of overtly political cases, and in Wetherhead's view most of its members were "determined at all events to do wrong." But by his "fixt Resolution and steady Firmness," he had persuaded them to "do right" instead. Wetherhead, as much as a James DeLancey or a Cadwallader Colden, made his choice in terms of the public arena.[26]

Yet most of the great merchants were never active in public life, never openly committed to the British by what they had done and said in the forum. They were people whom a sympathetic Alexander Hamilton would call, as they prepared to leave in 1783, "characters of no political consequence."[27] The partners James Percy, Thomas Hope, and Miles Sherbrooke, who sought compensation for a business that had been worth £54,000 New York currency, had been too busy trading to hold office. So had Samuel Hake, John Dawson, and Catherine and James Thompson, who were in partnership as traders as well as husband and wife. At least one merchant-politician, Isaac Low, had made his reputation as a firebrand of resistance, going as far as a seat in the Continental Congress before he turned his coat.[28] Why did such men choose the British by the overwhelming ratio at which they did?

One reason may have been foreign origins. Most of them simply did not have roots that went deep in New York, no matter how well their presence there had been rewarded. Of a sample of seventeen merchants who filed claims for compensation, only one, Isaac Low, was from a family that was well settled in America, and he chose the crown at the eleventh hour. To cite some cases of immigrants, James Jauncey had come from Bermuda, James Thompson and the brothers Hugh and Alexander Wallace from Ireland, and Miles Sherbrooke, Samuel Hake, and John Dawson from Britain. Though Jauncey had been in the province since 1740, many of these men had had only a few years to get used to being New Yorkers. Samuel Hake, though married to a Livingston, had come in 1766. John Wetherhead had arrived in 1763, and John Dawson in 1770. The Albany royalist merchants Robert Hoakesley and Richard Minisie had settled in 1765 and 1773, respectively. All of these men had shaped their identities before coming to the province. They were closer to being transatlantic adventurers than the economic spokesman of a settled society. Even Isaac Low told his republican brother years later that his highest ambition "was and is to live and die a British subject."[29]

Such men faced eastward. Besides their families, they had partners and trading connections in Bristol, London, or Glasgow. The traders who did choose independence seem to have been of a different sort. Their connections were up and down the American coast and with the Caribbean—French and Spanish as well as British. The great sugar-refining patriot Isaac Roosevelt did not trade at all; he imported his raw sugar in other men's ships and had no lines with Britain to keep tied. People like Isaac Sears, Jacobus Van Zandt, or Alexander McDougall were too small to maintain trade with the metropolis. They dealt with other provinces.[30]

What rich men did with their fortunes may also have had an effect on their political decisions. The British claims commissioners demanded precise, detailed accounts, especially from men filing claims in the tens of thousands of pounds. For the merchant princes, that meant describing their investments. These men put their fortunes out at loan. They gave mortgages. They bought land for speculation rather than for direct development. They depended on credit's remaining good between themselves and both their American debtors and their British colleagues. They were enmeshed in a world where the conditions of legality and stability that the empire provided were necessary for survival.

Thus Samuel Hake submitted an itemized list of the debts that were owing to him and mentioned his ownership of a large speculation in the Mohawk Valley. Oliver DeLancey explained how he had sunk his fortune in land in New York, New Jersey, and the Green Mountains. Some of his land was tenanted, and some was not, but DeLancey was a city man who had been buying in, not an aspirant country gentleman. The enormously wealthy William Bayard was another city man who treated his rural holdings strictly as a business. Isaac Low, whose holdings were scattered almost as widely as DeLancey's and Bayard's, did the same. James Jauncey's fortune was largely in the form of outstanding debts; he reported that his real property was worth only about £14,000 currency but that he had loaned a total of £52,360, on which the interest due totaled £23,610. Such wealth, sunk in speculations, loans, and chains of credit, could be defended only in the courts and under a stable legal system. That need for stability pointed its owners towards royalism.[31]

The country landlords present a different problem, for they split roughly evenly between royalism and revolution. In objective terms, the world in which Frederick Philipse and Sir John Johnson lived was much the same as that inhabited by Robert Livingston, Jr., and Philip Schuyler. What, then, drove two of them in one direction and two in the other?

The way they ran their estates may have counted. Though the royalist Beverly Robinson seems the archetype of the rapacious landlord, most men of that sort became Whigs. The Livingstons, the Van Rensselaers, and Philip Schuyler were in the fore as personal relationships and mutual obligations gave way to ties of money. By contrast, the two men whose estates were most clearly paternalist, Frederick Philipse and Sir William Johnson, were unquestioningly royalist. Other factors also entered, however. Robert Livingston, together with the Van Rensselaers, the Schuylers, and the Ten Broecks, among whom his family had married, had a long list of reasons for doubting that Britain's cause in America could be his own. Livingston knew that London regarded the great estates with suspicion, and none more so than his. He knew that his enemy Cadwallader Colden had fed that suspicion zealously. He knew that his own tenants were aware of the enemies that he had in high places. Livingston could remember how slow Lieutenant Governor James DeLancey had been to help him during the troubles of the 1750s. He had seen the humiliation of his family's party at the hands of the DeLanceys in the elections of 1768 and 1769 and during the last assembly. He knew that those same DeLanceys were at the heart of royalism in the province.

Contrast Livingston's situation with that of Frederick Philipse, a member of the DeLancey group and the owner of an estate that was notable for how settled rather than how troubled it was. Contrast Livingston's deep roots in the province with the shallow ones of Philipse's royalist brothers-in-law, Roger Morris and Beverly Robinson, who shared the Highland patent. Both were former British officers who had done nothing more than marry well. Contrast Livingston's mere colonelcy in the militia with the titles that the crown had lavished on the upstart Irishman who had become his greatest rival, William Johnson. Contrast the way in which the first Robert Livingston had built his manor on sheer gall and fraud with the way a grateful government gave Johnson secure title to hundreds of thousands of acres, and that free of quitrent. No single factor was determinant, of course, but many things separated the group that centered on Livingston from the Johnsons to the west and the Philipses to the south. In 1775 Frederick Philipse and Sir William's heirs looked at everything the imperial tie meant and saw that for them it was good. Robert Livingston looked and could only doubt.

The mere fact of being rich did not determine the stance on independence of anybody in New York. But a rich man whose fortune depended on imperial stability and on the existing structure of legality, who had gained a landed estate from British favor, or who looked on the province more as a place to make a fortune than as a place in which to be a citizen was likely to choose the crown, as was a rich man who had taken part in politics with the DeLancey group, a group that had longstanding connections with dukes and archbishops in Britain and whose short-run decisions in the early 1770s would have made it highly embarrassing for them to join seriously in resistance. By contrast, a rich man whose trade routes ran north and south rather than east and west, whose landed estate had been secured in spite of British opposition rather than because of British favor, whose political connections were "out" rather than "in" after 1769, or who was tied by marriage to people of whom such things were true was more likely to stay with the movement.

In the end New York's rulers split over whether or not they dared to try to live through the Revolution, with all the threats that it posed to stability, order, legality, and even to property. The rich patriot decided, on the basis of who and what he was, that he did have the nerve, the rich royalist that he lacked it. A fair amount of the rest of this story is concerned with how those rich patriots tried to face the prospect of fundamental change, sometimes succeeding in staving it off and sometimes failing. But one well-known contrast can illustrate the point. Though he was a Whig politician, a pamphleteer, and a member by marriage of the Livingston family, William Smith made it clear in his diary that he did not believe either that the Americans could overcome British arms or that his own sort could remain on top if the British did lose. Gouverneur Morris spent the middle and late 1770s in almost as great a panic as did Smith. His ties to Britain were strong, including a Tory mother and a half-brother who was a British lieutenant general and who had married a dowager duchess. But though Morris was quick to predict mob rule as he watched revolutionary meetings, he never completely lost his nerve, never completely gave up his confidence that in the end his sort would make things go their way. He would, in other words, somehow live through the changes and the threats that revolution portended rather than run from them in terror.[32] What precise characteristic gave him—or Robert R. Livingston, John Jay, Philip Schuyler, or Isaac Roosevelt—that ultimate confidence cannot be established. But those characteristics that in general separated men like him from the Frederick Philipses, the James DeLanceys, and the Sir John Johnsons have been established.

III

New York's Tories numbered in the many thousands, and most of them were ordinary people rather than grandees. Among twenty men taken up by the revolutionary authorities in New York City in June 1776 were two tanners, five tavernkeepers, four who called themselves laborers or apprentices, two leatherworkers, two smiths, a teacher, a pensioner, and a constable. In the same year the committee of a Westchester County village, Salem, made inventories of the estates of men who had fled to the British. It found that most of them were middling farmers, like Ephraim Sanford. Sanford had a horse worth fifteen pounds, six cattle worth twenty-one pounds, five hogs and fifteen bushels of corn valued at seventeen pounds, twelve loads of hay worth eighteen pounds, and a forty-eight-acre farm valued at three hundred pounds. Sanford was thus in fair circumstances, but among the men who fled Salem there were also some like Ezra Morehouse, a young man who owned only an old mare, and Jacob Wallace, who possessed nothing at all.[33]

Ordinary people also filed claims for compensation after the loss of the war had forced them into exile. There were some very poor men among them, like John Chatterton, of Westchester County, who "used to move from one farm to another" working as a laborer and who "had some grain and two horses." The world Chatterton lost was minute; he sought a mere £68 in provincial currency to compensate for it. Many more claims came from people like John Robblee and Peter Angevine. Robblee had been born on Long Island, but in 1764 he had moved to the Great Nine Partners patent, in Dutchess County. There he bought 150 acres of land, and by the time the Revolution came he had cleared 110 acres of it and had built a house. He valued his farm at £400 currency and thought his animals and movable goods were worth another £170. Angevine inherited a Philipse tenancy of 158 acres in 1774. He thought it was worth £316 and claimed £188 more for his goods and animals, giving him a total of £504 in provincial currency.[34]

Why did such very ordinary men choose the crown? For some of them, at least, foreign birth and a continuing sense that they were something other than New Yorkers may have counted. The point applies for the New York City cartmen Thomas Ryan and Thomas Mills, who had come from Ireland and Scotland, respectively, to the Welsh gunsmith Henry Watkeys and to the German baker Frederick Brautigan. Ryan and Mills may have been typical laborers, and Watkeys and Brautigan representative artisans. The time they had spent in America varied from only a few months to twenty years. But none of them had subscribed to the way in which the radicals who spoke for most of their class were coming to see the world.[35]

The same point holds for the large number of royalist Scots. Many of them had migrated to the Mohawk Valley as tenants of the Johnson family, but there were others who had settled north of Albany. There they gave their hamlets names like Argyle and New Perth. They were highlanders who wore the kilt proudly. They were refugees from the misery that enclosures and anti-Jacobite repression had been making of highland life since the uprising of 1745, and that gave them good reason to hate the English. But they also learned quickly to fear the revolutionaries. The Scots who settled north of Albany found themselves fearing the fury of the Green Mountain insurgents; Otter Creek, the town sacked so thoroughly that even the stones in its mill were broken, was only one of the Scots settlements that Ethan Allen's people demolished. Moreover, many of these Scots were Catholics, and for intensely Protestant Dutchmen and Yankees that by itself was reason enough to fear them. Sir William Johnson, a man with a Catholic background, encouraged his Scots tenants to recreate as many of their old ways as they wanted. Part of what they recreated was their tradition of fierce loyalty to their military chieftains, and in the Mohawk Valley those chieftains were the Johnsons.[36]

These people were tenant farmers as well as Scots migrants. That tenancy was bound up with men's political decisions is well known. Farmers in western Massachusetts were radicalized in part by the fear that British policy was pushing them towards the loss of their farms and towards tenancy under great landlords. In the Hudson Valley the desire to escape tenancy impelled men in both political directions. The tenants of Whig landlords like the Van Rensselaers and the Livingstons became royalists because British agents led them to believe that if the mother country triumphed they would be given the freeholds they coveted. Though conservative in the strictly political sense, such men were intensely radical in social terms.[37] But the landlords of the western frontier and on the northern marches themselves chose royalism. Tenants who followed a John Johnson or a Philip Skene towards the crown cannot have expected that a British triumph would make freeholders of them, whatever secret promises were being made on Rensselaerwyck. If they wanted freeholds, their chances were far better with the American side than with the British. Moreover, these were not the only Tory tenants of Tory landlords, and for many such men the complications that grew out of being Catholic, Scottish, and an immigrant had no bearing. How can their choice be explained?

An answer can be found in the enormously detailed royalist claims that were filed by Frederick Philipse and Beverly Robinson. Chapter 1 showed that these brothers-in-law controlled their holdings in very different ways. But both landlords chose royalism, and each suffered the confiscation of his estate for it. The reactions of their respective tenants to their landlord's choice open a window on how tenant royalists and tenant revolutionaries were like and unlike one another, on the differences and the similarities between tenants who followed their landlord to disaster and other tenants who found in the Revolution their chance to get rid of him.

The political positions that most of the tenants on both estates took can be found. Some on Philipse Manor signed a "Protest of Inhabitants and Freeholders" that Colonel Philipse circulated in April 1775 against the calling of the Second Continental Congress. People on both estates were cited for their actions and their beliefs by the Commissioners for Detecting and Defeating Conspiracies, the Revolution's political police. These people can safely be regarded as royalists. The names of others appear on the muster roll of the state militia.[38] These we can call Whigs, patriots, or revolutionaries, unless their names also appear in one of the royalist sources. The trimmers whose names do appear on both sides and the many who avoided being mentioned in any of the political sources can be called neutrals. The listings cannot be perfect, for the neutral category without doubt includes both men who were too old for militia service and committed Tories who had the good luck never to be cited. Moreover, and more serious, the royalist category rests on two qualitatively different sorts of evidence. The Westchester protest and the militia muster roll are inclusive listings. They give the names of everyone who took the positive step of signing the protest or of joining up. But the only equivalent source for the Robinson tenants would be lists of people who signed and refused the Continental Association. Such lists were kept, but for the Highland patent they have not survived.[39] The identification of royalists there thus depends solely on the records of the conspiracies commissioners, which give only the names of the people who had the bad luck to be caught or reported. But this merely qualifies the evidence and does not destroy it.

Philipsburgh had 283 male tenants, and the Robinson estate 146. On both tracts the vast majority of the tenants avoided taking either side. One hundred and fifty of those on Philipsburgh appear in none of the political sources, and 14 more were listed on both sides. These account for 57.9 percent of the whole, not including the widows who worked their husbands' farms. Seventy-six Philipse tenants became royalists, and 43 took the revolutionary side, or 26.9 and 15.1 percent respectively. On the Robinson land 106 tenants, accounting for 61.2 percent of the whole, were neutral. But on that estate the percentages of revolutionaries and royalists reversed the figures for Philipsburgh. Only 19 of Robinson's tenants, 10.9 percent of the total, were cited by the conspiracies commissioners, despite the landlord's claim that he had raised a regiment of 500 men among them. Forty-eight, however, or 27.1 percent of the estate's adult male population, served in the revolutionary militia.

These remarkably complete records suggest several things about what the Revolution meant to the people of Philipsburgh and of Robinson's share of the Highland patent. Six tenants in every ten managed to avoid involvement on either side. As several scholars have suggested, the need is great for a more sophisticated understanding of what neutralism meant to the people whom the Revolution did not reach.[40] They may have been Quakers; many in the region were. They may have been old, or cripples. Perhaps their wish was that a pox descend on the houses of both George Washington and George III. Perhaps, since where they lived meant that they were caught between the American and British armies, they simply held still until the horror of living on a front line had passed. Perhaps, as for Boris Pasternak's Doctor Zhivago and for many men and women in Northern Ireland as I write this, they wanted only the private victory of keeping their own lives intact. We cannot tell.

But what of the ones who did choose? Though tenants were in debt to both landlords, their owing money had little to do with the choices they made. People listed on both Philipse's and Robinson's debt rolls are divided among three positions—Tory, neutral, and revolutionary. What seems more significant is a rough relationship between the quality of life on the two estates and the way that each fragmented. The Revolution reached only about two tenants in every five on either estate, but whereas on Philipsburgh some five in every eight of those who did take a stand followed the landlord, on Robinson's land only one in four did.

Colonel Philipse's royalist tenants were satisfied people. Rents there had been frozen for years, and if a Philipse tenant paid a high rent, it was more likely a sign that he was doing well than evidence that the landlord was pressing him hard. Among the nine tenants who both signed the Westchester protest and figured in the records of the conspiracies commissioners, only one paid a rental of less than five pounds per year. The rents of the other eight ranged between £5.4.6 and £11.11. Philipsburgh royalists included many tenants like Joshua Hart, who paid £6.10, or Gilbert Pugsley, who paid £6.12, but few like Richard Archer, whose farm cost him £3.4.6. Among the tenants who joined the revolutionary militia were men of fair comfort, paying rents of up to £12, but most of them paid under £5. The conclusion must be that whatever politicized Philipse tenants onto the revolutionary side, it worked more effectively among poor tenants than among prosperous ones.

On Robinson's estate the question was more involved. A rental that betokened prosperity for a Philipse tenant may well have been paid to Robinson by a man seething with resentment at the way the rent rose and rose. Robinson's Tories came from among his poorer tenants and from among those who were best off, but not from among those in the middle of his rent roll. Thomas Williamson had seen the price of his farm rise from £1.10 to only £3 between 1768 and 1775, and the cost of Isaac Haviland's actually fell by sixpence over the same period. Both became royalists. But Daniel Chase's rent had risen from £3 to £20; that for Malcolm Morison's farm from £4 to £40, and the cost of the three farms that Alexander Grant held, from £5 each to £100 for all of them. They became royalists as well. The revolutionaries among Robinson's tenants did not come from either of these extremes. Rather, they came from the men in the middle of the rent roll, from people who knew that their rent would rise again and that meeting the increase might be difficult.

The contrast between politics among the Philipsburgh tenants and politics on the Robinson holding shows that the ethnicity of the Scots who followed Sir John Johnson may not have been the only factor that kept them loyal. Their Scottishness drove a wedge between them and their German and English neighbors, and their being tenants, while the others were largely freeholders, drove it further. But Sir John was heir to a tradition of "good" landlordship. The important contrast is not between tenants who came from one cultural background and tenants who came from another. It is between estates where landlordism meant stability and security and estates where it meant insecurity and as much hard exploitation as the landlord dared to inflict. It was the tenants of the latter sort of landlord, whatever his actual politics, who grasped in the Revolution their chance to get rid of him.[41]

Philipsburgh and Robinson's estate are not the only places where a comparison is possible between humble royalists and equally obscure revolutionaries. In Albany County the conspiracies commissioners kept detailed records of their activities from 1778 to 1781. During those years they saw a cross section of the county's people: day laborers, yeomen, farmers, innkeepers, artisans, schoolteachers. They forced about 350 of the unfortunates who came before them to give bail to appear again. Some of them were merely witnesses being put under a nominal bond, but most of them were charged with disaffection or active royalism. Two hundred fifty-two of these people were farmers, yeomen, and farm laborers, and among the rest there were twelve innkeepers, thirty-one artisans and youths, nine professional men, and two merchants. Four were women, and the occupations of nineteen of the men were not given. Although the Albany area was full of prisoners of war taken when Burgoyne capitulated at Saratoga, they accounted for only nine of the men from whom the commissioners demanded bail. The rest were settled Albanians.[42]

These people had built up friendships and business relationships and acquaintances. They had parents and children and brothers and uncles who had signed the Continental Association, who had sworn allegiance, and who had enrolled in the militia. When they were arrested, such people suddenly found that they needed those ties, for rarely would the commissioners release them without someone else's standing surety for them. There were times when the board asked for the security not just of one person but of two or three, and there were times when it asked for sums as high as a thousand pounds. If an arrested man needed someone to stand up with him before the commissioners, or if he needed to raise a thousand pounds to gain his freedom, he did not turn to a stranger. He turned to people who knew him well enough to trust and care about him and to risk their money for him. He called, in other words, on someone who was already important in his life. Who were the people on whom these Tories called?

For thirteen months the commissioners recorded the occupations of the people who gave bail for their prisoners,[43] and this record provides a chance to see who counted in the prisoners' lives. The evidence must be used with care. Some of the men who put up bail had been arrested themselves, and there were instances that seem more like the impersonal functioning of a modern bail bondsman than the literal cashing in of a tie of friendship, interest, or blood. But in general the way that some men gave bail to free others shows that the prisoners turned for help to men of their own class, status, and family, and the men to whom they turned gave their help despite the bitterness that separated Tory and rebel. The prisoners and the men who helped them can be roughly divided into three main groups: farmers and farm laborers, artisans and innkeepers, and men of high status. A comparison shows how likely men in trouble were to go for help to someone of their own sort. One hundred ninety-one farm people were given bail by other farm people, but only twenty-nine by artisans or innkeepers and twenty-eight by men of high status. Nineteen of the artisan and publican prisoners were given bail by farm workers, twenty-two by other artisans or innkeepers, and only six by men of high status. Only four men of high status were given bail by farmers, and three by artisans or innkeepers, but seventeen of them received bail from other men of rank. The correlation is not perfect. It is not surprising that some farmers had developed ties with the local shoemaker or tavernkeeper. Some of the instances when a person of high status put up bail were clearly short-term favors while the man who had been freed searched for a more permanent surety. But the tendency within all three groups to turn to other men in the same group gives some sense of the dense network of obligations and connections that bound people even in strife-torn Albany.

Such ties could bind whole villages and families as well as individuals. At the end of the winter of 1780/81 the commissioners ordered the arrest of a large number of Rensselaerwyck men. Many of them lived in the village of Schodack, which lay inland on the east side of the Hudson, somewhat downstream from Albany. Almost all of the men who were taken up were soon freed on bail, and in several cases the bail for a number of prisoners was put up by one man. A cordwainer named Jacob J. Van Valkenburgh put up bail for three prisoners, and in two of the cases he was joined by another cordwainer named Philip Schermerhorne. Meanwhile Jacob Schermerhorne, who was a farmer, was standing bail for two more, one of them named Van Valkenburgh. Yet another Van Valkenburgh produced the money to release two more men.[44]

Perhaps everyone in Schodack secretly shared the hopes, the doubts, and the fears of the unlucky ones who had been caught. Perhaps they all felt threatened when the commissioners, who were great men with fearsome powers,[45] seized their neighbors. Perhaps the money that the various Van Valkenburghs and Schermerhornes put up had been collected house-to-house. It may also be that during the sleigh ride or the trudge from Albany back to Schodack the men who had put up the bail gave terrible tongue-lashings to the hapless ones whom they had rescued. We will never know. But the tangle of bailees and bailors, all of them bearing the same Dutch names, that grew out of the arrests in Schodack tells us that in that village deeper ties did run beneath political divisiveness.

Precisely what kind of ties survived the split into Tory and rebel can be seen in another sleepy Dutch community, Haverstraw, in Orange County. The town fronted on the river, below the mountains, in the area that had sent the bullying John DeNoyelles to the last provincial assembly, and what royalism there was in Orange was concentrated there. But despite having the worst Tory problem in the county, the area was still heavily revolutionary. Four hundred fifty-six of the men of Haverstraw signed the Continental Association, and only one hundred thirty-six refused it. Family connections counted heavily when a person there decided whether to sign. The men who refused included three of the four named Babcock, nine of thirteen Conklins, eight of thirteen Johnstons, seven of twelve Osborns, five of six Posts, all three Wanamakers, and both Bereas. But they numbered only four of the fourteen Ackersons; one of the twelve Blauvelts; and none of the eight Coopers, the eight Gurnees, the thirteen Onderdonks, or the twelve Van Houtens. Here was a town where the Revolution was an affair of families. Were they embittered by some small war about religion? Had some tried to grab land from others? Were the royalists closer to the river and thus more able to trade with New York City? Again, the sources do not tell. But the way in which whole families went to one side or the other shows that more was at work than happenstance and individual choice.[46]

The links, the connections, the relationships that made such ordinary men what they were have left much fainter traces than have those that defined their "betters." The provincial elite knew one another. They kept records and preserved letters and thought their stories important enough to recount them. They formed a class, albeit one so badly fractured that it could not maintain its cohesion when crisis confronted it. In objective terms, the tenants on Philipsburgh, those on Sir William Johnson's Kingsborough, and those in Schodack formed a class as well, but they had much less reason to know it. The people who figured large in their lives lived at distances of only a mile or two. Understanding them requires understanding the precise set of linkages and tensions that made each local group what it was. For these, as for the great men, such linkages and tensions can be found.

Little men as well as great ones sweated and agonized at the moment of decision. Decades ago, Carl Becker made immortal the pain that John Jay and his friend Peter Van Schaack felt as they went in their different directions. While Van Schaack and Jay were making up their well-educated minds, a group of frightened Rensselaerwyck farmers were debating the same problem. They had left their farms and gone into hiding among the rocks and pine trees of the rugged Helderbergh escarpment, west of Albany. There they discussed matters, turning the question over and over until one of them, John Commons, put it for decision. "Those who thought Congress were in the right," Commons told the meeting, "should go and those who thought the King was right should stay." But putting the question was easier than answering it, and Commons himself said that "he did not know who was right."[47]

IV

Within both the royalist and the revolutionary camps some led and others followed. Though militant royalism did bring some inexperienced men into the thick of events,[48] its leaders were generally the people who had stood out in the old order. The people to compare them with are the people who led the toppling of that order, the members of the revolutionary committees that began to appear in 1774 and that by 1776 were the effective government of all New York. These committees were "the novel structures of the Revolution and the proof that the times were truly revolutionary."[49] Understanding them is central to the purpose of this study, and how the committees emerged, ruled, and finally disappeared will be the cardinal problem of the next two chapters. But first, whom did the committees bring into the forum? The question cannot be answered in simple, static terms, for the committeemen established "who" they were by their actions. But the kinds of men they were when they became revolutionaries can be discovered.

The committees formed a movement, not a fixed structure, and for that reason the "typical" committeeman never existed. The men who gave form to the committees in 1774 were not the only men involved in them in 1776. The men involved in 1776, in turn, were not the sole ones to be found in them during their final phase, in 1779. Throughout revolutionary America, as committees gained power they became larger and more full of men new to affairs. Yet from the beginning to the end two things were true. One was that the committees spoke for people who had been outside the circles where decisions were made under the old order. The other was that they were the instruments of a revolutionary coalition rather than of a single class.[50]

The experience of the mechanics of New York City exemplifies both points. The mechanics were a source of driving energy throughout the decade before independence, and as they worked to give force to the revolutionary movement, they also expressed their own concerns. In doing both, they gained the self-awareness and self-confidence necessary to make themselves a separate group. It was shown in chapter 2 how their grievances and those of other workmen underlay the rioting between soldiers and civilians on Golden Hill in January 1770. The pamphleteer "Brutus" stimulated confrontation precisely in terms of the damage that the soldiers were doing to workmen by taking work from them. Later that year "Brutus" was in print again, this time inveighing not against the soldiers but rather against the city's great men. Nonimportation, adopted as a tactic to resist the Townshend Acts, was collapsing, and the merchants, who wanted trade to resume, were asserting that the decision to start importing again was for them alone to make. But "Brutus" warned his "Friends, Fellow Citizens, Fellow Countrymen and Fellow Freemen" that nothing could "be more flagrantly wrong than the assertion of some of our mercantile dons, that the Mechanics have no right to give their Sentiments." Thus was posed a problem that would run for twenty years and would be crucial within the committee movement.[51]

Three years later, when the issue of the East India Company's tea was breaking, William Smith discovered "by Hints that the Mechanics convene at Beer Houses," where Sons of Liberty like Isaac Sears and Alexander

McDougall were meeting them "to concert measures." Out of these discussions the Body of Mechanics emerged as a group with a public voice. Its members bought a meeting place and named it Mechanics Hall. As the crisis moved towards war, they found themselves gathering there in plenary sessions as often as every week, and at moments of high tension their leaders rushed into print flyers calling them out. Their committee acted as a steering body when radical actions were being planned, and if they did not like what they saw royalists or milder rebels doing, they acted. In March 1776 the printer Samuel Loudon was about to publish a pamphlet written in opposition to Tom Paine's *Common Sense*. But Paine had summed up exactly what mechanics were thinking, and when word of the pamphlet got out, the Body of Mechanics ordered Loudon to hold it back. Then some of them seized and burned the printed sheets and forced the hapless printer to swear that he accepted what they had done. The men who led the seizure included the chairman of the committee, a tavernkeeper, a carpenter, and a pewterer.[52]

The mechanics had a great deal to do with the genesis of the "official" committee movement as well. They may fairly be given credit for beginning it, for it was at their impetus that the city's first committee of correspondence was elected. They wanted that committee to have twenty-five members, but they acquiesced in a proposal by more conservative men to put fifty people (the number was later raised to fifty-one) on it. The times called, as they knew, for coalition, for the broadest possible base, not for the domination by one group and the alienation of all others. Even after its cautiousness and lack of responsiveness cost the fifty-one the mechanics' confidence, they cooperated with its successors, the committee of sixty and the committee of one hundred. Unity in the face of the British threat required of them that they work with men far more tepid than themselves.[53]

But the mechanics were engaging in coalition politics; they were not submerging themselves in an undefined "common interest." They wanted men like themselves to be at the center of affairs, and they made at least a symbolic gain by the active involvement of some of them in the city's committees. This gain was of a piece with two changes of much greater import. As Staughton Lynd has shown, the mechanics generated their own demands and their own concerns between 1774 and 1776. These demands and concerns went beyond "official" policy in a number of ways, and they reflected the particular situation of the men who were making them. The mechanics wanted New Yorkers to accept the revolutionary paper money that was beginning to come from New England. They wanted royalists to be silenced rather than tolerated. They wanted members of the Continental Congress to be elected directly by people like themselves. They had no illusions that such things would come merely from the good will of other men in the province. On the contrary, they were learning that they could gain what they wanted only if they acted assertively on their own.[54]

The other change under way was in the city's leading coalition, as the make-up of the successive committees shows. No attempt has been made here at a rigorous collective biography of the fifty-one, the sixty, and the one hundred, but Carl Becker showed long ago that each fresh election brought forth men who were more militant and less prominent. Becker found that nineteen members of the fifty-one became Tories, that only thirteen of the sixty did, and that eighteen of the one hundred finally opted for the crown. Royalists thus shrank from 37 percent of the first committee to 22 percent of the second to only 18 percent of the third. As the royalists were forced out, their places were taken by mechanics, small traders, and lesser professionals who had been outside the charmed circle of the old order. Committee politics was coalition politics just as much in 1776 as in 1774, but the coalition itself was markedly different. In New York, as in the Philadelphia committees studied by Richard Ryerson, the make-up after each new committee election moved downward socially and to the left politically.[55]

Something similar happened in the city of Albany. As in New York City, resistance there developed against a long history of conflict and posed the potential for more. But again as in New York, it posed a short-run need for as broad a coalition as could be held together. The elements in Albany's coalition were, on the one hand, the city's old Dutch oligarchy and, on the other, its Sons of Liberty. The prominence in the city's revolutionary movement of men like Philip Schuyler, Stephen and Jeremiah Van Rensselaer, Abraham Ten Broeck, Goose (or Gooje) Van Schaick, and Leonard Gansevoort shows that the oligarchy could hold its own.[56] But the city's Sons of Liberty were a different matter. Ninety-four men had signed the group's constitution in 1765, during the Stamp Act crisis, and the first name on the list was that of Dr. Thomas Young, the wandering physician whose career weaves into one skein radicalism in places as far apart as Philadelphia and the Green Mountains. A study of the Albany Sons of Liberty has shown that most of them were merchants, and their willingness to intimidate Albany's stamp distributor demonstrates that they were militant. In other words, they stood to the movement in Albany as men like Isaac Sears did to that in New York, and thirteen of them joined the old oligarchs on the committee.[57]

The Albany committee likewise moved from men of prominence to men of obscurity as election followed election. There were six committee elections between 1775 and 1777, and very few who were chosen at the first of them were still sitting after the last. Places that had been filled by Volkert P. Douw, a former mayor, Goose Van Schaick, an original Son of Liberty, Abraham Yates, an established if radical politician, and Leonard Gansevoort, scion of a great family, had been taken over by unknowns such as James Vernor, Nicholas Marselis, and Gerrit Groesbeck. There were exceptions: Abraham Ten Broeck, former assemblyman, landowner, militia general, Van Rensselaer son-in-law, and future state senator, sat on the committee throughout its history. But in Albany, as in New York and Philadelphia, the committee movement was bringing men of a different sort to power.[58]

That was as true in rural Albany County as in the city. One of the largest rural committees was that of the manor of Rensselaerwyck. It had twenty-three places, and over the six elections forty-five men were picked to fill them. Only six men were returned at all of the elections, and fifteen of the committeemen were elected but once. Twenty-five of them can be identified on a tax list made a decade earlier, in 1766, and their placing on that list shows how the committee changed. The first election produced a committee drawn from the better-off among the manor's residents. Though most of its people were assessed at well below £10, they picked as their committeemen one rated at £125, four more rated at between £30 and £40, and three rated at between £15 and £29. But of all the committeemen picked at subsequent polls, only two came from those levels. Among the newcomers at later elections there were five who had been rated at £10, one at £6, one at £5, and two at only £1. With each fresh election the percentage of men not mentioned at all on the tax list grew.[59]

Rensselaerwyck is the only place for which precise information about the property that committeemen held is available, but the rate at which each new committee election brought forth fresh faces shows that something similar was happening in other districts. In Hoosac, just north of Rensselaerwyck, thirty-two committeemen were chosen in all, twenty-one of whom were elected only once. King's District, near the Massachusetts border, picked twenty-one members altogether, choosing twelve of them only one time. In Schoharie, to the west, over the six elections twenty men were chosen, of whom eight were picked once and another six twice. The people of Saratoga elected thirty-one committeemen in all, twenty of them only one time. Altogether more than four hundred men served on the county's committees. The Revolution was not imposed on the people of Albany County. They made it for themselves.[60] Only on Livingston Manor, where the Livingston family dominated the committee throughout its history, was the picture different.[61]

The same picture applies in the other rural counties. To involve oneself in the committee movement in Tryon County was to make a public stand against all that the Johnson family stood for. There were some committeemen, like Nicholas Herkimer, the German-born hero of Oriskany, who had been among Sir Williams's friends, but there were many more who had not. Not one of the committeemen was among the county officials and grand jurors who published an ostentatious declaration of their loyalty just a month before the battle at Lexington.[62] But there were many like Isaac Paris and Jacob Klock, Indian traders who had long opposed the way that Sir William had restricted contact between red and white. If the Johnsons stood for a well-intentioned but hopeless vision of seigneurial society that would protect both red and white, Paris and Klock stood for a ruthless, acquisitive expansionism that would sweep Indians and Johnsons alike out of its way.

Some of the Tryon committeemen formed the nucleus of a new frontier elite, but there was also a large proportion of obscure farmers. Six of the members became full colonels in the revolutionary militia, and one a general, and all but one of those men also won a seat in the state legislature. So did several of the committeemen who remained civilians. But there were also many men who were genuinely small. Thus Andrew Reber, noted earlier in this chapter, was a militia private and a shareholder in a small patent. Daniel McDougall served as an ordinary soldier in a regiment commanded by his fellow committeeman Peter Waggoner. George Eader, Jr., was a private in the regiment led by Jacob Klock. Indeed, two-fifths of all the Tryon committeemen bore neither the military rank nor the civilian title that told who a man was in their world. About some of them no information survives at all.[63]

Even in Orange and Ulster, the counties of revolutionary consensus, the committee movement brought change. The men who made up the initial committees in eight towns there are known, and among them there was a sizable proportion of men wholly new to public affairs. The towns were Marlborough, Shawangunk, Rochester, Cornwall, Kingston, New Windsor, and Orange-Town. In social terms these places had much in common. Their people were freeholders, or at worst the tenants of small landlords. In none of them was there either great wealth or great poverty. They were, in other words, typical of these two counties, where most men agreed that the Revolution was a good thing. For all that, there were lines of possible division among them. Orange-Town, Newburgh, New Windsor, Kingston, and Cornwall were old river towns, but Marlborough, Shawangunk, and Rochester lay well back from the shore. The origins of Kingston and Orange-Town ran back to the seventeenth century, but Marlborough was formally organized only in 1772. Kingston, Rochester, Shawangunk, and Orange-Town were heavily Dutch, and their committees were full of men called Andries, Johannes, and Jacobus. But Marlborough, Cornwall, and New Windsor were peopled by Britons and New Englanders, and their committees were studded with men bearing such names as Jonathan, Nathaniel, and Hezekiah. These differences, however, counted for little in political terms.

The greatest influx of new men came in Newburgh, where eight of the eleven committeemen had held only a minor post or no post at all before the Revolution. New Windsor was dominated by the Clinton family, and through George Clinton it had a major link with the outside world. Clinton's brother James, who had been town clerk before independence and who finished the Revolution with a Continental generalship, became the first chairman of New Windsor's committee, and the board over which he presided included two former supervisors. But the other six committeemen were either complete novices or veterans of only minor positions. One of those men succeeded James Clinton in the chair. The founding chairman in Cornwall was wholly new to power, and three men who were equally without experience sat at his board. Two of that town's nine committeemen had held minor offices, two had been supervisor, and one had been a justice of the peace.

Rochester was not very different. There, too, the chairman was a novice, and four other committeemen likewise had held no posts. Of the three who had held office, one had been supervisor, one an assessor, and one only a fence-viewer. In Marlborough the chairman had been supervisor, and another member had been town clerk. Three committeemen had held minor posts, and the other six had never held office. In Orange-Town, too, men without experience outnumbered men used to wielding local power. Only in Shawangunk and Kingston did the committeemen bring wide political experience to the board. Five of the seven committeemen in Shawangunk had been either supervisor or town clerk, and in Kingston the committee included the county sheriff, the county surrogate, a justice of the peace, two former supervisors, and five former trustees. Only three of the committeemen there had held no office.[64]

In social terms the committee movement thus had many implications. The primary reason why men formed committees was the stark need to win and coordinate support for the Grand Cause, but how New Yorkers responded to that need varied. At one extreme there was Tryon, where to become involved was to challenge the whole world one had lived in. At the other was Livingston Manor, where to do the same thing was to declare allegiance to a very similar world. Only in those two places did the local situation make the committees overt instruments of class conflict. But throughout New York the make-up of the committees signified profound internal change. The committees became the most broadly representative government that New Yorkers had ever known, and the involvement in them of so many new men suggests that they were the means not simply of broadened representation but of a new kind of direct involvement.

The available evidence about the committeemen is sketchy and fragmented. It allows us to know only one kind of information about one group and another kind about another. But stitched together, these different sorts of information present a picture that makes sense. The old order in New York had been dominated by men who expected to rule, but the committee movement brought out men of a different kind. The shifts in New York City from well-known figures to mechanics and small traders, in Albany from the Dutch oligarchy to men of obscurity, and in Rensselaerwyck from men who were prosperous to men who were much less so all point towards one conclusion. So do the number of committeemen in rural Albany County who served only once and then gave way to others, and the way that men in placid Orange and Ulster came to the committees with little political experience, and the way in which the Tryon committee drew its membership from the Johnsons' enemies and from privates as well as colonels. Something profoundly unsettling was going on, and the name for it is revolution.

V

The issue of independence reduced all complexities to one simple question: Did one support it or did one not? In 1776 the revolutionaries were insistent that everyone give his answer, no matter what the cost. Though at first they drew a distinction between outright royalism and mere disaffection, they soon stopped bothering and acted on the principle that everyone who was not fully with them was against them. But how men made their choices was by no means so simple. The positions that people took grew out of the lives they had led and out of what the people who counted in those lives were doing. Some acted in terms of the class they knew they belonged to, and others in opposition to a class they hated. Some forgot their domestic problems, or tried to, and joined in coalition with men very different from themselves. Some chose a side because their family was choosing it, and some simply went the way their whole community was going. Without doubt some switched back and forth, hoping to end up backing whoever might win. No single factor guaranteed that a man would become either a royalist or a revolutionary, and for most men choice meant heartache. But people made their choices as members of a tangled, complicated society, not simply as individuals or colonists or Americans. They became rebels or Tories or they tried to stay out of it by reference to the whole set of material, cultural, geographical, economic, and political complexities that had been their world, even if their choice meant that that world had to come apart.

Chapter 5

The Rending of New York

During the first months of 1774 the British government responded with vigor to the challenge that Bostonians had posed by means of their Tea Party. It closed Boston Harbor; it altered the structure of the government of Massachusetts; it permitted legal cases involving colonial officials to be transferred to courts in Nova Scotia or Britain; it loosened the regulations that governed the billeting of troops in the Colonies; it appointed General Gage, its American commander in chief, as governor of Massachusetts. Ministers and Parliamentarians in London were sure that so clear a show of determination would force the Bostonians to back down quickly.

But the effect was to spread the American crisis rather than to contain it. Direct resistance in Massachusetts itself made a nullity of the new government, as angry crowds forced the "mandamus" councillors named by General Gage to resign their seats, closed county courts, and forced the jurists to go through public rituals of submission to popular rather than royal sovereignty. In June the provincial assembly debated resistance behind barred doors while the provincial secretary stood outside proclaiming the assembly's dissolution. Over the months that followed, militia units went into training, and men began to gather stores of arms and ammunition. By the end of the year, Gage's writ ran no further than the reach of the regulars to whom he gave orders.[1]

Outside Massachusetts, people rallied to support Boston, collecting funds and sending shipload after shipload of food and fuel. Organizing that aid program posed problems that shook the established order and led to the calling of the First Continental Congress. The congress called not only for coordination of the relief for Boston but for an escalating program of economic resistance by all the colonies. Meanwhile, men of passion and men of moderation jostled for position and power. In Philadelphia, for instance, the summer of 1774 was frantic with maneuvers and ploys, and by July "a new force" of popular committees "dominated Pennsylvania politics." The men whom this new force embodied were "a new elite for a new society, chosen (and self chosen) to perform unprecedented public services."[2]

Only New York seemed to lag behind. There the crown courts still did their business. The provincial assembly bubbled as usual with the bickerings of the Livingstons and the DeLanceys. No one opposed either Governor Tryon or Lieutenant Governor Colden, and while Colden was administering the province that year, he worried less about imperial matters than about land grants in the Green Mountains and offices for his sons. The royalist printer James Rivington published his newspaper without hindrance, and the Reverend Samuel Seabury began bringing out his arch-Tory *Letters of a Westchester Farmer.* Small wonder that Joseph Reed, of Pennsylvania, writing to Josiah Quincy, of Massachusetts, scorned the timid province that lay between them: "While they are attending to the little paltry debates which their own parties have produced, the Great Cause is suffering in their hands."[3]

Reed was both right and wrong in his perception. New York's "official" revolutionary leaders were cautious about resistance, independence, and republicanism, and they were the ones who spoke for the province to the rest of America. Their timidity, however, reflected not a general lethargy or petty-mindedness among their people but rather their own recognition of how volatile those people were. Even by the time that Reed made his caustic comments street turmoil was renewing itself in New York City. Though there were only faint noises in the countryside, no landlord was going to be quick to do anything that might encourage his tenants to try again what they had attempted in 1766. Nor did either landlords or speculators want to encourage the Green Mountain Boys. It was better by far to go slowly and let others take the lead. But despite the leaders' foot-dragging, revolution came, bringing with it changes and upheavals as full as those experienced anywhere in America.

I

Establishing how those changes and upheavals happened means first of all confronting the concept of *revolution.* The word is perhaps the most complex and the most abused in the modern historian's vocabulary. Its use here is specific and limited, for my primary concern is with the *process* of the *political revolution* that took place between 1774 and 1780. The process of a massive revolution can be grasped only if fragments of evidence from many different sources are put together. But such fragments cannot form anything more than a historical crazy quilt unless a coherent structure of ideas gives them meaning and shape.

There is no shortage of theories about revolution,[4] but the most sophisticated thought on how political revolution takes place in Western society comes from an unlikely combination of practicing Marxist revolutionaries and American policy scientists. Lenin, writing his *State and Revolution* in hiding in 1917, argued that the task confronting the Bolsheviks and the Russian workers and peasants was not to gain control of existing Russian institutions, such as they were; rather, it was to smash them, and with them the whole apparatus of the old order, and to create something wholly new in their place. In his vision, that new order would be based on a participatory democracy of workers', soldiers', and peasants' councils, or soviets, rather than on parliamentary representation. Years later, Trotsky refined the analysis in his history of the revolution that Lenin and he had helped to make. He brought out the significance in a revolutionary situation of a period of dual power, or dyarchy, in which no single set of political institutions can claim the monopoly of coercive authority that is the basis of politics in normal times. That had been Russia's condition in 1917. Only in such a situation could a call like Lenin's for the smashing of the old order present a feasible strategy.[5]

To marry the ideas of Lenin and Trotsky with those of Peter Amann, Samuel P. Huntington, Ted Robert Gurr, and J. P. Nettl requires an unusual notion of intellectual romance. But these political sociologists, like the famous Russians, concentrate on the problem of revolutionary power. In 1962 Amann tried to cut through the thicket of theorizing on revolution by developing Trotsky's point that a revolutionary situation is one in which there is no accepted claimant to power. Six years later Huntington, openly acknowledging his debt to Lenin, expanded Amann's insight at length. He laid great stress on the importance of understanding revolutionary coalitions and on the concept of political mobilization. By *mobilization* Huntington meant a sudden surge into public affairs of people who had previously taken no part in them. If enough people push forward, and if their interests are opposed to those of the people who have been running things, the old order is doomed.[6]

Meanwhile, Nettl was developing the same concept in the language of Parsonian sociology. He defined mobilization as "essentially (1) attitudinal—a commitment to action and (2) a means of translating this commitment into action or observed behaviour." Nettl noted that mobilization involves a number of different factors, including values and goals that require it, action by leaders, collective and institutional means of achieving it, and symbols and references by which the need for it and the goals it seeks are communicated. As Nettl used it, the term has many overtones of otherwise passive people's being manipulated. The result is to lose the stress on active lower-class involvement that is so important in Lenin and Trotsky and even in Huntington. But Nettl also pointed out the need to grasp "the process by which mobilization takes place in terms of individual interaction, the creation and change of collectivities and structures, the crystallization of roles, the effect on subsystems and their boundaries." Translated, this makes almost the same point that Trotsky put more eloquently and more romantically when he said that "the most indubitable feature of a revolution is the direct interference of the masses in historical events."[7]

The great strength of such analysis, whatever its language, is that it comes to grips with the fundamental difference between how people behave in normal times and how they act during a revolution. To understand the difference, one might use David Easton's metaphor of the "political system" operating on its "environment" and maintaining a sharp boundary around itself.[8] The essence of political revolution is to smash the system and destroy the boundary. The mechanistic quality of the metaphor hides the fact that the system is in reality the pattern of power relationships, legitimizing beliefs, and predictable political roles that ensures that some govern and others are governed. To "smash the system" is to end those relationships, beliefs, and roles and to place the people whom Easton relegated to the "environment" in a position where it is up to them to make public decisions and to undertake public business. Even in placid times the metaphor has its limitations, for the difference is more than semantic if we abandon it and speak instead of "the ruling class" and "the masses" or of "the elite" and "the plebs." But the central point is that there is a difference between revolutionary and nonrevolutionary political life. It is the difference between "the environment's" putting pressure on "the system" to act and people's acting for themselves. Hannah Arendt once described the latter condition as one in which public liberty ("the *right* to a *share* in the government," in Alexander Hamilton's astute phrase of 1784)[9] is real for the many, not simply for the few.[10]

But if we have learned anything from the collapse of the synthesis made by the progressive historians,[11] it is that for revolutionary America broad categories like the few and the many, the rulers and the people, or the rich and the poor are too clumsy. They do not describe what was happening. A general view can be valid only if it explains many local situations, and Ted Robert Gurr has offered a way to understand the balance between the particular and the general during struggles over power. His schema distinguishes types of rebellion in terms of their magnitude. At one end of his spectrum is *internal war* ("large-scale, organized, focused civil strife, almost always accompanied by extensive violence, including large-scale revolts"), and at the other is *conspiracy* ("intensively organized, relatively small-scale civil strife, including political assassinations, small-scale terrorism, small-scale guerrilla wars, coups, mutinies, and plots and purges"). Between these extremes comes *turmoil*, or "relatively spontaneous, unstructured mass strife, including demonstrations, political strikes, riots, political clashes and localized rebellions." The magnitude of conflict must of course be assessed in relative terms; insurgents whose numbers could represent a massive revolt in one society might be able to cause only minor strife in another. One of the most important factors in determining which form will issue from a rebellion is the "coercive balance." The chances of internal war are greatest if the contenders are nearly equal in strength; those of conspiracy when a dissident group is heavily outmatched; and those of turmoil when angry people form a weighty minority.[12]

Neither Lenin and Trotsky nor Huntington, Amann, Nettl, and Gurr had the American Revolution in mind when they formulated their concepts.[13] To impose their ideas on one another is to risk distorting them all; to impose a homemade synthesis of them on eighteenth-century New York is to risk crude anachronism. Nonetheless, the upheaval that went with independence presents a vast mass of evidence whose arrangement around such a conceptual structure can give a deeper understanding of what the Revolution did and meant. It also implies at least some testing of the ideas that have been borrowed. Actually using the concept of mobilization leads one to realize that, crudely put, it is not enough. People mobilized themselves and turned out because "leaders" and "radicals" were stimulating them. The metaphor of the political system likewise proves inadequate. After independence as before it, there were institutions, roles, and accepted patterns of behavior. Many of them look remarkably similar to what had gone before. A governor, still styled "His Excellency," presided over New York and saw to the enforcement of its laws. Elected legislators made those laws and received petitions. Ordinary people voted and paid taxes. The system, one might say, had simply made some adjustments. But the similarity is deceptive, for by 1784 the interests represented by policy makers and the way in which men in power related to men not in power were both very different from what they had been the eve of independence. The differences stemmed directly from the ten years of revolutionary change that lay between.

II

Between 1775 and 1782 the claimants to power in New York were many. Besides politicians in office and voters out of it, there were militant royalists, Vermont separatists, and armed Indians, as well as the armies of three powers. There were people who accepted that they were New Yorkers but denied republican independence, as well as people who accepted the break with Britain but denied that they were New Yorkers. There were still others who accepted New York as their political society, and republicanism as the way to run that society's affairs. There were guerrillas on all sides, as well as men who fled to the wilderness when their civilization came to pieces. There were men who were firmly republican and firmly for independence but who denied that the meaning of either was to be found in the constitution of 1777. The only mercy is that rarely were all of these people on stage at the same time.

New Yorkers entered the revolutionary crisis from many different directions, and they brought with them many different, often conflicting goals. People who stayed with the Revolution as it gathered force were in an overall majority, but the balance between them and royalists varied widely. What each group did varied as well. In the six counties of consensus the minority, whether revolutionary or Tory, was reduced to conspiracy and to symbolic gestures. In New York City the royalists were few in number, but they made up for this by their heavy representation among old men of power and by the closeness of British might. In Albany, Dutchess, Charlotte, and Westchester the revolutionaries were the larger group, but the royalists were strong enough to generate turmoil that lasted for years. In Tryon the forces were evenly matched, and the result was devastation. In Cumberland, Gloucester, and parts of Charlotte royalism was no serious problem by itself, but there the adherents of New York were heavily overbalanced by Vermont separatists.

Time, too, made a difference: the British occupation of the city in 1776 changed its royalists from a small minority to its only politically significant Americans. The closeness of the redcoats greatly strengthened upstate royalists as well. It enabled Tories in Westchester to shift from merely resisting the revolutionaries to active guerrilla warfare. Further up the Hudson the expectation of British aid moved royalist tenants on Livingston Manor to rise against their landlords in May 1777. But time hurt them as well as helped them: Tories in Albany County were enabled by their own numbers to render their community profoundly unstable between 1777 and 1779, but by 1781 they could do no more than form conspiracies. Understanding what the Revolution did thus requires a model that allows for royalism, neutralism, revolutionary militance, the emergence of Vermont, and time.

To understand how the old order got into such a mess requires taking the revolutionaries, the royalists, and the Vermonters separately. The revolutionaries would be the winners, and they must be treated first. The independence coalition that took shape after the Boston Tea Party was complex. It included firebrand militants and calculating men who bet their survival on astute footwork. The movement drew much of its energy from people in crowds, but that energy was guided, if not wholly controlled, by a system of popular committees. Those committees are the heart of the matter, both in the disintegration of the royal government and in the founding of the power of the state.

Half a century ago Alexander Flick pointed out that committees of public safety had had a long history in early New York. As early as 1689, when America's version of the Glorious Revolution brought the Dominion of New England to an inglorious end, a committee took on the functions of provincial government. It opened letters, raised a militia, and appointed Jacob Leisler to command it. It took charge of the customs house and put out a call for elections to a provincial assembly.[14] But the more immediate background to the committees of the mid-1770s is to be found among the Sons of Liberty in Albany and New York City. In 1766 the Albany group wrote and published a set of rules for itself. The Sons set up a leading committee of thirteen of their members. The committee chose its own president and clerk, but each officer was liable to instant recall. The men who signed their constitution pledged that only with the group's guidance would they carry out actions to oppose the Stamp Act "or anything that shall be thought by us unconstitutional and oppressive." They promised to act only for the general cause and to stand together against anyone who used the crisis as a pretext for private injury. They vowed to "discourage. . .and oppose the mean practice of dropping Letters on the Streets, setting up scandalous Libels, Verses, or any other thing detractive of any person's Character." They also swore to treat "as cold Friends to Liberty" any of their members who neglected or refused the association's discipline. If anyone "subscribing or publicly assenting and behaving agreeable" to their articles should be "arrested, taken, prosecuted by any force civil or military," they would do "the uttermost" for his relief. They would treat anyone who drew back at such point as "a perjured Traytor to LIBERTY."[15]

In 1769 Sons of Liberty in New York City adopted and published another organizing agreement. Their purpose was to defend "rights which as Men, we derived from Nature." "It must appear obvious," they wrote, "that supineness would prove as fatal to us as a Disunion." Like the Albanians, they would concern themselves wholly with the imperial problem and would "not as a Society. . .engage in any other Matter whatever." They promised to meet every week, and more often if they had to, to support nonimportation as a tactic against the Townshend Acts, and to blacklist anyone who violated it. Between them, these two documents raised nearly every question and every problem that emerged during the half-decade from 1775 to 1779, when the revolutionary committees were at the center of the struggle for power in New York.[16]

The revolutionary committees took shape during the twelve months between the news of the coercive acts and the outbreak of war. The first steps were taken in New York City, where on 16 May 1774 a mass meeting gathered in the Merchants' Exchange. Its purpose was to consider a proposal to name a committee of correspondence. Such committees were nothing new; the provincial assembly, the chamber of commerce, and the Sons of Liberty all had had them. What was new was the idea of a committee that would be responsible to the town itself. The idea had come from the Sons of Liberty and the mechanics, and they had a list of twenty-five men ready for election.

The first part of their plan worked: a committee was elected. The second did not. Instead of picking the twenty-five men put up by the radicals, the meeting elected a committee twice that size, about a third of whose members would become royalists and whose sponsors were a coalition of future Tories and future conservative politicians. The reasons for the conservative victory are easy to see. The meeting that elected the committee was the one that prompted a panic-stricken Gouverneur Morris to write of how "the mob" were beginning "to think and to reason," and on that tumultuous day men of Morris's kind made the first of their many successful attempts at making sure that action, if not thinking and reasoning, went their way. A committee there must be, but better a large one under conservative control than a small one run by hotheads. Let the angry men be on it, of course: Alexander McDougall, Isaac Sears, Abraham Brasher, and several other Sons of Liberty were given seats. But appeal for unity in a time of crisis, make the committee a symbol of how all New Yorkers were coming together, and use it to keep control. It worked. The election of the fifty, later increased to fifty-one, was the first of many successful essays at coalition politics by the city's conservatives. Their victory received its seal when James Duane, John Jay, and Peter Van Schaack, cool heads all, were given the important task of drafting the rules by which the committee's business would be done.[17]

Roughly the same thing happened on two more occasions. The fifty-one split in July, when eleven radicals resigned rather than go along with its condemnation of a popular meeting. The rump that remained would have been happy to stay in business indefinitely, but it came to its end when the First Continental Congress called in November for committees "in every county, city and town" to enforce the Continental Association. The city mechanics called a public meeting to protest a plan proffered by the fifty-one stating that they themselves should take on the task, and a new committee of sixty men was picked to take their place. The new committee claimed broader powers than its predecessor had had. It could call on merchants to countermand orders; it could inspect incoming ships, seize "contraband" and auction it for the public benefit; it could order economic boycotts and social ostracism of people who broke ranks. This committee too was a study in coalition. It included most of the men who had resigned from the fifty-one four months earlier, but it also had places for many men who ultimately became royalists. The presence of Alexander Wallace, James Jauncey, William Bayard, and Peter Van Schaack provided an adequate balance to the presence of Isaac Sears, Abraham P. Lott, and Alexander McDougall, especially with Philip Livingston, James Duane, and John Jay to sit in the middle.[18]

A committee of one hundred men replaced the sixty after the arrival of the news from Lexington in April 1775. The election was noisy and confused, but once again adroit coalition building forestalled any question of full radical control. That there had to be a fresh election was certain: the outbreak of war had raised issues that ran well beyond the mandate of the sixty. The sixty themselves put forward one slate of candidates, and radicals led by Isaac Sears named another. The old committee admitted openly that they were reaching towards the right and that some of their candidates were "objects of distrust and suspicion," but they called for their election for the sake of unity. During the election, rumors began to fly that that five prominent New Yorkers, Lieutenant Governor Colden among them, had invited the British government to send troops to the province. The possibility of both serious violence and a radical victory suddenly became acute. The sixty, however, brought matters under control. They convinced two of the five to issue public denials that the rumors were true and then hurriedly cobbled together a new association for the city's people to sign. People who signed it pledged to refrain from violence, to support the new committee, and to stand together with the rest of America in the face of war. In the midst of the excitement the candidates that the sixty had put forward for the new committee won.[19]

Two different processes were underway as the people of the city elected their three committees. The need for coalition was real. Radicals as well as conservatives agreed that the broader the base, the better. But coalition politics also gave immense benefit to the men who recognized that if there was no stopping the resistance movement, they ought for their own sakes to try to control it. Both sides, radicals and conservatives, were winning. The radicals got committees that enjoyed broader and broader support and that could claim wider and wider powers. The cooler men kept alive a situation in which they could maintain working control and in which *moderation* rather than *vehemence* would be the leadership's watchword. The lesson they learned over those twelve months would serve them well at many points during the years that followed.

Meanwhile people in the rural counties were starting to get involved. There as in the cities, the development of committees was a response to local conditions and initiatives as well as to the Continental Association. During August 1774 committees began to take form in places as far from one another as Rye, in Westchester, and Palatine District, in Tryon. At the end of the year, Kingston elected a committee to enforce the Association, and in March 1775 a committee "of observation" was chosen in New Windsor, in Ulster. During late March and early April there were committee elections in most of the towns in Orange County, and in April a county committee was picked in Westchester.[20] The committee of Albany County, which would be one of the most important outside New York City, had its beginnings in small, half-clandestine gatherings over that winter. After some preliminary meetings at the end of 1774, eleven Albanians gathered early in 1775 to discuss the mounting crisis. Four of them were from the city, and the other seven had come in from outlying districts, and they probably had no greater mandate than their mutual worries. They moved quickly, however, to gain greater legitimacy, sending throughout the county a circular letter in which they asked each district supervisor "if no Committee be appointed, to charge the District thereto, and should a committee be already appointed, that they the supervisors will be good enough to send this Letter to them."[21]

A provincewide movement was getting underway, but it was hampered by caution, as well as by powerful resistance. The committee in Tryon had to function through the winter of 1774/75 in secrecy, for the Johnson family still ruled. As late as mid-May, Tryon revolutionaries had to explain to the Albany committee that "this county has for a series of years been ruled by one Family, the different Branches of which are still strenious in dissuading people from coming into Congressional Measures." Militants in Westchester met similar difficulties. In 1774 Colonel Frederick Philipse and men who agreed with him blocked any serious support from the county for the First Continental Congress, and in April 1775 the colonel got more than three hundred people to sign a protest against establishing a committee.[22] Even in Albany things moved slowly. When the county committee met to debate sending delegates to the Second Continental Congress, it could muster only fifteen members, and more than a third of these came from the city of Albany. More than half of the county's eighteen rural districts still were unrepresented.[23]

It was the news of war that made the difference. When word of what had happened in Massachusetts arrived in Albany, the members of the existing committee met immediately. They resolved that they did not "conceive themselves fully invested with the Power to do every Matter which in this critical Hour may become necessary" and called for an election for a new "Committee of Safety, Protection and Correspondence," with power to "transact all such matters as they shall conceive may tend to the welfare of the American Cause." The new committeemen would be picked at mass meetings that would "take the sense of the Citizens." When the word arrived in Tryon, such a meeting was immediately called in Palatine District. It resolved to repudiate a royalist statement that the county's officials had issued only the month before, lest its being "passed over in Silence" lead to its being taken as "the sense of the County in General." The meeting elected a local committee of twelve men, and by the end of May three other districts in the county had followed its lead. Meanwhile similar events were occurring in Ulster, Orange, Dutchess, Westchester, and Suffolk.[24]

Something quite new emerged over the year between the New York Tea Party and the outbreak of the war. No one intended that the committees that began to spring up should form a countergovernment. No one set out to create a situation of dual power. But the radicals realized what each new step meant as they took it, and they showed it in their words. At first they spoke of committees of "correspondence," whose charge was only to circulate information. Then they became committees of "inspection" and of "observation," and the new terms betokened a new mandate, one that empowered the committees to extract pledges from people to honor the boycott of British commerce and allowed them to humiliate and to seize the goods of people who broke ranks.

After the war broke out, the titles changed again. Now they were committees of "safety," and the new title symbolized a great deal. One was in the committees' size. The elections that followed Lexington produced much larger committees than the ones that had been meeting up to that point. In New York City the 60 gave way to the 100. In Tryon a body that had begun with only 4 men now comprised at least 30. The Westchester committee had 90 members, and there were at least 64 on the committee in Orange and 63 on the committee in Ulster. The elections held in Albany County early in May produced a committee of 153 men, more than ten times the size of its predecessor.[25]

A second difference was that now the committees were part of a structure that spread over the whole province. As the new committees of safety convened, delegates to the first of New York's four provincial congresses were making their way to New York City, and these congresses, in turn, were linked to the Continental Congress in Philadelphia. Never again would the movement be without leadership at the provincial or the continental level. If the provincial congress went into recess, it appointed a committee of safety to act in its name. Congresses and committees alike acted on the principle that refusal to associate "by committees" deserved ostracism. The Albany committee warned that that would be the fate of a district that wanted to name only a single man to correspond for it. The first provincial congress said the same thing to Tryon County when delays kept the congress from learning that a committee had been chosen there. Later, the refusal of the people of Queens and of Richmond to pick committees would be the congress's justification for cutting them off from contact and for sending military forces to disarm their people.[26]

Most important of all, the new title announced that the committees were doing something larger, more sweeping, more daring. A war had begun in Massachusetts, and it would be the committees' task to support it and to prepare their own people when it came to them. This could not be done without challenging the institutions of the old order; it could not be done unless the committees began in important ways to act as a government; it could not be done without dual power.

The committee in Albany learned that lesson quickly. On 3 May 1775, only a day after its election, the committee asked the mayor and the common council to institute a "burghers' watch." But the city officials refused, and since the committee still thought it "prudent and advisable to have a Strict and Strong Watch well Armed and under proper Discipline," it called on the city's men to organize themselves into companies. The watch would be neither an extralegal crowd nor a sheriff's posse. It would be a peoples' militia, and by forming it the committee had begun to take power.[27]

What did committee power mean over the following year? Let us look at what the Albany committee was doing over two separate weeks, one late in May, when it was just beginning to be the dominant force in the city's life, and the other about a year later. On 25 May 1775 the committee began to meet in its own "committee chamber" rather than in the private homes and the taverns where it had previously gathered. On that day it also decreed that two additional delegates be picked in each of the city's three wards. Albany was a small place, where a drumroll or the tolling of a bell was enough to gather an election meeting, and the new members were in their seats by that afternoon. On the same day, the committee intercepted a packet of mail bound for Canada and appointed two men to open it. The next day these censors reported, and the committee named one man as its treasurer and another as its commissary of stores. It also began to pressure Albanians to sign the military association that it was circulating and asked doctors to stop inoculating for smallpox until it gave them permission. On 27 May it met in plenary session. This meant not that all 153 members were there but rather that every district was expected to have a delegate or two present. Forty-six men jammed into the committee room in the morning, and 41 in the afternoon. Most of what it did that day was concerned with the prospect of war on the northern frontier. The next day it resolved that it would record in its minutes divisions on "anything of Importance," and on 29 May it received a report that included a draft of an oath for militia officers. The thirtieth saw it "request" the captains of all the companies in the county to start holding training sessions every fortnight. It also named a "town serjeant" to oversee its "burghers' watch."[28]

By April 1776 the committee was much less concerned with war preparations and military matters than about affairs within Albany. On 18 April it named a subcommittee to "rate the price of such merchandise as they shall think proper and make report to this board with all convenient speed." Two days later the subcommittee presented its report, and the list of goods on which it set maximum prices shows what was running low: rum, Jamaica spirits, molasses, coffee, sugar, chocolate, salt, pepper, and tea. Of those, only salt was a necessity rather than a luxury, but the committee had decided that what happened in the marketplace was a matter for its concern. On 24 April it listened to charges that were being brought against one of its own members, a merchant named Robert McClellan. People had complained that McClellan was selling cloth at "an advanced Price. . . higher than three or four years ago." But the committee postponed acting on the charge until it had received advice from the Continental Congress. On the twenty-sixth it was dealing with a different matter, counting votes in the election that had just taken place for the third provincial congress.[29]

The minutes of these two short periods suggest what the emergence of the Albany committee meant in practice. No other committee's records have survived in such detail, but there is no reason to think that the Albany group's experience was unique. Its records show it trying to cooperate with the established government, failing to get cooperation, and then acting on its own, even though its decision to raise an armed force could be taken as treason. After establishing that police force, it began to name officials to serve it, took command of the militia, made preparations for war, and interfered with the royal mail. It arranged elections for one superior body, the provincial congress, and waited for advice from another, the Continental Congress. As it developed, it shifted its attention away from military concerns to such civilian questions as the control of prices and the practice of medicine. By the end of their first year, its members considered all of these matters to be fit for their consideration.

III

Who mobilized whom? Enemies of this American Revolution ascribed it all to manipulation by radicals. A friend of the Johnson family, writing in 1776, explained the loss of the family's hegemony in the Mohawk Valley by pointing out that Sir John Johnson and Colonel Guy Johnson foolishly left the valley just before the war broke out, leaving hotheads free "to sow the seeds of discontent and sedition."[30] But far from being mastermanipulators who could stir up trouble when they wanted, militants knew that their revolutionary committees could function only if they had wide popular support. It was the existence of such support that enabled radicals and committees alike to act.

The New York City committees emerged directly out of street turmoil. As early as October 1773 William Smith noted that "a new Flame is apparently kindling," and in December he recorded with horror a conversation in which Alexander McDougall baited him by asking, "What if we prevent the landing [of the East India Company's tea] and kill [the] Govr. and all the Council?" Tea came in April 1774 when a ship captain tried to sneak some in on his own account. An official party of "Mohawks" were still donning their warpaint to repeat the events in Boston when people standing on the shore boarded the ship and dumped the tea themselves. Then they carried the empty casks to the Fields and burned them, in the same way that another crowd had paraded and burned the wreckage of the Chapel Street theater eight years before.[31]

That began it. In June a crowd hung effigies of Lord North, the British prime minister, Thomas Hutchinson, the governor of Massachusetts, and Alexander Wedderburn, the British ministry's parliamentary spokesman. In September reports that arrived of fighting at Boston had the "lower classes" calling the king "*a knave* or *a fool*." Early in 1775 only the intervention of "principal Gentlemen and Merchants" thwarted a crowd's attempt to seize arms held by the collector of the port. Three days before Lexington itself, another crowd rescued Isaac Sears and Marinus Willett when the mayor had them arrested. Sears and Willett were paraded triumphantly through the streets, riding on other men's shoulders.[32]

When the news arrived shortly afterwards that fighting had really begun, Sears led marchers through the city while fifes and drums played. For nearly a week the crowd, armed with muskets that its members had seized from the arsenal, ruled. By the beginning of the summer the British garrison had retreated from its barracks to the safety of a warship in the harbor. Reports to other places caught the city's excitement. As early as May one correspondent announced that "there never was a more total revolution than at *New-York*. The tories have been obliged to fly. The Province is arming; and the Governour dares not call his prostituted assembly." In July another correspondent was writing to London that "all authority, power and government (though I cannot say government, as there is none) is in the hands of the lower class of people."[33]

Crowd action during the crisis meant more than just riots, rescues, and parades. It involved street theater and public rituals of commitment as much as it did actual violence. People in crowds were doing things that were more consciously political, more consciously focused on the disposition and use of power, than previous demonstrations had ever been. Mass meetings in the two cities and town, precinct, and county meetings in the countryside were one form. Another was direct action against royalist propaganda. In the towns of Ulster County, people responded over the winter of 1774/75 to the publication of Samuel Seabury's *Letters of a Westchester Farmer* by holding public burnings of the text. In New Windsor the people who gathered for the burning also pledged to boycott James Rivington's Tory newspaper and to slaughter no more sheep, knowing that soon wool would be worth more than mutton. One of the most important rituals was the circulation of associations, first to support the Continental Congress's program of economic resistance, then to obey the committees, and finally to support the war. Signing an association was serious. The Albany committee would not allow an association to circulate unless it had been approved by the provincial and continental congresses. Though within the terms of the old order an association had no legal standing, a man who signed one was committing himself. He had taken a long step towards repudiating the legitimacy of a political order based on kingship and obedience and towards affirming the idea of one based on participation and consent.[34]

Radical writers explained the meaning of what the crowds and the committees were doing. As early as 1774, writers began developing the argument that direct popular involvement was the basis of superior political forms, and that these were rendering unnecessary the institutions of the old order. A broadside that circulated in Pennsylvania and in New York condemned a proposal that delegates to the First Continental Congress be appointed by the provincial assemblies. The legislatures, it explained, were part of the structure of British authority and therefore were necessarily hostile to the American cause. "Cannot an appeal be made to the People?" it asked, adding that "if there are counties or districts who choose to lessen the weight of our common country, by taking themselves out of the scale. . . let them instantly declare themselves." If each county elected delegates to a special convention, those men would, in effect, be its county committee. Then to form connections with "every small district, township, hundred, etc." would be simple. In June "A Citizen" stressed again that the provincial assembly could have no claim to speak for the whole people. Some "spurious Zealots" maintained that the congressional delegates should be elected by the assembly's committee of correspondence, since it was a small group of wise, experienced men. But the pamphleteer pointed out that the men who said this were the same men who had succeeded only a month before in choosing a committee of fifty-one members instead of one of twenty-five, claiming that "there would be wisdom and safety in Numbers." The writer asked his "Fellow Citizens" whether this was not "an insult to your understanding."[35]

At the end of the following year, "A Poor Man" went much further. He explained that although regular institutions were good enough "in ordinary cases in the calms of government," the times had made them wholly inadequate. New Yorkers had been "obliged to suspend the use of them, and have recourse to other forms." The writer stressed that "in our new method, the people have all the weight and influence they ought to have, and are effectually represented." Another broadside writer took the same line: "The whole *people* are oppressed—*They* must relieve themselves—and therefore *they* must *act*." When the Albany committee announced its members' expectation that "no Person whatsoever able to attend will be absent" from a public meeting, it was against the background of arguments such as these and of the willingness that people all over the province were showing to throw themselves into public events.[36]

The more moderate men in the emerging leadership learned quickly enough to use the devices and the language of revolution in order to achieve their own goal of keeping things under control. In 1776 James Duane summed up their strategy when he warned men of like mind to himself to "let [the people] be rather followed than driven." Associations could serve to cool things off as well as to stimulate involvement. Thus in June 1774 the cool-headed men on the committee of fifty-one, worried by the parading and hanging of the effigies of Lord North, Thomas Hutchinson, and Alexander Wedderburn, issued a statement that the demonstration had violated an association to support and obey the committee. They used the same trick to regain the initiative during the tumult that followed the news from Lexington.[37]

Meanwhile, others were stressing how important it was to maintain as much respect as possible for regular magistrates and for legal ways of doing things. The Albany committee was asked in June 1775 whether law and justice should still be executed by the courts and in the king's name. It replied that they should, "for otherwise, we conceive the whole country will be reduced to. . .anarchy and confusion." When it heard at the end of July of violent conflict in Tryon County between supporters of the committee and people loyal to the Johnsons, it reproved the radicals. They could find legal remedies for their grievances and should never give "our Enemies" any reason "to upbraid us with an infringement of the Laws and Constitution which we are studiously trying to preserve."[38] At their first mass meeting, the people of King's District, in eastern Albany County, announced that they were against any closing of the courts and promised "strict obedience" to proper authority. The mayors of both New York City and Albany continued in office until the very moment of independence, though clearly they were the tools of the governor. So did many judges and sheriffs whose royalism could not be mistaken. In the summer of 1775, Tryon County revolutionaries ran their Tory sheriff out. When they asked the provincial congress what they should do next, the congress passed their message straight to Governor Tryon, who responded that the sheriff must be allowed to return. In most of the Hudson Valley townships, there was never a time when the supervisor, the town clerk, the roadmasters, the assessors, and the overseers of the poor did not work side by side with the committeemen. Of such obedience, determination to break no law until need forced it, and agreement on local leadership, we have often been told, was the orderly American Revolution made.[39]

But in much of New York the Revolution was by no means so orderly. As the moderates who worked so hard to keep things under control knew, popular involvement was explosive. Its rituals and street theater were challenges to a crumbling political and social order, not playlets with tightly written scripts. The committees were establishing a situation of dual power; the crowds were exalting the ideas of popular sovereignty and direct involvement above that of established legality. However much the Albany committeemen wanted to avoid "the least slander of pretence. . .that we forcibly set aside the law," they established their own town watch when the city fathers refused. Meanwhile, judges in Orange County were refusing to take the oath that would qualify them for office and thus were avoiding the decision of whether to enforce the king's law. In Skenesborough, on the northern frontier, a man named Eleazer Bartholomew, newly elected commander of a revolutionary militia company, instructed the local magistrate to close his court and "to grant no process whatever in the King's name." Bartholomew "would not suffer any civil law to take place," and he had the support of his townsmen, who had voted in a meeting that "the ordinary courts of justice should be stayed."[40]

Nowhere was the problem posed more starkly than in Tryon County. It is easy to see why committeemen there, where the great ruling family went so far as to claim ownership of the jail and the courthouse, met in secret.

But in August 1774, even to organize the committee of Palatine District was to begin to undermine the Johnsons' power, and when the people of the same district met after Lexington to repudiate the royalism of their county's officials and to elect an open committee, it was a direct challenge to the Johnsons. No one doubted how they would react. "All" of their "dependents" turned up to harass "a numerous Meeting of the Mohawk District" in May and, "their Number being so Large, and the people unarmed, struck Terror into most of them and they dispersed." In June, Sir John himself chanced upon another gathering, in the district of Caughnawaga. There people "were met to choose a Captain agreeable to the resolution of their committee." The baronet was the commanding officer of the provincial militia in the county, and seeing the election, he alighted from his coach and told the crowd that "the Duty he owed to his King obliged him to interfere." But Johnson found himself contradicted by "one Mr. Visher who was a candidate" for the captaincy that was being filled. As a friend of the baronet put it, Visher "became so very impertinent that Sir John could not bear it—but gave him a hearty Horsewhipping at the head of these brave fellows and then very cooly got into his carriage and drove" off. Visher might have phrased the story differently, but Johnson's father would never have needed to do such a thing. The heir was showing his weakness, not his strength.[41]

Matters between the Johnsons and the revolutionaries finally came to a head in July. A servant of county sheriff Alexander White chanced to cross a newly sown field that belonged to a rebel named John Fonda. Fonda scuffled with the intruder and was arrested; as Fonda went off to jail, the servant told him that "he would be the death of him." As word of the arrest circulated, a crowd of about a hundred rebels gathered to free the prisoner. The crowd and the sheriff's men exchanged fire, and White fled to the protection of Johnson Hall, which Sir John had fortified with light artillery. There the baronet assembled between four hundred and five hundred tenants and other "people who had not forgot the Benevolence of his much lamented father." Meanwhile, the other crowd swelled to about the same size. The rebel "army" sent delegates to the mansion, who threatened that if White were not released to them, they would burn down the mansion and the surrounding village. When Johnson refused to meet their demand, the besiegers sent an express to Schenectady for the cannon they would need to break Sir John's defenses. Schenectady passed the message on to Albany, and at a midnight meeting the committee there heard what was going on. They sent not cannon but negotiators, who cooked up a truce. But the truce lasted only until autumn, when the Johnsons and their allies fled to the Niagara frontier. Their flight marked the beginning of seven years of civil war.[42]

A phrase like "political mobilization" seems too bland, too flat to serve as a blanket description of such events. Over 1774 and 1775 the general goal of resisting Britain brought men to do and say things that not long before would have been unthinkable to them. For some, it was a matter of joining in the Grand Cause once involvement could no longer be avoided honorably. The timing of events in Orange, Ulster, and Suffolk counties and the way in which local government and revolutionary committees coexisted there tell us that the whole focus of their people was on the imperial problem. For others, it was a matter of trying hard to preserve legality despite their being pushed further and further into the crucible where one way of doing things was dissolving and another was only starting to crystallize. Events in Albany County and in New York City followed this course. In both places, moderate men worried about what was happening and did all they could to keep events under control; more adventurous souls exulted, proclaiming that direct involvement represented the best form politics could take. In the Mohawk Valley the rebels had neither time nor energy for either worry or exultation. There the crisis meant immediate confrontation between the Revolution and its enemies. The result would be bitter for everyone who had the bad luck to be involved.

IV

For men who still revered the king as much as for men learning to repudiate him, the independence crisis was a time to choose. Just as supporting the American movement meant different things in different parts of New York, so did royalists find their separate courses charted by their strength or lack of it, by their cultural and economic heritage, and by the course of the war. In Kings, Queens, and Richmond counties in 1775 and early 1776 the Tory majority needed only to dissociate itself from the movement, to endure what the revolutionaries might do in response, and to wait for the British to come. Some radicals in Queens chose a county committee at the end of 1774, but a meeting of the county's people repudiated the action immediately. At about the same time, a popular meeting in Oyster Bay resolved that it was itself illegal and dissolved. Late in January 1775 136 of Jamaica's freeholders, or about 60 percent, signed a statement against forming a committee. By autumn, one of the few pockets of radical enthusiasm in Queens, the district of Cow Neck and Great Neck, had been driven to the point of seceding from royalist Hempstead and electing its own committee. Royalists in Hempstead itself were holding military drills and avowing that they would resist anyone who might try to disarm them.[43]

When a new provincial congress was elected in November 1775 the voters of Queens rejected taking part by a majority of nearly four to one. A Continental force led by General Charles Lee disarmed the Queens Tories in January 1776, but neither that nor the arrest of eighteen of their leaders broke the county's spirit. The most that Lee's troops could exact by way of compliance was to force the people who had been disarmed either to swear not to aid the British or to swear that the arms taken were all they had. The former oath, which fell somewhere between neutrality and mild support for the Revolution, was taken by 462 men. The latter, which was no more than acceptance of something that could not be avoided, was taken by 340. After the British conquest in August, more than 1,300 Queens people signed an address congratulating the brothers Howe on what they had done, and when the first militia muster was held under the renewed British authority, some 800 men turned out. With evident satisfaction, Governor Tryon wrote home that the people of Queens were firmly for the crown. Meanwhile Kings and Richmond were following much the same course.[44]

The predicament of royalists in Ulster, Orange, and Suffolk was identical to that of rebels in Kings, Queens, and Richmond. The revolutionaries of Great Neck had their Tory counterparts among residents of Brookhaven, Suffolk County, who signed a royalist statement in March 1775, and among people in Shawangunk, Ulster County, who in January of that year raised a loyalty pole bearing the king's standard. The actual number of committed royalists in Ulster was small, possibly totaling less than 100, and they could do little more than carry on covert trade with New York City after it was occupied, drink the king's health, distribute British proclamations, and give shelter to couriers and spies.[45] There were more in Suffolk; there 236 men are known to have refused the military association in 1775. They represented about 10 percent of those to whom it was offered. These people ran a supply network for the British fleet that lay offshore through the summer of 1776, but as long as power grew from numbers, their situation was hopeless. Even after the conquest, when as many people turned out in Suffolk as in Queens for a Tory militia muster, Governor Tryon lamented that only small parts of the county were really pacified.[46]

In Orange the royalists were marginally stronger. Out of approximately 1,700 men to whom the military association was offered, 228 refused it. This was five times as many as refused it in neighboring Ulster, and the nonsigners were 13 percent of the men to whom it was tendered. More than half of the refusals came from the town of Haverstraw, south of the highlands, where British agents circulated freely, promising land and money to any who would take the king's side. In June 1776 a Haverstraw farmer named John Clark recruited five of his neighbors with promises of two hundred acres of land, a bounty of five guineas, and soldier's pay when the British came. Orange royalists grew bolder after the British seized the southern district. In December 1776 the American general William Heath found that revolutionaries there were "in the utmost distress; the tories are joining the enemy, and insulting and disarming the Whigs, stripping them of their cattle effects etc." One Orange County militia company was so disaffected that seven men in it were imprisoned and the rest disarmed. As late as 1778 William Smith was giving credence to reports that a hundred Orange Tories had broken into the jail and freed eighty of their fellows. But though these were serious problems, they were not of the same order as those elsewhere in the state.[47]

Whether royalist or revolutionary, the counties of consensus had in common relatively little dissent. But whatever it was that made revolutionaries out of quiet farmers and traders in the Mohawk Valley reached only about half of the people there. The two sides were evenly matched during the confrontation at Johnson Hall, and they remained so in the seven years of war that followed. The rebels had the worst of it in 1777, when they were decimated stopping Barry St. Leger's force of British, royalists, and Indians at Oriskany, and in 1780 and 1781, when Sir John Johnson, Walter Butler, and Joseph Brant led raiding parties up and down the valleys of the Schoharie and the Mohawk. The other side suffered most in 1779, when an expedition of militia and Continental troops swept westward, pillaging and burning as far as the upper Susquehanna Valley. By the time the war was over, according to one estimate, seven hundred buildings had been burned, twelve thousand farms abandoned, hundreds of thousands of bushels of grain destroyed, nearly four hundred rebel women made widows, and some two thousand children of revolutionaries orphaned.[48] Historical markers at Cobleskill, Springfield, Schoharie, Middleburg, Andrustown, German Flats, Cherry Valley, Unadilla, and other quiet places west of Schenectady mutely tell bits of the story. As Piers Mackesy has suggested, the most vicious fighting of the war was between American and American, and in Tryon both sides had the numbers and the secure hinterland needed to carry on until both were exhausted and broken.[49]

Royalists in Westchester, Dutchess, and Albany counties were neither so few as to be impotent nor so many as to be capable of full civil war. There were enough of them, however, to make a powerful force. In Westchester more than three hundred men signed Frederick Philipse's statement of opposition to forming a committee in April 1775. Many of these must also have been in the town meeting of the borough of Westchester that in the same month voted against further resistance. Later that year, observers in Connecticut reported that in southern Westchester the revolutionaries were vastly outnumbered and royalists were supplying British ships with impunity. Meanwhile the provincial congress heard that groups of armed Tories were marauding in Mamaroneck. The situation remained unstable until the British invasion threw a military front across the county; thereafter royalist guerrilla groups, such as James DeLancey's Westchester Refugees, waged war nearly as they chose.[50]

Some twenty-three hundred men were disarmed for disaffection in 1776 in the four Hudson Valley counties, and nearly two thousand of them lived in Westchester and Dutchess. More than nine hundred men in Dutchess are known to have refused the military association in 1775, and though they numbered only half as many as those who are known to have signed it, they, their friends, and their families formed a formidable group. Recruiting for the British service went on apace among them; the recruiters used the same promises of land and money that they employed in southern Orange. When a draft was called for the revolutionary army in June 1776 the captains of two Dutchess companies forbade their colonel to take any of their men and dismissed the troops to keep the colonel from acting. By that time, the county committee was asking for a full-time garrison for anti-Tory duty. Just after independence, 150 royalists in eastern Dutchess disarmed the local radicals and occupied their committee room; only the intervention of a massive force from Connecticut defeated them. But even before the war forced the question, people in Dutchess were choosing the crown. Voters in Poughkeepsie decided in August 1774 not to create a local committee, and early in 1775 a popular convention resolved that despite the Continental Association, it would support free consumption. In April of that year, 175 men in the precinct called Charlotte voted against sending delegates to the Second Continental Congress.[51]

People in Albany County divided in about the same way. No area of the county was immune from royalism; as late as 1779 people in the city of Albany were drinking the king's health, and in 1777, while Burgoyne's army was advancing on them, some three hundred royalists gathered in Schenectady and disarmed the town watchmen. The local committee was so frightened that it ordered a heavy watch to patrol the town by day and night and detained a militia unit that Philip Schuyler had ordered to march to meet Burgoyne. Large numbers of people in northern Albany County actually joined Burgoyne, and still more sent supplies to his troops. Many of these fled to Canada after the capitulation at Saratoga.[52]

But the centers of militant royalism in Albany were to be found on the manors of Rensselaerwyck and Livingston. As early as 1776 the rugged Helderbergh escarpment in the western reaches of Rensselaerwyck became a haven for people avoiding military duty. In the spring of 1777 tenants on Livingston Manor and Clermont broke into open revolt. Some five hundred of them, thinking wrongly that a British force was on its way to their aid, roamed the manor under arms for a week, frightening the manor lord and his family and skirmishing with soldiers of the Revolution. One of the skirmishes cost five men their lives. As Staughton Lynd points out, the tenants had no more chance against the revolutionary militiamen who were called out than they had had in 1766 against the British regulars who put down the great rising. Both times the result was defeat for the tenants rather than the overthrow of the Livingstons, and in 1777 the defeat meant deaths and imprisonments.[53]

The crushing of the rising at Livingston Manor ended any chance that the Hudson Valley would have to suffer full-scale civil war, but in 1778 and 1779 royalists on Rensselaerwyck and Livingston joined with deserters from the armies of both sides in bands that marauded through both manors and into Dutchess. What they did hovered somewhere between social banditry and guerrilla warfare. The revolutionaries called them robbers, and they never openly maintained that they were serving under direct military discipline.[54] That set them apart from Tories further south who were organized in military form as the Westchester Refugees. But though they spent most of their time stealing money and goods, they chose their targets with fine political precision: revolutionary militia officers who fined Tories for missing muster, "hot committeemen" who harassed them for their coolness about fighting in units led by Livingstons and Van Rensselaers, and state legislators who passed laws to punish them.

William Smith saw this banditry at close range while he was under house arrest on Livingston Manor, and he commented that while the bands roamed free, "all the high Whiggs are in Terror and cry out for Law and Safety." The bandits told one of their victims that they wanted reimbursement for fines that his son, a Continental captain, had exacted. The band that roamed on the east bank, through Livingston Manor, northern Dutchess, and eastern Rensselaerwyck, advertised that it would bring "murder and fire to all rebels," and when its members were captured they said they had been fighting for the king. There were rumors that the robbers were led by a regular British officer. In western Rensselaerwyck, the bandits found a secure base in the Helderbergh range. In 1778 the band that was based there began forcing militiamen who fell into its power to swear neutrality for the duration of the war, imitating the practice of the state authorities towards captured Tories. The guerrillas even offered to negotiate with the revolutionaries, promising that they would end their campaign if the revolutionaries would let royalist exiles come home. Alarms and fright spread when the bandits were on the move, but when revolutionary leaders tried to capture them, they found they could not see them. Like guerrillas in many other times and places, they enjoyed the support and protection of people who looked, sounded, and acted like them and who could give them shelter and sustenance.[55]

Such militancy faded by the winter of 1780/81, for reasons that will be discussed in chapter 6. But as their numbers dwindled, the more determined Albany County Tories turned to conspiracy and especially to kidnap. As early as January 1777 royalists in eastern Rensselaerwyck were stopped while on their way to seize "Col. Whiting, Col. Van Ness and Esqr. Adgate," the radical leaders in King's District. In August 1781 a group of royalists in the city of Albany tried to capture Philip Schuyler. They failed, and while they escaped in the direction of Schenectady, the militia pursued them amidst general excitement. Not long afterwards, a militia lieutenant reported that armed men had come to his house to make off with him and had abused his wife. At about the same time, an Indian woman lured the mayor of Albany into the woods with a story about finding a corpse. But the mayor learned in time that her report was a ruse, intended to bring him out to where he could be taken.[56]

Historians have long debated the actual number of people who chose royalism in New York, but thanks to Bernard Mason's careful research, it now seems clear that it was the revolutionaries who had the overall majority. The debate has not always been purely academic; Alexander McDougall, writing just after the British seized the southern district, was desperately afraid of what would happen should conquest and free choice return a majority to British allegiance. He told the state committee of safety that New York had only fourteen counties and that the enemy now controlled five of them totally and parts of two more. If their conquests extended any further, they would "get a representation of the majority of the State and make a surrender of our rights."[57]

But the central problem was not sheerly one of numbers. Royalists and revolutionaries were not parties competing in an election. They could not expect to resign themselves to a victory by the other side, in the hope that the next poll might reverse things. They had divided on problems of the most basic import. The middle and late 1770s were a time of upheaval, dissolution, and forcible conflict, not a time when a politics of majority rule was in smooth operation. Once raised, the basic questions of the dispute could not have been settled by any plebiscite. Rather, their resolution required either the full capitulation or the exile of one of the two sides. The actual numbers of royalists are important not for themselves but for the way they fed into the balance of power that determined the shape and the course of the struggle. There were other elements in the balance, including both geography and time. Without the Helderbergh Mountains, there might not have been social banditry in Rensselaerwyck. Without the Niagara frontier, there might not have been civil war in Tryon. Without rumors about British strategy, the tenants might have staged their rising, not in May 1777, when it proved fruitless, but five months later, when it could have been of real help to Burgoyne.

The number of people who chose royalism is thus not as important as what those people did once they had made their choice. Some merely undermined the rebels, whether by refusing American currency, spreading rumors, talking of defeat, praying for the king, or weakening the militia. But others went much further, traveling themselves and guiding others on the underground railroad that linked New York City to Montreal, resisting the revolutionary authorities, boycotting committee elections, electing committeemen of their own sort,[58] "skulking in the woods," plotting kidnaps, waging guerrilla war, and openly rising in arms. In their different ways they did an enormous amount; in Albany County alone, the conspiracies commissioners recorded nearly six hundred incidents between 1778 and 1781.[59]

These people too were "politically mobilized." Popular royalism was perfectly compatible with social radicalism; what, after all, were the Livingston Manor tenant rising and the social banditry of Albany and Dutchess counties but continuations of the land rioting of the 1750s and the 1760s?[60]

But not all popular Toryism was revolution in the name of the crown. For some, the attraction may have been simply mercenary; still others affirmed rather than denied the ways of the old order. It was the tenants of Sir John Johnson who protected Johnson Hall from angry freeholders in 1775. But all the royalists agreed that they denied the legitimacy of the revolutionary movement and of the republican order towards which it was leading. Their agreement posed a problem of the utmost gravity for both the movement and the new order.

V

During the two years after the Boston Tea Party, leaders of the Revolution kept proclaiming how important it was that Americans show perfect harmony among themselves. The Grand Cause was too important to let lesser issues divide them. Even New Yorkers who leaned towards royalism responded, particularly in the second half of 1775. Scots tenants of Sir John Johnson repented before the Tryon County Committee of the support they had given the baronet. Committees and patriot militia units appeared briefly in Queens and Richmond. Leaders elsewhere happily reported that their people stood united and that all factionalism had disappeared. Sociologists tell us that that is precisely the result to be expected from so searing an experience as getting the news from Lexington.[61]

War with Britain likewise damped the insurgency in the Green Mountains. But there, just as in the counties of heavy royalism, the effect was only temporary. By the beginning of 1777 the Green Mountain people had finally broken free of New York and created their own state of Vermont. Both their short-term reconciliation and the final break were among the changes that the Revolution wrought in New York. The one stemmed from the run of events as the war was breaking out, and the other from the long-term problem of land and authority within the grants.

By the time of the crisis at the Cumberland County courthouse in March 1775[62] both Green Mountain Boys and their enemies were insisting that the insurgents' cause and America's cause were the same. Cadwallader Colden wrote that the Westminster rioters had been inspired to close the Cumberland court by the way the people of western Massachusetts had closed their courts to nullify the Massachusetts Government Act. The rioters defended what they had done in terms of the imperial question, writing to the committee of New York City that their county officials had tried to close off their communication with it, that local officials did nothing for the movement save make excuses for doing nothing, and that two officers of the court had kept a county convention from choosing a committee. Enemies of the cause, they said, were using the court to harass the movement's friends by prosecuting them for debt. The court closers insisted that they were "The People of the County of Cumberland and Province of New-York," despite nearly a decade of bitterness against the province. County committees appeared after Lexington in both Cumberland and Charlotte counties, and by June the one in Cumberland was asking the New York provincial congress how it might restore order and regularity.[63]

In May 1775, two months after the court closing, the Green Mountain Boys and a force of Connecticut militia captured Fort Ticonderoga. The fort was a key to the route from Albany to Montreal, and its cannon provided invaluable artillery for the ragtag American army that was besieging the British in Boston. No longer could any revolutionary dismiss the people of the grants as lawless vagabonds, and in July, two months after the coup, Ethan Allen and Seth Warner were admitted to speak before the New York provincial congress. Both men were condemned by name to die in the Bloody Act, as the grants people called the riot act of 1774. The congress accepted the Green Mountain Boys as a formal unit of New York's revolutionary militia. It gave them the right to name their own junior officers, and in August it called on the Continental officer commanding the northern theater to name field officers for them. That commander was Philip Schuyler, whom Allen's followers had hated as the presiding judge of Charlotte County only a year before. The congress also put up money to buy them tents and uniform coats. In September, New York's military association was circulating freely in the three counties, and committees had been chosen "agreeable to the desire" of the New York congress. Even Ethan Allen had promised to use his influence to help reconcile his people and revolutionary New Yorkers.[64]

Yet even in these months omens began to appear that the reconciliation would not last. In September 1775, the committee of Charlotte County reported to the provincial leaders that disputes about land titles had led to disputes about committee elections. As a result, "it was thought proper by the committees on the Grants to divide the County in two parts." The grants people did not "choose to join the other part of the county." At the end of the year, people in Putney, Westminster, and Fulham published objections to the higher militia officers who had been appointed for them and demanded that they be consulted about who would command them in battle. In June 1776, when elections were called for the provincial congress that would write a republican constitution, the committee of Cumberland County announced that it reserved the right to reject whatever document might be written and that it might go ahead in any case with plans for joining Massachusetts. By this time local committees in the grants were getting their military supplies from New England, while making no mention in their correspondence of owing allegiance to New York.[65]

The final split followed hard on independence. A convention met in July 1776 at Dorset and declared that further obedience to New York was impossible. It drafted new articles of association for internal defense and commanded that this be the only association to circulate in the region. In August and September townspeople met to debate secession, and in September another convention declared that the grants and New York were completely separated. Early in 1777 the insurgents adopted the name of Vermont, and with it their own state constitution, modeled on that of Pennsylvania.[66]

Many factors contributed to Vermont's decision to make the break, and the Vermonters themselves said what most of them were. Land was the fundamental question; the secessionists cited New York's long history of "disingeneus Conduct" and its "seaveral illeagual unjustifiable and unwarrantable meashures. . .to Deprive by frawd viollance and oppression those inhabitants of thire property and in particular thire Landed intrest." They cited the massive illegal land grants that New York's governors had made in defiance of the order-in-council of 1767. They maintained that New Yorkers, not they, had initiated the violence of the past decade. They saw little reason to believe that independence would change New York's policies. Drawing on both Locke and Jefferson, they wrote that "whenever the lives and properties of a part of a community have been manifestly aimed at by either the legislature or executive authority. . .necessity requires a separation."[67]

The long conflict had left wounds too deep to be cauterized even by the iron of war with Britain. One of the deepest had been left by the Bloody Act of 1774. The Green Mountain poet Thomas Rowley thought no law like it had ever existed, and though his history was as faulty as his verses were crude, he caught the mood of his neighbors. Ethan Allen wrote a furious denunciation of the law, concluding that it was in no way an aberration but rather was the natural outcome of the power that land jobbers held within the New York government. Made as early as 1774, his argument presaged the way in which Tom Paine's *Common Sense* would persuade Americans that their troubles sprang from a basic flaw in the empire rather than from the mere malevolence of evil men. In 1776 the Vermonters could see that among the most important leaders of New York's revolution were James Duane and George Clinton. Duane, for them, was so much the archetype of the New York speculator that pamphlets singled him out for direct reference. Clinton, in his turn, had been chairman of the committee of the provincial assembly that had drafted the Bloody Act.[68]

The Vermonters also realized that they were living through one of those rare moments when the structure of affairs, of institutions, and of legality itself had come loose. Things were possible that could not be contemplated in ordinary times, and the day had to be seized before it was lost. Heman Allen, Ethan's brother, saw the issue clearly. Propagandizing for separation, he told the people of the village of Westminster that a petition for recognition had been sent to Congress. Allen was too astute to expect that recognition would be granted immediately, but that was not the point. Rather, it was to establish publicly that the Vermonters were refusing to be bound by the New York constitution, for "if we submitted to the mode of Government now forming in the State of New York we should be so tied that we could not get off in a future day." In the same spirit, the Vermont declaration of independence announced that the severance of America's connection with Britain meant that "the Arbitrary Acts of the Crown are null and void [and] consequently the jurisdiction by the said Crown granted to New York government over the people of the New Hampshire Grants is totally dissolved." It was up to the people of the grants, being now "without law or government," to create for themselves whatever new form they might choose.[69]

The Vermont conventions that met late in 1776 and early in 1777 cited all of these causes and added still others. New York had decided to continue charging the heavy quitrents once due to the crown. Cumberland and Gloucester counties had been set up not for the benefit of their citizens but rather for that of the outsiders who sat on their courts and pocketed heavy fees. The province had imposed taxes to build the Cumberland courthouse, even though it was known that the people there wanted no county court at all. The Vermonters were so far from New York City that effective communication was impossible. These "people of the Lord" knew that New Yorkers were notorious for "breaking of *Sabbaths*" and "neglect of publick worship."[70]

The grants people had always run ahead of dominant New Yorkers in their understanding of what the Revolution meant. As early as 1774, when the committee movement in New York was still half-clandestine and when no one there was thinking of independence, Ethan Allen was boldly lumping together the principle of kingship and the hated provincial authorities. "Every opposition to their monarchical government," he complained, "is deemed felony." In the summer of 1775, when the bravest spirits in New York City were shrinking from more than defensive preparations, Allen planned and led the capture of Fort Ticonderoga. When Allen was admitted to speak to the New York convention, the motion was put by Isaac Sears, one of the few New York leaders whose vehemence could match Allen's own.[71]

The state constitution that the Vermonters wrote was very different from the moderate, carefully balanced document that New York eventually adopted. The Vermonters had a perfect chance to realize their ideas about public life, and they used it to define the outer limits of radical American republicanism. Their constitution is usually dismissed as no more than a copy of the Pennsylvania constitution of 1776. It was indeed a copy, but that itself is significant. One of the main figures in Pennsylvania radicalism, and the man who suggested the document to the Vermonters, was Dr. Thomas Young, physician, sometime New Yorker, and wandering revolutionary. Young came from Ulster County, springing from the same Scotch-Irish yeoman milieu that gave rise to George Clinton. His career had led him to the study of both medicine and deism, and on his way to Philadelphia he had lived in the Dutchess County town of Amenia, as well as in Albany, Boston, and Newport. In Amenia he had seen landlordism and tenant resistance firsthand. Until his death, Young would try to weave the practice of his profession, the development of his heterodoxy, his hostility to landlords, and his militancy on the British issue into a single fabric. Young was where the action was from the Stamp Act to independence, and his travels show better than a shelf of pamphlets how radical insights developed and circulated.[72]

Young's political education began during his time in the Dutchess borderland, where he saw New England rural culture as well as the strife of landlords and tenants. While he was in Amenia, he made friends with Ethan Allen, who was living just across the Connecticut line. One result of their friendship was collaboration on the rationalist tract known to posterity as Ethan Allen's bible.[73] Another was Young's involvement in a Green Mountain land scheme that was being floated under Massachusetts auspices. The scheme centered on an Albany speculator named John Henry Lydius, who had a long history of getting Indians drunk and then buying their lands.

In 1764 Lydius's Green Mountain operation ran into trouble with the New York government, and Young published a tract in its defense. In this, his first publication, Young fell back to basic principles. His working premise was that in America the only sound land title was one derived from an Indian purchase. Coming from one defending a man notorious for making his Indian purchases by fraud, the argument sounds ill, but Young's point was that the land belonged neither to the king nor to the "gentlemen in the province of *New-York*" who stood in Lydius's way. These New Yorkers, he wrote, were merely speculators who for the sake of their own capital gains wanted to keep industrious settlers out. Young's understanding of the relationship between landlordism and the process of development was ill-informed. His association with Lydius casts a shadow over his pieties about respecting land titles derived from the Indians. But in his mind, intense hostility for New York's land grandees was already blending with an absence of any great reverence for the crown. By all evidence, he quickly dropped his connection with Lydius, but throughout the decade that followed he supported the grants people in their struggle with New York.[74]

This was the man who became a Son of Liberty in Albany and Boston and a firebrand of radicalism in Philadelphia, and who recommended Pennsylvania's constitution to the Vermonters. That document was democratic, not Whiggish. Its single-house legislature, its lack of a governorship, and its procedures for direct popular involvement establish it at the Revolution's radical extreme, and Young advised the Vermonters to model their own constitution upon it. "With very little alteration," he told the Vermonters it would "come as near perfection as anything yet concerted by mankind." It was most especially preferable to the colonial charters that

Connecticut and Rhode Island carried into independence, those two documents beloved by historians who see nothing revolutionary about the Revolution. The Connecticut charter had a good claim to the Vermonters' emotional allegiance, for many of them had grown up under it. But compared with the Pennsylvania constitution, it had the great defect that "in the one case the Executive power can advise and in the other compel." Young favored advice, not compulsion, and he believed that "the people at large" ought to be "the true proprietors of governmental power." Thus he cast away the whole intellectual baggage of Whiggism, the whole set of ideas about depraved human nature and a "senatorial part of society" that many American leaders carried into independence with them. At the same time, he was condemning the plans of "men of some rank" in America to recreate "the system of Lord and Vassal or *principal* and *dependent*."[75] Young's hostility to New York's land system, his experience as a revolutionary, and his ideas about radical democracy were never far from one another.

It would be wrong to give Young sole credit for the adoption by the Vermonters of the Pennsylvania document. Tom Paine, the mechanics of New York City, and villagers scattered across Massachusetts all were dealing with the ideas that the Pennsylvania and Vermont constitutions encapsulated, and there is no reason why the Vermonters should not have developed them on their own.[76] But in Young's career, as well as in his writings, one can see a linkage that gives a larger importance to Vermont's own separatism. Hostility to landlordism, urban radicalism, republican ideology, and that separatism itself were all part of the revolutionary crisis. By linking them together, Young and his allies in Vermont brought them into a single chain. Vermont's radicalism was no aberration; rather, it was the measure of what the Revolution could do.

VI

At the end of the year in which independence was declared, New York was a very different place from what it had been only three years earlier. The southern district was under military occupation. Civil war was destroying the society of the western frontier. The counties on the east bank of the Hudson were seething with discontent that blended loyalty to the crown with hostility to landlordism. The small farmers of Vermont were making their own state in their own way. Throughout New York the old political system had collapsed. Local officials might still hold office in Orange and Ulster, but the royal governor and his council, the provincial assembly, the mayors and corporations of New York City and Albany, the county courts, the justices of the peace, and the sheriffs were no more. Power among the revolutionaries was in the hands of a pyramidal structure of local committees, county committees, and revolutionary congresses, and the decisions of the committees were enforced by consent and by the power of a revolutionized militia. The province had been so thoroughly shattered that there was no longer agreement even on what New York was in geographical terms, let alone in political ones. It was from this rubble that a new order had to be constructed.

Chapter 6

Defining the New Order

On 10 September 1777 the legislature of the state of New York had a quorum for the first time. About half of the members of each house had made their ways to Kingston, where the governor had summoned them; of the rest, some were in Congress, some had died or been captured after Oriskany, some were marching to Saratoga, and some were tied up with local affairs. One was wearing George III's uniform. In British eyes all save that one were traitors, and all the more culpable for being leaders of the rebellion.[1]

In the eyes of the people who had made up provincial New York their position was more complex. The new constitution was clear enough. It apportioned membership in the senate and the assembly. It declared who could vote in elections for each house and for the governorship. It stated that every year the voters would choose a whole new assembly and one-third of the senate, and it vested in the two houses together "the supreme legislative power within this state." It prescribed the procedure for making public policy, and it set up elaborate machinery for the final passage of bills and for naming officials. As a document, it was specific and matter-of-fact. It created a set of institutions that would endure for decades and that would be a model for those set up by the Federal Constitution a decade later.[2]

But other things were less certain. Even while the first legislature was gathering, Burgoyne's army threatened the state's existence. Sixty miles below Kingston independent New York came to an abrupt end, and the occupied zone began. The British forces there showed their power less than a month after the legislature began business when a pillaging expedition sailed up the Hudson, captured and destroyed Kingston, and sailed back down—all virtually without opposition. As the redcoats advanced, the legislators scattered to their homes and militia units, leaving the state once more without regular government. For the time being, a few of them gathered in an utterly irregular Convention of the Members of the Senate and Assembly and took the little power there was to take.[3]

The constitution declared that Cumberland and Gloucester counties were part of the state, but by the time the legislature finally met, those counties, and parts of Charlotte and Albany, had become Vermont. Within revolutionary New York there was serious royalism in Westchester, Tryon, Dutchess, and Albany, and there were difficulties in Orange. Neither Tories nor Vermonters wanted to be numbered among the "good people of this state" in whom the constitution placed final sovereignty.

Those "good people" had ample grounds to be confused as well. The source of their new rulers' authority was to be regular elections, but the many rebels who had fled the southern district were represented by men named to their seats by the same "Convention of the People" that had written and promulgated the constitution. Despite protests, these "ordinance members" would serve until the British evacuation at the end of 1783. If one of them left his seat, his replacement was chosen by a vote in the other legislative house. The constitution announced that the new government had been created because of the "many and great inconveniences" that had attended informal government by congresses and committees. But those committees refused to disappear. The legitimacy of a political or social order can be challenged on many levels, and to deny the rightfulness of a ruler, or even of a governmental structure, is not necessarily to deny the legitimacy of the society that lies behind it.[4] But the independence crisis had shattered old New York, both politically and socially. Some whom men in the new positions of authority called New Yorkers denied the name. Others who called themselves New Yorkers denied those men and what they stood for. Many who accepted both the name and the facts of independence and republicanism were unsure about the relationship between the new authorities and themselves. In such an atmosphere, making the new order stable would require widespread, fundamental internal change.

I

Early in 1776 the most likely sources of the energy needed for change were in New York City, and the foremost of these was the city's Body of Mechanics. These artisans were organized, articulate, and militant; they were also thinking seriously about the new order. They expressed the core of their ideas in a message that they sent in May to the third of the four provincial congresses. The mechanics were concerned about two things: first, that any constitution that might be written be submitted for popular ratification; and second, that it include provision for people like themselves to continue their direct involvement in public affairs.

The mechanics raised the question of ratification because the congress was calling for elections to its successor, elections that would empower that new congress to write and implement a constitution. The mechanics objected; they could not believe "that the future delegates. . .could be vested with the power of framing a new constitution. . .and that [the] inhabitants. . .should not exercise the right which *God* has given them, in common with all men, to judge whether it be consistent with their interest to accept or reject" it. Only if the document were submitted to the people would it be "truly binding" on them. The mechanics were thus among the first in America to raise the idea of popular ratification, and they not only raised it but went beyond it. They wanted the people at large to retain "an uncontrolled power to alter the constitution in the same manner that it shall have been received," and thus they proposed that localities should retain the right "occasionally to renew their Deputies to Committees and Congresses." This should be whenever "the majority of such district shall think fit," and it should be without interference by any "power foreign to the body of the respective electors." Only through this eighteenth-century version of permanent revolution could the people be sure that the government would always stem from their own "voluntary choice."[5]

It was for and to such men that Tom Paine had written *Common Sense*, with its destruction of the pieties of royalism and Whiggery and its call for simple, responsive republican institutions. Paine's call was echoed in New York. "Spartanus," who wrote a series of essays called *The Interest of America*, wanted, "so far as private property will allow," to "form our government. . .just as if we had never had any form of government before." He called for a single-house legislature, annual elections, and the most rudimentary public administration. Local officers would be chosen by mass meetings, and officials bearing larger responsibilities would be chosen by the general assembly. But such ideas, and the people who held them, became less rather than more weighty in New York in the months immediately before and after independence.[6]

The situation in New York during the first half of 1776 stood in direct contrast to that in Pennsylvania, where radicalism did triumph in the making of the constitution. Pennsylvanians faced little immediate military danger, and the conservatives among them, based in the provincial assembly, made the strategic mistake of trying to stand fast against independence. The result was a coalescence of urban and rural radicals who were committed not just to independence but also to simple republicanism. The province's cooler heads, men like John Dickinson and James Wilson, simply were not involved during the hectic months when the provincial government's power was toppled and the constitution of 1776 was written.[7]

But in New York no such coalition emerged. For one thing, the military danger was real, both from royalists and from a British invasion that everyone knew was inevitable. Radicals like Isaac Sears, John Lamb, and Alexander McDougall began withdrawing from street and committee politics over the winter of 1775/76 and taking up army posts instead. Sears, for instance, associated himself with Charles Lee, and though Lee was the most radical of George Washington's generals, this association meant the removal of one of the city's most militant and dynamic men. When war actually came to New York, it had the same effect on the whole Body of Mechanics, and on other urban radicals who might have aligned with them. The British occupation scattered and broke them, and not until the end of 1783 would they again be in a position to intervene collectively.[8]

Another reason why nothing like the Pennsylvania coalition developed in New York was that there was no focus for anger comparable to the one that the Pennsylvania assembly provided right up to independence. The New York assembly never met again after the war broke out. The province's equivalents of the Wilsons and the Dickinsons based themselves in the provincial congresses. There they concentrated, not on stopping independence, but on putting it off for as long as they could. Meanwhile, the energy of rural radicals was taking a different course from the one it took in the commonwealth to the south. The Vermonters were debating among themselves, not contributing to struggles in New York. So were the Hudson Valley tenants, whichever way they leaned on the independence issue. In the landlord counties—Albany, Dutchess, and Westchester—*coalition* was the watchword among all who agreed on resistance. There were men there who were more than suspicious of the "better sort," but if they were with the movement, they were not yet ready to coalesce with the yeomen of Orange and Ulster, with the city mechanics, or with tenants against them.

New York's coalition for independence thus formed along lines quite different from those of the one in Pennsylvania. Its members agreed on resistance, but they did not agree that independence, if it had to be, should mean sharp internal change. The newspaper debates of the first six months of 1776 reflected the fact that what was taking place was coalition rather than confrontation. The debates were focused on the problem of what to do once an inevitable break was made. A republican constitution there would have to be, but save for the mechanics and for "Spartanus," the writers who contributed called for continuity and for piecemeal tinkering. Thus "Essex" wanted to broaden the suffrage laws, though not to the extent of instituting either manhood suffrage or the secret ballot. An "Independent Whig" believed that the existing structure was good enough, if only the council were chosen by the assembly, and the governor and assembly by popular elections. Another writer wanted simply to borrow the charter of Connecticut. "Columbus" was more concerned about men than about measures; whoever was chosen to establish the new government should be "remarkable" for "true wisdom, integrity, an extensive political knowledge, fortitude of mind, and an uniform steadiness to the *American* cause.[9]

The make-up of the four revolutionary congresses that ruled New York from 1775 to 1777 demonstrates the same point. The congresses were large: the first had ninety-three members, the second seventy-one, the third ninety-nine, and the fourth, whose records are incomplete, at least fifty-three. Among their members could be found most of the individual firebrands of New York City who had led the crowds that had driven the Revolution forward since 1765, men like Sears, McDougall, and Jacobus Van Zandt. There were mechanics: Joseph Hallett, Abraham Brasher, Isaac Stoutenburgh, William Denning. There were up-province politicians who had been outside the charmed circle of the old order: Abraham Yates and Matthew Adgate of Albany, Cornelius Humfrey and Zephaniah Platt of Dutchess. Though some, like Isaac Low of New York City, became royalists, these were never significant, and they lost what hold they had by 1776.[10]

But the congresses never included anyone who spoke for the Green Mountain movement. Charlotte and Cumberland sent delegates, but most of them would be Yorker loyalists after the Vermont break. One of these was William Duer, an immigrant speculator and entrepreneur who stood for the opposite of all that the Green Mountain Boys wanted. There were never delegates to speak for discontented Hudson Valley tenants. Instead, Westchester sent Lewis and Gouverneur Morris, Dutchess sent Robert R. Livingston and at least two others who bore his family name, and Albany sent Abraham Ten Broeck, Leonard Gansevoort, and John Van Rensselaer. Only the delegates for Tryon had reached the convention by directly confronting domestic enemies. The men new to politics who came to the congresses entered in the name of facing the British danger, not of changing New York. They wanted to coalesce with everyone who agreed, not to found parties among themselves. Both change and parties would come, but this was not the time for them.

Only one group among the delegates had a coherent sense of itself as made up not just of New Yorkers but of New Yorkers who had certain things in common. This group comprised the conservative professionals, the Whig landlords, and those city merchants who had not chosen royalism. They had begun in 1774 to learn to accommodate themselves to a mass movement rather than to resist it. Robert R. Livingston summed up their perspective and their methods with a telling metaphor in 1777 when he wrote of "swimming with a stream it is impossible to stem" and of yielding "to the Torrent" in order to "direct its course." The measure of what his sort achieved, in terms of their development as political tacticians, can be seen in the contrast between the confidence that lay behind Livingston's image and the intense fear displayed only three years earlier by Gouverneur Morris. Morris, watching the first committee election in New York City, had not written of directing torrents that could not be stopped. He had compared the people to reptiles that would soon bite, and had foreseen "with fear and trembling" that "we shall be under the worst of all possible dominions; we shall be under the domination of a riotous mob."[11]

During 1776 and early 1777 the conservative leaders handled things exactly as they should, from their point of view, and events over which they had no control helped them. They put off proposals for independence and a state constitution in May 1776 by arguing that the newly elected provincial congress had no mandate to decide on either. The delay that was involved in dissolving that congress and electing its successor gained them about two months. Moreover, by the time the new congress did convene, the imminence of a British invasion had neutralized the mechanics as a political force. The immediate danger of a radical solution like Pennsylvania's had been averted, and it had been done not by resistance but rather by appeal to the revolutionary principle that the people ought to give their direct consent before a congress could go forward on matters so important. It was the same trick that had produced a committee of fifty-one instead of twenty-five in 1774, and this time the stakes were much higher. A year later, after the long delaying game was over and the constitution they wanted was written, Livingston wrote of the "well-timed delays, indefatigible industry and minute . . . attention to every favourable circumstance" that his sort had practiced. Meanwhile, William Duer reminisced to John Jay of how they had collaborated on the "Council of *Conspiracy*." Such men had understood William Smith's warning that at such a time the place for men of property was "rather to the Cabinet than the field."[12]

The war aided them. From the British landing on Long Island in August 1776 to the descent of winter, the fourth congress, renamed "Convention of the People," was a government in flight. It moved from New York City to White Plains, from White Plains to Fishkill, and from Fishkill to Kingston. It did its business in abandoned churches and in private homes. Its members burdened the ablest among them with staggering loads. Robert R. Livingston's is illustrative. He was a member of the committee to draft a constitution and a delegate to the Continental Congress. He served on a committee to plan harassment of the British and on the convention's committee of correspondence. His friend Edward Rutledge pressed him to drop his affairs in New York and attend Congress, but Livingston replied that he could not, and complained that he was so "sick of politics and power" that he would not "give one scene of Shakespeare for a 1000 Harringtons, Lockes, Sidneys and Adams to boot."[13] By the end of the winter, such men found that most members of the convention felt the same way they did. John Jay observed that "the difficulty of getting any Government at all [had] long been an apprehension of little influence" on his mind. Such fears had "always appeared to be founded less in fact than in a design of quickening the pace of the House."[14]

Outsiders as well as members of the convention took part in its debates that winter. A soldier named Ebenezer Hazard told the Dutchess County delegate Nathaniel Sackett that "the great matter seems to be to secure a free Representation of the People and to keep the Purse strings of the State in their hands." Hazard wanted elections to be held every year and the legislature's proceedings to be always open, their journals being published at frequent intervals. But he also thought that most of the old ways would be best kept, because "people are strongly prejudiced in favor of them, being accustomed to them." Hazard wanted a council, which would be the special preserve of the better sort, as well as an assembly. Together the assembly and the council would elect the governor; and the governor, though liable to impeachment, would continue in office while his behavior remained good. Delegates from Suffolk County presented a plan much like Hazard's. According to the Suffolk plan, the assembly would choose the councillors from among citizens who held land worth at least £10,000 and who were resident in "the Metropolis at least 7 months in the year." The position would be for life. Assemblymen and councillors would elect a member of the upper house to a three-year term as governor, and he would have all the powers of the old royal governors, including an absolute veto on bills.[15]

A first draft of a constitution was circulating by October 1776. The draft, like the Pennsylvania constitution, styled the chief executive as president rather than as governor and denied him a veto on laws. But in other ways he would be stronger than his Pennsylvania counterpart. He would serve a three-year term after being chosen by the assembly; he would make military appointments from among candidates nominated by the assembly; he would be "Captain General, Commander in Chief and Ordinary." The legislature would have two houses, and the upper house would serve both legislative and executive functions. Local officials and delegates to Congress would be chosen annually by popular election. John McKesson, political confidant to George Clinton, told Clinton that the draft was "a child of Heaven," but William Smith, who also saw it, feared that it would put private property at risk by giving too much power to "the peasantry."[16]

Hazard's ideas and the Suffolk proposals defined one extreme of the debate, and the first draft defined the other. Over the ensuing winter a drafting committee and then the whole convention worked towards the final document. The drafting committee included a representative of every tendency that was represented in the convention. Its chairman was the querulous politician Abraham Yates, of Albany, and among its members were two representatives of the west-bank yeomanry of the Hudson Valley, Henry Wisner of Orange and Charles DeWitt of Ulster. But the core of the committee was made up of James Duane, John Jay, Gouverneur Morris, and Robert R. Livingston.[17]

Only a few records survive from the committee's work, but they are enough to bring out some important points. One is that the constitution was not simply the work of John Jay. A second is that conventional ideas of who was radical and who was not can be misleading. Thus the supposed radical John Morin Scott joined James Duane in support of the idea that the upper legislative house ought not to be based on any form of representation. Moreover, in floor session the convention seriously revised what the committee finally produced. Much of the debate turned on the suffrage, for the committee's draft instituted secret ballots and gave the vote to everyone who paid taxes. The reforms were tied to each other; taxpayer suffrage meant enfranchising people whose dependence on their landlords and employers made them likely pawns in such men's hands. But the secret ballot lessened the danger of that.[18] The greatest gain from the reforms would have been felt by the tenants of Frederick Philipse, whose tenure-at-will had not qualified them for the vote under colonial law. Most of the Livingston, Van Rensselaer, and Schuyler tenants did qualify, since they held their farms on long leases, and it was these big patriot landlords that the secret ballot threatened. Perhaps for that reason, the convention rejected the whole package. It substituted a requirement that assembly electors have a freehold worth twenty pounds or a renthold valued at forty shillings, or that they be men who had gained the freemanship of one of the cities before 1775. Voters for the senate and the governorship would have to have freeholds worth one hundred pounds, and only for the governorship would voting be by ballot, though the constitution did permit an experiment with ballot voting for the legislature once the war was over.[19]

The other major change that took place on the floor was the creation of the council of revision and the council of appointment. The former was made up of the governor, the chancellor, and the justices of the supreme court; together they could veto laws, unless two thirds of both the senate and the assembly overrode their veto. The council of appointment was made up of the governor and a senator from each of the four great senatorial districts, the senators to be chosen by the assembly. It could grant civil and military offices above the lowest level. The council of revision originated when a delegate moved to give the governor an absolute veto on laws, which the draft did not grant. John Jay offered the council as an alternative, and the convention accepted it. The council of appointment came about when the convention rejected a draft clause for vesting the power of civil appointments in the legislature alone. Again it was Jay who made the counterproposal. The governor's presence on these two councils gave him some of the power that the royal governors had enjoyed, for they had possessed an absolute veto on laws and wide powers of patronage. But had the convention not altered the committee's draft, neither council would have existed, and the governor would have had no share in either legislation or appointments. Denying him any such share was the drafting committee's original intention.[20]

The prime task of the makers of the constitution was to define the new political society. They could write a document that would alter the terms of political participation radically, or they could write one that would continue and rationalize what had gone on before. They did neither. Their constitution enlarged the political community in practical terms by creating an assembly that was two and a half times the size of the old one, was roughly apportioned by counties, was annually elected by the many adult males who could meet the twenty-pound property requirement, and could expand freely as population grew. It enlarged it by creating a governorship and a senate that were to be filled by election, and by opening every public office to any freeholder of the state. It enlarged the community in principle by declaring that the people were the source of all sovereignty and by requiring that laws be enacted in their name alone.[21] But it deliberately excluded the rootless of New York: the seamen, the farm laborers, and the urban poor. By creating an elaborate structure in which public action could be slowed down or halted by the assembly, the senate, or the council of revision, it tried to guarantee that there would be no direct equation between popular desire and what the government did. The hope of the framers was that this would lead to political and social stability. In fact, stability would be achieved only when these restrictions were overcome and when New York approached in practice the working popular sovereignty that radical Pennsylvanians were seeking in principle.

II

During the first years of independence New Yorkers often had to ask who, for political purposes, was to count as one of themselves. The constitution declared that everyone who lived within the old provincial boundaries was a citizen, or "subject," of the state.[22] In practice, citizenship, if not subjection, was denied to women, slaves, minors, and men who did not meet the property requirement for the vote. These were held only to owe obedience to laws that they had no part in shaping. But defining the state as the continuation of the province was mere bluster, for the New York over which the constitution was proclaimed comprised only the counties of Orange, Ulster, Dutchess, Albany, and Tryon and parts of Westchester and Charlotte.

The most pressing aspect of the problem was royalism. It was met differently at every level of the revolutionary movement. Crowds harassed Tories; local committees controlled and punished them; the conspiracies commissioners operated as a police force against them; the laws forced them to identify themselves, and then they were placed under bonds and penalties.

From the beginning of the war, militant patriots took direct and often violent action against royalists, beginning with the siege of Johnson Hall in the summer of 1775. In September of that year a crowd in Poughkeepsie tarred and feathered a judge of the county court because he had ordered the recovery of arms that the county committee had seized and the imprisonment of one of the committeemen. In New York City antiroyalist riots erupted in June 1776. Crowds stripped Tories of their clothes, rode them through the streets on rails, and put them in jail.[23] Such actions continued after independence. During the winter of 1777/78 many Tories were free on bail in the district of Cambridge, Albany County. Releasing them under surety was normal when the jails were full, but a crowd of people gathered, formed itself into two ranks and made the royalists run between while the people standing on each side beat them. In 1778 people in Tryon began seizing the goods of royalists who had not fled; meanwhile, citizens of Albany County formed "a Combination to lessen the Number of the Disaffected by sending them Orders to move off and threatening them to abide by the consequences in Case of Neglect." Militants elsewhere in Albany claimed the authority of the conspiracies commissioners in order "to examine into the Conduct of Persons by them supposed to have been unfriendly to the American Cause." Catherine Simpson, wife of a royalist in Schoharie, Albany County, complained to the commissioners in July 1779 that a crowd had pulled down her home and destroyed her goods and clothes.[24]

Repression by local committees ran parallel to these outbursts. At the end of June 1776 the fourth provincial congress resolved that committees should search out people who had gone into hiding in the woods "with a design to join the enemy." The committees could make arrests and call out the militia if necessary. But weeks earlier, people in the city of Albany had petitioned their committee to put notorious royalists under heavy restraint. When a committee did not respond to such pressures, popular anger might turn against the committee itself. The crowd that made royalists in Cambridge run the gauntlet inflicted the same humiliation on the town's committeemen, whom they blamed for the Tories being at large. The committeemen were not beaten, however.[25]

Committeemen learned how to terrorize the Revolution's enemies. When the "Hickey Plot," to kidnap George Washington, was discovered in July 1776 the militia were deliberately sent in the small hours of the morning to arrest the people involved. One of the suspects proved unwilling to talk, but "Young Mr. Livingston" persuaded him to confess by advising him to prepare to die. At the same time, outstanding royalists were being rounded up in the counties of Albany and Ulster. The arrest of the Ulster sheriff, who was the son of Lieutenant Governor Colden, was carried out by armed men at midnight. Though the sheriff lived in the precinct of Hanover, the capture was directed by the committees of New Windsor and Newburgh, lest his neighbors be too easy on him.[26]

In March 1776 the committee of the breakaway rebel district of Cow Neck, Queens County, forbade people to enter the district without a certificate from the committee of the last place they had been. The county committee in Westchester adopted the same policy in June. Also in June, the committees in Newburgh and New Windsor begged for gunpowder for their militia to use in putting down royalists, and the committee of Dutchess asked for a force of 150 men for full-time anti-Tory duty. The committee of Salem, Westchester County, wanted to make Tories pay the costs of their own persecution, reasoning that they had made "all the trouble" and that dealing with them had been the committee's "whole business ever since we have been formed." Exile of royalists, like armed suppression of them, began in the month before independence, when the Tryon committee sent sixty-nine people to New Hampshire. Meanwhile, the Albany committee was planning the expulsion of the mayor of the city, the sheriff and the clerk of the county, and a number of others. The charges ranged from merely being "suspicious" to secretly warning Sir John Johnson of a plan to arrest him.[27]

Fragmentary records from Livingston Manor show a hard-pressed committee trying to cope with royalism. Here there was no question of popular pressure driving the committee forward, for on the manor the Revolution's enemies outnumbered its friends. Between October 1776 and April 1777 the committee tried to quell the royalist feeling that was building towards the tenant rising that took place in May. It appealed for militiamen from Dutchess; it sent men to jail; it tried to raise soldiers in the manor; it imposed fines; it required bonds for good behavior. The very lightness of some of the punishments it imposed is a measure of its weakness, and its records have a tone of bleak desperation. Prisoners were rescued from its custody; armed men roamed freely and took pot shots at rebels; a "king's book" circulated among the tenants; royalists told waverers that the British would reimburse them for any fines; men damned the committee, boasting that because British victory was certain, they could ignore the committee's orders. The committee's weakness was such that when, at one point, a militia lieutenant who was "executing his orders" was "abused" by three men of his company, the committee could do no more than reprimand them.[28]

Though the manor was the most Tory-ridden part of the county, the district of Kinderhook elected known royalists to the county committee in May 1776. But the county committee had the strength to deal with such problems; it purged the Kinderhook Tories when they refused to sign a test oath. At about the same time, its members stopped worrying about recruiting people to the cause and began instead to deal forcibly with those who would not be recruited. The committee had been running a Tory jail since 1775, and now it began arresting so many people that there were up to sixty prisoners in just one of the jail's rooms. In June 1776 it gave its subcommittees the power to punish anyone who denied their authority. In August it demanded that magistrates let it know whether they would execute their offices under the convention's authority. Knowing that blacks had good reason to be less than enthusiastic about this white man's revolution, the committee required the corporal punishment of any slave found outdoors at night. In May 1777, during the Livingston Manor rising, Tory problems filled the committee's agenda. It empowered the subcommittee of Rensselaerwyck to call out the militia, lest tenants rise there too. It required all subcommittees to collect information about people who were away from home, such as the cause of each journey and how long the person had been traveling. It named a special board to supply commanders of troops in the field with local political information. On its own authority, it began to confiscate the estates of the disaffected.[29]

During the summer of 1777 the Albany committee arrested people who refused Continental money. It ordered the militia to go after the social bandits of Livingston and Rensselaerwyck. Learning that "the greatest part of the Inhabitants on the Schenectady Road are disaffected," it directed its chairman to have them removed if necessary. It ordered the closure of a tavern whose royalist keeper was encouraging soldiers to desert, arresting the publican and turning his family out of their house. It forbade a trader who was refusing the state's paper currency to carry on her business.[30]

Tory policy developed and changed at higher levels as well. The decisions of the provincial congresses and the state legislature and the actions of the conspiracies commissioners show that what leaders thought needed doing varied with the Revolution's course. From the summer of 1775 until independence, they used moral force and the pressure of opinion to bring people into the movement. This was the primary function of the associations that circulated in the province, for failure to sign meant ostracism. After independence, the revolutionaries could call themselves a government and could require people not just to associate but to swear by the God they worshiped. The effect was the same: one showed the world where one stood. But an oath was more serious, and for many New Yorkers who had already sworn to the king the demand forced a serious crisis of conscience.[31]

Oaths, like associations, served two purposes: to identify the Revolution's enemies and to put its friends through one more ritual of commitment. In one of its earliest actions, the legislature required its members to swear "true faith and Allegiance to the State" and to vow that they would do their "Duty as a good Subject. . .ought to do." In June 1778 the legislature passed an act "more effectually to Prevent the Mischiefs Arising from the Influence and Example of Persons of Equivocal and Suspected Character." This act cited the danger posed by people who "affected to maintain a neutrality" and who had "advocated the American cause until it became serious." It required citizens to swear that they acknowledged New York's right to independence and their own obligations to the state. An act of 1781 "for the better securing the Independence of this State" required a test oath of voters who were suspected of not having "taken an active and decisive Part in Favour of the United States." A law granting relief to debtors who owed money to royalists denied any benefits to people who had not abjured their fealty to the king and sworn it to the state. The same condition was required of anyone who wanted to take advantage of a law that tried to settle the Vermont problem by confirming New England land titles.[32]

In June 1776, as local committees were starting to punish royalists, the third provincial congress set up a committee for detecting conspiracies and gave it a broad brief: it could arrest people, confine them to their homes, and order their exile. It could exile individuals by name and groups by general description. It could do such things for as nebulous a reason as the suspect's being of "a suspicious and equivocal character." The constitutional legislature transformed the committee into a commission and gave the commissioners even broader powers. They could confine "under such Restrictions and Limitations as to them shall appear Necessary, for the public Safety, all Persons whose going at large shall. . .appear dangerous." They could imprison their suspects, exile them, and put them under bond for good behavior. No court could interfere with their decisions or grant bail to the men and women they held. The only real limit on their power was that they were forbidden to impose corporal or capital punishment.[33]

The actions of the commissioners varied. The board that operated in Albany imposed a bond on nearly everyone who came before it, even if the person was found innocent of the charge against him. The commissioners and local committees exiled hundreds of people to New Hampshire, to the disused mines of Connecticut, and to occupied New York City. They forced the removal from places near sensitive military positions of the families of men who had fled to the enemy. After 1780 it was possible to remove such families from any district, whether it was militarily sensitive or not.[34] The primary concern of the commissioners was to keep the Tories in control rather than to punish them, and the Tory laws passed by the first two sessions of the legislature had the same intent. The only exception was a law that imposed double taxation on the property of royalists sent into exile and that rendered those exiles who returned guilty of misprision of treason.[35]

In the third session, held in late 1779 and early 1780, the legislature changed that policy and began passing acts to punish the Revolution's enemies. The first suspended all licenses to practice law that had been granted prior to 1776 and allowed readmission to the bar only after a jury had investigated an attorney's opinions and behavior. Then came the Forfeitures Act, passed in October 1779. This law justified itself on the ground that royalists had "forfeited all Right to the Protection of this State," and it directly attainted more than seventy of them with treason. These it banished forever; they would be liable to the death penalty if they returned. Their property, both real and personal, was seized by the state. People who had escaped being named in the act could be indicted under its provisions by a grand jury in any county, and failure to answer the publication of the indictment would be taken as a plea of guilty. The act also extended the common law of treason to cover people who had willingly gone into the British zone or who had broken engagements they had made with revolutionary committees, with local officials, or with the conspiracies commissioners. The crime carried a capital penalty.[36]

That set the pace for subsequent laws. "An Act More Effectually to Punish Adherents of the King" made it a felony to propagate royalist opinion or to undermine the revolutionary cause, whether by "preaching, teaching, speaking, writing, [or] printing." It also became felonious to seduce citizens away from their duty. The crime carried a death sentence, but that might be commuted to three years' service on a ship of war in the American or the French fleet. Meanwhile, the legislature struck at the social bandits of the Hudson Valley by imposing a special tax on known royalists to raise a fund that would provide restitution for the bandits' victims.[37]

As the war ended and the British withdrew, the legislature passed a series of laws intended to put the Revolution's enemies on a different footing from that of its friends. One of the most notable was the Citation Act, passed for the benefit of people in the free zone who were in debt to people behind the British lines. The act suspended all suits that such creditors might have against their debtors. It provided that if "any special Problem" affected a revolutionary debtor and a royalist creditor, the creditor would be unable to invoke the normal law of debt. Instead, the dispute would be referred to a panel of laymen drawn from the Revolution's supporters. The Trespass Act followed. It allowed people who had fled the southern district to bring damage suits against anyone who had used property that they had left behind. The act denied to defendants the right to plead that they had used the property at the order of the British authorities and were thus excused under the laws of war.[38]

Another law dealt with the chaos along the front that ran through Westchester County. Raiders from both sides operated freely there, and their status was somewhere between that of soldiers and that of freebooters. The legislature responded to this land-bound privateering by extending New York jurisdiction to include cases of plundering in the war zone. But the law announced that it was not intended "to give Protection to the Disaffected, who have fled to the Enemy," and denied them coverage. Another law of the sixth session recognized the fact that "many zealous Friends to the Freedom and Independence of the United States. . . have. . . committed and done acts. . . which were not conformable to the strict letter of the law." The return of peace posed the danger that royalists who had been the victims of such acts might bring damage suits. To prevent it, the act forbade them to undertake legal action "for any Imprisonment, Escape, Assault, Battery or Trespass done or committed. . . with Intent to further the Common Cause of America."[39]

As a final gesture, the seventh session, the first after the British evacuated, passed "An Act to Preserve the Freedom and Independence of this State." It declared the great importance "to the Safety of a Free Government, that Persons holding Principles inimical to the Constitution, should not be admitted into Offices or Places of Trust." The law continued the disqualification from voting and officeholding of the long list of offenders to whom previous election laws had denied political rights. It also allowed the bringing of a charge of misprision of treason against anyone who since independence had held office under the British, privateered for them, or served them under arms.[40]

New York earned the reputation that it acquired for being hard on the enemies of the Revolution. The Forfeitures Act, the Trespass Act, the Citation Act, and the thirty-odd other laws that were passed formed a rigorous body of legislation. These laws ruined people's lives and estates, and as the Revolution ended, they ensured that its enemies would not stand equal to its friends under the new order. But it would be a mistake to equate their harshness with mere vindictiveness. On the contrary, the Tory laws served important functions in securing the Revolution's triumph. One was to separate its friends from its enemies, and to render the enemies unable to harm it. By their rigor, these laws forced royalism's hard core into exile and saved New York's republicans from having to live with men who wanted to undo all they had achieved. Royalists who did remain knew that they did so on an unequal footing, that the Revolution had won and could not be turned back. Independence, republicanism, and the confiscation of the great Tory estates would be permanent, not because there had been no opposition, but because opposition had been crushed. The other function these laws served was felt by the revolutionaries. Their punitive aspect simply extended the treatment rebels had been giving Tories in the streets since as early as 1775. But men in power turned to a policy of punishment only in 1779, after four years of trying to do no more to the Tories than control and convert them. The last part of this chapter will show how that change was of crucial importance in getting a revolutionized people to accept their revolutionary government.

III

Vermonters, like royalists, denied the legitimacy of revolutionary New York, but they denied it from a different perspective and with different results. At one point in 1781 the two issues drew together, as news leaked that Ethan Allen and other Vermont leaders were flirting with General Frederick Haldimand, the British commander in Montreal. Haldimand was offering Allen's followers recognition as a self-governing British province and confirmation of their land titles if they would switch sides. Nothing serious came of it, save that New York leaders had a chance to score propaganda points.[41]

The Vermonters had their own problems in consolidating power. They enjoy a clearly defined border with neither New York nor New Hampshire.

There were times during the war when their ambitions seemed to reach both east and west. A few isolated New Hampshire towns on the east bank of the Connecticut River actually joined them briefly, and there were towns west of what became the Vermont-New York line where pressure to adhere to Thomas Chittenden's government rather than George Clinton's was strong. Such pressure sometimes became violent. John Younglove, an ardent revolutionary in the Albany County village of Cambridge, was once kidnapped and shot, though not mortally, by neighbors who wanted to take the district into Vermont. Yorker loyalists in Vermont itself kept up correspondence with Governor Clinton, sometimes sent deputies to the New York legislature, and asked for offices. But a judge who tried to open a court under New York authority was likely to find himself the defendant in a Vermont court for doing so. Even committed Yorkers told the governor that they were raising troops under Vermont authority and that they could only dare accept a New York commission if he could promise indemnity for what it might cost them.[42]

As late as 1788 New York kept up its pretense of including the counties of Cumberland and Gloucester. In official parlance, the Vermonters remained "revolted subjects of this state," and their community was the "pretended state of Vermont," but there was no question of either subduing them by force or punishing them by law. Partly because Vermont was geographically secure and politically united and partly from military necessity, throughout the war Yorker officials found that they had to collaborate on matters of security with their secessionist counterparts. The best example came in 1777 when the victory of Vermont militiamen at Bennington began the death agony of General Burgoyne's army.[43]

If New York had any chance of reincorporating the Green Mountains, it would be by persuasion and by extending its political community rather than by harsh action. The first legislative session took a long symbolic step in that direction by nullifying the hated Bloody Act of 1774. The act of repeal made no attempt to exculpate what the provincial legislature had done; instead it condemned the law itself as a massive injustice. In 1779 the state referred the whole dispute to Congress, empowering it to resolve the problem as seemed fit. But Congress did nothing, and in 1782 two laws were passed to cajole the Vermonters back to allegiance. One cited nameless "inhabitants residing in the Northeastern Parts" who had "by their humble Petition to the Legislature, represented that they were seduced and misled by artful and designing men from their Duty and Allegiance." These people had professed "a sincere Repentence," and the law gave them full amnesty.[44]

The other act, "for Quieting the Minds of the Inhabitants" of the region, confirmed all New Hampshire land grants that had been made prior to New York grants for the same land. It provided that no New Hampshire grants were to be made void because the conditions of the grant had not been met. It allowed squatter rights for up to five hundred acres of land that had not been granted, and it even confirmed Vermont grants predating New York ones. The only condition for enjoying its benefits was to renounce Vermont authority.[45] The act is reminiscent of the wartime attempts that Britain itself made to lure the Colonies by offering whatever they wanted short of independence. The legislators were trying, at last, to resolve the problem that lay at the heart of the matter. But by 1782 the main issue for Vermonters, and for the United States as a whole, was independence. Serious compromise on the original question became an option for the old rulers, or their heirs, only when their own intransigence had turned a movement of resistance into a separate community.

The withdrawal of royalists and of Vermonters meant a fundamental redefinition of New York both as a political society and as a geographical entity. The redefinition resulted from the release during the independence crisis of class, ethnic, ideological, and geographical tensions that had their own momentum and that were only half-tied to the trouble between Britain and America. Without the imperial crisis, neither problem would have exploded as it did, but thanks to these domestic tensions, independence brought changes far beyond a simple cutting of the imperial tie. The state government responded to the problems posed as well as might have been expected. It lost no face with its replacement of sticks by carrots in its dealings with Vermonters; it recognized the problem of royalism for what it was and acted accordingly.

IV

The most serious problem of all, and the surest sign that a popular revolution was underway, was among republican New Yorkers. Its central aspect was the emergence of the committees of safety, first as contestants for power and then as wielders of it. The committee movement gave focus and more permanent expression to the concerns that brought people into active involvement in the Revolution. A crowd would dissolve, but a committee could adjourn. A crowd could act, but a committee could make and execute a policy. Chapter 5 and Section II of this chapter showed how the committees operated against Britain and against royalists. They also showed that though the committees were the instruments of revolutionary coalitions rather than of a revolutionary class, they were still the means by which more and more people were drawn into "direct interference in historic events." They showed that those people were men who under the old order never would have gotten so close to the center of affairs. Now let us turn to how those committees operated within New York itself.

On paper, the structure of power was very simple as the committees were emerging. The committees were to prepare for war. They would be responsible to the provincial congress and to the Continental Congress.

They would not interfere with the ordinary affairs of either local government or the provincial authorities. In a few places it worked that way. Thus in Orange-Town, Orange County, people elected both committeemen and local officers in 1775 and 1776. The two groups overlapped only slightly, the one dealing with the war and the other with the routine of local government. But such examples were rare. In Tryon County the committee adopted its own rules for government after it expelled the county sheriff in August 1775. In Albany the last session of the court of common pleas was held in January 1776. The chief judge was already a committeeman, and six months later the other high officials of the county would be on their way to exile and imprisonment. The corporation of New York City likewise collapsed with independence, and in August 1776 the committee there was complaining that it was clogged by the judicial business it had taken on when the courts closed. In October 1776, the clerk of Dutchess County asked the convention whether he should convene a grand jury in preparation for a new court session, and it told him he should not.[46]

The records of the Albany committee show how it took on more and more civil functions. Even before it deposed and arrested the mayor and the sheriff, the committee seized the county archives and put them under guard. It told the royalist county clerk that he might use them, but only when his business required. In November 1776 it took on responsibility for the city's water supply, and by March 1777 it was in command of the fire companies and had appointed a "goaler to this Committee" to run its prison. It delegated a man to keep the town clock in good order and ordered chimney viewers to carry out their tasks under its authority until a new city corporation could take up its duties. Even when a new regular government came into effect, the committee remained the real source of initiatives. As late as November 1777 it called on the aldermen to see to the repair of the city's bridges, wells, and pumps, promising that it would cover their expenses.[47]

Power shifted in the same way in Schenectady. There too the committee was forbidding smallpox inoculations within weeks of its emergence. At the start of 1776 it resolved that conserving gunpowder was more important than firing off charges to celebrate the new year and asked the magistrates to put a stop to useless shooting. The magistrates complied. By the middle of 1777 the committee had all power in Schenectady. It named a ferryman for the Mohawk River crossing; established a town watch; licensed inns; arbitrated petty disputes; ordered road supervisors to see to their tasks. The committee fined illicit tavernkeepers and resolved a dispute between an estranged couple over the custody of their child. It even ordered the arrest of the town constable, whom it had appointed as part of a return to normality, when he refused to answer a summons.[48]

Nor did the committeemen necessarily do what a provincial congress ordered them to do. As early as 1775 the committee of Tryon County flatly refused to have Sheriff White back, even though the congress endorsed

Governor Tryon's command that he be allowed to return. A year later the congress ordered county committees to begin sending it two nominations for every post that fell vacant. This was an old provincial custom, and it served to make appointment by a higher authority something more than a mere ratification of a decision taken at a lower level. But when two county committees objected and refused to comply the congress dropped the idea. The fullest statement of this tendency came in the spring of 1776, when the New York City mechanics issued their call for the continuation of committee power even after any new constitution went into effect. Let it be stressed again that for the mechanics the source of committee power was below, not above. The "majority of such district" would decide when "to renew their Deputies to Committees and Congresses," without interference "from any power foreign to the body of the respective electors."[49] In practice, of course, the local committees and the provincial congresses cooperated far more than they clashed. With a war underway, they had to. But both the actions of committeemen and the arguments of such as the mechanics show that the committee movement was defining itself and asserting its power against the Revolution's "official" leadership in the same way that it did against the provincial authorities.

The 1777 constitution contained no provision for any renewal of committees. On the contrary, its preamble declared that popular committees and congresses had been "temporary expedients...to exist no longer than the grievances of the people should remain without redress" and that "many and great inconveniences attend the said mode of government by congresses and committees, as of necessity legislative, judicial and executive powers have been vested therein." Despite the constitution, however, circumstances kept the committee system alive until the middle of 1778, more than a year after the constitution was proclaimed, and a fresh crisis revived it in 1779.

As one of its very first acts, the new state legislature moved to contradict the constitution by providing for the continuation of the committees. Meanwhile, local committees were declaring on their own authority that they would not disband immediately. The new government began operations in September 1777, but it ceased them again a month later, when the British expedition captured and sacked Kingston. From then until early in 1778 central power was in the hands of a self-appointed "Convention of the Members of the Senate and Assembly" and of a committee of safety that the convention named. The legislature reassembled in January 1778, but the local committees, given a fresh mandate by an election held while the convention was in power, continued to operate at least until June. William Smith noted that these latest committee elections were held despite their "direct Repugnancy to the New Model."[50]

There were many reasons why the committees stayed alive. The lack of any other institution to take their place was one, as the legislature recognized in its act to continue their powers. The Tory problem was another.

But economic difficulties were also involved, and these gained greater and greater importance. By the end of 1775 committee power was becoming identified with corporatist interventions in the marketplace. The committee of New York City tried in November of that year to found a manufactory to employ the poor, harking back to the schemes put up a decade before by the "Society for Promoting Oeconomy." In May 1776 the Albany committee began to punish people who violated the price regulations that it was establishing. A merchant accused of selling tea at an excessive price "contrary to the Resolution of the Continental Congress and this Committee" was hauled before the committee. The committee found him guilty and held him up "to the public view as an Enemy to his Country." A second trader who was charged replied that he had merely been following normal practice; the committee ordered a boycott of his business. It imposed the same punishment on a merchant who pleaded that he did sell his tea at the set price but admitted that he charged a fee of two shillings "for his trouble in weighing." In August, finally, the committee ordered that a merchant go to jail for charging too much.[51]

At the same time, the committee turned its attention to the supply of salt. Salt was an absolute necessity in a pre-refrigeration society, and the British occupation of the state's only seaport meant that it would soon be in short supply. The committee set a maximum price and decreed that no customer could buy more than a bushel of salt at one time. In September the committee changed tactics, promising that anyone who exposed salt and other scarce commodities for sale would receive its protection. Its aim was still to see that the market was adequately supplied. By July 1777 grain also was becoming scarce. The committee resolved that "divers ill-minded Persons and Enemies to the Liberties of this State" were hoarding it, and promised to imprison anyone it caught doing so. In the autumn of 1777 it limited the distribution of salt to known patriots, and early in 1778 it forbade distilling to conserve grain. When the state legislature reassembled in January 1778 after its forced dissolution, the committee put pressure on it to regulate prices throughout the state.[52]

Economic concerns such as these were what revived the committees in 1779. During that year, the northern states went through a major crisis as the Continental dollar spiraled in wild inflation. The crisis struck harder at people who bought their food than at people who produced it; it was, in other words, an "urban" phenomenon, afflicting town dwellers, tradesmen, and refugees more than it did farmers.[53] The traditional way to cope with such a problem was to impose price controls, and at every level, from local committees to interstate conventions, northerners had been trying since 1777 to use controls to bring relief. But earlier efforts had failed, and in 1779 inflation was worse rather than better.

The crisis was not peculiar to New York; the movement to cope with it through the efforts of popular committees actually began in Philadelphia and Boston. In May, Philadelphia issued a call for the reestablishment of committees "in every State and County," and New Yorkers heeded it. The movement's focal points in the state were the city of Albany and the Dutchess town of Fishkill, but committees also appeared elsewhere in Dutchess and in Ulster, Tryon, and probably Orange.[54] The revived Albany committee first met on 20 June 1779, and its activities petered out sometime in August. During the two months it interested itself in most of the questions that had concerned the earlier committee movement, calling for harmony with the rest of America, hectoring slow districts to send delegates, and searching out royalists. There were, however, differences. When it discovered Tories, it sent them to the conspiracies commissioners instead of dealing with them itself. When it called for unanimity, it did so in the name of controlling inflation rather than in that of resisting Britain.

The committee's actions in regard to inflation were straightforward. At its very first meeting it resolved to search out supplies hidden in the county. On 3 July it considered the case of a man charged with selling a scythe at too high a price. A week later it was debating the export of wheat to Massachusetts. It named a subcommittee to see that the city of Albany was supplied with fresh produce at acceptable prices.[55] Committees elsewhere forbade distilling, took over police functions, and called out the militia. Not all were militant: the Ulster County committee *demanded* of its county's legislators that they act to reduce prices, but the one in Poughkeepsie contented itself with milder language and stressed its belief that the legislators could handle the situation. The movement culminated with a state convention at Claverack, in Albany County, in August. The convention sent a message to the legislature calling for heavier taxation and for voluntary public loans to soak up excess money, for statewide price controls, and for "the confiscation and disposition of the real estate of traitors and enemies to the country."[56]

The situation that summer was serious. Though the Albany committeemen were sure that "the institution of Committees will not clash but [be] perfectly conformable to the sentiments of the grand Council of the United States," any of them who had read the state constitution knew that what they were doing violated it. The Albanians recognized that "nothing can be effected by Committees unless their Fellow Citizens and Constituents generously support" them, and they branded their enemies as "designing and mercenary Individuals." Others went further. The Ulster committeemen pledged to support "our young Government to the Utmost of our Power" but warned that "if the Legislature does not take decisive measures this session the Virtue and Patriotism of the People at Large must once more be roused." "W. D. in Orange County" told newspaper readers that "as soon as the authority of your [earlier] committees ended, knavery showed its head, villains of every class came forth and practiced with impunity."[57] A new situation of dual power was being created as the committees punished men who violated their decrees and took up the functions of government. These writers knew it, and at least some of them liked it.

Parallel to the domestic committee concerns of 1776 and 1777 and to the revival of 1779 came less formal, less structured outbursts of popular energy. Committeemen were ambivalent about truly informal action. They might announce that they needed their "Fellow Citizens and Constituents" to "generously support" them, but they knew that popular action could threaten even them. When the committeemen of Cambridge, Albany County, were driven through the gauntlet together with the local Tories, the county committee resolved that the people there had done wrong and that it would suppress everything of the kind. The danger was there when the committees faced economic problems as much as when they faced political ones. As early as October 1775, Albanians warned their committee that if their demands were not answered within twenty-four hours, "we shall look upon it that you will not consider our oppression; and if we find that you will not vindicate our doleful Circumstances, we will without doubt be obliged to remove these ruinous circumstances ourselves."[58]

Direct action on economic questions meant acting in terms of corporatist political economy. The Ulster committee reported to the state convention in November 1776 that "we are daily alarmed, and our streets filled with mobs. . .breaking of doors and committing of outrages." The reason was "the misfortune of having that detestable article called tea stored here, which is taken by them and divided or distributed in such manner as they think fit." In Dutchess County, exiles from New York City were at the same time stopping wagons and searching them for food. People there believed that the developing shortage of flour was the fault of engrossers and resolved to stop flour exports and to detain would-be exporters until the state's council of safety could act. The Albany committee noted at the end of 1777 that food was scarce, that "the disaffected" were engrossing supplies, that the poor could buy neither at the high prices nor in the bulk quantities required, and that the "cities begin to be alarmed."[59]

In both Ulster and Dutchess counties there were outbursts of popular price-setting. This was something that Europeans knew well. It was the basis of most crowd action in eighteenth-century England, and the French called it *taxation populaire*. In England, France, and America alike it was a legitimate form of behavior with recognized rules. Price-setting often involved women, and it always meant a crowd's taking a needed commodity at what it considered a fair price. In one instance, in Nine Partners Precinct, Dutchess County, the crowd was led by the local committee. In another, in Ulster, the victim was a future speaker of the state assembly, John Hathorn. In both of these cases the commodity in question was salt. There are full descriptions of several outbursts in 1777, all involving tea. Two, in May, centered on the storekeeper Peter Messier, who wanted to sell his supply at four dollars per pound. A crowd of women, under the protection of two

Continental soldiers, invaded Messier's shop. "The women said they would. . .have [the tea] at their own price, and brought a Hammer and Scales." They took a hundredweight of it and left seventeen pounds in payment. The second time, the crowd got Messier to weigh out several parcels on promise that they would pay, and then offered him their price rather than his. Like the women in the first crowd, they had the protection of armed men. Many of the same women returned a few days later, telling Messier that "they had orders from the Committee to search his house." In July the same thing happened at an absentee-owned store in New Windsor. The partners learned from their manager that "the women! in this place have risen in a mob, and are now selling a box of tea of yours at 6s per lb." The women had learned of the tea from the drover who had brought it to the store.[60]

Unlike royalism and the Vermont insurgency, the continuation of the committees and of direct popular action did not challenge New York's basic republican integrity. It did, however, militate against the stabilization of the new government. These committees were "revolutionary manifestations of the most fundamental sort," and the emergence of their like seems characteristic of what Samuel P. Huntington has called the "Western" model of revolution. Their creation is a major step towards dissolving the power of an old order, as happened in 1774 and 1775. Their operations provide both a bulwark against revolution's becoming chaos and a way of structuring and directing the energy of people whom the Revolution has brought into public events. In New York they served that function from 1775 to 1778 and again in 1779. In every revolution where such committees have appeared, thinkers have speculated about their political meaning. Some have merely floated the idea that popular councils might become the basis of a better order; enough people did so in New York between 1775 and 1779 to show that the idea was at least in the air. Elsewhere and at other times men and women have explored the meaning of such committees much more thoroughly.[61]

Some of that exploration has been academic. Scholars have considered the emergence and the actions of such councils in the revolutions of eighteenth-century France and of twentieth-century Russia, Germany, and Eastern Europe.[62] But academics have not been the only people interested in them. Radical thinkers have looked and do look to such councils as the structural basis of an alternative to parliamentary democracy or corporate capitalism or both. Marx developed his ideas about politics after the socialist revolution from his observations of the Paris Commune. Lenin argued in *State and Revolution* that the soviets of Russia in 1917 should have all power and that the new order should be built around them. Both stressed that a system based on councils ought to be closely accountable to its constituents and that it ought to involve directly as many people as possible. Both held that the power of councils ought to combine the functions of lawmaking, law enforcement, and judgment. Ideas of the same sort became a dominant theme for the continental European New Left of the 1960s and have even had some echoes in Britain and the United States.

The foremost academic student of popular revolutionary councils, the German Oskar Anweiler, doubts that they can ever be the basis of a lasting social and political order. He points in particular to the problematic relationship between council democracy and party politics, a question that this study will explore in part III. But Anweiler also stresses the tension between councils and more orthodox political formations and the way in which council movements again and again articulate social protest under "ever-different concrete historical circumstances." To borrow Anweiler's categories, there developed in revolutionary New York both a widespread and persistent committee movement and significant if only half-formed elements of the "council thought" that would flourish in later writings.[63] It would be overstating the case to suggest that the committee movement compares directly to the soviets of revolutionary Russia; the latter were far more powerful, far more aware of themselves, and too bound up with the future of the Bolsheviks. Yet in practice, New York's committees did approach what Marx saw in the Commune, and Lenin in the soviets. They demonstrate how revolutionary the American Revolution was. Realizing what they signified and portended leads us to pose the question of how they finally ended and how New York's regular institutions finally gained a hegemony and a legitimacy that in their earliest years they most decidedly lacked.

V

There were men among New York's revolutionary leaders who recognized that establishing a general acceptance of the new state government would require more than simply proclaiming the constitution. They were the same men who had delayed the making of that constitution so that it would embody their ideas rather than the radical ones that triumphed in Pennsylvania; they were the same men who would be at the core of New York federalism in 1787 and 1788. They were men like John Jay, Robert R. Livingston, and Egbert Benson, each of whom held a strategic position during the first republican years. Jay was the chief justice of the state supreme court, and Livingston the chancellor, and each had a seat on the council of revision by virtue of his main office. Benson, sitting for Dutchess County in the assembly, was one of the legislature's leading figures from 1777 to 1781. These "constitutionalist patriots," as they may be called, bent every effort in 1777, 1778, and 1779 to restore the sharp boundary between the political system and its environment, to guarantee that only official rulers would exercise public power. Their old friend William Smith summed up their thought on direct public participation when he commented in 1776 that "the essential Properties of Civil Government are Power in the Magistracy. . . and the Establishment of that Power free from the arbitrary Exertions of a Few or the capricious Wantoness of the Multitude."[64]

Of particular concern, in the view of men like Jay and Benson, was a series of bills that went through the first session of the legislature, bills that recognized the existence and the power of the committee system. Jay and his colleagues confronted the problem as soon as they took their seats on the high court. They had been appointed by the convention that had written the constitution rather than by the constitutional council of appointment, and the fact worried them. They refused to exercise their functions until the council reappointed them, and they asked the legislature to approve what they had done. Jay and Livingston used their places on the council of revision to force it to reject such bills as one to continue an embargo on grain that had been imposed as an emergency measure by the extraordinary convention of late 1777. Jay wrote the veto message, stressing in it that the council objected to the bill because it "recognized the late supposed Council of Safety as a Legislative Body" and acknowledged the committee system, both of which were unknown to the constitution.

Meanwhile, Benson was working in the assembly to expunge mention of extralegal authority from bills that were being drafted. He even brought in a bill to indemnify the legislators who had taken part in the emergency convention. He and Jay were playing a complicated game, since both of them had been members of the Convention of the People, to whose action in appointing the supreme court Jay objected, and since Benson had taken a willing part in the emergency convention.[65] But their position was clear: it would be dangerous folly for the laws to recognize the committees in any way, for such a recognition would mean their acceptance of a continuing right of revolution. The right had been needed and used, but now it had to be securely enshrined in phrases like the "constitutional sovereignty of the people." It had, in other words, to be shifted from a working basis of action to a mythic basis of order. Such men greeted the revived committees of 1779 with similar attitudes. Benson, sure that they threatened the "subversion of the Constitution," wrote letter after letter expressing his hope that the movement for "*limitation* [of prices] may be *limited* to the city of Albany." One anxious official even tried to obtain a court indictment against the Albany committee in order to force it to disband. Yet the efforts of such men met little success. Only on the least significant points would the assembly accept Benson's efforts to redraft laws so they would not mention the committees, and the legislature overrode most of the vetoes that the council of revision sent down.[66]

The end of popular direct action came not from principled constitutional argument but rather from a dramatic demonstration by the new government that it could and would respond to popular pressure. During its first two sessions, in 1777, 1778, and early 1779, the legislature confined itself almost exclusively to war measures; needless to say, it had good reason for doing so. But in the third session, which followed the resurgence of the popular committees, there were sweeping changes in areas of intense popular concern. One was the royalist problem, in particular the question of whether to punish the Tories and confiscate what they owned. A confiscation bill passed the legislature in the second session, but its opponents were strong enough to delay it by forcing division after division, and when the council of revision rejected it, its supporters lacked the strength to override the veto. The whole affair was one of the most prolonged parliamentary fights of the early years of independence. But in the third session a new confiscation bill was approved almost without opposition by both the legislature and the council. In a similar vein, the legislature passed the law to recompense robbery victims out of a special tax on Tories. The highly political nature of the robberies in question has been shown; the response was appropriate. The transition in New York's official Tory policy from identifying and controlling them to punishing them was, in other words, the result of popular demand.[67]

The concerns of town dwellers and nonproducers of food, that is, the people directly responsible for the committee resurgence, were met by a fresh effort to impose statewide price controls. These had been tried before and had been found inadequate to the task of ending inflation; they were no more successful this time.[68] The point, however, was not so much the material achievement as the demonstration of responsiveness. As Huntington suggests, revolutionary governments can lead their people through the most dire economic straits if they can bring about a popular awareness (not "sense") of identification with the government, of possession and control of the institutions of power.[69]

Price controls, however, were anathema to the farmers who grew the grain, and the rural population's support was vital if the new institutions were to stand. Few farmers had become involved in the committee resurgence—a fact that distinguishes it from the popular conventions of Massachusetts in the 1780s—but rural discontent was very real. The legislature coped with it and, in a sense, brought consumers and small producers under one umbrella by means of a drastic change in the mode of taxation. Collecting taxes had proven no easy matter, given that none had been imposed directly for years, and the initial tax laws of 1778 and early 1779 imposed different rates on personal and real property. These generated enough division, for they marked the first time that New York tried to tax unimproved land. But in the third session, the legislature abandoned them and returned to the older practice of taxing on the basis of a quota for each county. Before independence this had been at the center of a tax system that hit the rich much more lightly than it did the middling sort and the poor. What was new now was that the law required assessors to make their decisions "according to the Estate and other Circumstances and Abilities to pay Taxes, of each respective Person, collectively considered." Whether "collectively considered" referred to a person's whole estate or whether it referred to her or his known place in the community, this was a radical piece of work. It gave elected assessors a license to soak the rich, and that they proceeded to do.[70] As a system of taxation this blend of old and new was far from elegant; observers in succeeding years regularly noted the logrolling that took place when the legislature was deciding each county's quota and bemoaned the class basis on which assessors did their work.[71] But of its popularity there can be no doubt.

The Forfeitures Act also was important in winning rural support. Whether it was rooted in class antagonism or simply in the desire to punish Tories, it was a direct response to the demands of groups like the Claverack Convention. It destroyed the estates and the power of men such as Frederick Philipse, Beverly Robinson, and Sir John Johnson, and the effect was to go a long way towards endearing the Revolution to tenant farmers. Not every tenant of a republican landlord had been willing to listen to British agents; not every tenant of a royalist was automatically a revolutionary. But it was in the landlord-ridden counties of Albany, Dutchess, Tryon, and Westchester that the state met its most severe problems of popular royalism and indifference. Now, at the same time that it was turning to punishment as its means of dealing with royalists, it was taking a general stance of hostility to landlords by expropriating the royalists among them and allowing punitive taxation of the rest. All three policies—repression, radical taxation, and confiscation—must be seen together if their impact is to be appreciated. Staughton Lynd has shown that the confiscation and sale of the great estates was a potent factor in turning tenants of Tory landlords from reluctant rebels to enthusiastic ones, and it seems a fair surmise that radical taxation, combined, perhaps, with the faint hope of more confiscations, began the process that turned tenants on the Whigs' estates from unashamed royalists to people who could live with the new order.[72]

In retrospect, then, it seems that the twelve months following May 1779 were crucial; it was during those months that the new institutions "took hold" among the people of the free counties. The problems faced by the republican government were great. The simultaneous upsurge of royalist militancy in Albany and Dutchess counties, the deterioration of the paper money accompanied by soaring prices, the outbursts of popular energy, and the rebirth of the revolutionary committees were the elements of a general social and political crisis. The strength that the new political system gained in coping, or in visibly trying to cope, with these problems can be seen in the events of subsequent years. Active royalism persisted, but after 1779 it worked at the level of conspiracy. The conspiracies commissioners even found time for such minor problems as sectarian pacifists whose stance was religious rather than political.[73] The economy remained in such frightful shape that in 1781 there was another brief flurry of committee activity. But this time it was confined to southern Albany County, and although it scared

Robert R. Livingston, it was different from the movement of two years before. Although the people involved declared, in words echoing 1779, that their grievances "unless soon remedied will tend to alienate the minds of the people from the Legislature," they were working on the assumption that the legislature would act. There is no evidence that they attempted or seriously considered direct action themselves, and they met little response from elsewhere in the state. The people behind this movement were Livingston Manor tenants; their forming a committee at all instead of a guerrilla group seems evidence that their confidence in the legislature was growing rather than waning.[74]

Consolidating the power of the new institutions was thus a process of great complexity. The state in which the process took place, redefined by the loss of Vermont and the southern district, by the migrations of royalists to Canada, New York City, and New England, and by civil war on the western frontier was very different from the pre-Revolution province. The people who were politically relevant for the new institutions were those royalists and neutrals who remained in the republican zone, together with upstate revolutionaries and with refugees from the southern district. In a way, this fragmentation of what had been New York made the task easier, for it saved the new institutions from having to deal with several large concentrations of people who denied the legitimacy of either the political community or the Revolution. The Vermonters were gone for good, and when the southern district was restored to the state at the end of 1783, large-scale emigration and the unquestionability of the Revolution's triumph made its reintegration easy. And ultimately, repression proved able to cope with the most serious of the royalists who remained upstate.

The immediate problem thus lay with the republicans who neither denied the propriety of the Revolution nor threatened the state's basic integrity and with royalists and neutrals whom the new system could "reach" in one way or another. That a problem existed, that legitimizing the regime was a different matter from legitimizing the state, was recognized by the men whom this chapter has identified as "constitutionalist patriots," but it was the actions of the legislature rather than the arguments of Benson and Jay that resolved it. The creation of a workable boundary between the new system and the citizens among whom and on whom it operated grew out of a recognition, forced on men in office by people out of it, that the boundary ought to be an open means of two-way communication rather than a fixed barrier.

But the people whose support was vital if the new order was to stand were not thinking in terms of the abstractions suggested by the terminology of systemic political science. Rather, they took to the streets, the fields, and the committee rooms because they had real interests at stake. The "constitutionalist patriots" in 1777, 1778, and 1779 used language akin to that of modern theorists in order to describe and to justify their hostility to committees and crowds, and there is no reason to doubt their sincerity. Yet Benson was worried about interference in the disposal of private property and in the course of commerce, as well as about constitutional irregularity. The Livingstons were plagued in the 1780s with radical taxation as the price for not being plagued, at least for a time, with radicalized tenants. What member of the old upper class would not have been worried when in 1779 a Poughkeepsie newspaper essayist called for a state monopoly of foreign trade and for special favoritism for the yeomanry? "A more equal distribution of property" was the essayist's goal.[75]

As we have seen, internal tensions of the sort that Benson feared had played a significant part in the creation of the committee movement and the major role in its continuation. The relationship between men in committee chambers and people outside them can be demonstrated by pointing to the congruent complexities of committee and crowd behavior and by reinforcing the point that the appearance of the committees gave new meaning to crowds themselves. It was, after all, the thinking and reasoning demonstrated in one of the earliest committee elections that inspired Gouverneur Morris to write his famous analysis of the class dynamics of 1774. Like their committeemen, New Yorkers in the late 1770s could be militant against the British enemy, Tories, landlords, hoarders, and aggrandizing merchants. The colonial predecessors of those crowds, especially the urban ones, had a long tradition and an accepted social role, but that acceptance had turned on a general acceptance of a corporatist social ideal. By the time of the war, many members of the elite were beginning to rationalize the values that they had manifested by their conspicuous consumption in the 1760s, and their new economic ideas accorded ill with corporatist practice.

People whose sort once would have responded to crowd action about matters of supply with efforts to control the market were now becoming free traders. They were convinced that relying on anything other than a free market to shape economic life was folly; they were moving out of the world of controls on prices and assizes of bread and into the fluid, jostling world of Adam Smith and James Madison. Egbert Benson said as much in 1779; hence one reason for the worry that the crowds and the committees of that year gave him. A food riot in New Windsor or popular price controls in Albany did not necessarily mean internal revolution, but they did betoken profound popular disagreement with the economic ideas of men who fancied themselves fit to lead. Thus they posed a significant threat to the social and political dominance of those men.

But if their dominance was challenged by the persistence of the popular movement after independence, it was also challenged by the positive and creative way in which the legislature responded to that movement. The same process of political innovation that was shoring up the power of New York's new government was also destroying the cohesion of the coalition that had led New York into independence. A partisan culture of a new sort began to emerge in the winter of 1779/80, and its maturation during the eight years that followed would complete the revolutionary transformation of New York's public life.

Part III

The Making of a Partisan Culture, 1777–1788

The right wing of its revolutionary coalition led New York into independence and republicanism. When the Convention of the People finally adjourned in 1777, the conservatives' fight seemed won. Besides the constitution itself, the offices that men of their sort held could be counted among their gains. Philip Schuyler spoke for them from the eminence of his major-generalship in the Continental army. John Jay would be chief justice of the state supreme court. Robert R. Livingston would be chancellor. It seemed certain that people like them would fill the governorship, the legislature, and New York's seats in Congress. There should be no wonder at the air of relief and of self-congratulation that fills their correspondence at the time.

But the spring of 1777 marked the high point rather than the consolidation of conservative control of New York's revolution. Though the people whom they had guided through the independence crisis had agreed most of all that they should stick together, they nonetheless had many distinct interests and perspectives. They had among them the raw material for other coalitions, different in form and in goals from the one of the mid-1770s. Between 1777 and 1781 the conservative politicians fought a losing battle to stay in power and to have the state adopt policies that they wanted. Meanwhile, others began to acquire the awareness of themselves as men with distinct interests that the conservatives had gained at the time of the coercive acts, and they began to act accordingly. Between 1782 and 1786 that "other side" developed from an inchoate group of political novices into a coherent force that dominated the state's political life.

The conservatives did not begin to reorganize until the war's end. When they did regroup, they found that gaining power was no longer a matter of "riding the torrent." Rather, they had to struggle against an opposition that could match them in its coherence and its self-awareness and that enjoyed a much broader popular base. The conservatives responded by displaying as much creativity and astuteness as they had shown at independence. They set out to make a popular base and to define a public agenda of their own. Recognizing that they could not defeat the radical party on ground that it had made its own, they built a by-pass around that ground in the form of the movement for the Federal Constitution. It was the interplay of all of these forces—the people, both rural and urban, whose energy gave punch to the revolutionary movement; the conservative politicians, who saw in the popular movement the gravest of dangers but who learned to accept it as something with which they had to live; and the radical politicians, who emerged from the movement and who believed by 1788 that they spoke for it—that completed the transformation of New York's political society.

Chapter 7

The Conservative Retreat, 1777–1782

New York's conservative leadership began to lose control of the Revolution almost as soon as the constitution of 1777 was promulgated. The loss took place on a number of levels and for a number of reasons. The earliest and the most visible sign came in the first election, when the Ulster County lawyer George Clinton defeated Philip Schuyler for the governorship. Clinton was an astute politician, and a "new man" of the Revolution, but by itself his victory did not betoken that the conservatives' world had turned upside down. His importance for the internal revolution lies rather in his gradual emergence as the representative of other, deeper changes. The most important of these lay outside the world of the politicians, for, as chapter 6 showed, the popular revolutionary movement persisted in full force for a good two years after the new state constitution supposedly was in effect. But there were other factors as well. The state legislature was full of men new to power, and though it took time, indeed years, for them to become a coherent bloc, they were from the beginning less than fully amenable to the leadership that the conservatives sought to give them. They showed their resistance in the policies they enacted, in their voting behavior. They gradually discovered that they could use the talents of their supposed betters for their own ends, and finally they realized that they could find such talents among themselves. It was they, not the conservatives, who responded positively and creatively to the fact that the revolutionary movement did not end when the constitutional government came into force. That response was at the heart of the conservative defeat. In practical terms, it meant the adoption by the state of policy after policy that they loathed. In power terms, it meant that the initiative was theirs no longer. What it amounted to was the achievment in New York on the level of policy-making and position-holding of the radicalism that triumphed in Pennsylvania in 1776 on the level of constitutionality.

I

During the spring of 1777 men all over New York jostled for public office. Some posts, such as the chancellorship and the three places on the supreme court, were filled by the Convention of the People, and that those posts went to men like Robert R. Livingston and John Jay is as full a measure as the state constitution itself of who held sway within the convention. Other posts, lesser ones like shrievalties and seats on county courts, would have to wait until the assembly elected four senators as a council of appointment and until the legislature passed acts to organize the detailed structure of the state government. Interest and competition thus focused on the governorship, the lieutenant-governorship, the senate, and the assembly. Even within the legislature not all seats would be filled by the voters. Because the southern district had been held by the British for months, the convention chose the district's members in both houses of the legislature and decreed that vacancies among these "ordinance" members would be filled by vote of the other house.

Many men either put themselves forward or were put up by others for the posts that remained available. The governorship was the great prize, and four men seriously considered it. One was John Jay, prime author of the state constitution and already chief justice. Jay realistically played down his chances of winning. Despite offers of support and assistance in Albany County, where he was weak, he told Philip Schuyler that he looked forward to addressing him as "your excellency" and advised his would-be supporters that when he considered "how well General Schuyler is qualified for that important office," he thought the Albanian "ought in justice to the public to be preferred."[1] Schuyler was the other conservative candidate, and he had more on which to base his hopes than just Jay's good opinion of him. The Livingston family agreed that William Livingston's accession to the governorship of New Jersey and their own unpopularity debarred any of them, and so they gave their support to their fellow landholder. Perhaps from reasons of local patriotism, perhaps because landlordism was well represented within it, the Albany committee likewise endorsed Schuyler, and it recommended his fellow Albanian Abraham Ten Broeck for lieutenant governor. Schuyler's candidacy thus represented the concerns of Albany as a sizable town and as the prime trading center of the free zone, those of the conservative professionals for whom Jay could speak, and those of the patriot fraction of the great landholders. The candidate himself thought the combination unbeatable: "They may chuse who they will," he boasted in private, "I will command them all."[2]

But Schuyler was challenged by two other men. One was John Morin Scott, the former radical Whig lawyer from New York City. Scott's candidacies for the provincial assembly had produced the nastiest politics of the late 1760s, and he was determined to make up for his humiliation then by obtaining a high office in the new order. While the convention still sat, he sought in vain for the chancellorship and the chief-justiceship, and his quest for the governor's chair proved as futile. The reasons for his defeat were complicated. He had already been smeared as homosexual, and his heavy drinking was well known. It was also true that as a man from occupied New York City who had participated in the trial of William Prendergast after the tenant rising of 1766, he had to cope with having no immediate power base and with the direct hostility of many upstaters. Moreover, though Scott cultivated the image of a radical and a democrat, his behavior both before and after independence was mercurial and opportunistic. Thus on the committee that drafted the state constitution he joined James Duane in wanting an upper house that would be completely divorced from the principle of representation, and during his service in the state senate his behavior would repeatedly dismay others.[3]

The fourth candidate was Clinton, Ulster lawyer, former assemblyman, defender of Alexander McDougall during McDougall's ordeal before the provincial assembly, and by 1777 a brigadier general in both the state militia and the Continental army. Clinton had all of Schuyler's advantages and many more. He could count on the support of the yeomen of Orange and Ulster counties. His prewar record placed him firmly in the revolutionary camp, and he suffered from none of the popular suspicion of secret royalism that plagued Schuyler. Questions of royalism aside, as a ranking officer he enjoyed a prominence almost as great as Schuyler's, but his plain manner meant that he did not suffer from the Albanian's well-earned reputation for arrogance. Finally, though he came from outside the circles in which the powerbrokers of New York traditionally had operated, the great men knew that Clinton was someone with whom they could work. He had contacts with the best professionals through William Smith, his teacher in the law. As assemblymen during the DeLancey period, he and Schuyler had worked together closely. As the best politician that the west-bank counties had ever produced, he had come to know well the magnates across the river.[4]

Clinton won, taking both the governorship and the lieutenant-governorship. His victory rested on the support of farmers in his own Ulster County and neighboring Orange and on that of small freeholders and tenants in Dutchess, of a significant minority even in Schuyler's Albany stronghold, and of soldiers. That it shocked the patriciate is clear. Schuyler wrote Jay that the Ulsterman had "played his cards better than was expected" and that "his family and connections do not entitle him to so distinguished a predominance." William Smith, making up his mind during his house arrest on Livingston Manor to move from neutrality to outright royalism, could not bring himself to address his former clerk as "your excellency." In an age of formality, he continued to address him in correspondence as "Dear George" and spoke disparagingly of him behind his back as "George the Governor." The combination of yeoman suspicion of the east bank, tenant discontent, and soldiers' preference for a popular general over a haughty one had given the conservatives their first serious defeat. A man whom the Revolution had made was in power.[5]

When the assembly and the senate finally gathered in September 1777, they, too, were full of new men. Among all 290 assemblymen who served during the Confederation period, only 6 had been members of the provincial assembly. But 85 were veterans of at least one of the revolutionary congresses, and 94 had served on a revolutionary committee. Fully 161 had no experience at any of these levels. The senate differed only in the relative absence of such totally inexperienced men. A mere 6 of the 55 senators of the Confederation era had been provincial assemblymen, but 34 had sat in at least one provincial congress and 31 had been county committeemen. "The rulers of this state," as Alexander Hamilton would call them in 1782, were either men who had acquired their high-level political experience in the heat of the Revolution or men who began gaining it in the state legislature itself.[6]

Part of the reason for this influx of novices was that only a few of the old order's legislators in fact chose independence; the *Pennsylvania Journal and Weekly Advertiser* was correct in 1775 when it attributed New York's sloth in joining the resistance to the many ties of interest and family that bound the province's leaders to Britain. Of those who did not move to royalism most followed the path to glory taken by Philip Schuyler and Philip Livingston, who became, respectively, a Continental general and a signer of the Declaration of Independence. Only a few, like state senators Abraham Ten Broeck of Albany and Lewis Morris of Westchester or assemblymen Charles DeWitt and Johannes G. Hardenbergh of Ulster, appeared in the new legislature.[7]

Quite apart from the fate of the old elite, another reason for the predominance of new men was the size of the new institutions. There had been thirty-one seats in the provincial assembly at its largest, and only twenty-seven for most of the half-century that preceded independence. The electorate filled those seats at intervals that might stretch to as long as eleven years. By contrast, even without the counties that seceded to form Vermont, there were sixty-five state assemblymen, all, save the ordinance members, elected annually, and twenty-four senators, each serving a three-year term. The numbers in themselves indicated that the new institutions would be filled by men whom the Revolution itself had politicized.

Jackson Turner Main has shown that these men, whether members of the senate or the assembly, were markedly less wealthy, less educated, and less cosmopolitan than their predecessors had been. Many of them were honest nonentities, people who had gained enough of the respect of their neighbors to win a term or two and who then drifted back to obscurity. To call them nonentities is not to belittle them; the very fact that people like Teunis Kuyper and Roeluff Van Houten of Orange, John Rowen of Charlotte, or Michael Etdick of Tryon could be members of the first state legislature is evidence that that legislature had been born in revolution. William Smith recognized as much. He dismissed one of them as "one Rowen of Charlotte County. . . a Farmer of New Perth & tenant of Oliver DeLanceys" who had "been 7 years in the Country." Smith, one of the first men of the province, was more than perplexed at having to beg such a man to explain a decision of the emergency council of safety.[8]

In the case of many counties, it is possible to see not only a haphazard emergence of new men but also the make-up of the county's revolutionary coalition. The counties of consensus, Orange and Ulster, were the most likely to send veterans of the old assembly. Orange County senator Henry Wisner and assemblyman John Coe and the Ulster assemblymen Johannes G. Hardenbergh, Abraham Hasbrouck, and Charles DeWitt had all been members before. Together, they accounted for five of the eleven state legislators—the assemblymen among them for four of the six in the lower house—who had been. Even in these counties, of course, many newcomers found their way to power, and it seems significant that while their voters were sending familiar men to the assembly, they were electing new men to the senate. William Smith knew the Hardenberghs, the DeWitts, and the Hasbroucks, but he was unfamiliar with such west-bank senators as Levi Pawling, Arthur Parks ("a senator Arthur Parks," as he archly put it),[9] and Jesse Woodhull.

These were men who had been town supervisors and clerks, assessors, and committeemen. They were farmers who were prosperous but by no means wealthy, small merchants, and professionals. Before the Revolution, most of them had been content with their private lives, but now thay had become public figures. Some of them found it enjoyable: Jesse Woodhull, with patent pride, told his sometime neighbor St. John de Crevecoeur of how he carried out his duties as county sheriff and colonel of the state militia. Nor were they necessarily provincial clods; the same Woodhull had journeyed to Surinam, and he had a brother who was a Yale professor.[10] But they were not climbers, and they represented constituencies that remained as stable as it was possible to remain in their time. Their constituents were well pleased with their service, and when they replaced them it was one at a time, not wholesale, and then with men of similar stripe. When Woodhull stepped down from the senate, the seat went to his hand-picked successor, Thomas Palmer. When Wisner left, his place was taken by his former colleague in the provincial assembly John Haring. And though by the fifth session Ulster had only one man in its delegation who had been there in the first—Hardenbergh—the delegation still included two others who had sat in the old assembly. Men like this were "chieftains," much like their famous neighbor George Clinton. They were farmers, country lawyers, shopkeepers, surveyors, and schoolmasters who were well placed in their narrow, secure societies.

The counties of conflict sent different sorts of men and replaced them in a different way. The initial Dutchess delegation told the story of how the Revolution had been made in that county. It included Dirck Brinckerhoff, whose defeat of the senior Robert R. Livingston for an assembly seat in 1768 had signaled the start of the Livingston family's political decline. Brinckerhoff was joined by a self-made militia colonel named Jacobus Swartwout. But the voters also chose Gilbert Livingston, of a minor branch of the great family, and in Egbert Benson and Anthony Hoffman they picked two men closely associated with the landlord class. Roughly the same delegation went to the second session, but in the third four men new to politics came forth. One was Henry Luddington, a ranking militia officer and a tenant on the Beverly Robinson estate who did not become owner of his farm until after the turn of the nineteenth century. Albany sent a similar mixture. Its first ten-man delegation included three Van Rensselaers and Walter Livingston, of Livingston Manor, but the lines of stress within the county could be seen from the start. Livingston was given only a seat in the assembly, but the county made senators of Abraham Yates and Dirck W. Ten Broeck. Yates would become a cardinal figure in the legislative radicalism of the 1780s (we will look at him in the next chapter). Of Ten Broeck's election William Smith said, "It is a proof of the Fears or Disaffection of the Wealthy that the Great Offices go to meaner Hands—From Albany they recommend a Mr. Ten Broeck for a Senator—Peter [Livingston] or Walter L[ivingston] for an Assemblyman. Ten Broeck was a Justice of the Peace who would not be perswaded formerly to act till Mr. L promised to assist him...the Jealousy of a Spirit of Levellism never rests till every Elevation is depressed."[11] Among the Albany assemblymen of the first session, there was one, William B. Whiting, of King's District, whose presence represented a clear challenge to the right to rule of the Livingstons, the Van Rensselaers, and the Schuylers. Most of the members of that delegation were reelected to the second assembly, but Whiting was one of only two who survived from that to the third. In the third session the men of great family were replaced by such people as Flores Bancker, Cornelius Humfrey, and Phineas Whiteside, whose names tell their stories. There, as in Dutchess, a politics based on coalescence was giving way to one based on competition.

The make-up of the southern district delegations reflected not the will of any electorate but rather that of the revolutionary convention. Nonetheless, it crystallized the state of the region's politics at the point of independence. The New York City ordinance members included at least three mechanics, the silversmith Abraham Brasher, the cooper Daniel Dunscomb, and the baker Abraham P. Lott. Dunscomb and Brasher has been members of the intensely radical Body of Mechanics, and Dunscomb its chairman. The delegation also included small merchants like John Berrien, Jacobus Van Zandt, and Van Zandt's nephew Peter Pra Van Zandt. Both Van Zandts, Brasher, and Lott had been active Sons of Liberty. But coalition politics was at work among the city people too. Besides these radicals and men of humble origin, the assemblymen included John Jay's brother Frederick and such newly politicized figures as the merchant Evert Bancker and Robert Harpur, a professor at King's College. The ordinance senators included Philip Livingston, the prominent sugar manufacturer Isaac Roosevelt, the brothers Lewis and Richard Morris, and William Smith's friend John Jones.[12]

The coalition politics that brought this mixture of men to power was based on local awareness and local circumstances rather than on statewide partisanship. From the beginning, men did try to manage elections, but during the first years, they went about it in a local, haphazard way. Their efforts reflected more than anything else their sense of what had gone into the making of the revolutionary movement in each separate county. Before the 1777 election the Albany committee decided that four of the western district's six senate seats should be filled by men from its own county. It picked its candidates and offered the other two seats to the Tryon committee to fill as it chose. The six men whom the committees then jointly put forward were elected.[13] At the same time a handbill was circulated in Newburgh, Ulster County, nominating candidates for five of the county's assembly seats, putting up Ulstermen for two of the six middle-district senate seats and asking for support for those two from the other two counties in the district, Dutchess and Orange. Meanwhile, George Clinton was learning that Charles DeWitt and Levi Pawling were likely to obtain the senate seats which belonged informally to Ulster and that the county's assembly seats had been divided between its northern and southern parts. Two separate slates were running in the north, but in the south there was only one.[14]

The very make-up of the Dutchess assembly delegation, comprising as it did both insurgent politicians and spokesmen for the landlords, is evidence that similar arrangements had been made there, in all probability by the county committee. Only in Tryon did these first elections provoke outspoken, angry conflict. The two men whom the committee there put forward for the senate were Isaac Paris, a country merchant and old enemy of the Johnson family, and Nicholas Herkimer, commander of the county militia. Paris was challenged for the seat by Jelles Fonda, a landholder and a Johnson ally, and Paris's friends responded by spreading charges that Fonda was a secret royalist. Fonda lost dismally, receiving only twelve votes in all of Tryon, but because of Herkimer's death at the Battle of Oriskany he did in fact become a senator. During his tenure, however, his enemies made his life as miserable as they could.[15]

The assemblymen and senators who listened to George Clinton's opening address in September 1777 were thus at the vortex of a complicated political process. The governor himself had won his post in a statewide election by one-hundred-pound freeholders. Restriction of the gubernatorial and senatorial electorate to such men had been part of the conservatives' plan for keeping the Revolution in control. That Clinton (rather than Schuyler or Jay) had won was evidence that the plan had been ill-conceived;[16] nevertheless, Clinton was a man with whom the magnates could work. The legislature was full of new men who could never have approached the center of power in the old order and whose very presence pointed out that the Revolution had politicized the anger of whole groups of men. But most of them were there as partners in coalitions, and they were more concerned to keep together what was left of New York than to carry on an internal struggle. There was, after all, a war to be won against the British and against the many Yorkers whose taking of the British side made that struggle itself an internal one.

II

Though most of the new legislators were novices in both personal and social terms, they lived in a culture that had long experience of parliamentary institutions and practices. Among those practices was the way that legislators sorted themselves into the few and the many, the leaders and the led. The frontbenchers in the colonial assemblies had been the men who held such positions as the speakership or the chairmanship of a standing committee. When their assemblies gave them such honors, they usually were putting a visible seal on the recipient's combination of recognizable skill, superior education, and social standing. Such practices were not peculiar to America, nor did they end with the Revolution. Sir Robert Walpole in the Georgian House of Commons, John Robinson in the eighteenth-century House of Burgesses, William Pitt Fessenden in the Civil War United States Senate, and Lyndon Johnson and Sam Rayburn in the twentieth-century Congress were men who would have recognized one another readily and who bore their visible marks of distinction with pride.[17]

The legislature in revolutionary New York organized itself differently. The assembly did name a speaker, and each house did appoint standing committees, but the evidence is strong that the members, particularly the assemblymen, went to great lengths to prevent specialization of function, concentration of power, and differentiation of honor among themselves. That they went to these lengths is as much an indication as is their make-up that the legislature was a revolutionary body as well as a parliamentary one.

The assembly's speakership had long been the grand prize in provincial politics. When John Cruger replaced Philip Livingston in the chair after the election of 1769, the change marked with finality the DeLancey victory over the Livingston party. But for most of the Confederation period, and especially during the war years, holding the speakership symbolized not the triumph of party but the fragility of coalition. The first speaker was Walter Livingston, a man terrified by the Revolution and reluctant to accept even his nomination to the assembly, let alone his elevation to its chief position. It seems clear that the assembly gave him the chair as a gesture of consolation for the privileges his family had lost and of respect for its record in the struggle against Britain.[18] Livingston held the speakership through two sessions, and when he lost his seat at the end of the second the House chose in his place Evert Bancker. The new speaker was a minor New York City merchant and an ordinance member who had entered politics seriously only during the final crisis with Britain. As speaker, he acted in the manner of a neutral presiding officer rather than in that of a partisan leader. One incumbent disliking even to be an assemblyman and another being a nonentity, the wartime speakership was a shadow of what the provincial office had been.[19]

Though the legislature named standing committees in every session, it did not in any way allow its committeemen to form an internal elite. The assembly appointed a heavy majority of its members actually in attendance to committee seats; thus in the opening days of the first session attendance hovered at around thirty-eight members, and twenty-eight of them became committeemen. The house never formally designated any member as a committee chairman. The inference is fair that the first-named on each list of committeemen was in fact chairman, but he received no public honor or distinction for it. The house never gave tenure from session to session of either the putative chairmanships or of seats on particular committees. A man whose name came first on a committee in one session might be a member of another committee or of no committee at all in the next.

For all the care that each new legislature took in naming its standing committees, it gave them very little to do. The assembly's normal practice in making public policy was to name an ad hoc committee for each problem that came before it and to charge that committee with framing a proposal. The proposal would then go before a committee of the whole house, whose debates in turn would be considered again in normal floor session. Weighing the relative importance of the drafting committees would involve a host of subjective judgments, though some distinctions can be drawn between committees of major significance and those of little import.[20] But the noteworthy point is that with very few exceptions,[21] the assembly originated its policies not via an established structure that accorded recognition to the movers and the shakers but rather in a fluid way that gave every member a chance to take part actively in most of the process.

The legislature established these procedures during its first session. The way it did so shows that this avoidance of a rigid internal structure was a matter of the members' choice rather than simply one of unthinking continuation of pre-Revolution practice. In its first weeks, during September and

October 1777, the assembly jostled continuously over procedure, the jostling again and again pitting men who wanted to set up an inegalitarian structure against men who did not. Much of the battling was over patronage, for the house had a number of posts either fully or partly to give. It was charged to name four senators to the council of appointment at the start of every session. These senators would, with the governor, fill the state's civil and military offices. Together with the senate, the assembly named New York's delegates to Congress. If a vacancy fell among the ordinance senators, it was the assemblymen who chose a replacement.

In one of the earliest meetings, assemblyman Egbert Benson, of Dutchess County, tried to preempt the questions both of how the councillors of appointment would be named and of who they would actually be by nominating four senators for service. Instead of taking Benson's nominations to a vote, the house resolved that it would take a complete set of four nominations from each of the members in turn and then vote on all the senators whose names had been put forward. It adopted the same method for electing both congressmen and ordinance senators, resolving the issue each time by a formal division. Its records do not indicate how it chose its own committeemen, whether for the standing committees or the ad hoc ones. They may have been elected from the floor, or they may have been chosen by the speaker. But it did rebuff an attempt by Gouverneur Morris to have it name its standing committees immediately. Morris made that attempt four days after Benson's motion on the councillors of appointment, and on the same day that he made it, he tried again to preempt the council issue by putting forward a nomination out of his turn.[22]

It is clear that the assembly was refusing to let Morris and Benson seize the initiative. It is also clear that their attempt to seize it was of a piece with their larger concerns. Both of them represented the Whig fraction of the Hudson Valley landlord class. It was Morris who in 1774 had seen the "poor reptiles" in the "mob" beginning "to think and to reason." Benson, despite his chairmanship of the revolutionary committee in Dutchess, was central in the group of "constitutionalist patriots" identified in the last chapter. In their view, a situation in which every legislator held a working equivalence to every other legislator was almost as bad as one in which crowds and committees were the places where power was to be found. They correctly saw that that situation was just as much an element in the Revolution as were the crowds and committees themselves.

In practice, however, some men did emerge even in the earliest sessions as at least potential wielders of extraordinary power. These were the men whom each house named to committees much more frequently than their fellows, and in the assembly Benson found himself the foremost among them. He was the only assemblyman to serve on more than one standing committee during all of the four sessions of which he was a member, and in the third session he held the probable chairmanship of two of them. The house also put him on many more ad hoc committees than it did any of his colleagues. He sat on nine altogether over the first two sessions, on thirty-one in the third, and on forty-one in the fourth. During those last two sessions especially he worked at a rate that must have been staggering. To take just one example, over 27 and 28 January 1780 the house put him on two drafting committees, both of major policy importance, heard his report on behalf of one of them, and received a bill that he brought in on his own.[23]

Benson aspired to be leader of the house, and he came close to achieving his goal. The conditions and constraints under which the house let him wield his influence, however, underscore the revolutionary quality of the time through which he was living. From his first intervention, when he joined Morris in trying to "de-democratize" the house's internal procedure, Benson struggled for the principles and the policies that he thought desirable. As chapter 6 showed, he worked throughout the first session to keep the laws from legitimating the revolutionary committees, and that was part of a larger program that he and his associates acted consistently to realize. Their first concern was that the written state constitution be established in practice as superior to the immediate will of either the people or the legislators. Their second was that the state's economic life be organized around an uncontrolled private sector rather than around public regulation of commerce. Their third was that "radicalism" be held down and moderated in any way.

Benson's group had already learned that what was most important to conserve was not any of these goals but rather their own ability to influence measures at all. Robert R. Livingston summed up their project in 1777 with his metaphor of swimming with a stream that could not be stemmed. In practical terms, this meant not just the adroit delays that had permitted them to write the kind of state constitution they wanted but also their acceptance that they would have to take part in and even lead attacks on positions they would have preferred to defend. Their strategy through the first years of statehood was to give way on as much as they had to when they had to, but to recoup whatever they could whenever they could.

They had to give away a great deal, and often they regained little. An illustration can be seen in their approach to managing the economy. Benson's four years in the legislature coincided with both long-term and short-term crises in American economic history. The long-range crisis turned on the transition from a corporatist to a free-market economy, and the short-term crisis on the wild inflation that accompanied the collapse of the Continental dollar. Benson and his associates, firmly committed to the coming order rather than to the waning order, believed that it was futile to fight the inflation by such corporatist devices as embargoes on trade, wage and price regulation, or, especially, by the continuation and then the revival of the revolutionary committees. Chapter 6 showed the steps they took against the committees, and it needs to be stressed again that they opposed them on grounds of both constitutionality and political economy. Benson was sure in 1779 that the revived committee threatened "the subversion of the constitution," but he was equally sure as the price-control movement was getting under way in Albany that he wanted "the *limitation*" to be "*limited*" to that city.[24]

The "constitutionalist patriots" stood firm on the issue of the committees, but they proved willing to compromise on other aspects of the problem. Early in the second legislative session, after the first flare-up of the committee issue had died down, Benson himself wrote a bill to post guards at the borders of the state in order to prevent the export of flour and grain to places where it could fetch a higher price. Later he served on a committee that the assembly appointed to investigate violations of that embargo. In 1780 he drafted a law to reinstitute the very price controls that he loathed. These, however, must be read as a tactical concession. The prime alternative to price controls in the fight against inflation was heavy taxation, and in every debate on a tax bill, Benson led the efforts to collect as much as possible and to impose the most demanding terms. His proposals for the sums to be collected consistently were the highest that any member put forward, often running to twice as high as others wanted. In the second session, he proposed a rate on real estate of two shillings to the pound instead of the one shilling that the house adopted. In the third, when the voting was on a lump sum rather than on a general rate, he wanted it set at three million dollars instead of the two-and-a-half-million-dollar figure that was finally settled upon. During debates on another tax bill later in the session, Benson wanted to raise three million more than the two million dollars to which the house agreed. He worked against taxation on the principle of assessment by "circumstances and abilities." He even opposed a stay of taxes for hard-pressed people who were already creditors to the government as a result of loans or impressment of their animals, wagons, and crops.[25]

Roughly the same point, namely, that they stood fast when they could and yielded when they had to, holds for the response of Benson's group to the Tory problem. They faced two separate dimensions of the issue, one being the danger that royalists actually posed to the state and the other the anger that was mounting against them among the patriot population. The former was purely a question of policing, for no one denied that the Tories had to be kept from interfering with the war,[26] but the latter was more divisive. Over the first two legislative sessions, policy on royalists was aimed at keeping them in control and was encapsulated in only three laws. One established the commissioners for conspiracies. A second, passed in response to a request from Governor Clinton, allowed the removal of Tories from places near sensitive military positions. A third, aimed at stopping illicit trade with the British zone, was "to prevent abuses of Flags of Truce."[27]

Chapter 6 showed how the basis of the state's policy shifted from control and conversion of the Tories to punishment of them. It showed, as well, that the shift came about in response to heavy pressure from angry republicans. The centerpiece of the new policy was the Confiscation Act of 1779, and the way it was passed illustrates the predicament in which Benson and his friends found themselves. The act was the second attempt to seize the royalists' property, the first having been made in the previous session. On that first occasion the bill had met little opposition in the assembly, but its passage through the senate was stormy, and when the council of revision vetoed it, the attempt to override the veto failed. The veto had the support of the entire council, that is, of Governor Clinton as well as the four high judges who sat on it with him. The governor observed privately that he thought the bill "neither founded on Justice or warranted by good Policy or the Spirit of the Constitution." But on the same day that the first bill finally died, the assembly named a committee to draw up a new one. Benson himself drafted it, and two weeks after the start of the next session he introduced it. This revised act passed with hardly any resistance.[28]

A surface reading of these events would suggest that the difference was simply Benson's skillful revision. Observers commented, after all, that he was one of the few men in the legislature who could draft a bill in proper legislative form.[29] But deeper forces were at work, and Benson himself had great doubts about confiscation. He knew how central confiscation was as a popular concern, most especially in his own county of Dutchess, and he knew that his own chances of reelection would be small if he opposed it publicly. After the defeat of the first bill, he told John Jay that it had been "the most important matter" of the session and that though it was "far from being unexceptionable," he wished it had passed. Public stands against confiscation could be left to Jay and Livingston, secure in their tenure on the bench and in the council, and to the ordinance legislators, who faced no electorate. Livingston himself thought that "never was there a greater compound of folly, avarice and injustice, than our new Confiscation Bill, to which Bensons compromising genius not a little contributed."[30] But the difference was simply that Benson had understood more quickly than Livingston that in political terms confiscation was becoming a necessity. By the third session, Livingston and the ordinance legislators were finally understanding that fact, and as a result they gave the bill no opposition. It was public anger that changed their minds.

When Benson could either postpone or weaken the process of seizure, he did. Even before the first bill was introduced, the house put him on a committee to deal with a massive petition demanding that a confiscation act be passed before that meeting rose. Though his name came last among the committeemen, he brought in their report. In it he maintained that the petition ought to be rejected, for the time remaining before adjournment was too short for a bill to be drafted and passed. Time indeed was short, and it was not until the following meeting that a bill was introduced. But Benson's argument contrasts oddly with his riposte one session later when another member moved for a quick adjournment. Then his position would be that the assemblymen should remain in session until their work was done "in Pursuance of the Trust reposed in them by their constituents."[31]

The real sign that a member was a radical friend of confiscation was his position on whether and how to sell the forfeitures. The pressure for confiscation had been most powerful among small farmers who had learned to hate the overweening ways of the great landlords, and especially among tenants. But as long as the confiscated land remained in the state's hands, a chance remained open to restore it to its pre-Revolution owners. Benson consistently acted to postpone sales and to see that they took place on the most demanding terms, if they had to take place at all. While the second bill was under debate he voted against allowing sales of unimproved lands. Later, after the bill had passed, he opposed altogether the introduction of a bill for selling the land. Despite his opposition to sales, the assembly named him to a committee to draft a sales bill, but in February 1780 he again voted not to sell unimproved property. In March of that year the senate sent down a resolution for postponing sales, and Benson was one of the minority of assemblymen who wanted to concur in it. A full year later, at the very end of his legislative career, he voted against a proposal to double the time that the law allowed purchasers to pay for what they had bought. For Benson, confiscation had to be, but the line could be drawn at redistribution.[32]

Benson's role in the first years of the legislature is important because in effect he was the sole representative of the Hudson Valley landlords. Although Walter Livingston was speaker during the first two sessions, he proved ineffectual. So did Gouverneur Morris during his single term. Philip Livingston died before he could make his influence felt in the senate, and the new head of the family, Robert R. Livingston, was busy with higher things, as chancellor. So were John Jay, as chief justice, and Pierre Van Cortlandt, as lieutenant governor. Frederick Philipse, Beverly Robinson, Roger Morris, Philip Skene, and Sir John Johnson were royalists. The brother senators Lewis and Richard Morris were possibly the only legislators giving extended service during Benson's assembly tenure who really can be counted as grandees.[33]

The task that Benson took upon himself thus formed an essential part of the strategy with which New York's elite coped with the revolutionary crisis. Using his skills as a lawyer and his eminently sound sense as a politician and drawing on seemingly inexhaustible reserves of energy, he battled against radical policies, for the absolute supremacy of the constitution, and for a working set of institutions that would enable men like himself to have far more power than the farmers, artisans, old radicals, and other newcomers by whom he found himself surrounded. He and his associates were adroit, acting in a flexible, intelligent manner to conserve their own position of power. In contrast with their Pennsylvania colleagues, they did not suffer a rout either at the point of independence or during the first few years after it. Benson remained an assemblyman for four terms, despite Robert R. Livingston's prediction that he would lose his seat at the end of the second term.[34] Livingston held onto the chancellorship, and Jay to the chief justiceship. New York's seats in Congress were filled by men like Philip Livingston, Philip Schuyler, James Duane, John Jay, William Duer, and Gouverneur Morris. Yet by the end of Benson's time in the assembly most of what he and his friends had fought for was lost.

They had lost on the committee question, for the laws recognized the committees and granted legitimacy to much of what they had done. They had lost on the Tory question, for royalist property had been seized and was on its way to redistribution. They had lost on economic affairs. In tax policy, the state had begun by taxing unimproved property as well as improved land and had moved to taxing on a principle that let an assessor rate anyone—landlord, yeoman, artisan, merchant, or tenant—on the basis of what his community thought of him. Moreover, laws derived from corporatist political economy formed the basis of the state's response to the inflation crisis. The conservatives had lost on internal procedure. Throughout the war, the legislature chose congressmen, councillors of appointment, and ordinance legislators in a way that gave no member a chance to seize the initiative. The daily business of the assembly, with its endless parade of drafting committees and committees of the whole, worked to the same effect. And the fact that Benson found himself forced to actually draft and introduce much of the legislation that reflected the losses his group was suffering suggests that rather than being the leader who took his less sophisticated colleagues along a path he had chosen, he became their servant, following where they wanted to go.

III

Benson's inability to manage the legislature sprang from the magnitude of the problems that he faced rather than from organized opposition to what he stood for. Neither in the genesis of public policies nor in their enactment did the legislators of the first four sessions show the persistent regular opposition that must be present if we are to speak of real parties among them. What they showed instead was that both among themselves and among their people existed the elements of a partisanship that would mature over the next decade. These elements included the most fundamental political, social, and economic questions of the time. They began with the constitutional problem of the relationship between regular institutions and popular action. They included the two questions of policy most bound up with the committee revival, those concerning the state's economic life and the position that the government ought to take on royalism. The problems also included the presence of all those new men who surrounded Benson in the assembly chamber. Principles, policies, and people in power—these are the very stuff of partisanship in a politically conscious society. Two things, however, kept that partisanship from maturing in the very first years. The most important was the awareness of all republican New Yorkers that they had more important things to do than brawl with one another. The second was that however aware Benson and his associates were that their interests were in danger and that concerted action was needed to defend them, the new men had not developed anything like that self-consciousness or that organization.

Governor Clinton's role during the war years illustrates both of these points. That his election was a surprise and a defeat for the magnates is beyond question. That by the time of the debate on the Federal Constitution he would be the clear focus of opposition to them is also beyond doubt. But as a war governor, he was more concerned with preserving what was left of New York than with enacting a partisan program within it.

Constitutionally, Clinton bore the responsibility to "inform the Legislature, at every session, of the condition of the state. . . [and] to recommend such matters to their consideration as shall appear to him to concern its good government, welfare, and prosperity." Clinton took that charge seriously, recommending policy after policy in his messages to the legislature. The editor of those messages finds that some 170 laws were passed and 40 other actions taken during the Confederation period in response to the governor's suggestions.[35] In the first years of his governorship, however, the "Clintonian program" was to hold the state together.

The governor's main concerns were three. The first was to keep the army and the militia in the field and to use them to prevent the loss of any more territory to the British. The second was to raise the supplies the military needed. The third was to undo the secession of Vermont. Clinton's links with the militia and with the Continental army were strong. While Jay, Livingston, Duer, and Gouverneur Morris were playing their delaying game so they could write a state constitution that would suit them Clinton was taking primary responsibility for fortifying the Hudson Highlands. He had been brigadier general of the Ulster and Orange militia since the end of 1775, and in March 1777 Congress gave him the same rank in the Continental service and made him commandant of the Highland posts. He offered to resign his state commission at that point, but the convention refused to let him do it. Clinton remained an officer on active duty throughout the war, and at its end Congress gave him a second star as a gesture of thanks. In addition, his brother James, also a Continental brigadier general, gained distinction as second-in-command of the expedition that Congress and the state jointly sent against the Iroquois and the western royalists in 1779.[36]

Clinton's close involvement with the military struggle, and perhaps his awareness that his first election had been based on the votes of soldiers, explains his attitude toward the state's economic problems throughout the war. His worry, quite simply, was that if the economic crisis went far enough, New York's ability to resist the enemy would collapse. With British armies in New York and Montreal, and with militant royalists in the Hudson Valley and on the western frontier, his fears were justified. He had, after all, stood at the center of things while St. Leger's troops were pushing east from Oswego, and Burgoyne's south from Canada, and he personally had organized what little defense the state put up against the expedition that his distant cousin Sir Henry Clinton had sent up the Hudson at the same time.[37]

What Clinton wanted most of all was to tax, since he knew that only through heavy taxation could the money be raised to buy arms and to pay, clothe, house, and feed the troops. He recognized, as did most politicians, that the tax laws of the provincial era were hopelessly inequitable and inefficient, and early in his first term he passed to the legislature those of another state to provide a model for reform. As the economic crisis deepened, he pleaded with the legislature to cope by taxing surplus money out of circulation rather than by trying to fix prices. During the second session, he poured scorn on a senator who campaigned against a tough tax law, and he told Gouverneur Morris that though he wished that bill "could meet the Approbation of Senate, this I despair of." Like most men who wanted hard taxation, he regretted the decision made by the third legislature to abandon statewide tax rates in favor of county quotas and radical assessment. After the first bill written along those lines had been passed, he told Chancellor Livingston that he hoped the next would be based on better principles. It was actions of this sort that Alexander Hamilton had in mind when in 1782 he explained what he saw as a decline in the governor's popularity. It was due, Hamilton thought, to "causes that do him honor—the vigorous execution of some necessary laws that bore hard upon the people."[38]

The other issue in which Clinton took a direct and active interest was Vermont. He saw the secessionist movement as posing as grave a threat to New York's integrity as the war, and he acted accordingly. The governor always spoke of the Green Mountain people with phrases like "revolted subjects of this state" and "rebellious northeastern districts," even when others had begun conceding the verbal point and simply calling the region Vermont. He corresponded with Yorker loyalists there, and they carefully tended his ire by telling him of their sufferings. He spoke to the legislature on the problem, and when a set of conciliatory resolutions had no effect, he told it that "all claims on the justice and even the generosity of this State have been fully satisfied." He pressed the delegates in Congress so hard that they corresponded among themselves about how to mollify him. In 1781, when the senate gave way and passed a resolution conceding Vermont's independence, he threatened that he would prorogue the legislature if the assembly so much as considered it.[39] Vermont, for him, assumed the qualities of an *idée fixe*, but his unbending determination that the secessionist movement should not succeed was of a piece with his situation as a war governor.

For the period of actual warfare, Clinton must be regarded as the major leader but not the only key figure in a coalition. He knew and could work with the state's conservative politicians, though whether he was aware of the correspondence and the strategy-making that they carried on among themselves is doubtful. He recognized that the state needed the talents of men like Benson and Jay and that these men shared his prime concern. But it was still a fact that on some deep level his very presence in the governorship was an affront to them. The knew that; whether he did cannot be said.

Within the legislature and among the politicized people outside it, the politics of coalescence was far less stable. During the first four sessions, from 1777 to 1781, both the public arena and the legislative chambers were places of conflict, often angry conflict, rather than of agreement. It was this conflict that gave rise to the radical quality that the state's laws began to take on in the third session and to attempts at radical policies even before then.

Evidence of popular opinion about what the state government should do is extremely hard to find for the first two sessions, but evidence of divisiveness among the legislators is not at all difficult to find. The first session of the assembly took sixty roll calls, and the second fifty-four, and though these included many divisions that were merely trivial, they also covered many important matters. Among such matters were the whole question of the committees, taxation, economic controls, Tory policy in general, and the first attempt at confiscation. Some of these issues were forced on the legislature by its own members, and some by events outside it, but none of them arose as aspects of a developed partisan program.[40]

William Smith did think otherwise while the votes were taking place. Commenting on the first session's debates on taxation, he saw "sharp Dissentions arising between the Levellers led by [John Morin] Scott & the Few Men of Property" and believed that "there is undoubtedly a Party already formed in the New Legislature." He thought it "strange that the Landed Interest have been so blind to the Consequences of a Separation from Great Britain—they now begin to perceive their Danger and that a Land Tax is inevitable without a Reconciliation."[41] As usual, Smith's eye was sharp. The first session's debates did pose a threat to the way that the land grandees had long safeguarded themselves. General rates on all kinds of property were being established. There would be taxes on personal belongings, on improved real estate, and on unimproved land. Although tenants would pay the taxes on most improved estates, only the owner could pay them on unimproved property.[42]

But when the legislature actually voted on taxation, the question that worried it was not how to tax but rather how much to tax, especially on personal property. Egbert Benson was at the center of the debate. He had no difficulty in persuading his colleagues to set the rate on improved real estate at three pence in the pound, and then in persuading them to set that on unimproved land at a lower level. The assembly likewise voted against setting equal rates for personal property and for improved real property, which again was what Benson wanted.

On two levels these votes make nonsense of Smith's glib assurance that the men of property and the levelers were drawing up against each other. First, men of property took some surprising positions on the votes. Speaker Livingston, for instance, voted in committee of the whole to set the rate on personal property at the same level as the rate on improved real estate. So did Killian Van Rensselaer. They voted on the same side as the Dutchess challengers Dirck Brinckerhoff and Jacobus Swartwout and Daniel Dunscomb, once chairman of the Body of Mechanics in New York City. The men who opposed taxing personal property at stiff rates included Benson and the Dutchess grandee Anthony Hoffman, as one might expect, but they also included all save one of the members from yeoman Ulster County. If this was partisanship, politics had made some strange bedfellows.[43]

The second reason why Smith had not grasped the whole picture is that the line-up on taxation had little or nothing to do with the line-up on the other main issue, legitimacy. This was the question that the "constitutionalist patriots" forced upon the legislature – Jay and his colleagues on the supreme court by their vetoes and their refusal to act until they were constitutionally reappointed, and Benson by his campaign against the laws mentioning the committees. In the eight roll calls taken on the subject in the first session, men tended to take the same position time after time. On one side were those who accepted the constitutionalist position that the written document must be the only source of legitimate political authority; on the other side were the assemblymen who proved less concerned about the issue. The hard core of constitutionalists were only a small minority of the house. Five of them were from Benson's own county of Dutchess, and though they included, besides Benson himself, Anthony Hoffman and Gilbert Livingston, they also included Jacobus Swartwout and Dirck Brinckerhoff. The other seven on whom Benson could count were scattered across several constituencies, including New York, Albany, Queens, Kings, Orange, and Tryon. The group that rejected Benson's argument included fully thirty assemblymen. They too were scattered among many constituencies, including eight members from the west-bank counties, six from New York City, and others from Queens, Suffolk, Tryon, Charlotte, Albany, and Westchester.[44]

The point is that the votes on this, the issue that the conservative leaders considered the most serious facing the first session, showed no congruence at all with the votes on taxation, which William Smith thought most salient. The members themselves regarded both questions as important; otherwise they would not have taken a total of twenty votes on problems of constitutionality and five more on the taxing of personal property. Most of them thought the issues important in different ways, however, and did not see them as complementary aspects of the larger problem of the direction in which the Revolution should go. Benson was not, in other words, faced with a united opposition. But it was also true that he did face opposition. On the legitimacy issue, he could get the assembly to take his point only on the least significant issues.[45] On taxation, the aristocrats at last had to face the land tax they had dreaded.

The legitimacy issue died at the end of the first session, at least as a subject for legislative debate,[46] but taxation, of course, persisted. During the second session, the assembly took many votes dealing with taxes, and on ten of them its members formed into roughly congruent groups. These ten roll calls isolated a small minority of members who wanted tough tax policies from a much larger group who wanted softer ones. The core that sought demanding taxes wanted to see them imposed on the salaries of officers in the service of Congress, higher rates on both personal and real property, and taxes on income from commerce, trade, and the professions. All seven of the assemblymen who voted consistently on this side came from the southern district, as did five of the eight who swung to them on some votes. The point is easy to make that they could afford to favor hard taxation because they faced no constituents themselves. Overall, the second session saw a marked fall-off in internal divisiveness from that of the first. Only a third of all of the roll calls that the session took gave prima facie evidence of being related to more than one or two others, which was fully 10 percent fewer than those that did so in the first session. Though in crude terms the number of legislators who voted in close harmony with others—more than 70 percent of the time—rose, the rise indicated a general high level of agreement rather than the emergence of competing blocs.[47]

The same overall pattern continued in the third session, when the assemblymen proved more divisive, taking roll call after roll call. Often the votes were on matters of social importance, indeed of considerably more importance than the issues that were debated in the second session. On these roll calls, as on those of the first two sessions, the assemblymen showed neither the continuity of alignment from issue to issue nor the class and sectional patterns that traditional sources would lead us to expect among them. Two characteristics, however, did set this session off from its two predecessors. One was the explosion of militant popular opinion, which became a factor in the way the legislature made its decisions. The other, tied to the first, was the way that policy changed in a number of sensitive fields.

Anger at the way the Revolution's leaders had been handling internal issues had been growing since the second half of 1778. State Senator Ebenezer Russell, of Charlotte County, heard in August of that year that a free "pardon" would be given to Tories who took the oath of allegiance, and he protested fiercely to the governor. He did not "desine to retaleate," but he was sure he heard "the blod of those Noble men who fell a Prey to these unhuman villins, crying aloud for justis." He warned that clemency would cause "a grate Deel of Defuculty. . .as the People in this Country are very unesy." What "defuculty" meant on the northern frontier had been shown a few months earlier by the people of the nearby town of Cambridge when they had run Tories and committeemen alike through the gauntlet.[48]

By the end of 1778 such feeling was congealing into a desire that the state punish the Tories and seize and redistribute their property. This desire became strongest in places like Westchester, southern Dutchess, and Tryon counties, where most great landlords had chosen the crown. Tenants on the Philipse Highland patent petitioned the second session of the legislature for a confiscation act at the end of 1778. They were sure that it was through the Tories' "wicked practices" that "the War with all its horrors, calamities and consequent charges, was brought upon us and is continued." The Tories' property no longer deserved society's protection, and both the principle of just retribution and the distressed condition of the patriots justified seizing it. "We doubt not," said the petitioners, "in the completion of so important an Act, but you will readily forgo every private conveniency to your selves and particular families."

Pressure for a confiscation act was a major theme in the committee revival of the subsequent year, and the Claverack Convention, in which the movement culminated, called for "the Confiscation and disposition of the real estate of traitors and enemies to the country."[49] This was the pressure that led the senate and the council of revision to turn around on confiscation, to pass other laws that punished royalists, to start taxing by "circumstances and abilities," and to try again to solve the economy's problems in a corporatist way. It also led to significant divisions within the legislature. But it did not yet lead to straightforward partisanship.

The third assembly took 105 roll calls. About 4 in every 10 showed marked congruence with other votes, and these tended to fall into relatively small groups rather than to show order and structure across issues. As in the first session, the assemblymen were factious rather than partisan, willing enough to quarrel with their colleagues and placing no great emphasis on maintaining a veneer of agreement but not organizing their squabbles around a clear polarity of organization and opinion. The return to a tax system based on county quotas reinforced this, for it led directly to debates in which whole county delegations jockeyed against other counties in order to reduce the bill that would finally be sent to their own constituents.

But two issues did start to cut through this otherwise tangled pattern of divisiveness. One of these was the principle of assessing according to "circumstances and abilities." In its whole history, this issue never dovetailed directly with others in any given session, but it did show how deeply the upheaval of 1778 and 1779 affected the coalition politics that had been the basis of the state's public life. The prime symbol of that government by coalition had been the influence that Egbert Benson held over his colleagues from Dutchess County. In the first session the Dutchess members were among his foremost supporters in his battle against legal recognition of the committees, and throughout the first two sessions they often voted together. But on radical taxation the Dutchess coalition finally split. The proposal won the support of the insurgents Dirck Brinckerhoff, Henry Luddington, and Brinton Paine, but it was opposed by Benson himself and by Samuel Dodge.

Much the same thing happened in the votes on selling the forfeitures. That the seizure would occur was assured by the time the third session convened, but what would take place then was another matter. During the session, the assembly took eight votes on selling the forfeitures, and these confirmed that the Dutchess coalition was breaking. Again, Benson found himself in opposition to his colleagues rather than in control of them. Brinckerhoff, Luddington, Paine, and Nathaniel Sackett all voted in favor of sales, leaving Benson virtually alone. The result of the two issues, taxation and sales, was once again to bring into the open the internal questions of class that had wracked not only the politics but the whole public life of the county for decades but that to that point had been smothered successfully within the independence movement.[50]

The fourth session of the legislature, the last in which Benson served, is of little interest in terms of the development of the state's political society. The session took only forty-four roll calls, and of these a mere eleven fell into obvious groups. But the session's votes did ratify the major behavioral development of the previous session: the collapse of the Dutchess coalition. Again, the prime issue was radical taxation. This time the proposal failed in the house, and support for it shrank to a hard minority. Among the Dutchess members that minority comprised the insurgent politicians Guisbert Schenck and Jacobus Swartwout, and the majority that opposed it was made up of Benson, his old ally Samuel Dodge, and Ebenezer Cary.

The history of the Dutchess members over the first four sessions is the history of only one of the county coalitions that made and unmade themselves during this period. The Dutchess coalition is particularly noteworthy, however, both because the social factors that lay behind the behavior of the county's members are well understood[51] and because the coalition's short history illustrates the larger nature of legislative politics during those first republican years. Men as diverse as Brinckerhoff and Luddington and Benson and Hoffman did not cooperate between 1774 and 1779 out of mere good will. They joined together because, whatever else separated them, they had come to share a commitment first to resistance and then to independence. They recognized that the most important thing to do was to work for these against Britain and its American supporters. Many of those royalists had been friends, neighbors, and colleagues of the coalition's members, but for the moment it was more important that one side had chosen Revolution and the other had not than that on each side there were landlords, tenants, and yeomen. By 1779, however, when Benson was bemoaning the revival of the committee movement, Swartwout was taking an active part in it.[52] The politics of coalition was starting to give way to a new formation, one that reflected a new reality, different from that of 1775 or 1776.

One other bit of evidence reflected that new reality. Despite their factiousness, legislators throughout these four sessions tended to agree overall at high rates. Only a few can be found who did not vote with the majority on at least half of the roll calls in which they took part. But if we look at the members who were to be found in the majority disproportionately often, we find that they were a different group by the fourth session from what they had been in the first or the second. Defining such men as those who took part in at least 70 percent of all roll calls and who voted on the winning side of at least 70 percent of those in which they voted at all, it can be seen that they shifted from being a group centered largely on New York City to one based largely in the upstate counties. In the first session there were eighteen men in the category, and in the second there were twenty. Thirteen of the eighteen came from the occupied counties or Westchester, as did eleven of the twenty. In the third session, when the state turned its policies around on so many matters, only three men were in the group, and each of them represented an unoccupied constituency. One was from Dutchess, one from Westchester, and one from Albany. In the fourth session there were fourteen men in the group, and only one of them came from downstate. Now it was the upstate members who were most likely to be voting on the winning side.[53]

The conclusion to which these figures lead is that during the war years legislative politics was marked by three qualities. One was that men were willing to argue and to quarrel, not anxious to agree. A second was that their quarreling was unstructured. It was coalition politics both in the sense that the men involved believed that ultimately there were more important questions at stake than their own disputes and in the sense that a majority that joined together on one issue was unlikely to come together on another. But the third, reflected both in the break-up of the Dutchess group and in the shift from downstate to upstate among those who voted together very often, whatever the issue, is that this was a situation that could not last.

IV

By the summer of 1781, when Egbert Benson completed his four sessions as an assemblyman, the conservatives whom he had represented there had lost control of the Revolution in New York. Their loss did not result from a simple defeat in a straightforward confrontation. On the contrary, it grew out of the complexity of the Revolution and out of certain choices that the conservatives made themselves. Moveover, the men who defeated them were only half-aware of what they had accomplished. But the loss was almost complete.

It began with the election of George Clinton as governor. Clinton was no novice politically; he had learned his trade in the bitter disputes that marked the final years of the old order. He was, as has been suggested, eminently "sound" on most issues, and during the war he knew that his main task was to cooperate—with Congress, with the other states, with General Washington, and with the whole republican coalition in his own state. But he was still a man whose "family and connections" did not "intitle him to so distinguished a predominance," and that never ceased to rankle the likes of Philip Schuyler. Moreover, however lacking in organization statewide politics may have been in 1777, Clinton not only played his cards right that year but had the whole deck in his hands when he came up for reelection in 1780. He faced no serious opposition, and his own situation was so strong that a candidate in a local squabble in Orange County found the best tactic for smearing his opponent was to charge him with conspiring to unseat the governor.[54]

At other levels of the state government also the conservatives found themselves in a retreat will they, nill they. For all his skills and maneuvering, Egbert Benson proved unable to stop the legislature from passing law after law that he considered anathema. For all the close reasoning that John Jay and Robert R. Livingston put into veto messages, the council of revision emerged equally powerless. Even Governor Clinton's quiet association with many of the positions that the council was taking had no effect.

At the level of patronage, too, the old rulers found themselves unable to control events. Civil and military offices were the gift of the council of appointment, and it is significant that Egbert Benson's very first act as an assemblyman was to try to seize control both of how the council would be chosen and of who the first councillors would be. Two of the senators whom Benson tried to nominate did get seats: Abraham Yates for the western district and Alexander Webster for the eastern. But for the middle district, the house chose Jesse Woodhull, the self-made farmer of Orange, instead of Benson's Dutchess colleague Zephaniah Platt, and it chose John Morin Scott for the southern district instead of Philip Livingston. Scott had been Benson's teacher in the law, but his former pupil knew that he was an uncontrollable opportunist. A senator was supposed to serve on the council for a single session, and over the next years the assembly's choices ran in the same direction. It did find places for the wealthy merchant Isaac Roosevelt in the second session, and for the Albany magnate Abraham Ten Broeck in the fourth, but their presence was balanced by that of obscure senators like Dirck W. Ten Broeck of Albany, Levi Pawling of Ulster, Rinier Mynderse, former chairman of the Schenectady committee, Stephen Ward of Westchester, and Ebenezer Russell of Charlotte.[55]

But the main reason that the conservatives lost control was that at last the Revolution caught up with them. Their astuteness and far-sightedness had enabled them to remain the dominant force throughout the independence crisis, and they had emerged from it not only with the constitution they wanted but, more important, with general agreement that it was as good a constitution as the state could have.[56] But the entry of new men into the political elite, the persistence and then the revival of the committees, the continuing crowd action against royalists, monopolizers, and hoarders, and the publication of such arguments as the one that the state's commerce ought to become the state's business forced them to retreat so far that they found themselves off the battlefield. Rather than controlling the legislature and the legislature controlling the people, Egbert Benson ended up in a situation where his skills were at the legislature's disposal and where the legislature increasingly regarded itself as an agent to accomplish what its constituents wanted.

The legitimation of the idea of direct popular involvement in the making of policy was completed during the fourth session, Benson's last. When the assembly received a letter from the Albany county militia complaining against the militia law, it treated it with respect instead of scorn, sending it immediately to a committee of the whole. It accorded similar treatment to a petition from Albany County, one that had 176 signatures, which complained about procedures in four separate areas. It was protests and petitions like these that led the senate and the assembly jointly to publish in March 1781 an "Address from the Legislature to their Constituents." Hailing them as "Friends and Fellow Citizens," the legislators told the people that "while government is without corruption, the representatives of a free people cannot be inattentive to the opinions of their constituents; they will hear their complaints and examine into the causes of them; if they proceed from errors in government, they will endeavor to correct such errors; if they originate in evils which arise from their particular situation, they will explain the necessity which gives birth to them."[57]

Throughout the third and the fourth sessions the legislature had shown that it could be responsive in practice as well as in theory, and in the address its members presented a detailed explanation of the problems before them. Taxation, the public debt, relations with other states and with Congress, "the extraordinary powers given to commissioners for defeating conspiracies," frontier defense, and the presence in the senate and the assembly of the ordinance members were all discussed. Throughout the address, the tone was one of equals addressing equals. It was, of course, a superb exercise in propaganda, but it symbolized the changes that had taken place. It endorsed on the level of principle the policy of responsiveness that the legislature had developed on the level of practice. As chapter 6 showed, it was that responsiveness that in the end consolidated the power of the new order, enabled it to "take hold," and kept the continuing revolutionary ferment from erupting into outright internal rebellion. But on the level of policy, on the level of principle, and on the level of who was in power, that responsiveness, that thrust towards practical democratization, meant that the conservatives of the state were losing their position.

By the end of 1779, it seems, they had recognized that fact. John Jay had already left the supreme court to become president of Congress, and from that post he moved to the sensitive post of envoy to Spain. Robert R. Livingston, though he remained chancellor, became Congress's secretary for foreign affairs, throwing his considerable energy into resolving the problems between America and her allies. James Duane, though a state senator, put much of his energy into Congress, of which he has been called the "near boss."[58] Gouverneur Morris and William Duer both withdrew early from state-level politics via a seat in Congress. Even Egbert Benson moved from the legislature to Congress at the end of 1780.

The sudden interest of these men in national rather than state affairs reflected several trends. One was their own and other men's awareness that they were needed at the center. But they cannot have been unaware that it had been in Congress that they had won their tactical victories over New York radicals in 1775 and 1776. The moderation of New York, which is to say the moderation of these men, its delegates, on the independence issue had been due to their own anxiousness to keep their province under control. They had returned to the state en masse after independence because they knew, as William Smith told Philip Schuyler, that while the constitution was being framed their call was "rather to the Cabinet than the field."[59] Without a base in Congress, concentrating almost exclusively on state affairs, they found themselves unable to maintain their control. Neither the tactics of delay and retreat nor their dominance of the council of revision kept the state government from taking step after step that they hated. In their move from state back to federal affairs as the decade changed they themselves took their own first step towards regaining the control of events that they had kept for so long but had finally lost.

Chapter 8

The Radical Ascendancy, 1781–1786

During the half-decade that spanned the end of the war and the beginning of reconstruction New York fell into the hands of what had been the left wing of its revolutionary coalition. Both in the assembly and in the senate,[1] the men who had dominated the streets and the committee chambers between 1774 and 1779 came now to constitutional power. They came to it without either full self-consciousness or an organization, but they generated both during the five years when they ruled the state. Leaders and astute politicians emerged among them, and they did their leading and their politicking according to the code of behavior that legislators and people had worked out between 1777 and 1780. One of the most important of those leaders was Governor Clinton, who repudiated his ties with the conservative elite and moved towards an open identification with what legislative and popular radicals stood for. While Clinton was doing this, the radicals themselves were developing positions on the new issues that the successful conclusion of the war had raised. These issues concerned the future of royalists and neutrals, the reconstruction of the liberated southern district, the state's economic situation, the development of the western and northern lands that the war had opened for settlement, and the permanent place in the new order of the groups that the revolution had brought into the public arena. In the eighth session of the legislature, during the winter of 1784–85, the consciousness and organization of these radicals bore fruit in the form of a remarkable demonstration of disciplined voting on a very wide range of issues. The politics of coalition with which New York's republicans had confronted the British and the Tories had given way to a politics of party as republican New Yorkers confronted one another.

I

This radicalism emerged from the anger of people throughout the state, but it had three main sources, each represented in the legislature by a different group of men. The most important were the insurgent politicians who stepped forward in the midst of landlord-tenant strife in the counties of conflict, Albany, Dutchess, and Westchester. By 1780 the republican coalitions within which these men had operated were in tatters, and the magnates and challengers who had formed them had begun again to struggle for control. The second source of legislative radicalism lay among the representatives of the west-bank counties of consensus. Until 1780 these men had little reason to identify with the insurgents across the Hudson, but in the new decade the two groups found that they had more and more in common. The third source was New York City. Radicalism there was to be found among the former Sons of Liberty, the artisans, the small merchants, and the people in crowds whose energy and commitment had driven the revolutionary movement forward from 1765 to 1776. The coalition of these men with conservative politicians lasted longest of all, but it finally cracked when the British evacuated the city at the end of 1783. It was from these elements that a statewide radicalism made itself.

These three groups themselves formed a new coalition, of course, and that coalition contained its own lines of stress and its own sources of instability. The west-bank legislators represented yeoman farmers, whose basic situation did not change during the Revolution but who came to see themselves in a new light vis-à-vis the grandees. The Hudson Valley insurgents stood for an assemblage of tenants, ex-tenants, and yeomen who joined in confronting the landlords. Some of these people had been militant popular royalists; others had used the Revolution to make the jump from tenantry to freehold; still others remained occupants of land they would never own. The third group picked up where the Sons of Liberty and the organized mechanics had left off in 1776. They wanted most of all to restore the southern district in a way that would smash the vestiges of British power, that would punish harshly the city people who had chosen the ease of life under the British rather than the rigors of a seven-year exile, and that would put the mechanics and the small merchants who had endured that exile in a position to dominate the city's development.

Radicalism emerged first among the representatives of the counties of conflict. Perhaps the first politician, other than the quixotic John Morin Scott, to espouse it was Abraham Yates, a senator from Albany, who in his life moved from licking the boots of the grandees to being the prime focus of their fears. Fifty-two years old at independence, Yates was no "young man of the revolution."[2] Nor was he new to serious politics, for he had sat for two decades on the Albany common council, had been his county's high sheriff in the mid-1750's, and had stood for the assembly in 1761. Yates was angry in 1776, but he had not always been. During his shrievalty he had given firm support to Robert Livingston, Jr., and the Van Rensselaers against their tenants, so much that in 1755 tenants had kidnapped him and imprisoned him in Massachusetts. When Yates ran for the provincial assembly, it was on the basis of having Livingston's support. But his anger may have begun with that election, for determined opposition to him by Sir William Johnson cost him first the backing of the Rensselaerwyck politician Abraham Ten Broeck, then that of Livingston, and finally the election itself.

Yates's anger waxed during the fifteen years between then and the formation of the Albany committee of safety. He began to write privately on the evils of landlordism. He built up the law practice that had long since replaced cobbling as his main source of income. In 1773 he lost his seat on the common council to a candidate sponsored by Abraham Ten Broeck and by the younger magnate Leonard Gansevoort. By this time his feelings about such men were blending with a longstanding hatred for British imperialism. He had begun to develop that hatred during his time as sheriff, which coincided with the early stages of the Seven Years' War, for the job had given him ample opportunity to witness British troops mistreating his people. When those people made him the foundation chairman of the Albany committee, they thus chose a thoroughly politicized and thoroughly angry man.[3]

Yates moved from the county committee to seats in several provincial congresses, to the chairmanship of the committee that drafted the state constitution, and, by the Albany committee's nomination, to a seat in the state senate. He held that seat throughout the Confederation period, and he was a delegate to Congress in 1787 and 1788. Twice he was a councillor of appointment, and he was also temporary president of the senate several times in the 1780s. If worldly honors came to him late, they came nevertheless.

But from the beginning of his senate tenure, conservatives feared the anger they knew he had in him and scorned him because of his humble origins. Early in 1778, William Smith reported that "new fears are rising in Albany on a Project of the Leaders at Poghkeepsing to put each County under a Lieutenant General & the appointment of Ab: Yates to that Station. He is one of the Council of Appointments & so hated that all Officers tis supposed will resign. He is a coadjutor of [John Morin] Scotts & obnoxious to the Renselaers, Schuylers and Livingstons."[4] At the same time, John Jay was guardedly hopeful that if Yates carried through on plans to run for lieutenant governor, he would find himself with no office at all. At the end of the first legislative session, Yates's enemies in Albany banded together to put Philip Schuyler into his senate seat. The effort failed, but it cannot have endeared to him those partners in an increasingly frail coalition. Yates never ceased to draw the magnates' hatred. In 1782 Alexander Hamilton called him "a staunch Whig, that deserves to be pensioned by the British Ministry." Philip Schuyler could never forget that he had once mended shoes. Thomas Tillotson, a mediocrity who had Livingston connections, dismissed him as an "old Booby." As Lynd suggests, such comments tell more about Yates's politics than would a pile of information about his investments.[5]

If Yates spoke in the senate for angry Albanians, Matthew Adgate and Jacob Ford did so in the assembly. Adgate entered the house in the fourth session, elected in June 1780, and Ford in the fifth, picked a year later. Adgate was a lawyer, though probably a self-made one, and Ford a major in the militia. They came from the eastern part of the county, close to the Massachusetts border, and were themselves part of the Yankee overspill that had helped to inflame class relations on the Albany County manors. Theirs was a society where the radical traditions of the Puritan Revolution lived on. Anne Grant had people like them in mind when she wrote of Yankee migrants who would invade a landowner's home, try to buy land, and talk politics in a way that would have done honor to the seventeenth-century English radical leader Praise-God Barebones. Their Massachusetts neighbor Asa Douglass did address Washington as "Great Cromwell" in 1776. Adgate was three times a member of the Albany committee, and Ford twice, and Adgate also went to the Convention of the People of 1776 and 1777. They used to travel down to meetings of the legislature together, and within it they both took active parts. Adgate was on two standing committees in the fifth session and was probably chairman of the committee on ways and means in the eighth. Ford was likewise appointed to standing committees in both of those sessions. By 1785 Hamilton was sure that they were the central figures in the legislature's radicalism, calling them a "couple of New England Adventurers. . .who make tools of the Yates and their Associates."[6]

Radicalism in Dutchess County in the early 1780s focused increasingly on Ephraim Paine, a middle-district senator in the fourth session and again in the sixth, seventh, and eighth sessions. Paine had been shaped by the same Yankee remembrance of revolutionary England that produced Matthew Adgate, and for that matter, Ethan Allen. But in contrast to the deist Allen,[7] he expressed his radicalism in intensely religious terms. Born in Connecticut, he had been so strongly influenced by the Great Awakening that throughout his life he preached to Baptist and New Light Presbyterian congregations. He became the sort of evangelical Protestant for whom religion and politics alike point towards human equality. He showed how much he scorned rank and hierarchy by his dress, for he habitually wore homespun, even to the senate. He showed it by his demeanor, for he refused so angrily to submit to the senate's discipline that it expelled him for dereliction of duty in his first year. Hamilton called him a "man of strong natural parts and as strong prejudices; his zeal is fiery, his obstinacy unconquerable. He is as primitive in his notions as in his appearance." But Paine was a man of talent, and his constituents reelected him after the expulsion. In his very first session the assembly made him a councillor of appointment. Even Hamilton had to concede in 1782 that he had his "share of influence."[8]

Neither in Albany nor in Dutchess, however, was radicalism confined to New England migrants. The Yates family were descended from a Yorkshireman who came to Albany in the seventeenth century. Their in-laws and allies, the Lansings, were Dutch, and so were the Bleeckers, the Visschers, and the Winnes.[9] In Dutchess, Ephraim Paine and his kinsman, the assemblyman Brinton Paine, allied themselves with Dutchmen like Jacobus Swartwout and Dirck Brinckerhoff and with Long Island migrants like Zephaniah Platt and Henry Luddington. These men built up ties of family and interest among themselves. Thus the Yateses were kin of long standing to the Lansings. Similarly, by the end of the Confederation period, most of the Dutchess insurgents had joined Zephaniah Platt in promoting the Plattsburgh speculation in the Champlain Valley.[10] But what made a political group of them was their situation as challengers in a stratified society and as men who formed themselves in the Revolution. They were as close as rural New York came to producing *enragés*, and they showed it in their style. Every time that Ephraim Paine wore his homespun suit to the senate, every time that Abraham Yates penned an essay as "Rough Hewer" or contemned his enemies for being "high flyers," every time that Matthew Adgate, Nathaniel Sackett, Henry Luddington, and Jacobus Swartwout voted for radical taxation and for the sale of confiscated land, they were defining their position on what the Revolution should mean.

The first alliance that they forged was with men from across the river, the chieftains of Orange and Ulster counties. As chapter 7 showed, many of these men had been prominent in local affairs for years, even decades. Their archetype was Johannes G. Hardenbergh, son of the patentee of the two-million-acre Great Hardenbergh patent, which sprawled over the Catskill Mountains in western Ulster county. Its distance from the river, its rugged terrain, and its openness to Indian attack meant that the patent was practically worthless for development, and Hardenbergh, a mere co-owner, reaped no great fortune from it. But though by no means rich, he was the west bank's elder statesman. As early as 1737 he was an assemblyman, and for two decades he commanded the Ulster militia. He filled the whole range of local offices, from common pounder to supervisor, and he was seventy-one years old when he began his four terms in the state assembly. Abraham Hasbrouck, who joined him in the assembly in the fifth session, was comparable. The grandson of one of the first patentees of Newburgh, he served in the provincial assembly on and off for twenty years. He kept a store in Kingston, where he was the town supervisor in years as far apart as 1747 and 1784. He was long lieutenant colonel of Hardenbergh's militia regiment. Either of these could have been the original for Abraham Van Valkenburgh, the "colonel and memper" of Cooper's *Satanstoe*.[11]

Men like these were joined in the legislature by many others. The newcomers included migrants such as John Hathorn, who came from New England to the Orange County village of Warwick. There he taught school, practiced surveying, and got involved. He became a captain in the colonial militia and eventually a major general in the state's service. His political career progressed from the assembly floor to the speakership, the state senate, and finally the House of Representatives. There were other immigrants among the west bank's revolutionary politicians, such as David Pye, an Englishman who made the most of finding himself stranded in America by becoming an Orange County assemblyman, or Ebenezer Clarke, the son of a migrant from northern Ireland, who represented at different times both Charlotte County, where his father had settled, and Ulster, to which he moved.[12] The newcomers also included men whose west-bank roots ran deep, men of English descent, like the middle-district senator Jesse Woodhull, or of Dutch background, like the Ulster assemblymen Cornelius C. Schoonmaker, Dirck Wynkoop, and Johannes Bruyn. But whether migrant or native, Irish, English, or Dutch, almost all of them were men who never would have been heard of outside their towns under the old order.

In terms of the property they held and the career lines they followed, such men looked much like the insurgents across the river, but there were some significant differences. The basic one was that the west-bank men stood atop their own social structures and thus had no need to challenge grander folk for power and position. By contrast, the need to make such a challenge was exactly what made the insurgents what they were. In many instances, the west-bank leaders had better personal relations with the grandees than they did with such men's opponents. Sometimes these sprang from long-shared political experience. Charles DeWitt, George Clinton's kin by marriage, had joined Clinton as an assemblyman during the early 1770s. Both men had found that to oppose the DeLanceys and defend the American cause was to give their support to the Livingstons. The friendships that DeWitt built in those years lasted, and as late as the mid-1780s he was still exchanging friendly correspondence with Walter Livingston. Meanwhile, he was roundly rebuffing overtures of friendship that Ephraim Paine had begun to make to him.[13] The difference between the chieftains and the insurgents showed itself in political terms, as well as in who corresponded with whom, for in the late 1770s legislators of the two sorts were no more likely to vote together than were men of any other two groups.[14]

For a number of reasons, however, they began to move into a new coalition about 1780. One reason certainly was that they shared a perspective on the world that marked them off from the grandees. To measure precisely how their sense of themselves differed from that of the great men is not simple. How and where they lived tells some of the story. Men of two different sorts dwelt amidst the elegance of the Schuyler mansion in Albany, on the one hand, and in the rough comfort of the stone Schoonmaker house in Saugerties, on the other, as the political behavior of Philip Schuyler and Cornelius Schoonmaker showed. It would be less predictable that Schoonmaker was a politician of a different kind from Leonard Bronck, who had an equally homey stone house at Coxsackie. Yet during the 1780s, while Schoonmaker consistently was taking anti-magnate positions, Bronck was in close contact with the great in Albany and at Livingston Manor.[15]

The difference in perspective, style, or tone that marked the west-bank leaders off from the great men is best seen in the experience of Charles DeWitt. A trained lawyer, possibly the second most powerful man in Ulster, and a former provincial assemblyman, DeWitt was neither a novice nor an innocent when he entered the legislature. Besides his seat in the assembly, he gained the colonelcy of a regiment of minutemen, sat in two provincial congresses, was on the committee that drafted the state constitution, and became a commissioner for conspiracies. His fellow Ulstermen elected and reelected him to the state assembly.[16]

The legislature, in turn, sent DeWitt to Congress in 1784, and it was during his tenure there that he learned what he was made of. Congress was sitting in Annapolis, and he set off to take his seat with the greatest reluctance. As soon as he left New York he realized that he was overstepping his limitations. Awestruck by the elegance of Philadelphia, he reported to his son that it was "a place the most magnificent that ever I saw and perhaps it may be ranked among the finest cities in the world." Even the sidewalks were "as clean as a house floor." He was astonished to find himself hobnobbing there with the envoys of France and the Netherlands. His strong sense that he did not belong persisted after he arrived in Annapolis. Walter Livingston heard from him that "there is no pleasure in being in Congress" and that he had "not been able to oppose thoughts . . . that [Congress] are as corrupt as the British Parliament." He told another correspondent that he did not "think it more honorable to be a member of Congress than of the Assembly of my native state of New York." He became so homesick that when a packet of letters arrived, he "read them over and over, and kissed every one of them instead of the dear lips that have dropped the affectionate language contained in them."[17] DeWitt had learned that he had gone too far. He had come by a different route to almost the same perspective on the large world of affairs as that of Abraham Yates, who had been convinced from the Revolution's beginning that great men and great institutions brought only great evil.

Chieftains and insurgents were likewise brought together during their experience of the crisis of 1779. The Dutchess members had been Egbert Benson's strongest supporters in his drive on 1777 and early 1778 against the committees. Only one west-bank member, John Hathorn of Orange, took Benson's point then, and the other eight Orange and Ulster assemblymen opposed him steadfastly. But the Dutchess challengers found in 1779 that to their constituents, as "to many a perplexed householder, not only in New York but throughout the struggling states, the revival of the local committees seemed. . .to be the way to check the monopolistic practices of merchants and the dishonesty of public officials."[18] The insurgents involved themselves actively in the revival. Jacobus Swartwout chaired the committee at Fishkill; the antifederalist-to-be Gilbert Livingston led the one at Poughkeepsie; the tenant-assemblyman Henry Luddington helped to organize the one at Fredericksburgh. As committeemen, they found themselves working parallel with men elsewhere who would also be radical legislators during the next decade: James Hunter in Ulster County, Matthew Adgate, Matthew Visscher, James Gordon, John Lansing, and Philip Frisbie in Albany, and others in Orange. Some of these men were already legislators by 1779. Most of them would never go so far as the Poughkeepsie call for socialized foreign trade and a redistribution of property, or as the Orange County declaration that committees were simply a better way of doing things than were constitutional institutions.[19] But they formed part of the movement from which such sentiments sprang, and it was as a result of that movement that they began to come together.

The point was encapsulated in the respective ways that magnates and members of the coalition that was forming against them reacted to later spasms of committee activity. Though after 1779 there was never again a statewide movement, people did make gestures here and there. The most notable were one that occurred on Livingston Manor in 1781 and one in Poughkeepsie in 1783. The former grew out of the aftermath of the economic crisis, and like the committees of 1779, it was concerned largely with regulating prices. The latter emerged as former royalists began trying to reenter Hudson Valley society, and thus harked back to the committees of 1775 and 1776. The flurry of 1781 gave Robert R. Livingston a bad fright. Exaggerating what was really happening, he told Gouverneur Morris that "the people are clamorous [and] the whole County of Dutchess have chosen precinct & County committees." But the brief revival in Poughkeepsie produced another reaction in Frederick Weissenfels, a radical army officer and an intimate of John Lamb. He told Lamb how a meeting was called "to form Committees, to prevent the plunderers, and murderers. . . from worming themselves in the Company of worthy Citizens." But "some men in power" had damped down the movement, and Weissenfels regretted it. He thought it was "dangerous to slacken any zeal for the public welfare, and to trow [*sic*] Cold Water on the Spirit of Liberty."[20] The fright of the one man and the sanguinity of the other provide a measure of what divided the two sides that were forming.

The third radical element emerged later, not becoming a serious factor until the seventh legislative session, early in 1784. The members of this group were the representatives of the artisans, small traders, laborers, and sailors of New York City. Their people were the ones whom Gouverneur Morris had scorned in 1774 as "poor reptiles." They were the ones who had joined Isaac Sears in seizing control of the streets after the Battle of Lexington and whose committee had wanted popular ratification of the state constitution and provision in it for reestablishing committees whenever the people thought they needed them. They were the ones who had ridden the city's royalists on rails and who had pulled down King George's statue at the Battery. They were the ones who fled the king's armies rather than submit to them.

What they and the men who represented them did after that flight remains largely unknown. Some, like the printers John Holt and Samuel Loudon or the blacksmith Robert Boyd, established themselves upstate and there carried on their trades. Others followed John Lamb, Alexander McDougall, Marinus Willett and Isaac Sears into the Continental army. These men were given their share of the "ordinance" seats in the wartime legislature, and their position within it improved after 1777. The assembly sent the candlemaker Isaac Stoutenburgh to the senate in 1779. Robert Boyd won election from Ulster County to the assembly in the same year. From 1780 to 1782 the ardently political mechanic John Stagg held a seat from Orange.

Whether the votes that elected Boyd and Stagg were those of natives of the two counties or those of other refugees cannot be said, but their victories show that there were real links between urban and rural radicals. That is not surprising. When John Morin Scott failed to win a New York City assembly seat in 1768, it may have been due to voters' awareness of the part he had taken in persecuting the Hudson Valley levelers two years before. The whole career of Thomas Young wove into a single fabric radicalism in Dutchess County, Albany, Boston, Philadelphia, and Vermont. When the Vermonters involved themselves with the larger American cause in 1775, it was Isaac Sears who moved that Ethan Allen be admitted to speak to the New York provincial congress.[21]

Nonetheless, the urban radicals were missing as a force during the war years. Though few of their men among the ordinance legislators supported Egbert Benson's drive against the committees, they were not notable for their part in the reversal of state policies after 1779. During the second session's debates over confiscation, two mechanics, Abraham Brasher and Daniel Dunscomb, were among the few assemblymen who opposed overriding the council of revision's veto. In the first meeting of the third session, Brasher, Robert Boyd, Peter Pra Van Zandt, and Abraham P. Lott accepted Benson's position in favor of hard taxation. Brasher, Boyd, Lott, and Dunscomb took the same position in the second. Boyd and Dunscomb voted against radical taxation in the third session; Boyd and John Stagg did so in the fourth; Lott and Stagg in the fifth; and Dunscomb and Stagg in the sixth. Similar comments could be made about their performance on most of the other issues that were separating radicals and their enemies between 1779 and 1782.[22]

Things changed when the downstaters were at last able to elect their representatives. Though in the upstate counties the elections for the seventh session took place in June 1783, in the southern district they were not held until December, when the British finally left. Regular government was not reestablished there until 1784, when the legislature modified the city's charter to suit the new situation, when the council of appointment made James Duane mayor, and when local elections were held. Until then an enormous council held provisional power. Appointed under a law of 1779, the council comprised the governor, the high judges, the judges of the southern-district county courts, the attorney general, the secretary of state, and the legislators. In arranging elections, the council was required to "prevent Persons charged with, or suspected of Disaffection to the Freedom and Independence of this State, from electing, or being elected."[23]

The revolutionaries began drifting back to the city early in 1783, and during that year tension built up between them and the royalists. In February it was reported "that a number of 'determined Whigs' had agreed that any Tory Printer in New York who...uses the term 'rebel' in his paper shall have his ears cropt." During the spring and summer, while the twenty thousand Tories who eventually fled the city prepared their exit, the British took their time at returning to its owners property they had commandeered. As British authority waned, both a wave of robberies and a series of demonstrations broke out. On 20 October a royalist "canaille" of "negroes, sailors and loyal leathern apron'd statesmen" tore the American colors from a ship in the harbor. About a month later, the British inspector of markets stole the bell of the Fly Market and threatened to have the building itself torn down, from sheer spite. In response to such outbursts, Governor Clinton issued a proclamation ordering that the decrees of the provisional council be obeyed.[24]

The liberated city's first elections took place in this atmosphere of bitterness. John Jay, in Spain, heard of the situation from Robert R. Livingston, who told him that "our parties are, first, the tories, who still hope for power...Secondly, the violent Whigs, who are for expelling all tories from the state...the third are those who wish to suppress all violences, to soften the rigor of the laws against the loyalists, and not to banish them from... social intercourse." Both the law and the anger of the returned refugees ensured that at the first poll the electorate was restricted to people whose commitment to the Revolution was undoubtable. Hamilton reported that the determining voice in the question of who might vote was that of "the returning citizen," and if they were "not at this juncture gratified, tumults were by some apprehended." In such circumstances, the Tories made no showing at all, and the moderate third group likewise had little impact.[25]

The victory, by an overwhelming margin, went to a slate nominated by a committee of mechanics. This ticket marked the revival of the coalition of artisans and small merchants that had been the Sons of Liberty. It included Isaac Sears, Marinus Willett, Peter Pra Van Zandt, and John Lamb, traders all, but it also had places for the mechanics John Stagg and Hugh Hughes. What united these men early in 1784 was agreement that the royalists had to be crushed. They showed as much the day before the election, when Sears, Lamb, and Willett led a crowd that put a finish to James Rivington's royalist printing house.[26]

In contrast with the Hudson Valley, and for reasons that chapter 9 will discuss, the city did not settle into a period of prolonged radical dominion. Instead, a ticket made up of men who had been defeated in December won the elections for the eighth assembly, in June. There were three mechanics on it—William Denning, William Goforth, and Daniel Dunscomb—none of whom had been involved in the radical ticket the previous session. Dunscomb, in particular, had a record of moderation that extended back to pre-Revolution days. They associated themselves with a Livingston, with the anti-mechanic politician Aaron Burr, and with the conservative merchants John Lawrence, Henry Remsen, and Comfort Sands.[27] A year later, however, in the election for the ninth assembly, this group gave way to another slate put up by the mechanics. Though it marked a fusion, giving places to Denning, Goforth, and former speaker Evert Bancker, it had a much more radical cast, including Isaac Sears, John Stagg, and the blacksmith and former Ulster member Robert Boyd.[28]

This third element in the radicalism of the 1780s thus rested on a different base from that of the other two. Hostility to royalists and a belief that they ought to be punished was one tenet that the three did hold in common. All of them supported confiscation, punitive taxation, political and economic disabilities, and forced exile for the Tories. But by 1783 many upstaters had come to think that the whole southern district was a nest of Toryism and to believe that all of its people needed punishing. Some of the downstate radicals agreed, but most did not, if only because they had to live with the result. Moreover, their constituencies had a markedly different make-up from those of the Hudson Valley members. These men represented, not tenants and former tenants and yeomen, but the volatile combination of small merchants and artisans who had pushed their way into public life in the street politics of the 1760s and 1770s. Among themselves, those two groups had reason to disagree if not to quarrel. Whether their coalition could last, and whether it could form a lasting larger coalition with the upstate members, was uncertain. But it was the representatives of all of these groups—the old Sons of Liberty, the west-bank chieftains, and the east-bank insurgents—that made up New York's radicalism at the end of the war.

II

The practices, customs, and habits that formed the sinews of political society during the five years of radical power were the ones that the people and their representatives had worked out between 1777 and 1780. By their way of doing things, the radicals confirmed that responsiveness, fluidity, and the avoidance of rigid structures were the essence of their style. The legislature continued to appoint standing committees and then to give them little to do. It continued to deny distinctions, honors, and titles to its committee chairmen. It continued to do most of its business in temporary drafting committees and committees of the whole. It continued to elect members of Congress and of the council of appointment by open nominations from every member present rather than by allowing one or a few to take the initiative.

The legislators bound these internal practices up with an express responsiveness to what their constituents wanted. One way the people showed what they wanted was by giving their members instructions, treating them not as "the rulers of this state," which is how Hamilton described them in 1782, but rather as the bound "representatives of a free people," which had been the legislators' self-description in 1780. The committee that formed on Livingston Manor in 1781 made the framing of such instructions its prime task. So did "late exiled Mechanics, Grocers, Retailers and Innholders" who met in New York City in 1784. People who avoided using the militant term "instructions" produced much the same effect by publishing copies of their demands and thus ensuring that the dialogue of represented and representative was a matter for the public record rather than a private affair. Refugees from the southern district published such a statement in 1783, describing their own piteous condition and calling on the provisional council to help them. In 1786, when patriot merchants in the city were conducting a campaign for relief from the debts they owed to British creditors, they appealed for support both to the legislature and the public. Even the chamber of commerce, campaigning to strengthen the economic powers of Congress, sent out a public letter urging people to frame "pointed instructions" to their members.[29]

During the radical ascendancy, people petitioned their representatives constantly. Hardly ever did they send their petitions to the senate, but they deluged the assembly with them. In the fifth session the house received about 120 petitions and memorials, and in the sixth a few more. The seventh session saw an enormous jump, with more than 330 petitions coming to the house. In the eighth session the number surged again, to nearly 600.[30] Petitions came on the largest matters and on the smallest. They came on taxation, the powers of Congress, royalism, the need for a bridge across a minor stream, the settlement of an intestate's property. They came from inside

New York and from outside. They came from former soldiers and former Tories; from debtors in jail and rich men; from people wanting to encourage immigration, to open the Mohawk River to navigation, to settle western townships, to become citizens. The petitions that the assembly received often bore just one signature, but some had as many as a thousand, and not infrequently they had several hundred. The names of major figures and of serving legislators appeared on some of them, but most of the petitioners were humble. The quickness with which these people signed petitions suggests that they knew the legislature had learned the lesson of responsiveness they had taught it in 1779.

Dealing with these petitions took up a great deal of the assembly's time, and their sheer volume imposed a need for some systematic practices. Most petitions went to specially chosen committees, but with increasing frequency a committee would be expected to handle several requests or even a large number of them. It became practice for all petitions for naturalization to go to one board, for petitions from imprisoned debtors to go to another, for petitions for land grants to go to a third. By the sixth session, the assembly began setting aside days for receiving petitions and for naming committees to deal with them. At the same time, those committees began to vary in weight and importance. A normal petition was sent to a committee of three men, but one of greater import might go to a committee of five or more. Usually the committeemen were picked at random, but not infrequently a petition would go to all the members from a county, or to a committee whose chairman came from the petitioner's district. Only very rarely did the assembly reject petitions out-of-hand or order them to "lie on the table."[31]

Petitions were often the origin of major policy commitments. The Citation Act of 1782, dealing with the problem of royalist creditors and rebel debtors, sprang from a petition from one of the assembly's own members, Ebenezer Husted, of Dutchess. The repeal of the law establishing the conspiracies commissioners originated in a petition from Westchester. The time allowed for buyers of forfeited land to pay off the purchase price was extended in the fifth session because a man named George Kidd petitioned for it. Petitions from Albany and Kingston for the right to establish colleges helped shape the act that modified the charter of King's College and established a state university. A dispute over Trinity Church in 1784 produced petitions and counterpetitions. So did an attempt in 1785 to carve out a new county between Albany and Dutchess. The reincorporation of the chamber of commerce in the seventh session and an attempt to incorporate the Body of Mechanics in the eighth were the result of petitions. Former royalists sometimes found that a petition could win them the right to return, particularly if known revolutionaries supported them.[32] These are only a few instances, for the mid-1780s petitions and the responses to them became the main means by which legislators and their constituents maintained contact.

Legislators actively courted public opinion as well. Alexander Hamilton said unkindly that Abraham Yates was "a preacher" to the popular taste and that "he *assures*" his constituents that "they are too poor to pay taxes." Ephraim Paine, seeking in 1782 to return to the senate, published a political creed in which he declared that people trading with the British ought "to be reduced to atoms, and made the sport of the wind." By 1786 a popular politician could be expected to keep up a careful correspondence about affairs at home while he was away at the legislature, with his informants telling him what maneuvers and what groups lay behind the petitions that his constituents sent.[33]

With popular interest running high, and with little internal structure to either channel or smother that interest, the legislature became a place that no single person could dominate. Alexander Hamilton spelled out the result in a report on New York affairs that he wrote for Robert Morris in 1782. As far as he could see, the man "of a most uniform influence" was his father-in-law, Philip Schuyler, sitting in the senate for the western district. But even Schuyler did not have so much power "as not to be exposed to the mortification of seeing important measures patronized by him frequently miscarry." Of the other senators, James Duane, John Morin Scott, Zephaniah Platt, Ephraim Paine, and Abraham Yates had "each their share of influence." In the assembly, William Malcolm, John Lawrence, John Lansing, Thomas Tredwell, and Cornelius Humfrey all could bring weight to bear.[34]

More objective evidence bears out both Hamilton's judgment that these were the most notable men in that particular session and his opinion that none of them wielded preponderant influence. No single member in the whole radical period ever made himself so necessary that he was always at the center of affairs, as Egbert Benson had been. Hamilton wrote his report to Morris during the sixth session, when two of the men whom he mentioned, John Lansing of Albany and John Lawrence of New York City, were among the three assemblymen who held seats on more than one standing committee. Both Lansing and Lawrence served on a sizable number of temporary committees as well, but neither came even close to the rate at which Benson had been named to such boards.[35]

It would be tedious to work through the legislative records of all the people whom Hamilton singled out, but that of Governor Clinton does need attention. Hamilton characterized the governor as having "declined in popularity, partly from a defect of qualifications for his station and partly from causes that do him honor—the vigorous execution of some necessary laws that bore hard upon the people, and severity of discipline among the militia." Hamilton thought him "a man of integrity" and knew that his "particular friends" considered him "a statesman." But he also recognized that the governor was a man who wanted to stay in office. That, he thought, explained Clinton's style, which was either to flatter "prevailing prejudice" or to temporize, "especially when a new election approaches."[36]

When he penned his sketch of Clinton, Hamilton and the governor were still in fairly close liaison. Clinton could expect occasionally to find in his mail one of the letter-essays in which Hamilton developed his ideas on public affairs.[37] Nonetheless, Hamilton had both put his finger on the secret of the governor's success and had exposed the issue over which they would confront each other six years later, in the ratification debates at Poughkeepsie. Between 1779 and 1783, Clinton successfully detached himself from most of the conservative figures who had surrounded him early in his governorship. During the same years, he identified himself with the issues that underlay the state's popular and legislative radicalism. It was not until the end of the 1780s that he publicly took a position as the leader of a party, but throughout the decade he moved towards it.

He began the move with his response to the crisis of 1779. While Egbert Benson and Robert R. Livingston were turning pale at the revival of the committees and at crowd action, Clinton was realizing that the people involved wanted most of all to be heard and to know that what they said would have effect. His advice to the legislature at the opening of the third session was that they should recognize the currency crisis as a "subject of the first importance," worthy of their "most serious deliberation." He told them that the "sense that your constituents loudly express of the necessity of applying some suitable remedy. . .gives you the strongest assurances of their acquiescence" in any serious effort to meet the crisis. He had realized, in other words, that if the government was to survive, it first had to prove that it could hear what people said and could then act.[38]

From that, Clinton went on to endorse one by one the other aspects of what was becoming the radical position. He left behind his belief that the state needed only to control the royalists, not punish them, a belief that had led him to oppose the first attempt at confiscation and to work closely with the conservative judges on the council of revision. In February 1779 he had been willing to defend alone what such men stood for. He reported to John Jay that in the absence of the rest of the council, he was without "aid in warding off a wicked factious Measure which might perhaps be more easily defeated now than at later Period." But he flattered himself that he would be "able to render the present Attempt abortive."[39] Over the next five years, however, Clinton moved away from such close cooperation and towards the position on the Tories that enabled both the Marquis de Chastellux and the royalist historian Thomas Jones to identify him as the most angry of Tory-haters.[40] In that, his reputation may be exaggerated; never in his policy speeches during the war years did he give mention to the royalists as a problem that needed special attention. But when he finally did raise the issue in January 1784 it was in terms that, though oblique, aligned him with the radicals who believed the Tories needed punishing.

Speaking at the opening of the seventh session, Clinton recalled the "cruelty and rapine" with which the royalists and the British had waged the war. He looked around New York and saw "the calamities which have reduced so many of our virtuous fellow citizens to want and distress." He singled out for praise the "obedience to the laws and. . .care to preserve peace and good order" of "those patriots. . .who have returned to this city." The governor said those things to an audience that included assemblymen Isaac Sears, Marinus Willett, and John Lamb. Only the day before, those three had led the violent silencing of James Rivington, the voice of the city's royalists. Clinton was telling them and their followers that as far as Tories were concerned, their definition of "peace and good order" was his as well.[41]

The governor broke with the conservatives on economic policy in the same way. He had given firm support to the heavy taxation that was the center of their response to the wartime economic crisis, but he never gave any evidence that he joined the likes of Egbert Benson, Robert R. Livingston, and John Sloss Hobart in their commitment to the idea of a free market. Instead, Clinton was always willing to accept that it could be proper and necessary for the government to interfere in the economy. After an interstate convention met in Hartford at the end of 1779 to deal with inflation, Clinton called a special meeting of the legislature to consider its proposals. He advised the meeting that the need for "a general limitation of prices, was the immediate occasion of my calling you" and that it was a subject "of great importance" which demanded "a suitable attention." By 1782 he was also endorsing the radical position on taxation. Opening the sixth session of the legislature, he called on it to undertake a general revision of the tax laws. But he stressed that though their structure was ramshackle, their general basis was "founded in justice," for they were "calculated to compel the members of the community to contribute towards the public burthen, according to their respective abilities."[42]

Hamilton's assessment of how Clinton did things was thus astute. The governor was no fire-eating tribune of the people, but again and again he displayed a sympathy and a responsiveness to angry public opinion and a willingness to turn to radical policies that the conservative politicians could never show. It may have sprung, as Hamilton thought, from his anxiousness to be reelected. Or it may have been tied to the plain republican manner which observers noted about him throughout his life. He was, after all, the one who had said that the public would judge the provincial assembly's persecution of Alexander McDougall.[43] Whatever it was, it worked. In the election of 1780, the year after his first gesture towards the sources of popular anger, he faced no opponent. In 1783 two other candidates set themselves up. One was Philip Schuyler, and the other was Ephraim Paine. The Dutchess senator's candidacy showed that the governor by no means represented the left extreme in the state. The Albany general was still smarting from the humiliation that Clinton had inflicted on him in 1777, and now that the war was won, he wanted to turn the Revolution to the right. But neither candidacy was ever a serious threat, and one observer sarcastically predicted that Clinton was certain of victory, "although he has the distinguished talents of Schuyler and Paine to parry, which by the bye is no small matter, when you consider that two to one is odds even at football." Clinton was again without opposition at the next election, in 1786. Not until 1789, when the issue of the Federal Constitution had transformed state politics, would he face a serious challenge, and not until 1792 would he finally be defeated.[44]

Much of Clinton's success was due to the effectiveness of what Peter W. Yates once called "his private Irish ways." Those ways can be seen at their least private in the matter of patronage. Clinton shared the disposal of the state's public offices with the four senators whom the assembly elected each session as a council of appointment. With very few exceptions, those senators were men of Clinton's own sort. He could count on working in the council with radical senators like William B. Whiting, Abraham Yates, Henry Oothoudt, Zephaniah Platt, and Ebenezer Russell. The only times when the assembly picked grandees rather than plain men were in the eighth session, when it named Isaac Roosevelt, the ninth, when it picked Philip Schuyler and Lewis Morris, and the eleventh, when Schuyler was again a member. Never did such men control the council; even in the ninth session, when Clinton faced Schuyler and Morris across the table, he could count on the support of the radical Jacobus Swartwout and the frontier senator David Hopkins.

By no means did the council follow a policy of strict spoilsmanship under Clinton's domination. It made James Duane mayor of New York in 1784. It was happy enough for Egbert Benson to continue as attorney general. But the county judges, the justices of the peace, the sheriffs, and the militia officers whom it chose were by and large far from being like Benson or Duane. The council offered, in other words, a magnificent opportunity for Clinton to create an interest loyal to himself. Philip Schuyler, full of envy but still displaying accurate insight, recognized what was going on. He observed in 1785 that the governor's secure position was more and more a matter of patronage and that though he dispensed it "privately as he thinks," it was "sufficiently notorious to those who have taken some pains to be informed."[45]

Clinton's story between 1777 and 1788 encapsulates the internal dynamics of New York's revolution. The people from whom he sprang were west-bank yeomen. They had not been a major factor in the pre-Revolution life of the province. Their leaders had been overshadowed by the great men across the river and in the two cities. They had far less reason than either tenants or city folk for discontent. They were drawn into revolutionary politics as part of a coalition with magnates and urban radicals, but once involved, they developed an identity and a radicalism of their own, an identity and a radicalism that Clinton came to share. The governor had always been an astute politician; he would not have become an assemblyman at twenty-nine and chief magistrate at thirty-eight otherwise. But his greatest political achievement was to realize between 1779 and the mid-1780s the potential that had been there in his first election but which others had seen far more clearly than he. Like the radicalism for which his name came to stand, he made himself during those years, developing from a partner in a coalition for independence to the leader of a democratic party.

III

The radical policies that the people and their legislators developed and that Clinton made his own centered on three broad areas: the treatment of the royalists, the reconstruction of the southern district, and the future development of the state. Though analytically separate, the three were thoroughly bound up with one another. The royalist issue, in particular, underlay not only the other two but also other questions that began appearing on the public agenda later in the 1780s. The central radical tenet was that royalism deserved punishment, and by the time the set of punishments was completed, the laws that enacted it filled a sizable volume.[46] They began with the laws passed in the third session to seize the great Tory estates, to impose a special tax on Tories for the victims of royalist banditry, and to allow the expulsion from the state of the Tories' families.[47] A second wave followed during the fifth, sixth, and seventh sessions, from 1781 to 1784. The Citation Act of 1782 applied a stay to all suits brought by residents of the occupied zone against debtors who lived in the free area. It provided that the cases of such debtors should be settled by referees drawn from the patriot population rather than by court trials. It discharged all interest for the period of the war, allowed the debtor to make his payment in paper rather than specie, and permitted him to pay the debt into the state treasury if the creditor refused the paper. The Trespass Act of 1783 allowed refugees to sue people who had used their property during the occupation. Only a veto by the council of revision prevented "An Act Declaring the Alienism of the Persons therein Described," which would have stripped citizenship from everyone who either remained in the southern district or went there freely during the occupation.[48]

A Trading-with-the-Enemy Act, passed in 1782, allowed anyone to seize suspected goods and the vehicles or boats in which they were being transported. If the case were proven, the informant could claim half the value of both. Another law of that year allowed people whose buildings had been destroyed by the enemy to replace the timber from confiscated lands. "Zealous Friends" of the Revolution who had "done Acts. . .not conformable to the Strict Letter of the Law" were assured by an act of 1783 that their royalist victims would not be allowed to sue them. Though the end of the war brought the abolition of the conspiracies commissioners and the repeal of the act for recompensing robbery victims, passage of anti-Tory laws continued. Most notably, the seventh session's act "to preserve the Freedom and Independence of this State" imposed a conviction for misprision of treason on all who had actually aided the British and disqualified them from voting and officeholding. The result of these and the many other acts made in the same spirit was that no state "passed harsher laws against the Loyalists than New York."[49]

The reconstruction of the southern district was bound up with the royalist issue, if only because so many Tories had lived there or fled there. A dispassionate observer could see that there were distinctions to be made, for the district had been a conquered province and not everyone who remained in it either chose to do so or became a collaborator. International law recognized the plight of such people, but the laws that New York passed blurred both that distinction and the one between people who stayed behind when the British came and people who fled them and only returned in 1783. Thus any southern-district creditor was affected by the Citation Act, and anyone who obeyed a British order to live in a certain house was liable to suit under the Trespass Act. Similarly, towards the end of the seventh session, the legislature passed an act to raise a tax of one hundred thousand pounds in the counties that had been occupied. The act's stated reason was that the people of the free zone had "sustained many and heavy Burthens and Expences" and that it was "just and equitable that all who participate in the Blessings" of "Freedom and Independence" should contribute to their cost. It stated that the "citizens of the Southern District" were ready to "afford a testimonial of the Sense they have" of "the Exertions and Sufferings of their brethren" and that they agreed that the tax would be "such a compensation to the other Districts as would prove satisfactory to the Citizens thereof." The law was passed despite the facts that the southern district itself had been devastated and that its exiles had borne their share of the burden in the free counties. It summed up the spirit in which the reconstruction of the occupied counties was carried out.[50]

The other acts that dealt with reconstruction were concerned not with retribution but rather with de-Anglicizing three institutions that had symbolized the old order. These were the established Anglican Church, and particularly Trinity Church in New York City, King's College, and the chamber of commerce. In all three cases part of the problem was simply institutional, for Trinity, the college, and the chamber of commerce were all chartered corporations whose autonomy was derived directly from the crown. But there was more to it than legal formulae. The case of Trinity Church was especially complicated. It was just one of a large number of Anglican parishes in the southern counties that had enjoyed legal establishment in the colonial period, and throughout the southern district the benefits that establishment brought had long been a sensitive political issue. But Trinity was also a major landholding institution and one of the places where the old elite had gathered to proclaim its preeminence. As such, it had served major social and economic functions.[51]

King's College was likewise bound up with Anglicanism as well as with the crown. The "New York Triumvirate" of William Livingston, William Smith, and John Morin Scott had entered the public arena in the early 1750s over precisely the issue of whether the college should have a royal charter and an Anglican tie, and it has been argued that the debate they provoked marked the beginning of a separation in the province between Tory ideology and Whig.[52] As for the chamber of commerce, its founding in 1770 articulated the growing belief of the city's merchants that they were different from the rest of its citizens, different enough that they deserved a special, privileged place of their own. The problems that that belief had raised ran through the angry street politics of the decade from the Stamp Act to independence. Moreover, a sizable proportion of the men who had founded the chamber had become royalists.[53]

The legislature responded to all three problems by continuing the institution but at the same time modifying it. The chamber of commerce was reestablished as an incorporated institution by an act of the seventh session. The former royalist John Alsop replaced John Cruger as president, and the radical Isaac Sears took the place once held by Hugh Wallace as vice president; their selection was an indication that a new merchant coalition was starting to form. The renewal of the charter confirmed that even radicals like Sears wanted New York to be a commercial society dominated by its merchants. Sears himself, now a wealthy man, was on the point of launching the first American trading expedition to China. In fact, renewal of the charter was never in doubt; the question being raised even by people who mistrusted any merchant, whatever his politics, was not how to extirpate them but rather how other New Yorkers might defend their own interests against them.[54]

The legislature performed more drastic surgery on the churches and the college. The Church of England was disestablished by a law making null every act of the colonial government that either gave benefit to Anglicans or disadvantaged other faiths. Disestablishment was tied to an act that allowed the incorporation of non-Anglican churches and provided a mode for dividing a congregation's property, should it split. But the issue surrounding Trinity Church proved more thorny, both because of its special royal charter and because of the land that it owned. Its most important real property comprised the tracts on Manhattan Island known as the King's Farm and the King's Garden. It claimed these from a series of grants made by royal governors, beginning with the notoriously corrupt Benjamin Fletcher in the seventeenth century. The church's charter specified that it was subject to the authority of the Bishop of London, and it gave to the royal governor the right to induct its rector. These two matters were easily changed, but the internal control of the church and the property it held were other matters.

Two groups jousted for control of the church in the spring of 1784. One was made up of ex-royalists and the other of Anglicans who had taken the Revolution's side. The latter group was a cross section of the city's revolutionary coalition. It included figures as diverse as William Duer, James Duane, Robert R. Livingston, Isaac Sears, Daniel Dunscomb, and the old street leader Hercules Mulligan. With such men in it, the patriot group could not of course lose, and the law that modified Trinity's charter confirmed these men as the church's vestry.[55] But on the matter of the land, efforts to change the church's situation failed. The question began as a legislative issue in November 1784, when Matthew Adgate moved the establishment of an assembly committee to investigate the land's title. In February 1785 the committee presented a long historical report, intended to show that the land belonged to the state rather than to Trinity. The assembly printed the full text in its journal, which was most unusual, and instructed the committee to prepare a bill to vindicate the state's claim. In March the house overwhelmingly rejected a memorial from the church asking that the entire matter be stricken from the journal. But there the matter ended. No law was ever passed reclaiming the land, and Trinity was left free to become the enormously wealthy institution that it is today. Whether the effort to seize the land failed because of a lack of time or because of backstage maneuvers cannot be known. But it marked one high point of the radical attempt to link the Americanization of New York's old institutions with serious internal change.[56]

King's College proved another area of difficulty. From its beginning it had served as a bastion of Anglicanism, and its rector, Myles Cooper, had been an outspoken opponent of the Revolution.[57] But the college also had produced many of the men who led New York's revolution and who were in positions of power and eminence because of it. Among them were John Jay, Robert R. Livingston, Alexander Hamilton, and Egbert Benson. At the point of independence, Myles Cooper had been advocating a plan to transform King's into the center of a network of colleges that together would form a university for the province. This plan became the basis of the reestablishment of the college after the war. By a law of the seventh session, the college was renamed Columbia, and it retained its endowment and estates. Its governors became the board of regents of the new state university that the law established, and they were given the right to found and oversee colleges and academies throughout the state.

As Jurgen Herbst has shown, the change had its genesis not in the Revolution but rather in the brain of a high Tory. Moreover, the regents functioned initially "not as the administrators of a state system of preparatory and collegiate education, but as the governors of Columbia College." The law itself was modified severely in 1785 and again in 1787, and it was not until the second change that the University of the State of New York was divorced from the college. The spirit of even the initial law, however, was in tune with what radical republicanism meant in New York. It began the transformation of higher education from something that was the monopoly of one institution and the business of an established church to something in which any group or place could involve itself and something that was the business of the state.[58]

The third great problem, New York's future course of development, was necessarily more diffuse. It involved the remaining great estates, the vast areas of public land that the Revolution had opened to settlement, and the political economy of urban society. The most contentious question was the last, and it turned on the organized mechanics of New York City. In the eighth session, the legislature passed a bill to incorporate them, thus giving them approximately the same collective status as the merchants, with their chamber of commerce. The act originated with a petition from the mechanics themselves, and their desire for incorporation had several aspects. They had gained a collective consciousness during the struggle with Britain, and incorporation would seal their emergence as a major social and political factor. But it would also give them material benefits: it could provide a legal basis for a loan fund, thus freeing them from dependence on banks or on rich men for credit; it could give them an institution that they could use to defend their interests, especially vis-à-vis the merchants.[59]

Their effort met hard resistance. Aaron Burr spoke against it in the assembly, saying that it would "give them too much *political importance,* and that they ought to be *'kept down'* or *'under.'*" Pamphleteers speculated that designing men were using the mechanics "as mere Ladders to their ungovernable ambition." Though the bill passed the legislature, it was successfully vetoed by the council of revision. The veto message raised fourteen points in objection, some of them merely technical. But its primary position was that of Burr: the mechanics were not fit men for the privilege of incorporation. The message maintained that incorporating them would put them on a distinct footing from that of other citizens, that it would make them a quasi state within the state, and that it would transform New York from "a community of free citizens pursuing the public interest" to "a community of corporations, influenced by partial views." Ignoring two decades of history, the council told the mechanics that they had long "happily prospered" without incorporation and that they ought not to change so good a thing. At this point, the council was taking a general line against incorporations; using many of the same arguments,[60] it vetoed acts to incorporate the city of Hudson and a society for encouraging German immigration. But its particular hostility to the mechanics did not sit well with the sympathy it had shown to reincorporating the chamber of commerce. It fitted not at all with the fact that rich men already had a number of corporations either at their disposal or on the way to establishment, corporations such as the chamber itself, the Bank of North America, and the Bank of New York. The mechanics sought parity, and most of the legislators agreed with the request. But the council denied it.

On land policy and rural development, the legislation of the 1780s was far too varied for any quick review. There were several guiding principles, however. One was hostility to the idea that great landholdings should bring special privileges to their holders. This hostility did not take the form of a flat attack on the remaining great estates. On the contrary, Livingston and Rensselaerwyck survived, and new estates were founded. James Fenimore Cooper, writing from a landlord's point of view, recounted the trials of setting one up in his novel *The Pioneers*. Sometime after 1800, and from a different perspective, a minister traveling in what had been Iroquois country noted that "the same evil operates here. . . as in many parts of this country—the lands are most of them leased."[61]

But the legislature of the 1780s did abolish primogeniture and entail, thus opening the estates to division by inheritance. It did abrogate all remnants of feudal legal privilege. It did guarantee in the bill of rights which it adopted in 1787 that tenants would enjoy the same rights at law as landlords. Moreover, it adopted a policy for distributing public lands that contrasted in three ways with colonial policy. One way was that land would be handed out openly rather than in secret deals. The maps on which grants were to be recorded were to be accessible, and land was to be sold at vendue. Another was that the fees involved were reduced to almost nothing; thus a law of 1784 limited fees to three pounds to the governor and five pounds to the surveyor. Third, a chance was provided for smaller people to get land directly from the state. The land law of 1785 allowed locations of up to 500 acres at only four shillings per acre, which meant a payment of only one hundred pounds for the maximum grant. The law of 1786 divided land into townships of 64,000 acres and provided that every fourth township would be sold in individual lots of 640 acres each. Surveys, too, were regularized; a pattern of townships, as nearly square as possible, replaced the haphazard irregularities that had made colonial grants a surveyor's nightmare and a lawyer's bonanza. Such things helped balance the way that Clintonian land policy still delivered vast tracts to speculators and the way in which after 1791 the governor and his followers "proceeded to dispose of land on a scale that might have made the most generous royal governor. . . blush."[62]

The essence of radical policy, on matters other than royalism, was that citizens' opportunity should replace gentlemen's privilege. Abolishing the rights of the Church of England, making higher education the state's business, opening up western lands directly to small men as well as to large ones, and wanting mechanics as well as merchants to be able to incorporate themselves were all aspects of that general orientation. Two friends of John Lamb, Hugh Hughes and Charles Tillinghast, summed up their radicalism's meaning in 1785 in an exchange of views on what the legislature was doing.

Tillinghast reported to Hughes that the senate was upset and insulted when the assembly began sending messages to it by only one messenger rather than by the customary two. He told him that whatever their former politics, New York City Anglicans were coalescing to defend the land claims of Trinity Church and that the bill to incorporate the mechanics had met opposition from Aaron Burr in the assembly and was likely to fail in the senate or the council. He also told him that Quakers had petitioned for an act to end slavery.

Tillinghast and Hughes alike thought that all of these problems fitted together. Tillinghast dreaded an Anglican coalition that would weaken the Revolution. He wrote with sarcasm of the council of revision, "that last *resort of state wisdom*." He disliked Burr's arrogance on the subject of the mechanics. Hughes, himself a former assemblyman, carried the analysis further. Sending two assemblymen with messages to the upper house when it sent only one "always appeared ridiculous" to him, and he had tried to end it while he was a member. The Anglican Church had "much the same *Right* to *some of the Property* it holds as the Senate has to *two Members* of the Assembly, and will give it up as willingly." The conduct of "our Church and the Senate" made him see how necessary was constant vigilance against "Property or Prerogative," but he thought that candid Anglicans would not press a claim they could see was unjust. He contrasted what before the Revolution was "deemed legality" with the better ways that New Yorkers had developed. Though "not greatly in favour of corporate bodies," Hughes was sure that "the Mechanicks have as good a Right to be incorporated as any Class of Citizens whatever, and, were it asserted that they have a better, it might not, perhaps, be deviating an iota from the truth." Both men wanted to see a quick end to slavery, Hughes calling it "*cruelty in the extreme*" and the "*severest reproach*" to the country. But they recognized that most of the country representatives themselves owned slaves and that "masters will, *generally,* give them up. . . as freely *as the Church & Senate relinquish their claims.*"[63]

Here was the radical mentality of the 1780s. For both of these men, the central task was to establish an egalitarian democracy, one in which slavery would be ended; the unequal power of the church, the senate, the council, and "haughty men" would be brought down; and groups like the mechanics would be able to maintain what they had won in the Revolution. The questions on which they expressed their radicalism were of course urban ones. They showed no interest at all in such problems as the future of landlordism or dividing the state's lands, for as city people they were not affected by these questions. They realized that even radicals in the countryside were unlikely to go against their own interests by freeing their slaves. But they shared with country radicals like Adgate, Paine, DeWitt and Swartwout a commitment to a democracy of equal, productive men and a hostility to whatever seemed to oppose it. This was the core of the radicalism that shaped itself and then ruled in New York during the so-called critical period.

IV

Between 1780 and 1785 radicalism became a coherent position in the minds of many men besides Tillinghast and Hughes. The legislators who represented those men demonstrated that development by the way they learned to vote with one another. In the first years of independence the only people who maintained a coherent position and acted on it were the conservatives whom this study has been calling "constitutionalist patriots." The rest of the legislators were factious enough, but hardly ever did the votes in which they expressed their thoughts on one issue match those on another. By the eighth session, in 1784/85, that had changed. Partisanship split that session along the same lines on vote after vote, almost without regard to issue. Such sharp definition was without clear precedent, but it was not without background, for it marked the culmination of trends and tendencies that had been developing since the crisis of 1779.

This tendency towards radical coherence gave the first unmistakable evidence of its existence in the fifth session, late in 1781 and early in 1782. This session was different from its four predecessors in a number of ways. First, it contained a remarkable number of new people. About 72 percent of the members for the free counties had not been present the year before. Albany County, with a delegation of ten men, sent only three from the previous session. Ulster, Westchester, and Tryon, which each had six, reelected one, two, and two, respectively. Dutchess chose only one man of the seven whom it had sent to the fourth session. Orange and Ulster each reelected only one of their four. So high a rate of turnover was matched during the Confederation period only in the election for the third session, during the crisis of 1779.

The men whom the upstate voters sent were the radicals whom this chapter has discussed. For the first time, Dutchess did not elect Egbert Benson or anyone like him; instead it chose men like Dirck Brinckerhoff, Cornelius Humfrey, Brinton Paine, and Jacobus Swartwout. Albany sent no Livingstons or Schuylers or Van Rensselaers. It elected men like Matthew Adgate, Jacob Ford, and John Lansing. Ulster County picked its two venerable chieftains, Johannes C. Hardenbergh and Abraham Hasbrouck, and James Hunter, who had been the most prominent man in its committee revival two years before. Hunter was only one of many fifth-session assemblymen who had figured prominently in the revival.

During the session, the assemblymen took fifty-one roll calls. Their voting behavior in these roll calls is notable for two reasons. First, in gross, overall terms they sorted themselves into blocs that clung together and opposed each other. Second, for the first time, agreement among groups of assemblymen extended not only from division to division on a single issue but also from issue to issue.

About a quarter of the session's members fell into groups whose members agreed with one another on more than 70 percent of all divisions in which they took part. More than 40 percent of the house formed into groups whose members voted together at least 60 percent of the time. In the second session, about as many assemblymen had formed into such groups, but the blocs were not antagonistic, for agreement within pairs of members across bloc lines had ranged to as high as 87 percent. In the fifth session, the rate of agreement within pairs whose members were in the two different blocs was typically at the level of only 20 percent or 25 percent. One of the groups was dominated by members from the mid-Hudson counties, on both sides of the river. Its members included the Dutchess representatives Dirck Brinckerhoff, Jonathan Dennis, and Cornelius Humfrey and the Ulstermen Johannes Hardenbergh, Abraham Hasbrouck, and Charles DeWitt. The members of the other group came from the periphery, from both the southern district and the frontier counties of Charlotte and Tryon. The group included Thomas Wickes and Ezra L'Hommedieu of Suffolk, John Berrien and Daniel Dunscomb of New York, Jonathan G. Tompkins and Thomas Thomas of Westchester, William Petry and Isaac Paris of Tryon, and John Williams of Charlotte.[64]

The issues on which these two groups defined themselves most clearly were the governor's salary and the Citation Act. The debates on the Citation Act formed the central discussion in the session's consideration of how to punish royalists, and as was shown above, the problem blended royalism itself, regional antagonism, and debtor-creditor relations. The assembly divided twelve times during the debate, and on each division the split was sharp. Twenty-six members were firmly in support of the act, fifteen unequivocally against it, and only three in between. Of the twenty-six who favored it, twenty-one came from upstate constituencies. Of the fifteen who opposed it, eight came from the occupied zone, and three more from neighboring Westchester.

A split that was almost identical, in terms of the core on each side, developed over the governor's salary. The fifth session was the first in which the assembly quarreled over what the governor ought to be paid, and it took five roll calls to resolve the question. These separated a group of fifteen members who wanted to keep the salary low from nineteen others who wanted to be generous. Seven men remained in the middle. The fifteen who believed in a low salary all took part in the larger group that passed the Citation Act. They included Dennis, Brinckerhoff, Swartwout, Husted, Paine, and Humfrey of Dutchess; Bruyn, Hasbrouck, Hardenbergh, DeWitt, and Hunter of Ulster; and Frisbie, Palmer, and Adgate of Albany. The other side included eleven ordinance members and eight from a scattering of upstate constituencies.

Clearly, the assemblymen themselves saw a connection between the salary of the governor and the payment of debts owed by rebels to people below the enemy lines. Was the connection ideological, linking memories of the old American dislike of royal governors with a new-found dislike of Tories? Was it just pocketbook economics, tying together unhappiness about paying taxes and paying debts? In the absence of documentary evidence, there is no way of knowing, but the important point is that on both sides the legislators themselves drew a connection between the issues. Whatever their reason, the people who drew the connection had taken a long step towards partisan coherence. That the cores of the two sides were the same on both questions is more important than the fact that some men swung, allowing the radicals to win on the Citation Act but giving the victory to their opponents on the salary bill.

Over the sixth and seventh sessions such divisiveness dropped. These were the sessions when the legislature completed the passage of its laws punishing the royalists, and resistance to their passage was minimal. Turnover during these sessions was much lower than it had been between the fourth and the fifth. Between the fifth and sixth sessions barely more than half of the assemblymen were replaced,[65] a rate lower than that of all other elections of the Confederation period save one. Albany sent back five of the ten men who had represented it the session before, Ulster and Westchester each three of their six, and Dutchess five of its seven. The men who were reelected were the Matthew Adgates, the Jacobus Swartwouts, and the Charles DeWitts. The men who joined them were typified by Christopher Yates, an assemblyman for Albany and a nephew of the senator.

In the election for the seventh session, turnover rose to 57 percent, but this reflected the fact that this first free election in the formerly occupied counties returned hardly anyone who had been an ordinance member. In those counties two such men returned among the nine members for New York City. Suffolk and Queens each chose only one. Kings and Richmond counties chose none. In Albany, by contrast, six of the previous session's members were elected again, and in Ulster four. Westchester and Dutchess each reelected five. Orange picked three of its four men again, and Charlotte, which would soon become Washington, two of its four. Only in Tryon, shortly to be renamed Montgomery, was there a massive turnover, the county returning to the seventh session none of the men who had served it in the sixth.

The seventh was thus the session when radicals were most easy to find in the legislature. Albany once again elected Matthew Adgate and Jacob Ford. Although Philip Schuyler held one of the western-district senate seats, the others were filled by old Tryon and Albany figures like Andrew Finck and Jacob G. Klock, long enemies of the Johnson family, Henry Oothoudt, a Hudson Valley farmer, William B. Whiting, from the same township as Adgate, and Abraham Yates. Dirck Brinckerhoff was in the assembly for Dutchess, and Jacobus Swartwout had joined Ephraim Paine in the senate. The men representing New York City in the assembly were old urban radicals: Hugh Hughes, John Stagg, Isaac Sears, Marinus Willett, John Lamb, and Peter Pra Van Zandt. Though James Duane, Isaac Roosevelt, and Lewis Morris were among the southern-district senators, so were Alexander McDougall and the candlemaker Isaac Stoutenburgh.

The defeat that the conservatives suffered on the Citation Act had thus opened the way for even greater defeats, both at the polls and in the legislature, over the next two sessions. Without serious opposition to force them into disciplined coherence, however, the radicals splintered and fractured. Their votes during these sessions, especially the seventh, reflected unstructured agreement, not antagonism. The assemblymen who voted together more than 70 percent of the whole time fell to only 10 percent of the house in the sixth session and only 12 percent in the seventh. Assemblymen voting together at the 60-percent level fell from 37 percent in the fifth session to 34 percent in the sixth and 25 percent in the seventh. In both sessions, agreement between members of different blocs was markedly higher than it had been in the fifth. During the sixth session it ranged between a low of 8 percent in the case of one pair and highs above 50 percent in the cases of several. In the seventh session it ran from a low of 28 percent to a high of 61 percent.

A similar pattern developed on particular roll calls. Though the assembly divided often enough—sixty-two times in the sixth session and eighty-one in the seventh—the divisions usually had little to do with one another. This was particularly true in the seventh session, when men formed coherent groups across roll calls on only 30 percent of the votes. The members of that session changed their alignments rapidly from issue to issue. Only on the ten votes that the assembly took on the punitive tax law that it imposed on the southern district was there a run of roll calls that separated one group clearly from another. But in contrast to the votes of earlier sessions, what these votes showed was not that partisanship was in abeyance but rather that one group was triumphant. The radicals' position was so secure that they could allow themselves the same luxury of internal factiousness that had once been the privilege of the provincial ruling class.

The eighth session was very different. The assembly took 148 divisions, more than any other in the Confederation years. On those divisions, the assemblymen lined up time after time into two opposing groups. Almost half of all the roll calls taken showed congruence with other divisions, and this time congruence ran not simply from one issue to another but from problem to problem to problem. On only one major question was there a long run of votes on which the assemblymen took positions that did not fit with the overall pattern that they were defining: the abolition of slavery. The distinction between the votes on that issue, which split the radical group, and the many others that consistently sorted radicals out from conservatives gives emphasis to the point made by Hugh Hughes and Charles Tillinghast in their correspondence of 1785, that the "country members" were the representatives of slaveholders and were often slaveholders themselves.

The reason for the difference between the factious seventh session and the partisan eighth lies largely in the make-up of the two sessions. After the radical triumph in the first southern-district election, conservatives in New York City organized themselves to regain power. As a result, not a single member was carried over from the one session to the next. But in the upstate counties continuity was far greater. Albany reelected six men, and though Walter Livingston was among its new members his presence was balanced by that of Matthew Visscher, former secretary of the committee of safety, and other known radicals like Dirck Swart, Abraham Becker, Matthew Adgate, and Jacob Ford. Dutchess reelected five of its seven men, including two Brinckerhoffs, Cornelius Humfrey, and Brinton Paine. Ulster's delegates were men like Charles DeWitt and Cornelius C. Schoonmaker, who by this time were used to cooperating with Dutchess and Albany insurgents. Montgomery County sent old enemies of the Johnson family, such as William Harper, Isaac Paris, Volkert Veeder, and Christopher P. Yates.

The presence of conservative downstate and radical upstate members explains the confrontation that ran through vote after vote in that session. Fully 30 percent of the assemblymen formed into groups whose members agreed with one another more than 70 percent of the time. Almost half of the members were in groups that voted together on at least 60 percent of all roll calls. The level of agreement between members of the opposing groups was minimal, ranging, for different pairs, between 13 percent and about 30 percent. One group was dominated by Matthew Adgate, Jacob Ford, William Harper of Montgomery, Edward Savage of Westchester, Israel Thompson and Abraham Becker of Albany, and Brinton Paine of Dutchess. The other centered on Cornelius Corsen and Joshua Mercereau of Richmond, Charles Doughty and John Vanderbilt of Kings, Thomas Randall, Peter Van Brugh Livingston, and Comfort Sands of New York, and John Sands of Queens.

The roll calls of the eighth session present the problem of finding not divisions that show congruence but rather those that do not. Divisions can be grouped in dozens according to the way the legislators lined up on them, and the alignments persisted almost without regard to issue, save that of slavery. One of the largest groups of roll calls centered on the assembly's response to the decision that James Duane handed down in the Mayor's Court of New York City in the lawsuit that Elizabeth Rutgers brought against Joshua Waddington. Mrs. Rutgers sued Waddington for damages under the Trespass Act of 1783, and the trial turned into a test case on the state's punitive Tory laws. Alexander Hamilton argued for Waddington, and Egbert Benson, as attorney general, for the state and for Mrs. Rutgers. Duane's ruling effectively nullified the law by construing it so as not to conflict with the 1783 Treaty of Paris and with the international law of warfare. It thus struck both at the legislature's claim that as New York's sovereign authority it might do as it chose and at the policies that it had established on the Tory question.[66]

Radical assemblymen responded to the decision with anger. The house took a total of nine divisions on it, with motions ranging from mere condemnation of the decision to a proposal to change the mode of the mayor's appointment, as a way of getting rid of Duane. The more hostile a member's position toward Duane, the greater his radicalism. But what is more important is that the men who were most angry about what Duane had done were also coming together on other issues. They wanted to appoint only a minimal staff to the customs house that was being set up in New York City. They favored a facetious motion in the same debate to name a customs collector for the nonexistent "Port of Claverack." They voted to emit a new supply of bills of credit and to pass a bill "for the relief of certain tenants." They opposed allowing people who owed debts to the state dating from the colonial period to pay those debts off in paper rather than in specie. Overwhelmingly, the radical position on these votes was taken by the upstate members who had begun to come to power at the turn of the decade and who now, at last, formed a coherent group. The conservative side was made up of the men who had come to the assembly as the victors in an explicitly antiradical campaign.

The same pattern was evident on many other issues. One set of congruent votes brought together roll calls on the lands that were claimed by both the state and Trinity Church, on how to collect the punitive tax that the previous session had imposed on the southern district, on whether to impose import duties, and on land policy. The men who favored the claim of the state rather than that of Trinity Church also wanted to pass the bill for collecting the tax. They wanted to impose duties on European foodstuffs that competed with what their own constituents produced. They favored recognizing the land claims of some kinds of squatters. They wanted the state to limit the charges payable in the supreme court to the level of those payable in county courts. They saw no reason why the law should give a second chance to the holder of a land grant who lost it because he failed to meet the conditions that the state had imposed. They favored distributing land in ways that pointed towards a society of yeoman freeholders rather than towards one of landlords and tenants. They fought against every attempt to repeal or weaken the anti-Tory laws. The men who took these positions were of course the upstate representatives whose names are by now familiar and who had by this point made themselves into a party.

V

This was New York's post-Revolution radicalism at high tide. The presence in the eighth session of a markedly and consciously conservative delegation from New York City and the other southern counties forced the upstate radicals to form a coherent and disciplined bloc. In their votes, the members of that bloc mingled the remnants of the old issues of the 1770s with the new problems of development that the 1780s were presenting.

The assemblymen whose votes expressed this radicalism were in a position to cast them in that way because their constituents were telling them to do so. Since the time that legislators like themselves had adopted the principle of responsiveness to what their constituents wanted, a remarkable relationship had developed between them and their people. It showed itself in the populist content of the votes that defined the radical position but also in the dialogue from 1780 to 1785 between the representatives and their "fellow citizens." The dialogue was carried on at the polls; when the voters reelected a Matthew Adgate, a Dirck Brinckerhoff, an Abraham Yates, or an Ephraim Paine, they were saying that they approved of what such men had been doing. It was carried on in the hundreds of petitions that the assemblymen received. It expressed itself in the statements, declarations, and speeches in which legislators spoke to their constituents and in the addresses and instructions in which the constituents spoke back to them. It was a dialogue not just about how the political system should function but about the whole past and future of the state. The central belief of the people who took part in it was that New York ought to be a society of free and equal men. By autumn 1784 and spring 1785 the state was controlled by men who believed that and acted accordingly. But even as the radicals were realizing and enjoying their triumph, their enemies were beginning a campaign not just to drive them from office and annul their policies but to establish a new set of conditions in which the likes of their untrammeled ascendancy would never happen again.

Chapter 9

The Rise of Conservative Nationalism, 1784–1788

As the war ended, New York's conservatives began to regroup in order to recapture what they had lost. They faced a host of new problems. People like John Jay, Robert R. Livingston, James Duane, and Philip Schuyler had gained prominence and power in the independence coalition because others valued their obvious talents, because they agreed with those others about resistance and ultimately about independence, because it was vital to keep as much of old New York together as possible, and because of the remnants of the deference with which their sort had long expected common people to treat them. By 1784 they could count on none of those things save their talents. They disagreed vehemently with their former partners in coalition about what independence should mean. Those former partners had learned that they could advance their own interests by struggling with their fellow New Yorkers. Tenants, yeomen, and mechanics no longer thought of the elite as men to whom they ought to defer; they had learned otherwise in crowds, as committeemen, as voters, and as militiamen and guerrillas.

Consequently, the return of the conservatives to power had to be by some means other than a frontal assault on the radical position. Some aspects of their style remained the same; in 1786 just as much as in 1775, their core was a small group of people who knew one another and who based their cooperation on shared interests, shared experiences, and a shared perspective. If anything, it was more so, for this remnant of the factious New York elite had taken some long steps towards becoming a cohesive class. But there were differences as well. The conservatives recognized that they needed a popular base and that creating one would mean coming to terms with the changes in political society that the Revolution had wrought. "Usquebaugh and beer," "No Lawyers, No Presbyterians," and condescending attention at election time would do no longer. They found that they could win popular support in the southern district and, to a lesser extent, in Albany, but they also found that that support would never be great enough to overcome the other side fully. Their realization of that fact was part—though only part—of their decision to transform state politics into a branch of national politics. Establishing the federal republic was their way of changing the rules so as to end the conditions that had enabled the radicals to triumph.

They scored a magnificent success but did not quite achieve what they intended. Between 1784 and 1787 they transformed the public agenda from the one the radicals had written to one of their choice. They won significant victories in elections. They prevented the immediate completion of the coalition between New York City militants and upstate radicals that had seemed to be building at the end of the war. Most of all, they brought New York into the federal union. But what they did forced the other side to complete its own formation and to reach out from the legislature to the public whose anger had begun that formation. The result was that both sides, conservatives become nationalists and radicals become democrats, won Pyrrhic victories. Despite the Constitution's being an issue that the conservatives had raised, the radicals won the election for the Poughkeepsie ratifying convention in 1788 and were in as good a position to dominate it as they had been in the eighth legislature. The conservatives deftly undid that domination and achieved New York's ratification. But rather than accepting the finality of their loss, the radicals were in a position to turn it to at least some of their own purposes. How and to what extent they did that is outside the scope of this study,[1] but the basis on which they did it was laid by 1788.

I

Radicalism in revolutionary New York cannot be measured by the actions or the concerns of any one man. By contrast, much of the credit for both the rise and the partial triumph of nationalism must go to Alexander Hamilton. The way in which Hamilton, an outsider of dubious background, enrolled himself among New York's first gentlemen demonstrates that those first gentlemen were no closed circle, but then no successful aristocracy ever has been. Hamilton's contribution to the aristocracy was twofold. He conceptualized and gave first expression to most of the issues around which its recovery took place, and he convinced its divergent elements to begin cooperating and acting as a whole. By doing so, he forced the aristocrats to accept the political and social realities of the Revolution and to act on the basis of them rather than simply in reaction against them.

Hamilton was in a position to do these things because by 1782 he had turned his full attention to New York. Jay was in Spain, Duane and Benson were in Congress, Livingston was busy as secretary for foreign affairs, and Schuyler was sulking in his elegant tent south of Albany, but Hamilton was paying close attention to New York's problems and affairs. He had left Washington's official family after a tiff with the general, had fought gallantly as a commander at Yorktown, and then had returned to New York to study law and consider America's future. He brought with him the perspective from the heights that he had gained in five years as Washington's aide-de-camp, and he added to it the social point of view that went with marrying Schuyler's daughter.

Radical New Yorkers as well as conservative ones adopted Hamilton quickly. Privately, they sought his talents as an advocate in their court cases. Publicly, they sent him to Congress in 1782, choosing him in preference to his father-in-law.[2] While in Congress, he served the state with energy and exchanged lengthy letters with Governor Clinton. But during his year there he came to several conclusions. The first was that the people in power in the various states, New York not least, did not deserve their positions. He etched the portrait gallery of New York leaders that he sent to Robert Morris in 1782 in strong acid; the highest praise he could muster for most of them was that one man intended "to do well whenever he can hit upon what is right" or that another was "esteemed a sensible and an honest man." His contempt for ordinary men's abilities and for their limited concerns became clear while he was in Congress. He distinguished his fellows into "two classes...one attached to state, the other to Continental politics."[3] He watched the frightened response of the government of Pennsylvania to a militia mutiny in 1783 and poured equal scorn upon the government, the mutineers, and "the Multitude," who would "lean to the speciousness of a professed humanity rather than to the necessary harshness of authority." Government, he was coming to think, had rights "as essential to be defended as the rights of individuals." Congress offered the best hope of defending those rights, and it was for that reason that Hamilton busied himself there with efforts to secure its finances. That would be the first step towards securing and strengthening its power.[4]

Sure finance, however, demanded a sure income, and Hamilton believed that that income could come only from a merchant economy. What was important, now that the war was won, was to secure commercial prosperity. Securing such prosperity required a political economy in which credit would be readily available and in which taxation would be carried out in as regular and predictable a way as possible. Private property had to be safe from public intervention so that it would be invested and developed as its owners saw most fit. The persecution of merchant royalists had to end, for it put credit in jeopardy; it involved irregular taxation and even the seizure of the merchants' property; it presented the danger that they would take their talents, connections, and capital elsewhere; and by violating the treaty of 1783, it destroyed the international climate of confidence on which commercial prosperity had to rest.

Hamilton took high ground in most of the public arguments that he made on behalf of congressional power and against persecution of the Tories. In the "Phocion" letters of 1784 and in his defense of Joshua Waddington in the lawsuit that Waddington faced that year under the Trespass Act, he argued on the basis of abstract constitutionality and of the superior quality of treaties and international law over state law.[5] But it is important to note that these themes emerged in his thought after a long period during which he expressed his concerns largely in terms of political economy. In the "Continentalist" essays of 1781 and 1782 he argued that Congress ought to have the supreme power of regulating trade, and he wrote specifically against the "injudicious attempts made at different times to effect a REGULATION OF PRICES." Though he rejected the "cant phrase among the opposers of these attempts that TRADE MUST REGULATE ITSELF," he nonetheless believed in the free market rather than in governmental intervention. No amount of political action could overcome the "strong reciprocal influence between the prices of all commodities in a state, by which they, sooner or later, attain a pretty exact ballance and proportion to each other."[6]

His earliest statements on the royalist problem were phrased in similar terms. In August 1783 he wrote to Robert R. Livingston about the Tory emigration from New York City that was underway: "Many merchants of the second class, characters of no political consequence, each of whom may carry away eight or ten thousand guineas have I am told lately applied for shipping to convey them away. Our state will feel for twenty years, at least, the effects of the popular phrenzy." He had already expressed similar views to Governor Clinton, mingling constitutionality, hostility to any form of popular action, concern for the treaty's supremacy, and the belief that persecuting the Tories could only drive out "a great number of useful citizens, whose situations do not make them a proper object of resentment." These refugees would "abandon the country to form settlements that will hereafter become our rivals. . .nothing. . .can be more unwise than to contribute as we are doing to people the shores and wilderness of Nova-Scotia." He wrote James Duane that "many who have all along talked of staying now talk of going. We have already lost too large a number of valuable citizens."[7]

Meanwhile, Hamilton was developing ideas about the state's political economy. By June 1782 he had concluded that "the whole system (if it may be so called) of taxation in this state is radically vicious." He elaborated on that conclusion in the set of notes on the state of New York that he wrote for Robert Morris two months later. He criticized the method of taxing by county quotas and according to "circumstances and abilities." The "evil" began at the point of assigning the quotas, for "the members cabal and intrigue to throw the burden off their respective constituents." It continued in the actual assessment, for "the exterior figure a man makes, the decency or meanness of his manner of living, the personal friendships, or dislikes of the assessors have much more share in determining what individuals shall pay, than the proportion of property." Worst of all, though this system was based on the "ostensible reason" of "a desire of equality," in fact it rested on "a desire to discriminate between the *whigs* and *tories*."[8]

Hamilton said such things in public as well as to his friends. In the sixth "Continentalist" essay, published in July 1782, he wrote of "that worst of all modes" of taxation, which was "by assessment." He criticized the supposed egalitarianism of the system, asking, "Do we imagine that our assessments opperate equally? Nothing could be more contrary to the fact." What he wrote when he argued for a fixed Continental impost, which he did again and again, must be read against the background of the openly political and highly flexible taxation that was the rule in his own state and of his belief that it must be replaced by "the establishment of permanent funds."[9]

Hamilton insisted that the application of his ideas would benefit everyone, not just the few. A permanent tax system "would be the most effectual way of easing the people," for "with this basis for procuring credit, the amount of present taxes might be greatly diminished." He dismissed the idea that there was bound to be "collision and rivalship . . . between the landed and trading interests, for the truth is they are so inseparably interwoven, that one cannot be injured, without injury, nor benefitted, without benefit to the other." Land did not form the basis of a way of life that was different and superior to what went on in cities; rather, it was a commodity, to be traded like any other. He believed that if trade was depressed, land would sink in value, but that if trade flourished, land's value would rise. Men who worked with their hands ought likewise to realize that "the only object of concern with an industrious artisan, as such, ought to be, that there be plenty of money in the community, and a brisk commerce to give it circulation and activity." Whether farmers, merchants, or craftsmen, New Yorkers were "a commercial people."[10]

From these assumptions, Hamilton worked up an elaborate set of ideas about the liberty that Americans had won in the Revolution. Though on one occasion he defined the concept in public, participatory terms, calling it "the *right* to a *share* in the government," in general he was at pains to defend not the liberty to take part but rather the liberty to be left alone. He insisted that "the nature of our popular constitutions requires a numerous magistracy" to check the people. He wrote that "the true sense" of liberty "must be the enjoyment of the common privileges of subjects under the same government." Paraphrasing Saint Paul on charity, he declared that "the spirit of Whiggism cherishes legal liberty, holds the rights of each individual sacred, condemns or punishes no man without regular trial."[11]

Such a definition of liberty implied that people whose class made them unfit to conduct the great affairs of state ought to remain quietly in their station. Arguing against the active involvement in politics of the New York

City mechanics, Hamilton wrote that "there is a certain proportion or level in all the departments of industry. It is folly to think to raise any of them, and keep them long above their natural height. . . . By attempting to do it the oeconomy of the political machine is disturbed, and till things return to their proper state, the society at large suffers."[12] Liberty meant the freedom to enjoy a climate of general prosperity under laws that were fixed and impartial in their operations, laws made by society's "best" men. It did not mean the right to join with others to advance a shared interest by political means. To Hamilton, the interest of the merchant was the interest of all. New York's future would be as a society of private men who pursued their private concerns and resolved their conflicts of interest in the marketplace rather than in the political arena. The dollar, not the vote, would be the deciding factor among them.

Hamilton's program for a thriving merchant society thus contained many different elements held together by a dominant vision. He wanted a market as free as possible from the government's interference, but he also wanted a government strong enough to give that market maximum encouragement and protection. He wanted an end to political harassment of the Tory merchants, whom he considered to be the men most qualified to make the market work. He wanted taxation that would be predictable from year to year rather than open to change with each new legislature. He wanted secure credit for American commerce both at home and abroad. He wanted men who shared his vision to be in power, and he wanted the rest of the citizenry to accept such men's taking care of everyone's interest and to remain quiet, save when they cast their votes. To secure all these things, he wanted to establish the twin principles that Congress, not the states, held sovereignty in America and that international law was paramount to even Congress's will.

Never content as a mere analyst, Hamilton acted to realize his ideas throughout the time that he was shaping them. All of his political writing was intended to intervene in the world, as well as to explain it. As soon as he left the army, he busied himself in active politics, first as receiver of Continental taxes for the state and then, in 1783, as a member of Congress. He used both positions to promote his ends. In July 1782 he was promising Robert Morris that he would lobby the legislature for a change in the state's tax system. Shortly afterwards, he got the legislature to pass a resolution he had written calling for a convention to strengthen the Articles of Confederation. He met the legislators and urged them to revise the tax laws. In September 1782 he ghostwrote an address "To the Public Creditors of the State of New York," which was adopted by a meeting over which his father-in-law presided. Even as he left the post of Continental receiver, he was still lobbying for a more demanding tax system. As a congressman, he argued incessantly for strengthening the central government and for enforcing the treaty's clauses against victimizing the royalists.[13]

Though he held no public office between the time of his leaving Congress, in September 1783, and his election to the state assembly, in June 1787, Hamilton's career in those years was centered on political action. The many defense arguments that he undertook for Tories accused under New York's punitive laws showed that he supported with deeds what he had written on the subject. He was closely bound up with the Bank of North America venture in Philadelphia, and he encouraged efforts to support it there and to spread it to New York. He drafted the charter and the constitution of the Bank of New York. He intended his bank projects to be oriented around circulating capital and the needs of merchants rather than around land and the needs of farmers, and when Robert R. Livingston mooted a counterplan for a bank based on land, he joined a group of merchants that opposed it. He convinced his fellow founders of the Bank of New York to accept the principle that the greater an investor's share, the greater ought to be his power in influencing decisions, in place of their original plan to limit all shareholders to a maximum number of votes.[14]

When Hamilton entered the legislature in 1787, he organized his actions on the same principles. One of his first steps was to support the petition of a British general for a land grant. He spoke against continuing the disqualification from public office of people who had been involved in anti-American privateering during the war. Throughout the session, he worked to transform the basis of public life from constant struggle to predictable order and regularity. This became most clear when he tried to bring about a sweeping change in the tax system. He drafted a set of resolutions and then a bill that were intended to do away finally with the system of county quotas and political assessment. He proposed instead an elaborate set of procedures in which taxation would be based on specific kinds of land and other property and in which the law set the rates on everything taxed. The assessors' task would be merely to count the number of items and acres and compute the proper rate. The text of his draft bill runs in print to fifteen detailed pages, and though the attempt failed, it illustrates perfectly his concern to substitute regularity and order for struggle and endless political decisions. He was sure that "the principles of the present bill will approach much nearer to equality than the former system" and that "it will have the great advantage of certainty—it leaves nothing to discretion."[15]

Hamilton's passion for putting regularity in the place of open political struggle extended to other realms. Divorces in New York traditionally had taken the form of private laws, but he used a petition for such a law as an excuse to introduce a general divorce bill. Legislative sessions since independence had decided by vote where their successors would meet, and often the votes went on for several divisions while supporters of Poughkeepsie vied with those of Newburgh and Kingston. Hamilton proposed to substitute a plan fixing the meetings of alternate sessions in New York and Albany. Continuing his battle for the supremacy of the peace treaty, he brought in bills to repeal the Trespass Act, the Citation Act, and, finally, all laws that were inconsistent with the pact.[16] There were limits, of course, even to his zeal for regularity. When a bill was brought in to set the fees that lawyers might charge, he spoke against putting them too low. Whatever the law said, if it "did not allow a proper compensation, it would be evaded."[17] Regularity meant ending open political struggle in the interest of guaranteeing the conditions necessary for mercantile prosperity. It did not extend to political intervention in the profits that merchants and their associated professionals, such as lawyers, might take. It was in support of these principles that Hamilton involved himself in the political life of the state and in the drive to render the state subordinate to the central government.

II

Though Thomas Jefferson once said that Hamilton was "without numbers...an host within himself,"[18] he could have achieved nothing had he stood alone. He gained political importance because around his ideas he built a political movement. He was able to build the movement because there were New Yorkers who were learning to think and act as he did. When Robert R. Livingston wrote with an audible sigh to John Jay of the radical victory in the New York City election of December 1783, he was associating himself with Hamilton's perspective. Hamilton knew what Livingston thought, for months earlier the chancellor had lamented with him "the violent spirit of persecution" and expressed his dread of "its consequences upon the wealth, commerce & future tranquilily [*sic*] of the state." Livingston concurred with Hamilton's judgment about persecution's cause: "one [man] wishes to possess the house of some wretched Tory another fears him as a rival in his trade or commerce & a forth [*sic*] wishes to get rid of his debts by shaking his creditor or to reduce the price of living by depopulating the town." Jay, far away in France, agreed as well: "What does it signify where nine tenths of these People are buried? I would rather see the Sweat of their Brows fertilize our Fields than those of our Neighbours."[19]

These men sometimes quarreled among themselves, as when Hamilton spotted the chancellor behind the move to create a land bank rather than a merchant bank. But they laid much of the groundwork for the nationalist movement that they were to lead as they rediscovered the agreement that had allowed them to control the independence movement. The Tory question and political economy were what brought them to do so. Their gathering and their realization of what they had to do amounted in the first stages to simply a renewal of old-style politics. They were, after all, great men who knew one another well.

More was needed than just the agreement of a few great men, and the raw materials were lying all around, at least in the southern district and the landlord counties. In the south Hamilton found no difficulty in gathering support from royalists who had not fled. A measure of the openness of his identification with their cause and with that of the British came in April 1786 when patriot merchants of New York City sought the legislature's interposition against their British creditors. These were men who had spent the war in exile; one of them, who had been Hamilton's brother officer, begged him in the name of old comradeship for aid in getting their case before the legislature. He sought especially the support in the senate of Philip Schuyler. Hamilton did give some help, but he wrote that this did not mean that he was abandoning the position for which he was known to stand. His situation was delicate, for he supported the merchant interest, whatever the former politics of the men who made it up. But not for nothing did one of his allies remember years later how "we permitted the Tories to enlist under our banners," how they "fought by our side in every important battle. . . with the democracy," and how "we ought not to forget their zealous and useful service in our great contest for the constitution."[20]

By themselves, however, the Tories could not win even New York City. Somehow an alliance had to be struck both with revolutionaries there and with people upstate. Some of the old radicals, particularly the merchants among them, began to drift towards particular conservative causes as a result of their connections, their wartime experience, and their self-interest. Alexander McDougall might never reconcile himself to an easy policy on royalists, but as a Continental major general he had seen the problems of organization and finance that made nationalists of most who reached such rank.[21] McDougall's daughter married John Lawrence, a New York merchant who played a conservative role both as an ordinance assemblyman and in later legislatures. Hamilton affectionally called Lawrence "my dear friend," lobbied him on behalf of tighter tax policies, and praised him to Robert Morris as "a man of good sense and good intentions" who had "just views of public affairs." Such were the connections that lay behind McDougall's acceptance of the presidency of Hamilton's Bank of New York.[22] Even the redoubtable Isaac Sears, who the day before he began his assembly service led the sacking of James Rivington's printing house, had become a rich man. Sears took the vice-presidency, under a Tory president, of the reconstituted chamber of commerce. Moreover, as a communicant of Trinity Church, he found himself mingling every Sunday with royalists and men of the better sort. His days of drinking in seamen's taverns were over.[23]

Sears and McDougall were both dead by 1788, but the overwhelming support of New York merchants for the Federal Constitution demonstrates that Hamilton had won his point among them. The mechanics represented a more difficult matter. By organizing their committee and pressing for its incorporation, by their lack of enthusiasm for the Bank of New York, and by the slates they ran for the legislature in 1784 and 1785, they showed that they saw themselves as men with a separate interest. Hamilton's own attempts to bring them to his side in 1784 were fumbling and smacked of the irritating condescension with which they had been treated under the old order. He talked down to them in the first "Phocion" letter, telling them that his "arguments, if they were understood, would be conclusive with the Mechanic," speaking archly of "those classes of the community who are to employ you," and telling them not to try to rise "above their natural height." He had enough sense, however, to keep quiet during their struggle in 1785 for incorporation. The points that he probably would have liked to make were put by, of all people, Aaron Burr.[24]

Others in his camp were more astute. The radical assembly delegation that won the first election in the city was swept out in June 1784 by a ticket that included the mechanics Daniel Dunscomb and William Goforth. The merchants and the conservative professionals were beginning to recognize the importance of the mechanics in any winning urban coalition. That the mechanics named both of these men to their own victorious slate in the election of April 1785 suggests that they were willing to reach to their right even while the conservatives were reaching to their left. Despite the condescending tone in which Hamilton first suggested it, many mechanics were accepting the idea that at least in the short run they stood to gain more from a détente with their fellow downstaters than from any alliance with upstate radicals.

Albany County was the other place where the conservative nucleus found some basis for a drive for power. Though thousands of ordinary Albanians and some great ones did choose the king's side, the county's leading families, the Ten Broecks, the Van Rensselaers, the Livingstons, the Gansevoorts, and the Schuylers, all supported independence. That did not retain for them control of Albany's revolution; instead, they played and lost the game of coalition politics. Though Philip Schuyler held a senate seat throughout the 1780s, for most of that time he was either isolated or possessed of few allies among the county's other members. As chapter 8 showed, Albany's legislators were very important in the group of upstate radicals.

Even in their worst moments, however, the great men had their supporters in the county. They tried in 1777 to make Schuyler governor and Abraham Ten Broeck lieutenant governor. The next year they again put Ten Broeck up for lieutenant governor, nominated Schuyler for the senate, and picked a slate for the assembly. Their prime goal was to "disappoint Abraham Yates," but though every one of their assembly candidates won, neither Schuyler nor Ten Broeck gained the office he sought. William Smith listed the twenty-five men who met to pick that slate. They included Schuyler and Ten Broeck themselves, James Duane, and a cross section of Beekmans, Van Rensselaers, and Livingstons. Here was the county's traditional politics in action.[25]

The measure of the great men's inability to control things can be seen in the one set of Albany election correspondence and returns that survives from the 1780s. These were recorded in the village of Coxsackie, on the west bank of the Hudson. Coxsackie lay just below the southern limit of Rensselaerwyck. In economic and cultural terms, the freehold farmers there had more in common with the men of Ulster and Orange than they did with most Albanians. They sent one of their own, Henry Oothoudt, to the legislature, and both as an assemblyman and later as a senator, Oothoudt behaved much the same as did members from further down the Hudson. But the election returns in question and the correspondence accompanying them were not collected by Oothoudt or one of his friends; rather, they were the work of Leonard Bronck, a young man who had ties to the county's upper crust.

In the early 1780s, as in 1777 and 1778, the magnates wanted to control the elections. In 1782 their coordinator was Leonard Gansevoort, and after "some residents of Albany City" proposed a ticket, he passed it on to Bronck. The "residents" were particularly worried about the way that King's District, the home of Matthew Adgate and William B. Whiting, had "for these two years past had such an unequal representation." Gansevoort advised Bronck to "solicit the attendance of everybody to your poll." But despite this opposition to him, Adgate won. The next year it was the turn of John Wigram, business manager of Livingston Manor, to arrange things, and in this election the great men virtually gave up. They nominated a slate, but after they had sent it out they resigned themselves to "the alteration that will here be made among the People" in favor of Adgate and Jacob Ford. Wigram advised Bronck "please to make the necessary Alteration on the Lists."[26]

Part of what was wrong resulted from simple sloppiness. Despite the Albany gentlemen's nomination of Abraham Ten Broeck for lieutenant governor in 1778, Peter R. Livingston handed out poll lists in Livingston Manor naming not Ten Broeck but the eventual victor, Pierre Van Cortlandt. Chancellor Robert R. Livingston convinced the election inspector to alter the list, but his cousin's error cannot have helped Ten Broeck's chances. The deeper problem, from the magnates' viewpoint, was that their old ways at election time were no longer working. Chancellor Livingston scoured Clermont, his estate, to bring in tenants for the election of 1778, but only forty persons turned out from the whole manor. Despite Leonard Bronck's efforts against Adgate in the election of 1782, less than half as many Coxsackie people turned out that year as had voted in 1780.[27]

But by the end of the war, the conservatives had begun to learn their lesson. The first results came in the spring of 1784, at the election in New York City for the eighth assembly. In that poll the radical slate nominated by the mechanics was defeated by a ticket of merchants such as Comfort Sands and Henry Remsen and politicians like Aaron Burr and John Lawrence. It was on the basis of this success that Alexander Hamilton ventured his first intervention in upstate politics. That came during the election of 1785, held immediately after the conclusion of the eighth legislative session.

That session had marked the high point of radicalism in state politics, and Hamilton and a number of others decided that enough was enough.

Hamilton confronted two problems. First he had to convince the men of his class that they had to work together not just within their own counties but across the whole state. Then he had to get them to stop bickering among themselves. The bickering most immediately in question was between the Livingstons of Livingston Manor, led by the manor lord Robert Livingston, Jr., and his sons Walter and Peter, and those of Clermont, led by the chancellor. Their feud sprang from the weighty matter of where to place gristmills along the Roeliff Jansen Kill, the stream that divided the two estates. The manor lord asked Hamilton for legal help, but Hamilton used the request as a pretext for lecturing him on the state's perilous politics. He told him that the "truly alarming" spirit of the "present legislature" appeared "evidently directed to the confusion of all property and principle." The time had come for "those who are concerned for the *security of property*...to endeavour to put men in the Legislature whose principles are not of the *levelling kind*." The "principal people" had for their "own defence" to "unite to overset" men like Jacob Ford and Matthew Adgate, whom Hamilton called "a couple of New England adventurers...who make tools of the Yates and their associates." The "safety of all those who have anything to lose" required them "to take care that the power of government is intrusted to proper hands."[28]

Hamilton was sure that the manor lord had "heared from other quarters...a like account of public affairs." Not long afterwards, Hamilton wrote William Duer, recently elected an assemblyman from New York City, that "there was every reason to believe General Schuyler with all his friends (whose views correspond with yours) would be elected in exclusion of Ford, Adgate, Yates &c." Hamilton was making suggestions to men who were ready to listen to them. Even before he wrote to the manor lord, one Livingston was telling another that "this Country never had such a hard tryal since the Revolution between Demo. and Aristo. as it will have this Election. All parties are alive, Letters and Lists contending...and every subterfuge invented by both parties." The aristocrats had taken the offensive; whereas in 1783 they had had to accept that "the People" would make an "alteration" in favor of Adgate and Ford, now they "could not agree" to place Ford on a compromise ticket that might produce "the happy effects of Harmony and Unanimity."[29]

The right won an unqualified victory. Only one member of Albany's delegation to the eighth assembly was returned to the ninth. In the place of the Adgates and Fords were figures such as John Livingston, Leonard Bronck, James Gordon, Peter Vrooman, and John Taylor. Livingston's name and Bronck's long connection with the great men speak for themselves, and three of the new members had been nominated as far back as

1778 by the cabal that tried to unseat Abraham Yates from the senate.[30] The radical dominion in Albany had been broken, and a gleeful manor lord reported to Hamilton that by "uniting the interests of the Rensselaer, Schuyler & our family, with other Gentm. of property in the County in our Interest. . . we carryed this last Election to a man." He trusted that "we shall always have the like Success provided we stick Close to Each other. . . [and] we should be Cautious of letting our Enemyes know anything while that may be dangerous."[31]

But all the Rensselaers, Schuylers, and Livingstons in the county could not have carried a single precinct even if every other "Gentm. of property" had joined them. The success of their "interest" depended on their ability to get their tenants to vote their way. By 1785 the two factors that had combined over the previous two decades to make precarious the political power of such men over their tenants had come to an end. Where confiscation and redistribution had broken the great estates most of the tenants were now yeomen, but none of the redistribution had taken place in Albany County. The popular royalism that had continued the strife of pre-Revolution days into the war was over, both because the radicalization of state policy had brought many of the people involved in it to the side of the Revolution and because the end of the war made further resistance futile.

On the estates that remained, the tenants confronted a new regimen, one that was in the spirit of Hamilton's advancing capitalism rather than in that of Sir William Johnson's seigneurial stasis. A series of state laws forced an end to entail and to all remnants of feudal privilege in the 1780s,[32] but these only required from the landlords a stance that the more forward-looking among them had already endorsed. Philip Schuyler's leases of the 1780s and 1790s illustrate the triumph of the cash nexus over the personal relationships and obligations which at their best had given stability to the old order. Some of Schuyler's leases continued to specify the obligations of service which had been normal before independence, and as late as 1805 some tenants found that he intended to exact his due of a day of riding, first refusal of the sale of a lease, or a quarter of the proceeds of a sale.

But after 1780 it was more and more Schuyler's practice to cross such clauses out on his printed lease forms. On the new forms that he introduced about 1790 they were not even to be found. By that year, Schuyler had taken decisive steps towards organizing his estates as rural capitalist enterprises rather than as manors. He began offering tenants the choice of paying a shilling per acre with the quarter-sale clause in effect or a shilling and sixpence without it. Even earlier, he had begun selling the freehold to people who could meet his terms, and he told tenants on his wife's land at Claverack that whatever their lease conditions, their land would soon be sold. Even before the war, Schuyler's leases had begun to specify that the landlord retained the right to flood a leasehold if he needed to for a mill pond.

Nineteenth-century American law would take the position that material development was more important than the security of any particular piece of property, and Schuyler was presaging that doctrine in his practice.[33] His whole purpose was to create a development in which capital gains and running profits would bring him the greatest possible income. His practice was not unique. The same practices came into being on Livingston Manor, Rensselaerwyck, and James Duane's estate west of Schenectady. Moreover, it, rather than the neofeudal ethos, governed the development of the speculative tracts that were beginning to open up farther west.[34]

The triumph of cash relations on the land did not lead to any spirit of equality between great men and small. Philip Schuyler expected and got obsequiousness from his tenants. One tenant wanted in 1784 to sell his lease "provided your Honnour consents." Another alternated between fawning ("your most affectionate friend and tennant") and cringing ("Honored Sir. . . Dear Landlord"). To awe such people, Schuyler had a complete set of the poll lists for Albany and Tryon counties made up in 1786; he would not have spent the ten pounds that the list cost had he not intended his agents to use it while tenants and other men beholden to him cast their open votes.[35] Even the introduction of ballots in 1787 made relatively little difference, for landlords concocted device after device to keep track of which party's ballot their tenants were casting.[36]

The conservative resurgence was thus based on several different factors. One was Hamilton's personal combination of astute analysis and careful party-building. Hamilton's genius in those years was to tie into one bundle the issues of royalism, a merchant-based political economy, the great estates, and nationalism and to convince former royalists, merchants, landlords, and men with a nationalist perspective to join their causes together. But he did not act alone. The ready response that his interventions provoked and such parallel actions as those of the Albany landlords in 1785 show that what was happening was the development of a class. The old New York elite had allowed itself to bicker and had broken apart in the Revolution. Now the "men of respectability," the people who had "anything to lose," the men "whose principles are not of the *levelling kind*" had realized the importance of cooperating among themselves and of using all the weapons at their behest to gain power. Those weapons included old-fashioned intimidation of tenants, but they also included urban support that had to be won by argument. In 1777 conservatism in republican New York had been centered in a small group of men who did as much as they dared as partners in a republican coalition. By 1786 conservatism was embodied in a partisan organization whose leaders recognized that they were defending the interests of a beleagured ruling class. Those leaders used both the traditional devices of their class's dominion and the new ones of coalition building to defend those interests.

III

During the last three years of the Confederation several things happened to the state's public agenda. The most important was the injection of the issue of nationalism into political debate, culminating in the decision of the Poughkeepsie convention to ratify the Federal Constitution. As Stephen Boyd and other scholars have shown, the conservatives won a major part of their case before the convention ever assembled, for in 1787 and 1788 the problem of the central government took precedence over all others, and they had made it so.[37] While that was happening, other changes, bound up with the question of nationalism, were taking place on the state level. The last three legislative sessions of the Confederation period—the ninth in 1786, the tenth in 1787, and the eleventh in 1788—saw a progressive dismantling of both the achievements and the methods of the radicalism of the previous years. They also saw a gradual diminution of the salience of state politics. It has been said that in the whole Confederation period New York politics was a matter of boring, petty tedium.[38] That is in no sense true for the first eight years of independence, but it is a fair description of state-level affairs between 1786 and 1788, while the federal question was in agitation. The contrast between the vital and sometimes spectacular quality of state politics during the radical years and its prosaic quality as the Confederation died underscores the conservatives' success in deciding what issues New Yorkers would debate.

Many of the characteristics of radical political practice remained during those three years. Legislative business was still done in ad hoc committees and in committees of the whole. Petitions continued to pour in by the hundreds, their numbers swollen especially in 1786 by missives from insolvent debtors and in all three years by land-seekers. Over just two days in 1786 fully a hundred debtors asked the legislature for relief, and the largest land petition presented that year bore 719 signatures.[39] On the basic issues of getting out of the debtors' prison and obtaining a farm to till, New Yorkers continued to look to their representatives.

Those representatives, however, showed themselves increasingly open to other petitioners, particularly to former royalists. Supplications from the king's friends had been treated with scorn during the two sessions immediately after the war ended, but by the tenth session that rigor was fading. Instead of tabling or giving an outright rejection to Tory requests, the assembly began naming committees to deal with them. Some of the royalists whom it treated kindly were small folk, such as Hannah Van Dyke, the widow of a Tory who had lost his estate. Her petition was given the normal treatment of being assigned to a three-man committee. But bigger folk also found sympathy. At the request of his wife, Miles Sherbrooke, a man attainted by name in the Confiscation Act of 1779, was given permission to return by a vote of the assembly. A petition signed by, among others, Sir John Johnson was sent to a grand committee of twelve among whose members was Alexander Hamilton. The assembly charged the same committee to report on a petition from Joanna Morris regarding the vast tract that she and her husband Roger Morris had once held in southern Dutchess.[40]

Even without petitions, the conservative-led sessions went steadily about the business of relaxing the Tory laws. On the motion of speaker David Gelston, the ninth session voted to repeal the act disqualifying royalists from the practice of law. Towards the end of the same session, full citizenship was restored to some of the men stripped of it by the act of 1784 preserving the state's "freedom and independence." The tenth session repealed all previous election laws, including those disqualifying Tories, and put a new act in their place. In that session, Hamilton and the former royalist Samuel Jones, of Queens, combined to lead a movement that brought the repeal of the Trespass Act, the Citation Act, and all laws that conflicted with the peace treaty. The end came the following year, when the legislature finally repealed the last of the Tory laws that it had passed, the 1784 act preserving the state's freedom and independence. The policy of putting Tories and patriots on unequal social, economic, political, and legal footings had come to an end.[41]

The ninth session saw a major debate on whether and how the state should issue bills of credit. The debate cut across several separate dimensions, and William Duer, sitting for New York City, provided a focus for much of it. Duer's main concern was to prevent the state from assuming Congress's debt, for that would weaken Congress itself. In a volley of motions in committee of the whole, he tried unsuccessfully to drive the bill towards continentalism and to remove all political considerations from the question of what kind of certificates the treasury would receive under the law. He could not persuade the house to take his points, but he and his friends did prevent it from making the bills a general legal tender on a par with gold and silver. The debate became even more complicated when the New York City Chamber of Commerce tried to intervene with a petition on the bill. Duer's ally William Malcom moved that the house take formal note of the petition in its debates, and, after that motion failed, he moved that the text of the petition be entered in the house journal. That second motion failed as well, as did one to order the state printer to make copies of the petition.[42] The significant point is not, however, whether particular motions failed or passed but that the debate illustrates the emergence of a coherent conservative position that cut across the separate problems of the supply of money, the political privileges of the merchants who were organized in the chamber, and the relationship between the state and Congress.

The real conservative gain over the last three years of the Confederation lay in the fact that such extended debates became rarer and rarer. The legislature was ceasing to be a place of excited and angry debate, which was exactly what the conservatives wanted to happen. The tenth and eleventh sessions, in particular, concentrated largely on a nondivisive policy of tidying up and codifying the laws. One of their major projects was to pass a long series of bills "pursuant to the law for revising the laws of this state." These bills were written by Samuel Jones, who had the best of all worlds. Jones was among the very few ex-Tories who got close to Governor Clinton, and as a lawyer he had the respect of Alexander Hamilton. He introduced his bills in batches of up to ten at a time, almost all of them concerned with matters of legal procedure and criminal justice. Though they went through the usual procedure of discussion in committee of the whole, hardly ever did one of them provoke a division.[43]

As early as the ninth session more and more assemblymen had begun to value the ordered regularity and the procedural certainty that were the mark of Hamilton's actions as an assemblyman and of Jones's codification of the laws. When the former royalist James Barclay sought permission to become a licensed auctioneer in New York City, speaker David Gelston convinced the assembly to grant the request in the form of a general repeal of the law that disqualified men like Barclay rather than as a particular favor. The speaker likewise convinced the house to turn a bill that allowed a particular Tory lawyer to resume his practice into a bill repealing the general disqualification of such men. The ninth assembly even entertained a motion to abandon its practice of each year setting afresh the salaries of the high judges and to grant them a permanent income instead.[44] The motion failed, but it showed the drift of opinion. That drift was not simply towards softness on Tories or strengthening Congress; both of those things were bound up with men's increasing willingness to value predictability and order rather than struggle and uncertainty. Not all of the men who began to value those things became nationalists. But that these policies were epitomized in Hamilton's actions of the tenth session, that they were of a piece with his total perspective, and that they occasioned little debate are measures of the extent to which he and his associates were taking the initiative.

It was the radical ascendancy in the legislature that had driven the conservative nationalists to organize themselves. Their goal was not simply to put an end to particular radical policies. Rather, it was to establish a different political climate, one in which would be found the conditions necessary for the realization of the conservatives' vision of the future. Their major triumph came at Philadelphia, and it is important that for years Hamilton, at least, had understood fully the importance of revision at the center. As early as July 1783 he drafted a long Congressional resolution calling for a convention to strengthen the Articles of Confederation. All of the elements in what became the conservative program were there: the problems of a commercial economy, the need to establish the peace treaty's supremacy over state law, the nation's impotence abroad, Congress's lack of power to tax and to enforce its will. All that was lacking was support, and recognizing that, Hamilton abandoned the resolution.[45]

The story of conservatism over the five years between then and the ratification of the Constitution is a story of building that support. Building support meant convincing other New Yorkers that at least part of the nationalist critique of radical democracy was valid. The waning of radicalism within the legislature, as measured by the ending of punishment of Tories, by the willingness of members to accept order rather than struggle, and by the falling off of both contentiousness and salience in what the legislators did, indicates that they were making their case.

IV

Seizing the initiative, however, was not the same thing as seizing control. The conservatives found that though they had stymied their opponents, they still lacked the strength to defeat them. Only a change in the conditions under which power was exercised could do that, which is why nationalism became the central element in their program. Within the state government, the story of the last three years of the Confederation is one of stalemate. In 1786, for instance, everyone, save perhaps Philip Schuyler, recognized that Governor Clinton could not be beaten. Though the governor was close to open identification with the radical party and though he had publicly endorsed much of the radical program, no one dared take him on. Even the conservative legislative ticket in Albany County was headed by his name.[46]

The conservatives stumbled repeatedly in their efforts to gain complete control. Their victory in the Albany assembly election of 1785 was impressive, but they were defeated in the New York City assembly election of the same year. In the city only two men were carried over from the eighth session, when the conservatives had controlled the delegation, to the ninth. These were the outsiders William Goforth and William Denning. The new delegation included Isaac Sears and the mechanics Robert Boyd and John Stagg. The former speaker Evert Bancker and the nationalists William Duer, William Malcom, and Robert Troup also were elected, but the poll meant that even while they were winning upstate, the conservatives were losing the hold that had made the city's members their center of resistance to the eighth session's radicalism. Hamilton recognized as much, telling Duer that he hoped he would not be "fettered by some of your Colleagues."[47]

Turnover in that election was high overall. Two thirds of the members of the ninth assembly had not been members of the eighth. But in most counties changes took place for local reasons rather than because of coordinated partisanship. Dutchess reelected only three of its seven members, but they were the radicals Dirck Brinckerhoff, Brinton Paine, and Matthew

Patterson. They were joined in the new session by four more of the same sort. Orange reelected only one, and Ulster only two, but radical dominion on the west bank remained secure. Westchester sent back four of its six, and all four had taken radical positions in the previous session. Montgomery reelected three of its six, and all three had voted radical the year before. The one man whom Washington County sent back had a similar voting record.

The net effect of the election was thus to deprive each side of the county that had been its centerpiece in the previous session. The radicals lost Albany, but the conservatives lost New York. This was not a simple trade-off. By the time the ninth assembly met in January 1786 there were many reasons for upstate and downstate radicals to take different perspectives. Most especially, the urban economy was in the depths of the trading depression that followed the return of peace.[48] As a result, the session's voting did not present the sharp, clear polarity that had separated radicalism from conservatism the year before. Instead, it shows a muzzier, much less defined division, one in which a basic polarity can be sensed but not precisely established.

As many members of the ninth session fell into blocs that held together at rates above 70 percent as had in the eighth, but there were two major differences. First, instead of pitting upstate against down, the blocs centered, respectively, on the members from Albany and on those from the mid-Hudson counties. At one core were six of the newly elected Albany representatives—John Taylor, John Livingston, Jacobus Schoonhoven, Leonard Bronck, Peter Vrooman, and Henry Glenn. The core of the other was a group of ten, including five from Dutchess, two each from Ulster and Orange, and one from Washington. The coalition of Dutchess insurgents and west-bank chieftains was holding, even if Albany had been lost. Second, these two groups did not face each other from positions of total hostility. In the eighth session the rates of agreement between members of the opposing blocs had been low, falling in most cases to well below 30 percent. But in this session they were much higher, ranging for most pairs between 40 percent and 60 percent.

Further evidence that politics had lost its precise quality appears in the separate roll calls. The number of divisions that can be grouped coherently fell dramatically from the eighth session to the ninth, from just short of half of those taken to only three-tenths. Twenty-four of the session's votes can be formed into one group in which the members lined up roughly the same way each time. That group included divisions on such disparate questions as the salaries of public officials, the privileges of the New York City Chamber of Commerce, the federal impost, the issuance of bills of credit, and a few Tory questions. By linking together many separate issues, the members behaved on these roll calls in much the same way that they had the previous session. But instead of pitting two sharply defined parties against each other, the votes sorted the members into three separate groups. One was made up of people from downstate. A second, opposed to the first on most of the divisions, was made up of the Albany delegates. In the middle was a huge group dominated by delegates from the Hudson Valley counties. The effect of the election, in other words, had been to splinter two previously solid groups. Despite the collaboration in the election of Hamilton and the upstate magnates, no single conservative legislative bloc emerged. Rather, radical New York City members and conservative Albanians defined themselves separately vis-à-vis the mid-Hudson radical coalition. In numerical terms, that last group remained the dominant factor in the legislature, even if it was losing the initiative in terms of setting the public agenda.[49]

The conservatives enjoyed much greater success in the election for the tenth session, held in the spring of 1786. Alexander Hamilton was chosen for New York City, and the other city members were largely men like himself. The overall proportion of new men in this session was much lower than that in the previous one, standing at only 48 percent of the house. In only one other session in the whole Confederation period did the percentage of the house that was newly elected drop below half. The upstate counties, in particular, sent back the men who had represented them the previous year, whether radical or conservative. Dutchess reelected all seven of its members. Ulster retained four of its six, Montgomery three of its six, and Albany six of its ten. By contrast, New York reelected only three of its nine-man contingent. Those whom it reelected were William Denning, who had been a radical and would be a Jeffersonian Republican,[50] and the conservatives Evert Bancker and William Malcom. They were joined by a battery of nationalists, including Hamilton, Nicholas Bayard, the ex-Tory Robert C. Livingston, and Richard Varick. Though a freshman member, Varick became speaker, the first elevation to the chair since independence that clearly carried partisan significance.

During the tenth session one measure of partisanship rose sharply in relation to the pattern in the ninth. This was the percentage of roll calls that fell into groups on which the members' behavior was roughly the same. The overall rate climbed by almost 15 points, to just short of 45 percent, the second highest figure of the Confederation period. Though voting patterns in this session did not show quite the sharp polarity that they had in the utterly divisive eighth, they were closer to those of that session than to the blurred quality of the ninth. The reason was certainly that the conservatives had recaptured New York City, for three main issues separated upstaters from downstaters in that session: the powers of the central government, relaxation of the Tory laws, and salaries of public officials. The downstate conservatives, as might be expected, wanted Congress's powers to be augmented, the Tory laws to be repealed, and salaries to be made permanent at a high level. Radicals wanted the opposite on each question.[51]

Partisanship was also pronounced in terms of voting overall, without regard to issue. Two sizable groups emerged whose members voted together on more than 70 percent of all votes. One was made up entirely of upstate members, including five of the seven from Dutchess, two each from Orange and Montgomery, and one from Washington. The other group included eight of the ten New York City members and one man from nearby Richmond. In contrast to the fairly high level of mutual agreement between the Albany and mid-Hudson cores in the ninth session, these two groups agreed on very little. The rate of agreement within pairs across the groups was less than 35 percent in every case and ran for some pairs to as low as 16 percent or even 11 percent.

The story of the eleventh session, the last of the Confederation period, is different. The number of newly elected men climbed to 55 percent of the house. The most dramatic change came in Dutchess, where at last the conservatives broke radical domination. In place of the Brinckerhoffs, Paines, and Luddingtons, whom the county had been sending since 1781, it elected a ticket that included Egbert Benson and Thomas Tillotson and Morris Graham, the last two connected to the Livingstons. Not much evidence survives about how the change took place, but there is enough to show that Dutchess conservatives used methods akin to the ones that brought the change of 1785 in Albany. Writing to Hamilton in March 1787, Robert R. Livingston explained how he was going to make himself "useful here by affecting some changes in the representation which I have good hopes of accomplishing in Dutchess County where I have conversed with most of the leading people." The chancellor predicted that five of the sitting Dutchess members would not survive the coming poll, and his prognosis proved correct.[52]

Breaking of the radical control in Dutchess meant the end of the mid-Hudson coalition. It also meant that conservatives finally gained control of the assembly. With the members from Dutchess, Albany, the newly created county of Columbia, and all of the southern-district counties on their side, they were in a situation analogous to that of the radicals in the seventh session. Then radical strength had been so strong that no persistent polarity emerged in the votes, whether overall or across particular issues. Now the same thing happened again. The year 1788, when the eleventh session met, can in no sense be called one when partisanship was low; indeed, the debates held that summer in the Poughkeepsie ratifying convention repeated almost perfectly those of the eighth assembly. But within the assembly, conservative control was so secure that there seemed nothing to quarrel about.

The result was that all objective measures of partisanship fell dramatically. With public attention focused on the question of ratification, few problems worth debating were raised in the legislature. Since the radicals held only the west-bank counties, they could offer no effective opposition. There was thus neither need nor opportunity for either party to present a united front. The number of assemblymen who voted together more than 70 percent of the time dropped to only half of what it had been the year before, from 30 percent to 15 percent. Those voting together on more than 60 percent of all roll calls fell from two-fifths of the house to only three-tenths. Agreement within pairs across those blocs was high, running to over 50 percent in some cases. Only 15 percent of all divisions showed voting alignments that were congruent with those on any significant number of others. This was by far the lowest percentage of interrelated votes of the entire Confederate era.

A perspective from within the legislature would take such figures as evidence that consensus ruled among New Yorkers in the year the Constitution was ratified. In fact they indicate no such thing. They betoken the triumph within the legislature in that year of one side, a triumph that was as much the result of astute analysis and hard politics as was the ratification of the Constitution itself. The conservatives had achieved what they wanted, save capture of the governorship. But the opposition that they faced the same year in the ratification convention shows that the democrats had mastered the same things.

V

As the members of New York's ratifying convention gathered in Poughkeepsie in the summer of 1788, it seemed a certainty that they would reject the new Federal Constitution. The delegates had been elected a full year after those who had made up the conservative assembly that had just risen, and opinion had changed. The line-up of delegations repeated that of the eighth assembly, when rural radicalism had been supreme. The counties of Albany, Columbia, Dutchess, Montgomery, Orange, Ulster, and Washington were all antifederalist, as they had been radical three years before, and they were joined now by Suffolk and Queens. Federalists held only Kings, New York, Richmond, and Westchester. Many of the familiar radicals of the 1780s were members: Matthew Adgate for Columbia, Jacobus Swartwout for Dutchess, John Lansing and Henry Oothoudt for Albany, Jesse Woodhull and John Haring for Orange, Cornelius Schoonmaker for Ulster. At their head was George Clinton, an Ulster delegate and an open opponent of the Constitution.[53]

The election in which the voters chose these men was the first ever held in New York on the basis of manhood suffrage. The radicals won it because they organized, campaigned, and got out the vote as they had never done before. Only a year after losing not just the initiative but even numerical control in the legislature, they won a sweeping victory in what everyone recognized as the most important election in the state's history. Their victory proved ironic, for by campaigning as they did, they accepted the federalist position that the new constitution was the issue above all others, and acceptance of that pointed the way towards the antifederalists' split and ultimate defeat within the convention itself. But even though they finally lost on ratification, the antifederalists had gained enough organization and self-consciousness to challenge and ultimately defeat the federalists on the new ground that the Federal Constitution defined. Thus they repeated their unintended triumph of a decade earlier, for the state constitution under which they had first triumphed also had been meant to stymie them. This time they did it with full intent.

The difference was that now the radicals knew exactly whom they opposed, exactly how to defeat them, and exactly why they needed to do so. A first glance at the split on ratification suggests that its causes lay in regionalism and in economic geography. The farther a county was from New York City, the more likely were its delegates to be uncompromising on the Constitution; the closer an antifederalist county was to the city, the more willing were its members to accept the compromise formula of ratification "in full confidence" of subsequent amendments, which was the basis on which the state entered the union. Thus Albany, Montgomery, Washington, Ulster, and Columbia held fast to antifederalism; Orange, Dutchess, and Suffolk split; and Queens changed sides completely.[54]

But the antifederalists saw matters differently at the time. They did not speak and write in terms of upstate versus down or of agriculture versus commerce. Rather, they continually posed the question as one of republicanism versus its enemies and of ordinary men against the self-styled great. In April 1787 a radical Albany politician was describing his own group as "the Republican party." In 1788 the old Son of Liberty Hugh Hughes was writing of "the patriotic side." An out-of-state correspondent of John Lamb's likened the struggle to the one that the Sons of Liberty had waged against the British and their minions. He spoke of the federalists as a "junto" of "Ciceroes as they think themselves and others of superior rank, as they call themselves." As the convention was gathering, another of Lamb's correspondents reported that there had "not been a time since the Revolution in which the *Well Born*. . . have felt and appeared so uneffectual as they feel and appear at this time and Place—*How are the Mighty Fallen*!" George Clinton himself described to Lamb how the "Friends to the Rights of Mankind outnumber the Advocates for Despotism" in Poughkeepsie, and Charles Tillinghast told him of how Hamilton posed in debate as an "amazing Republican. . . but he is known." As the antifederalist leaders saw it, the issue turned not on geography but rather on a mixture of class, revolutionary history, and republicanism. They believed that their own side represented ordinary but politically active citizens. They saw its origins as lying deep in two and a half decades of struggle. They saw themselves as standing for the gains that the Revolution had won. They were sure that the Constitution and its advocates threatened all of these things.[55]

Around this perspective, the antifederalists created a powerful and sophisticated organization. By 1787 they were masters of the nuts-and-bolts politics of their own areas, and through that year and 1788 they shared that mastery with one another. During the assembly election of 1787, Henry Oothoudt wrote from Albany to Governor Clinton's closest advisor of how pleased he was that in "the City and the Manor of Rensselaerwyck the elections come on sparingly which indicates in favor of the Republican Party." Meanwhile, Abraham Yates was performing a lapidary analysis of the senatorial poll in the county. By the following year Yates was showing the same interest in returns elsewhere, noting that in Columbia his allies had won "by a majority of above 300 of the lowest anti to the highest Federal."[56]

In 1788 the antifederalists organized committees and coordinated their actions throughout the state. Out-of-state observers knew that their leaders were to be found as much in the enemy territory of New York City as in the upstate counties. Governor Clinton, the New York merchant Melancton Smith, the old Sons of Liberty Marinus Willett, Hugh Hughes, and John Lamb, and the Albanians Abraham Yates and John Lansing were known as the party's informal central organizers. They carried on a campaign of letter and essay writing to counter the federalist propaganda that poured from downstate presses. Their methods reflected the experience that they had gained as Sons of Liberty and in the committee movement. In both, they had learned that popular politics meant leading people but not forcing them, and now, rather than calling on landlords to pressure their tenants into voting the right way, they agitated among citizens to pay attention to "the cause of Liberty." Their committee in New York City kept its eye on developments throughout the southern district. It reported that "by accounts from Queens & Suffolk it appears the people begin to pay attention to the subject of the proposed Constitution and the opposition is formidable and increasing."[57]

The antifederalists knew that George Clinton stood to their cause almost as George Washington did to that of federalism. During the election for the convention, Melancton Smith and John Lamb schemed to make sure that the governor would be one of its members, whatever happened. Smith traveled back and forth between Poughkeepsie and New York City, sounded opinion upstate and down, and flattered himself that his party's strength in the city was "greater than we expected." He was sure that even federalists in the city would vote for Clinton "notwithstanding he differs in sentiment with them," but he still advised Lamb that the governor should run upstate as well. "He had better be chosen in two places, than not to be elected at all."[58]

Meanwhile, the New York committee forwarded copies of antifederalist pamphlets to committees elsewhere, noting how many went to every antifederalist leader in the state. It kept a list of antifederalist committeemen, and the roster of their names, each with its quota of pamphlets, reads like a roll call of the state's radicals. In New York were John Lamb and Marinus Willett; in Suffolk Thomas Tredwell, Thomas Hickes, David Hedges, and

Jonathan Havens; in Westchester Philip Pell, Jonathan G. Tompkins, Abijah Gilbert, Thomas Thomas, Joseph Strang, and Joseph Drake. On the list went: John Hathorn and John Suffern in Orange; Matthew Adgate, William B. Whiting, John Bay, and Peter Van Ness in Columbia; Nathan Smith, Johannes Snyder, Cornelius C. Schoonmaker, and Dirck Wynkoop in Ulster; John Lansing, Peter W. Yates, and Henry Oothoudt in Albany; David Hopkins, Ebenezer Russell, John Williams, and Alexander Webster in Washington; and Christopher P. Yates, Volkert Veeder, John Frey, and William Harper in Montgomery. Even solidly federalist Kings was represented by Charles Doughty and Hendrick Wyckoff, former legislators both. These men, with their obscure Dutch, English, Gaelic, and Yankee names, their work as farmers and artisans and traders, and their experience as committeemen and radical legislators, were the men who spoke for the groups that the Revolution had hurled into public life. At the highest level, Governor Clinton himself reported that "the Republican members of the convention have appointed a special committee of correspondence. . .of which the Honorable Judge Yates is Chairman."[59] The Yates in question was Robert, not Abraham, but for any Yates to be an honorable judge of the supreme court was a measure of how times had changed.

Among the federalists, Hamilton, Jay, and Robert R. Livingston ran things tightly, mingling the methods of condescending attention which their sort had long employed with the powerful arguments that they developed in such writings as *The Federalist*. Charles Tillinghast reported to John Lamb how the trio "are continually singling out the Members in Opposition (when out of convention) and conversing with them on the subject." He thought that their "manners and mode of address would probably do much mischief, were the members not as firm as they are." George Clinton noted, once debates got underway, that the federalist arguments amounted to "a second Edition of Publius, well delivered." By contrast, the antifederalists carried on a lively internal debate about tactics and arguments. Much of their printed propaganda originated in New York City or out of state, but local committees decided what they would actually circulate. After the city committee sent a large batch of pamphlets to Albany, the committee there told it not to bother sending any more. The pamphlet was "in a Stile too sublime & florid for the Common People in this Part of the Country." But they advised the New Yorkers that "the publication of Luther Martin's speech in a Pamphlet would be of great service and tend to open the Eyes of our Country more than anything yet published."[60] The contrast between the antifederalists' carefully adjusting their arguments to the mood, the concerns, and the culture of their supporters and federalists' relying on grand theory, the flattery of a great man offering his friendship, and the forced support of tenants is one measure of what the two parties stood for. The one endorsed and acted within the egalitarian participatory political society that had emerged from the Revolution. The other group opposed it.

The antifederalists recognized that difference, and they laid heavy stress on it in their arguments. For them, the state legislature was important not because it was the place of their own power but because they and their constituents had made it the central element in a good state of affairs. Abraham Yates began developing the point even before 1787. Always suspicious of the "high flyers," Yates saw nothing but evil in their attempts of the mid-1780s to strengthen Congress and give it an independent income. For New Yorkers, that matter came to a head in 1786 when the legislature's refusal to grant Congress an impost unless the tax was administered by state officers blocked the last attempt at revising the Articles of Confederation. Yates wrote a series of "Political Papers" on the question in which he placed the impost issue squarely against the background of the struggle with Britain. For him, Congress was in no way a body of representatives. It was an irresponsible, uncontrollable executive, and the state legislatures stood to it as the colonial assemblies had stood to George III. Granting it financial independence would mean the legislature's divesting itself "of sovereignty, that most precious and inestimable jewel." It would mean a future not of the vital state politics that had been going on for the past decade but rather of legislating for roads, blackbirds, crows, and hogs. That, it seems from what happened in the legislature in 1787 and 1788, was exactly what the federalists wanted.[61]

During the ratification controversy itself the antifederalists went further. They developed the argument that the reason for defending the state governments was that they stood for working popular control of public life. Speaking in the Poughkeepsie convention, Melancton Smith asked, "How was the will of the community to be expressed?" His answer was that the only possible way was through the state governments. The pamphleteer "Cato," whom different scholars have identified as Abraham Yates and as George Clinton, said that the point of republicanism was not simply that officials draw their power from the people's consent in some remote way but that the government be readily accountable and that the opportunity to exercise power directly be spread as widely as possible. "The safety of the people in a republic," he explained, "depends on the share or proportion they have in the government."

Alexander Hamilton had said similar things once, but when he wrote in 1784 that liberty was "the *right* to a *share* in the government," he was already drawing distinctions between the rights of the people and the rights of their rulers. He meant the people's share to be exercised only at the polls. For "Cato," by contrast, voting was only the beginning. He thought it equally important that "many" have "the opportunity to be advanced to the supreme command." His republic was not an ideal utopia, but one that already existed at the state level and in which no distinction was to be drawn between the citizenship of the ordinary man and the statesmanship of the man of power. Liberty was active participation, and widespread participation was "one of the principal securities of a free people."[62] It was because the state government offered just such participation and the federal government would not that New York's antifederalists fought the Constitution. Or so, at least, they said.

VI

The confrontation between the federalists and the antifederalists in 1787 and 1788 was thus the culmination of a development that had been going on for a full decade. New York's politics in those two years was not consensual, not a matter of a passing dispute among friends. It met every test of whether parties existed. Both sides were recognized—by themselves, by their opponents, and by the people at large. Each had a name that it was not ashamed to use in public. Each had well-known leaders and an internal structure. Each tried to gain public support by nominating attractive candidates and by putting its case openly. Each drew its strength from definable interests. Each articulated the beliefs of its ideologues and advanced the interests of its supporters as if they were the beliefs and interests of all who mattered in society. Each drew its organizational strength and know-how and its ideas from experience that two and a half decades of revolution had given it. Each quite explicitly saw the other as the enemy.

Though New Yorkers had always been a factious people, they had not always been partisan. New Yorkers were used to disputes among their rulers, used to those rulers' inviting lesser men to choose sides. They were used to rough play. Generating a partisan political culture among them did not require either the breaking of a consensual social model, as it did in much of New England, or the shattering of a ruling class's hegemony, as it did in Virginia or South Carolina. But it did require that an end be put to the coalition politics with which revolutionary New Yorkers had gained their independence.

There had been good reasons for coalescence rather than conflict among New York's rebels. The great cause of resisting Britain had required the burying of as many hatchets as possible. Massive royalism, Vermont secession, and the British occupation of five whole counties had required that those hatchets remain in their graves. But the movement had always been a coalition that men consciously created rather than a solid front that they took for granted. It had always incorporated the elements of the partisanship that split it. The fundamental problems on which it split concerned what sort of men should be in power; how they should act vis-à-vis the people and how the people should act vis-à-vis them; and what the rulers ought to do with their power. These questions were thoroughly intertwined; none was separable from any of the others. All of them were discussed and acted upon between the crisis of 1779 and the ratification campaign. Each side in the emerging party system made itself—as it gained a separate perspective, developed its organization, and reached out for popular support—but in relation to the other. During the independence crisis the conservatives had the advantage of sharper insight, but they could not do without radical support. Though they "rode the torrent" successfully until 1779, they lost control in that year. They lost it not because of concerted opposition but because of the magnitude of the problems that faced them. The radicals who gained power in their place were only half-aware of what they had won, but their behavior in the legislature and the public's behavior towards them between then and 1785 shows that radicalism was becoming a coherent position and that the radicals themselves were becoming a disciplined group.

The conservative response was as creative as it was reactionary. In several major senses, the conservatives did seek between 1783 and 1788 to turn back the clock. They wanted to drive out the rough, grubby men whom the Revolution had brought forth. They wanted to undo their policies. They wanted to substitute predictable order for untidy participation. But they could not regain either the clear position of control which they thought their kind had enjoyed before independence or the leadership-in-coalition that they knew they had had in the mid-1770s. By turning themselves from an embattled elite into a political party, and by establishing a new public agenda to replace the issues of the war years, they thus stimulated the completion of New York's partisan culture. It was in response to these things that the radicals pinned such labels as antifederalist and republican on themselves, that Governor Clinton became their acknowledged leader, and that they developed their permanent structure.

New York's partisanship in the 1780s thus involved many elements. Class, sectionalism, economics, royalism, and the whole problem of the people's involvement in government were all bound up with it. But most of all it involved time. It took time for the independence coalition to crack. It took time for the radicals to come to full control. It took time for their opponents to confront the full extent of their loss, to chart another course, and to organize themselves so that they could turn their map of the future into a new reality. All of these developments were as much a part of the Revolution as were the crowds of the 1760s, the break with Britain, and the writing of a new constitution. It was all of them together that defined the new order under which New Yorkers would develop as the eighteenth century became the nineteenth and that transformed New York from a troubled, unstable, class-ridden province to a partisan liberal state.

Part IV

Conclusion

Chapter 10

The Revolutionary Transformation

I

By 1790 the Revolution was settled for New York, as it was for the rest of the former Colonies. The prime fruit of independence was the national republic, resting its claim to resolve the old problem of American legitimacy on several bases.[1] One was the charisma of General Washington, embodying as he did the way the states had fought the war together. Another was the half-realized myth of an ultimate popular sovereignty, superior to both the republic and the separate states. A third, as Madison so astutely saw, was the suitability of the republic's political structure to the needs of a competitive, individualistic, expanding bourgeois society.

Settlement at the national level was coeval with settlement at the state level, but the two processes were by no means identical. Instead, the end of the Revolution in New York came with the resolution of the problems that had plagued its people at the end of the colonial period. Independence and stable republicanism had required massive changes, and those changes had been achieved.

The most spectacular change was the forcible separation from New York of whole groups of people who stood opposed either to what the province had been or to what the state was becoming. One of those groups was the Vermonters. Not until after 1790 did the state and federal governments recognize Vermont's independence, and throughout the previous decade George Clinton had spoken of the Vermonters in terms that George III might have used for Clinton's own people. Yet from the end of the war the issue was dead, and at the Poughkeepsie convention even Clinton's allies showed that they knew it.[2] The question had arisen from two conflicting sets of ideas and practices about property and society, and it had been resolved by a fundamental redefinition of the geography of New York. Cumberland and Gloucester counties had ceased to exist, as had the eastern part of Charlotte and a small corner of Albany. In their place, defined on the west by that rough line that might have been drawn on Sauthier's map from Williamstown, Massachusetts, to Lake Champlain and on the east by the Connecticut River, which New York had once claimed as its own boundary, lay a whole new political entity. Compared with other eighteenth-century land rioters, the Vermonters had been fortunate. Their remoteness, the difficulties of their mountainous country, and the merger of their cause with the movement for independence had saved them from the fate of the Hudson Valley tenants, the New Jersey rioters, and the Carolina Regulators. Though the Allen brothers flirted with the British general Frederick Haldimand in 1781, the Vermonters never experienced the repression at the hands of Whig leaders that had made king's men of rural insurgents elsewhere.

Here was the one occasion in early America when agrarian rebels got what they wanted, and the genesis by those rebels' descendants of the Oneida Community, of Mormonism, of Seventh-Day Adventism, and of all sorts of other social ferment[3] suggests that America's nineteenth-century cultural history would have been much poorer had they not. That Ethan Allen and Remember Baker gave way to Joseph Smith and William Miller suggests the long-term fate of the radicalism of the Revolution itself. But the immediate point is that though their separation cost New York two whole counties and parts of two more, it freed the state of the liability of trying to incorporate and govern a people who had shaped their own distinct identity and who did not want to lose it. Thanks to the success of the Vermonters, to the Treaty of Paris, and to the negotiators who during the revolutionary era worked out boundary agreements with Massachusetts, New Jersey, and Pennsylvania,[4] New York's outline assumed the familiar shape that it has today.

The working out of that outline redefined New York in political as well as geographical terms, and political redefinition was extended by the way that the state resolved the Tory problem. However much they had shared before the Revolution with Yorkers who became republicans,[5] Tories ultimately decided that they themselves could not be republicans. Nor could they accept a society in which individualistic egalitarianism was becoming the dominant tone. Royalist claimants like John Wetherhead, Isaac Low, William Axtell, and Sir John Johnson demonstrated their attitude by repeatedly speaking of themselves in such phrases as "the principal people." That language would remain in use in English county society until well into the twentieth century, but in America it was obsolescent in these men's own time.

Royalists looked eastward towards Britain and upward towards the crown. For this reason, Esmond Wright is persuasive in his judgment that "it is false to Loyalism to see it only as a variant of Whiggism. The Loyalist was in essence a man or woman with a strong...devotion to the Mother Country and to the Establishment...'I Believe,' 'I obey,' these were part of the Loyalist code." Perhaps as many as thirty-five thousand New Yorkers were serious enough about royalism to leave when their cause was lost rather than try to pick up their lives where the Revolution had broken them. They were driven out, both by warfare and by the vindictive laws that marked the second, popular phase of New York's Tory policy. Their exile confirmed that henceforward to be a New Yorker was to be a republican. Isaac Low put the point perfectly in 1788. Writing from London to his brother, just elected to the state legislature, he said that he should never "envy the Happiness of others, who are advocates for republican Government. The height of my Ambition was and is to live and die a British subject."[6]

Alexander Hamilton and his allies bemoaned the Tory exodus; in their view it was simply depriving the state of valuable capital and of even more valuable mercantile skill. But given the dimensions and the nature of the quarrel, neither the vindictive laws nor the forced exiles are surprising. Moreover, they made good political sense. Not all former Tories left, and within three years of the British departure some would be reentering both the economic and the public life of the state. Many who reentered politics would do so behind Hamilton's banner, though some, like Samuel Jones, would become Clintonians. But the unquestionability of the Revolution's triumph and the permanent fate of their exiled former comrades meant that Tories who remained knew they would have to act within a republican scheme of things. The repression, the exile, and the submission of its enemies meant that New York's revolution would not have to suffer the enmity of people who remained Yorkers but still disputed its rightfulness. Two basic problems that had helped to tear the old order apart, one of men who would not be Yorkers and the other of Yorkers who would not be republicans, had come to an end.

What remained as an area of dispute was the internal order of republican New York. Even here, some matters were in question no longer. New York did not, for instance, have to endure the continuing constitutional debates that Pennsylvania's radical constitution of 1776 provoked. This was due in good part to the nature of the New York constitution of 1777, which, though often regarded as conservative, is better understood as middle-of-the-road.[7] The contrast between it and Maryland's constitution of 1776 illustrates what might have happened had the right really had its way. In Maryland, property requirements for officeholding, long intervals between elections, and an elaborate structure of indirect electoral machinery all served effectively to annul popular sovereignty. Seen against Maryland's constitution, the New York document, with its broadening of the assembly suffrage, its creation of a senatorial and a gubernatorial electorate, its opening of office to all citizens, and its annual assembly elections, seems almost radical. Yet the New York governorship was independent of the legislature, and the senate was equal in power to the assembly. Though the chairman of the constitution committee had been Abraham Yates, a fair amount of the work had been done by John Jay. What is more, Yates and Jay had agreed that what they had turned out was right for the state. When, from the right wing's viewpoint, things started to go wrong, the constitution could not be blamed.

Conservatives realized in the 1780s that they had misread the state when they wrote the constitution. The attempt to balance property against people by setting the freehold requirement for voting for the governor and for senators at a hundred pounds had failed. The hundred-pound electorate had made George Clinton the chief magistrate and had put Ephraim Paine, Jacobus Swartwout, Dirck Brinckerhoff, and Henry Oothoudt in the senate. Nor were such men a minority, as the policies of the 1780s show. Landowners tried to remedy their mistake by turning to open coercion of their tenants. Robert Livingston, Jr., did it. So did Philip Schuyler. So did James Duane, and Stephen Van Rensselaer, and Chancellor Robert R. Livingston and his mother, Margaret Beekman Livingston. Among the tenants whom they coerced, an appreciable portion were qualified as hundred-pound voters, thanks to rising land values. It seems that the landlords' power in the senate in the 1780s rested not just on agreement among better-off men to send one of their own but also on pressure put by rich men upon their dependents. But once the constitution of 1777 was established, there could be no question, as there was in Pennsylvania, of conservative men trying to change it.

The problem after 1777 was not the structure of the new political order but what men did with that structure. "They may chuse who they will," smugly thought Philip Schuyler in 1777, "I will command them all." And when "they" chose George Clinton instead of himself, Schulyer could do the gracious thing and pledge his support.[8] But five years later Schuyler's son-in-law, who never let either connections or wishful thinking interfere with his political judgments, knew that the general could not be sure of having enough power to get his measures through the senate. Schuyler was nothing if not a proud man, and there lies one reason for his eagerness to get Clinton out of the governorship, even when his friends knew that for him to stand in opposition was foolish. But there was more to it on Schuyler's part than pique. Clinton may have studied law under William Smith, and he may have been Schuyler's close colleague in the colonial assembly, but he was still a new man whose "family and connections" did not "entitle him to so distinguished a predominance."[9]

There were new men too among the senators, the assemblymen, the judges, and the sheriffs. Voters in Dutchess were happy enough in 1777 to elect to the legislature Egbert Benson and Anthony Hoffman as well as Dirck Brinckerhoff and Jacobus Swartwout. The new assemblymen were happy enough to make Walter Livingston their first speaker. The Livingstons, the Bensons, and the Hoffmans gained power because in 1777 the revolutionary movement was a coalition of all who agreed on independence, however timorously, as in the case of Mr. Speaker Livingston. But the coalition foundered on the domestic issues of the late 1770s, and by 1784 pre-Revolution hands or names were hard to find in either house. An Orange County schoolteacher named John Hathorn was speaker, whereas before the war that post had been the preserve of men like Philip Livingston and Adolph Philipse. The old order had seen its moments of intense competition, and old-style politicians had realized the wisdom of "usquebaugh and beer" at election time. Sometimes they even lost, as did the elder Robert R. Livingston to Dirck Brinckerhoff in 1768 and 1769. But the make-up of the legislature in the 1780s marked the coming of new men and the driving out of old in a massive way. The old elite was not completely driven out, let alone destroyed. It still held great strength, for instance, at the highest level of the court system. But its losses were serious enough that to regain power it both had to drag out its old techniques and master a set of new ones.

Worse from the old elite's viewpoint was how the new men used their power. Radical taxation, Tory policy, New York's attitude towards the Continental impost, postwar policy on land distribution, and the state's determination to control its own Indian relations[10] all flew in the face of the old elite's interests and sensibilities. Those interests and sensibilities included the prevention of the threat to their own estates that was implied in confiscation of Tory ones and in radical taxation, the protection from postwar victimization of their own kind who had chosen royalism, a commitment to a free market, and, increasingly, the augmentation of national power. All of these elements fitted together into their understanding of what the political economy of the new nation should be. Each of them was threatened by what the state government did after 1779. The radicalism of New York's revolution expressed itself in policies rather than in structural experimentation.

But it was precisely the combination of new men, radical policies, and unexceptionable institutions that stabilized the new order within New York. The radicalism of the legislature between 1779 and 1785 was a response to the immediate complaints and demands of the active, self-conscious, articulate groups that made up the popular wing of the revolutionary coalition. It was also a manifestation of the democratic bourgeois character of that wing. As such, its basic goal was to replace stratified privilege by egalitarian opportunity. Some of the men who made this radicalism harked back to what they thought had been a more cooperative society. A few, such as the writer of 1779 who called for a state monopoly on foreign trade, challenged the coming order on its own ground. But by the end of the 1780s most Clintonians were anxious to be counted in—as artisan-businessmen, as buyers and sellers of land, as developers of the north and the west.

Their radicalism was in some ways parochial and in some ways shortsighted. It was in many ways intensely selfish. The votes of the eighth session showed that as a group its proponents had little room for a principled attack on slavery and even less for egalitarian ideas about race relations. But many of those proponents themselves held both slaves and racist ideas. Clintonian land policy had no room for justice towards the Indians. But the Iroquois held land that Governor Clinton's followers wanted; moreover, many of them had chosen to be the Revolution's enemies. The laws of the 1780s began to use the phrase "he or she" instead of the generic "he," and elsewhere such figures as Abigail Adams and Judith Sergeant Murray were drawing feminist conclusions from American revolutionary thought. But the time for organized feminism had not yet come, and the radicalism of Elizabeth Cady Stanton's grandfather, a Clintonian politician, could not envisage it. Neither blacks, Indians, nor women took part as a group in the revolutionary coalition, and none of them got much that they wanted out of its radicalism.[11]

Other groups made partial gains. The Confiscation Act gave tenants on the Tory estates a chance to gain the freeholds for which their sort had long struggled, and that helped win them to the Revolution. Tenants on the estates of republicans were less fortunate. In the end, radical taxation proved a mirage as a means of attacking landlordism. Eventually Clintonian politicians found themselves trying to deprive tenants of the vote, thus signifying both their recognition that landlord coercion was once again operating and their own lack of sympathy for the tenant cause. That lack of sympathy was shown more forcefully in 1791 when Clinton's government moved swiftly to put down a tenant rising in Columbia County.[12] Urban mechanics did better, partly because, unlike tenants, they were neither dependent on overlords nor tainted with royalism. They successfully endorsed three sets of candidates for the postwar legislature, once at the end of 1783, once in 1785, and once, as part of a coalition with merchants, in 1786. The federalists of 1787 recognized their importance and courted their support for the new constitution. But the mechanics had to struggle against determined opposition in order to gain recognition as a group with full membership in the new order, as their unhappy experience when they tried to incorporate themselves in 1785 showed.

The situation of tenants and mechanics was still vastly different in 1790 from that of blacks, Indians, and women. It was to these artisans, white laborers, small farmers, and expectant small capitalists that the policies of the 1780s appealed. It was these groups that tax, Tory, economic, and land policies brought to the Revolution's support, and it was their support that was vital if the new order was to stand. Groups that had established their political identity in the Revolution, and no others, were in a position to struggle for their concerns in the liberal "new order of the ages."

II

New York was not the only state where a combination of conservative institutions and radical policies led to the stabilizing of the new order. Consolidating the power of the new state regimes was a problem throughout America, as the troubled history of Massachusetts and the wrangles between Republicans and Constitutionalists in Pennsylvania show. Ronald Hoffman has demonstrated that Maryland achieved stability in a way remarkably similar to that of New York. There too a group of astute men who had much to lose learned the importance of swimming with a tide they could not stem. They wrote a constitution far more conservative than New York's, and they had to establish its power in a state that like New York was exposed to British military power and riddled with "disaffection." There too the "lesser sort," both black and white, feared that the Revolution would only solidify the power of a hated elite. There too was heard talk of murdering the Revolution's leaders and expropriating their land. There too militia units would not muster, salt rioters responded to shortage in traditional style, and courts could do no more than hold symbolic sessions. There too, radical changes in tax and currency policy helped to tame the Revolution's wild men.

In Maryland these policies were engineered by the very figures who created the state constitution. Understanding the "wisdom of sacrifice," such men as Charles Carroll of Carrollton and Samuel Chase thought it preferable that their class should pay heavier taxes and see book debts erode through inflation rather than lose control of the centers of power. Their strategy worked, for the laws they wrote proved popular, and "as the years of 1778 and 1779 went by and the social convulsions diminished. . . the establishment of independence and stability was insured."[13] The end result was the same, but in New York it happened differently. Egbert Benson finally voted for confiscation and for price controls, and John Jay and Robert R. Livingston began to let radical laws pass the council of revision. But these laws were not, as they were in Maryland, the calculated response of a threatened elite to inchoate popular demands. What the people of New York were demanding in those same years was clear enough, and the immediate energy behind both the radical policies and the Clintonian group that began to form as a result of them came from the new men, whose very presence at the higher levels of power was a challenge to the old leaders.

Many of the legislators who became Clintonians in the 1780s were directly involved in the popular upsurge of the mid and late 1770s. From the original Tryon County committeemen, secretly laying the groundwork in 1774 for the armed assault on Sir John Johnson's mansion, to Gilbert Livingston, Jacobus Swartwout, and Melancton Smith in Dutchess, James Hunter in Ulster, and Matthew Adgate and John Lansing of Albany, playing their roles on the committees of 1779, one finds men who would be the governor's supporters involved in the internal aspects of the political mobilization of New York. Despite that Poughkeepsie call for socialized foreign trade, there were few Gracchus Babeufs among them. But unlike the architects of Maryland's policies, they were in fundamental sympathy with the popular movement to which radical policies appealed. It was in response to that movement that they began to come together. As a result of their coalescence the "governing class on the defensive"[14] that opposed popular action in 1777, 1778, and 1779 found that its problems had not ended with the subsiding of the popular movement. The old elite had neither the policies that it wanted nor the satisfaction that policies that it disliked were the price it paid for retaining power.

Instead, power fell into the hands of a legislative party that provided effective linkage between popular feeling and the formal institutions of government. If stabilization began with a constitution that was acceptable to all, it continued with policies that were loathed by the few. The partisanship that emerged from those policies finished the process, for it regularized the popular upsurge that had been the revolutionary movement and reflected the social aspects of that movement even as it tamed them. The emerging Clintonians probably did not intend to produce any such effect. The Maryland group have very much of the air of modern "nation builders," consciously confronting the social dimensions of establishing a new political order.[15] The equivalent men in New York—Jay, Hamilton, Schuyler, Benson, Robert R. Livingston—would play the role of genuine nation builders in the establishment of the federal republic. They would assume that role precisely because of the way in which their interests were offended by the way in which stability came to their own state. But the point is that in New York stability was achieved, and its achievement required creative radical politics as well as consensual constitution-writing.

Stabilization and the partisanship that brought it and resulted from it were part of a basic reinterpretation of relationships, both formal and informal, between men in and out of power. The old order had been characterized by archaic concepts of representation and by the legislative arrogance that had imprisoned an Alexander McDougall in 1771. Neither survived the Declaration of Independence. The state constitution replaced special constituencies and county equality as the basis of representation with a system that gave counties as few as two seats and as many as ten. Elections, which under the old order might take place only at long intervals, became annual. The appointive royal council, with its maximum of twelve members, was replaced by a senate of twenty-four, and the constitution required a census and reapportionment septennially. The assembly could grow with reapportionment to a maximum of three hundred members, and the senate to one hundred. These structural changes were a necessary condition for the emergence of the Revolution's "new men" into public affairs.[16]

The state constitution abolished acts of attainder, save for the duration of the War of Independence. Though the assembly briefly continued the old practice of appointing an official printer and warning lest others "presume to print" its journals, that practice soon was dropped. A state bill of rights adopted in 1787 forbade the imprisonment of people save under indictment or presentment by a grand jury. By declaring the sanctity of the right of petition, the same bill of rights safeguarded citizens from legislative persecution for daring to ask for what they wanted.[17] These changes, and a new sense of self-restraint on the part of legislators, provided the climate in which Hamilton's "Phocion" letters and *The Federalist* could be freely published and in which he and his allies could organize to undo the "truly alarming" spirit of the legislature.[18] The old government would have seen the men behind such actions and writings as worthy of imprisonment. No longer, moreover, did its constituents address the legislature in the language of servility.

There had been tendencies towards more open government in the last years of the old order; independence transformed these into a torrent and virtually wiped out the old order's elitism. The secret deliberations of the council were replaced by open senate sessions recorded in a published journal. The assembly's journal continued to be published as well, of course. As a result of the war, the legislature met between 1777 and 1783 not in its traditional venue of New York City but rather in Peekskill, Newburgh, Poughkeepsie, Kingston, and Albany, and it may be inferred that its close presence helped to demythologize it in the minds of townsmen and of farmers in the neighboring countryside. By the late 1780s newspapers were reporting the proceedings and even the actual debates of the members.[19] In 1788 New York antifederalists made a point of attacking the "genius of aristocracy" which had prompted the Philadelphia convention "to enjoin secrecy on their members, to keep their doors shut, their journals locked up, and none of their members to take any extracts."[20]

There were parallel changes in the spirit of the government's operations. Public appointments, both military and civilian, were vested by the constitution in the council of appointment, made up of the governor and of four senators elected afresh each session. This was not the direct popular election that some radical opinion had demanded,[21] but the council acted as if people had a right to a say about their officials. The first time the question arose, a militia colonel who also held a senate seat was charged with gross corruption and misuse of his powers. The council resolved that it was "reduced to an absolute Necessity in Point of Duty to hear every Complaint of Misbehaviour in Officers of the Militia and to displace where there are just grounds for it." And when the council did order a dismissal, it was on the ground that "the Pleasure of the People of this State. . .determines the tenure of his office."[22] The day when office was a piece of private property was over. Two years after the crisis of 1779 the legislature's address to its constituents demonstrated that the men who occupied it believed they had a duty to be responsive, even if responsiveness meant telling the people why what they wanted could not be done. As an outstanding political scientist suggests, "The acceptance by superordinates of the obligation to be responsive, in however limited a way, is probably as great a watershed in democratic political development as the right of people to choose representatives, which is to say to participate at all."[23] In New York the Revolution established that principle.

III

Their revolutionary experience permanently altered the way in which mechanics and other ordinary folk took part in the public life of New York City. The late 1780s, like the late 1760s, were years of depression and economic difficulty, but they saw little crowd action of the sort that had been commonplace in the decade before independence. That is not to say that there were no urban riots; the "Doctors' Riot" of 1788, the sacking by a federalist crowd of the office of the antifederalist *New York Journal*, the advance of the same crowd on the houses of Governor Clinton and John Lamb, and a street brawl after ratification in Albany would refute any such contention. But the real story of workingmen's public involvement after the liberation of New York City is told in terms of purely political action rather than in terms of riots.

The new consciousness can be seen most clearly in two street actions of a sort far removed from traditional rioting. The first, in 1788, celebrated the ratification of the Federal Constitution. No mechanics had sat in the Poughkeepsie convention, let alone in the one at Philadelphia, and their willingness to gather behind the federalist ship Hamilton on its progress through the streets might be taken as a sign that deference had been reestablished. But only three years earlier, mechanic spokesmen had been warning of the "powerful mercantile interest" that mechanics had "to struggle with."[24] In May and June 1794 there came further evidence that what mechanics did was a matter of their own choice. Each morning during those months one company of craftsmen after another marched with fifes, drums, and banners to take boats to Governor's Island. There they would spend the day working without pay on fortifications to protect the city. As Alfred Young comments, it was "the Constitutional parade of 1788 all over again, except this time the parade was under Republican leadership."[25] Mechanic enthusiasm for both the Constitution and the work of fortification rested on mechanics' ability to judge matters from their own viewpoint and to act accordingly. Just as they had little doubt in 1788 that the Constitution would be to their benefit, so they had a great deal of doubt in 1794 that they would gain anything from federalist policies on relations with Britain as represented by Jay's Treaty. Through symbolic gestures, through efforts to elect their own men to the legislature and to get their charter, through the writings of their spokesmen, and through their willingness to enter into coalition politics, the mechanics of the Confederation and early national periods were asserting their equality in the process of controlling their world.

By the mid-1790s the language used to describe common people was quite different from that of the 1760s. Then, terms like "the people," "the many," "the mob," and "the rabble" had been satisfactory; post-Revolution practice made it necessary to be much more precise. The economic and professional elite, who had been "the few" and "the better sort" under the old order, had started the process even before the Revolution. When lawyers formed their "moot society" to discuss matters of common interest, when the bar association began requiring a college degree as well as a law clerk's training of aspirants,[26] when the chamber of commerce acknowledged by its own existence that merchants had distinct interests, they were striking at the idea that New Yorkers were either an undifferentiated community or an organic if hierarchical one. Even before independence, mechanics had begun to act in the same spirit. Their eagerness to win incorporation, despite rebuffs in 1785 and again in 1791, reflects their sense that they were as legitimate an interest group as any other. In both the ratification parade of 1788 and the volunteer fortification work of 1794 mechanics stressed their proud identification as members of particular trades. As one observer described the march to Governor's Island, "today, the whole trade of carpenters and joiners; yesterday the body of masons; before this, the grocers, school-masters, coopers and barbers. . .handle the mattock and shovel, the whole day, and carry their provisions with them."[27] Such group consciousness would remain alive for decades, showing itself at the celebrations in 1825 to mark the opening of the Erie Canal and in 1842 to mark that of the Croton Aqueduct. That nothing like it appeared in 1883 when "the people" gathered to celebrate the Brooklyn Bridge was a sign that New York had entered another era.[28]

In some ways this proliferation of group sensibilities in the late eighteenth century was part of a rush by New Yorkers to form societies that would embody every conceivable interest. Ethnic organizations like the St.

Andrew's Society, political clubs like the Democratic-Republican societies, benevolent and friendly groups like the Society of Tammany, and philanthropic bodies like the New York Society for Promoting the Manumission of Slaves all took form. They gathered in small villages in upstate counties as well as in the metropolis. Such societies were very different in orientation from the committees of the revolutionary years. Though they had claimed to represent whole communities, the committees had been the means by which people excluded under the old order entered fully into politics. They exercised power directly, and in ways fundamentally opposed to the politics of normal times. In some ways, the associations sharpened class awareness, especially in the case of the General Society of Mechanics and Tradesmen and of the craft groups that marched in 1788 and 1794. But they made no claim to power, acting instead as pressure groups. Moreover, many associations drew on ethnic and cultural consciousness rather than on class consciousness. Radical politics and nascent class consciousness foundered on electoral participation and on the spirit of voluntary association, of which Alexis de Tocqueville would make so much.

But the ability, even anxiousness, of lower- and middle-class New Yorkers to form organizations centered on their occupations, their religions, their backgrounds, and their interests was thoroughly congruent with the competitive, interest-based capitalism whose prophets were Adam Smith and James Madison. The "moral economy of the crowd" which had underlain pre-Revolution urban crowd action, like classical Whig politics, had postulated a single public striving to achieve a single good.[29] The classic example, both in Europe and America, was the regulation of prices, as in the assize of bread, so as to protect both consumers and producers. That concept did not die in 1776, in 1785, or in 1790. New York City did not abolished the assize until 1821, and as late as 1837 it experienced a perfect example of an eighteenth-century grain riot.[30] Both Madison and the free-market economists assumed, however, that self-disciplined interest groups would be central in future social organization and that the public good would be the outcome of competition rather than of harmonization. However many or few of them read it, the mechanics showed by their behavior that they understood what number 10 of *The Federalist* was about.

The essence of the Revolution in political society was bound up in that understanding. Life in New York in the 1760s had been dominated by three great problems. One was the British challenge to provincial autonomy. A second was deteriorating class relations. The third was an ethos, held more by the lower classes than by the upper classes, that stressed the desirability and the possibility of community and harmony. The conjuncture of these gave rise to both the revolutionary crowds of the cities and the land rioters of the countryside. In the 1770s New York was dominated by war and by the increasing strain to which its coalition for independence was subjected, as different groups realized that their interests stood opposed. The result was the emergence of the revolutionary committees in 1774 and 1775 and their continuance as arenas of internal struggle after 1776. New York in the late 1780s was independent. It was as politicized as it had been in 1766 or 1779, but now politicization meant partisanship and competition for control of the state's republican institutions. A political economy based, however tenuously, on the idea that a single public good might be achieved had given way to one in which American faced American in an unending struggle for the maximum possible gain.

The nineteenth century would show how illusory was the notion that shared republican citizenship made poor and middling Americans the equals of rich ones. It would see some people gain to a degree undreamed of at the time of the Revolution, other people made happy by modest achievements, and still others whose lot would be to endure far worse poverty and exploitation than the eighteenth century ever saw. It would see the emergence of two new lower classes, in the form of industrial workers and freed slaves, and it would see their first gropings towards the organization and the ideas necessary to cope in their demanding society. These people would create and face new problems, different from those of the Revolution and in many ways the fruits of the Revolution itself. But because all would not be perfect in republican America does not mean that the Revolution had made no difference, that George Washington's New York in 1790 was much the same as George III's in 1765. However much the bare outline of political institutions may have looked like what had gone before, the reality was very different.

Social tensions and class conflict were only part of the American Revolution in New York; it was, after all, a struggle *for* home rule as well as *over* the nature and practice of rule at home. But it can be seen how Huntington's—and Lenin's—model of the revolutionary process in terms of an explosion of political participation aids in understanding events as they unfolded and how the explosion that took place in New York can be understood only in terms of its own society. Scholars from Carl Becker to Patricia Bonomi have shown that the political life of the late colonial period was marked by the mobilization of new groups, a mobilization which had its origins in the existing social system and with which the existing political system could not cope. The final upheaval, following the tea crisis, completed the process. It led to a fundamental redefinition of New York's political community, to an enlarged and rationalized set of formal institutions, and to the stabilization of a participatory political culture. Social practice likewise changed, through both political partisanship and the generation of permanent group feelings among artisans and farmers who had learned to think for themselves. The whole process was violent and rapid, and by the time it finished it had created a New York that was new in leadership, institutions, population, consciousness, and geography. This was done at the price of great human suffering, of which by 1795 the most poignant victims were not

Tory exiles but rather the Seneca Indians, huddling in their rural slums on the Niagara frontier.[31] The success story that would be New York's history for the next century and more would be achieved at the price of more human suffering. Nonetheless, a revolution had been wrought, firmly laying the foundations of a liberal bourgeois society and sweeping away the contradictions of the past. Little more than the name of New York, and the continuing fact of private property within it, remained the same.

Appendixes

Appendix 1

Fifty Thousand Choices: A Note on Quantitative Method

The cumulative argument that I develop in section III of chapter 7, section IV of chapter 8, and section IV of chapter 9, is based on a quantitative analysis of all roll-call votes taken in the state legislature during its first eleven sessions. The clerks of the two houses recorded 1,260 divisions altogether during those years. More than two-thirds of them, 852 to be precise, were taken in the sixty-five man assembly, whose members were elected each year. The other 408 were taken in the twenty-four man senate, whose members were chosen in rotation over a three-year cycle. If each house had always been at full strength, these divisions would have meant the recording of 65,172 individual decisions, and even allowing for absences, the number taken was in the region of 50,000. This represents the largest body of early American legislative voting data ever analyzed. I have made use during this project of every one of the decisions that the clerks recorded.

The argument in part III, however, is drawn solely from the assembly data. I have done this for several reasons. First, using a single point of focus gives clarity and prevents the confusion that would result from jumping back and forth in the text from one house to the other. Second, the assembly data provide a better index of probable changes in public opinion. As Lee Benson has pointed out,[1] no elected assembly is truly a microcosm of its public, but the state assembly's larger size and its being elected annually rather than triennially, and by a broader electorate, mean together that the assembly was more likely than was the senate to be affected by political formations "outside." Third, the choices made in the assembly outnumbered those made in the senate by roughly six to one. Finally, previous scholarship, in the form of two books by Jackson Turner Main and my own doctoral thesis, indicates that in fact from year to year there was relatively little difference between the voting behavior of the senators and that of the assemblymen.[2]

My concern in part III is to show that partisanship both in the legislature and among the electorate developed out of the coalition politics that patriot New Yorkers adopted during the independence crisis. In this I build on, but go farther than, the argument of Alfred F. Young,[3] who also sees partisanship as something that developed rather than something that existed. I have some points of quibbling disagreement with Young, most especially in my emphasis on the coalition basis of politics in the 1770s and in my handling of Governor Clinton, but my chief concern is to steer a course between the accounts of two other historians, Linda Grant DePauw and Jackson Turner Main. In DePauw's reading, politics in the Confederation era was concerned largely with questions that held no more than local interest and with voting patterns that represented only shifting factionalism. She maintains that "the business of the legislature during the Confederation period was rarely dramatic," that "there were few issues that could arouse strong feelings," that "personalities rather than principles dominated the political alliances of New York in the 1780s," and that legislative politics was highly unstable, with neither continuity from year to year nor predictive power on the matter of the Federal Constitution.[4]

Main argues that in both the senate and the assembly precisely the opposite was the case, that a flat, hard conflict between "Clintonians" and "Anti-Clintonians" extended throughout the Confederation years. DePauw is correct in noting that those terms were never used during that time.[5] But Main's analysis, especially in his second study, rests on a use of the legislative voting data that is much more thorough and rigorous than that of any previous scholar. He shows with overwhelming evidence that pattern and regularity were indeed to be found among the legislators. His demonstration makes one wonder whether DePauw bothered to read the legislative journals for any session other than the uncontentious eleventh.[6] My difference with Main is simply that he leaves out the dimension of time.

The reason why Main, like most quantitative political historians, ignores the dimension of time is that all rigorous analysis of legislative voting data requires the use of methods that make it difficult to take time into account. These methods presuppose a static situation, and their effect is to sort out the elements in such a situation. The two most commonly used are cluster-bloc and Guttman scale analysis. Applied in the conventional way, each eventually produces lists of legislators who took different voting positions and gives some details of the voting behavior that separated them. Cluster blocs are discovered by making matrices on which the percentage of agreement and the number of votes in agreement are given for each pair of members in a house. The blocs are identified by grouping together on the matrices all those members who had levels of agreement above a defined cutoff line. The result gives a crude indication of alignments, without regard to the issues that lay behind them. It also allows comparison across bloc lines. Such comparison permits one to say that given blocs were antagonistic, their members showing only low agreement with members of the other bloc, or nonantagonistic, the members of the blocs showing higher levels of agreement.

Guttman scaling separates men according to their behavior on certain issues. These issues can be picked out either by their known content or by statistical means, but the end result is the identification of a group of roll calls on which the behavior of the members indicates the presence of a single issue-dimension, and the placement of those roll calls and members according to that behavior. That placement is spectral rather than polar. That is, rather than dividing the members into flatly opposing groups, scaling sorts them by their behavior from those who were most extreme to those who were least extreme on a given issue. The major criterion is that once the roll calls are properly arranged on the scale, only a small number of members must take an "easy" position after having taken a "hard" one. The spread of roll calls should show a core group taking a certain stand (such as hostility to royalists) and not deviating from it, that core being joined by more and more members as the position becomes easier to take, and the isolation at the other extreme of the core that is totally opposed. The arrangement of the roll calls in the spectrum is according to the members' behavior rather than according to their chronology.

Both scales and cluster blocs thus give lists of names. These lists can be broken down according to the personal and political characteristics of the men on them. What is the relationship between taking a certain scale or cluster position and being from a certain region, being a member of a particular party, being of a given religion, ethnic group, or class? If adequate biographical data are given, simple correlations can answer such questions, and it is towards that end that most historical analysis using these tools has worked. For the early American period, the work of Main and Owen Stephen Ireland provides good evidence of the gains that can be made in this way.[7]

But such study usually presupposes the existence of known partisan groups: Democrats and Republicans in Congress, Constitutionalists and Republicans in Pennsylvania, Liberals and Tories in Parliament. It seeks to establish the defining characteristics of those groups. A more recent tendency in quantitative legislative study of early America has regarded the existence of such groups as either wholly problematic or a matter of development rather than of stasis.[8] In this study, which reflects that tendency, I have faced a number of problems in using methods that are essentially *static* for understanding partisan *dynamics.* Because to my knowledge these methods have not been employed in this way before, I will report in some detail on my use of them.

I have used three separate kinds of legislative data. One is simply the amount of turnover from session to session, both in the assembly as a whole and in particular county delegations. For the first six sessions, I have calculated the overall figure without reference to the southern-district counties, which were under enemy occupation and were continuously represented by the "ordinance" members. Figure 1 shows the curve of overall variation from session to session. Table 1 shows the number of reelections for each county in each new session. These figures are the basis of the comments made about reelection in the main text.

The second sort of data comprises cluster blocs for each of the first eleven sessions. The matrices on which these cluster blocs were found were built by hand in 1969–70, during the dissertation stage of this project. They were based on a computation of the rate of agreement for every pair of members in every session, using a program written and tested for me by Rachel Countryman, then of the Cornell University chemistry department and now of the Warwick University computer unit. I built the matrices by isolating at each end of each sheet pairs of members with extremely high percentages of agreement and with relatively low levels across pair lines. I then added to each core pair other members who showed high agreement with them. This was continued with decreasing levels of agreement until all the voting members of a session had been placed on the matrix. Each matrix showed both the overall percentage of voting agreement for all pairs of members and the raw number

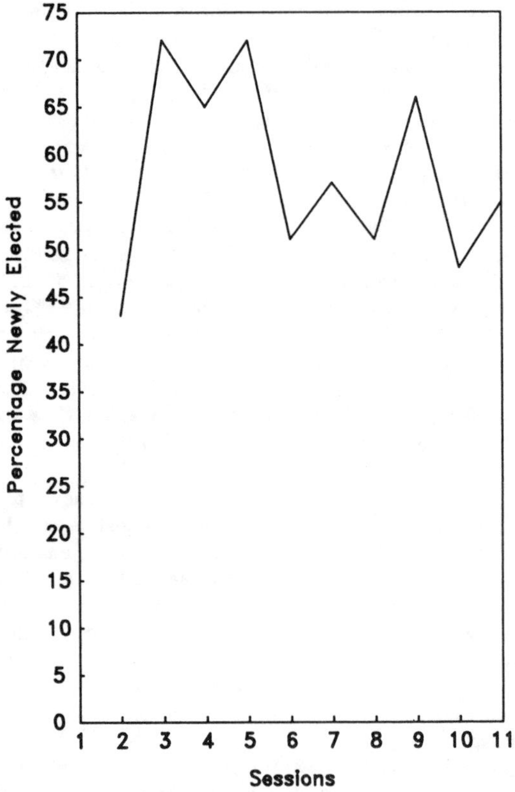

Figure 1. Percentage of Assemblymen Newly Elected, Sessions 2–11

of votes on which each pair agreed. I could thus sort out those with a percentage that was based on many agreements from those with a percentage based on only a few.

These matrices could be used in several ways. They provided conventional lists of members in mutually high agreement. They allowed me to check cohesion among members from different counties or senatorial districts.[9] Such analysis is wholly static and conventional. But the matrices also permitted me to compare the extent of cohesion in different sessions. To do that, I graphed the percentages in each session of members of two sorts: those who formed into blocs that cohered at rates above 70 percent for all pairs within the bloc and those who cohered at rates above 60 percent. A legislator who failed to agree with even a single member of a bloc at the defined minimum was automatically excluded. The resulting curves show the *total* percentage of members in the 70- and 60-percent blocs for each session against the number of voting members (see figures 2 and 3). I based my calculations on the blocs that revealed themselves at the diagonal extremes of each matrix and made no attempt to find other blocs in the middle. The curves show nothing about the issues on which members divided. Neither do they show the size of the separate blocs in each session.

Table 1. Numbers of Assemblymen Reelected in Sessions 2–11, by County

County	Numbers of Assemblymen in 1st Session	Numbers of Assemblymen reelected in Session									
		2	3	4	5	6	7	8	9	10	11
New York	9	x	x	x	x	x	1	0	2	2	4
Suffolk	5	x	x	x	x	x	1	4	2	2	4
Queens	4	x	x	x	x	x	1	1	1	2	1
Kings	2	x	x	x	x	x	0	0	2	1	2
Richmond	2	x	x	x	x	x	0	0	1	1	1
Albany	10	8	2	2	3	5	6	4	0	6	2
Ulster	6	4	3	4	1	3	4	5	2	4	3
Westchester	6	3	1	2	2	3	5	4	4	3	4
Dutchess	7	5	3	4	1	5	5	3	3	7	2
Orange	4	2	1	2	1	1	3	4	1	1	2
Tryon / Montgomery	6	1	1	2	2	2	0	5	3	3	2
Charlotte / Washington	4	1	1	0	1	0	2	2	1	2	2

But the varying percentages of members in blocs do indicate the extent to which the members of each session were cohering without regard to issue. It will be recognized that each 60-percent bloc includes the members of the corresponding 70-percent bloc, plus those in the next decile down. To illustrate the data from which these curves are drawn, table 2 shows the 70-percent blocs and the percentage of agreement across blocs for the eighth session, when partisanship was high. Table 3 shows the equivalent data for the eleventh session, when it was seemingly low.

Using Guttman scaling to study the dynamics of partisanship presented more serious problems. One difficulty was to decide which roll calls to select for scale treatment. Conventional methods could not be used, either because of lack of data or from logical faults in the methods themselves. One commonly used method is to select the votes that seem to reflect a given issue. This, however, is a totally subjective judgment, and it presents the risk of both leaving out roll calls that in fact bear on the question and missing connections between seemingly separate issues. It is precisely those connections that are the important element in a developing partisan situation. It was precisely those connections, their absence, or their presence at one time but not at another for which I was looking.

A second method is to pick votes that are identified as part of a presidential, prime ministerial, or gubernatorial program. I have seen no evidence, however, that would have permitted me to identify any roll calls as part of a program identified explicitly with Governor Clinton, in the way that bills in the modern Congress are associated with the White House. DePauw is correct when she argues that Clinton did not function publicly in the ways characteristic of a modern partisan leader.[10] A third method is to pick bills associated with the leadership of a legislative party and to test the leaders' ability to influence backbenchers. Such a method cannot be used in a situation in which the development of party is itself the central problem and in which no publicly recognized party leaders can be found. I demonstrate the futility of this method in chapter 7, and with more detail in a separate essay that shows that

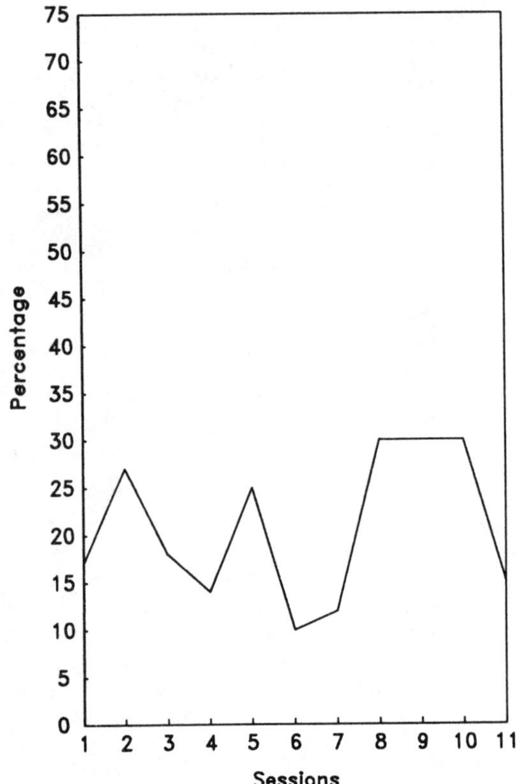

Figure 2. Percentage of Assemblymen in Cluster Blocs with Agreement above 70 Percent, Sessions 1-11

the evidence that would normally identify such leaders cannot be relied upon in this context to actually pick out powerful men.[11]

Accordingly, picking roll calls to subject to scaling had to be done by purely statistical methods. The standard handbook *Legislative Roll Call Analysis,* by Lee Anderson and his associates,[12] suggests that this can be done by computing Yule's Q for all pairs of roll calls in a session. Q is the standard statistical measure for finding correlation between two bipolar variables, such as roll calls on which one voted either yea or nay. Computing it is the normal technique for establishing whether a given roll call is "scalable" with the other roll calls in a set. "Scalability" means the lack on a roll call of any significant number of responses that indicate inconsistency in voting, for a scale can be built only if those voting on the roll calls in it took consistent or nearly consistent positions. Since perfect consistency cannot be expected, computing Q allows one to see how close a putative set of scalable votes approaches it. Q can vary between 1.0 and -1.0, and if there is a statistical relationship between a pair of roll calls, Q for that pair will be close to one of the extreme values. If there is no rela-

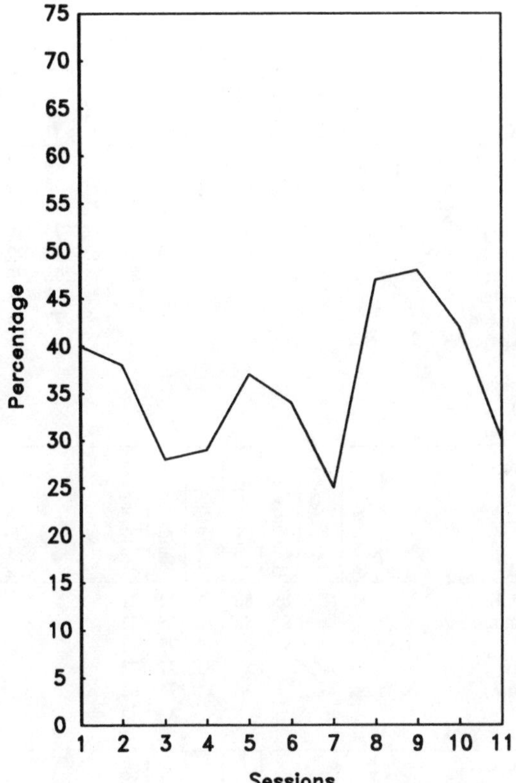

Figure 3. Percentage of Assemblymen in Cluster Blocs with Agreement above 60 Percent, Sessions 1-11

tionship at all, it will stand at 0.0. The value below or above which one discounts a pair of roll calls can vary with one's purpose, but in general the more extreme the cut-off value, the more reliable the scale.

Anderson and his associates, however, discuss the use of *Q* in a way that caused me, and perhaps has caused others, considerable confusion. Though they note in one place that "the value of *Q* ranges from −1.0 to 1.0," their central point is that "the *higher* the *Q* value, the greater the association or scalability of the roll calls. Thus, if two votes are perfectly scalar. . . then *Q* equals 1.0."[13] The analytical problem they pose is how to find a *positive* position on each roll call. If that is done, they imply, *Q* will vary only from 0.0 to 1.0, and high values will be the determining evidence.

Their discussion is an utter muddle, because the problem of how to assign that "positive" position cannot be resolved. They cite a study by the political scientist Duncan MacRae, Jr., in which the positive side is identified with the position taken in Congress by the Republican party, but it can be seen readily that where the development of party is the problem and where party labels are not in use such a method is

Table 2. 70 Percent Cores in the Eighth Assembly

A) The Radical Core	Adgate	Ford	Harper	Savage	Thompson	Becker	Deygart	Hopkins	Younglove	Burling	Patterson	Cooper	Purdy
Adgate (Albany)	x	90	88	85	80	82	81	75	74	74	72	80	77
Ford (Albany)		x	87	82	78	79	75	71	78	71	76	78	72
Harper (Albany)			x	81	83	82	82	82	74	73	75	73	79
Savage (Washington)				x	84	85	84	78	75	79	76	78	81
Thompson (Albany)					x	84	84	83	77	77	76	78	80
Becker (Albany)						x	82	79	78	70	77	76	77
Deygart (Montgomery)							x	88	75	78	79	81	82
Hopkins (Washington)								x	77	75	81	77	79
Younglove (Albany)									x	71	79	70	75
Burling (Albany)										x	75	70	87
Patterson (Dutchess)											x	75	78
Cooper (Orange)												x	76
Purdy (Westchester)													x

B) The Conservative Core	Corsen	Mercereau	Doughty	Vanderbilt	Randall	Sands	P. Livingston
Corsen (Richmond)	x	86	85	80	77	72	71
Mercereau (Richmond)		x	81	80	78	75	73
Doughty (Kings)			x	86	73	75	72
Vanderbilt (Kings)				x	85	77	72
Randall (New York)					x	75	82
Sands (Queens)						x	75
P. Livingston (New York)							x

C) Cross-Core Agreement	Corsen	Mercereau	Doughty	Vanderbilt	Randall	Sands	P. Livingston
Adgate	32	25	27	21	19	30	29
Ford	29	25	28	22	23	30	32
Harper	23	23	23	20	20	25	28
Savage	24	26	32	20	13	28	28
Thompson	26	28	29	22	17	28	28
Becker	25	27	23	20	20	31	28
Deygart	30	29	30	26	22	31	28
Hopkins	30	31	30	27	18	31	25
Younglove	35	30	32	28	24	36	31
Burling	31	29	35	30	24	36	27
Patterson	34	31	28	28	23	32	26
Cooper	35	41	35	30	27	37	34
Purdy	27	27	31	30	20	40	31

Note: All figures given represent percentages.

Table 3. 70 Percent Cores in the Eleventh Assembly

A) The Upstate Core	Bruyn	Wisner	Bloom	
Bruyn (Ulster)	x	90	89	
Wisner (Ulster)		x	85	
Bloom (Dutchess)			x	

B) The Downstate Core	Brooks	Niven	Lewis	Ver Planck	Sands
Brooks (New York)	x	84	83	71	86
Niven (New York)		x	82	73	72
Lewis (Queens)			x	85	87
Ver Planck (New York)				x	83
Sands (New York)					x

C) Cross-Core Agreement	Brooks	Niven	Lewis	Ver Planck	Sands
Bruyn	39	30	48	56	56
Wisner	38	28	37	48	45
Bloom	34	36	40	44	50

Note: All figures given represent percentages.

of no use. Indeed, however it is picked, any attempt to assign a "positive" quality to one side on each of a long series of roll calls must be subjective. It thus negates this method's claim to total objectivity.

A third reason for rejecting this approach is that the complications that it presents are not only illogical but needless. Given that Q can vary over two whole integers, relationships between roll calls can be found by computing it for every pair of roll calls and then searching not for *high* but for *extreme* values. Negative values of Q, approaching -1.0, simply indicate that a group that voted yea on one question was voting nay on another and that the two votes both reflect the same basic position. I did this using a program written for me by Keith Halstead, of the Warwick University computer unit, which printed matrices showing the value of Q for each pair of roll calls in each session. Extreme values were sorted out first by having the computer suppress them below or above a given cutoff line and then by visual searches of the matrices. Table 4 shows a sample of the matrix for the eighth assembly.

These matrices permitted ready identification of groups of roll calls that gave prima facie evidence of being related to one another. Clusters of votes could be found that shared extreme values of Q in roughly the same way that clusters of members who had mutually high rates of agreement could be found on the hand-built matrices. I did not analyze any clusters containing fewer than five roll calls. I calculated and graphed the percentage of roll calls in each session that fell into clusters containing more than five, and the resulting curve could be taken as evidence of in-

Table 4. Part of the Eighth-Session *Q*-Matrix

Roll Call	1	2	3	4	5	6	7	8
1	1.000							
2	0.7578	1.000						
3	0.8214	0.8828	1.0000					
4	0.7546	0.8958	0.9277	1.0000				
5	−0.736	−0.940	−0.948	−0.978	1.0000			
6	0.7561	0.8592	0.9075	0.9732	−1.000	1.0000		
7	−0.807	−0.936	−0.906	−0.966	1.0000	−0.955	1.0000	
8	0.8605	0.9200	0.9664	0.9669	−1.000	0.9298	−0.973	1.0000

creases and decreases in the rate of regular, ordered divisiveness within the legislature (see figure 4).

Three curves were thus established for the assemblymen's behavior. One shows crude cohesion at the 70-percent level; a second, crude cohesion at the 60-percent level; and the third, the percentage of each session's roll calls falling into sizable groups. If they are graphed together, it can be seen that these curves display rough, though by no means perfect congruence (see figure 5). It can be noted that by all three measures, ordered internal divisiveness rose and fell rather than remained steady, and it reached peaks in the fifth and eighth sessions. Several long steps had been taken, in other words, towards a rigorous analysis of the dynamics of party development.

None of these curves, however, shows either who was opposing whom or the issues on which they faced each other. The first could be discovered in broad terms from the cluster-bloc matrices, but these showed nothing about issues. Moreover, in a fair number of sessions agreement ran at fairly high levels across bloc lines. In those cases, the matrices showed groups that cohered but not groups that stood in opposition. Moreover, the hand-built matrices were based on the responses of members on all roll calls, whether or not these roll calls in fact were related to any others.

These problems were resolved by building Guttman scales on the basis of the *Q* matrices. The scales were built using the program BMD05S in the *Biomedical Data* computing package. This is the simpler of two scaling programs available in that series.[14] It permits the construction of scales based on up to twenty-five roll calls and using data, such as I had, in which *Q* takes negative as well as positive values. Those scales were constructed to give a position to every member who made even a single response on one of the roll calls in question. Normally, members failing to respond on more than a certain percentage of roll calls are dismissed from scale analysis, but I chose to include all save those who did not vote at all, for two reasons. First, with a group considerably smaller than, say, Congress or the House of Commons, I wanted to have as full a body of evidence as possible, even if some of it were known to be doubtful. Second, on BMD05S printouts, respondents for whom the program has "supplied" responses on the basis of other responses that are known are listed *after* those who were given their position on the basis of a full or more complete set of data. It is thus an easy matter to separate men whose positions in a scale are certain from men whose positions are only probable. Only rarely did the method lead me into difficulties.[15]

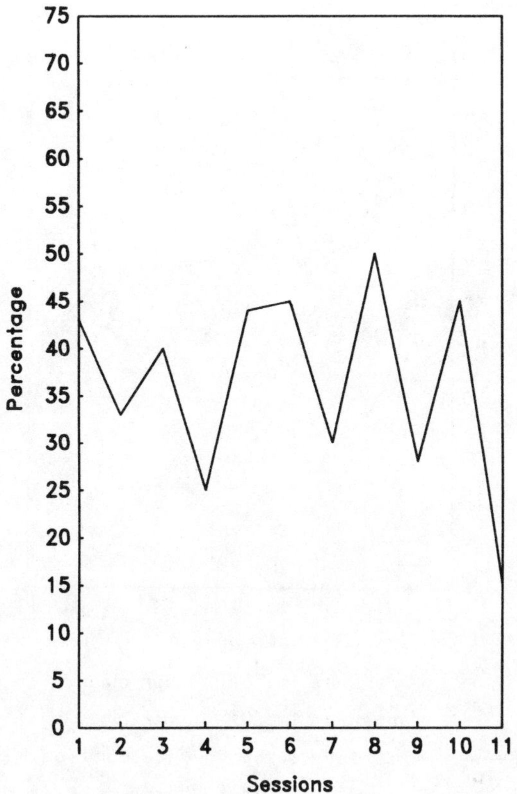

Figure 4. Percentage of Roll Calls Susceptible to Scale Analysis, Sessions 1–11

The printouts also gave each scale's coefficient of reproducibility. This measures the accuracy with which a known vote on any roll call predicts a member's response on another roll call within the scale. As a matter of convention, I discarded scales with a coefficient below 0.9. I made only one exception to this rule, that being a scale for the ninth session, which showed muzzy rather than clear partisanship. The coefficient of reproducibility for that scale stood at barely more than 0.8. It would have been possible to break it into a number of smaller scales, each with a higher coefficient, but the large scale did point to an underlying single dimension, even if it was a blurred one. The correctness of staying with that scale was borne out when the results of the elections for that session, when the conservatives lost New York and the radicals lost Albany, were brought into analysis.

Using the coefficients of reproducibility provided a check on the prima facie evidence of interrelatedness that was to be found in the *Q* matrices. It also allowed me to test the whole method. Testing was done by running BMD05S for several sets of roll calls that were either chosen at random or picked from among those not shown as interrelated by the *Q* matrices. Setting my minimum / maximum value of

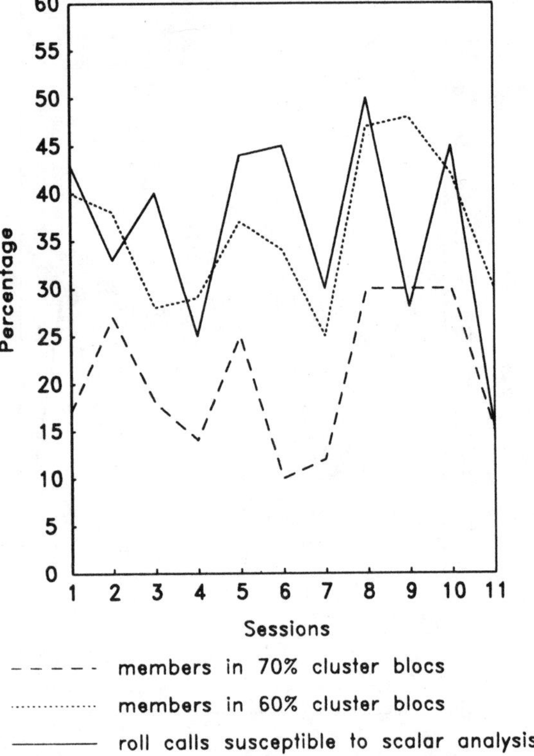

Figure 5. Percentage of Assemblymen Voting in 70 Percent and 60 Percent Cluster Blocs, and Percentage of Roll Calls Susceptible to Analysis, Sessions 1-11

Q at 0.8 / −0.8, I picked one test set from roll calls with shared values of Q between 0.5 / −0.5 and 0.8 / −0.8, another set from those with values between 0.5 and −0.5, and a third set at random. I did this for roll calls from both the seventh session and the eighth session, since the voting characteristics of those two sessions were very different. In all six cases, the result was a scale with a low coefficient. Had high coefficients been produced in the test runs, it would have thrown my method into doubt.

The scale programs done, I then checked the "content" of the particular roll calls on which scales were built by referring back to data collected at the time of recording the roll call behavior from the legislative records; this was the first point at which nonstatistical evidence entered the analysis. Not to my surprise, most scalable sets of votes were found to turn on a single issue, such as Tories, taxes, the abolition of slavery, or salaries. My concern, however, was to find relationships between votes on seemingly disparate issues, and analysis using this method made it possible, even easy, to find such connections. Sometimes the connections turned on the presence of a single dimension underlying the surface question. My discovery of the first-session votes on the "legitimacy" issue, from which my whole interpretation has sprung, represents a case of this. But more important, the discovery of the congruence of the fifth-session votes on the Citation Act and on salaries and the repeated line-up on issue after issue in the eighth session permitted me to make my argument that partisanship was a matter of development rather than of existence.

In both of those sessions, divisiveness transcended particular issues, and in the eighth there can be no doubt that two self-conscious parties confronted each other. The limited partisanship of the fifth session directly prefigured the full-blown partisanship of the eighth, and together they pointed towards the division on the Federal Constitution. Demonstrating these things provides as much "proof" as I can muster that politics in the Confederation period was neither the empty shadow game that DePauw depicts nor the flat confrontation that Main presents, but rather a matter of development and change.

My other point, that this development was away from a situation of coalition and towards one of confrontation, is supported by the data for the earliest sessions and from those on turnover in assembly elections. There are several troughs in the curves in figure 5, but they are there for different reasons. The votes in the earliest sessions, the first through the fourth, do reflect a politics based on shifting alliances from issue to issue, which is exactly the voting pattern that one would expect in open voting among coalition members. None of the particular issues of that period prefigure the politics of the fifth session, the eighth sesion, and the ratification controversy. None of them displayed any particular congruence with others. Thus, for instance, there was no relationship in the first session between members' behavior on the taxation issue and their behavior on the "legitimacy" question. Though the third session saw a rise in the percentage of votes that were prima facie subject to scale analysis, it saw falls in the percentages of members voting together at the 60- and 70-percent levels. It was not until the fifth session, the first that saw partisanship transcending particular issues, that all three measures rose together. All of these things support my contention that the previous years had been a time of coalition, even if the coalition began to fray during the crisis of 1779.

That contention is supported as well by the way that the assemblymen were replaced from one session to another. The overall curve of replacements shown in figure 1 is useful in places. It shows a massive entry of new men in the elections for the third and the fifth assembly sessions, a low figure in that for the eighth, and a sharp jump in that for the ninth. The peak in the third session indicates the first serious cracks in the independence coalition. The peak in the fifth represents the end of the coalition, as men like Egbert Benson finally made their exit. The trough in the sixth session represents electors' endorsement of what the fifth session had done. The slight rise in the seventh stems from the presence, for the first time, of elected southern-district members. The trough in the eighth session indicates general rural approval of radical members, the new men that year being the downstate conservatives whose opposition to rural radicalism caused the session's massive division. The rise in new men in the ninth session represents the combination of conservative victory in Albany and radical resurgence in New York City. The lower figures for the last two years show the conservatives consolidating their hold.

The overall curve, in other words, needs to be read against a variety of backgrounds. Real statewide partisanship at the polls did not occur until the election in 1788 for the ratifying convention. Serious efforts at cross-county coordination did not occur before Hamilton's half-abortive intervention in 1785. Instead, for most of the period, the county is the important unit of electoral analysis. Deciding for each county when a coalition was collapsing (Albany in 1779, Dutchess in 1781), when an emergent party group was holding on (Albany, Westchester, and Orange in 1783, Ulster and Tryon in 1784), or when another group was mounting a challenge (New York in the second election of 1784, Albany in 1785, Dutchess in 1787) is a matter for "feel" and for more conventional sources. But combining feel and conventional sources with the hard analysis done on the roll calls completes the story of how, when, where, and why New York's post-Revolution parties took shape.

I believe that this represents the most completely quantitative study of early American roll-call data ever done. I also believe that it breaks through the bias towards static discussion that is built into both cluster-bloc and scale analysis and that it permits a discussion of the dynamics of development rather than the dissection of a static situation.

Appendix 2

The Structure of the State Legislature, 1777–1788

FIRST SESSION

First meeting: Called for 1 September 1777 by proclamation of the council of safety and the governor; several delays due to military situation; held at Kingston; quorum reached 10 September 1777; scattered without adjournment by approach of a British expedition on 7 October 1777.

Second meeting: Called for 2 January 1778 by proclamation of the governor; held at Poughkeepsie; quorum reached 15 January 1778; adjourned 4 April 1778.

Third meeting: Called for second Tuesday in June 1778 by adjournment of second meeting; held at Poughkeepsie; quorum reached 22 June 1778; adjourned 30 June 1778.

Senate[1]

President: Pierre Van Cortlandt

Southern District:[2] William Floyd, John Jones,[3] Jonathan Lawrence, Philip Livingston,[4] Lewis Morris, Richard Morris,[5] Isaac Roosevelt, William Smith of Suffolk, Pierre Van Cortlandt[6]

Middle District: Jonathan Landon, Arthur Parks, Levi Pawling, Zephaniah Platt, Henry Wisner, Jesse Woodhull

Eastern District: William Duer,[7] Alexander Webster, John Williams

Western District: Jelles Fonda, Rinier Mynderse, Isaac Paris, Dirck W. Ten Broeck, Anthony Van Schaick, Abraham Yates, Jr.

Assembly

Speaker: Walter Livingston (Albany)
Albany County: Jacob Cuyler, John Cuyler, Jr., James Gordon, Walter Livingston, Stephen J. Schuyler, John Taylor, Killian Van Rensselaer, Robert Van Rensselaer, Peter Vrooman, William B. Whiting
Charlotte County: John Barns, Ebenezer Clarke, John Rowen, Ebenezer Russell
Dutchess County: Egbert Benson, Dirck Brinckerhoff, Anthony Hoffman, Gilbert Livingston, Andrew Morehouse, John Schenck, Jacobus Swartwout
Kings County: William Boerum, Henry Williams
New York County: Evert Bancker, Abraham Brasher, Daniel Dunscomb, Robert Harpur, Frederick Jay, Abraham P. Lott, Henry Rutgers,[8] Jacobus Van Zandt, Peter Pra Van Zandt
Orange County: Jeremiah Clark, John Hathorn, Tunis Kuyper, Roeluff Van Houten
Queens County: Benjamin Birdsall, Benjamin Coe, Philip Edsall, Daniel Lawrence
Richmond County: Abraham Jones, Joshua Mercereau
Suffolk County: David Gelston, Ezra L'Hommedieu, Burnet Miller, Thomas Tredwell, Thomas Wickes
Tryon County: Samuel Clyde, Michael Etdick, Jacob G. Klock, Jacob Snell, Abraham Van Horne, Johannes Veeder
Ulster County: John Cantine, Johannes G. Hardenbergh, Matthew Rea, Cornelius C. Schoonmaker, Johannes Snyder, Henry Wisner, Jr.
Westchester County: Thaddeus Crane, Samuel Drake, Robert Graham, Israel Honeywell, Jr., Zebediah Mills, Gouverneur Morris

Council of Appointment[9]

John Morin Scott (southern), Jesse Woodhull (middle), Alexander Webster (eastern), Abraham Yates, Jr. (western)

SECOND SESSION

First meeting: Called from 1 October 1778 by proclamation of the governor; held at Poughkeepsie; quorum reached 13 October 1778; adjourned 6 November 1778.
Second meeting: Called for second Tuesday in January 1779 by adjournment of first meeting; held at Poughkeepsie; quorum reached 28 January 1779; adjourned 16 March 1779.

Senate

Lieutenant governor and president: Pierre Van Cortlandt
Southern District: William Floyd, Sir James Jay,[10] Jonathan Lawrence, Lewis Morris, Richard Morris,[11] Isaac Roosevelt, John Morin Scott, William Smith of Suffolk, Isaac Stoutenburgh[12]
Middle District: Jonathan Landon, Arthur Parks, Levi Pawling, Zephaniah Platt, Henry Wisner, Jesse Woodhull

Eastern District: Ebenezer Russell, Alexander Webster, John Williams[13]
Western District: Jelles Fonda, Jacob G. Klock, Rinier Mynderse, Dirck W. Ten Broeck, Anthony Van Schaick, Abraham Yates, Jr.

Assembly

Speaker: Walter Livingston (Albany)
Albany County: Leonard Gansevoort, James Gordon, Walter Livingston, Stephen J. Schuyler, John Taylor, Jacobus Teller, Killian Van Rensselaer, Robert Van Rensselaer, Peter Vrooman, William B. Whiting
Charlotte County: Albert Baker, Ebenezer Clarke, David Hopkins, Elishamer Tozer
Dutchess County: Egbert Benson, Dirck Brinckerhoff, Joseph Crane, Samuel Dodge, Anthony Hoffman, Andrew Morehouse, Jacobus Swartwout
Kings County: William Boerum, Henry Williams
New York County: Evert Bancker, Abraham Brasher, John Berrien,[14] Daniel Dunscomb, Robert Harpur, Frederick Jay, Abraham P. Lott, Jacobus Van Zandt, Peter Pra Van Zandt
Orange County: Jeremiah Clark, John Coe, Peter Ogilvie, Roeluff Van Houten
Queens County: Benjamin Birdsall, Benjamin Coe, Philip Edsall, Daniel Lawrence
Richmond County: Joshua Mercereau
Suffolk County: David Gelston, Ezra L'Hommedieu, Burnet Miller, Thomas Tredwell, Thomas Wickes
Tryon County: George Henry Bell, John Newkirk, Abraham Van Horne, Peter Waggoner, Moses Younglove
Ulster County: John Cantine, Matthew Rea, Cornelius C. Schoonmaker, Nathan Smith, Johannis Snyder
Westchester County: Joseph Benedict, Thaddeus Crane, Israel Honeywell, Ebenezer Lockwood, Zebediah Mills, Stephen Ward

Council of Appointment

Jonathan Lawrence (southern), Zephaniah Platt (middle), Alexander Webster (eastern), Dirck W. Ten Broeck (western)

THIRD SESSION

First meeting: Called for 9 August 1779 by proclamation of the governor; held at Kingston; quorum reached 18 August 1779; adjourned 25 October 1779.
Second meeting: Called for 4 January 1780 by adjournment of first meeting; held at Albany; quorum reached 25 January 1780; adjourned 14 March 1780.
Third meeting: Called for 9 May 1780 by proclamation of the governor, supplanting adjournment to 1 June 1780; held at Kingston; quorum reached 25 May 1780; adjourned 2 July 1780.

Senate

Lieutenant governor and president: Pierre Van Cortlandt
Southern District: William Floyd, Sir James Jay, Jonathan Lawrence, Lewis Morris,

Isaac Roosevelt, John Morin Scott, William Smith of Suffolk, Isaac Stoutenburgh, Stephen Ward[15]

Middle District: Ephraim Paine, Arthur Parks, Levi Pawling, Zephaniah Platt, Henry Wisner, Jesse Woodhull

Eastern District: Ebenezer Russell, Elishamer Tozer, Alexander Webster

Western District: Jelles Fonda, Jacob G. Klock, Rinier Mynderse, Dirck W. Ten Broeck, Anthony Van Schaick, Abraham Yates, Jr.

Assembly

Speaker: Evert Bancker (New York)

Albany County: Flores Bancker, John Bay, James Gordon, Cornelius Humfrey, Hugh Mitchell, Henry Oothoudt, Henry Quackenbos, Isaac Vrooman, Phineas Whiteside, William B. Whiting

Charlotte County: Albert Baker, John Grover, Noah Payn

Cumberland County: (Vermont): Elkanah Day, John Sessions, Micah Townsend

Dutchess County: Egbert Benson, Dirck Brinckerhoff, Ananias Cooper, Samuel Dodge, Henry Luddington, Brinton Paine, Nathaniel Sackett

Kings County: William Boerum, Henry Williams

New York County: Evert Bancker, John Berrien, Abraham Brasher, Daniel Dunscomb, Robert Harpur, Frederick Jay, Abraham P. Lott, Jacobus Van Zandt, Peter Pra Van Zandt

Orange County: John Coe, Thomas Moffat, Bezaleel Seely, Jr.

Queens County: Benjamin Birdsall, Benjamin Coe, Philip Edsall, Daniel Lawrence

Richmond County: Joshua Mercereau

Suffolk County: David Gelston, Ezra L'Hommedieu, Burnet Miller, Thomas Tredwell, Thomas Wickes

Tryon County: Abraham Copeman, Peter S. Deygart, Frederick Fox, Jacob Gardinier, Melkert Van Deusen, Peter Waggoner

Ulster County: Robert Boyd, Jr., John Cantine, Johannes C. Hardenbergh, Thomas Palmer, Cornelius C. Schoonmaker, Nathan Smith

Westchester County: Samuel Drake, Abijah Gilbert, Zebediah Mills, William Paulding, Philip Pell, Jr., Ebenezer Purdy

Council of Appointment

Isaac Roosevelt (southern), Levi Pawling (middle), Alexander Webster (eastern), Rinier Mynderse (western)

FOURTH SESSION

First meeting: Called for 4 September 1780 by proclamation of the governor; held at Poughkeepsie; quorum reached 7 September 1780; adjourned 10 October 1780.

Second meeting: Called for 2 January 1781 by proclamation of the governor, supplanting adjournment to second Wednesday in January; held at Albany; quorum reached 31 January 1781; adjourned 28 March 1781.

Third meeting: Called for 6 June 1781 by adjournment of second meeting; held at Poughkeepsie; quorum reached 16 June 1781; adjourned 1 July 1781.

Senate

Lieutenant governor and president: Pierre Van Cortlandt
Southern District: William Floyd, Sir James Jay, Jonathan Lawrence, Lewis Morris, Isaac Roosevelt, John Morin Scott, William Smith of Suffolk, Isaac Stoutenburgh, Stephen Ward
Middle District: Ephraim Paine,[16] Arthur Parks, Levi Pawling, Zephaniah Platt, Henry Wisner, Jesse Woodhull
Eastern District: Ebenezer Russell, Alexander Webster
Western District: Jelles Fonda, Jacob G. Klock, Rinier Mynderse, Philip Schuyler, Abraham Ten Broeck, Abraham Yates, Jr.

Assembly

Speaker: Evert Bancker (New York)
Albany County: Matthew Adgate, John H. Beekman, James Gordon, John Lansing, Jr., Peter R. Livingston, Dirck Swart, John Taylor, John Van Rensselaer, Jr., Robert Van Rensselaer, Isaac Vrooman
Charlotte County: David Hopkins, Hamilton McCollister, Matthew McWhorter, Ichabod Parker
Dutchess County: Egbert Benson, Ebenezer Cary, Samuel Dodge, Henry Luddington, Brinton Paine, Guisbert Schenck, Jacobus Swartwout
Kings County: William Boerum, Henry Williams
New York County: Evert Bancker, John Berrien, Abraham Brasher, Daniel Dunscomb, Robert Harpur, Frederick Jay, Abraham P. Lott, Jacobus Van Zandt, Peter Pra Van Zandt
Orange County: Jeremiah Clark, David Pye, Bezaleel Seely, Jr., John Stagg
Queens County: Benjamin Birdsall, Benjamin Coe, Philip Edsall, Daniel Lawrence
Richmond County: Joshua Mercereau
Suffolk County: David Gelston, Ezra L'Hommedieu, Burnet Miller, Thomas Tredwell, Thomas Wickes
Tryon County: Zephaniah Batchelor, Jacob Gardinier, Abraham Gerrison, John Moore, Abraham Van Horne, Peter Waggoner
Ulster County: Robert Boyd, Jr., John Cantine, Johannes C. Hardenbergh, Cornelius C. Schoonmaker, Nathan Smith, Dirck Wynkoop
Westchester County: Samuel Drake, Philip Pell, Nathan Rockwell, Joseph Strang, Thomas Thomas, Jonathan G. Tompkins

Council of Appointment

Stephen Ward (southern), Ephraim Paine (middle), Arthur Parks (middle),[17] Ebenezer Russell (eastern), Abraham Ten Broeck (western)

FIFTH SESSION

First meeting: Called for 1 October 1781 by proclamation of the governor; held at Poughkeepsie; quorum reached 24 October 1781; adjourned 23 November 1781.
Second meeting: Called for 11 February 1782 by proclamation of the governor, supplanting adjournment to third Wednesday in May; held at Poughkeepsie; quorum reached 21 February 1782; adjourned 14 April 1782.

Senate

Lieutenant governor and president: Pierre Van Cortlandt
Southern District: William Floyd, Sir James Jay,[18] Jonathan Lawrence, Lewis Morris, Isaac Roosevelt, John Morin Scott, William Smith of Suffolk, Isaac Stoutenburgh, Stephen Ward
Middle District: John Haring, Thomas Palmer, Arthur Parks, Levi Pawling, Zephaniah Platt, Henry Wisner
Eastern District: Alexander Webster
Western District: Jacob G. Klock, Henry Oothoudt, Philip Schuyler, Abraham Ten Broeck, William B. Whiting, Abraham Yates, Jr.

Assembly

Speaker: Evert Bancker (New York)[19]
Albany County: Matthew Adgate, Jacob Ford, Philip Frisbie, John Lansing, Jr., George Palmer, Dirck Swart, Samuel Ten Broeck, Israel Thompson, Isaac Vrooman, Edmund Wells
Charlotte County: Matthew McWhorter, John Williams
Dutchess County: Dirck Brinckerhoff, Jonathan Dennis, Cornelius Humfrey, Ebenezer Husted, Brinton Paine, Thomas Storm, Jacobus Swartwout
Kings County: William Boerum, Henry Williams
New York County: Evert Bancker, John Berrien, Abraham Brasher, Daniel Dunscomb, Robert Harpur, Frederick Jay, Abraham P. Lott, Jacobus Van Zandt, Peter Pra Van Zandt
Orange County: Jeremiah Clark, John Hathorn, John Stagg, John Suffern
Queens County: Benjamin Birdsall, Benjamin Coe, Philip Edsall, Daniel Lawrence
Richmond County: Joshua Mercereau
Suffolk County: David Gelston, Ezra L'Hommedieu, Burnet Miller, Thomas Tredwell, Thomas Wickes
Tryon County: Zephaniah Batchelor, William Harper, John Moore, William Petry
Ulster County: Johannes Bruyn, Charles DeWitt, Johannes C. Hardenbergh, Abraham Hasbrouck, James Hunter
Westchester County: Nathaniel Delivan, Abijah Gilbert, Zebediah Mills, Nathan Rockwell, Thomas Thomas, Jonathan G. Tompkins

Council of Appointment

Isaac Stoutenburgh (southern), Zephaniah Platt (middle), Alexander Webster (eastern), Henry Oothoudt (western)

SIXTH SESSION

First meeting: Called for 3 July 1782 by proclamation of the governor; held at Poughkeepsie; quorum reached 11 July 1782; adjourned 25 July 1782.

Second meeting: Called for first Tuesday in January 1783 by adjournment of first meeting; held at Kingston; quorum reached 27 January 1783; adjourned 28 March 1783.

Senate

Lieutenant governor and president: Pierre Van Cortlandt

President pro hac vice: Abraham Ten Broeck (Western)[20]

Southern District: James Duane,[21] William Floyd, Jonathan Lawrence, Lewis Morris, Isaac Roosevelt, John Morin Scott, William Smith of Suffolk, Isaac Stoutenburgh, Stephen Ward

Middle District: William Allison, John Haring, Ephraim Paine, Thomas Palmer, Arthur Parks, Zephaniah Platt

Eastern District: Alexander Webster, John Williams

Western District: Jacob G. Klock, Henry Oothoudt, Philip Schuyler, Abraham Ten Broeck, William B. Whiting, Abraham Yates, Jr.

Assembly

Speaker: Evert Bancker (New York)

Albany County: Matthew Adgate, John H. Beekman, John Ja. Beekman, Jacob Ford, John Lansing, Jr., Dirck Swart, Samuel Ten Broeck, Peter Van Ness, Christopher Yates, John Younglove

Charlotte County: Benjamin Baker, David Hopkins, Hamilton McCollister, Joseph McCracken

Dutchess County: Benjamin Birdsall, Jr., Jonathan Dennis, Cornelius Humfrey, Ebenezer Husted, Matthew Patterson, Thomas Storm, Jacobus Swartwout

Kings County: William Boerum, Henry Williams

New York County: Evert Bancker, John Berrien, Abraham Brasher, Daniel Dunscomb, Robert Harpur, Frederick Jay, Abraham P. Lott, Jacobus Van Zandt, Peter Pra Van Zandt

Orange County: Jeremiah Clark, Gilbert Cooper, John Hathorn, John Stagg

Queens County: Benjamin Birdsall, Benjamin Coe, Daniel Lawrence, Nathaniel Tom[22]

Richmond County: Joshua Mercereau

Suffolk County: David Gelston, Ezra L'Hommedieu, Burnet Miller, Thomas Tredwell, Thomas Wickes

Tryon County: Zephaniah Batchelor, Andrew Finck, Jr., Frederick Fischer, John Frey, Christian Nellis, William Petry

Ulster County: Johannes Bruyn, Charles DeWitt, James Hunter, William Malcom, John Nicholson, Cornelius C. Schoonmaker

Westchester County: Abijah Gilbert, Samuel Haight, John Lawrence, Zebediah Mills, Ebenezer Purdy, Thomas Thomas

Council of Appointment

Jonathan Lawrence (southern), John Haring (middle), Elkanah Day (eastern), William B. Whiting (western)

SEVENTH SESSION

Meeting: Called for 6 January 1784 by proclamation of the governor; held at New York City; quorum reached 21 January 1784; adjourned 12 May 1784.

Senate

Lieutenant governor and president: Pierre Van Cortlandt
Southern District:[23] James Duane, William Floyd, Ezra L'Hommedieu, Alexander McDougall, Lewis Morris, Isaac Roosevelt, Isaac Stoutenburgh, Stephen Ward
Middle District: William Allison, Joseph Gasherie, John Haring, Ephraim Paine, Arthur Parks, Jacobus Swartwout
Eastern District: Alexander Webster, John Williams
Western District: Andrew Finck, Jelles Fonda, Jacob G. Klock, Henry Oothoudt, Philip Schuyler, William B. Whiting, Abraham Yates, Jr.

Assembly

Speaker: John Hathorn (Orange)
Albany County: Matthew Adgate, Abraham Becker, Abraham Cuyler, Jacob Ford, James Gordon, John Lansing, Jr., Peter Schuyler, Dirck Swart, Peter Van Ness, Christopher Yates
Charlotte County: David Hopkins, Hamilton McCollister, Ebenezer Russell, Edward Savage
Dutchess County: Dirck Brinckerhoff, Jonathan Dennis, Anthony Hoffman, Cornelius Humfrey, Ebenezer Husted, Matthew Patterson, Thomas Storm
Kings County: Johannes E. Lott, Rutger Van Brunt
New York County: Robert Harpur, Hugh Hughes, John Lamb, William Malcom, Henry Rutgers, Isaac Sears, John Stagg, Peter P. Van Zandt, Marinus Willet
Orange County: Jeremiah Clark, Gilbert Cooper, John Hathorn, William Sickles
Queens County: Benjamin Coe, Hendrick Onderdonck, Samuel Riker, James Townsend
Richmond County: Adrian Bancker, Johannes Van Wagenen
Suffolk County: John Brush, David Gelston, Ebenezer Platt, Jeffrey Smith, Thomas Youngs
Tryon County: Abraham Copeman, William Harper, James Livingston, Isaac Paris, Volkert Veeder, Christopher P. Yates
Ulster County: John Cantine, Charles DeWitt, James Hunter, John Nicholson, Cornelius C. Schoonmaker, Nathan Smith
Westchester County: Abijah Gilbert, Samuel Haight, Zebediah Mills, Philip Pell, Ebenezer Purdy, Thomas Thomas

Council of Appointment

Ezra L'Hommedieu (southern), Jacobus Swartwout (middle), Alexander Webster (eastern), Abraham Yates, Jr. (western)

EIGHTH SESSION

First meeting: Called for 4 October 1784 by proclamation of the governor; held at New York City; quorum reached 12 October 1784; adjourned 27 November 1784.

Second meeting: Called for third Tuesday in January 1785 by adjournment of first meeting; held at New York City; quorum reached 27 January 1785; adjourned 27 April 1785.

Senate

Lieutenant governor and president: Pierre Van Cortlandt

President pro hac vice: Abraham Yates, Jr. (western)[24]

Southern District: James Duane, William Floyd, Ezra L'Hommedieu, Alexander McDougall, Lewis Morris, Isaac Roosevelt, Isaac Stoutenburgh, Stephen Ward

Middle District: William Allison, Jospeh Gasherie, John Haring, Ephraim Paine, Arthur Parks, Jacobus Swartwout

Eastern District: Ebenezer Russell, Alexander Webster

Western District: Andrew Finck, Philip Schuyler, William B. Whiting, Abraham Yates, Jr.

Assembly

Speaker: John Hathorn (Orange) and David Gelston (Suffolk)[25]

Albany County: Matthew Adgate, Abraham Becker, Jacob Ford, Walter Livingston, Dirck Swart, Israel Thompson, Matthew Visscher, Peter W. Yates, John Younglove

Dutchess County: Abraham Brinckerhoff, Dirck Brinckerhoff, Ebenezer Cary, Cornelius Humfrey, Brinton Paine, Matthew Patterson, James Talmadge

Kings County: Charles Doughty, John Vanderbilt

Montgomery County:[26] Frederick C. Fox, William Harper, James Livingston, Isaac Paris, Volkert Veeder, Christopher P. Yates

New York County: Aaron Burr, William Denning, Daniel Dunscomb, William Goforth, John Lawrence, Peter V. B. Livingston, Thomas Randall, Henry Remsen, Comfort Sands

Orange County: Jeremiah Clark, Gilbert Cooper, John Hathorn, William Sickles

Queens County: Joseph Lawrence, John Sands, Abraham Skinner, James Townsend

Richmond County: Cornelius Corsen, Joshua Mercereau

Suffolk County: David Gelston, Ebenezer Platt, Jeffrey Smith, John Smith, Thomas Youngs

Ulster County: John Cantine, Charles DeWitt, Johannes C. Hardenbergh, John Nicholson, Cornelius C. Schoonmaker, Nathan Smith
Washington County:[27] Albert Baker, David Hopkins, Edward Savage, Adiel Sherwood
Westchester County: Ebenezer S. Burling, Abijah Gilbert, Ebenezer Lockwood, Philip Pell, Jr., Ebenezer Purdy, Thomas Thomas

Council of Appointment

Isaac Roosevelt (southern), Joseph Gasherie (middle), Ebenezer Russell (eastern), William B. Whiting (western)

NINTH SESSION

Meeting: Called for 6 January 1786 by proclamation of the governor; held at New York City; quorum reached 12 January 1786; adjourned 5 May 1786.

Senate

Lieutenant governor and president: Pierre Van Cortlandt
President pro hac vice: Abraham Yates, Jr. (Western)[28]
Southern District: William Floyd, Ezra L'Hommedieu, Alexander McDougall, Lewis Morris, Isaac Roosevelt, Isaac Stoutenburgh, Samuel Townsend, Thomas Tredwell, Stephen Ward
Middle District: Joseph Gasherie, John Haring, Arthur Parks, Jacobus Swartwout
Eastern District: David Hopkins, Ebenezer Russell, John Williams
Western District: Volkert P. Douw, Andrew Finck, Philip Schuyler, Abraham Yates, Jr.

Assembly

Speaker: John Lansing, Jr. (Albany)
Albany County: Leonard Bronck, Henry Glenn, James Gordon, Lawrence Hogeboom, John Lansing, Jr., John Livingston, Jacobus Schoonhoven, John Taylor, Abraham Van Alstyne, Peter Vrooman
Dutchess County: Dirck Brinckerhoff, John DeWitt, Lewis DuBoys, Jacob Griffin, Henry Luddington, Brinton Paine, Matthew Patterson
Kings County: Charles Doughty, John Vanderbilt
Montgomery County: Abraham Arndt, John Frey, William Harper, James Livingston, Abraham Van Horne, Volkert Veeder
New York County: Evert Bancker, Robert Boyd, William Denning, William Duer, William Goforth, William Malcolm, Isaac Sears, John Stagg, Robert Troup
Orange County: John Bradner, Gilbert Cooper, Nathaniel Satterly, Henry Wisner III
Queens County: Daniel Duryea, Samuel Jones, Daniel Whitehead Kissam, James Townsend
Richmond County: John Dongan, Joshua Mercereau

Suffolk County: Nathaniel Gardner, Jonathan Nicoll Havens, David Hedges, Jeffrey Smith, Thomas Youngs
Ulster County: David Galatian, Joseph Hasbrouck, Thomas Jansen, Cornelius Schoonmaker, Nathan Smith, Johannis Snyder
Washington County: Albert Baker, Joseph McCracken
Westchester County: Samuel Drake, Abijah Gilbert, Ebenezer Lockwood, Philip Pell, Jr., Thomas Thomas, Jonathan G. Tompkins

Council of Appointment

Lewis Morris (southern), Jacobus Swartwout (middle), David Hopkins (eastern), Philip Schuyler (western)

TENTH SESSION

Meeting: Called for 2 January 1787 according to date set by law; held at New York City; quorum reached 12 January 1787; adjourned 21 April 1787.

Senate

Lieutenant governor and president: Pierre Van Cortlandt
Southern District: William Floyd, Ezra L'Hommedieu, Isaac Stoutenburgh, Samuel Townsend, Thomas Tredwell, John Vanderbilt, Stephen Ward
Middle District: Joseph Gasherie, John Haring, John Hathorn, Arthur Parks, Jacobus Swartwout
Eastern District: David Hopkins, Ebenezer Russell, John Williams
Western District: Volkert P. Douw, Andrew Finck, Peter Schuyler, Philip Schuyler, Peter Van Ness, Abraham Yates, Jr.

Assembly

Speaker: Richard Varick (New York)
Albany County: Leonard Bronck, Henry Glenn, James Gordon, John Lansing, Jr., John Livingston, Thomas Sickles, John Taylor, Matthew Visscher, Peter Vrooman
Dutchess County: Dirck Brinckerhoff, John DeWitt, Lewis DuBoys, Jacob Griffin, Henry Luddington, Brinton Paine, Matthew Patterson
Kings County: Charles Doughty, Cornelius Wyckoff
Montgomery County: Zephaniah Batchelor, James Cannan, Josiah Crane, John Frey, William Harper, James Livingston
New York County: Evert Bancker, Nicholas Bayard, David Brooks, William Denning, Alexander Hamilton, Robert C. Livingston, William Malcom, John Ray, Richard Varick
Orange County: Robert Armstrong, Jeremiah Clark, Gilbert Cooper, Peter Taulman
Queens County: Samuel Jones, John Schenck, Richard Thorne, James Townsend
Richmond County: John C. Dongan, Thomas Frost

Suffolk County: Jonathan Nicoll Havens, David Hedges, Daniel Osborn, Caleb Smith, John Smith

Ulster County: John Cantine, Ebenezer Clark, David Galatian, Cornelius Schoonmaker, Nathan Smith, Johannis Snyder

Washington County: Adam Martin, Ichabod Parker, Edward Savage, Peter B. Tierce

Westchester County: Ebenezer Lockwood, Ebenezer Purdy, Nathan Rockwell, Joseph Strang, Thomas Thomas, Jonathan G. Tompkins

Council of Appointment

William Floyd (southern), John Hathorn (middle), Ebenezer Russell (eastern), Peter Schuyler (western)

ELEVENTH SESSION

Meeting: Called for 1 January 1788 according to date set by law; held at New York City; quorum reached 9 January 1788; adjourned 22 March 1788.

Senate

Lieutenant governor and president: Pierre Van Cortlandt

Southern District: James Duane, William Floyd, Jonathan Lawrence, Ezra L'Hommedieu, Lewis Morris, Samuel Townsend, Thomas Tredwell, John Vanderbilt

Middle District: John Haring, John Hathorn, Anthony Hoffman, Cornelius Hoffman, Arthur Parks, Jacobus Swartwout

Eastern District: David Hopkins, Ebenezer Russell, John Williams

Western District: Volkert P. Douw, Jelles Fonda, Peter Schuyler, Philip Schuyler, Abraham Yates, Jr.

Assembly

Speaker: Richard Varick (New York)

Albany County: Leonard Gansevoort, James Gordon, Thomas Sickels, John De Peyster Ten Eyck, Hezekiah Van Arden, Dirck Van Ingen, John Younglove

Columbia County: John Livingston, William Powers, Peter Silvester

Dutchess County: Egbert Benson, Isaac Bloom, Peter Cantine, Jr., John DeWitt, Jr., Morris Graham, Matthew Paterson, Thomas Tillotson

Kings County: Charles Doughty, Cornelius Wyckoff

Montgomery County: Abraham Arndt, John Frey, James Livingston, Isaac Paris, Volkert Veeder, John Winn

New York County: Evert Bancker, Nicholas Bayard, David Brooks, Richard Harison, Nicholas Low, Daniel Niven, Comfort Sands, Richard Varick, Gulian Ver Planck

Orange County: Jeremiah Clark, Peter Taulman, William Thompson, Henry Wisner, Jr.

Queens County: Stephen Carman, Whitehead Cornwel, Samuel Jones, Francis Lewis, Jr.

Richmond County: John C. Dongan, Peter Winant

Suffolk County: Jonathan Nicoll Havens, David Hedges, Daniel Osborn, John Smith

Ulster County: James Bruyn, John Cantine, James Clinton, Charles DeWitt, Cornelius C. Schoonmaker, Nathan Smith

Washington County: Albert Baker, Edward Savage, Peter B. Tierce, Alexander Webster

Westchester County: Samuel Drake, Abijah Gilbert, Ebenezer Lockwood, Joseph Strang, Thomas Thomas, Jonathan G. Tompkins

Council of Appointment

John Vanderbilt (southern), Anthony Hoffman (middle), David Hopkins (eastern), Philip Schuyler (western)

Notes

PREFACE

1. Dirk Hoerder, *Crowd Action in Revolutionary Massachusetts, 1765–1780* (New York: Academic Press, 1977).

2. Pauline Maier, *From Resistance to Revolution: Colonial Radicals and the Development of American Opposition to Britain, 1765–1776* (New York: Alfred A. Knopf, 1972); and idem, *The Old Revolutionaries: Political Lives in the Age of Samuel Adams* (New York: Alfred A. Knopf, 1980).

3. Gary B. Nash, *The Urban Crucible: Social Change, Political Consciousness and the Origins of the American Revolution* (Cambridge, Mass.: Harvard University Press, 1979).

4. Richard Alan Ryerson, *The Revolution Is Now Begun: The Radical Committees of Philadelphia, 1765–1776* (Philadelphia: University of Pennsylvania Press, 1978).

5. Eric Foner, *Tom Paine and Revolutionary America* (New York: Oxford University Press, 1976).

6. Ronald Hoffman, *A Spirit of Dissension: Economics, Politics and the Revolution in Maryland* (Baltimore: Johns Hopkins University Press, 1973).

7. Stephen E. Patterson, *Political Parties in Revolutionary Massachusetts* (Madison: University of Wisconsin Press, 1973); Jackson Turner Main, *Political Parties before the Constitution* (Chapel Hill: University of North Carolina Press, 1973).

8. Gordon S. Wood, *The Creation of the American Republic, 1776–1787* (Chapel Hill: University of North Carolina Press, 1969).

9. Alfred F. Young, ed., *The American Revolution: Explorations in the History of American Radicalism* (DeKalb: Northern Illinois University Press, 1976); Jack P. Greene and Pauline Maier, eds., *Interdisciplinary Studies of the American Revolution* (Beverly Hills: Sage, 1976); Erich Angermann et al., eds., *New Wine in Old Skins: A Comparative View of Socio-political Structures and Values Affecting the American Revolution* (Stuttgart: Ernst Klett Verlag, 1976).

10. Leon Trotsky, *The History of the Russian Revolution*, trans. Max Eastman, 3 vols. in 1 (London: Victor Gollancz, 1932-33); Oskar Anweiler, *The Soviets: The Russian Workers, Peasants and Soldiers Councils, 1905-1921*, trans. Ruth Hein (New York: Pantheon, 1975).

11. Daniel Calhoun, *The Intelligence of a People* (Princeton: Princeton University Press, 1973), p. xii.

CHAPTER 1

1. The Ratzer Map, as it is called, was based on surveys done in 1766; it had two editions, one published in 1770 and the other in 1776. My comments are drawn from a full-color, full-size reproduction of the 1770 edition, published by the British Museum in 1975.

2. William Smith, Jr., *The History of the Province of New York*, ed. Michael Kammen, 2 vols. (Cambridge, Mass.: Harvard University Press, Belknap Press, 1972), 1:202, 228.

3. For DeLancey as a merchant, see his memorial and testimony for loyalist compensation, Audit Office Papers, Series 12, vol. 19, Public Records Office, London (hereafter cited as A.O. 12 and by volume); and Michael Kammen, *Colonial New York: A History* (New York: Charles Scribner's Sons, 1975), p. 332. On Elliott, see Robert Ernst, "Andrew Elliott, Forgotten Loyalist of Occupied New York," *New York History* 57 (1976): 285-320. On Scott, see Dorothy M. Dillon, *The New York Triumvirate: A Study of the Legal and Political Careers of William Livingston, John Morin Scott and William Smith, Jr.* (New York: Columbia University Press, 1949).

4. Smith, *History of New York*, 1:221.

5. Loyalist claim of Rapalje, A.O. 12, vol. 22; for more detail, see below, chap. 4.

6. Table of British imports and provincial exports, 1715-23, British Library, Manuscript Division, Add. Ms. 14035; records of colonial shipping, 1760-62, Liverpool Papers, vol. 146, British Library, Manuscript Division, Add. Ms. 38335; "An Account of the Amount of the Value of the Exports from England to the North American Colonies from Christmas, 1763 to Christmas, 1767," British Library, Manuscript Division, Add. Ms. 8133C.

7. "Accounts of Colonial Imports and Exports, 1768-69," British Library, Manuscript Division, Add. Ms. 15485.

8. For staves hewn by slave labor, see Mrs. Ann Grant, *Memoirs of an American Lady*, 2 vols. in 1 (1808; reprint ed., Freeport, N.Y.: Books for Libraries Press, 1972), 1:272-73; for Albany ladies and their gardens, see ibid., pp. 71-72.

9. See Julian Gwyn, "Private Credit in Colonial New York: The Warren Portfolio, 1731-95," *New York History* 54 (1973):268-93.

10. Loyalist claim of Wetherhead, A.O. 12, vol. 22; claim of Axtell, ibid.. See also claims of Isaac Low and Samuel Hake, both in ibid., vol. 19.

11. Kammen, *Colonial New York*, p. 292.

12. See Brautigan's loyalist claim, A.O. 12, vol. 22, and below, chap. 4.

13. Kammen, *Colonial New York*, pp. 287-88; Douglas Greenberg, *Crime and Law Enforcement in the Colony of New York, 1691-1776* (Ithaca: Cornell University Press, 1976), pp. 138-46, 188-95.

14. These figures are drawn from Gary B. Nash, "Urban Wealth and Poverty in Pre-Revolutionary America," *Journal of Interdisciplinary History* 6 (1975-76):545-84.

15. Ibid.; see also Jacob M. Price, "Quantifying Colonial America: A Comment on Nash and Warden," ibid., p. 709.

16. Nash, "Urban Wealth and Poverty," p. 549; Jackson Turner Main, *The Social Structure of Revolutionary America* (Princeton: Princeton University Press, 1965), pp. 158-59; Staughton Lynd, "The Revolution and the Common Man: Farm Tenants and Artisans in New York Politics, 1777-88" (Ph.D. diss., Columbia University, 1962), pp. 179, 200-202, 209; Edmund P. Willis, "Social Origins of Political Leadership in New York City from the Revolution to 1815" (Ph.D. diss., University of California, Berkeley, 1967), pp. 18, 149-50, 345, 354; Carl Lotus Becker, *The History of Political Parties in the Province of New York, 1760-76* (Madison: University of Wisconsin Press, 1909), pp. 113, 114, 126-27, 168, 197, 206, 226, 232, 257-58; Roger J. Champagne, "The Sons of Liberty and the Aristocracy in New York Politics, 1765-90" (Ph.D. diss., University of Wisconsin, 1961), p. 386; Robert Jay Christen, "King Sears: Politician and Patriot in a Decade of Revolution" (Ph.D. diss., Columbia University, 1968), pp. 157, 160, 163, 183, 206.

17. Pauline Maier, *From Resistance to Revolution: Colonial Radicals and the Development of American Opposition to Britain, 1765–76* (New York: Alfred A. Knopf, 1972), p. 58; Roger J. Champagne, *Alexander McDougall and the American Revolution in New York* (Schenectady, N.Y.: Union College Press, 1975), chap. 1.

18. Raymond A. Mohl, "Poverty in Early America, A Reappraisal: The Case of Eighteenth-Century New York City," *New York History* 50 (1969):19; Staughton Lynd, "The Mechanics in New York Politics, 1774–85," in his *Class Conflict, Slavery and the United States Constitution: Ten Essays* (Indianapolis: Bobbs-Merrill, 1967), pp. 79–108.

19. Philip L. White, *The Beekmans of New York in Politics and Commerce, 1647–1877* (New York: New-York Historical Society, 1956), pp. 442, 433; Christen, "King Sears," chap. 1.

20. Cf. William Smith, Jr., William Livingston, and John Morin Scott, *The Independent Reflector: or, Weekly Essays on Sundry Important Subjects More Particularly Adapted to the Province of New-York*, ed. Milton M. Klein (Cambridge, Mass.: Harvard University Press, Belknap Press, 1963). For European and New England opinion, see the comments of Peter Kalm (1750) and John Singleton Copley (1771), quoted in Kammen, *Colonial New York*, pp. 290, 292.

21. I have worked from the reduced, black-and-white reproduction of the Sauthier Map inserted in Edmund B. O'Callaghan, ed., *The Documentary History of the State of New York*, 4 vols. (Albany: Weed, Parsons & Co., Public Printers, 1849– 51). The legend gives the color code used on the original.

22. Colden attacked New York's land system many times. See Patricia U. Bonomi, *A Factious People: Politics and Society in Colonial New York* (New York: Columbia University Press, 1971), p. 205; and Carole Shammas, "Cadwallader Colden and the Role of the King's Prerogative," *New-York Historical Society Quarterly* 53 (1969):106–8. For studies influenced by Colden, see Irving Mark, *Agrarian Conflicts in Colonial New York, 1711–1775* (New York: Columbia University Press, 1940); and Lynd, *Class Conflict, Slavery and the Constitution*.

23. J. Hector St. John de Crevecoeur, *Letters from an American Farmer and Sketches of Eighteenth-Century America* (New York: Signet, 1963). For studies influenced by Crevecoeur, see Dixon Ryan Fox, *Yankees and Yorkers* (New York: New York University Press, 1940); Bonomi, *A Factious People*, chap. 6; and Sung Bok Kim, *Landlord and Tenant in Colonial New York: Manorial Society, 1664–1775* (Chapel Hill: University of North Carolina Press, 1978).

24. Rowland Berthoff and John M. Murrin, "Feudalism, Communalism and the Yeoman Freeholder: The American Revolution Considered As a Social Accident," in *Essays on the American Revolution*, ed. Stephen G. Kurtz and James H. Hutson (Chapel Hill: University of North Carolina Press; New York: W. W. Norton, 1973), pp. 256–88.

25. See below, chap. 2; see also Bonomi, *A Factious People*, pp. 204–5.

26. Cadwallader Colden to Sir William Johnson, 26 February 1769, in *The Papers of Sir William Johnson*, 14 vols. (Albany: University of the State of New York, 1921–65), vol. 12 (1957), ed. Milton W. Hamilton, p. 699; *The Minute Book of the Committee of Safety of Tryon County*, ed. J. Howard Hanson and Samuel Ludlow Frey (New York: Dodd, Mead and Company, 1905), pp. 81–85; John C. Guzzardo, "The Superintendent and the Ministers: The Battle for Oneida Allegiances, 1761–1775," *New York History* 57 (1976):265.

27. Loyalist claims of Sir John Johnson, A.O. 12, vol. 20, and of Colonel Guy Johnson, ibid., vol. 22.

28. Petitions for the erection of Skenesborough as county town of Charlotte County, in O'Callaghan, *Documentary History*, 4:818–21; Philip Skene to Sir William Johnson, 23 January 1773, *Papers of Sir William Johnson*, 12:1011.

29. The number of Skene tenants is drawn from petitions for the erection of Skenesborough as county town of Charlotte County, in O'Callaghan, *Documentary History*, 4:818–21; the number of Johnson tenants is taken from the Sir John Johnson and Colonel Guy Johnson loyalist claims, A.O. 12, vols. 20 and 22, respectively; the Beverly Robinson figure is taken from Robinson's loyalist claim, A.O. 12, vol. 21.

30. Cf. the rent roll in the Frederick Philipse loyalist claim, A.O. 12, vol. 19. The whole of this valuable record is published as Jacob Judd, ed., "Appendix: A Loyalist Claim: The Philipse Estate," in *The Loyalist Americans: A View from Greater New York*, ed. Robert A. East and Jacob Judd (Tarrytown, N.Y.: Sleepy Hollow Restorations, 1976), pp. 95–119.

31. These estimates of total population are based on a minimum average family size of 4 persons and a maximum average size of 5.4 persons; the latter figure is deliberately conservative, but no universal multiplier for early New York families exists. For the best available figures, see Robert V. Wells, *The Population of the British Colonies in America before 1776* (Princeton: Princeton University Press, 1975), table 4-5, p. 124.

32. Loyalist claims of Houghton, A.O. 12, vol. 20, and of Low, ibid., vol. 21; Armand LaPotin, "The Minisink Grant: Partnerships, Patents and Processing Fees in Eighteenth Century New York," *New York History* 56 (1975):29–50.

33. All the above information is drawn from the rent rolls, debt rolls, and testimony in Philipse's loyalist claim, A.O. 12, vol. 19.

34. E. Marie Becker, "The 801 Westchester County Freeholders of 1763 and the Cortlandt Manor Land-Case which Occasioned Their Listing," *New-York Historical Society Quarterly* 35 (1951):300–301; the quote is from the testimony of Beverly Robinson, Philipse claim, A.O. 12, vol. 19.

35. Testimony of John Watts, James DeLancey, and John Tabor Kempe, Philipse claim, A.O. 12, vol. 19; see also the discussion in Kim, *Landlord and Tenant*, chap. 5, esp. pp. 178–80.

36. Testimony of Frederick Philipse, James DeLancey, Beverly Robinson, Rev. Samuel Peters, and John Watts, and Philipse debt roll, Philipse claim, A.O. 12, vol. 19.

37. Testimony of Beverly Robinson and John Watts, ibid.

38. The figures, including the amount of the increases, are drawn from Beverly Robinson's rent roll, provided in his loyalist claim, ibid., vol. 21; the point about his indebtedness is from William Smith's testimony, ibid.

39. Figures in ibid.; testimony of John Kane, ibid.

40. Testimony of Robinson, Philipse claim, ibid., vol. 19; testimony of Robinson and John Kane, Robinson claim, ibid., vol. 21.

41. Robinson debt roll, testimony of John Kane, and list of persons paying rent in money rather than in kind, Robinson claim, ibid., vol. 21; Bonomi, *A Factious People*, p. 220; Mark, *Agrarian Conflicts*, pp. 131–32.

42. Testimony of Colonel Guy Johnson, Guy Johnson loyalist claim, A.O. 12, vol. 20.

43. On Livingston Manor and Rensselaerwyck, see Staughton Lynd, "The Tenant Rising at Livingston Manor, May, 1777," in his *Class Conflict, Slavery and the Constitution*, pp. 63–77, and Mark, *Agrarian Conflicts*; for a different argument, see Kim, *Landlord and Tenant*. For the Johnson points, see testimony of Sir John Johnson, Sir John Johnson loyalist claim, A.O. 12, vol. 19, and testimony of Colonel Guy Johnson, ibid.; for Bayard, see his testimony on his loyalist claim, ibid., vol. 20; for John Kane, see his testimony on his loyalist claim, ibid., vol. 22.

44. Staughton Lynd, *Anti-Federalism in Dutchess County, New York: A Study of Democracy and Class Conflict in the Revolutionary Era* (Chicago: Loyola University Press, 1962), p. 39.

45. Lease of Joseph Simson, 4 December 1750, Beekman Patent Land Papers, Box 20, Philip Schuyler Papers, Manuscript Division, New York Public Library, The Astor, Lenox and Tilden Foundations; see also leases of Jacobus DeLong, 15 January 1750, and Joseph Kosten, 3 June 1751, both in ibid.

46. Lease of Henry Mynert, 15 November 1764, Schuyler Papers.

47. Leases of William Hagerty and Andrew Brown, 15 September 1773, and of Alexander Simpson, n.d., ibid.

48. See Bonomi, *A Factious People*, pp. 196–200; and Kim, *Landlord and Tenant*, p. 246.

49. Testimony of Guy Johnson, loyalist claim of Sir John Johnson, A.O. 12, vol. 20;

leases of William Hagerty and Andrew Brown, 15 September 1773, and of Henry O'Hara, 10 February 1774, Schuyler Papers; Beekman Patent Memorandum Book, Box 20, ibid.

50. Handwritten lease, 9 October 1765, Beekman Patent Land Papers, Schuyler Papers.

51. See Mark, *Agrarian Conflicts.*

52. For the overall rate of population growth, see Wells, *Population of the British Colonies*, p. 111. I have calculated the growth rates for the different counties using the census figures given in O'Callaghan, *Documentary History*, 1:686–97. My analysis follows the method for the analysis of time series presented in Roderick Floud, *An Introduction to Quantitative Methods for Historians* (London: Methuen, 1973), chap. 6. I have calculated the compounding growth rate for each county at each census against both the figure for the first census, which gives the overall rate of growth, and the figure for the immediately preceding census. I used the formula:

$$r = \left(\sqrt[m]{\left(\frac{x_n}{x_t} \right)} - 1 \right) 100,$$

where m is the difference in years, x_n is the later population figure, and x_t is the earlier figure. Calculations were done by hand, using four-figure log tables. A check of the validity of the rates calculated was done by extrapolating the New York City population of 1771 from the 1756 census figures, using an annual compounding rate of 3.4 percent, as arrived at by the formula. The actual figure for 1771 was 21,863, and the figure arrived at by extrapolation was 21,453, an error of 1.8 percent.

53. That the tenants were "simply bourgeois" is the final conclusion of Kim, *Landlord and Tenant.*

54. For the Westchester freeholders see Becker, "The 801 Westchester Freeholders."

55. Max Mintz, *Gouverneur Morris and the American Revolution* (Norman: University of Oklahoma Press, 1970), pp. 4–7.

56. Main, *Social Structure of Revolutionary America*, p. 24.

57. Rensselaerwyck tax rolls, Schuyler Papers.

58. Newburgh assessment roll, 1767, in *Historical Society of Newburgh Bay and the Highlands Publication* 28 (1942):16–22; Goshen assessment roll, 1775, in E. M. Ruttenber and L. H. Clark, *History of Orange County, New York* (Philadelphia: Everts & Peck, 1881), pp. 521ff.

59. Alice Curtis Desmond, "Mary Philipse: Heiress," *New York History* 28 (1947):26, quoted in Lynd, *Anti-Federalism in Dutchess County*, p. 37; Carl Nordstrom, *Frontier Elements in a Hudson River Village* (Port Washington, N.Y.: Kennikat Press, 1973), p. 25.

60. Thomas Hunt, *A Historical Sketch of the Town of Clermont* (Hudson, N.Y.: Hudson Press, 1928), p. 33. My thanks to Mother Mary Gabriel, O. Carm., of St. Teresa's Motherhouse, Germantown, New York, for bringing this to my attention.

61. For Philipse, see Stefan Bielinski, *An American Loyalist: The Ordeal of Frederick Philipse III* (Albany: New York State Education Department, 1976), pp. 8–10; for Johnson Hall, see Milton W. Hamilton, *Sir William Johnson, Colonial American, 1715–1763* (Port Washington, N.Y.: Kennikat Press, 1976), chap. 25; for Clermont, see George Dangerfield, *Chancellor Robert R. Livingston of New York, 1746–1813* (New York: Harcourt, Brace and Company, 1960), p. 423.

62. LaPotin, "The Minisink Tract"; Dangerfield, *Chancellor Robert R. Livingston*, 190–91.

63. Stuart Blumin, *The Urban Threshold: Growth and Change in a Nineteenth-Century American Community* (Chicago: University of Chicago Press, 1976); Patricia U. Bonomi, "Local Government in Colonial New York: A Base for Republicanism," in *Aspects of Early New York Society and Politics*, ed. Jacob Judd and Irwin H. Polishook (Tarrytown, N.Y.: Sleepy Hollow Restorations, 1974), pp. 29–50; Nordstrom, *Frontier Elements in a Hudson River Village.*

64. Edward M. Ruttenber, *History of the County of Orange* (Newburgh, N.Y.: E. M. Ruttenber and Son, Printers, 1875), pp. 369–70; Russel Headley, ed., *The History of Orange County, New York* (Middletown, N.Y.: Van Deusen and Elms, 1908), p. 342; Kammen, *Colonial New York*, p. 222; Samuel W. Eager, *Outline History of Orange County* (Newburgh, N.Y.: S. S. Callahan, 1846–47), pp. 92–94.

65. Nordstrom, *Frontier Elements in a Hudson River Village*, pp. 40–41; Main, *Social Structure of Revolutionary America*; "Tappan Patent v. McEvers and Symes," item 71, p. 183, Budke Collection, Manuscript Division, New York Public Library, The Astor, Lenox and Tilden Foundations.

66. Alphonso T. Clearwater, *History of Ulster County, New York* (Kingston, N.Y.: W. J. Van Deusen, 1907), pp. 277, 314.

67. Nathaniel Bartlett Sylvester, *History of Ulster County, New York* (Philadelphia: Everts & Peck, 1880), pt. 2, p. 215.

68. Nordstrom, *Frontier Elements in a Hudson River Village*, p. 33; "Orange-Town Ordinance of 1786," in item 36, Budke Collection.

69. On New England communalism, see the following: Kenneth Lockridge, *A New England Town: The First Hundred Years; Dedham, Massachusetts, 1636–1736* (New York: W. W. Norton, 1970); Philip J. Greven, Jr., *Four Generations: Population, Land and Family in Colonial Andover, Massachusetts* (Ithaca: Cornell University Press, 1970); and Michael Zuckerman, *Peaceable Kingdoms: New England Towns in the Eighteenth Century* (New York: Alfred A. Knopf, 1970). On equivalent Dutch traditions, see Alice P. Kenney, *Stubborn for Liberty: The Dutch in New York* (Syracuse: Syracuse University Press, 1975). On literacy, see Kammen, *Colonial New York*, p. 130.

70. Records of the Kakiate-Tappan dispute, item 71, Budke Collection.

71. Bonomi, *A Factious People*, pp. 28–39.

72. Bonomi, "Local Government in Colonial New York."

73. Zuckerman, *Peaceable Kingdoms*; Robert E. Brown, *Middle-Class Democracy and the Revolution in Massachusetts* (Ithaca: Cornell University Press, 1955); John M. Murrin, "Review Essay," *History and Theory* 11 (1972):226–75; idem, "The Myths of Colonial Democracy and Royal Decline in Eighteenth-Century America: A Review Essay," *Cithara* 5 (1965):53–69.

74. One measure of the difference between factious New York and the New England provinces was the amount of crime that the two societies could endure. Douglas Greenberg has recently shown that in New York the rate of prosecutions per 100,000 population was 12–24 times the rate in Massachusetts (see Greenberg, *Crime and Law Enforcement in New York*, pp. 135–36).

75. Bonomi, "Local Government in Colonial New York," p. 42; idem, *A Factious People*, p. 33; see also above, sec. III.

76. Order of the King's College Board of Governors, 17 February 1772, in O'Callaghan, *Documentary History*, 4:767–68.

77. These comments and data are drawn from Becker, "The 801 Westchester Freeholders."

78. Cf. Milton M. Klein, "Democracy and Politics in Colonial New York," in his *The Politics of Diversity: Essays in the History of Colonial New York* (Port Washington, N.Y.: Kennikat Press, 1974), p. 24.

79. See the following: Klein, "Democracy and Politics in Colonial New York"; idem, "Detachment and the Writing of American History: The Dilemma of Carl Becker," in *Perspectives on Early American History: Essays in Honor of Richard B. Morris*, ed. Alden T. Vaughan and George A. Billias (New York: Columbia University Press, 1973), pp. 120–66; Bonomi, *A Factious People*, chap. 1; Robert E. Brown, *Carl Becker on History and the American Revolution* (East Lansing, Mich.: Spartan Press, 1970).

80. John C. Guzzardo, "Democracy along the Mohawk: An Election Return, 1773," *New York History* 57 (1976):30–52; the quote is from Samuel Edge to Johnson, 18 August 1772, *Papers of Sir William Johnson*, 12:980–81.

CHAPTER 2

1. See the following: Gordon S. Wood, "A Note on Mobs in the American Revolution," *William and Mary Quarterly* 23 (1966): 635–42; Pauline Maier, *From Resistance to Revolution: Colonial Radicals and the Development of American Opposition to Britain, 1765–1776* (New York: Alfred A. Knopf, 1972), esp. chap. 1; and Dirk Hoerder, *Crowd Action in Revolutionary Massachusetts, 1765–1780* (New York: Academic Press, 1977). For European origins and counterparts, see George Rudé, *The Crowd in History, 1730–1848* (New York: John Wiley and Sons, 1964); and E. P. Thompson, "The Moral Economy of the English Crowd in the Eighteenth Century," *Past and Present*, no. 50 (February 1971):76–136.

2. Jesse Lemisch, "Radical Plot in Boston (1770): A Study in the Use of Evidence," *Harvard Law Review* 84 (1970–71):501.

3. *New-York Gazette or the Weekly Post-Boy* (John Holt), 19, 26 January 1764, cited in Isaac Newton Phelps Stokes, ed. *The Iconography of Manhattan Island*, 6 vols. (New York: R. H. Dodd, 1915–28), 4:739; *New-York Gazette* (W. Weyman), 16–23 January 1764.

4. *New-York Post-Boy* (Holt), 12 July 1764, cited in Stokes, *Iconography*, 4:742.

5. Sheriff Schuyler to Lieutenant Governor Colden, 17 August 1764, in Edmund B. O'Callaghan, ed., *The Documentary History of the State of New York*, 4 vols. (Albany: Weed, Parsons & Co., Public Printers, 1849–51), 4:575–76; extract from minutes of the New York Provincial Council, 4 September 1764, in ibid., pp. 576–77.

6. *New York Mercury*, 13 June 1765, cited in Stokes, *Iconography*, 4:748.

7. *New York Mercury*, 22 July 1765, cited in Stokes, *Iconography*, 4:749.

8. G. D. Scull, ed., *The Montresor Journals*, Collections of the New-York Historical Society, vol. 14 (New York: Printed for the Society, 1882), entries for 22–23 October 1765, pp. 335–36.

9. Ibid., 31 October 1765, p. 336.

10. Ibid., 1 November 1765, p. 337; précis of letter from General Gage, 4 November 1765, British Library, Manuscript Division, Add. Ms. 33030 (Newcastle Mss.).

11. *Montresor Journals*, 3–5 November 1765, pp. 337–39; excerpt from the papers of Cadwallader Colden, in Stokes, *Iconography*, 4:754.

12. *New-York Post-Boy* (Holt), 28 November 1765; *New-York Gazette* (Weyman), 2 December 1765; *Montresor Journals*, 27 November–1 December 1765, pp. 340–41; L. Jesse Lemisch, "New York's Petitions and Resolves of December, 1765: Liberals vs. Radicals," *New-York Historical Society Quarterly* 49 (1965):313–26.

13. *Montresor Journals*, 16–17 December 1765, pp. 342–43; *New-York Post-Boy* (Holt), 19 December 1765.

14. *Montresor Journals*, 23–31 December 1765, pp. 343–44; *New-York Post-Boy* (Holt), 26 December 1765.

15. *Montresor Journals*, 7 January 1766, p. 345.

16. Ibid., 14 January 1766, p. 346.

17. *New York Gazette* (Weyman), 20 January 1766; *New-York Post-Boy* (Holt), 23 January 1766.

18. *Montresor Journals*, 14–15 February 1766, pp. 349–50.

19. Ibid., 6 March 1766, p. 351.

20. Ibid., 19–21 March 1766, pp. 353–54.

21. *New-York Post-Boy* (Holt), 27 March 1766; *Montresor Journals*, 14 January, 5 February, 4 April 1766, pp. 346–57.

22. *Montresor Journals*, 24–30 April 1766, pp. 361–63; Sir Henry Moore to Secretary Conway, 30 April 1766, in E. B. O'Callaghan, ed., *Documents Relative to the Colonial History of the State of New York: Procured in Holland, England and France*, 14 vols. (Albany: Weed Parsons, Printers, 1856–83), 7:825; Patricia U. Bonomi, *A Factious People: Politics and Society in Colonial New York* (New York: Columbia University Press, 1971), pp. 218–24;

Staughton Lynd, *Anti-Federalism in Dutchess County, New York: A Study of Democracy and Class Conflict in the Revolutionary Era* (Chicago: Loyola University Press, 1962), chap. 3; Sung Bok Kim, *Landlord and Tenant in Colonial New York: Manorial Society, 1664–1775* (Chapel Hill: University of North Carolina Press, 1978), chap. 8.

23. *New-York Post-Boy* (Holt), 1–8 May 1766; *New-York Gazette* (Weyman), 12 May 1766; *Montresor Journals*, 5 May 1766, p. 364.

24. *Montresor Journals*, 17–20 May 1766, pp. 366–67.

25. Ibid., 8 June 1766, p. 372.

26. Ibid., 28 June–2 July 1766, pp. 375–76.

27. Ibid., 21 July 1766, p. 378.

28. Ibid., 11–21 August 1766, pp. 382–85; *New-York Post-Boy* (Holt), 27 August 1766.

29. *New-York Gazette* (Weyman), 29 September 1766.

30. *New-York Journal* (Holt), 23 October–6 November 1766; *New-York Gazette* (Weyman), 27 October 1766.

31. *New-York Journal* (Holt), 26 March 1767.

32. Ibid., 4 February 1768.

33. Michael Kammen, *Colonial New York: A History* (New York: Charles Scribner's Sons, 1975), p. 360; Bonomi, *A Factious People*, pp. 239–46, 248–57; Roger J. Champagne, "Liberty Boys and Mechanics of New York City, 1764–1774," *Labor History* 8 (1967):115–35; idem, "Family Politics versus Constitutional Principles: The New York Assembly Elections of 1768 and 1769," *William and Mary Quarterly* 20 (1963):57–79; Lawrence H. Leder, "The New York Elections of 1769: An Assault on Privilege," *Mississippi Valley Historical Review* 49 (1962–63): 675–82.

34. *New-York Journal* (Holt), 7, 21 April 1768.

35. William Smith, Jr., *Historical Memoirs from 16 March, 1763 to 25 July, 1778*, ed. William H. W. Sabine, 2 vols. in 1 (New York: New York Times and Arno Press, 1969), entry for 18 November 1768, 1:46–48; *New York Mercury*, 28 November 1768, and journal of the provincial assembly, 1768–69, pp. 28–31, both cited in Stokes, *Iconography*, 4:788–89.

36. Proclamation of Lieutenant Governor Colden, 12 December 1769, in O'Callaghan, *Documentary History*, 4:615–16; affidavit of James Breakenridge and Samll Robinson, 14 February 1770, ibid., pp. 617–19.

37. Memorial of John Wentworth to Lieutenant Governor Colden, 10 February 1770; affidavit of Benjamin Whiting, 1 January 1770; deposition of Benjamin Wait, 15 November 1769—all in ibid., pp. 624–32.

38. *New-York Post-Boy*, 5 February 1770, cited in Stokes, *Iconography*, 4:802–3; "To the Public," broadside, New York, 1770, Evans no. 11589; Lee R. Boyer, "Lobster Backs, Liberty Boys and Laborers in the Streets: New York's Golden Hill and Nassau Street Riots," *New-York Historical Society Quarterly* 57 (1973):280–308; Smith, *Historical Memoirs*, 23 January 1770, 1:72–73.

39. Affidavit of John Grout, 9 August 1770, in O'Callaghan, *Documentary History*, 4: 637–40.

40. Deposition of John Munro, 27 February 1771, ibid., pp. 685–91.

41. Munro to Goldsbrow Baynard [Banyar], 30 May 1771, ibid., p. 710; affidavit of Samuel Willoughby, 17 May 1771, ibid., pp. 710–11.

42. *New-York Journal* (Holt), 20 June 1771, cited in Stokes, *Iconography*, 4:820.

43. Governor Tryon to Philip Skene et al., 24 August 1771, in O'Callaghan, *Documentary History*, 4:720.

44. Deposition of Samuel Gardinier, 21 September 1771, ibid., pp. 724–29.

45. Deposition of an unnamed witness and extract from minutes of the provincial council, 30 September 1771, ibid., pp. 729–31; affidavits of Robert Yates and other witnesses, August–October 1771, ibid., pp. 732–44.

46. Warrant by Alexander McNaughton, J.P., for the arrest of New Perth rioters, 12 November 1771; Esqr. McNachton to Col. Fanning, 12 November 1771, ibid., pp. 745–47.

47. Judge Joseph Lord to Tryon, 29 January 1772, ibid., pp. 757-59; Thomas Chandler to Tryon, 6 February 1772, ibid., pp. 759-61.

48. Tryon to Rev. Mr. Dewey and inhabitants of Bennington, 19 May 1772, and People of Bennington to Tryon, 5 June 1772, *Vermont State Papers*, comp. William Slade, Jr. (Middlebury, Vt.: J. W. Copeland, 1823), pp. 22-24.

49. Munro to Tryon, 24 November 1772, in O'Callaghan, *Documentary History*, 4:800-801.

50. Deposition of David Wooster, 20 February 1773, ibid., pp. 825-27.

51. Deposition of Philip Nichols, [April] 1773, ibid., p. 830.

52. James Henderson to Mr. McIntosh, 12 August 1773, ibid., pp. 842-43; affidavit of John Cameron, 25 September 1773, affidavit of James Henderson, 28 September 1773, and affidavit of Angus McBean, 28 September 1773, in ibid., pp. 846-54; Ethan Allen to Tryon, 25 August 1773, *Vermont State Papers* (1823), pp. 30-33.

53. Munro to Tryon, 22 August 1773, in O'Callaghan, *Documentary History*, 4:843; affidavit of James Henderson, 28 September 1773, ibid., p. 852.

54. Records of trials of Benjamin Spencer, J.P., and Jacob Marsh, J.P., 6 December 1773, and affidavit of Benjamin Hough, 6 December 1773, ibid., pp. 859-68.

55. Petition of Benjamin Hough and others to Tryon, 2 February 1774, ibid., pp. 856-59.

56. Smith, *Historical Memoirs*, 22 April 1774, 1:184-85; Arthur M. Schlesinger, *The Colonial Merchants and the American Revolution* (1918; reprint ed., New York: Atheneum, 1968), pp. 291-94; Thomas Jefferson Wertenbaker, *Father Knickerbocker Rebels: New York City during the American Revolution* (New York: Charles Scribner's Sons, 1948), pp. 32-34.

57. Affidavit of Benjamin Hough, 24 August 1774, in O'Callaghan, *Documentary History*, 4:880-84.

58. Deposition of Benjamin Hough, 7 March 1775, in Peter Force, comp., *American Archives*, 9 vols. (Washington, D.C.: M. St. Clair Clarke and Peter Force, 1837-53), 4th ser., 2:215-18.

59. Deposition of Benjamin Hough and Daniel Walker, 18 March 1775, in O'Callaghan, *Documentary History*, 4:902-3; affidavit of Oliver Church and Joseph Hancock, 22 March 1775, deposition of John Griffin, 27 March 1775, Lieutenant Governor Colden to Lord Dartmouth, 5 April 1775, in ibid., pp. 904-16; Colden to New York Assembly, 23 March 1775, in Force, *American Archives*, 4th ser., 1:1308; Smith, *Historical Memoirs*, 21-23 March 1775, 1:215; newspaper account of Cumberland court closing, 23 March 1775, deposition of Benjamin Hough, 7 March 1775, "A Relation of the Proceedings of the People of the County of Cumberland and Province of New York," 1775, in Force, *American Archives*, 4th ser., 2:218-22.

60. George Rudé, Review of *From Resistance to Revolution* by Pauline Maier, *William and Mary Quarterly* 30 (1973):153; Thompson, "The Moral Economy of the English Crowd"; idem, *Whigs and Hunters: The Origins of the Black Act* (Harmondsworth, Middlesex: Penguin Books, 1976); George Rudé, *Wilkes and Liberty: A Social Study of 1763 to 1774* (Oxford: Clarendon Press, 1962).

61. Samuel P. Huntington, *Political Order in Changing Societies* (New Haven: Yale University Press, 1968), p. 277.

62. For factors weakening the claims of the great landlords, see Bonomi, *A Factious People*, pp. 200-211; and Kim, *Landlord and Tenant*, pp. 346-67. For the Indian claims, see petition of Benjamin Kokkkowenaunaut et al. to Sir Henry Moore, 1 April 1765, Kokkkowenaunaut to Volkert Douw, mayor of Albany, 30 June 1766, Kokkkowenaunaut et al. to Governor Bernard, 1 July 1766, and Sir William Johnson to Governor Moore, 20 July 1768, all in British Library, Manuscript Division, Add. Ms. 22679; and "Narrative of the Controversy between Daniel Ninham . . . and Messrs. Roger Morris, Beverly Robinson and Philip Philipse," British Library, Manuscript Division, Lansdowne Ms. 707.

63. Hiland Hall, "New York Land Grants in Vermont, 1765-1776," *Collections of the Vermont Historical Society*, 2 vols. (Montpelier, Vt.: Printed for the Society, 1870-71), 1:145-59;

Lord Shelburne to Sir Henry Moore, 11 April 1767, in O'Callaghan, *Documentary History*, 4:589-90; Order in Council, 24 June 1767, ibid., pp. 609-11. The New York quitrent was 2s. 6d. sterling per hundred acres; that of New Hampshire was one ear of Indian corn from the town for ten years and thereafter a shilling proclamation money per hundred acres.

64. Petitions for the erection of Skenesborough as county town of Charlotte County, in O'Callaghan, *Documentary History*, 4:818-21; Mrs. Anne Grant, *Memoirs of an American Lady*, 2 vols. in 1 (1808, reprint ed., Freeport, N.Y.: Books for Libraries Press, 1972), 2:131.

65. *Montresor Journals*, 28 June and 29 April 1766, pp. 375-76 and 363.

66. Petition of Robert Livingston, Jr., 16 April 1752, in O'Callaghan, *Documentary History*, 3:729; memorial of Robert Livingston, Jr., 31 May 1753, ibid., pp. 740-48; report of New York boundary commissioners, 16 November 1753, ibid., p. 764; Livingston to Lieutenant Governor DeLancey, 12 February 1754, ibid., p. 767; affidavit of John Van Rensselaer, 22 February 1755, ibid., p. 780; Livingston to Governor Hardy, 22 November 1755, ibid., pp. 814-16; Dirck Swart to Livingston, 6 May 1755, ibid., pp. 791-92; DeLancey to Lt. Gov. Phips, 12 May 1755, ibid., pp. 793-95.

67. Grant, *Memoirs of an American Lady*, 2:136-39, 147-56.

68. Cf. Herbert Gutman, *Work, Culture and Society in Industrializing America: Essays in American Working Class and Social History* (New York: Alfred A. Knopf, 1976), chap. 1.

69. Charles A. Jellison, *Ethan Allen, Frontier Rebel* (Syracuse: Syracuse University Press, 1969); Irving Mark, *Agrarian Conflicts in Colonial New York, 1711-1775* (New York: Columbia University Press, 1940), p. 175; Alford Family Records, collected by C. Edmund Alford, Delmar, N.Y.; James A. Henretta, "Families and Farms: *Mentalité* in Pre-Industrial America," *William and Mary Quarterly* 35 (1978):3-32.

70. Irving Mark and Oscar Handlin, eds., "Land Cases in Colonial New York, 1765-1767: The King v. William Prendergast," *New York University Law Quarterly Review* 9 (1942):175, 191; Ethan Allen, Seth Warner, Remember Baker, and Robert Cochran to Tryon, 5 June 1774, *Vermont State Papers* (1823), pp. 24-29.

71. This argument was begun in Hudson Valley landlords' own accounts of the tenant insurgency of the 1750s and in writings by their friends (cf. Livingston to DeLancey, 29 May 1755, in O'Callaghan, *Documentary History*, 3:802; and the various discussions of New Englanders in Grant, *Memoirs of an American Lady*). The argument was first developed in modern historiography by Dixon Ryan Fox in *Yankees and Yorkers* (New York: New York University Press, 1940) and has been elaborated more recently by Bonomi in *A Factious People* and by Kim in *Landlord and Tenant*; Kim's point about a Massachusetts conspiracy is made in chap. 7, esp. pp. 290-315.

72. Bonomi, *A Factious People*, p. 221n; O'Callaghan, *Documentary History*, vol. 3; on the Westonhook patent, see Kim, *Landlord and Tenant*, pp. 283ff. See also Alice P. Kenney, "The Albany Dutch, Loyalists and Patriots," *New York History* 42 (1961):331-50; and Staughton Lynd, "The Tenant Rising at Livingston Manor, May, 1777," in his *Class Conflict, Slavery and the United States Constitution: Ten Essays* (Indianapolis: Bobbs-Merrill, 1967), pp. 63-77. It is also noteworthy that ethnicity lost its salience in New York City politics between 1700 and 1760 (see Gary B. Nash, "The Transformation of Urban Politics, 1700-1765," *Journal of American History* 60 [1973-74]:611).

73. See the discussion in Edward Countryman, " 'Out of the Bounds of the Law': Northern Land Rioters in the Eighteenth Century," in *The American Revolution: Explorations in the History of American Radicalism*, ed. Alfred F. Young (DeKalb: Northern Illinois University Press, 1976), pp. 37-69.

74. James A. Henretta, "The Morphology of New England Society in the Colonial Period," *Journal of Interdisciplinary History* 2 (1971-72):391.

75. This discussion is based on the following: Kenneth Lockridge, *A New England Town: The First Hundred Years, Dedham, Massachusetts, 1636-1736* (New York: W. W. Norton, 1970), esp. pt. 1; Stephen J. Foster and Timothy H. Breen, "The Puritans' Greatest Achieve-

ment: A Study of Social Cohesion in Seventeenth-Century Massachusetts," *Journal of American History* 60 (1973–74):5–22; Edward M. Cook, Jr., "Social Behavior and Changing Values in Dedham, Massachusetts, 1700 to 1775," *William and Mary Quarterly* 27 (1970):546–80; Philip J. Greven, Jr., *Four Generations: Population, Land and Family in Colonial Andover, Massachusetts* (Ithaca: Cornell University Press, 1970); Kenneth Lockridge and Alan H. Kreider, "The Evolution of Massachusetts Town Government, 1640 to 1740," *William and Mary Quarterly* 23 (1966):549–74; John M. Murrin, "Review Essay," *History and Theory* 11 (1972): 226–75; Charles S. Grant, *Democracy in the Connecticut Frontier Town of Kent* (New York: Columbia University Press, 1961); William F. Willingham, "Deference Democracy and Town Government in Windham, Connecticut, 1755 to 1786," *William and Mary Quarterly* 30 (1973): 401–22; Alan Heimert, *Religion and the American Mind, From the Great Awakening to the Revolution* (Cambridge, Mass.: Harvard University Press, 1966). None of these authors bears the slightest responsibility for my attempt at a synthesis of their work.

76. Grant, *Memoirs of an American Lady*, 2:147–48; the transmission of the radicalism of the English revolution to America is a subject in need of much more study. See Alfred F. Young, Afterword, in Young, *The American Revolution*, pp. 455–56, 458; and J. F. Maclear, "New England and the Fifth Monarchy: The Quest for the Millennium in Early American Puritanism," *William and Mary Quarterly* 32 (1975):223–60.

77. Chittenden town land records, copies in Alford Family Records.

78. Schuyler, Skene, and Duer made up the first bench of Charlotte County after its creation by the colonial government. For the Dutch, see Alice P. Kenney, *Stubborn for Liberty: The Dutch in New York* (Syracuse: Syracuse University Press, 1975), pp. 2–3, 11, 36–37; for the rural mentality, see Henretta, "Families and Farms."

79. Mark and Handlin, "Land Cases in Colonial New York," p. 181; "The Vision of Junus, the Benningtonite," *Connecticut Courant*, 22 September 1772, reprinted in *Collections of the Vermont Historical Society*, 1:105–8; Aaron Hutchinson, "A Well Tempered Self-Love, A Rule of Conduct Towards Others," a sermon preached on 2 July 1777 before the Vermont State convention at Windsor, *Collections of the Vermont Historical Society*, 1:67–101; Michael Zuckerman, *Peaceable Kingdoms: New England Towns in the Eighteenth Century* (New York: Alfred A. Knopf, 1970).

80. Huntington, *Political Order in Changing Societies*, pp. 298–99 (emphasis in the original).

81. Lockridge, *A New England Town*, chap. 1; resolutions of a meeting at Bennington, 14 April 1774, *Vermont State Papers* (1823), p. 40; "The Vision of Junus," *Collections of the Vermont Historical Society*, 1:106; Lynd, *Anti-Federalism in Dutchess County*, pp. 37–38, 50–51.

82. James Elliott to Robert Livingston, Esq., 20 March 1762, in O'Callaghan, *Documentary History*, 3:826–27; Lynd, *Anti-Federalism in Dutchess County*, 49; Kim, *Landlord and Tenant*, pp. 381–83; Bonomi, *A Factious People*, pp. 221–22; Mark and Handlin, "Land Cases in Colonial New York," p. 178.

83. Affidavit of James Breakenridge and Samll Robinson, 14 February 1770, in O'Callaghan, *Documentary History*, 4:617–19; depositions of Ebenezer Cole, 27 February 1771, and Samll Wells, 2 March 1771, ibid., pp. 679–85 and 696–99, respectively; Jellison, *Ethan Allen*, p. 43; deposition of Benjamin Hough, 7 March 1775, in Force, *American Archives*, 4th ser., 2:215–18.

84. *Montresor Journals*, 5 May 1766, p. 364.

85. On the depression and its effect on American society, see Merrill Jensen, *The Founding of a Nation: A History of the American Revolution, 1763–1776* (New York: Oxford University Press, 1968). Holt's newspaper was called *The New-York Gazette or the Weekly Post-Boy* until October 1766, when he surrendered the title to another publisher; thereafter it was called *The New-York Journal, or General Advertiser*.

86. On corporatist economic ideas, see Thompson, "The Moral Economy of the English

Crowd"; Eric Foner, *Tom Paine and Revolutionary America* (New York: Oxford University Press, 1976), chaps. 2 and 5; and Sam Bass Warner, Jr., *The Private City: Philadelphia in Three Periods of Its Growth* (Philadelphia: University of Pennsylvania Press, 1968), pt. 1.

87. Laws and ordinances of New Netherland, quoted in Stokes, *Iconography*, 4:113–14, 119; entries for the years 1683 and 1684 in ibid., pp. 327, 961; entries for the years 1741 and 1742, ibid., pp. 571ff.; *The Colonial Laws of New York from the Year 1664 to the Revolution*, 5 vols. (Albany: James B. Lyon, State Printer, 1894), chap. 747 (1743), 3:296–309; entries for January–March 1771, in Stokes, *Iconography*, 4:817–18; entry for the year 1763, ibid., p. 737.

88. For causes other than social welfare behind market controls, see the following: Calendar of council minutes, 24 May 1754, 29 December 1756, and 2 March 1757, cited in Stokes, *Iconography*, 4:680, 687, 689; *New-York Post Boy* and colonial assembly journal, 24, 28 October 1750, cited in ibid., 4:623. For controls in the interests of the poor, see Records of New Amsterdam, cited in ibid., pp. 175–76; William Smith, Jr., *The History of the Province of New York*, ed. Michael Kammen, 2 vols. (Cambridge, Mass.: Harvard University Press, Belknap Press, 1972), 2:49; Calendar of council minutes, cited in Stokes, *Iconography*, 4:565; entry for the year 1748, in ibid., 4:613; *New-York Gazette* (Weyman), 21 January 1760; *New-York Gazette* (Weyman) and *New-York Weekly Journal*, (J. P. Zenger) 26 May 1740, cited in Stokes, *Iconography*, 4:564.

89. *New-York Gazette; or the Weekly Post-Boy* (J. Parker and W. Weyman), 3, 18 December 1753, 14, 21 January and 22 April 1754, cited in Stokes, *Iconography*, 4:645–646, 648; *New-York Post-Boy* (Holt), 6 April 1765; Thompson, "The Moral Economy of the English Crowd."

90. Stanley Nider Katz, *Newcastle's New York: Anglo-American Politics, 1732–1753* (Cambridge, Mass.: Harvard University Press, 1968), pp. 44–49. See also the essays by Milton Klein collected as *The Politics of Diversity: Essays in the History of Colonial New York* (Port Washington, N.Y.: Kennikat Press, 1974).

91. *New-York Weekly Journal* (Zenger), quoted in "appendix A" of James Alexander, *A Brief Narrative of the Case and Trial of John Peter Zenger, Printer of the New-York Weekly Journal*, ed. Stanley Nider Katz (Cambridge, Mass.: Harvard University Press, Belknap Press, 1963), pp. 109–10.

92. Katz, *Newcastle's New York*, p. 49.

93. Maier, *From Resistance to Revolution*; Roger J. Champagne, *Alexander McDougall and the American Revolution in New York* (Schenectady, N.Y.: Union College Press, 1975); and Robert Jay Christen, "King Sears: Politician and Patriot in a Decade of Revolution" (Ph.D. diss., Columbia University, 1968). See also Stefan Bielinski, *Abraham Yates, Jr., and the New Political Order in Revolutionary New York* (Albany: New York State American Revolution Bicentennial Commission, 1975).

94. Christen, "King Sears," pp. 12–13; Foner, *Tom Paine and Revolutionary America*, chap. 3; *New York Mercury*, 21 October 1765.

95. *New-York Gazette* (Weyman), 3, 10, 24 December 1764, 7 January 1765; *New-York Post-Boy* (Holt), 14 March, 17, 24 October 1765.

96. *New-York Post-Boy* (Holt), 10 October 1765, cited in Stokes, *Iconography*, 4:751; *London Chronicle*, 10–12 December 1767, cited in ibid., p. 778; report of the officers' ball, *New-York Gazette* (Weyman), 26 January 1767; *New-York Gazette* (Weyman), 14 December 1767; entry for the year 1770, Stokes, *Iconography*, 4:801.

97. *Montresor Journals*, 27 April 1766, pp. 362–63; "Thoughts on Usury," *New-York Post-Boy* (Holt), 6 February 1766.

98. "A Tradesman," *New-York Journal* (Holt), 17 December 1767; "Philander," ibid., 7 January 1768.

99. *New-York Post-Boy* (Holt), 1–8 May 1766, cited in Stokes, *Iconography*, 4:764; Milton S. Klein, "Prelude to Revolution in New York: Jury Trials and Judicial Tenure," in his *Politics of Diversity*, pp. 154–77; Kim, *Landlord and Tenant*, pp. 350–63; John C. Miller, *Ori-*

gins of the American Revolution (Boston: Little, Brown, 1943), pp. 142–43; Cadwallader Colden to General Conway, 23 September 1765, in O'Callaghan, *New York Colonial Documents*, 7:759–61.

100. Gouverneur Morris to Mr. Penn, 20 May 1774, in Force, *American Archives*, 4th ser., 1:342; *Montresor Journals*, 6 November 1765 and 4 February 1766, pp. 339, 348; Colden, letter of 9 November 1765, British Library, Manuscript Division, Add. Ms. 33030 (Newcastle Mss.).

101. *Montresor Journals*, 15 February and 11 August 1766, pp. 349–50, 382; Smith, *Historical Memoirs*, 18 November 1768, 1:46.

102. *Montresor Journals*, 27 November 1765, p. 340; précis of a letter from General Gage, 8 November 1765, British Library, Manuscript Division, Add. Ms. 33030 (Newcastle Mss.); *Montresor Journals*, 28 November 1765, p. 340.

103. Boyer, "Lobster Backs, Liberty Boys and Laborers," pp. 281–82.

104. See above, nn. 4, 7, 11, 12, 14, 28.

105. Boyer, "Lobster Backs, Liberty Boys and Laborers"; the soldiers' broadside is reproduced in Boyer's text.

106. *Montresor Journals*, 14 January 1766, p. 346; "To the Public." Boyer identifies "Brutus" as Lamb in his "Lobster Backs, Liberty Boys and Laborers," and Pauline Maier identifies him as McDougall in *The Old Revolutionaries: Political Lives in the Age of Samuel Adams* (New York: Alfred A. Knopf, 1980).

107. Normand MacLeod to Sir William Johnson, 27 January 1770, in *The Papers of Sir William Johnson*, 14 vols. (Albany: University of the State of New York, 1921–65), vol. 12 (1957), ed. Milton W. Hamilton, pp. 772–73; "To the Public."

108. [Alexander McDougall], "To the Betrayed Inhabitants of the City and Colony of New York," broadside, New York, 1769, Evans no. 11710.

109. See Maier, *From Resistance to Revolution*, chap. 3.

110. Testimony of Moss Kent, in Mark and Handlin, "Land Cases in Colonial New York," p. 175; *Montresor Journals*, 1 May 1766, p. 363; Lynd, *Anti-Federalism in Dutchess County*, pp. 51, 53; Kim, *Landlord and Tenant*, p. 389.

111. Moore to Conway, 30 April 1766, in O'Callaghan, *New York Colonial Documents*, 7:825; *New-York Post-Boy* (Holt), 6 February, 15 May, 3 July, 11, 4 September, 21 August 1766.

112. Maier, *From Resistance to Revolution*, chap. 1; Thompson, "The Moral Economy of the English Crowd"; Hoerder, *Crowd Action in Revolutionary Massachusetts*, chap. 1. For the weakness of the New York provincial government, see Douglass Greenberg, *Crime and Law Enforcement in the Colony of New York 1691–1776* (Ithaca: Cornell University Press, 1976). For gentlemen rioting in the costume of working men, see Maier, *From Resistance to Revolution*, p. 58.

113. *Montresor Journals*, 18–19 January 1766, p. 347.

114. Smith, *Historical Memoirs*, 18–21 November 1768, 1:46–48; *New York Mercury*, 28 November 1768, and assembly journal for 1768–69, pp. 28–31, both cited in Stokes, *Iconography*, 4:788–89.

115. Deposition of Ebenezer Salter, 20 July 1749, in William A. Whitehead, ed., *Documents Relating to the Colonial History of the State of New Jersey, 1746–1751*, New Jersey Archives, 1st ser., vol. 7 (Newark: Daily Advertiser Printing House, 1883), pp. 450–52 (emphasis in the original); Mark and Handlin, "Land Cases in Colonial New York," p. 187; deposition of Benjamin Hough, 7 March 1775, in Force, *American Archives*, 4th ser., 2:216; Mark, *Agrarian Conflicts*, p. 184; warrant by Alexander McNaughton, J.P., 12 November 1771, in O'Callaghan, *Documentary History*, 4:745–47.

116. Kim, *Landlord and Tenant*, pp. 394–408; the quotations are from pp. 395 and 400.

117. Resolution of the provincial council, 31 August 1773, and General Haldimand to Governor Tryon, 1 September 1773, in O'Callaghan, *Documentary History*, 4:843–45; New

York Colonial Laws, chap. 1660, *Colonial Laws,* 5:647–55; excerpt from minutes of general meetings in Manchester, 1 March 1774, and in Arlington, third Wednesday in March 1774, and remonstrance of Ethan Allen et al., *Vermont State Papers* (1823), pp. 38–42, 49–54. A local versifyer named Thomas Rowley wrote the following poem about the act:

> When *Caesar* reigned King at *Rome*
> *St. Paul* was sent to hear his doom;
> But *Roman* laws in a criminal case,
> Must have the accuser face to face,
> Or *Caesar* gives a flat denial.
> But here's a law made now of late,
> Which destines men to awful fate,
> And hangs and damns without a trial.
> Which made me view all nature through,
> To find a law where men were ti'd,
> By legal act which doth exact,
> Men's lives before they're try'd,
> Then down I took the sacred book,
> And turn'd the pages O'er,
> But could not find one of this kind,
> By God or man before.

Ibid., p. 54.

CHAPTER 3

1. James Fenimore Cooper, *Satanstoe* (New York: Leatherstocking Edition, n.d.), pp. 24–28.

2. See Richard F. Fenno, Jr., *The Power of the Purse: Appropriations Politics in Congress* (Boston: Little, Brown, 1966).

3. Taken by itself the debate on what percentage of the early American white adult male population had the vote is sterile. Thomas J. Archdeacon estimates that 55–60 percent of the potential electorate voted in the New York City election of 1701, but he also correctly points out that "voting was not designed to promote popular control of the government" and that "colonials theoretically did not hold political leaders responsible to their constituents" ("The Age of Leisler – New York City, 1689–1710: A Social and Demographic Interpretation," in *Aspects of Early New York Society and Politics,* ed. Jacob Judd and Irwin H. Polishook [Tarrytown, N.Y.: Sleepy Hollow Restorations, 1974]). For further discussion, see below in this chapter.

4. These comments are drawn from a reading of the assembly journal from 1750 to 1775, Colonial Office Papers, Series 5, vols. 1216–20, Public Records Office, London (hereafter cited as C.O. 5 and by volume). On assemblymen's pay, see Guy Johnson to Sir William Johnson, 23 February 1773, in *The Papers of Sir William Johnson,* 14 vols. (Albany: University of the State of New York, 1921–65), vol. 8 (1933), ed. Alexander C. Flick, p. 772.

5. Robert R. Palmer, *The Age of the Democratic Revolution: A Political History of Europe and America, 1760–1800,* 2 vols. (Princeton: Princeton University Press, 1959–64), 1:29.

6. On the council's judicial role, see Milton M. Klein, "Prelude to Revolution in New York: Jury Trials and Judicial Tenure," *William and Mary Quarterly* 17 (1960):439–62.

7. See William Smith, Jr., *The History of the Province of New York,* ed. Michael Kammen, 2 vols. (Cambridge, Mass.: Harvard University Press, Belknap Press, 1972), 1:254–55.

8. William Smith, Jr., *Historical Memoirs from 16 March, 1763 to 25 July, 1778,* ed. William H. W. Sabine, 2 vols. in 1 (New York: New York Times and Arno Press, 1969), entry for 13 October 1766 and accompanying documents, 1:34–39.

9. Removal of an imperial official could be accomplished if the right connections were carefully cultivated and skilfully used. The odds, however, were against success for even a worldly-wise petitioner (see Stanley Nider Katz, *Newcastle's New York: Anglo-American Politics, 1732–1753* [Cambridge, Mass.: Harvard University Press, 1968], pp. 91–132).

10. On DeLancey, see Patricia U. Bonomi, *A Factious People: Politics and Society in Colonial New York* (New York: Columbia University Press, 1971), pp. 140–78.

11. Thomas Whately, "The Regulations Lately Made...Considered," in *Prologue to Revolution: Sources and Documents on the Stamp Act Crisis, 1764–1766,* ed. Edmund S. Morgan, (Chapel Hill: University of North Carolina Press, 1959), pp. 17–23.

12. Smith, *Historical Memoirs*, 23 December 1772, 1:135.

13. Assembly journal, entries for 26 November 1754 and 16 January–18 February 1756, C.O. 5, vol. 1216. See also the correspondence of Sir William Johnson with Hugh Wallace, James DeLancey, and John Watts on a proposed division of Albany County, *Papers of Sir William Johnson*, vols. 7 (1931) and 8 (1933).

14. For the rules governing assembly visitors, see the assembly journal, 6 December 1769, C.O. 5, vol. 1219; on McDougall as a visitor, see Roger J. Champagne, *Alexander McDougall and the American Revolution in New York* (Schenectady, N.Y.: Union College Press, 1975), p. 18.

15. See assembly journal, 7–8 April, 19 May 1769, C.O. 5, vol. 1218.

16. Nicholas Varga, "Election Procedures and Practices in Colonial New York," *New York History* 41 (1960): 249–77; Milton M. Klein, "Democracy and Politics in Colonial New York," in his *The Politics of Diversity: Essays in the History of Colonial New York* (Port Washington, N.Y.: Kennikat Press, 1974); Staughton Lynd, "The Mechanics in New York Politics, 1774–1785," in his *Class Conflict, Slavery and the United States Constitution: Ten Essays* (Indianapolis: Bobbs-Merrill, 1967), pp. 79–108, esp. pp. 85–87; Roger J. Champagne, "Liberty Boys and Mechanics of New York City, 1764–1774," *Labor History* 8 (1967): 115–35. For the reasons why the number of the disenfranchised was growing, see above, chap. 1.

17. Varga, "Election Procedures and Practices," pp. 251, 260–61; Staughton Lynd, *Anti-Federalism in Dutchess County, New York: A Study of Democracy and Class Conflict in the Revolutionary Era* (Chicago: Loyola University Press, 1962), pp. 51–53; assembly journal, 4–29 April 1769, C.O. 5, vol. 1218.

18. Bonomi, *A Factious People*, pp. 237–39.

19. Varga, "Election Procedures and Practices," pp. 260–61; Stefan Bielinski, *Abraham Yates, Jr., and the New Political Order in Revolutionary New York* (Albany: New York State American Revolution Bicentennial Commission, 1975), pp. 8–9; Bonomi, *A Factious People*, pp. 251–52.

20. Chilton Williamson, *American Suffrage from Property to Democracy, 1760–1860* (Princeton: Princeton University Press, 1960), pp. 41–42; John C. Guzzardo, "Democracy along the Mohawk: An Election Return, 1773," *New York History* 57 (1976): 30–52; Staughton Lynd, "Who Should Rule at Home? Dutchess County, New York, in the American Revolution," in his *Class Conflict, Slavery and the Constitution*, 39.

21. Sir William Johnson to Hugh Wallace, 12 February 1771, *Papers of Sir William Johnson*, 7: 1136; Johnson to James DeLancey, 17 August 1769, ibid., pp. 100–101.

22. See Mary Patterson Clarke, *Parliamentary Privilege in the American Colonies* (New Haven: Yale University Press, 1943); and Leonard Levy, "Did the Zenger Case Really Matter? Freedom of the Press in Colonial New York," *William and Mary Quarterly* 17 (1960): 35–50.

23. Assembly journal, 10–30 March 1765, C.O. 5, vol. 1216.

24. Ibid., 16–24 March 1758.

25. Ibid., 29 November 1765, vol. 1217.

26. Ibid., 30 December 1767, vol. 1218.

27. Ibid., 15–16 February 1771, vol. 1219.

28. On Smith, see L.F.S. Upton, *The Loyal Whig: William Smith of New York* (Toronto: University of Toronto Press, 1969); Dorothy M. Dillon, *The New York Triumvirate: A Study*

of the Legal and Political Careers of William Livingston, John Morin Scott and William Smith, Jr. (New York: Columbia University Press, 1949); and Michael Kammen, "A Character of William Smith, Jr.," in Smith, *History of New York*, 1: xvii–xxxvii.

29. Smith, *Historical Memoirs*, 7 March 1772, 29 September 1769, 5 March and 16 December 1772, 6 March 1775, 1:55, 118, 119, 132, 212.

30. Colden to R. Monckton, 20 January 1764, *The Colden Letter Books, I,* Collections of the New-York Historical Society, vol. 9 (New York: Printed for the Society, 1877), p. 281.

31. Colden to Arthur Mairs, 12 November 1770, *The Colden Letter Books, II,* Collections of the New-York Historical Society, vol. 10 (New York: Printed for the Society, 1878), pp. 235–36.

32. Smith, *Historical Memoirs*, 9 July 1771, 1:106–7.

33. Ibid., following 2 May 1774, 1:185ff.

34. Smith to Schuyler, 9 July 1774, ibid., 1:188–89.

35. Assembly journal, 23 November 1769, C.O. 5, vol. 1219; *The Address of Mr. Justice Livingston to the House of Assembly, in Support of his Right to a Seat* (New York: John Holt, 1769), Evans no. 11313.

36. Assembly journal, 12 May 1769, C.O. 5, vol. 1219; Lawrence H. Leder, "The New York Elections of 1769: An Assault on Privilege," *Mississippi Valley Historical Review* 49 (1962–63): 675–82; Smith, *Historical Memoirs,* 23 March 1775, 1:215.

37. Assembly journal, 29 April, 7, 21 December 1769, C.O. 5, vols. 1218–19.

38. Bonomi, *A Factious People,* pp. 265–66; Smith, *Historical Memoirs*, 20 November 1769, 1:68, and 13 October 1766 and accompanying documents, 1:34–39.

39. Assembly journal, 8–17 January 1770, C.O. 5, vol. 1219.

40. I use *corruption* here to mean the use by incumbents of institutions that ostensibly serve the public interest for the sake of other interests, in violation of publicly stated norms. It might be argued, however, that the practices I am describing were common knowledge and were condoned as "the way things were." On corruption, see J. R. Ravetz, *Scientific Knowledge and its Social Problems* (Oxford: Clarendon Press, 1972), pp. 418–22.

41. Robert Arthur Becker, "The Politics of Taxation in America, 1763–1783" (Ph.D. diss., University of Wisconsin, 1971), pp. 58–59, 68, 114.

42. *Tne Colonial Laws of New York from the Year 1664 to the Revolution*, 5 vols. (Albany: James B. Lyon, State Printer, 1894), chaps. 30 (1693), 1:315–21; 1059 (1758), 4:215–35. The law of 1693 taxed Ulster and Dutchess counties together at £630; that of 1759 taxed Dutchess at £642 and Ulster at £690.

43. For an example of a lease throwing the tax burden onto the tenant, see the lease of Philip Schuyler, William Hagerthy, and Andrew Brown, 15 September 1773, Philip Schuyler Papers, Manuscript Division, New York Public Library, The Astor, Lenox and Tilden Foundations.

44. *Colonial Laws*, chap. 1076 (1758), 4:306–9.

45. Ibid., chap. 1263 (1764), 4:826–27. Among those involved in Orange County land operations were assemblymen Vincent Mathews and John DeNoyelles, merchants Christopher Bancker and Gabriel Ludlow, and the lawyers John Alsop, John McEvers and John Morin Scott (see assembly journal, 22 November 1754, C.O. 5, vol. 1216). In 1765 a law provided for taxation of "every part" of the real estate of Orange, but by excepting "woodlands" it provided a continuing loophole (*Colonial Laws*, chap. 1289 [1765], 4:844–86). For the law of 1775, see ibid., chap. 1740 (1775), 5:858–62.

46. *Colonial Laws*, chap. 1652 (1774), 5:624–36.

47. Smith, *Historical Memoirs*, 8 March 1773, 1:142–43.

48. *Colonial Laws,* chap 1660 (1774), 5:647–55.

49. Ibid., chap. 1738 (1775), 5:850–56; on the crown's hostility, see Bonomi, *A Factious People*, p. 182.

50. James Alexander, *A Brief Narrative of the Case and Trial of John Peter Zenger,*

Printer of the New-York Weekly Journal, ed. Stanley Nider Katz (Cambridge, Mass.: Harvard University Press, Belknap Press, 1963), appendix A.

51. Ibid., pp. 80, 81.

52. "To Colonel Vincent Mathews," *New-York Weekly Journal* (J. P. Zenger), 7 October 1734, reprinted in Alexander, *Case and Trial of John Peter Zenger,* pp. 129-31.

53. See J.G.A. Pocock, *The Machiavellian Moment: Florentine Political Thought and the Atlantic Republican Tradition* (Princeton: Princeton University Press, 1975); "Memorandum of some Grounds and Reasons to hope that his Majesty will be graciously pleased to grant his Royal Assent to the Act for frequent Election of Representatives lately passed in the General Assembly of the Colony of New York," in *The Documentary History of the State of New York,* ed. Edmund B. O'Callaghan, 4 vols. (Albany: Weed, Parsons & Co., Public Printers, 1849-51), 4:245-54.

54. Dillon, *The New York Triumvirate.*

55. The emergence of a self-conscious group of lawyers steeped in both professionalism and local pride is a powerful sign that New York was coming of age. For a discussion of the meaning of a similar development in Massachusetts, see John M. Murrin, "The Legal Transformation: The Bench and Bar of Eighteenth-Century Massachusetts," in *Colonial America: Essays in Politics and Social Development,* ed. Stanley N. Katz, (Boston: Little, Brown, 1971).

56. [William Livingston, John Morin Scott, and William Smith, Jr.], *The Independent Reflector, or Weekly Essays on Sundry Important Subjects More Particularly Adapted to the Province of New York,* ed. Milton M. Klein (Cambridge, Mass.: Harvard University Press, Belknap Press, 1963); for optimism on New York, see esp. essays 8 and 52.

57. Ibid., essays 17-21, 33.

58. "Freeman" [John Morin Scott], in *New-York Gazette, or the Weekly Post-Boy* (John Holt), 6-13 June 1765; Scott is identified as "Freeman" in Richard B. Morris's capsule biography of him in the *Dictionary of American Biography.*

59. L. Jesse Lemisch, "New York's Petitions and Resolves of December, 1765: Liberals vs. Radicals," *New-York Historical Society Quarterly* 49 (1965): 313-26.

60. Assembly journal, 20 November 1765, C.O. 5, vol. 1217.

61. Smith, *Historical Memoirs,* 19 March 1774, 1:177.

62. Alexander McDougall, "To the Freeholders and Freemen of the City and Colony of New York," broadside, New York, 1770, Evans no. 11710.

63. In general on McDougall, see Champagne, *Alexander McDougall,* and Sister Anne Madeleine Shannon, "General Alexander McDougall, Citizen and Soldier, 1732-1786" (Ph.D. diss., Fordham University, 1957).

64. Assembly journal, 21 April, 12 May 1769, C.O. 5, vol. 1218; Roger Champagne, "Family Politics versus Constitutional Principles: The New York Assembly Elections of 1768 and 1769," *William and Mary Quarterly* 20 (1963):57-79; for the last repetition of the cycle, see assembly journal, 24 January 1774, C.O. 5, vol. 1220.

65. *The Address of Mr. Justice Livingston to the House of Assembly, in Support of his Right to a Seat; Speech of Mr. Justice Livingstone, Made on Friday the 25th of January in Support of His Claim to a Seat in the House of the General Assembly* (New York: John Holt, 1771), Evans no. 12096.

66. *A Letter to the Majority of the General Assembly of Liliput* (New York: John Holt, January-March 1772), Evans nos. 12433-35.

67. Undated petition of DeNoyelles to the Board of Trade, *Cadwallader Colden Papers,* 7 vols., Collections of the New-York Historical Society, vols. 50-56 (New York: Printed for the Society, 1918-23), 5 (1922): 394-95.

68. Assembly journal, 17 April 1769, C.O. 5, vol. 1218.

69. *The Case of the County of Orange*...(New York, 1774), Evans no. 13187.

70. He was called "Prince of Orange" in "To the People called, Freeholders and Freemen of the 'dirty Corporation' of the City of New-York," broadside, New York, 1772, Evans no.

12578. In the same year "A Farmer (and once a Grand Juror) of Orange County" published a bitter personal attack on him entitled "To the General Assembly," broadside, New York, 1772, Evans no. 12576. The "speech" is in "Debates on Dividing Orange County," broadside, New York, 1774, Evans no. 13239.

71. *Pennsylvania Journal and Weekly Advertiser*, 22 February 1775.

72. Bernard Mason, *The Road to Independence: The Revolutionary Movement in New York, 1773-1777* (Lexington: University of Kentucky Press, 1966), pp. 129-31.

73. New York committee of safety to members of the provincial congress, [January 1776], in Peter Force, comp., *American Archives*, 9 vols. (Washington, D.C.: M. St. Clair Clarke and Peter Force, 1837-53), 4th ser., 4: 1028-29.

74. " 'A Poor Man' to the Citizens of New York, 30 December, 1775," broadside, New York, 1775, Evans no. 14490.

75. See Samuel P. Huntington, "Political Development and Political Decay," *World Politics* 17 (1965):386-430.

76. See Douglas Greenberg, "The Effectiveness of Law Enforcement in Eighteenth-Century New York," *American Journal of Legal History* 19 (1975): 173-207.

CHAPTER 4

1. For the sources of these figures and the method by which they were calculated, see above, chap.1, n. 52.

2. William Smith, Jr., *Historical Memoirs from 16 March, 1763 to 25 July, 1778*, ed. William H. W. Sabine, 2 vols. in 1 (New York: New York Times and Arno Press, 1969), entry for 15 April 1769, 1:63; Journal of the provincial assembly, Colonial Office Papers, Series 5, vol. 1218, Public Records Office, London (hereafter cited as C.O. 5 and by volume), entries for 7 and 29 April 1769.

3. For arguments that stress ethnicity in New York history see, among many others, Patricia U. Bonomi, *A Factious People: Politics and Society in Colonial New York* (New York: Columbia University Press, 1971); and Milton M. Klein, *The Politics of Diversity: Essays in the History of Colonial New York* (Port Washington, N.Y.: Kennikat Press, 1974).

4. For travelers' accounts, see the following: Patrick M'Robert, *A Tour through Part of the North Provinces of America*, ed. Carl Bridenbaugh (New York: New York Times and Arno Press, 1968), pp. 11-12; Nicholas Cresswell, *The Journal of Nicholas Cresswell, 1774-1777* (Port Washington, N.Y.: Kennikat Press, 1968), entry for 25 May 1777, p. 223; and Journal of John Lee, Merchant, summer 1768, British Library, Manuscript Division, Add. Ms. 28605.

5. On the use of these claims, see Mary Beth Norton, "Essay on Sources," *The British-Americans: The Loyalist Exiles in England, 1774-1789* (London: Constable, 1974), pp. 260-72; and Eugene Fingerhut, "Uses and Abuses of the American Loyalists' Claims: A Critique of Quantitative Analysis," *William and Mary Quarterly* 25 (1968):245-58.

6. Claim of John Rapalje, Audit Office Papers, Series 12, vol. 22, Public Records Office, London (hereafter cited as A.O. 12 and by volume).

7. Claims in A.O. 12 are given indiscriminately in sterling and in New York currency, and conversion was at approximately the rate of £3 sterling to £5 currency. Thus the claim of James DeLancey, the sheriff of Westchester County, was given as £5,049 currency and £3,009 sterling. That of the New York City merchant and politician who bore the same name was £95,326 currency or £53,621 sterling. Both claims are in A.O. 12, vol. 19.

8. Claim of Christopher Billopp, ibid.

9. Claim of John Polhamus, ibid, vol. 23.

10. M'Robert, *Tour through the North Provinces*, p. 7; Jean-François, Marquis de Chastellux, *Travels in North America in the Years 1780, 1781 and 1782*, ed. Howard C. Rice, Jr., 2 vols. (Chapel Hill: University of North Carolina Press, 1963), 1:187-97; Journal of John

Lee; J. Hector St. John de Crevecoeur, *Letters from an American Farmer and Sketches of Eighteenth-Century America* (New York: Signet, 1963).

11. Carl Nordstrom, *Frontier Elements in a Hudson River Village* (Port Washington, N.Y.: Kennikat Press, 1973), esp. chap. 4; Stuart Blumin, *The Urban Threshold: Growth and Change in a Nineteenth-Century American Community* (Chicago: University of Chicago Press, 1976).

12. Patricia U. Bonomi, "Local Government in Colonial New York: A Base for Republicanism," in *Aspects of Early New York Society and Politics*, ed. Jacob Judd and Irwin H. Polishook (Tarrytown, N.Y.: Sleepy Hollow Restorations, 1974), pp. 29-50; Jessica Kross Erlich, "A Town Study in Colonial New York: Newtown, Queens County, 1642-1790" (Ph.D. diss., University of Michigan, 1974), esp. chap. 2.

13. For further discussion of local government, see Bonomi, *A Factious People*, pp. 28-38; and Robert C. Ritchie, *The Duke's Province: A Study of New York Politics and Society, 1664-1691* (Chapel Hill: University of North Carolina Press, 1977).

14. For the committee in Kingston, see Carl Lotus Becker, *The History of Political Parties in the Province of New York, 1760-1776* (Madison: University of Wisconsin Press, 1909), p. 171.

15. For the sources and analysis of these figures, see above, chap. 1, n. 52.

16. Claims of William Bayard, A.O. 12, vol. 20; Oliver DeLancey, ibid., vol. 19; Sir John Johnson, ibid., vol. 20; Roger Morris, ibid., vol. 21; Samuel Hake, ibid., vol. 19.

17. Stanley Nider Katz, *Newcastle's New York: Anglo-American Politics, 1732-1753* (Cambridge, Mass.: Harvard University Press, 1968), pp. 69, 82; Staughton Lynd, *Anti-Federalism in Dutchess County, New York: A Study of Democracy and Class Conflict in the Revolutionary Era* (Chicago: Loyola University Press, 1962), chap. 1; Stefan Bielinski, *Abraham Yates, Jr., and the New Political Order in Revolutionary New York* (Albany: New York State American Revolution Bicentennial Commission, 1975), pp. 8-9.

18. See above, chap. 2, and below, chaps. 5 and 6.

19. Claims of Thomas Ryan, A.O. 12, vol. 19; Peter Angevine, ibid., vol. 23; for Reber, *The Minute Book of the Committee of Safety of Tryon County*, ed. J. Howard Hanson and Samuel Ludlow Frey (New York: Dodd, Mead, 1905), p. 111, n. 11; for Sly, Russell Headley, ed., *The History of Orange County, New York* (Middletown, N.Y.: Van Deusen and Elms, 1908), p. 82, and E. M. Ruttenber and L. H. Clark, *History of Orange County, New York* (Philadelphia: Everts & Peck, 1881), p. 235.

20. *Pennsylvania Journal and Weekly Advertiser*, 22 February 1775.

21. Esmond Wright, "The New York Loyalists: A Cross-Section of Colonial Society," in *The Loyalist Americans: A Focus on Greater New York*, ed. Robert A. East and Jacob Judd (Tarrytown, N.Y.: Sleepy Hollow Restorations, 1975), pp. 83-84; James Kirby Martin, *Men in Rebellion: Higher Governmental Leaders and the Coming of the American Revolution* (New Brunswick, N.J.: Rutgers University Press, 1973), p. 44.

22. Claims of David Mathews, A.O. 12, vol. 19; George Duncan Ludlow, ibid.; J. H. Cruger, ibid., vol. 20.

23. Claims of Rapalje, ibid., vol. 22; Frederick Philipse, ibid., vol. 19; James DeLancey, ibid.; James Jauncey, ibid., vol. 21.

24. Claims of Christopher Billopp, ibid., vol. 19; John Rapalje, ibid., vol. 22; William Axtell, ibid.

25. Wright, "The New York Loyalists," p. 81.

26. Claim of John Wetherhead, A.O. 12, vol. 22.

27. Alexander Hamilton to Robert R. Livingston, 13 August 1783, *The Papers of Alexander Hamilton*, ed. Harold C. Syrett et al., 24 vols. to date (New York: Columbia University Press, 1961-), 3:431.

28. Claims of James Percy, Thomas Hayes, and Miles Sherbrooke, A.O. 12, vol. 22; Samuel Hake, ibid., vol. 19; James and Catherine Thompson, ibid.; Isaac Low, ibid., vol. 21.

29. Claims of James Jauncey, ibid., vol. 21; James and Catherine Thompson, ibid., vol.

19; Hugh Wallace, ibid., vol. 20; Alexander Wallace, ibid.; James Percy, Thomas Hayes, and Miles Sherbrooke, ibid., vol. 22; Samuel Hake, ibid., vol. 19; John Wetherhead, ibid., vol. 22; John Dawson, ibid., vol. 21; Robert Hoakesley, ibid., vol. 20; and Richard Minisie, ibid., vol. 21; Isaac Low to Nicholas Low, 8 March 1788, Nicholas Low Papers, Library of Congress.

30. On Sears as a merchant, see Robert J. Christen, "King Sears: Politician and Patriot in a Decade of Revolution" (Ph.D. diss., Columbia University, 1968), chap. 1; for McDougall, see Roger J. Champagne, *Alexander McDougall and the American Revolution in New York* (Schenectady, N.Y.: Union College Press, 1975), chap. 1; for Roosevelt, see Allen Churchill, *The Roosevelts* (London: Frederick Muller, 1965), chaps. 4-5; see also the account in Philip L. White, *The Beekmans of New York in Politics and Commerce, 1647-1877* (New York: New-York Historical Society, 1956).

31. Claims of Samuel Hake, A.O. 12, vol. 19; Oliver DeLancey, ibid.; William Bayard, ibid., vol. 20; Isaac Low, ibid., vol. 21; James Jauncey, ibid.

32. For Smith, see his *Historical Memoirs*, vol. 2; for Morris, see Max Mintz, *Gouverneur Morris and the American Revolution* (Norman: University of Oklahoma Press, 1970).

33. List of loyalists charged in New York City, June 1776, in Peter Force, comp., *American Archives*, 9 vols. (Washington, D.C.: M. St. Clair Clarke and Peter Force, 1837-53), 4th ser., 6:1157-58; committee of Salem, Westchester County, to New York Convention, 6 December 1776, ibid., 5th ser., 3:1100-1101.

34. Claims of John Chatterton; John Robblee; and Peter Angevine, all in A.O. 12, vol. 23.

35. Claims of Thomas Ryan, ibid., vol. 19; Thomas Mills, ibid., vol. 23; Henry Watkeys, ibid.; Frederick Brautigan, ibid., vol. 22.

36. On the problems of Scots in early America, see Ian Charles Cargill Graham, *Colonists from Scotland: Emigration to North America, 1707-1783* (Ithaca: Cornell University Press, 1956); for Sir William Johnson's efforts to settle them in the Mohawk Valley, see *The Papers of Sir William Johnson*, 14 vols. (Albany: University of the State of New York, 1921-65), vols. 4 (1925) and 7 (1931), ed. Alexander C. Flick, pp. 824 and 1026, respectively, and vol. 12 (1957), ed. Milton W. Hamilton, pp. 1023, 1111; for their difficulties with the Green Mountain Boys, see above, chap. 2; for fear of their Catholicism, see C. P. Yates et al. to Albany committee, 18 May 1775, *Journals of the Provincial Congress, Provincial Convention, Committee of Safety and Council of Safety of the State of New-York, 1775-1776-1777*, vol. 2 (Albany: T. Weed, 1842), pp. 33-34.

37. Richard M. Bushman, "Massachusetts Farmers and the Revolution," in *Society, Freedom and Conscience: The American Revolution in Virginia, Massachusetts and New York* ed. Richard M. Jellison, (New York: W. W. Norton, 1976); Staughton Lynd, "Who Should Rule at Home? Dutchess County, New York, in the American Revolution," and "The Tenant Rising at Livingston Manor, May, 1777," both in his *Class Conflict, Slavery and the United States Constitution: Ten Essays* (Indianapolis: Bobbs-Merrill, 1967).

38. For the records of the estates, see the claims of Frederick Philipse, A.O. 12, vol. 19, and Beverly Robinson, ibid., vol. 21; the Westchester loyalist protest is in Force, *American Archives*, 4th ser., 2:321-22; for the conspiracies records, see Dorothy C. Barck, ed., *Minutes of the Committee and of the First Commission for Detecting and Defeating Conspiracies in the State of New York, Dec. 11, 1776-Sept. 23, 1778,* Collections of the New-York Historical Society, Vols. 57 and 58 (New York: Printed for the Society, 1924-25); the muster roll of the militia is in Berthold Fernow, ed., *New York in the Revolution*, vol. 1 (Albany: Weed, Parsons and Company, 1887). Troops are listed on the muster roll in alphabetical order and are identified in regiments by the name of their commander. The geographical locations of the regiments can be identified from a separate listing in the same volume. I have included a tenant in the "revolutionary" category if a person with the identical name (allowing for spelling variations) appeared on the muster roll as a member of a regiment in Westchester or southern Dutchess.

39. See the records of persons taking and refusing the association in Dutchess County, summer 1775, in Force, *American Archives*, 4th ser., 3:597-608.

40. Michael Kammen, "The American Revolution as a *Crise de Conscience*: The Case of

New York," in Jellison, *Society, Freedom and Conscience*; Ronald Hoffman, "The 'Disaffected' in the Revolutionary South," and Alfred F. Young, Afterword, in *The American Revolution: Explorations in the History of American Radicalism,* ed. Alfred F. Young (DeKalb: Northern Illinois University Press, 1976).

41. These figures and examples are taken from the debt and rent rolls in the Robinson and Philipse loyalist claims.

42. This count is drawn from Victor Hugo Paltsits, ed., *Minutes of the Commissioners for Detecting and Defeating Conspiracies in the State of New York, Albany County Sessions, 1778–1781,* 3 vols., continuous pagination (Albany: State of New York, 1909–10).

43. The record of the occupations of persons putting up bail was kept from July 1780 to August 1781.

44. Paltsits, *Minutes of the Commissioners,* entries for 3–20 March 1781, pp. 638–63.

45. The practices and powers of the commissioners were among the grievances set forth in a petition to the legislature in January 1781, two months before the arrests in Schodack (see *New-York Packet and the American Advertiser* [Fishkill, Samuel London], 18 January 1781).

46. Records of associators and nonassociators in Haverstraw, Budke Collection, Manuscript Division, The New York Public Library, The Astor, Lenox and Tilden Foundations, vol. 67.

47. Carl Becker, "John Jay and Peter Van Schaack," *Every Man His Own Historian: Essays on History and Politics* (Chicago: Quadrangle Books, 1966); examination of John Vandenburgh by Albany committee, in Force, *American Archives,* 5th ser., 3:573–74.

48. For examples of inexperienced royalists coming to the fore, see claims of Thomas William Moore, A.O. 12, vol. 20; John Griffiths, ibid., vol. 22; Lawrence Van Buskirk, ibid., vol. 23; Benjamin Hunt, ibid.; John Stone, ibid., vol. 22; and Robert Gilmer, ibid., vol. 21.

49. Pauline Maier, "Review Article: Why Revolution? Why Democracy?" *Journal of Interdisciplinary History* 6 (1975–76):721, quoting Stephen E. Patterson, *Political Parties in Revolutionary Massachusetts* (Madison: University of Wisconsin Press, 1973), p. 289.

50. For the importance of understanding the revolutionary movement as a series of coalitions, see below, chaps. 5–9.

51. "To the Free and Loyal Inhabitants of the City and Colony of New York," Broadside, New York, 1770, Evans no. 11588.

52. Smith, *Historical Memoirs,* 22 December 1773, 1:163; Alexander McDougall, "To the Freeholders, Freemen and Inhabitants of the City and Colony of New-York," broadside, New York, 9 July 1774, Evans no. 13389; broadsides of the Mechanics, New York, 1, 18 May 1774, Evans nos. 13490 and 13491; minutes of the New York committee of safety, 20 March 1776, in Force, *American Archives,* 4th ser., 5:1389; memorial of Samuel Loudon to New York committee of safety, 13 April 1776, ibid., pp. 1441–42.

53. Staughton Lynd, "The Mechanics in New York Politics, 1774–1785," in his *Class Conflict, Slavery and the Constitution,* pp. 79–108; Becker, *History of Political Parties,* pp. 113–14.

54. Lynd, "The Mechanics in New York Politics," pp. 92–96.

55. Becker, *History of Political Parties,* pp. 113–16, 167–68, 197–98; Richard Alan Ryerson, *The Revolution Is Now Begun: The Radical Committees of Philadelphia, 1765–1776* (Philadelphia: University of Pennsylvania Press, 1978), chaps. 4 and 8.

56. For the Dutch oligarchy, see Bonomi, *A Factious People,* pp. 39–55; and Alice P. Kenney, "Patricians and Plebians in Colonial Albany, Part I—Historical Demography and the Hudson Valley Dutch," *De Halve Maen* 45, no. 1, (1970–71):7. My thanks to E. A. Wrigley for helping me to find a set of these essays in Britain.

57. "Constitution of the Sons of Liberty of Albany, and Names of the Signers," *American Historian and Quarterly Genealogical Record* 1 (1876): 145–52; Bruce M. Venter, "The Albany Sons of Liberty from the Stamp Act Crisis to the American Revolution" (Honors research paper, Manhattan College, 1969).

58. For the names of the Albany committeemen, see *Minutes of the Albany Committee of*

Correspondence, 1775-1778, ed. James Sullivan, 2 vols., continuous pagination (Albany: University of the State of New York, 1923-25).

59. Records of the members of the Rensselaerwyck subcommittee, in ibid.; tax lists for the manor of Rensselaerwyck, Philip Schuyler Papers, Manuscript Division, New York Public Library, The Astor, Lenox and Tilden Foundations.

60. Listings of the subcommittees of Hoosac, King's District, Schoharie and Saratoga, in Sullivan, *Minutes of the Albany Committee.*

61. "The Minutes of the Committee of Safety of the Manor of Livingston, Columbia County, New York, in 1776," *New York Genealogical and Biographical Record* 60 (1929):325-41.

62. Biographical information on the Tryon committeemen is given in the editors' footnotes, *Minute Book of Tryon County*; see also Washington Frothingham, *History of Montgomery County* (Syracuse: D. Mason and Co., 1892), pp. 82-83, 113-14, 319; and *History of Montgomery and Fulton Counties, New York* (New York: F. W. Beers and Co., 1878), p. 151; the declaration of the Tryon grand jury is in Force, *American Archives*, 4th ser., 2:151-52.

63. Editors' footnotes, *Minute Book of Tryon County.*

64. Orange County committeemen are listed in Headley, *History of Orange County*, p. 82; town officers are given in Ruttenber and Clark, *History of Orange County*, pp. 235 (New Windsor), 327-28 (Newburgh), and 761 (Cornwall). Committeemen and local officers of Orange-Town are in Budke Collection, vol. 36. Ulster County committeemen are listed in Alphonso T. Clearwater, *History of Ulster County, New York* (Kingston, N.Y.: W. J. Van Deusen, 1907), pp. 142-43. Town officers are given in Nathaniel Bartlett Sylvester, *History of Ulster County, New York* (Philadelphia: Everts & Peck, 1880), pt. 1, pp. 188-89 (Kingston); pt. 2, pp. 83 (Marlborough), 164 (Shawangunk), 191-92 (Marbletown), and 216-17 (Rochester). Information on Kingston local officers is also taken from the appendix to Bonomi, "Local Government in Colonial New York," in Judd and Polishook, *Aspects of Early New York Society and Politics*, pp. 118-31.

CHAPTER 5

1. Richard D. Brown, *Revolutionary Politics in Massachusetts: The Boston Committee of Correspondence and the Towns, 1772-1774* (New York: W. W. Norton, 1976), chap. 9; Benjamin Woods Labaree, *The Boston Tea Party* (New York: Oxford University Press, 1966), chaps. 11 and 12, esp. pp. 236-37.

2. Merrill Jensen, *The Founding of a Nation: A History of the American Revolution, 1763-1776* (New York: Oxford University Press, 1968), chaps. 18 and 19; Richard Alan Ryerson, *The Revolution Is Now Begun: The Radical Committees of Philadelphia, 1765-1776* (Philadelphia: University of Pennsylvania Press, 1978), pp. 64, 88, 99.

3. Joseph Reed to Josiah Quincy, 6 November 1774, in Peter Force, comp., *American Archives*, 9 vols. (Washington, D.C.: M. St. Clair Clarke and Peter Force, 1837-53), 4th ser., 1:964.

4. See the following: Harry Eckstein, "On the Etiology of Internal Wars," *History and Theory* 4 (1965):133-63; Eugene Kamenka, "Revolution—The History of an Idea," in Kamenka, ed., *A World in Revolution?* (Canberra: Australian National University, 1970), pp. 2-14; Isaac Kramnick, "Reflections on Revolution: Definition and Explanation in Recent Scholarship," *History and Theory* 11 (1972):26-63; Perez Zagorin, "Theories of Revolution in Contemporary Historiography," *Political Science Quarterly* 88 (1973):23-52.

5. V. I. Lenin, *State and Revolution* (1917; reprint ed., Moscow: Progress Publishers, 1972); Leon Trotsky, *The History of the Russian Revolution*, trans. Max Eastman, 3 vols. in 1 (London: Victor Gollancz, 1932-33), vol. 1, chap. 11.

6. Peter Amann, "Revolution: A Redefinition," *Political Science Quarterly* 77

(1962):36–53; Samuel P. Huntington, *Political Order in Changing Societies* (New Haven: Yale University Press, 1968), chap. 5.

7. J. P. Nettl, *Political Mobilization: A Sociological Analysis of Methods and Concepts* (London: Faber and Faber, 1967), pp. 32–33; Trotsky, *History of the Russian Revolution,* 1:17.

8. David Easton, *The Political System: An Enquiry into the State of Political Science* (New York: Alfred A. Knopf, 1953), and idem, *A Systems Analysis of Political Life* (New York: John Wiley and Sons, 1965). For a terse criticism of Easton's use of the concept, see Nettl, *Political Mobilization*, pp. 27–29.

9. Alexander Hamilton, "A Second Letter from Phocion to the Considerate Citizens of New York. Containing Remarks on Mentor's Reply" [1784], in *The Papers of Alexander Hamilton*, ed. Harold C. Syrett et al., 24 vols. to date (New York: Columbia University Press, 1961–), 3:545 (emphasis in the original).

10. Hannah Arendt, *On Revolution* (London: Faber and Faber, 1963), esp. chaps. 4 and 6.

11. For overviews, see Jack P. Greene, "The Reappraisal of the American Revolution in Recent Historical Literature," in Greene, ed., *The Reinterpretation of the American Revolution, 1763–1789* (New York: Harper and Row, 1968), pp. 2–74; and Robert E. Shalhope, "Toward a Republican Synthesis: The Emergence of an Understanding of Republicanism in American Historiography," *William and Mary Quarterly* 29 (1972):49–80.

12. Ted Robert Gurr, "A Causal Model of Civil Strife: A Comparative Analysis Using New Indices," in *Anger, Violence and Politics: Theories and Research,* ed. Ivo K. Feierabend et al. (Englewood Cliffs, N. J.: Prentice-Hall, 1972), p. 188; idem, *Why Men Rebel* (Princeton: Princeton University Press, 1970), chap. 8.

13. Huntington in fact denies that the American Revolution had any significant revolutionary content (see his *Political Order in Changing Societies,* pp. 134–35).

14. Alexander C. Flick, "Rise of the Revolutionary Committee System," in [Flick, ed.], *The American Revolution in New York: Its Political, Social and Economic Significance* (Albany: University of the State of New York, 1926), pp. 27–46.

15. "Constitution of the Sons of Liberty of Albany, and Names of the Signers," *American Historian and Quarterly Genealogical Record* 1 (1876):145–52.

16. "Draft of Constitution of New York Sons of Liberty, July 7, 1769," in [Flick], *The American Revolution in New York*, pp. 310–11.

17. Carl Lotus Becker, *The History of Political Parties in the Province of New York, 1760–1776* (Madison: University of Wisconsin Press, 1909), pp. 116–17.

18. Ibid., pp. 167–68.

19. Ibid., pp. 194–200.

20. Ibid., pp. 170–71; minutes of New Windsor town meeting, 14 March 1775, in Force, *American Archives*, 4th ser., 2:131–32; minutes of Ulster County committee, ibid., p. 298; minutes of Goshen and Cornwall town meetings, April 1775, ibid., pp. 275–76; report of Westchester County meeting, 11 April 1775, ibid., pp. 314–15; Frederick Shonnard and W. W. Spooner, *History of Westchester County* (New York: New York History Company, 1900), pp. 297, 301; Henry Dawson, "Westchester County in the Revolution," in *History of Westchester County* ed., John Thomas Scharf, 2 vols., (Philadelphia: L. E. Preston & Co., 1886), 1:248–55.

21. *Minutes of the Albany Committee of Correspondence, 1775–1778*, ed., James Sullivan, 2 vols., continuous pagination (Albany: University of the State of New York, 1923–25), entry for 24 January 1775, 1:5–6.

22. *The Minute Book of the Committee of Safety of Tryon County,* ed., J. Howard Hanson and Samuel Ludlow Frey (New York: Dodd, Mead, 1905), entry for 19 May 1775, pp. 6–9; report of Westchester County meeting, 11 April 1775, in Force, *American Archives*, 4th ser., 2:314–15; "Protest of Inhabitants and Freeholders of Westchester County," 13 April 1775, ibid., pp. 321–22.

23. *Minutes of the Albany Committee*, 21 March 1775, 1:8–10. The rural districts that were represented were Rensselaerwyck, Livingston Manor, Schaghticoke, Claverack, Schoharie, Duanesburgh, Half Moon, and Saratoga. Those not represented were Hoosac, King's District, Cambridge, German Camp, Coxsackie, Schenectady, Ballston, Kinderhook, and Grote Imboght.

24. Ibid., 29 April–7 May 1775, 1:14–45; *Minute Book of Tryon County*, early May, 24 May, and 3 June 1775, pp. 4–6, 12–15, 26.

25. Shonnard and Spooner, *History of Westchester County*, p. 305; Russel Headley, ed., *The History of Orange County, New York* (Middletown, N.Y.: Van Deusen and Elms, 1908), p. 82; Alphonso T. Clearwater, *History of Ulster County, New York* (Kingston, N.Y.: W. J. Van Deusen, 1907), pp. 142–43; *Minutes of the Albany Committee*, vol. 1.

26. *Minutes of the Albany Committee*, 7 June 1775, 1:68; New York provincial congress to John Frey et al., 3 June 1775, in Force, *American Archives*, 4th ser., 2:1274–75; report of Charles Lee's expedition, January 1776, ibid., 4:858–61.

27. *Minutes of the Albany Committee*, 3 May 1775, 1:24–26.

28. Ibid., 25–30 May 1775, 1:40–55.

29. Ibid., 18–26 April 1776, 1:384–91.

30. Joseph Chux [?] to unspecified addressee in London, 25 January 1776, British Library, Manuscript Division, Add. Ms. 29327.

31. William Smith, Jr., *Historical Memoirs from 16 March, 1763 to 25 July, 1778,* ed. William H. W. Sabine, 2 vols. in 1 (New York: New York Times and Arno Press, 1969), entries for 13 October, 13 December 1773, 22 April 1774, 1:156, 158, 184–85; Arthur M. Schlesinger, *The Colonial Merchants and the American Revolution, 1763–1776* (1918; reprint ed., New York: Atheneum, 1968), pp. 291–94. For the sacking of the theater, see above, chap. 2.

32. "To the Public" and "To the People of New York," broadsides, New York, 20 June 1774, Evans nos. 13670 and 13665; Smith, *Historical Memoirs*, 17 September 1774, 1:192 (emphasis in the original); Cadwallader Colden to Lord Dartmouth, 4 January 1775 in *Documents Relative to the Colonial History of the State of New York: Procured in Holland, England and France,* ed. Edmund B. O'Callaghan, 14 vols., (Albany: Weed, Parsons, Printers, 1856–83), 8:528; Smith, *Historical Memoirs*, 15 April 1775, 1:219–20.

33. Smith, *Historical Memoirs*, 25 June and 25 November 1775, 1:228c–228d, 242–43; Thomas Jefferson Wertenbaker, *Father Knickerbocker Rebels: New York City during the American Revolution* (New York: Charles Scribner's Sons, 1948), pp. 58, 61, 64; Becker, *History of Political Parties*, p. 193; Robert Jay Christen, "King Sears: Politician and Patriot in a Decade of Revolution" (Ph.D. diss., Columbia University, 1968), chap. 14; *London Chronicle*, 10–12 August 1775, cited in Isaac Newton Phelps Stokes, ed., *The Iconography of Manhattan Island*, 6 vols. (New York: R. H. Dodd, 1915–28), 4:896; letter from Philadelphia to Williamsburgh, 22 May 1775, in Force, *American Archives*, 4th ser., 2:668–69.

34. Samuel Seabury, *Letters of a Westchester Farmer*, ed. Clarence H. Vance (White Plains, N.Y.: Westchester County Historical Society, 1930); minutes of New Windsor town meeting, 14 March 1775, in Force, *American Archives*, 4th ser., 2:131–32; minutes of Ulster County committee, 7 April 1775, ibid., p. 298; resolutions of Westchester County Committee, 17–18 August 1775, ibid., 3:150; *Minutes of the Albany Committee,* 7 June 1775, 1:68. For the symbolic importance of the associations, see Michael Kammen, "The American Revolution as a *Crise de Conscience*: The Case of New York," in *Society, Freedom and Conscience: The American Revolution in Virginia, Massachusetts and New York,* ed., Richard M. Jellison, (New York: W. W. Norton, 1976), pp. 125–89.

35. "To the Inhabitants of the City and Colony of New-York," broadside, [1774], Evans no. 13660; " 'A Citizen' to the Inhabitants of the City and Colony of New-York," broadside, 30 June 1774, Evans no. 13659.

36. " 'A Poor Man' to the Citizens of New York," 30 December 1775, broadside, New York, 1775, Evans no. 14490; "To the Inhabitants of the City and Colony of New-York."

37. James Duane to John Jay, 18 May 1776, *The Correspondence and Public Papers of John Jay*, ed. Henry P. Johnston, 4 vols. (New York: G. P. Putnam's Sons, 1890–93), 1:61; "To the Public" and "To the People of New-York."

38. *Minutes of the Albany Committee*, 29 June, 22 July 1775, 1:114–15, 165–70.

39. King's District resolutions, 24 December 1774, in Force, *American Archives*, 4th ser., 1:1063; *Minute Book of Tryon County*, 12 August 1775, p. 47; Tryon committee to provincial congress, 7 September 1775, *Journals of the Provincial Congress, Provincial Convention, Committee of Safety and Council of Safety of the State of New-York, 1775–1776–1777*, vol. 2 (Albany: T. Weed, 1842), pp. 81–82; Tryon committee to provincial congress, 28 October 1775, ibid., pp. 96–97.

40. *Minutes of the Albany Committee*, 3 May 1775, 1:55; Smith, *Historical Memoirs*, 21 April 1775, 1:221; Garret Keating to Philip Schuyler, 21 July 1775, Robert Gordon to Philip Schuyler, 1 August 1775, copy of minutes of Skenesborough town meeting, 19 July 1775, all in Philip Schuyler Papers, Manuscript Division, New York Public Library, The Astor, Lenox and Tilden Foundations.

41. *Minute Book of Tryon County*, August 1774–May 1775, 1–6; ibid., 19 May 1775, p. 7; Joseph Chux [?] to unspecified addressee in London, 25 January 1776, British Library, Manuscript Division, Add. Ms. 29327.

42. *Minute Book of Tryon County*, 25 August 1775, pp. 48–51; *Minutes of the Albany Committee*, 22–29 July 1775, 1:165–72.

43. Report of 10 December 1774 and letter to James Rivington, in Force, *American Archives*, 4th ser., 1:1035, 1076–77; Jamaica committee to delegates in the Continental Congress, January 1775, ibid., pp. 1166–67; Jamaica Declaration, 27 January 1775, ibid., pp. 1191–92; letter to James Rivington, 4 April 1775, ibid., 2:273–74; minutes of New York provincial congress, 22 June 1775, ibid., pp. 1312, 1328; minutes of meeting of inhabitants of Cow-Neck, 23 September 1775, ibid., 3:777; Major William Williams to New York committee of safety, 26 September 1775, ibid., p. 912.

44. Poll list, 7 November 1775, ibid., 4th ser., 3:1389–92; report of Charles Lee's expedition, January 1776, ibid., 4:858–61; William Tryon to Lord George Germain, 24 December 1776, ibid., 5th ser., 3:1404–05; minutes of New York Convention, 10 August 1776, ibid., 1:911; New York Provincial Congress to committee of Richmond County, 2 December 1775, ibid., 4th ser., 3:1755.

45. Letter of 6 March 1775 and statement from Brookhaven of 10 March 1775, ibid., 4th ser., 2:36–37, 117–18; report from Shawangunk, Ulster County, 11 February 1775, ibid., 1:1230.

46. Investigation of Long Island loyalism by committees of Brookhaven, Manor of St. George and Moritches, May–June 1776, ibid., 4th ser., 6:569–73; Brookhaven committee to provincial congress, 3 August 1775, ibid., 3:16; Tryon to Lord George Germain, 24 December 1776, ibid., 5th ser., 3:1404–5; associators and nonassociators of Suffolk County, ibid., 4th ser., 3:608–18.

47. Associators and nonassociators of Orange County, summer 1775, ibid., 4th ser., 3:589–97; William Heath to George Washington, 11 December 1776, ibid., 5th ser., 3:1169; Smith, *Historical Memoirs,* 8 April 1778, 2:342.

48. Testimony of Sir John Johnson in support of his royalist claim, Audit Office Papers, Series 12, vol. 20, Public Records Office, London: [Flick], *The American Revolution in New York*, p. 173.

49. Piers Mackesy, *The War for America, 1775–1783* (Cambridge, Mass.: Harvard University Press, 1964), pp. 343–44.

50. Westchester loyalist protest, 13 April 1775, in Force, *American Archives*, 4th ser., 2:321–22; report from Greenwich, Conn., 26 December 1775, ibid., 4:590–91; examination of Colonel Gilbert Budd before the New York provincial congress, 3 November 1775, ibid., 3:1321–22; Catherine Snell Crary, "Guerilla Activities of James DeLancey's Cowboys in

Westchester County: Conventional Warfare or Self-Interested Freebooting?" in *The Loyalist Americans: A Focus on Greater New York*, ed. Robert A. East and Jacob Judd (Tarrytown, N.Y.: Sleepy Hollow Restorations, 1975), pp. 14–24.

51. Associators and nonassociators of Dutchess County, summer 1775, in Force, *American Archives*, 4th ser., 3:597–608; these returns do not include all precincts, and in particular they do not include the region of the Philipse Highland patent. Minutes of New York provincial congress, 2 November 1775, ibid., pp.1312–14; Dutchess County committee to New York provincial congress, 5 December 1775, ibid., 4:187–88; minutes of New York provincial congress, ibid., 6:1415–16; Colonel John Fields to New York provincial congress, 5 June 1776, ibid., p. 1429; report from Hartford, Conn., 15 July 1776, ibid., 5th ser., 1:360; report of convention at Poughkeepsie, 10 August 1774, ibid., 4th ser., 1:702–3; report of Dutchess County convention, 18 January 1775, ibid., p. 1164; report from Charlotte Precinct, 8 April 1775, ibid., 2:304.

52. Victor Hugo Paltsits, ed., *Minutes of the Commissioners for Detecting and Defeating Conspiracies in the State of New York, Albany County Sessions, 1778–1781*, 3 vols., continuous pagination (Albany: State of New York, 1909–10), entries for 1 April and 9 June 1779, pp. 325, 357; *Minutes of the Albany Committee*, 10 August 1777 in minutes of the Schenectady subcommittee, 2:1114–15.

53. Report of committee appointed to cooperate with General Schuyler, in Force, *American Archives*, 5th ser., 3:561–91; Staughton Lynd, "The Tenant Rising at Livingston Manor, May 1777," *Class Conflict, Slavery and the United States Constitution: Ten Essays* (Indianapolis: Bobbs-Merrill, 1967), pp. 63–77.

54. See Crary, "Guerrilla Activities of James DeLancey's Cowboys"; compare these social bandits with those described by E. J. Hobsbawm in *Primitive Rebels: Studies in Archaic Forms of Social Movement in the Nineteenth and Twentieth Centuries* (Manchester, England: Manchester University Press, 1959), esp. chaps. 2 and 3.

55. Paltsits, *Minutes of the Commissioners*, entries for 5, 15, 30 September, 3, 16 October 1778, 25 April, 18 June, 19 July 1779, pp. 233, 246–47, 252, 259, 331–32, 341, 354–55, 364–65, 388–89; Smith, *Historical Memoirs*, 6 May, 25 June 1778, 2:369–70, 404.

56. Dorothy C. Barck, ed., *Minutes of the Committee and of the First Commission for Detecting and Defeating Conspiracies in the State of New York, Dec. 11, 1776–Sept. 23, 1778*, Collections of the New-York Historical Society, vols. 57 and 58 (New York: Printed for the Society, 1924–25), entry for 21 August 1777, 2:362; Paltsits, *Minutes of the Commissioners*, 8, 11, 13 August 1781, 2:758–63.

57. Bernard Mason, *The Road to Independence: The Revolutionary Movement in New York, 1773–1777* (Lexington: University of Kentucky Press, 1966), pp. 62–99; see also John Shy, *A People Numerous and Armed: Reflections on the Military Struggle for American Independence* (New York: Oxford University Press, 1976), chaps. 8 and 9; Alexander McDougall to New York committee of safety, 9 December 1776, in Force, *American Archives*, 5th ser., 3:1123.

58. In May 1776, the Albany committee purged its members from the district of Kinderhook when they refused to subscribe to a test oath tendered to them (*Minutes of the Albany Committee*, 29 May 1776, 1:423).

59. Paltsits, *Minutes of the Commissioners*.

60. See above, chap. 2. The continuation of agrarian disturbances from the colonial period into and beyond the revolutionary era is the single most important element refuting Sung Bok Kim's argument that manorial society enjoyed internal stability and that its disturbances in the colonial period were caused merely by incoming New Englanders and by conspiracies to extend the territory of Massachusetts (Kim, *Landlord and Tenant in Colonial New York: Manorial Society, 1664–1775* [Chapel Hill: University of North Carolina Press, 1978]).

61. Kammen, "The American Revolution as a *Crise de Conscience*," p. 147; Queens County committee to New York provincial congress, 13 July 1776, in Force, *American*

Archives, 5th ser., 1:257-58; report of election of militia officers for Jamaica in minutes of New York committee of safety, March 1776, ibid., 4th ser., 5:1409; formation of militia company in Islip, 9 February 1776, ibid., pp. 256-57; election of Richmond County delegates to provincial congress, 19 January 1776, ibid., 4:1069-70; report from Ulster County, 9 May 1775, ibid., 2:543-44. For a sociological comment, see Ralph H. Turner, "Integrative Beliefs in Group Crisis," *Journal of Conflict Resolution* 16 (1972):25-40.

62. See above, chap. 2.

63. Colden to Lord Dartmouth, 5 April 1775, in *The Documentary History of the State of New York*, ed., Edmund B. O'Callaghan, 4 vols. (Albany: Weed, Parsons & Co., Public Printers, 1849-51), 4:914-16; "A Relation of the Proceedings of the People of the County of Cumberland, and Province of New York," 23 March 1775, in Force, *American Archives*, 4th ser., 2:218-22.

64. Minutes of the New York provincial congress, 4 July 1775, in Force, *American Archives*, 4th ser., 2:1338-39; minutes of the provincial congress, 15 August 1775, ibid., 3:530-31; Colonel James Rogers to New York provincial congress, 14 September 1775, ibid., pp. 708-9.

65. Charlotte County committee to New York provincial congress, 21 September 1775, ibid., 4th ser., 3:758-59; letters from Putney, Westminster, and Fulham, 6-13 December 1775, ibid., 4:429-31; minutes of provincial committee of safety, 4 January 1776, ibid., pp. 1022-23; New York committee of safety to committee of Cumberland County, 9 January 1776, ibid., p. 1031; committees of Newbury, Haverhill, Bath, and Mooretown to Massachusetts assembly and council, 25 June 1776, ibid., 6:1076; David Galusha to Governor Trumbull, 30 June 1776, ibid., pp. 1151-52; Cumberland County committee to New York provincial congress, 21 June 1776, ibid., p. 1014.

66. Votes and proceedings of the Dorset convention, 24 July 1776, ibid., 5th ser., 1:565-66; call for town meeting in New-Marlborough, 4 October 1776, ibid., 2:883; minutes of Vermont convention of 25-27 September 1776, ibid., pp. 526-30; minutes of Vermont convention of 30 October 1776, ibid., pp. 1300-1302.

67. Declaration of Dorset convention, 25 September 177[6], in O'Callaghan, *Documentary History*, 4:920-21 (a version with conventional spelling is in *Vermont State Papers*, comp., William Slade, Jr. [Middlebury, Vt.: J. W. Copeland, 1823], p. 67); Vermont declaration and petition to congress, 15 January 1777, *Vermont State Papers* (1823), pp. 70-73.

68. For Rowley's poem, see above, chap. 2, n. 117; remonstrance of Ethan Allen et al., 26 April 1774, *Vermont State Papers* (1823), pp. 49-54. For Clinton's role in the passage of the Bloody Act, see journal of the provincial assembly, 6 January 1774, Colonial Office Papers, Series 5, vol. 1220, Public Records Office, London.

69. Declaration of James Clay, Esq., 20 November 1776, in O'Callaghan, *Documentary History*, 4:923-24; Vermont declaration of independence, in *Collections of the Vermont Historical Society*, 2 vols. (Montpelier, Vt.: Printed for the Society, 1870-71), 1:46-47.

70. Minutes of the Windsor convention, 4 June 1777, *Collections of the Vermont Historical Society*, 1:51-53; minutes of Vermont convention, 25-27 September 1776, in Force, *American Archives*, 5th ser., 2:526-30; declaration by Vermont convention, 30 October 1776, ibid., pp. 1300-1302.

71. Remonstrance of Ethan Allen et al., p. 51; minutes of the New York provincial congress, 4 July 1775, in Force, *American Archives*, 4th ser., 2:1338-39.

72. The best study of Young is Pauline Maier, "Reason and Revolution: The Radicalism of Dr. Thomas Young," *American Quarterly* 28 (1976): 229-49. See also David Freeman Hawke, "Dr. Thomas Young—Eternal Fisher in Troubled Waters, Notes for a Biography," *New-York Historical Society Quarterly* 54 (1970): 7-29; and Henry Herbert Edes, "Memoir of Dr. Thomas Young, 1731-1777," *Publications of the Colonial Society of Massachusetts, Transactions, 1906-1909*, 11 (Boston: Published by the Society, 1910), pp. 2-54.

73. Ethan Allen, *Reason the Only Oracle of Man, Or a Compenduous System of Natural*

Religion (1784; reprint ed., New York: Scholars' Facsimiles and Reprints, 1940). For a discussion of the relationship between Allen's deism and other aspects of his radicalism, see Edward Countryman, "Rural Radical Thought in Eighteenth-Century America: The Case of Ethan Allen" (Paper presented at the II International Congress of North American History, Milan, June 1979).

74. [Thomas Young], *Some Reflections on the Disputes between New York, New Hampshire and Col. John Henry Lydius of Albany* (New Haven: Benjamin Mecom, 1764), Evans no. 9889. For Lydius as a defrauder of the Indians, see Milton W. Hamilton, *Sir William Johnson, Colonial American, 1715-1763* (Port Washington, N.Y.: Kennikat Press, 1976), pp. 110-12, 130-31.

75. Thomas Young, "To the Inhabitants of Vermont, A Free and Independent State, Bounding on the River Connecticut and Lake Champlain," broadside, Philadelphia, 11 April 1777, Evans no. 15649; Young's quote on "the system of Lord and Vassal" is in Eric Foner, "Tom Paine's Republic: Radical Ideology and Social Change," in *The American Revolution: Explorations in the History of American Radicalism,* ed. Alfred F. Young (DeKalb: Northern Illinois University Press, 1976), p. 208 (emphasis in the original).

76. For New York mechanics, see below, chap. 6; for Massachusetts villagers, see Dirk Hoerder, "Socio-Political Structures and Popular Ideologies, 1750s-1780s," in *New Wine in Old Skins: A Comparative View of Socio-Economic Structures and Values Affecting the American Revolution,* ed. Erich Angermann et al. (Stuttgart: Ernst Klett Verlag, 1976), pp. 41-65, esp. 52-57.

CHAPTER 6

1. *Journal of the Assembly of the State of New York,* microfilm ed., in *Records of the States of the United States,* ed. William Sumner Jenkins (Washington, D.C.: Library of Congress, 1949), N.Y., A.1b, reel 4, unit 1, entry for 10 September 1777 (hereinafter cited as *Assembly Journal*).

2. The text of the 1777 constitution can be found in [Alexander C. Flick, ed.], *The American Revolution in New York: Its Political, Social and Economic Significance* (Albany: University of the State of New York, 1926), pp. 326-39, and in William A. Polf, *1777: The Political Revolution and New York's First Constitution* (Albany: New York State Bicentennial Commission, 1977), pp. 43-61.

3. *Assembly Journal,* 1 September 1777-5 January 1778; William Smith, Jr., *Historical Memoirs from 16 March, 1763 to 25 July, 1778,* ed. William H. W. Sabine, 2 vols. in 1 (New York: New York Times and Arno Press, 1969), entries for summer and autumn 1777 and winter 1777/78, vol. 2.

4. On levels of legitimacy, see Ted Robert Gurr, *Why Men Rebel* (Princeton: Princeton University Press, 1970), chap. 6.

5. "The Respectful Address of the Mechanicks in Union, for the City and County of New York, represented by their General Committee," in Peter Force, comp., *American Archives,* 9 vols. (Washington, D.C.: M. St. Clair Clarke and Peter Force, 1837-53), 4th ser., 6:895-98.

6. On Paine, see Eric Foner, *Tom Paine and Revolutionary America* (New York: Oxford University Press, 1976); "The Interest of America," *New-York Journal; or General Advertiser* (John Holt), 6-20 June 1776.

7. On the politics of independence in Pennsylvania, see Foner, *Tom Paine and Revolutionary America*; Richard Alan Ryerson, *The Revolution Is Now Begun: The Radical Committees of Philadelphia, 1765-1776* (Philadelphia: University of Pennsylvania Press, 1978); and Charles S. Olton, *Artisans for Independence: Philadelphia Mechanics and the American Revolution* (Syracuse: Syracuse University Press, 1975).

8. For Sears, see Robert Jay Christen, "King Sears: Politician and Patriot in a Decade of

Revolution" (Ph.D. diss., Columbia University, 1968); for McDougall, see Roger J. Champagne, *Alexander McDougall and the American Revolution in New York* (Schenectady, N.Y.: Union College Press, 1975); for the mechanics, see Staughton Lynd, "The Mechanics in New York Politics, 1774-1785," in his *Class Conflict, Slavery and the United States Constitution: Ten Essays* (Indianapolis: Bobbs-Merrill, 1967), pp. 79–108.

9. "To the Inhabitants of New York," 11 April 1776, in Force, *American Archives*, 4th ser., 5:854–56; "Essex," in *New-York Journal* (Holt), 4 March–14 April 1776; "To the Freeborn Sons of America," *New-York Packet and the American Advertiser* (Samuel Loudon), 21 March 1776; "Independent Whig," *New-York Journal*, 29 February 1776; "To the Electors of the City and County of New-York," 12 June 1776, in Force, *American Archives*, 4th ser., 6:825–26.

10. The members of the provincial congresses are listed in Force, *American Archives*, as follows: 1st congress, 4th ser., 2:1241–43; 2d congress, ibid. 4:383 ff.; 3d congress, ibid., 6:1309–12; 4th congress, 5th ser., 1:1385 ff.

11. Livingston to William Duer, 12 June 1777, Robert R. Livingston Papers, New-York Historical Society, New York, quoted in Alfred F. Young, *The Democratic Republicans of New York: The Origins, 1763–1797* (Chapel Hill: University of North Carolina Press, 1967), p. 15; Morris to Mr. Penn, 20 June 1774, in Force, *American Archives*, 4th ser., 1:342–43; see also Staughton Lynd, "A Governing Class on the Defensive: The Case of New York," in his *Class Conflict, Slavery and the Constitution*.

12. See Bernard Mason, *The Road to Independence: The Revolutionary Movement in New York, 1773–1777* (Lexington: University of Kentucky Press, 1966), chap. 7; Livingston to Duer, 12 June 1777, quoted in Staughton Lynd, "Who Should Rule at Home? Dutchess County, New York in the American Revolution," in his *Class Conflict Slavery and the Constitution*, pp. 40–41; Duer to Jay, in *The Correspondence and Public Papers of John Jay*, ed. Henry P. Johnston, 4 vols. (New York: G. P. Putnam's Sons, 1890–93), 1:140; Smith to Philip Schuyler, 17 August 1776, in Smith, *Historical Memoirs*, 2:2–3.

13. Livingston, quoted in George Dangerfield, *Chancellor Robert R. Livingston of New York, 1746–1813* (New York: Harcourt, Brace and Company, 1960), p. 87.

14. Jay to Livingston and Morris, 29 April 1777, in *John Jay: The Making of a Revolutionary, Unpublished Papers, 1745–1780*, ed. Richard B. Morris (New York: Harper & Row, 1975), pp. 397–402.

15. Hazard to Sackett, 25 October 1776, Misc. Mss., George Washington's Headquarters Museum, Newburgh, N.Y.; *Calendar of Historical Manuscripts Relating to the War of the Revolution in the Office of the Secretary of State*, 2 vols. (Albany: Weed, Parsons and Company, 1868), 2:117–18.

16. McKesson to Clinton, 18 October 1776, *Public Papers of George Clinton, First Governor of New York*, ed. Hugh Hastings, 10 vols. (Albany: Published by the State of New York, 1911), 1:384; Smith, *Historical Memoirs*, 14 October 1776, 2:18–21.

17. Minutes of the drafting committee, *Calendar of Historical Manuscripts*, 1:552–53.

18. Ibid.; see also Mason, *The Road to Independence*, pp. 225–41. On the suffrage question, see Chilton Williamson, *American Suffrage from Property to Democracy, 1760–1860* (Princeton: Princeton University Press, 1960); and Milton M. Klein, "Democracy and Politics in Colonial New York," in his *The Politics of Diversity: Essays in the History of Colonial New York* (Port Washington, N.Y.: Kennikat Press, 1974).

19. Mason, *The Road to Independence*, p. 241; Beverly McAnear, "The Place of the Freeman in Old New York," *New York History* 21 (1940):418–30; Jay to Livingston and Morris, 29 April 1777, in Morris, *John Jay*, pp. 397–402.

20. McKesson to Clinton, 13 March 1777, *Clinton Papers*, 1:657–58; Smith, *Historical Memoirs*, 7 May 1777, 2:129; Mason, *The Road to Independence*, p. 243, n. 92; Dangerfield, *Chancellor Robert R. Livingston*, p. 90; Jay to Livingston and Morris, 29 April 1777, in Morris, *John Jay*, pp. 397–402; Hugh Flick, "The Council of Appointment in New York State," *New York History* 32 (1954):253–80.

21. During the very first years, public documents substituted "God Save the People" for "God Save the King" and used "the People" in place of "the King" in formulas of sovereignty.

22. Membership in the state continued to be described as a relationship of subjection for some years. It was not until the late 1780s that the word *citizen* completely replaced *subject* in official parlance.

23. *The Minute Book of the Committee of Safety of Tryon County*, ed. J. Howard Hanson and Samuel Ludlow Frey (New York: Dodd, Mead, 1905), entry for 25–26 August 1775, pp. 48–62; report from Dutchess County, 27 September 1775, in Force, *American Archives*, 4th ser., 3:823; entries for 10 and 11 June 1776, *The Iconography of Manhattan Island*, ed. Isaac Newton Phelps Stokes, 6 vols. (New York: R. H. Dodd, 1915–28), 4:932.

24. Victor Hugo Paltsits, ed., *Minutes of the Commissioners for Detecting and Defeating Conspiracies in the State of New York, Albany County Sessions, 1778–1781*, 3 vols., continuous pagination (Albany: State of New York, 1909–10), entries for 30 July, 8 August, 28 September 1778 and 19 July 1779, pp. 185, 197, 244, 388; John Younglove to Albany committee, and accompanying documents, 26 February 1778, *Clinton Papers*, 2:854–58.

25. Resolution of provincial congress, 30 June 1776, in Stokes, *Iconography* 4:936; petition of Albany inhabitants, 5 June 1776, in Force, *American Archives*, 4th ser., 6:715; Younglove to Albany committee, 26 February 1778, and accompanying documents, *Clinton Papers*, 2:854–58.

26. Reports of suppression of Tory plot, in Force, *American Archives*, 4th ser., 6:1054–55; Colden to Ulster committee, 27 June 1776, pp. 1112–13. Washington personally ordered that the mayor of New York be arrested at precisely 1:00 A.M. (reports of suppression of the plot, ibid., pp. 1152–83, esp. p. 1158).

27. Report from Cow-Neck, 18 March 1776, ibid., 5:405; minutes of Westchester committee, 11 June 1776, ibid., 6:816–17; reports of anti-Tory action, 24–25 June 1776, ibid., pp. 1055 ff.; testimony of Egbert Benson before the provincial congress, 19 June 1776, ibid., pp. 1415–16; Salem committee to provincial congress, 5 June 1776, ibid., pp. 1385–86; expulsions from Tryon and Albany counties, ibid., pp. 1072–73.

28. "The Minutes of the Committee of Safety of the Manor of Livingston, Columbia County, New York, in 1776," *New York Genealogical and Biographical Record* 60 (1929):325–41; 1 October 1776; committee to Col. Peter R. Livingston, in entry for 10 October 1776; 24 October 1776; 1 March 1777; 14 October 1776; 1 November 1776; 11 March 1777.

29. *Minutes of the Albany Committee of Correspondence, 1775–1778*, ed. James Sullivan, 2 vols., continuous pagination (Albany: University of the State of New York, 1923–25), vol. 1, entries for 29 May, 13–14 June, 23 August, 22 October 1776, 2 May, 13–18 June 1777, pp. 423, 445–50, 553, 585, 739 ff., 793–96; Smith, *Historical Memoirs*, 28 and 8 June 1778, 2:407 and 397.

30. *Minutes of the Albany Committee*, 30 July, 7–15, 29, 22 August, 3 December 1777, 1:816–17, 823–29, 833, 837, 874.

31. Provincial congress to inhabitants of Tryon County, 3 June 1775, in Force, *American Archives*, 4th ser., 2:1274–75; resolution of Continental Congress, 3 January 1776, ibid., 4:1630–32; Michael Kammen, "The American Revolution as a *Crise de Conscience*: The Case of New York," in *Society, Freedom and Conscience: The American Revolution in Virginia, Massachusetts, and New York*, ed. Richard M. Jellison, (New York: W. W. Norton, 1976).

32. *Laws of the State of New York*, microfilm ed., in *Records of the States*, N.Y. B.2, reel 6, unit 2, 1st sess., chaps. 7, 47; 4th sess., chap. 36; 6th sess., chap. 1; 5th sess., chap. 44.

33. Minutes of the provincial congress, 5 June 1776, in Force, *American Archives*, 4th ser., 6:1365–70; *Laws*, 1st sess., chap. 3; for the work of the commissioners, see Dorothy C. Barck, ed., *Minutes of the Committee and of the First Commission for Detecting and Defeating Conspiracies in the State of New York, Dec. 11, 1776–Sept. 23, 1778*, Collections of the New-York Historical Society, vols. 57 and 58, (New York: Printed for the Society, 1924–25); and Paltsits, *Minutes of the Commissioners*.

34. For the use of bonds, see above, chap. 4; for expulsions, see Force, *American Archives*, 5th ser., 3:466–71, as well as both Paltsits, *Minutes of the Commissioners*, and Barck, *Minutes*; for the law allowing expulsion by local officials, see *Laws*, 3d sess., chap. 76.

35. *Laws*, 1st sess., chap. 47.

36. Ibid., 3d sess., chaps. 12, 25.

37. Ibid., 4th sess., chap. 48; 3d sess., chap. 19.

38. Ibid., 6th sess., chaps. 1, 31.

39. Ibid., chaps. 38, 40.

40. Ibid., 7th sess., chap. 66.

41. On the Haldimand negotiations, see Robert McCluer Calhoon, *The Loyalists in Revolutionary America, 1760–1781* (New York: Harcourt, Brace, Jovanovich, 1973), pp. 331–32.

42. [William H. Hill, comp.], *History of Washington County, N.Y.: The Gibson Papers* (Fort Edward, N.Y.: Honeywood Press, 1932), pp. 92–96; Micah Townsend to Clinton, record of Brattleboro meeting, and Townsend and Israel Smith to Clinton, all 27 May 1778, Townsend to Clinton, 7 April 1779, Hilkiah Grout to Townsend, 21 April 1779, *Clinton Papers*, 3:363–67, 4:693–97; Micah Townsend to Clinton, 10, 12 April 1780, Ibid., 5:595–96, 616–17; John Williams to Clinton, 22 April 1778, John Williams Papers, New York State Library, Albany; Williams to Clinton, 21 July 1780, *Clinton Papers*, 6:39–43.

43. For an instance of cooperation, see Volkert Veeder to the conspiracies commissioners, 5 August 1778, Paltsits, *Minutes of the Commissioners*, p. 196.

44. *Laws*, 1st sess., chap. 11; 3d sess., chap. 24; 5th sess., chap. 43.

45. Ibid., 5th sess., chap. 44.

46. Election records of Orange-Town, Budke Collection, Manuscript Division, New York Public Library, The Astor, Lenox and Tilden Foundations, vol. 36; Tryon committee to provincial congress, 26 August 1775, in Force, *American Archives*, 4th ser., 3:439–40; [George R.] Howell and [Jonathan] Tenney, *History of the County of Albany, N.Y. from 1609 to 1886* (New York: W. W. Munsell, 1886), p. 128; McKesson to Robert Benson, July 1776, in Force, *American Archives*, 5th ser., 1:257; minutes of New York convention, 2 August 1776, ibid., pp. 1469–70; minutes of convention, 5 October 1776, ibid., 3:228.

47. *Minutes of the Albany Committee*, vol. 1, entries for 10 May, 14 June, 25 November 1776, 15 March, 28 August, 6, 15 November 1777, pp. 403, 450, 616–17, 700–702, 837, 861, 868.

48. Schenectady committee minutes, in ibid., vol. 2, entries for 31 May, 29 December 1775, 3 March, 14–19 April, 17, 23, 30 June 1777, 3 January 1778, pp. 1015, 1035, 1084–85, 1089–90, 1103, 1104, 1105, 1134–35.

49. *Minute Book of Tryon County*, 7 September 1775, pp. 66–68; Tryon committee to provincial congress, 7 September 1775, *Journals of the Provincial Congress, Provincial Convention, Committee of Safety and Council of Safety of the State of New-York, 1775–1776–1777*, vol. 2 (Albany: T. Weed, 1842), pp. 81–82; Tryon committee to provincial congress, 28 October 1775, ibid., p. 97; Benson to provincial congress, 8 February 1776, ibid., p. 136; Tryon committee to provincial congress, 17 February 1776, ibid., p. 191; "The Respectful Address of the Mechanicks," pp. 895–96.

50. Constitution of 1777, preamble; *Journal of the Senate of the State of New York*, microfilm ed., in *Records of the States*, N.Y., A.1a, reel 2, unit 1, entry for 30 September 1777 (hereinafter cited as *Senate Journal*); *Assembly Journal*, 29 September–7 October 1777; *Minutes of the Albany Committee*, 30 September 1777, 1:849; *Assembly Journal*, 5 January 1778; resolutions of the convention, and Pierre Van Cortlandt to Clinton, both 7 October 1777, *Clinton Papers*, 2:376–80; Smith, *Historical Memoirs*, 27 January 1778, 2:293. The last recorded meeting of the Albany committee was on 10 June 1778.

51. Minutes of the New York City committee, 10 November 1775, in Force, *American Archives*, 4th ser., 3:1423–26; Minutes of the Albany Committee, 2, 8 May, 23 August 1776, 1:395, 400, 533.

52. *Minutes of the Albany Committee*, 3 August, 19 September 1776, 16 July, 18 November 1777, 19 February 1778, 1:512, 556, 811–12, 869, 916–17, 926.

53. Critics of this argument have made the point that the committee movement must have involved farmers as much as it did consumers. The evidence is ambiguous, but it does not support the criticism. William Smith, for instance, noted repeatedly that price regulation was finding no favor among farmers in southern Albany and northern Dutchess (see his *Historical Memoirs*, 14, 15, 24 March 1778, 3, 7 May 1778, 2:321–22, 324, 330, 365, 373). It is also noteworthy that the district of Saratoga, as removed from the process of urbanization as any part of Albany County, declined to take part in the call for a state convention (Albany Committee Minutes, Matthew Visscher Folder, Albany Institute of History and Art, entry for 20 July 1779).

54. For the movement in Philadelphia, see Sam Bass Warner, Jr., *The Private City: Philadelphia in Three Periods of Its Growth* (Philadelphia: University of Pennsylvania Press, 1968), pp. 34–45; and John K. Alexander, "The Fort Wilson Incident of 1779: A Case Study of the Revolutionary Crowd," *William and Mary Quarterly* 31 (1974):589–612. For the movement's spread, see Richard B. Morris, *Government and Labor in Early America* (New York: Harper & Row, 1965), pp. 110–14.

55. Albany Committee Minutes, Matthew Visscher Folder, 20 June–14 July 1779.

56. Ulster County Association and instructions to assemblymen, Matthew Visscher Folder, Albany Institute; "Instructions Agreed to...by the Inhabitants of Poughkeepsie...to their Committee," broadside, 31 July 1779, New-York Historical Society; Schenectady committee minutes, 16 June–18 August 1779, *Minutes of the Albany Committee*, 2:1145–59; records of the Claverack Convention, Matthew Visscher Folder, Albany Institute.

57. Albany Committee Minutes, Matthew Visscher Folder, 20 June 1779; undated letter draft, ibid.; James Hunter to Albany committee, 7 September 1779, ibid.; Ulster County Association, ibid.; "W.D. in Orange County," *New-York Packet* (Loudon), 12 August 1779.

58. *Minutes of the Albany Committee*, 4 March 1778, 1:935; 31 October 1775, 1:282–83. See also James V. Downton, *Rebel Leadership: Commitment and Charisma in the Revolutionary Process* (New York: Collier-Macmillan, 1973).

59. Ulster County Committee to New York convention, 18 November 1776, *Journals of the Provincial Congress*, pp. 229–30; Albany committee to council of safety, 29 December 1777, ibid., p. 351; Andrew Billings and Peter Tappan to council of safety, 9 December 1777, ibid., pp. 354–55; letter from Henry Luddington et al., 3 December 1776[7], ibid., p. 355.

60. Abram P. Lott to council of safety, 2 and 9 December 1777, ibid., pp. 335 and 355; deposition of Peter Messier, storekeeper, 23 May 1777, in Paltsits, *Minutes of the Commissioners*, pp. 301–3; James H. Kip to James Caldwell and John Maley, New Windsor, 14 July 1777, *Journals of the Provincial Congress*, p. 506. On *taxation populaire*, see George Rudé, *The Crowd in History, 1730–1848* (New York: John Wiley and Sons, 1964), esp. chap 1.

61. Ted Robert Gurr emphatically made the point about "revolutionary manifestations of the most fundamental sort" at a conference on the interdisciplinary study of the American Revolution held at Harvard University in May 1975. Huntington says that "two general patterns [of revolution] can be identified. In the 'Western' pattern, the political institutions of the old regime collapse; this is followed by the mobilization of new groups into politics and then by the creation of new political institutions. The 'Eastern' revolution, in contrast, begins with the mobilization of new groups into politics and the creation of new political institutions and ends with the violent overthrow of the political institutions of the old order." (Samuel P. Huntington, *Political Order in Changing Societies* [New Haven: Yale University Press, 1968], p. 266). These categories must be taken as pure types; events in New York, at least, partook of both patterns.

62. Albert Soboul, *Les sans-culottes parisiens en l'an II: Mouvement populaire et Gouvernement Révolutionnaire, 2 Juin, 1793–9 thermidor, an II* (Paris: Librairie Clavreuil, 1962), pp. 21–175, 582–85; Oskar Anweiler, *The Soviets: The Russian Workers, Peasants and Sol-*

diers Councils, 1905-1921, trans. Ruth Hein (New York: Pantheon, 1975); idem, "Die Arbeit-erselbstverwaltung in Polen" and "Die Räte in der ungarnischen Revolution 1956," *Osteuropa* 7 (1958):224-32 and 393-400, respectively.

63. Karl Marx, "The Civil War in France," in *The Marx-Engels Reader*, ed. Robert C. Tucker (New York: W. W. Norton, 1972), pp. 526-76; V. I. Lenin, *State and Revolution* (1917; reprint ed., Moscow: Progress Publishers, 1972), esp. chap. 3. A full discussion of their position is in Anweiler, *The Soviets*, pp. 11-19, 144-60. See also Hannah Arendt, "Thoughts on Politics and Revolution," *New York Review of Books*, 22 April 1971, pp. 8-20, esp. p. 19; and Oskar Anweiler, "Der Revolutionsgeschichtliche Zusammenhang des Räteproblems," *Politische Vierteljahresschrift* 11 (1970):56-69, in which essay Anweiler distinguishes *council movements* ("the concrete political and social appearance of councils; their beginnings; their reality; and their conclusions"), *council thought* ("the articulated theoretical ideas which stand in relation to council movements"), and *council systems* ("either the political or legal form of a victorious and stabilized council movement [in Soviet Russia after 1918] or a structure traced out in theory for a social order based on councils") (p. 57, my translation).

64. Smith, *Historical memoirs*, 14 October 1776, 2:18.

65. *Assembly Journal*, 2 October 1777; *Minutes of the Council of Revision of the State of New York*, microfilm ed., in *Records of the States*, N.Y., E.1x, A.X., reel 8, unit 1, 20 and 4-5 February 1778.

66. John Lansing to Philip Schuyler, 4 August 1779, Philip Schuyler Papers, Manuscript Division, New York Public Library, The Astor, Lenox and Tilden Foundations; Benson to Jay, 6 July 1779, *Jay Papers*, 1:213 (emphasis in the originals); *Assembly Journal*, 5-10 March 1778.

67. *Laws*, 1st sess., chaps. 3, 27, 31, 47; 2d sess., chaps. 3, 10, 28; *Senate Journal*, 9-15 March 1779; *Assembly Journal*, 2 November 1778-15 March 1779, 14-18 September 1779; *Laws*, 3d sess., chap. 25; *Assembly Journal*, 28-29 September 1779; *Laws*, 3d sess., chap. 19.

68. *Laws*, 3d sess., chap. 43; Thomas C. Cochran, *New York in the Confederation: An Economic Study* (Port Washington, N.Y.: Kennikat Press, 1970), pp. 31-32.

69. Huntington, *Political Order in Changing Societies*, pp. 308-11.

70. *Assembly Journal*, 25 February-27 March 1778; 20 October 1778-6 February 1779; 21 October 1779; 31 January 1780; *Laws*, 1st sess., chap. 17, 2d sess., chap. 16, 3d sess., chap. 47; Lynd, "Who Should Rule at Home?" p. 49.

71. Alexander Hamilton to Robert Morris, 13 August 1782, *The Papers of Alexander Hamilton*, ed. Harold C. Syrett et al., 24 vols. to date (New York: Columbia University Press, 1961-), 3:135-37; Lynd, "Who Should Rule at Home?" p. 49; *Minutes of the Council of Revision*, 20 April 1784.

72. Lynd, "Who Should Rule at Home?" and "The Tenant Rising at Livingston Manor, May 1777," in his *Class Conflict, Slavery and the Constitution*.

73. This generalization is based on a reading of Paltsits, *Minutes of the Commissioners*, entries for 1780 and 1781.

74. Livingston to Morris, 18 January 1781, and to George Washington, 8 January 1781, Livingston Papers, quoted in Lynd, "Who Should Rule at Home?" p. 55.

75. "The Real Farmer," *The New-York Journal, and the General Advertiser*, 18, 25 January 1, 8, 15, February 1779.

CHAPTER 7

1. Peter W. Yates to Jay, 5 June 1777, in *John Jay: The Making of a Revolutionary, Unpublished Papers, 1745-1780*, ed. Richard B. Morris (New York: Harper & Row, 1975), p. 412; Jay to Schuyler, 20 June 1777, in *The Correspondence and Public Papers of John Jay*, ed.

Henry P. Johnston, 4 vols. (New York: G. P. Putnam's Sons, 1890–93), 1:142; Jay to Leonard Gansevoort, 5 June 1777, ibid., pp. 140–41; Jay to John Ten Broeck, 6 June 1777, in Morris, *John Jay*, p. 412.

2. George Dangerfield, *Chancellor Robert R. Livingston of New York, 1746–1813* (New York: Harcourt, Brace and Company, 1960), pp. 121–22; *Minutes of the Albany Committee of Correspondence, 1775–1778*, ed., James Sullivan, 2 vols., continuous pagination (Albany: University of the State of New York, 1923–25) 1:787–91; William Smith, Jr., *Historical Memoirs from 16 March, 1763 to 25 July, 1778*, ed. William H. W. Sabine, 2 vols. in 1 (New York: New York Times and Arno Press, 1969), entry for 3 June 1777, 2:151.

3. For Scott, see Dorothy M. Dillon, *The New York Triumvirate: A Study of the Legal and Political Careers of William Livingston, John Morin Scott and William Smith, Jr.* (New York: Columbia University Press, 1949); for his aligning with Duane, see *Calendar of Historical Manuscripts Relating to the War of the Revolution in the Office of the Secretary of State*, 2 vols. (Albany: Weed, Parsons and Company, 1868), 1:552–53; for judgments, see Alexander Hamilton to Robert Morris, 13 August 1782, in *The Papers of Alexander Hamilton*, ed. Harold C. Syrett et al., 24 vols. to date (New York: Columbia University Press, 1961–), 3:138–39; Clinton to Gouverneur Morris, 2 February 1779, *Public Papers of George Clinton, First Governor of New York*, ed. Hugh Hastings, 10 vols. (Albany: Published by the State of New York, 1911), 4:535–37.

4. E. Wilder Spaulding, *His Excellency George Clinton: Critic of the Constitution* (Port Washington, N.Y.: Ira J. Friedman, 1964), chap. 7.

5. Schuyler to Jay, 30 June and 14 July 1777, *Jay Papers*, 1:144 and 147; Smith to Clinton, 28 October 1777, in Smith, *Historical Memoirs*, 2:246; Smith to Schuyler, 6 December 1777, ibid., p. 266.

6. This information and information in the following two chapters is drawn from an exhaustive attempt at a collective biography of the legislators who served from 1777 to 1788. For greater detail, and for a full listing of sources, see Edward Francis Countryman, "Legislative Government in Revolutionary New York, 1777–1788" (Ph.D. diss., Cornell University, 1971). The Hamilton quote is from Hamilton to Robert Morris, 13 August 1782, *Papers of Alexander Hamilton*, 3:141.

7. *Pennsylvania Journal and Weekly Advertiser*, 22 February 1775. The members of the provincial assembly are listed in Patricia U. Bonomi, *A Factious People: Politics and Society in Colonial New York* (New York: Columbia University Press, 1971), appendix 1. The names of the state legislators for the years 1777–88 are given below, in Appendix 2.

8. Jackson Turner Main, "Government by the People: The American Revolution and the Democratization of the Legislatures," *William and Mary Quarterly* 23 (1966):391–407; idem, *The Upper House in Revolutionary America* (Madison: University of Wisconsin Press, 1967); idem, *Political Parties before the Constitution* (Chapel Hill: University of North Carolina Press, 1973); Smith, *Historical Memoirs*, 14–15 November 1777, 2:257–58; Smith to Philip Schuyler, 6 December 1777, ibid., pp. 266–67.

9. Smith, *Historical Memoirs*, 7 July 1778, 2:414.

10. Michel-Guillaume Jean de Crevecoeur, *Eighteenth-Century Travels in Pennsylvania and New York*, trans. and ed. Percy G. Adams (Lexington: University of Kentucky Press, 1961), pp. 20–23.

11. Smith, *Historical Memoirs*, 14 June 1777, 2:160.

12. For a full discussion of the backgrounds of revolutionary politicians in New York City, see Edmund P. Willis, "Social Origins of Political Leadership in New York City from the Revolution to 1815" (Ph.D. diss., University of California, Berkeley, 1967); see also Staughton Lynd, "The Mechanics in New York Politics, 1774–1785," in his *Class Conflict, Slavery and the United States Constitution: Ten Essays* (Indianapolis: Bobbs-Merrill, 1967), pp. 79–108.

13. *Minutes of the Albany Committee*, 11 June 1777, 1:790–91.

14. Resolution of the Newburgh committee, 14 June 1777, Misc. Mss., George Washing-

ton's Headquarters Museum, Newburgh, N.Y.; Dirck Wynkoop to Clinton, 14 June 1777, *Clinton Papers*, 2:31-32.

15. *Minutes of the Albany Committee*, 11 June 1777, 1:790-91; Tryon committee to Clinton, 7 September 1777, *Clinton Papers*. 2:283-86. The dispute even spilled over into the filling of appointive posts. (see "Loyal Persons in Tryon County Fitted for Civil Office under the New State Government," ibid., pp. 621-22).

16. William Smith saw as much. He commented that in framing the constitution the gentry should have "followed the example of Servius Tullius," who "constituted the Census & six Classes that the Power might fall into the Hands of Men of Property. Our People might at Least have given Voices for Govrs. Senators only to the higher Classes & made Men of great Property eligible—South Carolina had that in View...Amongst us a Beggar may be Govr. a Senator or Assemblyman" (*Historical Memoirs*, 14 June 1777, 2:160).

17. Compare the argument in this section with the following:
J. H. Plumb, *The Growth of Political Stability in England, 1675-1725* (Harmondsworth, Middlesex: Penguin, 1969); Jack P. Greene, "Foundations of Political Power in the Virginia House of Burgesses, 1720-1776," *William and Mary Quarterly* 16 (1959):485-506; Allan G. Bogue, "Some Dimensions of Power in the Thirty-Seventh Senate," in *The Dimensions of Quantitative Research in History*, ed. William O. Aydelotte et al. (London: Oxford University Press, 1972), pp. 285-318; and Nelson W. Polsby, "The Institutionalization of the U.S. House of Representatives," *American Political Science Review* 62 (1968):144-68. See also L. Ray Gunn, "The New York State Legislature, 1777-1846: A Developmental Perspective" (Paper presented at the 21st College Conference on New York History, Albany, N.Y., April 1977). A fuller and more technical statement of my argument here is in Edward Countryman, "Some Problems of Power in New York, 1777-1782" (Paper presented at the symposium "Sovereign States in the Age of Uncertainty," Washington, D.C., March 1979), to be published in an anthology edited by Ronald Hoffman.

18. Bonomi, *A Factious People*, pp. 257-58; Smith, *Historical Memoirs*, 8 April, 14, 27 June 1777 and 7 April 1778, 2:107-8, 160-61, 167, 341.

19. The first postwar speaker whose election indicates a partisan triumph was Richard Varick, a prominent federalist who held the chair in the tenth and eleventh sessions (1787 and 1788) (see below, chaps. 8 and 9).

20. For the elections of standing committees during the war, see *Journal of the Assembly of the State of New York*, microfilm ed., *Records of the States of the United States*, ed. William Sumner Jenkins (Washington, D.C.: Library of Congress, 1949), N.Y., A. 1b, reel 4, unit 1, entries for 17 September, 1777, 13 October 1778, 24 August 1779, 7 September 1780, and 24 October 1781 (hereinafter cited as *Assembly Journal*).

21. The unsuccessful attempt to seize Tory property in the second session stemmed from a report of one standing committee, and the third session's main tax bill originated in another (*Assembly Journal*, 15 October 1778, 25 August 1779.)

22. Ibid., 11, 16, 30 September, 2 October 1777.

23. Ibid., 27-28 January 1780.

24. John Lansing to Philip Schuyler, 4 August 1779, Philip Schuyler Papers, Manuscript Division, New York Public Library, The Astor, Lenox and Tilden Foundations; Benson to Jay, 6 July 1779, *Jay Papers*, 1:213. Early in 1780 Benson voted against going into a committee of the whole on "An Act to Prevent Monopoly And Extortion," whose very title placed it in the corporatist tradition, and tried to have the house establish "A Committee for Preserving the Constitution," which would have power to investigate any actions, such as a committee revival, that reflected on the constitution (*Assembly Journal*, 8-9 March 1780). For comments by other conservatives to the same effect, see Staughton Lynd, "Who Should Rule at Home? Dutchess County, New York in the American Revolution," in his *Class Conflict, Slavery and the Constitution*, pp. 45-46.

25. *Assembly Journal*, 19 October 1778, 27 February, 23 September, 6 October 1779; 9, 15-16 February 1780.

26. See Jay to Alexander McDougall, 21 March 1776, in Morris, *John Jay*, pp. 241–42; Hamilton to Jay, 26 November 1775, in *Papers of Alexander Hamilton*, 1:176–78; Hamilton to Gouverneur Morris, 12 May 1777, ibid., pp. 251–53; and Hamilton to committee of correspondence, 20 April 1777, ibid., pp. 233–34.

27. Messages of Governor Clinton, 21 March and 2 November 1778, in *Messages from the Governors,* ed. Charles Z. Lincoln, 11 vols. (Albany: J. B. Lyon, 1909), 2:33–34, 57–59; *Laws of the State of New York*, microfilm ed., *Records of the States,* N.Y., B.2, reel 6, unit 2, 1st sess., chap. 27, 2d sess., chap. 28.

28. *Assembly Journal*, 9 February–15 March, 6–18 September 1779; *Journal of the Senate of the State of New York*, microfilm ed., *Records of the States*, N.Y., A.1a, reel 2, unit 1, entries for 9–15 March 1779; *Laws*, 3d sess., chap. 25.

29. William Kent, *Memoirs and Letters of James Kent, LL.D.* (Boston: Little, Brown, 1898), p. 20; Smith, *Historical Memoirs*, 10 April and 1 July 1778, 2:345, 409–10.

30. Benson to Jay, 23 June 1779, in Morris, *John Jay*, p. 605; Livingston to Jay, 21 April 1779, ibid., pp. 583–84.

31. *Assembly Journal*, 2 November 1778, 12 October 1779.

32. Ibid., 4 February, 10 March 1780; 27 March 1781.

33. Gouverneur Morris and William Duer both had appalling attendance records during their one term in the assembly. Richard Morris left the senate in 1780 to become chief justice.

34. Livingston to Jay, 21 April 1779, in Morris, *John Jay*, pp. 583–84.

35. Constitution of 1777, Art. 19. For the text of the constitution, see William A. Polf, *1777: The Political Revolution and New York's First Constitution* (Albany: New York State Bicentennial Commission, 1977). For Clinton's recommendations and their results, see the footnotes in Lincoln, *Messages from the Governors*, vol. 2.

36. Spaulding, *George Clinton*, pp. 7–8, 52, 71, 158, and *passim.*

37. Ibid., chap. 6.

38. Lincoln, *Messages from the Governors*, 2:9, 18; Clinton to Livingston, 22 February, 9 March 1780, Robert R. Livingston Papers, New-York Historical Society, New York; Hamilton to Robert Morris, 13 August 1782, *Papers of Alexander Hamilton*, 3:137.

39. Lincoln, *Messages from the Governors*, 2:47; Livingston to Gouverneur Morris, 27 July 1778, Livingston Papers; Duane to Jay, 22–24 August 1778, in Morris, *John Jay*, pp. 493–94; Benson to Jay, 4 September 1779, ibid., pp. 632–33; Jay to Clinton, 16 September 1779, ibid., p. 635; Micah Townsend to Clinton, 27 May 1778, and accompanying documents, in *Clinton Papers*, 4:363–67; Townsend to Clinton, 7 April 1779, and Hilkiah Grout to Townsend, 21 April 1779, ibid., pp. 693–97; *Assembly Journal*, 27 February 1781.

40. For a fuller statement, see Countryman, "Legislative Government," chap. 6.

41. Smith, *Historical Memoirs*, 1 February 1778, 2:295–96.

42. For changes in American tax policy during the Revolution, see Robert Arthur Becker, "The Politics of Taxation in America, 1763–1783" (Ph.D. diss., University of Wisconsin, 1971). For New York's pre- and post-Revolution policies, see Edward Countryman, "The Revolutionary Transformation of New York," in *New Wine in Old Skins: A Comparative View of Socio-political Structures and Values Affecting the American Revolution*, ed. Erich Angermann et al. (Stuttgart: Ernst Klett Verlag, 1976), pp. 66–86.

43. For a detailed discussion of the votes in the legislature and of the method by which I analyzed them, see below, Appendix 1.

44. See ibid.

45. In March 1778, Benson scored one of his few successes when he persuaded the assembly to retitle the bill "An Act to authorize the several County Committees. . .to procure a Supply of Shoes and Stockings. . ." as "An Act to Procure a Supply of Shoes and Stockings for the Troops." All mention of the committees was obliterated from it (*Assembly Journal*, 5–10 March 1778).

46. The issue remained alive, however, as a measure of men's attitudes. See Frederick

Weissenfels to John Lamb, 23 May 1783, John Lamb Papers, New-York Historical Society; and below, chap. 8.

47. See below, Appendix 1.

48. Russell to Clinton, 17 August 1778, *Clinton Papers*, 3:688-89; John Younglove to Albany committee, 26 February 1778, and accompanying documents, in ibid., 2:854-58.

49. "Address of Citizens and Freeholders of Dutchess County to the Legislature, 1778" (dated 22 October 1778), in *Colonel Henry Luddington, a Memoir*, by Willis Fletcher Johnson (New York: Privately printed, 1907), pp. 153-56; minutes of the Claverack Convention, August 1779, Matthew Visscher Folder, Albany Institute of History and Art. See also Tryon committee to Clinton, 10 February 1778, *Clinton Papers*, 2:741-43; and letters of Tryon committee to Abraham Yates, Tryon Misc. Mss., New-York Historical Society.

50. See below, Appendix 1.

51. Cf. Lynd, "Who Should Rule at Home?"; and idem, *Anti-Federalism in Dutchess County, New York: A Study in Democracy and Class Conflict in the Revolutionary Era* (Chicago: Loyola University Press, 1962).

52. For Swartwout and the insurgent politicians Guisbert Schenck and Henry Luddington in the committee revival, see *New-York Packet and the American Advertiser* (Fishkill, Samuel Loudon), 29 July 1779.

53. For a fuller statement, see Countryman, "Some Problems of Power in New York;" and below, Appendix 1.

54. "Chester, the 17th of April, 1780, Dear Sir . . . [signed] Bezaleel Seely, Jun.," broadside, 1780, Evans no. 16991.

55. *Assembly Journal*, 11 September 1777; for elections to the council of appointment, see ibid., 16 September 1777, 17 October 1778, 11 September 1779, and 9 September 1780.

56. See Duer to Jay, 28 May 1777, *Jay Papers*, 1:137-40; Jay to William Livingston, 22 March 1777, ibid., pp. 122-24; McKesson to Clinton, 13 March 1777, *Clinton Papers*, 1:657-58.

57. *Assembly Journal*, 19 September 1780; 6, 13 March 1781.

58. Alfred F. Young, *The Democratic-Republicans of New York: The Origins, 1763-1797* (Chapel Hill: University of North Carolina Press, 1967), p. 31.

59. Smith to Schuyler, 17 August 1776, in Smith, *Historical Memoirs*, 2:2-3.

CHAPTER 8

1. Although the backgrounds and the political significance of particular senators will be discussed in this chapter, no attempt will be made to discuss their political behavior. For the reasons for this, see below, Appendix 1.

2. Stanley Elkins and Eric L. McKitrick, "The Founding Fathers: Young Men of the Revolution," *Political Science Quarterly* 76 (1961):181-216.

3. The best study of Yates is Stefan Bielinski, *Abraham Yates, Jr., and the New Political Order in Revolutionary New York* (Albany: New York State American Revolution Bicentennial Commission, 1975).

4. William Smith, Jr., *Historical Memoirs from 16 March 1763 to 25 July 1778*, ed. William H. W. Sabine, 2 vols. in 1 (New York: New York Times and Arno Press, 1969), entry for 21 February 1778, 2:306.

5. Schuyler to Jay, 1 February 1778, and Jay to Schuyler, 6 February 1778, in *John Jay: The Making of a Revolutionary, Unpublished Papers, 1745-1780*, ed. Richard B. Morris (New York: Harper & Row, 1975), pp. 463-65; Smith, *Historical Memoirs*, 20-21 April 1778, 2:353-54; Hamilton to Robert Morris, 13 August 1782, *The Papers of Alexander Hamilton*, ed.

Harold C. Syrett et al., 24 vols. to date (New York: Columbia University Press, 1961–), 3:139; Tillotson to Robert R. Livingston, May 1784, Robert R. Livingston Papers, New-York Historical Society, New York, quoted in Staughton Lynd, "Abraham Yates's History of the Movement for the United States Constitution," in his *Class Conflict, Slavery and the United States Constitution: Ten Essays* (Indianapolis: Bobbs-Merrill, 1967), p. 220.

6. For the background of Adgate and Ford, see *Minutes of the Albany Committee of Correspondence, 1775–1778*, ed. James Sullivan, 2 vols., continuous pagination (Albany: University of the State of New York, 1923–25), 1:4, 28, 280, 475; and *History of Columbia County, New York, with Illustrations and Biographical Sketches of Some of Its Prominent Men and Pioneers* (Philadelphia: Everts & Ensign, 1878), pp. 77, 79, 320, 321, 371, 380. For Grant's comments, see her *Memoirs of an American Lady*, 2 vols. in 1 (1808; reprint ed., Freeport, N.Y.: Books for Libraries Press, 1972), 2:147–48. See also Asa Douglass to George Washington, [June 1776], in Peter Force, comp., *American Archives*, 9 vols. (Washington, D.C.: M. St. Clair Clarke and Peter Force, 1837–53), 4th ser., 6:745–46; Hamilton to Robert Livingston, Jr., 25 April 1785, *Papers of Alexander Hamilton*, 3:609.

7. For a discussion of Allen's deism in relation to other aspects of his life, see Edward Countryman, "Rural Radical Thought in Eighteenth-Century America: The Case of Ethan Allen" (Paper presented at the II International Congress of North American History, Milan, June 1979).

8. For Paine, see Jackson Turner Main, *The Upper House in Revolutionary America* (Madison: University of Wisconsin Press, 1967), pp. 136–37; for his refusal to submit to the senate's discipline, see *Journal of the Senate of the State of New York*, microfilm ed., in *Records of the States of the United States*, ed. William Sumner Jenkins (Washington, D.C.: Library of Congress, 1949), N.Y., A.1a, reel 2, unit 1, entries for 27 May 1780–15 March 1781 (hereinafter cited as *Senate Journal*); Hamilton to Robert Morris, 13 August 1782, *Papers of Alexander Hamilton*, 3:139; and Frank Hasbrouck, *The History of Dutchess County, New York* (Poughkeepsie, N.Y.: S. A. Matthieu, 1909), pp. 67, 77.

9. Bielinski, *Abraham Yates*, p. 12.

10. Staughton Lynd, *Anti-Federalism in Dutchess County, New York: A Study of Democracy and Class Conflict in the Revolutionary Era* (Chicago: Loyola University Press, 1962), p. 27.

11. Alphonso T. Clearwater, *History of Ulster County, New York* (Kingston, N.Y.: W. J. Van Deusen, 1907), pp. 142, 145, 164, 247; Nathaniel Bartlett Sylvester, *History of Ulster County, New York* (Philadelphia: Everts & Peck, 1880), pt. 1, pp. 84, 86, 94, 199, 306, and pt. 2, pp. 3, 189, 190, 200, 215–17; "Family Record of Abraham Hasbrouck," *New York Genealogical and Biographical Record* (June–October 1940); "The Hasbrouck Diary," *Olde Ulster* 4 (1908):147–49.

12. Ferdinand V. Sanford, "Gen. John Hathorn," *Historical Society of Newburgh Bay and the Highlands Historical Papers* 40 (1904):91-97; Rev. A. A. Haines, "John Hathorn," *New York Genealogical and Biographical Record* 20 (1889):169–71; *Biographical Directory of the American Congress, 1774–1927* (Washington, D.C.: U.S. Government Printing Office, 1928), p. 1074; Russel Headley, ed., *The History of Orange County, New York* (Middletown, N.Y.: Van Deusen and Elms, 1908), pp. 82-83, 150; E. M. Ruttenber and L. H. Clark, *History of Orange County, New York* (Philadelphia: Everts & Peck, 1881), pp. 48, 202, 522, 523; Charles F. Stickney, *A History of the Minisink Region* (Middletown, N.Y.: Coe Finch and I. F. Gaiwits, 1867), p. 147; Rev. David Cole, *History of Rockland County, New York* (New York: J. H. Beers & Co., 1884), pp. 97, 129, 153; William H. Hill, *History of Washington County, N.Y., The Gibson Papers, Old Families* (Washington County Historical Society, 1954), pp. 215–19; *History of Washington County, New York* (Philadelphia: Everts & Ensign, 1878), pp. 112–15; *History and Biography of Washington County* (Chicago: Gresham Publishing Company, 1894), p. 42.

13. See the correspondence between DeWitt and Livingston in "Letters of Charles DeWitt,"

Olde Ulster 4 (1908) and 5 (1909); for DeWitt's rebuff to Paine, see DeWitt to Paine, 24 November 1784, DeWitt Typescripts, Senate House Museum, Kingston, N.Y.

14. See above, chap. 7.

15. See Leonard Gansevoort to Bronck, 28 March 1782, and John Wigram to Bronck, 16 April 1783, Bronck Mss., Bronck House Museum, Coxsackie, N.Y.

16. Sylvester, *History of Ulster County*, pt. 1, pp. 84, 102; Clearwater, *History of Ulster County*, p. 191; *Olde Ulster* 2 (1906):303.

17. DeWitt to Gerrett DeWitt, 16 March and 13 April 1784; DeWitt to Livingston, 18 May 1784; DeWitt to Mr. Eltinge, 21 April 1784; DeWitt to Gerrett DeWitt, 21 May 1784—all in "Letters of Charles DeWitt."

18. Staughton Lynd, "Who Should Rule at Home? Dutchess County, New York, in the American Revolution," in his *Class Conflict, Slavery and the Constitution*, p. 44.

19. For the committee service of these men, see above, chap. 6; for radical opinion on commerce and on the committee movement, see "W. D. in Orange County," *New-York Packet and the American Advertiser* (Fishkill, Samuel Loudon) 12 August 1779, and *New York Journal*, 18, 25 January, 1, 8, 15 February 1779.

20. Livingston to Morris, 18 January 1781, Livingston Papers, quoted in Lynd, "Who Should Rule at Home?" p. 55; Weissenfels to Lamb, 23 May 1783, John Lamb Papers, New-York Historical Society.

21. For urban sympathy with the Hudson Valley levelers, see above, chap. 2; for Young, see Pauline Maier, "Reason and Revolution: The Radicalism of Dr. Thomas Young," *American Quarterly* 28 (1976):229–49, and above, chap. 5; for Sears's introducing Allen to the provincial congress, see provincial congress minutes, 4 July 1775, in Force, *American Archives*, 4th ser., 2:1338–39.

22. For their votes, see Edward Francis Countryman, "Legislative Government in Revolutionary New York, 1777–1788" (Ph.D. diss., Cornell University, 1971), chap. 8; see also Staughton Lynd, "The Mechanics in New York Politics, 1774–1785," in his *Class Conflict, Slavery and the Constitution*, pp. 79–108, esp. pp. 98–99.

23. *Laws of the State of New York*, microfilm ed., *Records of the States*, N.Y., B.2, reel 6, unit 2, 3d sess. chap. 28.

24. Isaac Newton Phelps Stokes, ed., *The Iconography of Manhattan Island*, 6 vols. (New York: R. H. Dodd, 1915–28), entries for 27 February, 22–23 August, 1 September, 20 October, 14, 15 November 1783, 5:1157, 1165, 1167, 1169, 1170–71.

25. Livingston to Jay, 25 January 1784, *The Correspondence and Public Papers of John Jay*, ed. Henry P. Johnston, 4 vols. (New York: G. P. Putnam's Sons, 1890–93), 3:108; Alexander Hamilton, "A Second Letter from Phocion to the Considerate Citizens of New-York," *Papers of Alexander Hamilton*, 3:543.

26. Lynd, "The Mechanics in New York Politics," pp. 100–108; Stokes, *Iconography*, 12 January 1784, 5:1183.

27. For Burr's hostility to the mechanics, see Charles Tillinghast to Col. Hugh Hughes, [February 1785], and Hughes to Tillinghast, 7 March 1785, Lamb Papers.

28. *New York Journal*, 5 May 1785.

29. Hamilton to Robert Morris, 13 August 1782, *Papers of Alexander Hamilton*, 3:141; "Address of the Legislature to the People," *Journal of the Assembly of the State of New York*, microfilm ed., *Records of the States*, N.Y., A.1b, reel 4, unit 1, entry for 13 March 1781; Lynd, "The Mechanics in New York Politics," p. 101; "To his Excellency George Clinton," broadside, Fishkill, N.Y., 1783, Evans no. 18210; " 'A Citizen' to the Honorable the Legislature," broadside, New York, 1786, Evans no. 20024; "The Interest of the Landholder," broadside, New York, 1785, Evans no. 19136.

30. The journal entries are sometimes vague about the number of petitions received, so these figures are rough. Petitions for naturalization are not included; nor, for the last two sessions, are petitions from imprisoned debtors.

31. Among petitions flatly rejected were those for relief from the punitive tax law that the seventh session imposed on the southern district and, for the first several years after the British evacuation, most petitions for the return of royalist exiles.

32. *Assembly Journal*, 2, 19-20 March 1782; 5, 8 February 1783; 26 January, 21 February 1784; 31 March-1 April 1785; 6 February, 3 March, 22 October 1784.

33. Hamilton to Robert Morris, 13 August 1782, *Papers of Alexander Hamilton*, 3:139; *New-York Packet* (Loudon), 25 April 1782; Matthew Visscher to Abraham Yates, 6 March 1786, and Peter W. Yates to Abraham Yates et al., 21 January 1788, both in Abraham Yates Papers, Manuscript Division, New York Public Library, The Astor, Lenox and Tilden Foundations.

34. Hamilton to Morris, 13 August 1782, *Papers of Alexander Hamilton*, 3:138-40.

35. In the sixth session there were several members bearing the surname Lawrence, and the *Journal* is often unclear about which one is meant.

36. Hamilton to Morris, 13 August 1782, *Papers of Alexander Hamilton*, 3:137-38.

37. See Hamilton to Clinton, 24-27 February 1783; Hamilton to Clinton, 1 June; Hamilton to Clinton, 3 October, ibid., pp. 268-69, 367-72, 464-69.

38. Charles Z. Lincoln, ed., *Messages from the Governors*, 11 vols. (Albany: J. B. Lyon, 1909), 2:77.

39. Clinton to Jay, 2 February 1779, in Morris, *John Jay*, pp. 545-46.

40. E. Wilder Spaulding, *New York in the Critical Period, 1783-1789* (Port Washington, N.Y.: Ira J. Friedman, 1963), p. 122.

41. *Messages from the Governors*, 2:195-96.

42. Ibid., pp. 87, 183.

43. See the assessment of Clinton in Alfred F. Young, *The Democratic Republicans of New York: The Origins, 1763-1797* (Chapel Hill: University of North Carolina Press, 1967), pp. 33-39.

44. For the candidacies of Schuyler and Paine, see ibid., pp. 31, 34; and Spaulding, *New York in the Critical Period*, p. 101. The quote is from Thomas Tillotson to Robert R. Livingston, 24 March 1783, Livingston Papers.

45. Peter W. Yates to Joseph C. Yates, n.d., Yates Papers, quoted in Young, *Democratic Republicans*, p. 38; Schuyler to Jay, 30 May 1785, *Jay Papers*, 3:151.

46. See *Laws of the Legislature of the State of New York, in Force Against the Loyalists* (London: H. Reynell, 1786).

47. *Laws*, 3d sess., chaps. 19, 25, 76.

48. Ibid., 6th sess., chaps. 1, 20; *Senate Journal*, 11 February 1784; *Messages from the Governors*, 2:202-4.

49. *Laws*, 5th sess., chap. 39, 6th sess., chaps. 7, 21, 40, 41, 7th sess., chaps. 27, 66; Wallace Brown, *The King's Friends: The Composition and Motives of the American Loyalist Claimants* (Providence: Brown University Press, 1965), p. 78.

50. *Laws*, 7th sess., chap. 58.

51. For the background on Trinity Church, see *Old New York and Trinity Church*, Collections of the New-York Historical Society, vol. 3 (New York: Printed for the Society, 1871); Carl Bridenbaugh, *Mitre and Sceptre: Transatlantic Faiths, Ideas, Personalities and Politics, 1689-1775* (New York: Oxford University Press, 1962); and Edward Alexander, *A Revolutionary Conservative: James Duane of New York* (New York: Columbia University Press, 1938), pp. 176-80.

52. See [William Livingston, John Morin Scott, and William Smith, Jr.], *The Independent Reflector, or Weekly Essays on Sundry Important Subjects More Particularly Adapted to the Province of New York*, ed. Milton M. Klein (Cambridge, Mass.: Harvard University Press, Belknap Press, 1963); and Donald F. M. Gerardi, "The King's College Controversy 1753-1756 and the Ideological Roots of Toryism in New York," *Perspectives in American History* 11 (1977-78):145-96.

53. For my argument on the relationship between what the founding of the chamber of

commerce symbolized and crowd action, see above, chap. 2. For the royalism of the chamber's founders, see Alexander C. Flick, *Loyalism in New York during the American Revolution* (New York: Columbia University Press, 1901); and Bernard Mason, *The Road to Independence: The Revolutionary Movement in New York, 1773–1777* (Lexington: University of Kentucky Press, 1966). Mason finds that the "principal merchants of the province," whom the chamber embodied, were "largely in support of the administration" (p. 64).

54. *Laws*, 7th sess., chap. 38. For the attitudes of nonmerchants, see Lynd, "The Mechanics in New York Politics," pp. 102–8.

55. *Assembly Journal*, 21 February 1784; *Laws*, 7th sess., chap. 33.

56. *Assembly Journal*, 22 November 1784; 8 February, 14 March 1785.

57. Mason, *The Road to Independence*, pp. 53, 74.

58. *Laws*, 7th sess., chap. 51; Jurgen Herbst, "The American Revolution and the American University," *Perspectives in American History* 10 (1976):279–355, esp. pp. 301–9.

59. *Assembly Journal*, 7 May, 5 November 1784; 3, 9 February 1785.

60. Ibid., 15 February 1785; Charles Tillinghast to Col. Hugh Hughes, [February 1785], Lamb Papers (emphasis in the original).

61. James Fenimore Cooper, *The Pioneers* (1823; reprint ed., New York: Signet Books, 1964); "Journal of Rev. John Taylor's Missionary Tour through the Mohawk and Black River Countries in 1802," in *The Documentary History of the State of New York*, ed. Edmund B. O'Callaghan, 4 vols. (Albany: Weed, Parsons, & Co., 1849–51), 3:1136.

62. *Laws*, 10th sess., chap. 1, 7th sess., chap. 60, 8th sess., chap. 66, 9th sess., chap. 67; Young, *Democratic Republicans*, pp. 232, 243.

63. Tillinghast to Hughes [February 1785], and Hughes to Tillinghast, 7 March 1785, Lamb Papers (emphasis in the original).

64. For details on the voting patterns discussed in this section, see below, Appendix 1.

65. This refers to the free counties only.

66. For Duane's argument, see Alexander, *A Revolutionary Conservative*, pp. 161–64.

CHAPTER 9

1. On the details of ratification, see Linda Grant DePauw, *The Eleventh Pillar: New York State and the Federal Constitution* (Ithaca: Cornell University Press, 1966); on politics after ratification, see Dixon Ryan Fox, *The Decline of Aristocracy in the Politics of New York* (New York: Columbia University Press, 1919), and Alfred F. Young, *The Democratic Republicans of New York: The Origins, 1763–1797* (Chapel Hill: University of North Carolina Press, 1967).

2. Jacobus Swartwout to Hamilton, [1783], in *The Papers of Alexander Hamilton*, ed. Harold C. Syrett, et al., 24 vols. to date (New York: Columbia University Press, 1961–), 3:482; *Journal of the Assembly of the State of New York,* microfilm, ed., *Records of the States of the United States,* ed. William Sumner Jenkins (Washington, D.C.: Library of Congress, 1949), N.Y., A.1b, reel 4, unit 1, entry for 22 July 1782 (hereinafter cited as *Assembly Journal*). The election of Hamilton instead of Schuyler represented the third time in a row that the Albanian was defeated in the final choice of congressmen. He had previously lost to Ezra L'Hommedieu and Egbert Benson (see *Assembly Journal,* 12 November 1780 and 26 November 1781).

3. Hamilton to Morris, 13 August 1782, *Papers of Alexander Hamilton*, 3:138–41; Hamilton to George Washington, 8 April 1783, ibid., p. 318.

4. Hamilton to John Dickinson, 25–30 September 1783, ibid., pp. 438–58.

5. The letters from "Phocion" are printed in ibid., pp. 483–96, 530–58.

6. "The Continentalist No. V," [18 April 1782], ibid., pp. 76, 80 (emphasis in the original).

7. Hamilton to Livingston, 13 August 1783, ibid., p. 431; Hamilton to Clinton, 1 June 1783, ibid., pp. 367–72; Hamilton to Duane, 5 August 1783, ibid., pp. 430–31.

8. Hamilton to Morris, 17 June, 13 August 1782, ibid., pp. 93-94 and 135-36, respectively.

9. "The Continentalist No. VI," [4 July 1782], ibid., pp. 101-2.

10. Ibid., p. 102; "A Letter from Phocion to the Considerate Citizens of New York," [1-27 January 1784], ibid., p. 494.

11. "A Second Letter from Phocion to the Considerate Citizens of New-York, Containing Remarks on Mentor's Reply" [April 1784], ibid., p. 545; "A [first] Letter from Phocion," ibid., pp. 484, 487.

12. "A [first] Letter from Phocion," ibid., p. 494.

13. Hamilton to Morris, 12 July 1782, ibid., pp. 107-8; "Resolution of the New York Legislature Calling for a Convention" [20 July 1782], ibid., pp. 110-13; Hamilton to Morris, 22 July 1782, ibid., pp. 114-16; "To the Public Creditors of the State of New York" [30 September 1782], ibid., pp. 171-76; Hamilton to Morris, 26 October 1782, ibid., pp. 190-191.

14. For Hamilton's continuing interest in the defense of royalists, see Hamlton *et al.* to Thomas Mifflin, 10 December 1783, ibid., pp. 478-79; and Hamilton to Egbert Benson, 18 February 1784, ibid., p. 511. For his involvement with the Bank of North America, see John Chaloner to Hamilton, 26 November 1783 and 21 January 1784, ibid., pp. 477 and 497-98, respectively; Gouverneur Morris to Hamilton, 27 January 1784, ibid., pp. 498-503; and Hamilton to Jeremiah Wadsworth, 29 October 1785, ibid., pp. 625-26. For his involvement with he Bank of New York, see the bank's constitution and charter outline, ibid., 514-20; and Hamilton to John B. Church, 10 March 1784, ibid., pp. 520-21.

15. "Remarks on the Petition of John Maunsell" [16 January 1787], ibid., 4:1-2; "Remarks on an Act for Regulating Elections" [6 February 1787], ibid., pp. 34-37; outline and draft of a new tax law [February 1787], ibid., pp. 40-66; "Remarks on an Act for Raising Certain Yearly Taxes" [17 February 1787], ibid., pp. 94-96.

16. "Report on the Petition of Isaac Gouverneur, Junior" [14 February 1787], ibid., pp. 70-71; "Motion for Leave to Bring in a Bill on Places at Which the Legislature Shall Meet" [16 April 1787], ibid., pp. 146-47; "Report on a Letter from the Secretary for Foreign Affairs" [10 March 1787], ibid., p. 112; "Remarks on an Amendment to an Act Relative to Debts Due Persons within the Enemy's Lines" [12 April 1787], ibid., p. 145; "Remarks on an Act Repealing Laws Inconsistent with the Treaty of Peace" [17 April 1787], pp. 150-53.

17. "Remarks on an Act for Regulating the Fees of Offices and Ministers of the Courts" [21 February 1787], ibid., p. 98.

18. Jefferson to James Madison, 21 September 1795, quoted in Clinton Rossiter, *1787: The Grand Convention* (New York: Macmillan, 1966), plate facing p. 223.

19. Livingston to Jay, 25 January 1784, in *The Correspondence and Public Papers of John Jay*, ed. Henry P. Johnston, 4 vols. (New York: G. P. Putnam's Sons, 1890-93), 3:108; Livingston to Hamilton, 30 August 1783, *Papers of Alexander Hamilton*, 3:434-35; Jay to Hamilton, 28 September 1783, ibid., pp. 459-60.

20. Nathaniel Hazard to Hamilton, 21 April 1786, and Hamilton to Hazard, 24 April 1786, *Papers of Alexander Hamilton*, 3:661-65; Robert Troup to Rufus King, 4 April 1809, quoted in Young, *Democratic Republicans*, pp. 68-69.

21. For McDougall's military career and the politics that grew out of it, see Roger J. Champagne, *Alexander McDougall and the American Revolution in New York* (Schenectady, N.Y.: Union College Press, 1975).

22. For Lawrence as Hamilton's friend, see Hamilton to Lawrence, 12 December 1782, *Papers of Alexander Hamilton*, 3:211-12, and Hamilton to Robert Morris, 13 August 1782, ibid., p. 140.

23. For Sears as vice-president of the chamber of commerce, see *Laws of the State of New York*, microfilm ed., in *Records of the States*, N.Y., B.2, reel 6, unit 2, 7th sess., chap. 38. For his background, see Robert Jay Christen, "King Sears: Politician and Patriot in a Decade of Revolution" (Ph.D. diss., Columbia University, 1968).

24. For the attitude of the mechanics towards the Bank of New York, see Staughton Lynd,

"The Mechanics in New York Politics, 1774–1785," in his *Class Conflict, Slavery and the United States Constitution: Ten Essays* (Indianapolis: Bobbs-Merrill, 1967), pp. 102–6. Hamilton's comments appear in "A [first] Letter from Phocion," 493–94; for Burr's attitude towards incorporating the mechanics, see Charles Tillinghast to Hugh Hughes [February 1785], John Lamb Papers, New-York Historical Society.

25. *Minutes of the Albany Committee of Correspondence, 1775–1778*, ed. James Sullivan, 2 vols., continuous pagination (Albany: University of the State of New York, 1923–25), 1:787–91; William Smith, Jr., *Historical Memoirs from 16 March, 1763 to 25 July, 1778*, ed. William H. W. Sabine, 2 vols. in 1 (New York: New York Times and Arno Press, 1969), entry for 20 April 1778, 2:354.

26. Gansevoort to Bronck, 28 March 1782, and Wigram to Bronck, 16 April 1783, Bronck Mss., Bronck House Museum, Coxsackie, N.Y.

27. Smith, *Historical Memoirs*, 22 April 1778, 2:358; Coxsackie poll lists for 1780 and 1782, Bronck Mss.

28. Hamilton to Livingston, 25 April 1785, *Papers of Alexander Hamilton*, 3:608–9.

29. Hamilton to Duer, 14 May 1785, ibid., pp. 610–11; Henry Livingston to Walter Livingston, 24 April 1785, Robert R. Livingston Papers, New-York Historical Society, New York; Gansevoort to Bronck, 16 April 1785, Bronck Mss.

30. The three who were nominated in 1778 were John Taylor, James Gordon, and Peter Vrooman. Taylor also took part in the nomination cabal (Smith, *Historical Memoirs*, 20 April 1778, 2:354).

31. Robert Livingston, Jr., to Hamilton, 13 June 1785, *Papers of Alexander Hamilton*, 3:614–16.

32. See *Laws*, 6th sess., chap. 2; 9th sess., chap. 12; 10th sess., chaps. 1 and 36.

33. Lease of Thaddeus Lawrence, 23 September 1785; Andrew Stuart to Philip Schuyler, 1805; Schuyler to Elisha Challell, 16 May 1790; Schuyler to Hannah Brewer, 23 November 1784; Schuyler to Henry Carman, 26 May 1789—all in Philip Schuyler Papers, New York Public Library, The Astor, Lenox and Tilden Foundations. For the controversy over the rights of developers and those of property owners in 19th-century American law see J. R. Pole, "Property and Law in the American Republic," in his *Paths to the American Past* (New York: Oxford University Press, 1979), pp. 75–108.

34. See David Maldwyn Ellis, *Landlords and Tenants in the Hudson-Mohawk Region, 1790–1850* (Ithaca: Cornell University Press, 1946).

35. James Percy to Schuyler, 2 November 1784, Schuyler Papers; Aaron Forman to Schuyler, 5 May 1786, 13, 18 March 1787, ibid.; Robert Harpur to Schuyler, 2 August 1786, *Papers of Alexander Hamilton*, 3:679–80.

36. See Young, *Democratic Republicans*, pp. 95–98.

37. Stephen R. Boyd, "The Impact of the Constitution on State Politics: New York as a Test Case," in *The Human Dimensions of Nation Making: Essays in Colonial and Revolutionary History in Honor of Merrill Jensen*, ed. James Kirby Martin (Madison: State Historical Society of Wisconsin, 1976); see also DePauw, *The Eleventh Pillar*, and Young, *Democratic Republicans*.

38. DePauw, *The Eleventh Pillar*, p. 25.

39. *Assembly Journal*, 24–25 January, 6 February 1786.

40. Ibid., 24 February, 1, 26 March, 12 February 1787.

41. Ibid., 21 March, 26 April 1786; 27 January, 10 March, 13 April 1787; 26 February 1788.

42. Ibid., 15, 17 February, 2–4 March 1786.

43. Ibid., minutes of the 10th and 11th sessions.

44. Ibid., 11, 21, 7 March 1786.

45. "Unsubmitted Resolution Calling for a Convention to Amend the Articles of Confederation" [July 1783], *Papers of Alexander Hamilton*, 3:420–26.

46. "To the Public" [April 1786], Albany Miscellaneous Mss., New-York Historical Society.

47. Hamilton to Duer, 14 May 1785, *Papers of Alexander Hamilton*, 3:610–11.

48. See Thomas C. Cochran, *New York in the Confederation: An Economic Study*, 2d ed. (Port Washington, N.Y.: Kennikat Press, 1970); and Curtis P. Nettels, *The Emergence of a National Economy* (New York: Harper & Row, 1968).

49. For the figures and the method of analysis on which this section is based, see below, Appendix 1.

50. Carl Lotus Becker, *The History of Political Parties in the Province of New York, 1760–1776* (Madison: University of Wisconsin Press, 1909), p. 168, n. 36; Young, *Democratic Republicans*, p. 382.

51. See below, Appendix 1.

52. Livingston to Hamilton, 3 March 1787, *Papers of Alexander Hamilton*, 4:103–4.

53. The delegates to the convention and the votes they cast on the major questions are listed in DePauw, *The Eleventh Pillar*, table 4, pp. 248–49.

54. Ibid. No delegates from Albany, Columbia, Montgomery, or Ulster voted either for ratification "in full confidence" of amendments or for final ratification. One man from Washington voted for the first motion but against final ratification. No members from Orange accepted the "in full confidence" formula, but one voted to ratify. Three Dutchess members and three Suffolk members voted for the compromise formula, and four Dutchess members and three Suffolk members voted for final acceptance. The antifederalist members from Queens voted unanimously both for the compromise and for acceptance.

55. Henry Oothoudt to John McKesson, 25 April 1787, John McKesson Papers, New-York Historical Society; Hughes to Lamb, [1788], Lamb Papers; Hugh Ledley to Lamb, 15 January 1788, ibid.; James McHugh to Lamb, 18 June 1788, ibid.; Clinton to Lamb, 28 June 1788, ibid.; Tillinghast to Lamb, 27 June 1788, ibid.

56. Oothoudt to McKesson, 25 April 1787, McKesson Papers; Abraham Yates to Abraham G. Lansing, 27 May 1788, Abraham Yates Papers, Manuscript Division, New York Public Library, The Astor, Lenox and Tilden Foundations.

57. Ledley to Lamb, 15 January 1788, Lamb Papers; New York City committee to Albany committee, 6 April 1788, ibid.

58. Smith to Lamb, 6 April, 1788, Lamb Papers.

59. Record of distribution of "The Columbian Patriot," and Clinton to Lamb, 21 June 1788, both in ibid.

60. Tillinghast to Lamb, 21 June 1788; Clinton to Lamb, 21 June 1788; Albany committee to New York committee, 12 April 1788—all in ibid.

61. Abraham Yates, *Political Papers, Addressed to the Advocates for a Congressional Revenue in the State of New York* (New York: Shepard Kollock, 1786), Evans no. 20168, pp. 7, 8, 12–16.

62. Melancton Smith, comments in the New York ratifying convention, 1788, in *The Antifederalists,* ed. Cecilia M. Kenyon (Indianapolis: Bobbs-Merrill, 1966), pp. 375–76; " 'Cato' to the Citizens of New York," in ibid., pp. 306, 310–12. For the problem of Cato's identity, see DePauw, *The Eleventh Pillar*, appendix A. pp. 283–92.

CHAPTER 10

1. On the problem of pre-Revolution legitimacy, see Bernard Bailyn, *The Origins of American Politics* (New York: Alfred A. Knopf, 1968), and Michael Kammen, *People of Paradox: An Inquiry Concerning the Origins of American Civilization* (New York: Alfred A. Knopf, 1972).

2. See the comments made in the ratifying convention by Melancton Smith and Thomas

Tredwell, in *The Antifederalists,* ed. Cecilia M. Kenyon (Indianapolis: Bobbs-Merrill, 1966), pp. 371, 393–94.

3. See David Ludlum, *Social Ferment in Vermont, 1791–1850* (New York: Columbia University Press, 1939), and Alice Felt Tyler, *Freedom's Ferment: Phases of American Social History from the Colonial Period to the Outbreak of the Civil War* (New York: Harper & Row, 1962).

4. See Philip J. Schwarz, "New York's Provincial Boundaries: A Study of the Politics of Interest" (Ph.D. diss., Cornell University, 1973).

5. Leopold S. Launitz-Schurer, "Whig-Loyalists: The DeLanceys of New York," *New-York Historical Society Quarterly* 56 (1972):179–98; and William A. Benton, *Whig Loyalism: An Aspect of Political Ideology in the American Revolutionary Era* (Teaneck, N.J.: Fairleigh Dickinson University Press, 1969).

6. Esmond Wright, "The New York Loyalists: A Cross-Section of Colonial Society," in *The Loyalist Americans: A Focus on Greater New York,* ed. Robert A. East and Jacob Judd, (Tarrytown, N.Y.: Sleepy Hollow Restorations, 1975), p. 89; Isaac Low to Nicholas Low, 8 March 1788, Nicholas Low Papers, Library of Congress.

7. See Alfred F. Young, *The Democratic Republicans of New York: The Origins, 1763–1797* (Chapel Hill: University of North Carolina Press, 1967), p. 21.

8. William Smith, Jr., *Historical Memoirs from 16 March 1763 to 25 July, 1778,* ed. William H. W. Sabine, 2 vols. in 1 (New York: New York Times and Arno Press, 1969), 2:151; Schuyler to John Jay, 14 July 1777, *The Correspondence and Public Papers of John Jay,* ed. Henry P. Johnston, 4 vols. (New York: G. P. Putnam's Sons, 1890–93), 1:147.

9. Alexander Hamilton to Robert Morris, 13 August 1782, *The Papers of Alexander Hamilton,* ed. Harold C. Syrett et al., 24 vols. to date (New York: Columbia University Press, 1961–), 3:138.

10. On Indian policy as a source of tension between Congress and the state, see Barbara Graymont, "New York State Indian Policy after the Revolution," *New York History* 57 (1976):438–74.

11. Jack P. Greene succinctly summarizes the reason why women were excluded from the franchise in the Anglo-American world of the eighteenth century in his Oxford inaugural lecture *All Men Are Created Equal: Some Reflections on the Character of the American Revolution* (Oxford: Clarendon Press, 1976), pp. 15–16 and 37, n. 62. Daniel Calhoun offers the intriguing suggestion that eighteenth-century American fears about political tyranny gave way to nineteenth-century anxieties about masculinity and femininity (see his *The Intelligence of a People* [Princeton: Princeton University Press, 1973], pp. 188–205, esp. p. 201). That such anxieties were developing in one New York mind, presumably male, was revealed by a crude satire on the notion of women in politics that was published in New York City at the end of 1783. It described a legislature of women debating the need to raise a supply of husbands and voting on such resolutions as "that bewitching Kisses, bearing three and a half percent, be consolidated with pouting lips, and made transferable in the Currency of Rapture at the Exchequer of Bliss" ("A Female Legislator," *New York Gazetteer,* 3 December 1783).

12. Young, *Democratic Republicans,* pp. 84, n. 2, and 203–6.

13. These comments are drawn from Ronald Hoffman, *A Spirit of Dissension: Economics, Politics and the Revolution in Maryland* (Baltimore: Johns Hopkins University Press, 1973), esp. chaps. 6, 8, and 9; the quote is from p. 272.

14. See Staughton Lynd, "A Governing Class on the Defensive: The Case of New York," in his *Class Conflict, Slavery and the United States Constitution: Ten Essays* (Indianapolis: Bobbs-Merrill, 1967).

15. Hoffman, *A Spirit of Dissension.*

16. See the text of the constitution of 1777, in [Alexander C. Flick, ed.], *The American Revolution in New York: Its Political, Social and Economic Significance* (Albany: University of the State of New York, 1926), pp. 326–39.

17. *Laws of the State of New York*, microfilm ed., in *Records of the States of the United States*, ed. William Sumner Jenkins (Washington, D.C.: Library of Congress, 1949), N.Y., B.2, reel 6, unit 2, 10th sess., chap. 1.

18. Hamilton to Robert Livingston, Jr., 25 April 1785, *Papers of Alexander Hamilton*, 3:609.

19. For a different interpretation of the significance of newspaper publication of the debates, see Linda Grant DePauw, *The Eleventh Pillar: New York State and the Federal Constitution* (Ithaca: Cornell University Press, 1966), p. 25.

20. "A Manifesto of a Number of Gentlemen from Albany County," in Kenyon, *The Antifederalists*, p. 363.

21. For a constitutional plan calling for popular election of officials, see Smith, *Historical Memoirs*, 2:18–21.

22. *Minutes of the Council of Appointment, April 4, 1778–May 3, 1779*, Collections of the New-York Historical Society, vol. 58 (New York: Printed for the Society, 1925), pp. 18, 72.

23. "An Address from the Legislature of the State of New York to their Constituents," *Journal of the Assembly of the State of New York*, microfilm ed., in *Records of the States*, N.Y., A.1b, reel 4, unit 1, entry for 13 March 1781; Ted Robert Gurr, personal communication, 25 July 1975. See also Ted Robert Gurr and Harry Eckstein, *Patterns of Authority: A Structural Basis for Political Inquiry* (New York: Wiley-Interscience, 1975).

24. *New-York Packet and the American Advertiser* (Samuel Loudon), 7 April 1785.

25. Young, *Democratic Republicans*, pp. 100, 387.

26. See Milton M. Klein, "The Rise of the New York Bar: The Legal Career of William Livingston," in his *The Politics of Diversity: Essays in the History of Colonial New York* (Port Washington, N.Y.: Kennikat Press, 1974), pp. 145–46.

27. Henry Wansey, *The Journal of an Excursion to the United States of North America* (Salisbury, England: J. Easton, 1796), entry for 24 May 1794, quoted in Young, *Democratic Republicans*, p. 387.

28. Alan Trachtenberg, *Brooklyn Bridge: Fact and Symbol* (Chicago: University of Chicago Press, 1979), pp. 116–17.

29. Compare the Marxian argument of E. P. Thompson in "The Moral Economy of the English Crowd in the Eighteenth Century," *Past & Present*, no. 50 (February 1971):76–136, with the non-Marxian argument of Pauline Maier in "Popular Uprisings and Civil Authority in Eighteenth-Century America," *William and Mary Quarterly* 27 (1970):3–35. On the "Whig Science of Politics," see Gordon S. Wood, *The Creation of the American Republic, 1776–1787* (Chapel Hill: University of North Carolina Press, 1969), chap. 1.

30. For the abolition of the assize of bread, see Howard B. Rock, "The Perils of Laissez-Faire: The Aftermath of the New York Bakers' Strike of 1801," *Labor History* 17 (1976): 372–87; on the bread riot of 1837, see Joel Tyler Headley, *The Great Riots of New York, 1712–1873* (1873; reprint ed., New York: Dover Publications, 1971), chap. 7.

31. On the fate of the Indians after the Revolution, see Graymont, "New York State Indian Policy after the Revolution"; Francis Jennings, "The Indians' Revolution," in *The American Revolution: Explorations in the History of American Radicalism*, ed. Alfred F. Young (DeKalb: Northern Illinois University Press, 1976), pp. 319–48; and Anthony F. C. Wallace, *The Death and Rebirth of the Seneca* (New York: Random House, 1972), chaps. 5–7.

APPENDIX 1

1. Lee Benson, *Turner and Beard: American Historical Writing Reconsidered* (New York: The Free Press, 1960), pp. 160–74.

2. Jackson Turner Main, *The Upper House in Revolutionary America* (Madison: Univer-

sity of Wisconsin Press, 1967); idem, *Political Parties before the Constitution* (Chapel Hill: University of North Carolina Press, 1973); Edward Francis Countryman, "Legislative Government in Revolutionary New York, 1777–1788" (Ph.D. diss., Cornell University, 1971).

3. Alfred F. Young, *The Democratic Republicans of New York: The Origins, 1763–1797* (Chapel Hill: University of North Carolina Press, 1967).

4. Linda Grant DePauw, *The Eleventh Pillar: New York State and the Federal Constitution* (Ithaca: Cornell University Press, 1966), pp. 25–27.

5. Ibid., pp. 24–25.

6. Main, *Upper House* and *Political Parties.*

7. Besides Main's two books, see the following by Owen S. Ireland: "The Ratification of the Federal Constitution in Pennsylvania" (Ph.D. diss., University of Pittsburgh, 1966); "The Ethnic-Religious Dimension of Pennsylvania Politics, 1778–1779," *William and Mary Quarterly* 30 (1973):423–48; "Germans against Abolition: A Minority's View of Slavery in Revolutionary Pennsylvania," *Journal of Interdisciplinary History* 3 (1972–73):685–706.

8. See Edward C. Papenfuse, "Order out of Chaos: Efforts to Control the Economy and Attain Political Tranquility in Maryland, 1777–1789" (Paper presented at the symposium "Sovereign States in the Age of Uncertainty," Washington, D.C., March 1979).

9. See chapters 7 and 8 of Countryman, "Legislative Government."

10. DePauw, *The Eleventh Pillar*, p. 25.

11. Edward Countryman, "Some Problems of Power in New York, 1777–1782" (Paper presented at the symposium "Sovereign States in the Age of Uncertainty," Washington, D.C., March 1979).

12. Lee F. Anderson et al., *Legislative Roll-Call Analysis* (Evanston: Northwestern University Press, 1966), chap. 6.

13. Ibid., p. 103 (emphasis added).

14. W. J. Dixon, ed., *BMD: Biomedical Computer Programs* (Berkeley and Los Angeles: University of California Press, 1973).

15. Mary-Jo Kline, commenting on a preliminary study that I presented at the College Conference on New York History in Albany in April 1977, noted that by different measures I had placed one member as both a mild conservative and an extreme radical within one session. This, I found, was due to his being placed by the computer program in a position in which most of the data was "supplied."

APPENDIX 2

1. The lists of senators and assemblymen given in the official journals are incomplete. It was usual practice to name at the start of a session the members who were actually in attendance and to record the entry of others as they arrived. For most sessions my listing is thus based on attendance records rather than election records.

2. For the first six sessions, while their constituencies were occupied by the British, senators for the southern district and assemblymen for New York, Richmond, Kings, Queens, and Suffolk counties served without election. The first incumbents were chosen by the Convention of the People that wrote the constitution of 1777, and they served until they either resigned, were expelled, or died. Vacancies among these "ordinance members" were filled by vote of the other house.

3. Resigned due to ill health.

4. Died in office.

5. Chosen in place of John Jones.

6. Resigned to accept election as lieutenant governor.

7. Resigned to take a seat in Congress.

8. Resigned to accept a commission in the Continental army.

9. The council of appointment was made up of the governor and a senator from each senatorial district. The senators were chosen for one-year terms by the assembly.

10. Appointed in place of Philip Livingston.

11. Resigned to accept appointment as chief justice of the state.

12. Appointed in place of Pierre Van Cortlandt.

13. Expelled for misconduct in office.

14. Appointed in place of Henry Rutgers.

15. Appointed in place of Richard Morris.

16. Expelled for dereliction of duty and contempt of the senate.

17. Named to the council in place of Ephraim Paine.

18. Seat declared vacant after Jay's capture by the British and acceptance of a parole to go to Europe.

19. The page identifying the speaker is missing in the microfilm edition of the *Assembly Journal*. Bancker is assumed to be speaker because he held the post in both the preceding session and the following one and because he was a member of this session.

20. Twice named temporary president due to illness of the lieutenant governor.

21. Appointed in place of Sir James Jay.

22. Appointed in place of Philip Edsall.

23. From the seventh session onwards senators and assemblymen from the southern counties were elected as prescribed in the state constitution.

24. Served as temporary president throughout the second meeting of this session in the absence of the lieutenant governor.

25. Elected speaker when family difficulties kept Hathorn from punctual attendance.

26. Formerly Tryon County.

27. Formerly Charlotte County.

28. Served as temporary president from 8 April to 5 May while the lieutenant governor was absent on business.

Index